T0190479

Lecture Notes in Computer Science 11988

More information about this subseries at http://www.springer.com/series/7409

Marcin Wardaszko · Sebastiaan Meijer ·
Heide Lukosch · Hidehiko Kanegae ·
Willy Christian Kriz ·
Mariola Grzybowska-Brzezińska (Eds.)

Simulation Gaming Through Times and Disciplines

50th International Simulation and Gaming
Association Conference, ISAGA 2019
Warsaw, Poland, August 26–30, 2019
Revised Selected Papers

 Springer

effectiveness [8]. The chapter is closed by a paper analyzing the potential of escape rooms in an educational setting [9].

Chapter two is composed of papers on different aspects in design, implementation, and new directions for researchers to pursue. Four articles in this chapter discuss a variety of aspects of the theory of game design [12, 17, 18, 22]. Another interesting group of papers present a specific game with their implementation analysis [13–16, 19–23]. The third group of articles delivers papers on different analytical aspects of simulation gaming theory and practice [10, 11, 24].

The third chapter focuses on current issues. The first two papers are on the simulation gaming contribution to climate change education and perception [25, 26]. The other three papers focus on learning effectiveness with simulation gaming with an excellent paper from Mieko Nakamura [27], which won the Best Paper Award at the 50th Anniversary ISAGA Conference, followed by a paper on learning entrepreneurship skills [28] and an analysis of business simulation game courses [29].

The fourth chapter delivers a view with gamification in focus. All four papers deliver a unique view on different aspects of gamification and its connections to the field of simulation and gaming [30–33].

The final fifth chapter is a collection of papers that are connected to simulation gaming but offer a much broader perspective, from the point of view of video gaming [34], learning with location-based gaming [35], using AI and ML for content generation for games [36], using simulation to solve supply chain and logistic problems [37], and using VR to simulate real-world problems [38, 39].

All submissions went through a double-blind review process. We would like to thank our many reviewers for their hard work and dedication to the notion of increasing the quality of proposed papers. Their work is priceless and much underappreciated.

I want to thank the co-organizers JASAG, NASAGA, SAGANET, SAGSAGA, PTBG, and ThaiSIM for the continued support, promotion, and work put into delivering this conference and post-proceedings.

The success of this LNCS volume would not have been achieved without the hard work and cooperation of the editorial committee. I would like to thank them warmly. I'm grateful for their support. I hope that this collection of selected papers will serve as a reminder of the good times we had at the ISAGA conference in Warsaw in these difficult times we face right now.

On behalf of the Editorial Team

Marcin Wardaszko

Bibliography

1. Duke R.D. (1974), Gaming: The Future's Language, Sage Publications, New York, NY.
2. Leigh E., Tipton E. and de Wijse-van Heeswijk M. (2021), A Journey to the Role of Facilitator: Personal stories unfolding alongside world trends, (this issue).

3. Kikkawa T., Kriz W.C. and Sugiura J. (2021), Differences between Facilitator-guided and Self-guided Debriefing on the Attitudes of University Students, (this issue).
4. Kleiman F., Janssen M. and Meijer S. (2021), Evaluation of a pilot game to change civil servants' willingness towards open data policy making, (this issue).
5. Zhang C., Härenstam K.P., Nordquist J. and Meijer S. (2021) Structuring game design with active learning benefits: insights from logistical skills training in managing an emergency department, (this issue).
6. Goutx D., Sauvagnargues S. and Mermet L. (2021) Playing (in) a Crisis Simulation: What is the playful engagement in a serious simulation made of?
7. Köhler K., Röpke R. and Wolf M.R. (2021), Through a Mirror Darkly – On the Obscurity of Teaching Goals in Game-Based Learning in IT Security, (this issue).
8. Roungas B., Meijer S. and Verbraeck A. (2021), The Tacit Knowledge in Games: From Validation to Debriefing, (this issue).
9. Mijal M., Cieśla M. and Gromadzka M. (2021), Educational Escape Room – Challenges and Obstacles, (this issue)
10. Lobastova S. (2021), Simulated Construction of State's Intersubjective Reality in Virtual Games: An Emerging Tool of Social Power?, (this issue).
11. Nitisakunwut P. and Soranastaporn S. (2021), A Review of Game-Based Research for English Language Learning in S&G Interdiscipline Journal, (this issue).
12. Motzev M. and Pamukchieva O. (2021), Accuracy in Business Simulations, (this issue).
13. Chang S. and Deguchi H. (2021), Group-based learning and group composition on the provision of public goods: Incorporating agent-based simulation and gaming, (this issue).
14. Miki Yokoyama M., Ohnuma S. and Hirose Y. (2021), Can the Veil of Ignorance Create Consensus? A Qualitative Analysis Using the Siting for a Contaminated Waste Landfill Game, (this issue).
15. Kiattikomol P., Nimnual R. and Sittisanguansak P. (2021), The Development of the 3D Role-Playing Game on PC with an Assistive System for Deuteranopia, (this issue).
16. Kuijpers A., Lukosch H. and Verbraeck A. (2021), The Trust Game: The influence of Trust on Collaboration in the light of Technological Innovations, (this issue).
17 Freese M. and Lukoooh II.K. (2021), The funnel of game design - Proposing a new way to address a problem definition using the IDEAS approach, (this issue).
18. Teach R., Szot J. and Chasteen L. (2021), Little Things Mean a Lot in Simulations, (this issue).
19. Ogihara A., Suzuki K. and Nakai K. (2021), Impact of Competition in Energy Market on Promotion of Renewables: an Agent-Based Model Approach, (this issue).
20. Kowalik A. (2021), The perception of business wargaming practices among strategic and competitive intelligence professionals, (this issue).
21. Weber-Sabil J., Lalicic L. and Buijtenweg T. (2021), Managing Competing Values in Sustainable Urban Tourism: a Simulation-Gaming Approach, (this issue).
22. Ćwil M. (2021), Simulation games as a framework to conduct scientific experiments – the example of prospect theory research, (this issue).

23. Seita H. and Kurahashi S. (2021), Study on occurrence mechanism of quality scandal in enterprises by "Sontaku", "air" and "water" theory using business game, (this issue).
24. Dumblekar V. and Dhar U. (2021), Interpersonal Competitiveness in a Cohesive Team: Insights from a Business Simulation Game, (this issue).
25. Gerber A., Ulrich M. and Wäger P. (2021), Review of Haptic and Computerized (Simulation) Games on Climate Change, (this issue).
26. Goncalves M., Steenbeek J., Tomczak M., Romagnoni G., Puntilla R., Karvinen V., Santos C., Keijser X., Abspoel L., Warmelink H. and Mayer I. (2021), Food-web modeling in the Maritime Spatial Planning Challenge Simulation Platform: Results from the Baltic Sea Region, (this issue).
27. Nakamura M. (2021), Unpacking, Overconfidence, and Game Design, (this issue).
28. Titton L.A. and Jakubowski M. (2021), Authentic Learning in Entrepreneurship Education, (this issue).
29. Dumblekar V. and Dhar U. (2021), Learning from a Business Simulation Game: A Factor-Analytic Study, (this issue).
30. Hamada R., Iwasa N., Kaneko T. and Hiji M. (2021), Resolving Migrant Issues in Thailand Using the Framework of 'Simulation Game – Project PAL', (this issue).
31. Jakubowski M. (2021), Gamification Design Strategies - summary of research project, (this issue).
32. Wade D.W. (2021), Fostering Adaptive Organizations: Some Practical Lessons from Space Pirates, (this issue).
33. Pamula A., Patasius M. and Patasiene I. (2021), Comparison of Experience of Using Business Games in University of Lodz and Kaunas University of Technology, (this issue).
34. vanov M., Wittenzellner H. and Wardaszko M. (2021), Video game monetization mechanisms in triple A (AAA) video games, (this issue).
35. Vuorio J. and Harviainen T.J. (2021), Learning with Location-Based Gaming, (this issue).
36. Podgórski B. and Wardaszko M. (2021), Methodological challenges of creating a next-generation machine learning-based game engine for generating maps and vehicle behavior, (this issue).
37. Zaima Z. (2021), Agent-based Simulation for Sustainable Management of Supply Chain and Natural Resources: Basic Model, (this issue).
38. Deechuay N., Nimnual R., Makasorn P. and Permpoon S. (2021), Wonders of the World Simulation Program by Virtual Reality, (this issue).
39. Wang Z., Al-Shorji Y. and Zhang C. (2021), Framework and application of live video streaming as a virtual reality gaming technology: a study of function and performance, (this issue).

Organization

Local Organizational Committee

KOZMINSKI UNIVERSITY

Center for Simulation
Games and Gamification

Marcin Wardaszko (Organizational Committee Chair)
Błażej Podgórski
Małgorzata Ćwil
Anna Winniczuk
Michał Jakubowski
Wanda Widziszewska

ISAGA 2019 Conference Program Committee

Marcin Wardaszko (Program Chair)
Sebastiaan Meijer
Hidehiko Kanagae
Toshiko Kikkawa
Heide Lukosch
Willy C. Kriz
Karol Olejniczak
Marnix van Gisbergen
Yusuke Toyoda
Maria Garda
Błażej Podgórski
Elizabeth Tipton
Elyssebeth Leigh
Jayanth Raghothama
David Crookall
Vinod Dumblekar
Upinder Dhar
Małgorzata Ćwil
Michał Jakubowski
Anna Winniczuk

Track Chairs

The 50th Anniversary Track	Willy C. Kriz, F. H. Vorarlberg
Simulation & Gaming Track	Karol Olejniczak, SWPS University
Game Science Theory Track	Sebastiaan Meijer, KTH Royal Institute of Technology
Gamification Track	Michał Jakubowski, Kozminski University
Simulation gaming application in VR/AR	Małgorzata Ćwil, Kozminski University
Advances in Gaming Technology Track	Marcin Wardaszko, Kozminski University
Ethics of Simulation & Gaming, Special JASAG Track	Toshiko Kikkawa, Keio University
E-sports Science Track	Marnix van Gisbergen, Breda University of Applied Sciences
Simulation & Gaming for Logistics and Smart Infrastructure Track	Jayanth Raghothama, KTH Royal Institute of Technology
Gaming Cultures Track	Maria Berenika Garda, University of Tampere
Gaming for Individual Efficacy and Performance, Special Track	Vinod Dumblekar, MANTIS and Upinder Dhar, Shri Vaishnav Vidyapeeth Vishwavidyalaya
Gaming for Sustainable Development Goals, Special Track	David C. Crookall, UCA
Thematic Sessions Track	Marcin Wardaszko, Kozminski University
Poster Presentation Track	Marcin Wardaszko, Kozminski University

Contents

Simulation Gaming in the Science Space

A Journey to the Role of Facilitator: Personal Stories Unfolding Alongside World Trends

Elyssebeth Leigh[1]([⊠]), Elizabeth Tipton[2],
and Marieke de Wijse-van Heeswijk[3]

[1] University of Technology Sydney, Sydney, Australia
elyssebeth.leigh@icloud.com
[2] Eastern Washington University, Cheney, USA
[3] Radboud University, Nijmegen, The Netherlands

Abstract. Simulations and games for learning require expert management drawing on specialist skills and knowledge. Dick Duke's 1969 [1] invitation to a 'conversation about simulation', initiated a process that has generated 50 years of thoughtful analysis of the design and use of simulations. In the early stages, facilitation was not high on agendas for discussion or research. However, the role of the facilitator has been receiving more attention, as the importance of effective management of simulation events receives more recognition. Awareness of the complexity of human interactions, and the ways in which simulation can both replicate and unsettle them, is leading to more research and attention being paid to the role of the facilitator. Using a trajectory of personal experiences beginning in 1969, this paper uses an auto-ethnographic approach [2] to review our own development as facilitators of simulations and games, alongside an exploration of the broader, evolving understanding of the role, and the increasing complexity involved in ensuring facilitators contribute effectively to current learning contexts.

Keywords: Facilitation · Role of facilitator · Personal development ·
Simulations and games for learning

1 Introduction

Meanings attached to the terms 'simulations' and 'games', have evolved through time, as has greater understanding of their nature and potential as educational tools and strategies. In 1969 such activities were rarely used in formal education contexts, which makes Dick Duke's efforts to expand awareness of their potential especially important. Of course military and aviation trainers were familiar with the concept, and the American Management Association had introduced the Top Management Decision Game in 1956. However in the late 1960's as a means of educating the high school students, whom I (Elyssebeth) was learning to teach, the concept was simply not on any horizon I encountered.

This article uses an auto ethnographic approach to trace our development as educators. Beginning with a brief skirmish with school teaching, Elyssebeth became an adult educator in a tertiary college, worked in the finance and entertainments sectors,

© Springer Nature Switzerland AG 2021
M. Wardaszko et al. (Eds.): ISAGA 2019, LNCS 11988, pp. 3–13, 2021.
https://doi.org/10.1007/978-3-030-72132-9_1

and then as an academic. Beth became an educator after graduation and built her career over time. The unifying factor in all these varied contexts is my fascination with learning and education. Australia was not nearly as well connected to international trends at the beginning of this trajectory, as it is now. Most of the knowledge I acquired in those early years originated in Britain and I was blind to the paradox of applying knowledge developed on the other side of the world to my contexts, as if there was no difference.

2   Beginnings – 1969

When Dick Duke and his colleagues met in Bad Godesberg in July 1969 Elyssebeth was halfway through the second, and (while she did not know it) final year, of high school teaching, and Beth was beginning elementary school. In an interesting way those events have shaped all our subsequent learning and work. Drawing on the happenstance of timing, this article traces the personal development of two educators and facilitators of learning who are now using simulations and games for learning. Paralleling those journeys there have been extensive developments in the use of simulations and games for learning and changing expectations of, and understandings about, the capabilities required of people charged with managing such learning processes.

Elyssebeth - A Newly Qualified High School Teacher. When I began high school teaching in 1968 teachers were definitely 'in charge' of the learning process, students were not. Words like 'facilitation' had no part in the lexicon for training teachers, although the term already much in use in adult education and workplace learning contexts. While simulations and games (S&G) were coming into use for learning, they had not yet arrived in the Australian school system where I was teaching that year. In 1968 Australian school rooms had a clear power ratio - teachers were taught 'how to control the classroom' and students were taught how to obey. Their roles were respectively 'owner of knowledge' and 'passive recipient of it'. These expectations appeared not to bother the early adopters, elsewhere in the world, who were influencing the journey towards students being actively engaged in the process of their own learning. Bruner and his colleagues [26] for example, did not appear threatened by the idea of surrendering all/some of the teacher's power in the interests of creating engaging learning spaces to challenged support learners' efforts to play with ideas.

I was newly married, and in a strange and almost 'foreign' city more than 4,200 km from my birth town. My qualifications had been earned in New South Wales (NSW) and at that time there were few connections among the eight education systems in the states and territories forming the Australia nation. My first year of teaching was in a progressive school with a relatively (for its time) learner-focused environment, and this proved to be wildly inappropriate for how and what to teach in this new context.

The Darwin High School principal behaved as a narrow-minded disciplinarian, providing no support to a staff member unused to the South Australian education system. Despite passing the required 'teaching inspection' and receiving formal approval to teach in the South Australia system, my application for maternity leave (a relatively new phenomenon) submitted towards the end of the year provided an opportunity to ensure I never returned to secondary school teaching. The 'impregnable certainty' of hindsight suggests I was already on a 'facilitating learning' path in my clearly unacceptable use of practices counter to disciplinary-focused teaching, but that awareness was still some years away.

Beth – A Newly "Qualified?" Elementary School Student. My exposure to facilitation at this point has to be one of the worst facilitators ever, the PE teacher at my school. He was definitely of the mind that he was in charge and that we were not there to play games, which is somewhat absurd considering the purpose of the class was physical education through games. It sounds like a cliché, but I learned much at that tender age about what NOT to do in simulations and games from him. His chosen "pets" got to play whatever game we were playing in PE that day. The rest of us sat on the sideline waiting for our turn, which never came as the class period was too short. Eventually, the lack of participation there began to bleed over elsewhere and finally into other educational tasks in other classes that year. Simply put, what I learned there is "a facilitator must be aware of the entire group."

3 Facilitation Circa 1969

In the 1960's education was still largely seen as a teaching/learning dichotomy, although the work of researcher-practitioners like Malcolm Knowles [3, 4] Carl Rogers [5] and Vygotsky [6] were opening up awareness of learning as a 'social' networked process, rather than an 'individualised' power-ratio based exchange of information. The larger story of simulations and games for learning is much older than this, however 1969 provides a starting point for considering what was understood about the facilitation task as such knowledge has evolved through the years from 1969 to 2019.

Psychologists had been researching the concept of 'social facilitation' since the late 19th century [7], but the concept of a person occupying a formal role called 'facilitator' was not yet common. In particular Carl Rogers' therapeutic counselling approach *called client-centred therapy* [8] was opening up awareness of ways to engage with learning without any one person having a totally directive position in the process.

Of course, at that time, there were major differences between school, academic and workplace learning contexts, so it is useful to note that the changes were emerging in counselling and workplace contexts, rather than formal education ones. Research and practices in each domain were mostly confined to their own ways of 'knowing' with little awareness of, or interest in, the potential for connections among them. Work contexts were considered to be places that only became relevant *after* completing formal studies. Employers were more interested in 'quick results' and fast turn around, so it was natural to expect schools and academic settings would find workplace learning of little interest.

4   Professional Development - 1979

Elyssebeth - No Longer a Teacher Not Yet a Facilitator. In the New Year of 1970 I took my first job as a part-time adult educator (in evening classes) and for the next four years my students and I worked together to develop collaborative learning environments. At that time I was still fighting to clear my name and return to secondary teaching, so I was also working as a primary school teacher. When this was resolved by a surprise offer to become a full time adult educator late in 1973, I attended my first 'adult education' conference and met the word 'facilitation' for the first time. In 1974 I encountered my first educational board game, a SimCity-like design, and failed utterly to understand its principles.

By 1976, after a cyclone destroyed my home and my workplace, my family and I were back in NSW and I found my way to my first industry trainer role, catapulting me into an environment where facilitation of learning was the prime focus and simulations a key learning strategy. During the next four years I helped establish a local community of practice called ADSEGA - Australian Decision Support and Educational Gaming Association - whose members shared knowledge and skills about simulations and games, and somewhere along the way, introduced me to "Gaming the Futures Language" [1]. 'Teaching' had been left far behind and I was now an adult educator, a trainer, and a simulation and games practitioner. Not yet a facilitator nor a researcher, but beginning to dream about engaging with the international community in both capacities.

Beth – Becoming an Educator While Still in High School. I ended up "gamifying" a group of students into learning how to read. This happened because I knew absolutely nothing about how to help them learn how to read. This was a few years before the internet was to make information immediately available at our fingertips. The school library had nothing useful. The teacher of the reading class had gone AWOL (which is how I, who had study hall at the same time, ended up doing this) so there was no expert to ask. So, we as a group made up games throughout the semester to help with reading skills. What I learned here was "a facilitator must listen to the participants."

5   Facilitation Circa 1979

Simulations and games for learning were developing their capacity to educate and inform, and by the mid 1970's Pfeiffer and Jones were collating original designs and publishing their series of Annuals [9] including notes for facilitators alongside original resources. The term 'facilitator' had been in use for describing the persons who managed the immediacy of simulations and games for learning for a few years [10] but published research on simulations and games was still generally focused on their design and application.

As yet little attention was paid to the work expected of individual/s managing the moment to moment unfolding of particular activities. Moreover research being conducted, was mostly intent on 'comparing' learning acquired through conventional means with that acquired through active engagement in simulations. This approach privileged conventional teaching and assessment strategies for imparting, and measuring, content-based information. Researchers seemed mostly ignorant of the potential for acquiring - and assessing - knowledge and capabilities through engagement with, and exercise of, new skill sets.

6 Academic Contexts – 1989

Elyssebeth - Back in Academia - Exercising Facilitation Skills. I had now had 15 years experience in various workplaces in NSW with a deepening appreciation of simulations and games for learning. I had also completed courses of post-graduate tertiary study to support my evolution as a facilitator - no longer a 'teacher'. I knew about ISAGA but lacked the resources to travel to the conferences and inspired by the concept had co-organised and led several local smaller versions in Sydney to share knowledge. Facilitation as a learning process was now reinforced and informed by adult education theory (andragogy) and I was employed to lead learning programs for workplace trainers and educators learning to design and facilitate simulations and games in their particular contexts through public workshops and units of study in adult education degree programs.

Members of the ADSEGA community of practice had dispersed to various careers and roles and my energies were redirected to the Australian Consortium on Experiential Education [11] providing an opportunity to explore educational concepts underpinning the shape and form of simulations and games as educational tools and strategies. This period also expanded my knowledge of research and work in the field of adult learning including that of Jack Mezirow [12] David Boud [13] David Kolb [14] Stephen Brookfield [15] and Nod Miller [16] - all of whom I met at various times. Their interest in the role of educators of adults paralleled - but was not always seen to be pertinent to - my own continuing focus on use of simulations and games for learning.

Beth - Family, Study and Learning 'In situ'. I had completed the BS's and started the PhD, but was on a time-out with my kids at home. Try playing cards with friends who also have toddlers – more explicitly 5 kids between the ages of two and five, 2 husbands who cheat every time your back is turned, and a 1 canasta partner who is manic depressive. This was also a lesson in facilitation – in particular, the importance of situational awareness. By being aware of little stuff, it was possible to catch big disasters before they became big. I'll tell you some of the stories when I see you, but in short, it is amazing the mayhem 5 toddlers can create when your attention is distracted for 5 min. What I learned here was "a facilitator must pay attention to the entire space."

7 Facilitation Circa 1989

Wikipedia notes that the "role of facilitator emerged as a separate set of skills in the 1980s .... to actively participate and guide the group towards consensus." In a review of terms in use during this period Rees [17] identified an array of terms used, and a variety of types of roles now recognised as engaging in managing learning environments. Most of the available literature on facilitation at this time seems to have concerned business management, community and social consulting projects like Rees' - where a framework for practice was beginning to evolve. Clarity is emerging about the importance of breaking away from 'teacherly' modes of behaviour, but as yet simulations and games researchers are not paying much attention to the role - although there is, by now, an emerging body of literature about key tasks (e.g. briefing and debriefing) requiring focused attention from the person managing an activity.

Of course educators using simulations were already clear about the importance of the distinction between 'teaching' and facilitating' and while there was not yet a great deal of literature in the simulations and games field there was more discussion about it.

At the end of this decade John Heron had published The Facilitator's Handbook [18] creating a sound and well-balanced framework for the role in any context. While he did not pay specific attention to facilitating simulations and games, his frameworks and advice were - and still are - relevant for all in the field. Thus his book arriving at the turn of the century was a signal that facilitation - as a practice and a named role for educators - was well and truly part of the fabric of education. As I encountered the book through academic colleagues it was also signalling that those engaged in workplace and academic learning contexts were beginning to recognise the similarities in their interests.

8 Emergent New Roles and Study - 1999

Elyssebeth - PractitionerResearcher - Researching Facilitation Skills. I attended my first ISAGA conference in Riga in 1996, and was invited to host the 1999 conference in Sydney. Late in the decade, and parallel with the work towards the 1999 conference, I began part-time doctoral research. Initially my goal was to explore Peter Senge's concept of 'Team Learning'. However I was also now using an extended simulation to teach organisational behaviour, which was generating more complexity in regard to facilitating learning than I had ever previously encountered. When ISAGA 1999 arrived, my research was squarely focused on the special skills needed to facilitate what I was beginning to call an 'open-ended' [19], 'chaordic'[20]' simulation.

Becoming part of the ISAGA network was altering my perspective on every aspect of my own learning and teaching and I was beginning to engage in research focusing ever more closely on the role of the facilitator [21]. I was a member of the ISAGA Board and had begun publishing conference papers about simulations and facilitation.

Beth - Discovering the Traditions of My Practice. Just about finished with the PhD and teaching at ACC. One class in particular, informally known as "Math for Liberal Arts," I teach more as a facilitator rather than a typical educator. I just do not realize it until the math ed professor points it out to me. This results in a very interesting conversation, where she teases me for teaching "wrong" for decades. I realize that this is actually a compliment from her as she explains that I have always been what she tries to get her students to be...a facilitator/coach more than a lecturer at a podium. What I also take away from this is that facilitation has been around a long time, and that many teachers have been using it for a long time. But it seems to "fly under the radar." Perhaps we just did not talk about it? If not, I wonder why?

9   Facilitation Circa 1999

The International Association of Facilitators (IAF) was founded in 1993 to promote facilitation as a profession. By the end of the decade it was developing a Certified Professional Facilitator program which has now been in operation for nearly 20 years. Facilitation has become a recognised and viable role for educators. Thousands of articles are - or are on their way to - being published around the world and many educators are thinking differently about their role in education.

The IAF program does not directly address the particular set of skills required of facilitators of simulations and games although its general principles are relevant. By 1999, some researchers are taking a specific interest in 'how to manage' simulations and this work continues into the 21st century.

10   Seniority as Educators - 2009

Elyssebeth -Senior Lecturer and a Career Change. By 2009, I had served four years as General Secretary of ISAGA and seen the beginning of its transition from an informal international community of practice to a formally registered legal entity. My doctorate was completed. I had published two books and was working on the third one. I was also a member of Simulation Australia (SimAust) and had begun helping organise SimAust conferences and publish the proceedings.

I had also decided to leave my full time academic role and shift to a part-time role allowing for time to relax and travel. This has brought new adventures in research, and a change in my focus of attention such that I have been able to reflect on my own facilitator practices and research and write with new energy about simulation and facilitation. It has not, as yet, included much time for the kind of relaxing I had initially anticipated!

Beth – Tenured Associate Professor About to Host ISAGA 2010. Much had happened in the last decade as I had become active in the simulation and gaming academic community. Through a chance meeting about eight years earlier, I was publishing on the design of demand equations in business simulations. Through the unusual behaviors of some students in a game theory class, I had stumbled into the effects of culture attempting to override rules. While trying to figure out what was going on with these students, I had no formal framework so I fell back on my statistical training and treated it like a focus group. Sitting next to David Crookall at a conference lunch a few years later, I was informed that I was "wrong" again as I was really doing an important part of the simulation process...debriefing. I thought I was just finding out what the students had actually learned as it was quite different from what I had planned. What I learned here was "a facilitator must be prepared for emergent behavior and lessons to occur at any point in the simulation/game process."

11   Facilitation Circa 2009

In 2005 I collaborated on a review of Simulation&Gaming [22] that found "less than 10% of all articles made reference to requirements of the person/s facilitating a simulation or game." We noted then that: "It seemed that many writers did not regard facilitation as sufficiently important, or were unaware that its nature can be problematic." So while the role was now well known and widely accepted, at that point there still seemed to be assumptions that occupying it was unproblematic and did not need close attention. An alternative perspective is that facilitators are quintessential practitioners and disinclined to devote time and effort to the detail-driven task of researching what they do and how they do it [23].

In his dissertation exploring his own 'facilitator educator' practice Thomas [24, p.11] noted that "the role that a facilitator plays has been likened to the conductor of an orchestra ...; a catalyst, chameleon, and cabdriver ...; midwives ...; a choreographer ...; and a change agent ...". Perhaps it is this very complexity that is making the facilitator role not an easy subject for research.

12   Researching, Writing and Travelling - 2019

Elyssebeth. Theoretically I am 'retired' but am instead working on an engaging and fulfilling array of writing and teaching projects in Australia and Finland. Facilitation is now a key focus of my writing, and has similarly gained increasing attention as teaching methods slowly adapt to changing social and educational conditions. I have co-edited several books, published conference papers and book chapters and now work sessionally in Australia and Finland.
I was looking forward to being part of the 50th celebrations in Warsaw and to continuing my exploration of the tasks and role of the facilitator. There is still much to be explored.

Beth – Breaking Out All Over. As my travels were curtailed in the last few years for health reasons, I have been working on launching new degrees in analytics here at EWU. This has involved a ground-breaking partnership with Microsoft. It has also involved bringing much of what I have learned about experiential learning from simulations and games into the design of these degrees as we have treated them more as skill-transfer than rote-learning. We are constantly trying new things in the classes, learning what works and what doesn't, and adapting the curriculum to make it better. In one class last year, I gave students in one class the option of writing papers for an international conference. Two of seven groups did. What I learned was this was not a good idea as, while the students were capable of the research and presentation, they were not capable of writing such an academic paper in a 10-week quarter. Their writing skills were not up to the task and I had to rewrite the papers completely to fix the language and grammar. So, I adapted and worked with the conference this year to arrange for the students to present short workshops around a common theme – we eliminated the formal paper aspect and kept the rest of the experience. The students have since gone well beyond and have threaded the theme together into one coherent workshop that can be done in total or in individual parts. In another class, I had a student completely checked out of the learning process. So, I altered the rules of learning engagement on him, metaphorically changing the game from "Tic-Tac-Toe" to "Nomic". He took the lead role in organizing the final group presentation for the entire class. While lately I have not been facilitating in the usual simulation/game role, I have been helping students do this role. I have shifted into treating all of my classes as simulations/games themselves, even though they formally are not such. What I have learned is "A facilitator reflects and adapts continually."

Beth Still. I look forward to seeing everyone In Warsaw… who knows where we will end up next!

13 Facilitation Circa 2019

Reprising that 2005 search of the index of Simulation&Gaming issues a review of the issues between 2010 and 2019 and found only three additional articles that directly reference facilitation (only one mentions the facilitator). In addition there are four mentions of debriefing -which is one of the three key structural components that any facilitator must manage effectively to ensure learning intentions are achieved. A search of the Internet reveals numerous sites providing advice and information about how to be a facilitator of group work and other educational activities, and how to do the associated tasks well. There are not so many academic articles or research items. Thus it seems that the task of focusing on the skills and capabilities of the facilitator is still not a priority for researchers.

14 Concluding Comments

If - at graduation in 1968 - anyone had suggested that I (Elyssebeth) would only work in my chosen career for two years I may have been devastated. All that work and focus - not to be used! But in fact it has been in constant use, in roles and contexts that I would not have conceived of as possible or relevant at that time.

As John Lennon [25] noted 'Life is what happens to you while you're busy making other plans' and while education qualifications and passions have continued to shape work and life they have done so in entirely unexpected ways.

Similarly simulations and games for learning have travelled along an evolving trajectory from the 1960's. We know so much more about how to design them for effective learning outcomes, how to structure them to create particular replications of the real world, and how to manage them to achieve particular intentional results - while always being aware of their capacity to derail such intentions.

And, as always with human endeavour, there is so much more to be learned. I am looking forward to increasing attention - by way of research, analysis and thoughtful observation - being paid to the role of the facilitator in simulations and games, and of course, intend to continue my research and writing with collaborators from the ISAGA community who have travelled along this road with me.

If anyone had suggested that I (Beth) would work at my chosen career for the next fifty years (I wrote "teacher" as the answer to "what do you want to be when you grow up" on the first day of school in 1968 according to my mother), I would have laughed as I really wanted to be an astronaut but that was only for boys then – I was planning on changing that.

It is also amazing how, not setting out on the path to be where I am at now, just how straight line it actually has been. All of the pieces fit together neatly to give me the ability to do the things that I am doing.

As systems become more complex, emergent behavior becomes more likely. This is why the facilitator is so critical, akin to why airplanes need human pilots for when the autopilot hits a condition that it was not programmed to handle.

I look forward to continuing these travels, too!

References

1. Duke, R.: Gaming: The Futures Language. Sage Publications, New York (1974)
2. Ellis, C., Bochner, A.P.: Autoethnography, personal narrative, reflexivity: researcher as subject. In: Denzin, N.K., Lincoln, Y.S. (eds.) The Handbook of Qualitative Research. Sage Publications, California (2000)
3. Knowles, M.S.: Informal Adult Education: A Guide for Administrators, Leaders, and Teachers. Association Press, New York (1950)
4. Knowles, M.S.: Andragogy, not pedagogy. Adult Leadership 16(10), 350–352, 386 (1968)
5. Rogers, C.: Freedom to Learn for the 80's. Charles E. Merrill Publishing Company, Ohio (1982)
6. Vygotsky, L.S.: Mind in Society: The Development of Higher Psychological Processes. Harvard University Press ACEE, Harvard (1981). Newsletter. Australian Consortium on Experiential Education (1980)
7. Strauss, B.: Social facilitation in motor tasks: a review of research and theory. Psychol. Sport Exerc. 3(3), 237–256 (2002)
8. Cross, K.D.: An analysis of the concept facilitation. Nurse Educ. Today 16, 350–355 (1996)
9. Jones, J.E., Pfeiffer, J.W.: Introduction to the theory and practice section. In: Jones, J.E., Pfeiffer, J.W. (eds.) The 1975 Annual Handbook for Group Facilitators. Pfeiffer & Company, San Diego (1975)
10. Pfeiffer, J.W., Jones, J.E.: Design considerations in laboratory education. In: The 1973 Annual Handbook for Group Facilitators. Pfeiffer & Company, San Diego (1973)
11. ACEE: Newsletter. Australian Consortium on Experiential Education (1981)
12. Mezirow, J.: Transformative Dimensions of Adult Learning. Jossey-Bass, San Francisco (1991)
13. Boud, D.: The end of teaching as we know it. How can we assist people to learn what we don't know? UTS Public Research Lecture, Sydney (1996)

14. Kolb, D.: Experiential Learning: Experience as the Source of Learning and Development. Prentice Hall, Upper Saddle River (1984)
15. Brookfield, S.: Becoming a Critically Reflective Teacher. Jossey-Bass, San Francisco (1995)
16. Miller, N.: Shapeshifters, shadows, mentors and allies in a lifelong learning journey: lessons from television. Paper Presented at the SCUTREA, 31st Annual Conference, 3–5 July 2001, University of East London (2001)
17. Rees, P.L.: The role of the facilitator in management. Leadersh. Organ. Dev. J. **11**(7), 11–16 (1990). https://doi.org/10.1108/01437739010005334
18. Heron, J.: The Facilitator's Handbook. Kogan Page, London (1989)
19. Christopher, E.M., Smith, L.E.: Leadership Training Through Gaming: Power, People and Problem Solving. Kogan Page, London (1987)
20. Hock, D.: The Art of Chaordic Leadership. Leader to Leader, a Publication of the Leader to Leader Institute (2000)
21. Leigh, E., Spindler, L.: Vigilant observer: a role for facilitators of games/simulations. In: Geurts, J., Joldersma, C., Roelofs, E. (eds.) Gaming/Simulation for Policy Development and Organizational Change. Tilburg University Press, Tilburg (1998)
22. Leigh, E., Spindler, L.: Congruent facilitation of simulations and games. In: Shiratori, R., Arai, K., Kato, F. (eds.) Gaming, Simulations, and Society, pp. 189–198. Springer, Tokyo (2005). https://doi.org/10.1007/4-431-26797-2_20
23. Leigh, E.: A Practitioner Researcher Perspective on Facilitating an Open, Infinite, Chaordic Simulation. (EdD), University of Technology, Sydney, Sydney (2003). https://opus.lib.uts.edu.au/handle/2100/308
24. Thomas, G.: A Studty of the Theories and Practices of Facilitator Eduators. La Trobe University, Melbourne (2007)
25. Lennon, J.: Beautiful Boy (Darling Boy). On Double Fantasy. Geffen Records, London (1981)
26. Bruner, J.: Man a course of study. Occaiosnal paper No. 3 (1965). https://www.macosonline.org/research/Bruner_MACOS%20-Occasional%20Paper%203.pdf

Differences Between Facilitator-Guided and Self-guided Debriefing on the Attitudes of University Students

Toshiko Kikkawa[1]([envelope]) [iD], Willy Christian Kriz[2] [iD],
and Junkichi Sugiura[1] [iD]

[1] Keio University, 2-15-45, Mita, Minato-ku, Tokyo 108-8345, Japan
tompei22@keio.jp, jsugiura@flet.keio.ac.jp
[2] FHV University Vorarlberg, Hochschulstrasse 1, 6850 Dornbirn, Austria
Willy.kriz@fhv.at

Abstract. In this study, we investigated the effects of debriefing on 196 Japanese University students as part of an international collaboration between Austria and Japan. Based on the results of our previous studies [19–21], we showed that debriefing can bolster learning from the perspective of attitude changes and performance in games. However, there were weaknesses to previous studies in the sense that there were no facilitators to conduct the debriefings. In the experiments, all types of debriefing were carried out by students, i.e. self-guided. However, debriefing is usually conducted by a facilitator and carried out in a group. To address this weakness, we introduced facilitator-guided debriefing for the experimental conditions. Therefore, there were two experimental conditions: facilitator-guided debriefing and self-guided debriefing. After debriefing, groups of four participants played the *Highway Planning* game, which deals with co-operation and conflict. According to the results, the participants under facilitator-guided debriefing conditions showed more cooperative attitudes than did those under self-guided debriefing conditions, while participants in the self-guided debriefing group showed more competitive attitudes.

Keywords: Self-guided debriefing · Facilitator-guided debriefing · Attitudes · Conflict · Learning

1 Introduction

The process and effects of debriefing on learning have always been focal points of interest in the disciplines of simulation and gaming [1]. Debriefing can be defined as: "the process in which people who have had an experience are led through a purposive discussion of that experience." [2] (p. 146). As gaming simulations represent aspects of reality, the question arises about how participants' game experiences and results can be transferred back into their own real-life contexts. The term debriefing refers to the methods used to combine participants' reflections on their experiences with assessment of mental (cognition, emotion, etc.), social (action, communication, etc.), and reference systems processes (change of resources, structures, rules etc.) to deduce applications

© Springer Nature Switzerland AG 2021
M. Wardaszko et al. (Eds.): ISAGA 2019, LNCS 11988, pp. 14–22, 2021.
https://doi.org/10.1007/978-3-030-72132-9_2

for real situations beyond the gaming simulation experience [3]. Gaming simulations facilitate experiential learning. It has long been a tradition to link debriefing to Kolb's model of Experiential Learning [4], given that this connection is considered very important, especially in the case of reflective observation and abstract conceptualisation [5, 6]. Gaming with various debriefing methodologies has the potential to create learning opportunities that are interactive and engaging. Debriefing is not only important within the context of education and training but it is also relevant for the use of games in research, assessment and exploration [7, 8]. Furthermore, debriefing is considered to be ethically necessary because it provides opportunities to deal with stress, strained group dynamics and the emotional processes of the gaming experience itself [7, 9].

It is considered ineffective to conduct a simulation game without adequate debriefing and, according to the existing literature from various fields of application (e.g. business, education, health care etc.), there is a common understanding that effective learn ing only arises due to reflection through debriefing [10–13]. Crookall [14] (p. 419) even proposed a formula: "[(Simulation/game + proper debriefing) × engagement] = learning".

Although there are arguments (e.g. from theories of learning and instruction in the literature cited above) about why and how debriefing is an important factor for learning, it is remarkable that almost no attention has been paid so far to empirical research on this crucial element of gaming. For example, Crookall's formula has never been proven empirically. In the literature, several debriefing approaches and methods have been discussed (e.g. oral and written debriefing methods). There are examples of several structures, phase models, and proposals for concrete debriefing questions [2, 14–18]. However, there are no comprehensive empirical studies on the effects of the different debriefing methods.

We identified two major weaknesses of previous studies. First, few systematic studies were soundly designed. Second, many research initiatives focused only on questionnaire data to measure the effects of gaming, and performance data were missing. The aim of our research was to fill these gaps.

Therefore, we designed our study to overcome these weaknesses. We started a research project in 2016 and carried out our first experiments in 2017. In the previous studies, we investigated the effects of different types of debriefing, with no debriefing conditions as a control. We found significant empirical evidence that debriefing has positive effects on individual and group attitudes and behaviour (described in self-assessment questionnaires) and on group performance data (measured though performance indicators in experimental game-based scenarios). In our previous studies, with students in Japan and Austria, we also noticed cultural differences in the participants' attitudes, especially in terms of competition, conflict, and negotiation during game play [19–21].

Furthermore, as several experimental conditions were investigated at the same time among a large number of students in a class, i.e. with more than 100 students, all types of debriefing were carried out using a written sheet that was distributed to the participants. In other words, the debriefing was done by the participants themselves in our previous studies. They had to follow different types of written debriefing instructions. We are aware that, in practice, debriefing is more often used with forms of group discussion and is typically led by a facilitator [22]. In particular, direct communication, interactions and relationships between participants and facilitators seem to be important variables for the success of learning through facilitator-guided debriefing of simulation games [17, 23, 24]. Unfortunately, this discussion about the relevance of direct communication between facilitators and participants in game-based learning is more related to theoretical assumptions than the results of empirical studies. Some empirical studies support these arguments, such as the evaluation research on the learning outcomes of business games of Kriz & Auchter [25] who showed, based on the theory-oriented evaluation approach [26], that perceived facilitation quality through facilitator-guided debriefing has a significant influence on the learning process. However, there was no re search on different debriefing methods in this case. Therefore, in this study, we investigated the effects of self-guided vs. Facilitator-guided debriefing approaches.

2   Method

Participants. The present study included 196 university students from Tokyo, Japan, aged between 19 and 24 years (mean age = 20.65 ± .96 years); there were 105 females and 90 males (1 unknown). The experiments were carried out in two classes, each of which was allocated to one of the two experimental conditions.

Procedure. The procedure was identical under all experimental conditions. First, the participants filled out a questionnaire (hereafter referred to as the pre-test questionnaire), completed the activity for their condition, and were then debriefed either with guidance from a facilitator, or self-debriefed with written guidelines (hereafter referred to facilitator-guided debriefing and self-guided debriefing, respectively). Next, as a test scenario, the participants played the Highway Planning Game in groups of four, and individual and group performances were measured. Finally, the participants filled out another questionnaire (hereafter referred to as the post-test questionnaire). The overall length of the experiment was 90 min, which included the briefing and debriefing procedures (see Table 1).

Experimental Design and Manipulations. We used a between-subject design with two experimental conditions: self-guided debriefing and facilitator-guided debriefing.

Treatments. A Prisoner's Dilemma (PD) game was used as a treatment. The game used was a modified version of the Baregg Tunnel Game [27]. This educational game is concerned with conflict and cooperation and is played in pairs. After each pair played the game for 10 rounds, they joined the debriefing.

Debriefing. The study adopted two styles of debriefing: self-guided and facilitator-guided. Facilitator-guided debriefing involved debriefing guided by facilitators; self-guided debriefing was supported by written guidance, but without facilitators. In the self-guided debriefing condition, pairs of participants discussed the four questions, which were written on an instruction sheet.

The questions given to participants were the same for the two conditions. The four questions were adopted from Thiagarajan's six steps of debriefing [28]. They were: How do you feel?, What happened?, What did you learn? and How does this relate to the real world? In the facilitator-guided debriefing condition, facilitators ask these questions one by one, and the group participants discuss each question for several minutes. In so doing, the facilitators try to record the discussion as much as possible. In contrast, the participants discussed the same questions in the same order, but on their own, in the self-guided debriefing condition.

Seventeen trained students and the third author served as facilitators in the class with the facilitator-guided debriefing conditions. As there were many more pairs than facilitators (56 pairs and 18 facilitators), a facilitator debriefed three to four pairs simultaneously, meaning that there were eight to 10 people in each group for debriefing.

Test-Scenario-Game (*Highway Planning Game*): Groups of four participants played the Highway Planning Game [29], which requires communication, teamwork, cooperation, and conflict. The Highway Planning Game is played by groups of players with different roles (i.e. Archaeologist, Resident, Storekeeper, and City Engineer). Each of the four students in each group assumed one of the roles during the game, the ultimate goal of which was to agree on a common route for a highway that was advantageous for each individual. Each participant received a map featuring hexagons (representing land) and symbols (representing houses, shops, mountains, and cultural and archaeological sites). Each student was required to pay different penalties, according to their assumed role, for building the highway through hexagons with symbols that were more or less important from their particular perspective.

Dependent Variables. We measured two types of dependent variables to evaluate the effects of the games and debriefing. The first type of dependent variable encompassed performance indices, which were calculated according to the number of hexagons that the highway passed through (use of hexagons carried a land penalty), the route used, and the penalties (for destroying objects situated on the land) incurred. The second type of dependent variable encompassed the questionnaires assessing cooperation and leadership, which were completed before and after the activity, i.e. the pre- and post-test questionnaire.

The study also measured learning effects, teamwork behaviour, and satisfaction regarding the results of the game using a 5-point Likert scale ranging from 1 (*strongly disagree*) to 5 (*strongly agree*). Additionally, items assessing playing experience, the experience of the group, and several demographic variables were included in the post-test questionnaire.

Table 1. Summary of the experimental design

Condition	(5) Pre-test- questionnaire	(15) Treatment	(10) Debriefing	(30) Test- scenario game	(5) Post-test- questionnaire
1	Yes	PD Game	Facilitator-guided	Yes	Yes
2	Yes	PD Game	Self-guided with written guidelines	Yes	Yes

Note: Numbers in parentheses indicate time in minutes

3 Results

Regarding the teamwork-related questionnaires, participants in facilitator-guided debriefing conditions agreed with the following statements more: I think we acted more as a team rather than insisting on our own egoistic positions; We established a shared strategy to reach the shared goal. The results of t-test were $t(192) = 2.02$, $p < .05$, $t(191) = 2.18$, $p < .05$, respectively. As to the statement, "I think we were able to play with mutual concessions if necessary," in the facilitator-guided debriefing condition, participants agreed marginally more than those who were in the self-guided debriefing condition ($t = (191) = 1.78$, $.05 < p < .10$).

In contrast, participants under the self-guided debriefing condition agreed more with the following three statements, mainly regarding learning effects: I negotiated hard to win or to gain good results for my role; I think I will be able to transfer the knowledge gained into other group situations; I developed ideas about how to improve my own social competencies for group work. The t-values were $t = (193) = 2.36$, $p < .05$, $t = (190) = 2.40$, $p < .05$, $t = (191) = 2.02$, $p < .05$, respectively. The means and standard deviations in each condition were shown in Table 2.

We conducted an analysis of variance (ANOVA) for the pre- and post-test questionnaires. The measurement times of the questionnaires, i.e. pre- and post-treatment, were treated as within-subject factors. The debriefing condition was treated as a between-subject factor. As a result, we found two statistically significant results for two attitudinal items. Firstly, participants under the self-guided debriefing condition agreed with the statement that, when they work in a team, they trust in their colleagues (see Table 3), more than did those in the facilitator-guided debriefing conditions. Furthermore, there was a marginally significant effect of time of measurement, i.e. before- and after-treatment ($F(1,191) = 3.73$, $.05 < p < .10$). That is, trust slightly decreased after the game. There were also significant differences between experimental groups ($F(1,191) = 3.73$ $p < .05$), meaning that trust was higher in the self-guided debriefing condition than in the facilitator-guided debriefing condition. However, the results of these two debriefing conditions can be attributed to the relatively higher trust of the self-guided debriefing condition before treatment. There was no reason to expect any difference before the experiment, because no treatments had been carried out at that time. Therefore, we conducted an ANOVA of the after-treatment attitudes and two debriefing conditions using the pre-treatment trust as a covariate. The significant effects between the two experimental conditions disappeared, i.e. they were found to be not significant ($F < 1$, $M_{\text{self-guided}} = 3{,}75$, while $M_{\text{facilitator-guided}} = 4{.}01$.).

Table 2. Means and SDs (Standard Deviations) for facilitator-guided and self-guided-debriefing.

	Facilitator-guided		Self-guided	
	M	SD	M	SD
I negotiated hard in order to win or to have a good result for my role	2.77	1.11	3.15	1.14
I think we acted more as a team rather than insisting on own egoistic positions	4.12	0.93	3.83	0.99
We established a shared strategy to reach the shared goal	4.32	0.66	4.08	0.87
I think we were able to play with mutual concessions if necessary	4.18	0.66	4.03	0.82
I think I will be able to transfer gained knowledge into other group situations	3.58	0.87	3.89	0.83
I think I gained ideas how to develop my own social competencies for group work	3.60	0.81	3.84	0.81

Table 3. Means and SDs of trust.

	Facilitator-guided		Self-guided	
	M	SD	M	SD
Pre-test	3.77	0.97	4.24	0.74
Post-test	3.75	0.89	4.01	0.85

Table 4. Means and SDs of preference of the leadership.

	Facilitator-guided		Self-guided	
	M	SD	M	SD
Pre-test	2.98	1.00	3.22	1.06
Post-test	3.22	1.02	3.56	0.97

Secondly, participants under both conditions agreed with the statement, "When I work in a team, and I prefer to take a leadership role over being a follower," (see Table 4), more after playing the game ($F(1,192) = 17.33$ $p < .01$). Furthermore, the main effect of the type of debriefing was also significant ($F(1,192) = 4.78$, $p < .01$). That is, participants of the self-guided debriefing condition agreed more with the statement above than did those of the facilitator-guided debriefing condition.

4 Discussion

In terms of attitudes towards teamwork, participants in the facilitator-guided debriefing believed that they had acted more as a team, rather than insisting on their own egoistic positions. They also perceived that they had established a shared strategy to reach their shared goal. These results revealed that facilitator-guided debriefing could encourage the participants to engage in teamwork. This conclusion was indirectly supported by the fact that participants in facilitator-guided debriefing conditions were able to play with mutual concessions if necessary.

Participants in the self-guided debriefing condition can be characterised by the following two points. First, they seemed more competitive, according to the results of the questionnaire, because they negotiated hard to win or obtain good results for their roles. Secondly, in terms of the learning effects from the game, they believed that they would be able to transfer the knowledge gained to other group situations and that they had developed their ideas about how to improve their own social competencies for group work.

In terms of trust, we did not identify any changes arising due to having played the game, and the debriefing type had no effect. This may be due to the differences in the trust levels of the two experimental conditions before the game. The reason for this is still unclear, although demographic differences between the two classes may be a contributing factor. That is, the self-guided debriefing was carried out by the class studying organisational psychology, while the facilitator-guided debriefing was carried out in the class studying social psychology. The gender distribution also varied. Women were the majority in the facilitator-guided debriefing condition, while men were the majority in the self-guided debriefing condition. Although we do not have decisive evidence to support our contention that the gender or subject major could affect the results, these factors should be considered in future studies.

This study replicated the previous results regarding leadership [19, 21]. That is, students prefer to take leadership roles rather than take the role of being followers after playing the *Highway Planning* game. We also discovered that participants of the self-guided debriefing condition preferred to take leadership roles to a greater extent than did those of the facilitator-guided debriefing condition.

The above differences between the two experimental groups may be interpreted as follows: in the self-guided situation of debriefing students may feel more on their own responsibility and free to discuss what they want. They are less under control to act according to a supervisors or facilitators expectations. In oral facilitator-guided debriefing they may feel more dependent and under control of facilitator's expectations for "right" behaviour due to social group norms and values on teamwork. This could lead to some indirect pressure to behave more team-oriented.

We will discuss the performance data, which we did not include in this paper, in a future study, where we will compare it to data collected from Austrian students.

References

1. Crookall, D.: Serious games, debriefing, and simulation/gaming as a discipline. Simul. Gaming **41**, 898–920 (2010)
2. Lederman, L.C.: Debriefing: toward a systematic assessment of theory and practice. Simul. Gaming **23**, 145–160 (1992)
3. Kriz, W.C.: A systems-oriented constructivism approach to the facilitation and debriefing of simulations and games. Simul. Gaming **41**(5), 663–680 (2010)
4. Kolb, D.A.: Experiential Learning: Experience as the Source of Learning and Development. Prentice Hall, Englewood (1984)
5. Thatcher, D.C.: Promoting learning through games and simulations. Simul. Gaming **21**(3), 262–273 (1990)
6. Klabbers, J.H.G.: The Magic Circle: Principles of Gaming & Simulation. Rotterdam (2009)
7. Peters, V.A.M., Vissers, G.A.N.: A simple classification model for debriefing simulation games. Simul. Gaming **35**(1), 70–84 (2004)
8. Van den Hoogen, J., Lo, J., Meijer, S.: Debriefing research games: context substance and method. Simul. Gaming **47**(3), 368–388 (2016)
9. Stewart, L.P.: Ethical issues in postexperimental and postexperiential debriefing? Simul. Gaming **23**(2), 196–211 (1992)
10. Decker, S., et al.: Standards of best practice: simulation standard VI: the debriefing process. Clin. Simul. Nurs. **9**(6), S26–S29 (2013)
11. Pavlov, O.V., Saeed, K., Robinson, L.W.: Improving instructional simulation with structural debriefing. Simul. Gaming **46**(3–4), 383–403 (2015)
12. Sahakian, G.D., Alinier, G., Savoldelli, G., Oriot, D., Jaffrelot, M., Lecomte, F.: Setting conditions for productive debriefing. Simul. Gaming **46**(2), 197–208 (2015)
13. Tipton, E., Leigh, E., Kriz, W.C., Crookall, D.: Debriefing: the real learning begins when the game stops. In: Kaneda, T., Kanegae, H., Toyoda, Y., Rizzi, P. (eds.) Hybrid Simulation and Gaming in the Networked Society, pp. 1–3. Springer, Singapore (2016)
14. Crookall, D.: Engaging (in) gameplay and (in) debriefing. Simul. Gaming **45**(4–5), 416–427 (2014)
15. Thiagarajan, S.: How to maximize transfer from simulation games through systematic debriefing. In: Percival, F., Lodge, S., Saunders, D. (ed.) The Simulation and Gaming Year-Book 1993, pp. 45–52. Kogan Page, London (1993)
16. Petranek, C.F.: Written debriefing: the next vital step in learning with simulations. Simul. Gaming **31**(1), 108–118 (2000)
17. Clapper, T.C.: Situational interest and instructional design: a guide for simulation facilitators. Simul. Gaming **45**(2), 167–182 (2014)
18. Oertig, M.: Debriefing in Moodle: written feedback on trust and knowledge sharing in a social dilemma game. Simul. Gaming **41**(3), 374–389 (2010)
19 Kikkawa, T., Sugiura, J., Kriz, W.C.: The effects of debriefing on the performance and attitude of Japanese university students. In: Lukosch, H.K., Bekebrede, G., Kortmann, R. (eds.) ISAGA 2017. LNCS, vol. 10825, pp. 173–180. Springer, Cham (2018). https://doi.org/10.1007/978-3-319-91902-7_17
20. Kriz, W.C., Kikkawa, T., Sugiura, J.: The effects of debriefing on attitudes of Japanese university students. In: Proceedings of JASAG National Conference, Tokyo Institute of Technology, 26–27 May, pp. 58–59. Japan Association of Simulation and Gaming (2018)
21. Kikkawa, T., Kriz, W.C., Sugiura, J.: The Effects of Debriefing on the Performance and Attitude of Austrian University Students and Cultural Differences to Japanese Students (2019)

22. Leigh, E., Spindler, L.: Congruent facilitation of simulations and games. In: Shiratori, R., Arai, K., Kato, F. (eds.) Gaming, Simulations, and Society, pp. 189–198. Springer, Tokyo (2005). https://doi.org/10.1007/4-431-26797-2_20
23. Baker, A.C., Jensen, P.J., Kolb, D.A.: In conversation: transforming experience into learning. Simul. Gaming **28**(1), 6–12 (1997)
24. Hofstede, G.J., de Caluwé, L., Peters, V.: Why simulation games work-in search of the active substance: a synthesis. Simul. Gaming **41**(6), 824–843 (2010)
25. Kriz, W.C., Auchter, E.: 10 Years of evaluation research into gaming simulation for German entrepreneurship and a new study on its long-term effects. Simul. Gaming **47**(2), 179–205 (2016)
26. Hense, J., Kriz, W.C., Wolfe, J.: Putting theory oriented evaluation in practice: a logic model approach for the evaluation of Simgame. Simul. Gaming **40**(1), 110–133 (2009)
27. Capaul, R., Ulrich, M.: Planspiele: Simulationsspiele für Unterricht und Training mit Kurztheorie: Simulations- und Planspielmethodik. Tobler Verlag, AG., Altstätten, Switzerland (2003)
28. Thiagarajan, S., Tagliati, T., Richter, M.S., Thiagarajan, R.: Interactive Learning Techniques for Instructorled Training. The Thiagi Group, Inc. (2015)
29. Meadows, D., Seif, A.: Creating High Performance Teams for Sustainable Development: 58 Initiatives. The Institute for Policy and Social Science Research, University of New Hampshire, Durham, NH (1995)

Evaluation of a Pilot Game to Change Civil Servants' Willingness Towards Open Data Policy Making

Fernando Kleiman[1]([⊠]), Marijn Janssen[1], and Sebastiaan Meijer[2]

[1] University of Technology Delft, Jaffalaan, 5, 2628BX Delft, The Netherlands
f.kleiman@tudelft.nl
[2] Royal Institute of Technology, Hälsovägen 11 C, Huddinge, Sweden

Abstract. The adoption of open data policy-making by governments is limited due to different types of constraints. Civil servants are reluctant to open their data to the public for many reasons. The lack of knowledge of benefits that can be produced by the release of data and the overestimation of risks and operational complexity seems to decrease their willingness to support the opening of data. The idea that a serious game intervention can change awareness of participants in different domains is already known. Yet, games are domain dependent and concepts differ per domain. A game has never been used for the emerging domain of open data in which civil servants are operating in a bureaucratic environment having a risk-averse culture and strict institutional rules. A role-playing game prototype was designed for civil servants to experience open data policy-making. This paper analyses its first results aiming at changes of perception for the participants of the game and aims to understand the changes in behavior of civil servants that played it. For some participants, the game influenced their attitude, whereas others were not influenced. Suggesting that different approaches might be necessary for changing the attitude of different groups.

Keywords: Open data · Open government · Game · Design · Quasi-experiment · Survey

1 Introduction

Games can be seen as simulated (safe) environments for human interaction on (multi-variable) complex (wicked) problems that demands creative (participative) solutions from multi-stakeholders [1, 2]. As defined by Duke and Geurts [1]: "game-design is a combination of a disciplined design approach with a mimicry of existing game formats and styles; it is an elusive but real 'art'" (p. 273). A game is also "a communication mode that is capable of linking tacit knowledge to formal knowledge by provoking action and stimulating experience (p. 313). Meijer, Reich [3] uses openness and purpose as concepts to define objectives for the use of games. Games can be used for training, research, policy and design.

It is already known that game interventions can change its participants awareness on different topics [4]. Games are highly context dependent and different context

© Springer Nature Switzerland AG 2021
M. Wardaszko et al. (Eds.): ISAGA 2019, LNCS 11988, pp. 23–34, 2021.
https://doi.org/10.1007/978-3-030-72132-9_3

require games making use of different concepts. Still, it has never been tested with civil servants from governments that can provide governmental data to the public. These civil servants have particular characteristics to which a game intervention is complicated by the bureaucratic environment constrained by risk-averse cultures and norms and rules favoring not to open data [5]. This research focus at developing a game to change the willingness of local government's civil servants towards providing open data.

Governments are releasing more and more data in order to increase participation by the citizens, improve transparency, accountability and in order to deliver better policies [6]. Getting governments to release data implies in changing practices and routines. Many datasets remain closed [7] and civil servants resist to change and adopt open data as practice. Based on the literature [8], the main reasons found to explain the resistance for providing governmental data was listed in order to explore the triggers and incentives to overcome civil servants behavioral barriers for open data policy-making. Lack of knowledge of benefits and overestimation of risks by these professionals are defined as motives to decrease their open data policy-making adoption.

The goal of this paper is to present the evaluation results of the game. In an experimental set-up, a survey was applied before and after the game was played. The outcomes are compared in order to understand the game effects. The present paper aims at evaluating the pilot testing of this game.

2 Background

2.1 Open Government Data

Open Government Data (OGD) is the action by governments to get raw data to be available for manipulation by others [9]. Getting the public to access this data implies in open governmental data policies: "OGD can be used to help the public better understand what the government does and how well it performs, and to hold it accountable for wrongdoing or unachieved results" [10].

Described in Janssen, Charalabidis et. al. [8]: "Open data mends the traditional separation between public organizations and users. The opening of data leads to two important assumptions about government. First, it leads to an assumption of the readiness of public agencies for an opening process which considers influences, discourses and exchanges as constructive, and welcomes opposing views and inputs. Second, it leads to an assumption that government is to give up control, at least to some extent, demanding considerable transformations of the public sector" (p. 258). Achievable benefits for providing open data include reducing red tape burden and repeated demands by making data available, and benefits for society and government having more data used such as increasing economic activity, creating new products and services besides monitoring and control usages [8]. Still, there are barriers to get the data to be available and resistance to share data is common in the public sector.

The lack of knowledge of benefits that might be achieved by the opening of government data, such as increasing transparency and democratic accountability, is referred in the literature as a reason for low engagement in open data policies by civil servants [8, 11, 12]. These professionals themselves might also not be aware of benefits with the optimization of administrative processes or the increase in data sustainability (reducing data loss) by the creation of trustable databases based on combining data (with potential external quality checks of data and validation). The possibility to merge, integrate and mesh public and private data can also generate access to external problem-solving capacity.

On the other hand, Janssen, Charalabidis et. al. [8] also describe a set of constraints to open data policy making to happen and these can be overestimated by civil servants. Resistances can come from issues such as task complexity, when most workers lack the ability to deal with data. The common duplication of data and its availability in various forms makes it difficult to search and browse. There are also legal barriers related to open data. Privacy enhancement mechanisms can play a role in letting civil servants know better the risks and access tools on how to reduce them [13]. Finally, institutional barriers such as the stablished culture that emphasizes barriers and neglects opportunities or the unclear trade-off between public values (transparency vs. Privacy values) are explosive difficulties on the regular risk-averse environment of the public sector (lack of entrepreneurship).

Hardy and Maurushat [14] describes that: "fears of what might be exposed by releasing government information, with public servants reluctant to put decision-making processes down on paper for fear of these being released into the public domain (…) a generational preference amongst public service management for maintaining secrecy of information, whereas younger generations expect that data should be made freely available" (p. 35). Remarkably, while many of the perceptions described may vary from one government to another based on their context, a common group of benefits and barriers to open data policy-making can be defined for game design purposes.

A model was built to explore the variables that could influence civil servants behaviour towards open data [15]. Behavioral Intention (willingness to provide open data) was the main dependent variable defined which was to be influenced by other variables such as Performance Expectancy (benefits of open data) or Effort Expectancy (task complexities and risks). Hence, civil servants tend to decrease their adoption if not ad dressing the benefits that can be achieved providing open government data and overestimating the difficulties to put it into practice. The game intends to change their perception and increase the possibilities of getting government data to be accessible to the public by getting them to experience open data policy-making.

2.2 Game Description

A game was developed based on the list of expected unknown benefits and overestimated barriers to provide open government data [16, 17]. It simulates a public office where civil servants interact to deliver services to citizens. Different operations are performed producing datasets that needs to be managed. Data management options results in obstacles and performance boosters, mimicking the change in benefits and risks of data options in the office.

Different guidelines were referenced for the development of the game [2, 18–26]. First, a group of target behaviors were defined in order to decide the type of game to use. Then, a library of different entertainment game designs was built for the game design options that could work for the defined goal. A mobile digital game with time-management elements was selected. Three different prototypes were built before achieving the actual pilot tested prototype [16].

While developing the digital prototype, testing human behaviour assumptions before designing the digital game was suggested by specialists. Hence, the Role Playing version of the mobile digital project was designed [27, 28]. An specific data labelling activity was added and a new group of datasets with descriptions [29]. The pre-test conducted with PhD researchers (TUDelft) resulted in improving suggestions.

The game was designed to observe civil servants behavioural change when dealing with data management in a simulated office. It creates an environment for experiencing and learning the possibilities of opening data in different situations.

The game is played by four players that needs to role-play different positions in the office. The **Citizen** is the player that starts the processes by demanding services from the office. To do that he demands the **Civil Servant** (through a pre-set of cards with specific activities organized in routines that needs to be fulfilled). The Civil Servant walks across the office to distribute resources and deliver services to the Citizen. She is helped by a **Colleague** that has machines (dices) that produces certain codes for the demands to be delivered. A **Boss** stays in the middle of the office, monitoring the work and authorizing specific types of service deliveries.

Both Civil Servant and Colleague represents the operational workers in public service that needs to implement decisions in order to deliver services. In real life, they follow routines defined in law and the decisions made by the boss. In the game it is assumed that the law sets the task list which is to be executed by citizens demands. Supposedly the Boss has already defined the goal to deliver as many services as possible (maximizing recognition points).

Each round is set by a time-limit (5 min) that was designed to put some pressure on the players. After each round, the Game Master (**Facilitator** – an extra role played outside the "magic circle" [30]) announces the scores and prepares the upcoming week.

Each delivered service generates a dataset that has a sensibility. In between rounds, the players discuss the sensibility of these datasets and suggests how to label them (opened, shared or closed).

The Boss is the one to register a final position for labelling each dataset. Depending the labelling options, new resources or demands are added to the upcoming week. Certain combination of numbers on the machines generates Privacy or Security Crisis. Hence, the players also feel the risk of having data crisis to disturb their work.

The game is played in 5 rounds. It starts with a tutorial round for each player to learn the basic operations of their roles. Players get to switch roles every week, so they can experience different positions in each round.

3   Research Approach: Evaluation of the Game

The game was played using a quasi-experimental setting [31] to test the causal mechanisms for civil servants engagement in open data policies [32, 33]. It was aimed at comparing similar situations before and after the game as well as to understand how different variables affect outcomes for specific reasons [4, 31, 33]. The set-up aimed at providing these conditions to explore the outcomes of the gaming exercise.

The research is being developed based in Brazil which is a 200 million people Federal democracy in South America. Divided in 26 regions that contains 5,570 municipalities, it has the 6th largest area in the world. After a decade of national efforts to support open government policies, the country is ranked 8th in the Open Government Index[1]. Though differences remain between regions and local governments capacities for open data practice. Brazil is also a very unequal country. As the targeted research group is the Brazilian Local Public Service, the game was adjusted and translated to Portuguese.

3.1   The Survey

In order to assess civil servants perceptions, a survey was designed to be applied before and after the game was played. Different sets of questions were formulated in order to address the variables of influence and test their strength. A 7 points Likert scale was used varying from 1 (Strongly Disagree) to 7 (Strongly Agree). Debriefing sessions were conducted after each game play sessions in order to assess qualitative feedback from the participants. The present paper focus on the initial quantitative analysis of outcomes. A more complex data exploration and the discussions for the qualitative feedbacks are to be summarized in other papers.

Out of the 84 questions of the survey, 60 were repeated measures (30 before and 30 after the game was played) and 24 related to moderation variables – such as age, gender, previous experiences with open data and public service for a partial reference on the survey instrument. Three questions specifically addressed whether the civil servants were aware of their actual data provision situation in office, if they were willing to provide in the future and if they predicted if they would need to provide. These three approaches intended to stress different perception of their actual and future engagement in open data policy making.

The survey was applied before the game briefing avoiding to bias the respondents with concepts to be shared in the game explanation. The repeated measurement questions were applied immediately after the game session ended, before the debriefing session (Table 1).

---

[1] https://index.okfn.org/ accessed on March 22nd 2019.

Table 1. Survey questions

Question code (Before/After)	Questions
BI_11 BI_12	I already provide open public sector data in my work
BI_12 BI_22	I intend to provide open public sector data in the future
BI_13 BI_23	I predict that I will provide open public sector data in the future

The debriefing sessions focused on acquiring feedback on the game experience. Participants were invited to share comments and suggestions to improve the game.

3.2 Sample Description

The pilot testing happened in the city of Sao Paulo/Brazil. An invitation was sent by email and WhatsApp for all more than 100 civil servants from the Municipal Innovation and Technology Secretariat (SMIT)[2] and 011Lab[3] team organized the playtest groups. The sessions were developed in the public facility MobiLab, a co-working/incubator maintained by the municipality for start-ups that want to develop solutions for the city's transportation issues.

The 32 enrolled participants were majorly young with almost 40% under 25 years old and another 40% under 35 years old (80% of the total). About 53% were male, almost an equal gender distribution in the sample. In terms of work experience, the group was low experienced with more than 80% declaring less than 5 years' experience in public sector. Most of them (44%) declared to have the role of advisory as their main job and most of them had a permanent job relation to the municipality.

The group presented itself as an experienced sample with more than 80% declaring to have already heard of open data before playing the game and the same amount declared to have already studied the issue (even if just a little). About 47% declared to really already have used open data before (about 90% accused some kind of use).

The group showed some risk-taking attitude. Most of them declared themselves not to feel uncomfortable with sharing personal data in the internet (more than 70%, although they declared being aware of privacy concerns). The group was split between those who would "go against the law for reaching an important goal" but most of them (44%) would never do it. Most of them declared professional stability not to be a goal for their professional career and most of them declared to be excited with the unexpected (87%).

3.3 Methods for Data Analysis

The surveys were applied to the 32 subjects, before and after the playtest sessions. The aim of the experiment was to evaluate whether the game resulted in a change of

---

[2] The researchers thanks the Municipality of Sao Paulo and the SMIT team for their support.
[3] https://011lab.prefeitura.sp.gov.br/.

perception of the participants intentions. Hence, first, matched pair comparisons were conducted on the response of each participants before and after the game. Histograms were then crafted and analysed with paired sample t-tests for the repeated measures [34].

The intended statistical significance could not be reached by the sample. Still findings from the pilot testing were explored to improve the survey and the game. Mainly, the three Behavioral Intention questions were considered as the focus subject to which a deeper analysis needed to be conducted to explore the eventual effects of the game on its changes. Specifically, the analysis of these variables histograms showed a movement on the distributions for the before and after situation that could already inspire reflections for the game and survey improvement.

4   Findings

4.1   Analysis of the Behavioral Intention Change

A first operation of crafting histograms was conducted in order to analyse each of the three Behavioral Intention questions. It was possible to observe a change in their distribution and discuss whether the effects of the game in the sample were to be considered for the next steps of the research.

Already Providing Open Public Sector Data

The first question was related to individuals already providing public sector data in their work - Fig. 1. A clear movement happened in their perception after playing the game. More subjects were aware that they already work with public sector data and that by doing so they do provide it to the public.

It is interesting to observe that the increase of awareness that the civil servants already provide data can be an important game outcome. By being more aware, it is also possible to foster its practice in an active way, knowing better the risks and consequences. Even with a declared experienced (with open data) group, the effect appeared. It is expected that in less open data experienced groups the effects can be even greater.

Intention to Provide Public Sector Data in the Future

As shown in Fig. 2, after playing the game, more individuals were willing to provide more data (only one of them reduced its intention intensity, maybe an effect of awareness to be discussed).

One possible explanation for the resulting effect being weak may be the profile from the sample. As the Secretariat is responsible for fostering data policies in the municipality and most of the participants declared to already know about open data, the base measurement before the game was at a very high register. With other more diverse groups, with less open data knowledge or declared experience, the effects can be greater.

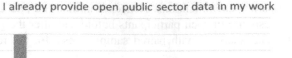

I already provide open public sector data in my work

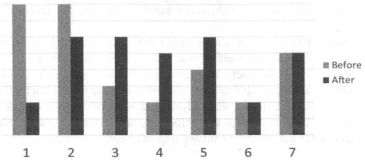

Fig. 1. BI_11 BI_21 (Likert Scale)

I intend to provide open public sector data in the future

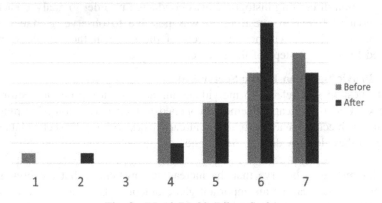

Fig. 2. BI_12 BI_22 (Likert Scale)

Prediction of Open Public Sector Data in the Future

Surprisingly, when predicting if they will provide public sector data - Fig. 3, more individuals were already very optimistic on the issue, making it difficult for the experience to improve their perception. Anyway, a small positive change is noticed towards a greater prediction of open data provision.

4.2 Matched Pair Analyses

The second method used to explore the produced change in Behavioral Intention was to analyse the differences for defined moderators: gender, age and public service previous experience [15].

In general, it came evident that 56% of the participants changed their perspective of being aware of already providing data by playing the game (44% changing positively,

I predict that I will provide open public sector data in the future

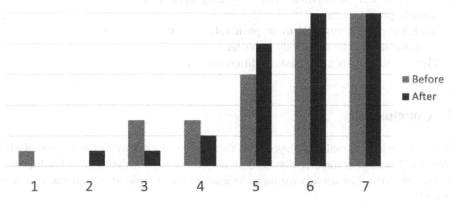

Fig. 3. DI_13 DI_23 (Likert Scale)

declaring to be more aware that they already provide). Gender was not a strong issue for change but the negative change was more impactful in men (9% against 6% for women). Both, absolute, negative and positive were greater on the less experienced civil servants (0 to 5 years in public sector) that lead us to the hypothesis that the less the participant experience, the greater is the potential impact of the game in changing their perception.

Changes promoted by the game in the intention to use open data were equal for positive and negative variations and there has been almost no evidence of gender differences. Younger civil servants also tended to have greater a positive variation (16% compared to 9%) while older participants had a greater negative change (13% compared to 9%). Age analysis shows that younger individuals and less experienced had more positive impact while the older were more negatively impacted.

Half of the participants inflicted in a score change related to their prediction of using open data in the future. The majority (31%) was in a positive direction. In between these positive change, more women changed (22% to men's 9%). Once more, the less experienced civil servants were, the more impacted in both, negative and positive effects. Older civil servants had more positive change whereas in between the younger, the effects were balanced.

4.3 Resulting Propositions from Data Analysis

As a result of the first data analysis from the collected data it is possible to explore some new propositions for further research with the improved versions of the survey and the game. These propositions can help to better define the focus of the research and how to use the designed game in order to explore the resulting knowledge.

1. The game shall fit better for civil servants with limited experience that might lead to higher attitude changes

2. Unexperienced civil servants tend to be more positively impacted by the game whereas it tends to have a negative impact in more experienced civil servants
3. The game has an important role in getting civil servants to be aware that they already provide data
4. Younger participants tend to be positively affected by the game while older participants tend to be negatively impacted
5. Gender doesn't seems to make a difference for the game.

5   Conclusions

The game was successfully played and surveys completed by the 8 groups of civil servants. The most common reaction when debriefing was for the game to last longer as it stopped when they usually managed to learn properly how to operate the resources (round 5).

From the data analysis, the most interesting outcome was to confirm the effect that the game increases awareness, even in a bureaucratic environment such as the public service. The awareness increase higher than the willingness change might have been caused by the sample bias of civil servants with previous experience with open data. As the group had prevailing high scores for the before the game Behavioral Intention questions, little room was left for improvement.

It will be important to test the game with more experienced civil servants. The bias from the group with a prevailing maximum of 5 years' experience seemed to show greater impact on people less influenced by stronger governmental routines.

For next rounds, it is already clear the need to include more direct questions related to the effects of the game. The post gameplay survey needs to assess more clearly if people felt effects of the game and if they declare to feel a different perception than they had before playing.

The game is still to show impacts for Behavioral Intention on broader and more diverse public. The outcomes of the exercise will improve the game and survey for the upcoming sessions.

References

1. Duke, R.D., Geurts, J.: Policy Games for Strategic Management. Rozenberg Publishers (2004)
2. McGonigal, J.: Reality is Broken: Why Games Make Us Better and How They can Change the World. Penguin (2011)
3. Meijer, S., Reich, Y., Subrahmanian, E.: The future of gaming for design of complex systems. Back to the Future of Gaming, pp. 154–167 (2014)
4. Kirriemuir, J., McFarlane, A.: Literature review in games and learning (2004). FUTURELAB: https://lchc.ucsd.edu/tclearninglounge/ROOT/Camille/readings/kirriemuir_lit%20on%20games.pdf. Accessed 10 Mar 2021
5. Bozeman, B., Kingsley, G.: Risk culture in public and private organizations. Public Administration Review, pp. 109–118 (1998)

6. Bertot, J.C., McDermott, P., Smith, T.: Measurement of open government: metrics and process. In: 2012 45th Hawaii International Conference on System Science (HICSS). IEEE (2012)
7. McDermott, P.: Building open government. Gov. Inf. Q. **27**(4), 401–413 (2010). https://doi.org/10.1016/j.giq.2010.07.002
8. Janssen, M., Charalabidis, Y., Zuiderwijk, A.: Benefits, adoption barriers and myths of open data and open government. Inf. Syst. Manag. **29**(4), 258–268 (2012)
9. Matheus, R., Ribeiro, M.M., Vaz, J.C.: Brazil towards government 2.0: strategies for adopting open government data in national and subnational governments. In: Boughzala, I., Janssen, M., Assar, S. (eds.) Case Studies in e-Government 2.0, pp. 121–138. Springer, Cham (2015). https://doi.org/10.1007/978-3-319-08081-9_8
10. Ubaldi, B.: Open government data: Towards empirical analysis of open government data initiatives. OECD Working Papers on Public Governance (22), p. 0_1 (2013)
11. Ed Parkes, T.K.-L., Wells, P., Hardinges, J., Vasileva, R.: Using open data to deliver public services (2018). https://theodi.org/article/using-open-data-for-public-services-report-2/. Accessed 05 Mar 2018
12. Attard, J., Orlandi, F., Scerri, S., Auer, S.: A systematic review of open government data initiatives. Gov. Inf. Q. **32**(4), 399–418 (2015). https://doi.org/10.1016/j.giq.2015.07.006
13. Luthfi, A., Janssen, M.: A conceptual model of decision-making support for opening data. In: Katsikas, S.K., Zorkadis, V. (eds.) e-Democracy 2017. CCIS, vol. 792, pp. 95–105. Springer, Cham (2017). https://doi.org/10.1007/978-3-319-71117-1_7
14. Hardy, K., Maurushat, A.: Opening up government data for Big Data analysis and public benefit. Comput. Law Secur. Rev. **33**(1), 30–37 (2017). https://doi.org/10.1016/j.clsr.2016.11.003
15. Zuiderwijk, A., Janssen, M., Dwivedi, Y.K.: Acceptance and use predictors of open data technologies: drawing upon the unified theory of acceptance and use of technology. Gov. Inf. Q. **32**(4), 429–440 (2015)
16. Kleiman, F., Janssen, M.: Gaming to improve public policies by engaging local governments in open data policy-making. In: Proceedings of the 19th Annual International Conference on Digital Government Research: Governance in the Data Age. ACM (2018)
17. Kleiman, F., Janssen, M., Meijer, S.: Serious gaming for developing open government data policies by local governments. In: Proceedings of the 11th International Conference on Theory and Practice of Electronic Governance. ACM (2018)
18. Almeida, M.S.O., da Silva, F.S.C.: A systematic review of game design methods and tools. In: Anacleto, J.C., Clua, E.W.G., da Silva, F.S.C., Fels, S., Yang, H.S. (eds.) ICEC 2013. LNCS, vol. 8215, pp. 17–29. Springer, Heidelberg (2013). https://doi.org/10.1007/978-3-642-41106-9_3
19. Bunchball, I.: Gamification 101: an introduction to the use of game dynamics to influence behavior. White paper, p. 9 (2010)
20. Chou, Y.-K.: Actionable gamification: beyond points, badges, and leaderboards. Octalysis Group (2016)
21. Fullerton, T.: Game Design Workshop: A Playcentric Approach to Creating Innovative Games. CRC Press (2014)
22. Greenblat, C.S.: Gaming-Simulation–Rationale, Design, and Applications: A Text with Parallel Readings for Social Scientists, Educators, and Community Workers. Wiley (1975)
23. Harteveld, C.: Triadic Game Design: Balancing Reality. Meaning and Play. Springer, Heidelberg (2011). https://doi.org/10.1007/978-1-84996-157-8
24. Salen, K., Zimmerman, E.: Rules of Play: Game Design Fundamentals. MIT Press (2004)
25. Werbach, K., Hunter, D.: The Gamification Toolkit: Dynamics, Mechanics, and Components for the Win. Wharton Digital Press (2015)

26. Walz, S.P., Deterding, S.: The Gameful World: Approaches, Issues, Applications. MIT Press (2015)
27. Meijer, S.: The power of sponges: comparing high-tech and low-tech gaming for innovation. Simul. Gaming **46**(5), 512–535 (2015). https://doi.org/10.1177/1046878115594520
28. Deen, M.: GAME games autonomy motivation & education: how autonomy-supportive game design may improve motivation to learn (2015)
29. Cordova, Y.: Indigenous communities and cloud-based Nations (2018). SSRN 3247287
30. Klabbers, J.: The Magic Circle. Sense Publishers Rotterdam (2006)
31. Shadish, W.R., Cook, T.D., Campbell, D.T.: Experimental and Quasi-Experimental Designs for Generalized Causal Inference. Houghton Mifflin Boston (2002)
32. Johansson, U., Woodilla, J.: Towards an epistemological merger of design thinking, strategy and innovation. In: 8th European Academy of Design Conference (2009)
33. Bichler, M.: Design science in information systems research. Wirtschaftsinformatik **48**(2), 133–135 (2006). https://doi.org/10.1007/s11576-006-0028-8
34. Field, A.: Discovering Statistics Using IBM SPSS Statistics. Sage (2013)

Structuring Game Design with Active Learning Benefits: Insights from Logistical Skills Training in Managing an Emergency Department

Cevin Zhang[1](✉) ⓘ, Karin Pukk Härenstam[2] ⓘ, Jonas Nordquist[3,4],
and Sebastiaan Meijer[1] ⓘ

[1] Division Logistics and Informatics, Royal Institute of Technology,
14157 Huddinge, Sweden
chenzh@kth.se
[2] Pediatric Emergency Department, Karolinska University Hospital,
14157 Huddinge, Sweden
[3] Department of Learning, Informatics, Management and Ethics,
Karolinska Institute, 17177 Stockholm, Sweden
[4] Department of Medicine, Karolinska Institute, 14157 Huddinge, Sweden

Abstract. Competency is central to a sustainable and resilient emergency department. Decision-makers, including clinicians, managers, and developers, would benefit from meaningful simulated scenarios in which their skills are trained. Among the various types of skills, non-technical skills are prioritized because the failure to communicate, coordinate and cooperate effectively are common contributing factors to adverse events and involving patients at the 'sharp-end' of the health system. For active learning of non-technical skills, simulation and gaming have been frequently used. From the methodology point of view, there is a need to clarify these two methods in order to improve their value in training and learning. This contribution presents the reflective methodology as an option of structuring game design compared to the mainstream service system modeling. The reflective methodology starts with the underlying assumption that it is still possible to achieve gaming effectiveness, even though the baseline layer is a simulation model instead of the service system. Based on a questionnaire investigating the activation of learning of logistical skills in managing an emergency department, results are illustrative of that active learning is much improved and is moving closer to achieving intended outcomes. Analyzing results from logistical experiments in the form of a statistical summary motivates to explore the middle ground of game design and gamification further, especially when the simulation model is the steering layer in scenario generations and debriefing. This aspect might have been less supervised in the philosophy of game science, let alone the application of simulation game for human resource management in emergency department logistics.

Keywords: Gaming · Simulation · Methodology · Logistical experiments

© Springer Nature Switzerland AG 2021
M. Wardaszko et al. (Eds.): ISAGA 2019, LNCS 11988, pp. 35–49, 2021.
https://doi.org/10.1007/978-3-030-72132-9_4

The health-related SDGs will not be achieved unless the global shortfall of 18 million health workers by 2030 is averted [1].

1 Introduction

Computer and board games are widely known and played for gaining entertainment. Examples are Monopoly, Warcraft, League of Legends, and Player Unknown's Battle Grounds that have become phenomenal digital games. That said, analog games are one of the most classic setups to discuss strategies and planning [2] and are continuously supported in modern multimodal technologies. Simulation and gaming are and more seen in a multimodal form where both board games and digitalization of industrial value chains can play a role in the understanding of systems, organizations, and complexity [3].

Simulation games hold a unique identity because they are a type of instrument that is crafted with dedicated purposes and functions and is built on the ground of being useful. Plays in simulation games are described as serious, which integrate 'an explicit and carefully thought-out educational purpose' [4]. For effective teamwork and coordination, simulation games demonstrate potentials for connecting cross-functional teams and for creating exact scenarios in which learning and understanding can activate. Meanwhile, behavioral aspects in the simulated environment can be explored and studied to exert influences on the reference system. Such kind of simulation games must follow a life-cycle like development and implementation in organizational studies, including game design [5], activation of learning, problem-solving, (meta-) debriefing, workplace-based analysis, and evaluation of the outcomes. Therefore simulation games design and gamification can be more challenging from the one for video games.

Simulation-based training is a powerful tool to grow competencies for safety engineering in hospitals, Sweden [6] and worldwide. Skills, knowledge, and attitudes are the abilities and characteristics that enable a job holder to accomplish the activities described in a task statement that explains what the job holder does [7]. According to the OECD, skills, classified as job-specific or generic/transversal, are generally a combination of ability, capacity, and knowledge acquired through deliberate, systematic, and sustained efforts to carry out complex tasks or jobs [8]. For improving medicine delivery, both management and non-technical skills are identified by EIT Health as essential but yet undeveloped areas of competencies [9]. Therefore, both faculty development and future workforces need training where simulation games can be central to providing collective learning experiences.

Game design is a fundamental problem for developing simulation games for job-oriented training. It is well-known that service systems are the baseline for simulation and gaming. However, in such a method, we have to rely on details for not under approaching reality. A new way of structuring game design is that the game is developed based on a simulation model.

This contribution compares two methods of the game based on the results of the Health Logistics Game. It explores whether or not applying the features of the simulation model could help participants activate learning on the indented outcomes as the game principal expects. Section 2 elaborates on the available gaming theories in which the *adopt* theory is suitable for guiding simulation game design that handles contemporary business management. Section 3 explains game design inclusive of how the game is played, debriefed, and evaluated, followed by Sect. 4 and Sect. 5 that discusses the statistics and correlation results based on the post-game user survey.

2 Simulation Game Theory

Computer simulations are in place for creating escapist immersion, triggering psychological state changes, and approaching reality. One of the theoretical tasks to validate the simulation side and the game side is a decent direction, provided that the logics could be different. The *adopt* theory is a conceptual framing of using simulation games in logistics [10]. This theoretical framework highlights that for better usage of simulation games to improve performances on safety and quality operations, the game shall be designed to encourage proactive planning, action and attitude out of the player, as Fig. 1 presents. Since gaming is the environment for learning and transfer, another big issue is the transfer between game and reality. As pointed out by Raghothama and Meijer, design should inherit a methodological rigor when any reference systems is being modeled [11]. The big issue in competency development is how predictable the performance on one level is for the performance on the next, documented in Miller's pyramid where simulations play a role equalling to the "show how" level [12]. This connection of performance in games and performance in reality needs to be explored with especially the Kolb's four-stage learning cycle [13]: from the active experimentation where ideas and strategies apply towards the concrete experimentation over a duration of time in the service system.

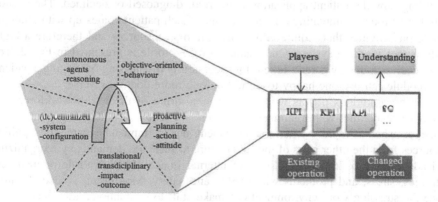

Fig. 1. *Adopt* simulation game theory, based on [10]

This contribution introduces a gaming methodology with a new way of structuring the design and debriefing to encourage knowledge transfer between the game and the simulation model. This differs from formalized reflection [14], but inspired by the mixed methods approach [15], given that the strengths of simulation and gaming can be clear and combined. It is applied in a game for training human resource and patient flow management in an emergency unit. The possibility of positioning the simulation model as the steering layer thoroughly is evaluated to answer the following investigative research question:

- How can structuring game design benefit from using a simulation model as the steering layer?

3 Game Design

3.1 What is Being Simulated

The gamified environment is a simulation model of a standard emergency department (ED), controlled by the Manchester Triage System which dedicates to ED organizational design in countries of Germany, Sweden, Norway, Netherlands, Austria and many others [16]. This simulated organization is a pediatric emergency department seeing a full range of patients from newborn to 18-year-old. The system is working towards the same capacity at all modules; during the daytime, the doctors can see both medical and orthopedic patients.

The game requires participation from 4 responsible teams mandating four modules, and one individual management nurse mandating the triage place in the ED. A team is formed by a leading doctor and an assistant management nurse that takes care of the competencies in their module. The module is assigned a couple of doctors and three nurses.

The ED receives predefined incoming patients into the triage place, and collective decisions need to be made by the module responsible person and the triage nurse regarding how the patient application is referred, diagnosed or declined. The session lasts for 12 rounds simulating 6 hours real time. Each patient comes up with a unique profile on activities that require allocation of human resources and therefore a high-performance working system. One example of the profile is presented in Fig. 2. The team receives a 'happy parents token' for successfully discharging or triaging a patient. The module can use one happy token to hire one more doctor or nurse.

The preconditions of this work are the monitoring of the health workforce performance, sometimes within minutes when there are surges of inflow of patients to the triage or when a rapidly deteriorating patient needs immediate care, thus pulling resources from the other parts of the ED. Failure to meet the demands by reorganizing and adapting work leads to build up of internal queues for diagnostic or treatment activities, stress, and problems with quality and safety. Monitoring is also impaired since the stressing work environment can make staff lose situational awareness.

In order to create the model of the described system, the Health Logistics Game was designed (see Fig. 2 and Fig. 3). The development was based on a series of tests with users and the simulation model. It was tested using observations of game participation, summaries of gaming experiences, and outcomes in the form of subjective evaluation.

According to Klabbers [17], rather than falling into absolute high-context or low-context games, this multiplayer analog game could be in a medium-context, because it provides well-defined game course; but more importantly, it improves player's tactic skills in a dynamic working environment that could be hard to codify.

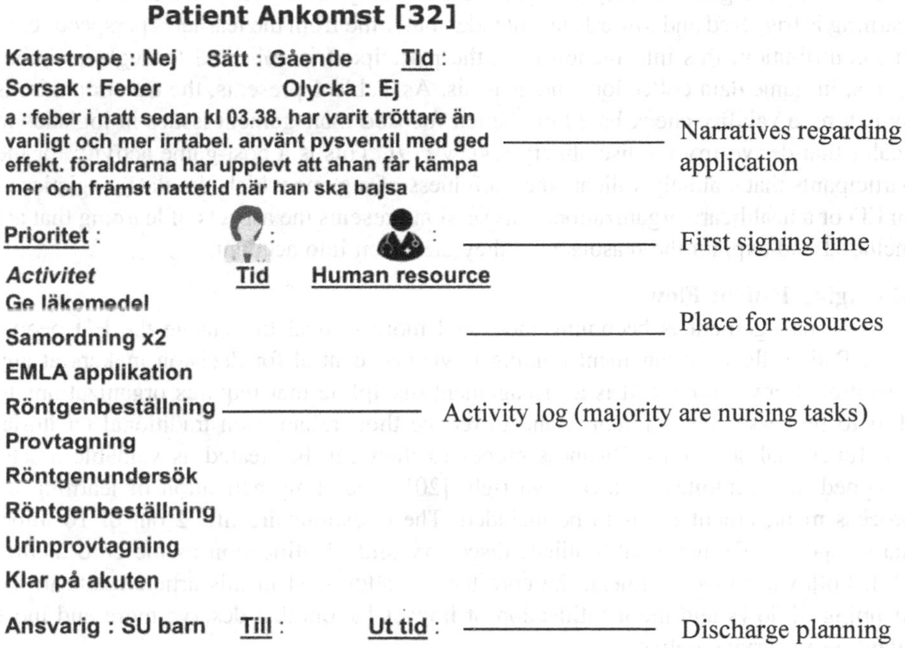

Patient Ankomst [32]
Katastrope : Nej
Sätt : Gående
Tid :
Sorsak : Feber
Olycka : Ej
a : feber i natt sedan kl 03.38. har varit tröttare än vanligt och mer irrtabel. använt pysventil med ged effekt. föraldrarna har upplevt att ahan får kämpa mer och främst nattetid när han ska bajsa
Narratives regarding application
Prioritet :
First signing time
Activitet
Tid
Human resource
Ge läkemedel
Samordning x2
Place for resources
EMLA applikation
Röntgenbeställning
Activity log (majority are nursing tasks)
Provtagning
Röntgenundersök
Röntgenbeställning
Urinprovtagning
Klar på akuten
Ansvarig : SU barn
Till :
Ut tid :
Discharge planning

Fig. 2. Logistical gaming suite: incoming patients

Logistical game for emergency department
Radiology dept
Biology dept
Round Tracker
1
2
3
4
5
6
7
8
9
10
11
12
Discharged
Incoming Flow
Obs area
Obs 1
Obs 2
Obs 3
Obs 4
väntrum
ICU
röd/rosa modules

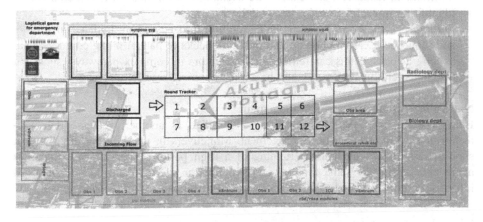

Fig. 3. Logistics Game suite for the emergency department

3.2 Intended Outcomes

The primary intended outcome is for participants to get familiar with the work of human resource and patient flow management in ED logistics. The best condition for doing this is through active learning. Active learning is a form of learning in which students are actively or experientially involved in the learning process and where there are different levels [18]. The game principal might want a reality check on whether or not active learning is triggered and towards the intended outcome from the learner's perspective. In this contribution, this information from the participant is collected through questionnaires, in-game data collection, and analysis. As Table 1 presents, the questionnaire is by nature, a validity check based on the ten focused management issues in logistics in health that derive from a disciplinary review [19]. This is a post-game activity for the participants that can help validate the usefulness of a game which simulates logistics in an ED or a healthcare organization. This session presents the aspects of learning that are included and explain the reasons why they are taken into account.

Managing Patient Flow
Process management is becoming more and more critical to manage the ED people flow. Patient flow management training is viewed central for decision makers at any operational environment. It is a management discipline that requires organizations to shift to process-centric thinking, and to reduce their reliance on traditional territorial and functional structures. Business processes then can be treated as valuable assets, designed and exploited in their own right [20]. Therefore, activation of learning on process management needs to be included. The questionnaire lifts 2 out of 10 information points. Dumas et al. outlines discovery and identification as the core themes [21]. Following this argument, the core themes addressed in this article relate to the mapping of flows and the identification of impact factors that deserve more and more attention in service delivery.

- Mapping information, resources and entities flow in the healthcare organization
  Mapping is a modeling practice. The ability of mapping flows serves as a basis of process analysis and redesign. The participants should start to understand how information, resources, and entities are exchanged with medical considerations.
- Identifying impact factors in service delivery
  ED logistics can be involved in which multiple procedures are initiated in parallel and sequence. Learning how to find the bottlenecks of patient piling could be ideal as long as participants can retrieve impact factors in complex pathways, such that flow intervention strategies could be explored.

Nature of Human Resource Management
Being able to exert tactical leadership is identified as another, yet essential, non-technical skill in ED logistics management. Maneuvers in the working environment should be trained such that the running of a high performance working system is achievable within the same capacity as possible. The questionnaire has 3 out of 10 information points related to the active learning of human resource management.

- Being influential in workload management
  The sustainable working environment is beneficial, not least to the staff. The workload might become an issue on quality in case that stressful situations spread. The timeline and activity line can be versatile to all the staff categories, see Fig. 4. Managing the workload of multipurpose ED staff is a logistical skill for preventing possible workflow problems.

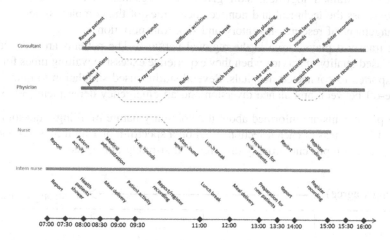

Fig. 4. Timeline and activity for working categories, based on [22]

- Cooperation in a networked society
  Being in a multilogue and the inter-professional situation is evident in all logistics systems. Organizational behaviors of members should be oriented to cooperation. Therefore, cooperation is another essential logistical skill to balance decisions among the actors and agencies.
- Negotiation and balancing at the individual level
  Negotiation and balancing in a point-to-point fashion that needs to be trained in patient-centered care. This practice is intense on the making between the service sender and receiver (patient). Since the patient would always supply a unique profile, whereas the doctor or nurse can be working with many patients at the same time, a logistical skill is needed here for the staff to strengthen the individual cohesion.

Ambient Factors
- Organize interior working environment
  The management of territorial spaces and ambiances poses a longstanding impact on the operation, satisfaction, and productivity [23]-inappropriate management might lead to unexpected human resource outcomes such as absenteeism and intention of leaving an organization [24]. The built environment issue in medicine administration might now become broader and more profound. World Healthcare Organization reports that the lack of healthcare capacity because of inadequate infrastructure for residents is an observatory and should be prevented [25]. Therefore, the ability to organize devices and interior working environment in the

broader infrastructure scope rises to be a logistical skill that is worthwhile to master if the benefit is shorten the proximity of communication between workers.

- Apply system thinking in health logistics design and management
  System improvement can be an output to reduce waiting time, lead time, or crowding. Supplying system improvement and implementing real changes are extensively researched by simulation studies, see [26–29]. System thinking is a must-to-be-trained logistical skill given that organizational boundaries trespass more across the technical and non-technical sides of the complex system.
- Management of resource inventory and sick transportation
  Sick transport plays a role in the regional network. The patients are subjective to decreased quality of service when they experience excessive waiting times for being transported to connected hospitals. Several studies used simulation to quantify the trade-off between ambulance diversion and an emergency department [30, 31].

The participants are informed about the voluntary nature of filling a questionnaire. The comfortableness of each selection is put on a spectrum of 1 until 5, where the ends of the spectrum represent strongly disagree and strongly agree, see Fig. 5.

Fig. 5. Likert scale for agreement

Table 1. Post-game user survey

Information point	Reference of agreement	ID
The game activates the player to map information, resources and entities flows in an organization	Likert scale	1
The game activates the player to identify impact factors in service procedures	Likert scale	2
The game activates the player to decision supporting of workload management	Likert scale	3
The game activates the player to understand cooperation in the networked society	Likert scale	4
The game activates the player to facilitate the negotiation and balancing between a service sender and the receiver	Likert scale	5
The game activates the player to design and select infrastructures to facilitate the management	Likert scale	6
The game activates the player to provide system improvement recommendations	Likert scale	7
The game activates the player to get acquainted with system design & management	Likert scale	8
The game activates the player to explore resources inventory or replacement policies	Likert scale	9
The game activates the player to know transport's spatial and temporal consequences	Likert scale	10

3.3 Debriefing

Debriefing is the phase where real learning triggers. The value of a simulation game or a logistical experiment based on simulation games mostly relies on this collaborative discussion and reflection. Debriefing is defined as 'the process in which people have had experience are led through a purposive discussion of that experience' [32]. Kriz outlined the phases in debriefing, encouraging the player to voice out the feeling of the game, explain what has happened and the connection with reality, think about the learning and future action plans [33]. Frameworks or debriefing models have been crafted to enable reflection between reality and the gamified environment [34, 35]. The connection between reality and the game is a precondition for meaningful indications for most organizational behavior, learning and management studies. In this contribution, we challenge this underlying assumption by encouraging the reflection between the game and simulation, shifting one layer away from the service system. This debriefing model is performed only in the experimental group. An overview of how the logistical experiments are performed is provided in Table 2.

3.4 Evaluation

Data for the evaluation of simulation gaming is collected from multiple sources of observation, in-game player behaviors, gaming outcomes, and survey. Performing this structure has twofold benefits: 1) providing the principal an opportunity to tailor the questionnaire and 2) reducing the risk of misanalysis for working with ED management leaders and content holders. Active learning is considered as a precondition for developing any training game in-complete, in case that there are uncertainties about what skills should be trained.

Table 2. Implemented debriefing models

Control group	Experimental group
1. The simulation model is hidden, and gamers are not aware of its existing	1. Via URL or standalone, the simulation model is accessible by gamers
2. The facilitator explains that the game is based on emergency department operation experiences	2. The facilitator explains that the game is based on the simulation model just presented
3. The facilitator elaborates on the convergence/divergence of what happened in the game with the one of ED	3. The facilitator elaborates on the convergence/divergence of what happened in the game compared to the one of the ED simulation
4. Open discussion	4. Open discussion

Sixty and above would be an excellent sampling size to seek for graduate students with management, social science, or engineering backgrounds. The confirmation of the sample size is in line with previous papers. Using board games, Huyakorn et al. met seventy residents and concluded positively on community capacity of accepting new cultural aspects [36]. Regarding the processing and interpretation of results, the method that has been followed for evaluation is Nakaruma framing with factor correlation analysis and statistical tests ($p < .01$) [37], which has shown a trendy formal analysis of gaming data in training situations of logistics, production, and service delivery [38, 39].

Questionnaires that are distributed will document on papers or digital protocols depending on the player's preference. Photographing applies in documenting the logistical experiment progress. In order to understand what gamers think, there is a need to coordinate workshops where the student group of various backgrounds can voluntarily participate in the early innovation phase of this two-stage game. The surveys are tailored not to infringe privacy.

4   Results

Eighty one graduate students from the Royal Institute of Technology (KTH) were able to voluntarily participate in the gaming workshops, as Fig. 6 illustrates. After roughly 5 out of the 12 rounds, the players established the willing of cooperation. The participants rarely encountered difficulties in navigating the logistical game suite and in understanding the questionnaire. The only questioned information point was about the meaning of inventory management. The facilitator replied that inventory management was more on the dispatching of non-capitalized health commodities in supply chain management. The survey aims for a statistical significance by following up with a hypothesis testing ($p < .01$) between the groups. A correlation analysis investigates the casual relationships of information points surveyed.

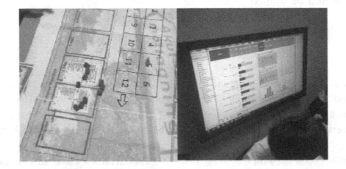

Fig. 6. Logistics Game in action (student group at KTH)

It is highly motivating that the questionnaire received 77 complete replies from 80 participants. The participants mainly came from an education background on the graduate level and from curriculum connected to engineering sciences. ED logistics management is a new area for the majority.

The averages and standard deviations of reply scores can be found in Table 3. The results show that active learning on the aspects of and business process and human resource management are higher regardless of the kind of logistical experiment performed. In a group sense, participants showed at least an 'agree' whereas any other aspects can vary between 'agree' and 'neutral' in the basic scenario.

Table 3. Survey result

Question ID	Control group (N = 39)		Experimental group (N = 38)		t-test	
	Mean	Standard deviation	Mean	Standard deviation	t-value	(p < .01)
1	4,28	0,31	4,55	0,25	−2,23	
2	4,26	0,30	4,61	0,25	−2,93	(**)
3	4,13	0,33	4,76	0,24	−5,25	(**)
4	3,95	0,31	4,26	0,36	−2,37	
5	4,15	0,24	4,32	0,44	−1,22	
6	4,15	0,40	4,74	0,25	−4,49	(**)
7	3,82	0,52	4,16	0,57	−2,01	
8	3,67	0,39	4,13	0,50	−3,07	(**)
9	3,85	0,77	4,00	0,49	−0,85	
10	4,15	0,24	4,73	0,20	−5,35	(**)

The activation of learning for mapping flows in the ED organization also receives a plausible score (Mean = 4,28 out of 5). In multimodal technology scenario, the score could be improved to 4,55 but without a statistical significance. It is evident that more skills in identifying service bottlenecks score high, especially in multimodal technology scenario (mean = 4,61 out of 5). Information points with lower scores (Mean = 4,0 or lower) are to the training in resource inventory and transport management.

In the board-gaming-only experiment, how the game performed illustrated some contradiction towards the principal's initial constructive alignment of the game (see Table 4), since the information points of Q4 and Q5 should have received a positive correlation score. In the multimodal technology scenario, however, unexpected scores are eliminated, and a positive correlation for metrics improves to be the majority.

Table 4. Correlation metrics (top: control group; bot: experimental group; red: non-positive value; green: positive value; yellow: positive value but larger than 0,5)

	Q1	Q2	Q3	Q4	Q5	Q6	Q7	Q8	Q9	Q10
Q1	1,00									
Q2	0,44	1,00								
Q3	0,46	0,23	1,00							
Q4	0,13	-0,04	0,19	1,00						
Q5	0,41	0,34	0,31	-0,07	1,00					
Q6	0,69	0,42	0,38	0,10	0,26	1,00				
Q7	0,32	0,32	0,12	0,11	0,30	0,47	1,00			
Q8	-0,03	0,26	0,05	0,33	0,00	0,07	0,16	1,00		
Q9	0,36	0,52	-0,01	0,09	0,12	0,38	0,21	0,44	1,00	
Q10	0,41	0,34	0,40	-0,07	0,34	0,52	0,45	0,17	0,43	1,00

	Q1	Q2	Q3	Q4	Q5	Q6	Q7	Q8	Q9	Q10
Q1	1,00									
Q2	0,28	1,00								
Q3	0,51	0,36	1,00							
Q4	0,48	0,41	0,14	1,00						
Q5	0,44	0,45	0,38	0,46	1,00					
Q6	0,27	0,44	0,44	0,29	0,48	1,00				
Q7	0,32	0,50	0,13	0,63	0,47	0,46	1,00			
Q8	0,42	0,44	0,24	0,57	0,52	0,42	0,54	1,00		
Q9	0,48	0,38	0,28	0,60	0,45	0,30	0,50	0,69	1,00	
Q10	0,39	0,38	0,57	0,31	0,31	0,54	0,31	0,38	0,46	1,00

5 Discussion and Conclusion

This study supplies evidence that the active learning on intended outcomes is positively affected when the computer and the board are connected for experiential learning and debriefing. This is done by plugging the computer simulation model as the steering layer in game design. We suggest such a new way of structuring game design by highlighting how a simulation model can improve the learning value of the game. An evidence is delivered on improved activation of learning on patient flow management, interior working environment management, workload management, and system design management.

It is worthwhile to note that the simulation model is developed with discrete-event simulation as the living environment of agents. The discrete-event simulation is primarily organizational flow charts that direct entities to the different places of the system. The participants admit that their interpretation of their behaviors in the artificial organization is supported after the background of the game is understood better. This message from gaming outcomes illustrates that participants with limited knowledge in logistics and non-technical skills can still approach the intended learning outcomes fast by such form of game design and organizing.

A possible explanation for not having a statistical significance among several information points is that the flowcharts directly affect the logistical flows of each ED module, therefore are influencing participant decision makings in the baseline scenario already. Moreover, the board game is not dedicated to providing an exact presentation of any transport network or parameters needed in a material supply chain.

The main output of this contribution is the reflective methodology pyramid where the foci of the gaming layer are the reflection of roles, as Table 5 presents. The closed part is for the learning aspect, requiring high-fidelity simulations. The open part is for principals to learn how the participants perceive their jobs. It is a pyramid where the game principal can continually add certain aspects. On the top layer, the game part is an enabler of how people think about their roles, which is impossible to simulate in computers. Different levels of validities and fidelities can, therefore, be evaluated by analyzing the outcome of playing.

A reservation of the pyramid is that gamification of the ED or health system is aiming everything but entertainment. Patient care is a serious topic that required sympathy, mutual considerations, and emotion management, particularly in escalating situations. Although the serious games are based on gamification of a hands-on problem-solving, the practice of simulation game sessions shall prioritize intended learning outcomes for the organization instead of the playfulness for participants. This is the reason that simulation-based training and courses are more frequently used as the interface names in institutional learning and teaching situations.

Table 5. Data-simulation-game triad for training game design

Actors → Game → Agency/roles	
Replicator of flexibility and social interactions that can not be simulated/represented by formal models in computers	↑
Modelling → Simulation → Scenarios	
1. Putting strategies/gamification mechanisms in a spreadsheet 2. Multi-method simulation model construction 3. Visualization, analysis and system evaluation	Validation
Machine learning → Data → Predictions	↓
Mechanical engineering details: Service time, intervals and shifts	

References

1. WHO | Framing the health workforce agenda for the Sustainable Development Goals. https://www.who.int/hrh/resources/bienium-report_16-17/en/. Accessed 30 Mar 2019

2. Masukawa, K.: The origins of board games and ancient game boards. In: Kaneda, T., Kanegae, H., Toyoda, Y., Rizzi, P. (eds.) Simulation and Gaming in the Network Society. TSS, vol. 9, pp. 3–11. Springer, Singapore (2016). https://doi.org/10.1007/978-981-10-0575-6_1

3. Stephens, R., Kaneda, T.: Urban planning games and simulations: from board games to artificial environments. In: Kaneda, T., Kanegae, H., Toyoda, Y., Rizzi, P. (eds.) Simulation and Gaming in the Network Society, pp. 253–273. Springer Singapore, Singapore (2016). https://doi.org/10.1007/978-981-10-0575-6_19

4. Abt, C.C.: Serious Games. University Press of America (1987)

5. van den Hoogen, J., Meijer, S.: Gaming and simulation for railway innovation: a case study of the Dutch railway system. Simul. Gaming 46(5), 489–511 (2015)

6. Hagiwara, M.A., Backlund, P., Söderholm, H.M., Lundberg, L., Lebram, M., Engström, H.: Measuring participants' immersion in healthcare simulation: the development of an instrument. Adv. Simul. 1(1) (2016)

7. Quinones, M.A., Ehrenstein, A. (eds.): Training for a Rapidly Changing Workplace: Applications of Psychological Research, 1st edn. Amer Psychological Assn, Washington, DC (1996)

8. OECD Health Division team: Feasibility Study on Health Workforce Skills Assessment - Supporting health workers achieve person-centred care. European Commission

9. Bakhshi, H., Downing, J.M., Osborne, M.A., Schneider, P.: The Future of Skills: Employment in 2030. Pearson, London (2017)

10. Zhang, C., Meijer, S.: A simulation game of patient transportation. In: Hamada, R., et al. (eds.) Neo-Simulation and Gaming Toward Active Learning. TSS, vol. 18, pp. 53–66. Springer, Singapore (2019). https://doi.org/10.1007/978-981-13-8039-6_5

11. Raghothama, J., Meijer, S.: Rigor in gaming for design: conditions for transfer between game and reality. Simul. Gaming 49(3), 246–262 (2018)

12. Miller, G.E.: The assessment of clinical skills/competence/performance. Acad. Med. 65(9 Suppl.), S63–S67 (1990)

13. Kolb, A., Kolb, D.: Eight important things to know about the experiential learning cycle. Aust. Educ. Leader 40(3), 8–14 (2018)

14. Mawdesley, M., Long, G., Al-jibouri, S., Scott, D.: The enhancement of simulation based learning exercises through formalised reflection, focus groups and group presentation. Comput. Educ. 56(1), 44–52 (2011)

15. Schoonenboom, J.: Designing mixed methods research by mixing and merging methodologies: a 13-step model. Am. Behav. Sci. 62(7), 998–1015 (2018)

16. Denton, B.T. (ed.): Handbook of Healthcare Operations Management: Methods and Applications. Springer, New York (2013). https://doi.org/10.1007/978-1-4614-5885-2

17. Klabbers, J.H.G.: Social problem solving: beyond method. In: Back to the Future of Gaming, Bertelsmann Verlag (2014)

18. Bonwell, C.C., Eison, J.A.: Active learning: creating excitement in the classroom. In: 1991 ASHE-ERIC Higher Education Reports. ERIC Clearinghouse on Higher Education, The George Washington University, One Dupont Circle, Suite 630, Washington, DC 20036-1183, $17 (1991)

19. Zhang, C., Grandits, T., Härenstam, K.P., Hauge, J.B., Meijer, S.: A systematic literature review of simulation models for non-technical skill training in healthcare logistics. Adv. Simul. 3(1), 15 (2018)

20. Thennakoon, D., Bandara, W., French, E., Mathiesen, P.: What do we know about business process management training? Current status of related research and a way forward. Bus. Process Manag. J. 24(2), 478–500 (2018)

21. Dumas, M., Rosa, M., Mendling, J., Reijers, H.: Fundamentals of Business Process Management. Springer, Heidelberg (2018). https://doi.org/10.1007/978-3-662-56509-4
22. Jarnheimer, A., Moustaid, E., Kendall, M., Sahin, S.: Klinikrapport, Avdelning 4, Norrtälje Sjukhus 2017–2018. Clinical Innovatoin Fellowships (2018)
23. Danielsson, C.B., Bodin, L.: Office type in relation to health, well-being, and job satisfaction among employees. Environ. Behav. **40**(5), 636–668 (2008)
24. Hardy, G.E., Woods, D., Wall, T.D.: The impact of psychological distress on absence from work. J. Appl. Psychol. **88**(2), 306–314 (2003)
25. WHO | Healthcare infrastructure. WHO. https://www.who.int/gho/health_technologies/medical_devices/healthcare_infrastructure/en/. Accessed 07 Mar 2019
26. Eskandari, H., Riyahifard, M., Khosravi, S., Geiger, C.D.: Improving the emergency department performance using simulation and MCDM methods. In: Proceedings of the Winter Simulation Conference, Phoenix, Arizona, pp. 1211–1222 (2011)
27. Pitt, M., Monks, T., Crowe, S., Vasilakis, C.: Systems modelling and simulation in health service design, delivery and decision making. BMJ Qual. Saf. **25**(1), 38–45 (2016)
28. Rashwan, W., Abo-Hamad, W., Arisha, A.: A system dynamics view of the acute bed blockage problem in the Irish healthcare system. Eur. J. Oper. Res. **247**(1), 276–293 (2015)
29. Zhao, Y., Peng, Q., Strome, T., Weldon, E., Zhang, M., Chochinov, A.: Bottleneck detection for improvement of Emergency Department efficiency. Bus. Process Manag. J. **21**(3), 564–585 (2015)
30. Aboueljinane, L., Jemai, Z., Sahin, E.: Reducing ambulance response time using simulation: the case of Val-de-Marne department Emergency Medical service. In: Proceedings of the 2012 Winter Simulation Conference (WSC), p. 12 (2012)
31. Delgado, M.K., Meng, L., Mercer, M., Pines, J., Owens, D., Zaric, G.: Reducing ambulance diversion at the hospital and regional levels: systemic review of insights from simulation models. Western J. Emerg. Med. **14**(5), 489–498 (2013)
32. Lederman, L.: Debriefing: toward a systematic assessment of theory and practice. Simul. Gaming **23**(2), 145–160 (1992)
33. Kriz, W.C.: A systemic-constructivist approach to the facilitation and debriefing of simulations and games. Simul. Gaming **41**(5), 663–680 (2010)
34. van den Hoogen, J., Lo, J., Meijer, S.: Debriefing research games: context, substance and method. Simul. Gaming **47**(3), 368–388 (2016)
35. Sawyer, T., Eppich, W., Brett-Fleegler, M., Grant, V., Cheng, A.: More than one way to debrief: a critical review of healthcare simulation debriefing methods. Simul. Healthcare J. Soc. Simul. Healthcare **11**(3), 209–217 (2016)
36. Huyakorn, P., Rizzi, P., Kanegae, H.: A study on gaming simulation as a key of meta-frame of planning for neighborhood immigrant integration and co-existing diversity. In: Naweed, A., Wardaszko, M., Leigh, E., Meijer, S. (eds.) ISAGA/SimTecT 2016. LNCS, vol. 10711, pp. 276–291. Springer, Cham (2018). https://doi.org/10.1007/978-3-319-78795-4_19
37. Nakaruma, M.: The impact of relevant experience and debriefing questions on participants' perception of gaming simulation. In: Back to the Future of Gaming (2014)
38. Mizuyama, H., Nonaka, T., Yoshikawa, Y., Miki, K.: ColPMan: a serious game for practicing collaborative production management. In: Kaneda, T., Kanegae, H., Toyoda, Y., Rizzi, P. (eds.) Simulation and Gaming in the Network Society, pp. 185–197. Springer, Singapore (2016). https://doi.org/10.1007/978-981-10-0575-6_15
39. Hamada, R., Kaneko, T., Hiji, M.: Development of BASE manufacturing business board game. In: Lukosch, H.K., Bekebrede, G., Kortmann, R. (eds.) ISAGA 2017. LNCS, vol. 10825, pp. 34–40. Springer, Cham (2018). https://doi.org/10.1007/978-3-319-91902-7_4

Playing (in) a Crisis Simulation

What is the Playful Engagement in a Serious Simulation Made of?

David Goutx[1]([✉]), Sophie Sauvagnargues[1], and Laurent Mermet[2]

[1] Institut Mines Alès, 6 Avenue de Clavières, 30100 Ales, France
david.goutx.pro@gmail.com
[2] MNHN (muséum national d'histoire naturelle), jardin des plantes,
57 rue Cuvier, 75005 Paris, France

Abstract. The nature and the varying levels of the engagement of participants with a crisis management exercise still cannot be described properly by the usual evaluation tools of the users' experiences nor does the application of the concept of flow help either.

The author proposes a protocol to do a qualitative analysis of video taken during crisis management exercises, based on the premise that emotional outbursts (laughter, swearwords,..) betray an excess of tension between the applied convention of pretending, by which the participants act like the simulation is a burdensome reality, and the always present knowledge that it is only a game.

This protocol is tested on two crisis management exercises played in a simulation room. It confirms the concept of ludicity - a component of the simulation, created by the participants on top of what is needed for the good progress of the simulation-, the proposal of a typology, which is used to analyse the impact on the simulation of the injection of new events and the possibility that the playfulness of the simulation is subject to entropy.

Keywords: Simulation · Ludicity · Engagement · Videoanalysis · Codification

1 Introduction

The learning benefits of engagement in a simulation are well known. The tools of play have been marshalled in various approaches mixing play and serious learnings, like serious games or gamification. They are the subject of a vast body of work which systematically shows, often thanks to evaluation *after the end of* the simulation, that learnings are heightened when playfulness is present.

Few works address what happens *during* the simulation, either to learnings or to the playful engagement, even though it is essential to determine if playing well in a simulation means learning well in the real world [1].

Using the exploration of two crisis management exercises, this article presents a way to analyse the components of the participants' playful engagement relying on a codification of the manifestations of playfulness and the proposal of a typology.

© Springer Nature Switzerland AG 2021
M. Wardaszko et al. (Eds.): ISAGA 2019, LNCS 11988, pp. 50–60, 2021.
https://doi.org/10.1007/978-3-030-72132-9_5

2   Theoretical Framework and Bibliographical Review

2.1   Play in Crisis Management Exercises

We are looking at crisis management exercises, which become games as soon as they require the participants to engage their imagination to believe they are in a real crisis.

The simulation's participants agree on the meaning they give to the information they interact with during the course of the simulation. This collective agreement forms a liminal space in which the simulation unfolds its reality with the active consent of the participants [2, 3].

The participants activate the procedures expected for the circumstances, but also, they create an original performance of the simulated crisis. As Klabbers [4] states: "*A game is not a neutral communication medium. The primary function of gaming is not information transfer, but influencing thought and action*". We give the name ludicity to this 'non-neutral' component of the simulation, created by the participants on top of what is needed for the good progress of the simulation [5]. It is close to the *jouabilité* of Henriot [6] or the lusory attitude of Suits [7].

Thus defined, ludicity is the part of the liminal space containing the emotions born in the simulation and unfolding during its development.

2.2   A Blind Spot in the Optimal Engagement in the Flow

The link between the presence of playful elements in a pedagogical exercise and the quality of the learnings, is regularly shown in publications, to the point that it is now usual to introduce playful elements in all types of activities – This is known as Gamification [8].

Numerous publications, influenced by the notion of flow -the optimal experience of total commitment to the task at hand [9, 10] are built on questionnaires given to players at the end of a session, appraising the components of the flow [15].

First described for athletes then extended to other situations which require a high performance, the concept of flow does not enable us to properly identify the pleasure created by play which is felt by the members of a group who face together a fictional situation without individual challenges. Furthermore, it is not well adapted to a game of simulation, in which the commitment, however intense, is always linked to a certain analytical distance as the participant plays while knowing he is playing [26].

2.3   Pleasures and Emotions from Play

The *pleasure* and the *emotions* created by play, even more than *commitment* itself - mentioned so often than its meaning is less clear [11] - play a key role in learning from a simulation. Faced with the failures of some Serious Games, Alvarez and Djaouti [12] reminds the creators of such games that they must not neglect the player's pleasure.

Paradoxically, the pleasure from play still is a rather vague concept, especially when compared to flow with its precise breakdown into nine components. From his observation of Live Action Role Playing (LARP) games, Kapp [13] defines it as the contentment the player derived from properly playing his role and assisting in the good development of the game.

The engagement of players with their characters, group and adventures has been evaluated in role playing games [14], after the end of the game. It is confronted with two intertwined problems [15]: first, a questionnaire at the end of the game does not capture the constant variation of the engagement during the game and second, measuring the engagement of a player during the game can unsettle the very engagement we were trying to observe.

Mullins & Sabherwal [16] propose a blueprint to explore the emotions linked to the player's engagement in a game. But it is difficult to observe emotions. It has been shown that protocols used to assign emotions when looking at pictures of faces were skewed by the subjectivity of the observers [17]. Most of the objective systems used to observe emotions, like heat sensors detecting changes in temperature of the hands or face, reduce the emotions captured to fear and stress [18].

Finally following Kapp [13], the best way to feel the emotions within a LARP game is to be playing among the players.

2.4   Selected Issue: From Fun in Games to Fun in Simulations

Rather than trying to continuously identify emotions during the simulation, our approach is to analyse the playful moments marked by emotional outbursts.

Indeed, during a crisis management exercise, mastering your emotions is recommended as they are seen to skew rational decisions. Emotions can even be feared for moving the simulation away from its objective of realism [19]. The sudden appearance of a smile, or even laughter or swearwords, is an incongruous sign that some tension pent-up inside the player has been released. This tension comes (according to Goffman [20]) from the efforts made by the player to keep up the appearances of the social (or here the game) convention he is part of, when he is conscious of an offset between this social convention and other realities.

We thus consider these smiles, laughs and swearwords as objective indicators of an emotional outburst (Goffman's *flooding*) revealing the tension accrued inside the player trying to maintain the convention of pretending in the simulation. These outbursts are also an attempt to push some other players to share in the outburst as a mean to reduce the tension.

3   Mechanism of the Experiment

3.1   Presentation of the Simulations and Simulation Room

The simulation room we used was built in 2011 in the IMT Mines d'Ales, following the work of Dautun [21], as a research platform in which it is possible to develop and test different devices, to immerse trainees in crisis situations, isolating them in a room representing a crisis unit.

Two rooms for the trainees are furnished like a town crisis management centre, while the facilitators stand in a control room (Fig. 1). The software Simul'Crises [22] enables the scenario of the simulated crisis to unfold, adapting the number of incidents to the level of mastery of the players, while maintaining some freedom of action for the players.

The simulations last for two hours. The team leading the simulation collects information on the players' actions through the phone calls it receives from the players but also thanks to observers present in the rooms.

The two simulations observed are based on the same scenario: the participants have been summoned to the crisis management centre because of a road traffic accident between a car and a heavy goods vehicle transporting chlorine cylinders which have spilled onto the road. The players must first make the local population under the threat of the toxic gas, take refuge inside, then face an accidental forest fire that forces the evacuation of the population. The two simulations differ only in the profiles of the participants (Table 1).

Table 1. General characteristics of the participants.

	Simulation 16V2017				Simulation 15VI2017			
	Average	Standard-deviation	Average (Male)	Average (Female)	Average	Standard-deviation	Average (Male)	Average (Female)
Age	21,32	0,75	21,00	22,00	33,7	9,6	34,80	31,50
Number	16		12	4	13		9	4

3.2 System of Observation

Observing the moment of ludicity relies on audio and video recording made -with the consent of the players - with tripod mounted stationary cameras (Fig. 1) which capture most of the players' activities from different angles without pre-selecting areas of interest [23].

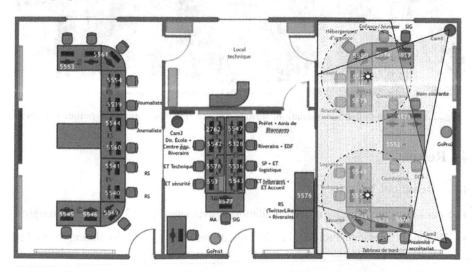

Fig. 1. Experimental installation with video cameras (red circles with field of view) and audio-recorders (black stars with approximate range). (Color figure online)

The machinary isn't hidden, but the players pay little attention to it during the simulation.

3.3   Methodology of the Analysis

The method retained to analyze the recordings is inspired by the qualitative analysis of video [23, 24]: using selection criteria chosen beforehand for their significance, the chosen recordings are screened several times, each time from a different point of view, then reconciling all the analysis of the same sequence.

Concretely the recording are analyzed as follow:

1. During the first viewing, the smiles, laughs, swearwords are detected and help define the sequences to be analyzed (Fig. 2).
2. Each defined sequence is then screened as many times as they are participants in the gameplay resulting in the emotional outburst.
3. Each defined sequence is described through *content logs* [23] in a way that enables us to infer the causes of the emotional outburst using the concept of ludicity [5].
4. The causes are written down trying to group what seems similar and their linking helps creates categories and subsequently a first attempt at a typology.
5. The typology is employed to codify minute per minute the emotional outburst throughout each simulation (Fig. 3) and to allow analysis.

Ludicity as we defined it has a collective component: the persons who manifest it try to share their emotions with the others around them by creating a form of fellowship. The codification of the ludicity bears that out: we analyse with the same system the player who creates this manifestation of ludicity and the players who share in it.

Fig. 2. Screenshots from a simulation: serious activity (left) vs. Emotional outburst (right).

4   Results

4.1   Density of Ludicity

The density of the ludicity in the simulation is evaluated (Fig. 3, Table 2) through:

- The one dimensional ludicity, i.e. the ratio of the length of the simulation marked by at least one player manifesting ludicity to the overall length of the simulation.

- The two dimensional ludicity, i.e. the ratio of the space of ludicity (number of players x the length of ludicity) to the overall space of the simulation.

These metrics (based on just two simulations) suggest that a significant part (around 13.5%) of the actions of the players is dedicated to the ludicity which does not participate in the rational crisis management.

Joueur	Rôle	Ludicité	72	73	74	75	76	77	78	79	80	81	82	83	84	85	86	87	88	89	90	91	92	93	94	95
Florence	DOS	22																								
François	Coordination	42																								
Jordan	Réseaux sociaux	17																								
Amandine	Communication	52																								
Vincent	Services techniques	8																								
Gunther	Sécurité	20																								
Mika	Education jeunesse	26																								
Manu	SIG	14																								
William	Main courante	11																								
Larbi	Accueil	7																								
Rachel	Hébergement / séc. ?	3																								
Camille	Tableau de bord	6																								
Séquence	*	228	38	39	40-	43		44	45		46	47		48		49	50	51	52	53-	55	56-		58-		60

Fig. 3. Example of codification template - zoom on the 72nd to 95th minute portion of the 15VI2017 simulation with a coloured codification of the types of ludicity detected (see Sect. 4.2 for details): players (with role played and total number of minutes of ludicity detected) in the three first columns on the left, each of the other columns corresponds to a minute of simulation; in white, the minutes without any occurrence of ludicity for a given player. Here, 1D-ludicity = 75% (18 columns out of 24 showing ludicity for at least one player), 2D-ludicity = 17% (48 cells out of 288 showing ludicity for a player within a minute).

Table 2. Basic metrics of ludicity detected in the simulations records.

	Simulation 16V2017	Simulation 15VI2017
Total duration recorded (min)	104	135
Cumulated playfulness sequences duration (min)	37	71
1-dimensional Rate of Ludicity	35.6%	52.6%
Total 2-dimensional game space recorded (players x min)	1040	1620
Cumulated 2-dimensional playfulness space (players x min)	134	228
2-dimensional Rate of Ludicity	12.9%	14.1%

4.2   Towards a Typology of Ludicity

As an attempt to make our ludicity concept as structured as the flow concept, we created a typology of the manifestations of ludicity, with two main categories:

- The ludicity linked to the game environment (A)
- The ludicity linked the in-game attitudes of the players (B)

Among the manifestations of (A), we distinguish between:

- The ones relating to the liminal space-time (A1), combining the start time of the simulation by which the players show their entry into the simulation, the agglutination of the collective liminal space from the individual agreement of each player to respect the convention of pretending, the integration of external information by which the players integrate in the liminal space, additional information coming from outside [3, 4] and the reunification of the liminal space after a schism;
- The ones relating to dissonances (A2), whether they are between the representation the players have of the fictional situation and the ones the people leading the simulation have [24], to the dislocation of the liminal space because of the disagreement on the interpretation of the fictional situation in the same simulation room, to a divergence in the assignment of meaning when a new external information is understood differently by two players [3, 4], to a defect in the game paraphernalia disturbing the fluid development of the simulation, to a subpar mastery of the game information when the player is not efficient at acting in the simulation, or to the loss of credibility of the simulation because of its perceived poor relationship to reality;
- The ones relating to stepping away from the game (A3) which encompass the corrosive manifestations of jests trying to amuse one's fellow players with the content of the simulation in reference to a context from outside the simulation [20], to the distraction game-in which uses an element of the simulation for a joke in a context internal to the simulation that distracts the other players [20], to the temptation of game breaker which reflect intentional acts of sabotage of the convention of pretending and of the liminal space [25] or to behaving as a spectator when the player sits there observing without participating in the game [26].

Among the manifestations of (B), we distinguish:

- The ones relating to the pleasure from play (B1) from the exploration of the limits of the game and the freedom to act within these limits, to a form of irony game-in when a player as his character teases another character for his actions in the game, to the exhilaration derived from the role-play when the role player becomes more of an actor and the character's actions start to feel real [13], to overcoming a difficulty which corresponds to a form of flow, or to the soothing of some anguish which is supposed to rise among the player;
- The ones relating to role-play disturbance (B2), it can be a difficulty in understanding the role assigned to oneself and especially the actions he should execute in the game [13], to erroneous actions for the assigned role when the player disturbs the realism of the simulation forcing the other players to ignore the mistake so as not to exit the simulation [20], to a conflict between the life experience of the player and the role assigned in the game when the player becomes recognized in the game more as the player rather than as his character [20], to a conflict of authority between players, or to a shift between the role assigned to a player and the role he

assumes when a player takes on consciously or not a role different to the one he was assigned;

- The ones relating to the level of difficulty (B3) which shows that the players stay conscious of the fact that the incidents they are dealing with are the results of the will of the team running the simulation, this level of difficulty can appear excessive or unrealistic, becomes a justification to enter gamer mode if the players bends their will to counteract the actions of the team running the simulation rather than act in a realistic manner, creates some attempts at cheating by using solution that are not in the scope of the game, or creates in the players a pressure to perform and make every effort to conform the supposed expectations of the team running the simulation.

		Simulation 16V2017		Simulation 15VI2017	
		Number	Percent	Number	Percent
A. Game environnement	A1. Liminal space-time	6	12%	1	1%
	A2. Dissonances	8	16%	28	28%
	A3. Stepping away from the game	10	20%	24	24%
B. In-game attitudes	B1. Pleasure from play	12	24%	15	15%
	B2. Role-play disturbance	9	18%	8	8%
	B3. Levels of difficulty	5	10%	21	21%
	Total	50	100%	100	100%

Fig. 4. Distribution of the manifestations of the ludicity in the two simulations observed

Some of these components stabilize the liminal space (A1 and B1), others destabilize it (A2 and B2) and the lasts drain it (A3 and B3).

4.3 Sensitivity of Ludicity to the Injection of an Event

The team running the simulation tries to optimise the involvement of the players in the simulation by injecting in it various events. We observe that these injections:

- Integrate a big part of the group of players in the same type of ludicity (73% on average over 5 injections) when the liminal space is little to not frayed (13% of A2-ludicity, 8% of A3-ludicity) but activate a reduced number of the players (45% on average over 7 injections) when the liminal space is frayed (24% of A2-ludicity, 24% of A3-ludicity),
- Create little in depth playful effects, the manifestations of ludicity lasting no more than a minute after the injection unless it brings information of extreme gravity (a child disappearance) then creating ludicity for the next 2 to 3 min,
- Create many stabilizing effects on the liminal space (41% of A1 and B1-ludicity within 1 min), many destabilizing effects (34% of A2 and B2-ludicity) and even destructive effects (25% of A3 and B3-ludicity) which leads to question the cost-benefit ratio of such interventions in the simulation,

- Are directly responsible for only 25% to 33% of the total 2D-ludicity detected, the remainder (67% to 75%) arising spontaneously during the simulation.

These results are not statistically significant enough to create a general rule but they should be seriously considered by the creators of simulation as to the undesirable side effects of the injection of events.

4.4 Entropy and the Persistence of Ludicity

The analysis of the simulations we observed shows (Fig. 5) that most of the stabilizing effects happen at the beginning (A1) and the end (B1) of the simulation but little in its middle half, whereas the destabilizing effects (A2 and B2) mainly happen in this middle half of the simulation. As for the effect draining the liminal space (A3 and B3) they tend to accumulate in the later half or later third of the simulation.

These analysis suggest a form of entropy is present in the organization of the liminal space. Once the liminal space is in place at the beginning of the simulation, it faces destabilizing effects which little by little drains and fragments it. Further investigations should be carried out to analyze how the disturbing events affect the players' engagement [27].

The ending of the simulation on a happy note wished by the team running the simulation (here the missing child is found) creates very different results among the players: it can restore the integrity of the liminal space or amplify its fragmentation.

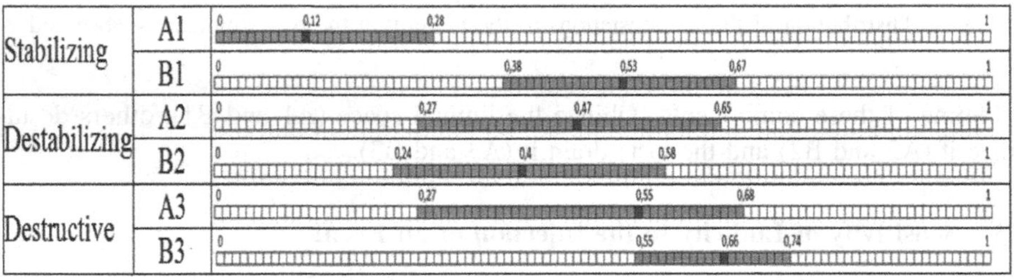

Fig. 5. Average parts of the simulation where ludicity appears (percent of the total legth)

5 Conclusions and Discussion

We have created a protocol to identify and do a qualitative analysis [24] of some recorded sequences of the crisis management exercise during which this ludicity, though emotional outbursts [20], manifests itself without any possible doubt. We have defined this ludicity as the emotional component of the simulation created by the players on top of what is needed for the good progress of the simulation [5].

This protocol, tested with two crisis management exercises, enabled us to verify the consistency of the ludicity which appears in at least a third of the total length of these simulations and to which close to an eighth of the ressources deployed by the players in the simulation, are dedicated. By the way our protocol is made, which identify only the emotional outbursts, these metrics underestimate the real consistency of ludicity. It also helped us to propose a typology of the components of ludicity with 6 main components further separated into 28 items helping us to codify the manifestations of lucidity.

The analysis done using this codification, without being statistically significant enough to create general rules, suggests that the injection of events in a simulation with which the team running the simulation hopes will influence its progress, have an effect on only a minor part of the simulation and may threaten the liminal space. To the extent that it is possible the effects created by the injection do not reflect an effort at crisis management but the effort of a group of players facing a problem with the assumed rules of the game.

They also suggest that the liminal space is built at the very beginning of the simulation, then is subject to a growing entropy which implacably disorganize it, up to the final crucial moment, the happy ending wished by the team running the simulation, when the credibility of the simulation is either mostly restored or annihilated.

We are deeply aware of the fact that we obviously by-passed the usual sophisticated definitions of emotions, extrasec or intrinsec motivation, engagement, presence,… that structure the theoric analysis of engagement. Our main objective was to focus on what could be observed in the simulation. The work should be carried on to refine the typology and take more benefit from theoric approachs.

Aknowledgements. The author thanks the LGEI team for recording the simulations and Matt Schoepfer for his precious support.

References

1. Raghothama, J., Meijer, S.: Rigor in gaming for design: conditions for transfer between game and reality. Simul. Gaming **49**, 246–262 (2018). https://doi.org/10.1177/1046878118770220
2. Harviainen, J.T., Lieberoth, A.: Similarity of social information processes in games and rituals: magical interfaces. Simul. Gaming **43**(4), 528–549 (2012). https://doi.org/10.1177/1046878110392703
3. Harviainen, J.T.: Ritualistic games, boundary control and information uncertainty. Simul. Gaming **43**(4), 506–527 (2012)
4. Klabbers, J.H.G.: On the architecture of game science. Simul. Gaming **49**(3), 207–245 (2018)
5. Goutx, D., Sauvagnargues, S., Mermet, L.: Managing the Game Within Crisis Exercises (2018). https://doi.org/10.1002/9781119557869.ch6
6. Henriot, J.: Sous couleur de jouer, la métaphore ludique. Ed. José Corti (1989)
7. Suits, B.: The Grasshopper. Games, Life, and Utopia. 3rd edn. Broadview Press (2014)
8. Alsawaier, R.S.: The effect of gamification on motivation and engagement. Int. J. Inf. Learn. Technol. **35**(1), 56–79 (2018). https://doi.org/10.1108/IJILT-02-2017-0009
9. Csikszentmihalyi, M.: Flow: The Psychology of Optimal Experience. Haper & Row, New York (1990)
10. Nakamura, J., Csikszentmihalyi, M.: The concept of flow. In: Snyder, C.R., Lopez, S. J. (eds.) Handbook of Positive Psychology, pp. 89–105. Oxford University Press, New York (2002)

11. Bonenfant, M., Philippette, T.: Rhétorique de l'engagement ludique dans des dispositifs de ludification. Sciences du jeu (en ligne), 10/2018, mis en ligne le 30 octobre 2018, consulté le 28 novembre 2018 (2018). https://journals.openedition.org/sdj/1422. https://doi.org/10.4000/sdj.1422

12. Alvarez, J., Djaouti, D.: Introduction au Serious game. Éditions: Questions théoriques (2010)

13. Kapp, S.: L'immersion fictionnelle collaborative. Une étude de la posture d'engagement dans les jeux de rôles grandeur nature. Sociologie. Ecole des Hautes Etudes en Sciences Sociales (EHESS); Université Libre de Bruxelles, Français (2013)

14. Tychsen, A., McIlwain, D., Brolund, T., Hitchens, M.: Player-character dynamics in multiplayer role playing games. In: Proceedings of the Digital Games Research Association Conference: Situated Play, pp. 40–49. Digital Games Research Association (DiGRA) (2007)

15. Shernoff, D., Tonks, S., Anderson, B.: The impact of the learning environment on student engagement in high school classrooms. Natl. Soc. Study Educ. 113(1), 166–177 (2014)

16. Mullins, J.K., Sabherwal, R.: Beyond enjoyment: a cognitive-emotional perspective of gamification. In: Proceedings of the 51st Hawaii International Conference on System Sciences (2018). https://hdl.handle.net/10125/50039

17. DiGirolamo, M.A., Russell, J.A.: The emotion seen in a face can be a methodological artifact: the process of elimination hypothesis. J. Am. Psychiol. Assoc. 17(3), 538–546 (2017)

18. Lonsdorf, T.B., et al.: Don't fear 'fear conditioning': methodological considerations for the design and analysis of studies on human fear acquisition, extinction, and return of fear. Neurosci. Behav. Rev. 77, 247–285 (2017)

19. Jones, K.: Fear of emotions. Simul. Gaming 35(4), 454–460 (2004)

20. Goffman, E.: Encounters: Two Studies in the Sociology of Interaction. Bobbs-Merrill Company, Inc., Indianapolis (1961)

21. Dautun, C.: Thesis: Contribution to the study of large-scale crises: Knowledge and Decision Support for Civil Security. Ecole Nationale Supérieure des Mines, Saint-Etienne, France, p. 271 (2007). (in French)

22. Tena-Chollet, F.: Elaboration d'un environnement semi-virtuel de formation à la gestion stratégique de crise basé sur la simulation multi-agents. Ph.D. thesis, Ecole Nationale Supérieure des Mines de Saint-Etienne, France (2012)

23. Schubert, C.: Video analysis of practice and the practice of video analysis. In: Knoblauch, H., Schnettler, B., Raab, J., Soeffner, H.G. (eds.) Video Analysis Methodology and Methods: Qualitative Audiovisual Data Analysis and Sociology. Peter Lang (2009)

24. Knoblauch, H., Schnettler, B., Raab, J., Soeffner, H.-G.: Video Analysis: Methodology and Methods. Qualitative Audiovisual Data Analysis in Sociology, 3rd edn. Peter Lang - Internationaler Verlag der Wissenschaften (2012)

25. Huizinga, J.: Homo ludens, essai sur la fonction sociale du jeu, Gallimard, 1988 (1938). ISBN 9782702204658

26. Laurent, M., Nathalie, Z.-R. (dir.): Au prisme du jeu. Concepts, pratiques, perspectives, Paris, Hermann, series: «Société» (2015)

27. Nygren, E.L., Laine, T.H., Suttinen, E.: Dynamics between disturbances and motivations in educational mobile games. Int. J. Interact. Mob. Technol. 12(3), 120–141 (2018)

Through a Mirror Darkly – On the Obscurity of Teaching Goals in Game-Based Learning in IT Security

Klemens Köhler[1]($^{(\boxtimes)}$) (ID), René Röpke[2] (ID), and Martin R. Wolf[1]

[1] FH Aachen University of Applied Sciences, Eupener Str. 70, 52064 Aachen, Germany
{k.koehler, m.wolf}@fh-aachen.de
[2] RWTH Aachen University, Ahornstr. 55, 52074 Aachen, Germany
roepke@cs.rwth-aachen.de

Abstract. Teachers and instructors use very specific language communicating teaching goals. The most widely used frameworks of common reference are the Bloom's Taxonomy and the Revised Bloom's Taxonomy. The latter provides distinction of 209 different teaching goals which are connected to methods. In Competence Developing Games (CDGs - serious games to convey knowledge) and in IT security education, a two- or three level typology exists, reducing possible learning outcomes to awareness, training, and education. This study explores whether this much simpler framework succeeds in achieving the same range of learning outcomes. Method wise a keyword analysis was conducted. The results were threefold: 1. The words used to describe teaching goals in CDGs on IT security education do not reflect the whole range of learning outcomes. 2. The word choice is nevertheless different from common language, indicating an intentional use of language. 3. IT security CDGs use different sets of terms to describe learning outcomes, depending on whether they are awareness, training, or education games. The interpretation of the findings is that the reduction to just three types of CDGs reduces the capacity to communicate and think about learning outcomes and consequently reduces the outcomes that are intentionally achieved.

Keywords: IT security education · Competence Developing Games · Game-based learning · Keyword analysis · Bloom's Taxonomy

1 Introduction

Game-based learning practices are increasingly used to convey or create knowledge (see for example [1–4]). There is little empirical data on how the properties of games influence learning, especially data not originating in self-reporting [5–7]. While there is a trove of practical knowledge, it is distributed and fragmented across several fields. The causal link between teaching goals and game characteristics is elusive and under-theorized since 30 years or more [8]. This is especially true with regard to teaching goals that are not knowledge-related, like motivation, sense of agency, etc. (see [6]). However, and this is probably more important, it seems that even for measurable and

© Springer Nature Switzerland AG 2021
M. Wardaszko et al. (Eds.): ISAGA 2019, LNCS 11988, pp. 61–73, 2021.
https://doi.org/10.1007/978-3-030-72132-9_6

quantifiable outcomes, like acquisition or retention of knowledge, there is a lack of theory to properly describe, differentiate, relate, and measure cause-effect relationships to specific game design decisions or mechanics.

Teaching interventions in IT security education are usually categorized into three types with different ambitions and target audiences: awareness, training, and education (later-on sometimes referred to as ATE terminology). The US National Institute of Standards and Technology (NIST) defines Awareness programs as enabling a general audience to recognize IT security concerns and respond accordingly [9, p. 28]. Training programs are specific to the role of the participants within their organization and should build knowledge and skills (ibd. p. 31). Education programs are aimed at professionals with prior formal education and constitute additional qualification (ibd. p. 35). The capacity to describe qualification programs and their goals is reduced to these three types, although the NIST definition actually mentions a fourth called "Cybersecurity Essentials". As the term yields 44 results in Google Scholar (as of March 29th 2019), it plays no role in actual IT security education.

Additionally, we often find only a weak distinction between training and awareness. Actually, we commonly find authors relying on the confounded term "awareness training", ignoring any possible distinction between training and awareness. By combining Awareness, Cybersecurity Essentials, and Training into one category, the initial idea of categories defined by audience and teaching goals is reduced to the audience dimension: "Awareness Training" for general audiences and "Education" for professionals. We will argue that this deteriorated state of discerning IT security education programs to the basic distinction of awareness, training, education, hurts our understanding. Focusing on the audience and not the intended outcome actually reduces our capacity to describe exactly what the aim of a specific learning intervention is, and therefore makes the goal-specific application of pedagogical theory impossible (see [10]).

Referring to serious games whose main function is to convey knowledge, we use the term Competence Developing Game [11]. Competence Developing Games (or CDGs) always include a narrative element and are conversely not pure "skill and drill" gamification implementations (see [12]). A usual subdivision sorts CDGs into training games and educational games (see [5]), which corresponds with the actual categorization of IT security education tools as described above[1]. Compared to well-defined pedagogical frameworks like Bloom's Taxonomy (BT) and the Revised Bloom's Taxonomy (RBT) [13] the distinction in two or three types found in IT security education and CDG research is severely underdeveloped. This lack of linguistic precision might hamper efforts to notice, understand, and research more nuanced differences.

---

[1] We acknowledge the existence of other definitions, distinctions and categories in the serious gaming community. However, using those definitions creates a bridge between IT security education programs in general and game-based approaches. Furthermore, the distinction into training games and education games represents a distinct part of our community: experts in International Relations, International Security, and military wargaming. This serves as further illustration of just how fragmented the serious gaming community is.

The Revised Bloom's Taxonomy is widely used in Education Science. It distinguishes 19 cognitive processes distributed over six categories, as well as a knowledge dimension with four categories and 11 subcategories. Each learning activity can be described by the cognitive activity expected of the learner and the type of knowledge the activity addresses. Educators relying on this taxonomy can precisely describe learning goals in 209 combinations of cognitive processes and depth of knowledge. For each of these combinations a precise definition has been developed and educators can rely on proven methods to teach and evaluate success for each goal. (Although, the original Bloom's Taxonomy is not as evolved, it is nevertheless still a trusted tool in pedagogic contexts.) This is a stark contrast to Serious Games and IT security education. Even adaptations like Bloom's Taxonomy for Information Security Education are not widely used [14].

This paper provides quantitative evidence that, analyzed at a more detailed level, Competence Developing Games for IT security education do not fully cover the pedagogical spectrum as described with the Revised Bloom's Taxonomy. Following this introduction, the research questions and hypothesis will be presented. Section 3 is a description of our method and the dataset we relied on. After the presentation of our results in Sect. 4, we discuss the problems with our data extraction and analysis methods. This paper closes with a section on our conclusions.

2 Research Question

2.1 Main Research Question

The range and complexity of necessary IT security related knowledge and behavior seems not to be represented by the ATE categorization used in conveying this knowledge. However, in order to efficiently apply game design and game mechanics to achieve specific learning goals, a sufficiently precise definition of these learning goals is necessary.

As argued above, we assume that publications on game-based learning do not reflect the whole spectrum of learning goals. If learning goals were intentionally addressed, it would reflect in the language used to describe them. Consequently, the use of terminology connected with learning goals should differ from common language.

To clarify further: If teaching goals were intentionally addressed, they would also be reported. If a combination of awareness, training, and education type CDGs cover the range of teaching goals, the language used to describe them would also reflect that. Therefore, a database of publications that contains several publications on each type of game would probably contain a comprehensive spread of teaching goal related terms. The main research question is:

Do we find the spectrum of learning-related language (LRL) in game-based learning applications on IT security?

To answer this main question, several inquiries into LRL used with regard to game-based learning applications in IT security education are necessary:

1. Do the publications about game-based learning applications in IT security use LRL similar to the RBT?

2. Do they us it intentionally or does the choice of word reflect common language?
3. Does the distinction between awareness, training, and education programs really reflect distinctive teaching goals?

2.2 Hypotheses

The hypotheses translate the questions into refutable claims. The hypotheses derived from the questions are in the same order: H_{a0} derives from question 1, H_{b0} from question 2, and H_{c0} from question 3.

- H_{a0}: The teaching goals described in the published articles do not reflect the whole spectrum of the revised Bloom's Taxonomy.
- H_{b0}: The word choice reflects the common use of language.
- H_{c0}: The categories awareness-training-education are predictors for divergent use of teaching goal related language.

3   Methods

3.1   Database

The database of the systematic review in Roepke & Schroeder [4] was created following a two-fold review process in which on the one hand, a systematic literature on academic publications was performed and on the other hand, a product search was executed with a search engine.

Based on two keyword sets, one covering all IT security related terms, and the other covering terms of the field of game-based learning and serious games, various search queries were generated for the following three digital libraries and/or search engines: IEEE Xplore, Google Scholar and ACM Digital Library. For each query, the first 100 results were extracted for further analysis (if less search results returned, all results were used). The same queries were used for the product search using the Google Search Engine.

Next, a multiple-step filtering and classification process was performed to systematically review all collected results. After removing all duplicates and discarding all results without online availability and open access, the third step was to filter all results based on whether the result is about IT security education or not. All off-topic results were irrelevant and hence discarded. Next, all results were sorted into the following categories: competition, game, gamification, review, and other. By adding all games referenced in the results categorized as reviews, the result set of games was extended. In the next step, the authors analyzed all games on their topic, target group and educational context. In addition, availability of the games was checked, to ensure that only games available to users would be reviewed further.

From this database, we extracted the set of games targeted at end-users, employees, teachers and students for further analysis. The analysis relies on published literature on several CDGs. The original database contains publications in academic journals, additional material for teachers who use specific games and in some cases the games themselves.

3.2   Methods

Data Extraction

To extract meaningful data, a classification framework was devised. Two lists of keywords were compiled, representing the knowledge dimension, and the cognitive process dimension of the Revised Bloom's Taxonomy. The first list (CP – cognitive processes) represents the cognitive process dimension of the Revised Bloom's Taxonomy. It has six classes, named after the categories of the RBT: remember, understand, apply, analyze, evaluate, and create. All subcategories of the RBT were included into these classes: the class remember has the subcategories recall and recognize. Additionally, terms from the original Bloom's Taxonomy, were added to the classes, according to the translation process between both taxonomies (see Table 1). The second list (K – knowledge) was created in the same way (see Table 2).

The elements of each class were then used as search strings after reducing them to their root words. The existence of different spellings, e.g. in case of analyse and analyze, lead to a further reduction of the search strings to the last common letter. In order to increase sensitivity, composite terms like factual knowledge, specific facts, self-knowledge were searched as disparate words. Furthermore, if one part of these composites appeared in more than one category, it was omitted. An example would be "knowledge" that appeared in combination with factual, conceptual, procedural, metacognitive, and self-. In the extreme case of "self-knowledge", the particle "self" was the search string. By not counting every word independently and instead counting them into bigger classes, oversensitivity was avoided.

Table 1. Categories of the Revised Bloom's Taxonomy cognitive process dimension and associated word search strings that constituted the class during analysis. The words in italic represent the original Bloom's Taxonomy.

Category	Search Strings in class
Remember	rememb recogni recall
Understand	understand explain compar infer summari classif exemplif interpret *comprehend translat extrapol*
Apply	apply implement execut
Analyze	analy attribut organi differentiat *relation*
Evaluate	evaluat critiqu check *criteria evidence*
Create	creat produc plan generat *communicat*

Table 2. Categories of the Revised Bloom's Taxonomy knowledge dimension and associated word search strings that constituted the class during analysis. The strings in italic represent the original Bloom's Taxonomy

Category	Search Strings in class
Factual Kn.	Element terminology detail *specific*
Conceptual Kn.	Convention structure model theor generalization principle category classification
Procedural Kn.	Decision criteria method technique algorithm skill *trend sequence*
Metacognitive Kn.	Self cognitive strategic

The items in the original database are either publications or the games themselves. In the latter case, an attempt was made to find accompanying publications. All items in the new list of publications were searched for all keywords and every instance of each keyword was counted sensitive to the context: Everytime a term was found, the whole sentence was assessed on its reference to teaching goals. If one sentence was not enough to clarify the context, the reading continued. This resulted in two datasets per category, one for all instances (A – all) and the other for the instances where the word was used to describe learning goals (C – context-sensitive). The criteria to get into the C-lists was that the term had to refer to a participant (player, user, student, etc.) and to the game.

In summary, the extracted data consisted of four lists: Cognitive Processes – All (CP-A), Cognitive Processes – context sensitive (CP-C), Knowledge - All (K-A), and Knowledge – context sensitive (K-C). To aquire additional data for comparisons, Google Ngram [15] was used to find out the frequency of use of each keyword in 2000. Newer data would have been preferable but is not available.

Finally, each publication was categorized as being either on an Awareness game, a Training game, or an Education game. To sort the publication into a type, we first checked whether the publications itself explicitly places the CDG into one of them. If not, two indicators were used: the intended audience and the behavior the intervention should enable. In case of discrepancies between the audience-based classification and the learning depth-based classification, the latter was regarded as more meaningful. In case of frameworks that are adaptable or teaching programs with consecutive parts, the respective game system was classified into a maximum of two types per publication.

Analysis and Statistics

The scale of measure for all data is nominal (while the ATE-continuum and the original Bloom's Taxonomy could arguably be ordered, the RBT has explicitly no hierarchy or order (see [13]). Therefore, statistical analysis is limited to descriptive statistics and Pearson's Chi-squared tests.

Since data extraction was largely manual and context specificity had to be ensured by reading portions of the texts, it was impossible to avoid preliminary, qualitative conclusions during this process.

After this unplanned preliminary analysis, the abundance of words in each category was visually inspected. Then, the relative abundance of the keywords for each category was compared to commonly used language. We used the Google NGRAM dataset. In order to extract the data of similar words, each possible variation of the word stem used for our analysis was looked up in NGRAM. We calculated the relative frequency of each root word for our datasets as well as the NGRAM data. Then, we calculated the deviation of word counts of our lists from the NGRAM data. A difference was relevant in case of differences of more than 50%.

Finally, in order to find out whether Awareness games, Training games, and Education games actually and intentionally have different teaching goals, a Pearson's Chi-squared test for independence was conducted on the cognitive process list.

In summary, there was a first preliminary analysis of the quality of the extracted data and possible implications, secondly a visual inspection. Thirdly, common usage of the keywords was compared to their usage within the database, and finally a Chi-squared test of independence was conducted in order to find out whether the attribution to a game type leads to a different language on teaching goals.

4 Results

4.1 Overview

Of the 53 entries of the original database, 36 became subject to the analysis (see Appendix Reviewed Literature). The rest was either not available as text (10), was considered an outlier because of its length (3), had technical issues with the publications or access requirements (3), or because the archive was no longer available (1).

Of the 36 publications on different games, 16 were classified as awareness games (4 of them also as training games), 19 were classified as training games (1 was also classified as education game 4 as training games, see above), and 6 as education games (again 1 was also a training game).

The cognitive process list (CP-A) had the categories (with word search findings in brackets) remember (86), understand (386), apply (300), analyze (464), evaluate (225), and create (700). The resulting context-specific counts (CP-C) in the same order were remember (58), understand (116), apply (46), analyze (21), evaluate (24), and create (51). Note that in 36 publications, only 21 instances of a class representing 5 different search strings were found. At least 15 publications do not contain even one of these words even once (Table 3).

Table 3. Results of the word search of the cognitive process dimension. Above all hits of the strings in each class, below corrected for context. Fields marked in red show counts below the number of publications analyzed for this study.

Category	Remember	Understand	Apply	Analyze	Evaluate	Create
Hits	86	386	300	464	225	700
Context-specific hits	58	116	46	21	24	51

The word search for the knowledge categories (K-A) revealed the following counts: factual knowledge (239), conceptual knowledge (727), procedural knowledge (499), and metacognitive knowledge (144). The contextualized counts (K-C) were: factual knowledge (20), conceptual knowledge (244), procedural knowledge (153), and metacognitive knowledge (13) (Table 4).

Table 4. Results of the word search of the knowledge dimension. Above all hits of the strings in each class, below corrected for context. Fields marked in red show counts below the number of publications analyzed for this study.

Category	Factual Kn.	Conceptual Kn.	Procedural Kn.	Metacognitive Kn.
Hits	239	727	499	144
Context-specific hits	20	244	153	13

4.2 Hypotheses

H_{a0}: The teaching goals described in the published articles do not reflect the whole spectrum of the revised Bloom's Taxonomy.

While there was no empty category in the CP-C list, terms associated with the cognitive processes of understanding where referred to often (116 times), analyzing and evaluating are underrepresented (21 and 24 mentions), while remembering, applying and creating came constitute the middle (58, 51, and 46). In other words, the underrepresented categories had about half as many mentions as the middle group, while the biggest category was roughly 5 times larger than the smallest. The absence of any words of the "analyze" and "evaluate" categories in education type CDGs is somewhat stunning.

The contrast is even more pronounced in the Knowledge Dimension of the Revised Bloom's Taxonomy (K-C): terms associated with factual and metacognitive knowledge were only mentioned 20 and 13 times. Conceptual and procedural knowledge on the other hand are overrepresented with 153 and 244 instances. This is one order of magnitude.

Supplementing the original methodical approach, the following interpretation relies on the preliminary impression during contextualization: The contextualization of the Knowledge categories suggested that the assumed connection between language and intention does not exist with regard to factual knowledge. In fact, the lack of terms on factual knowledge cannot mean that the designers of these games have not thought about which facts and details they want to teach. However, they seem to ignore these or take them for granted when analyzing their CDGs. Most publications do imply that factual knowledge is gained during play, as a base for conveying conceptual or procedural knowledge. On the other hand, metacognitive knowledge as a teaching goal is seldom implied and seldom found.

With regard to the CP-C list, we noticed a lack of words as well as implications that relate to analysis and evaluation. This is partly offset by the use of the term "recognize" (from the remember category), since a detection and recognition of certain IT threats implies an analysis of IT system. But the remember category (including the search string "recogni") is not especially large (see below). We would like to emphasize that the terms of this category are consistently used less than half as often in our dataset as in common language (see below).

In summary, there is little doubt that the publications in our dataset suggest a lack of communication and thinking about how to make participants in CDGs analyze and evaluate knowledge, and that the same is true about all learning activities on metacognitive knowledge.

H_{b0}: *The word choice reflects the common use of language.*

It does not. The relative use of the terms differs 50% and more in 5 of the 10 categories (CP-A and K-A). The same tendency was observed in the contextualized lists: all but 2 categories differed by more than 50% relative use. The lists show different patterns. In most cases, it looks as if all game types create the same pattern with gradual differences.

The language of publications on IT security CDGs thus differs from common language. This reflects choices made by the authors, whether they were intentional or not. That the effect is even stronger with contextualized language indicates that when reporting on teaching goals, authors chose different words (Figs. 1 and 2).

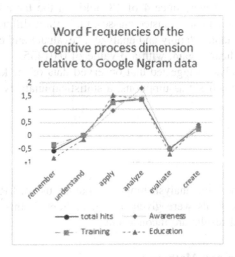

Fig. 1. Word frequencies of the cognitive process dimension relative to Google Ngram data shows that across all game types, the patterns of data are similar. The total count of 3 out of 6 categories deviated by more than 50% (above 0.5 or below −0.5), indicating a subject specific use of language.

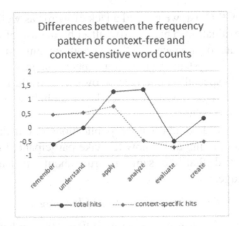

Fig. 2. Differences between the frequency patterns of context-free and context-specific word counts shows the different patterns of the data. Only deviations above 0.5 and below −0.5 are evaluated as relevant. Context-specific data shows a higher amount of relevant deviations, albeit in other classes.

H_{c0}: *The categories awareness-training-education are predictors for divergent use of teaching goal related language.*

Yes, they are. Our test-H0 that the use of language was independent of game-type is false. The calculated test statistic for the Pearson's Chi-squared test of independence was p = 0.0001535. However, since 4 of 18 fields in the table had values below 5, another test was conducted with adjusted classes. Only three different classes remained: "remember and understand", "apply and analyze", "evaluate and create". The resulting test statistic was significant again, with a p-value of 0.01435.

As preliminary analysis suggested that observed data of the knowledge dimension does not conform to our basic assumptions, a statistical analysis was omitted.

5   Discussion

5.1   Assumptions

The assumption on which the analysis hinges is that the use of LRL correlates with the consideration teaching goals were given by the authors. If this correlation does not exist, the methods and results are inconsistent.

5.2   Data Extraction and Methods

Less dramatic reductions of validity result from systematic biases due to methods used. Firstly, the analysis was limited to text passages that included a search string, the number of false negatives is unknown. The effect is unidirectional as it cannot produce false positives.

Another source of bias was the process of contextualization. Reading, interpreting, and evaluating whole passages of recurring texts introduces biases and increases chance as well as motivation to manipulate data. Taking breaks to self-reflect was the remedy of choice. Its effectiveness is uncertain.

One source of frustration as well as systematic bias was the CDG CyberCIEGE. It was mentioned or exclusively reported on in 15 of 36 publications of the dataset. Several of these 15 publications used the exact same sentences, most of the time not as quotes. Not in every instance, the re-use of a passage left the impression of being intentional and meaningful. The effect on our research is twofold: On one hand, the experience of repeatedly analyzing the same sentence is frustrating, introducing bias through affective states of the researcher. On the other hand, every word used in a standard sentence that is reused 6–7 times weighs as much in quantitative analysis. The effect was somewhat mitigated by the modularity of CyberCIEGE which led to the distribution over all three classes of games.

Another possible source of error is the use of the Google NGRAM dataset and the assumption that it reflects common language. An argument could be made, that publications for academic or teaching audiences dealing with computer science education will probably have divergent terminology compared to common language. It is also reasonable to assume that these effects persist even though the Google NGRAM data is known to over-represent scientific texts [15].

6 Conclusions

6.1 Summary and Conclusion

Our analysis of 36 publications on game-based learning in IT security indicates that the community lacks the means to communicate and strategically think about teaching goals. Although teaching goal-connected language differs from word frequencies in common language, indicating intentional wording and therefore strategic thinking about learning goals, it fails to reflect the whole range of learning objectives.

The available data suggests that participants of existing game-based learning programs are not expected to perform tasks from the categories "analyze" and "evaluate". Also, they do not convey metacognitive knowledge, i.e. self-reflection and insights about how cognitive processes work and how they can be used.

In summary, by using a simplified typology of IT security education types and CDGs, the community seems unable to cover the whole spectrum used in the Revised Bloom's Taxonomy to convey knowledge by default.

6.2 Future Research

A two-pronged approach to mitigate the simplicity of our thinking about game types is advised. On one hand, instead of concentrating on audiences, we should put the individual participant and his activities during gameplay in the center of our research. These learning activities can be precisely described with frameworks like the Revised Bloom's Taxonomy. This would allow us to build upon already developed refutable predictions. Secondly, instead of focusing on teaching goals derived from theory, game-based learning could be aligned with the motivational and cognitive challenges a participant would also face in a real situation. This would enable the development and testing of game mechanics that mirror real world circumstances (For the merits both approaches had in experimental economics, see [17]).

Acknowledgements. This research was supported by the research training group "Human Centered Systems Security" sponsored by the state of North-Rhine Westphalia.

References

1. Curry, J., Engle, C., Perla, P. (eds.): The Matrix Games Handbook - Professional Applications from Education to Analysis and Wargaming. The History of Wargaming Project, Wroclav (2018)
2. Curry, J., Price, T.: Dark guest - training games for cyber warfare - wargaming internet based attacks. In: History of Wargaming, 2nd edn., vol. 1 (2013)
3. Lahneman, W.J., Arcos, R. (eds.): The Art of Intelligence - Simulations, Exercises and Games, 1st edn. Rowman & Littlefield, New York (2014)
4. Roepke, R., Schroeder, U.: The problem with teaching defence against the dark arts - a review of game-based learning applications and serious games for cyber security education. In: Proceedings of the 11th International Conference on Computer Supported Education, vol. 1. SciTePress (2019)
5. Bartels, E., Hollingshed, D.: Can your Game Multi-task? Presented at the Military Operations and Research Society 81.1 Virtual Symposium, Washington D.C., June 2013. https://paxsims.wordpress.com/2013/06/14/virtual-mors-bartels-on-can-your-game-multi-task/. Accessed 16 May 2019
6. Butler, M.J.: The holy trinity? Connecting learning objectives, assessment, and debriefing in IR simulations. Presented at the International Studies Association Annual Conference, Atlanta, March 2016
7. Sabin, P.: Wargames as an academic instrument. In: Harrigan, P., Kirschenbaum, M.G. (eds.) Zones of Control - Perspectives on Wargaming, 1st edn., pp. 421–438. The MIT Press, London (2016)
8. Bartels, E.: Games as structured comparisons: a discussion of methods. Presented at the ISA's 59th Annual Convention, San Francisco, April 2018
9. Toth, P., Klein, P.: A role-based model for federal information technology/cybersecurity training. NIST Spec. Publ. **800**(16), 163 (2014)
10. Shostack, A.: Elevation of privilege: drawing developers into threat modeling. Presented at the 2014 USENIX Summit on Gaming, Games, and Gamification in Security Education, San Diego, 18 August 2014
11. König, J.A., Wolf, M.R.: A new definition of competence developing games - and a framework to assess them. Presented at the ACHI 2016: The Ninth International Conference on Advances in Computer-Human Interactions (2016)
12. Olano, M., et al.: SecurityEmpire: development and evaluation of a digital game to promote cybersecurity education. Presented at the 2014 USENIX Summit on Gaming, Games, and Gamification in Security Education, San Diego, August 2014
13. Krathwohl, D.R.: A revision of bloom's taxonomy - an overview. Theory Pract. **41**(4), 212–218 (2002)

14. van Niekerk, J., van Solms, R.: Bloom's Taxonomy for Information Security Education. ISSA (2008)
15. Michel, J.-B., et al.: Quantitative analysis of culture using millions of digitized books. Science **331**, 176–182 (2010)
16. Risi, S.: Google Ngrams: From Relative Frequencies to Absolute Counts (2016). https://stanford.edu/~risi/tutorials/absolute_ngram_counts.html. Accessed 30 Mar 2019
17. Smith, V.L., Wilson, B.J.: Humanomics - moral sentiments and the wealth of nations for the twenty-first century. In: Cambridge Studies in Economics, Choice, and Society, vol. 13. Cambridge University Press, Cambridge (2019)

The Tacit Knowledge in Games: From Validation to Debriefing

Bill Roungas[1]([⊠]), Sebastiaan Meijer[1], and Alexander Verbraeck[2]

[1] KTH Royal Institute of Technology, Huddinge, Sweden
sebastiaan.meijer@sth.kth.se
[2] Delft University of Technology, Delft, The Netherlands
a.verbraeck@tudelft.nl

Abstract. Game sessions consist of three phases: briefing, gameplay, and debriefing, with the latter being considered the most important feature of games. Nevertheless, given that games are considered by many to be more of an artistic form rather than a scientific artifact, a question that rises is: Can game sessions in general and debriefing in particular be analyzed and performed in a rigorous scientific way? In other words, can they be consistently structured, given the different characteristics of games, and can clear criteria on what would constitute a successful game session and debriefing be defined? The answer to these questions is yes. Yet, it remains a challenge to extract the knowledge of experts, which resides to a large extent in the tacit knowledge spectrum. Hence, the aim of this paper is to shed some light in this tacit knowledge possessed by experts and to gain understanding on why certain practices are more prone to success than others as well as bring into the surface other practices that have remained well hidden. In order to accomplish this goal, three rounds of interviews were conducted.

Keywords: Gaming simulation · Debriefing · Game sessions · Game validation

1 Introduction

In an era that the complexity of all things around us has dramatically increased, grasping, let alone fully comprehending, that complexity seems to be quite a challenging task. As a result, tools that used to provide insights on how certain parts of the world work a few decades ago in a satisfactory degree, can no longer address the complexity-derived challenges. There is a need for more rigorous methods that would enable the understanding of real-world problems within such an ever-changing complex environment. Gaming simulations (hereinafter referred to as games) is a discipline/method that has the potential to capture the complexity surrounding us and provide for a platform to better understand it. The primary reason is that games incorporate by definition the perpetrator of the aforementioned complexity, humans. Since human behavior cannot be characterized as 100% rational, systems involving

© Springer Nature Switzerland AG 2021
M. Wardaszko et al. (Eds.): ISAGA 2019, LNCS 11988, pp. 74–83, 2021.
https://doi.org/10.1007/978-3-030-72132-9_7

humans often tend to behave in a seemingly unpredictable way, or what is called bounded rationality [25], hence the complexity and the subsequent challenges.

The complexity of systems, and particularly the complexity of the decision-making process within those systems, can be explored through three levels: technical, actor, and context complexity [19]. Given these three levels, it becomes evident that complexity is not just the result of systems' increased size but is mainly caused by the numerous interdependencies among the different aspects of those systems. In turn, while these interdependencies are abstracted to a certain degree, they still bear a significant amount of complexity, which needs to be translated into game design choices. The result is artifacts, i.e. games for decision making, characterized by numerous and complex structures, which cause many challenges to game researchers and practitioners on how to understand and model them.

The core reason for which humans are interested in studying systems is their seemingly inherent need to understand and control these systems [4]. It is indeed a natural urge, not just out of curiosity, to deeply comprehend how certain systems work, in order to be able to improve them or at the very least adjust our behavior according to their boundaries. As a result, the increased complexity of modern systems, as it has been described so far, requires new methods that would be able to capture and adequately abstract the different elements of systems that cause this inflated complexity. While it seems to be easier said than done, gaming simulations as a discipline appear to possess that toolbox that would allow to tackle and understand complexity.

Therefore, the aim of this paper is initially, in Sect. 2, to debate on the nature of validation in games and particularly on the extent to which validation methods from simulations can be successfully applied in games and on the relationship of game validity to credibility and usability. Then, in Sect. 3, Sect. 4, and Sect. 5, a connection between validity, game sessions and debriefing is established, and results from multiple rounds of interviews of best practices on game sessions and debriefing are presented. Finally, in Sect. 6, final remarks are made.

2 Validation in Games

Before diving into the specifics, it is essential to first define what is validation in games. Adapting Schlesinger et al.'s [24] and Baloi's [3] definitions from simulations, validation in games can be defined as the degree to which the game imitates the underline system in a satisfactorily level, or in layman terms game validation addresses the question of whether the game is the "right" one. Yet, Peters et al. [17] argue that the scope of this definition is restrictive and it does not account for more abstract, perhaps even metaphorical, games. They instead adopt a more broad definition, initial proposed by Raser [18], who identified four criteria for the validation of games: psychological reality, structural validity, process validity, and predictive validity. In this thesis, while the importance of a strict definition, which would subsequently clearly provide an acceptability threshold, is acknowledged and supported, the need for a broader understanding of what the validation of games entails is also considered. The aim of this section is therefore not to propose one particular methodology for game validation but rather to pinpoint that in most cases game validation is not as straightforward as the validation of simulations.

With regards to validity in more broad terms, games can also be seen themselves as a mechanism for validation. Regardless the technology used or the area of application, games have been used as a means to validate certain hypotheses or future scenarios [16]. The concepts of validation and games are therefore intertwined, forming a more complex relationship than initially anticipated. In this thesis and particularly in this part, while several of the games examined have been used for validation purposes, the research is primarily concerned with the validation of games as opposed to how games can be used to validate artifacts or hypotheses.

2.1   From Simulations to Games

Unlike pure simulations, games have a distinct characteristic, which is the human participation, or in other words games have a Game Layer on top of the Simulation Layer. Game validation, due to its nature of including humans, usually depends more on the subjective opinion of experts [12], e.g. questionnaires, than formal methods. This limitation is related to the lack of design methods for games as well as to the usually low number of participants. The latter, i.e. the sample size, plays a significant role on the applicability of game results. A small sample size is easy to obtain but has limited possibilities for analytical conclusions thus limited possibilities for generalizing the observations from the game. A large sample size, while it solves the analytical problem and the generalizability of the results, it is usually expensive to obtain and difficult to coordinate.

Validation of the Simulation Layer has been vastly researched through the course of the last three decades [2, 23], where numerous formal methods and statistical techniques have been introduced. Moreover, methodologies for first verifying that indeed the sample size is small [14], then selecting the most appropriate validation methods and statistical techniques among the numerous existing ones [21], and finally automating validation [22], have been proposed. Though, the real contribution in games that the knowledge acquired from the validation of simulations has to offer is the ability of the validation methods from the simulation field to tackle and potentially address three of the criteria proposed by Raser [18], i.e. structural validity, process validity, and predictive validity.

Validation of the Game Layer due to its nature of including uncertainties pertaining to human activity, usually is not so straightforward. On the one hand, the formalization of game design can provide more structure on game validation. On the other hand, with regards to the sample size, the Game Layer would be benefited only through gradually extending the body of knowledge by building upon previous work. This aspect is directly linked with knowledge management, in the sense that the more game sessions are conducted the more evidences of a system's behavior are discovered and the cumulative sample size gradually becomes large enough to generalize the outcome of the game. Furthermore, it is the Game Layer the one that dictates the need for validating a game also with regards to its psychological reality, which is the degree to which a game provides an environment that seems realistic to the players.

2.2   Validity vs. Credibility and Usability

Apart from validity, two more terms are often associated with a game's successful implementation and application, credibility and usability. Credibility is defined as whether, and the degree to which, key stakeholders in a project consider the game, and subsequently its results, to be correct, always vis vis the particular objectives of the study [13]. While credibility does not conceptually has a 100% correspondence with prediction, this thesis posits that within the scope of games they are strongly correlated, in the sense that if a game has high predictive validity would provide credible results, and vice versa, a game that provides credible results has high predictive validity.

The second term, usability, is defined as the extent to which a product can be used by specified users to achieve specified goals with effectiveness, efficiency, and satisfaction in a specified context of use [8]. Given the nature of the games this thesis is covering, usability is strongly correlated with psychological reality, in the sense that games that aim to imitate a particular system, even in a metaphorical level, tend to be considered realistic when they provide a familiar to the users interface to interact with, which in turn this familiarity is perceived as a more usable artifact.

Given those two terms along with the different kinds of validity, proposed by Raser [18], validation of games should be seen as an extended version of simulation validation, incorporating psychological and user experience factors, as opposed to be seen as mutually exclusive to usability [7]. In that sense, the claim that a game is valid cannot be stated unless it has been established that the game is usable and its results credible, always for its intended purpose of use. In-deed, credibility has been recognized to be a validity criterion [15]. On the other hand, while to the best of our knowledge usability has not been explicitly identified to be a criterion for validity, there have been studies that acknowledge a strong connection between them in general [6] and in games as well [10].

2.3   Overview of Validation

While game validation can be strongly benefited from analytical methods, it cannot solely rely on them since it heavily depends on contextual and behavioral factors. These factors are not in conflict or even separate from validation, as the latter is defined in simulations, but rather complimentary, all of which in this thesis are put under the umbrella of validation in games. Moreover, game validation does not only depend on the game itself but also on how the game is executed. In other words, it depends on the briefing, game session, and debriefing, with particularly the latter being of paramount importance. Validation and game sessions have a reciprocal relationship. Increased validation is more likely to lead to a fruitful and more successful game session, and a successful game session boosts the game outcome and thus further increases its validity. But then the question that rises is: How is a successful game session defined particularly in games for decision making? A question that is further explored in the subsequent sections.

3   1st Round of Interviews: Debriefing Pitfalls

In 2016, a methodology was proposed and subsequently the first round of interviews was conducted for identifying the factors that inhibit debriefing because of problems on the design of the debriefing and for ascertaining whether these pitfalls depend on the different types of games [20]. The interviews included a questionnaire, which was answered by 8 game facilitation experts, and resulted in both quantitative and qualitative results. The answers complemented each other so the quantitative results could be interpreted and placed into the perspective in which an answer was given.

In more detail, the study was initially based on a literature review, from which 12 pitfalls occurring while debriefing games were identified. Then, the facilitation experts categorized the pitfalls based on two criteria: 1. Whether a pitfall occurred due to the design or the execution of the debriefing, and 2. Whether a pitfall occurred mostly in open (free play) or closed (rule based) games [9]. The 12 identified pitfalls can be found in more detail in [20], though briefly these pitfalls are:

1. The debriefers' level of involvement and style is not appropriate.
2. Debriefers have a lack of understanding of the debriefing process, which can lead into providing easy solutions and/or violating the debriefing process. This might occur due to lack of training and/or interest to improve.
3. Lack of plan and/or rules.
4. The allocated time for the debriefing is short and/or the complexity of the simulated scenarios, occurring during the debriefing, may require a repetition of the game, or lead into violating the planned time of the debriefing.
5. Ineffective use of audiovisual (A-V) material, which can lead to interruptions in finding relevant video segments.
6. Lack of emotional safety of the participant, probably revealed because of a. different levels of experience between the participants, b. a difference in education, and c. various other psychological reasons or due to the fact that debriefers might not take into account emotions.
7. Factors related to the actual physical environment, where the debriefing takes place.
8. Choosing the appropriate structure for debriefing.
9. The tendency of the participants to assign blame and antagonize each other.
10. Lack of trust of the participants towards the debriefers.
11. The simulation is not organized in a personal basis, which inhibits the effectiveness of debriefing.
12. Inappropriate timing/scheduling of the debriefing.

As the above list shows, pitfalls while debriefing vary significantly. By no means can this list be deemed complete as it was drawn out of specific contexts, but it was the product of an extensive literature review, and as such, it contains the majority of the most important factors that inhibit debriefing.

From the analysis of the interviews, the most noteworthy conclusions were:

– On the one hand, the pre-defined questions showed that most of the experts consider all pitfalls to be relevant to both closed and open games. On the other hand, the comments showed that some pitfalls (Pitfalls 1, 3, and 4) are more relevant either to closed or open games. This contradiction can characterize the results, with regards to this categorization, as inconclusive. If pitfalls prove to be independent of the rules of games, they will disprove the initial hypothesis. Thus, it is important and interesting to research this relationship until the point that it would be possible to support or disprove the initial hypothesis with statistical significance.

– Despite the fact that some pitfalls seem to occur mostly due to the design and others due to the execution of the debriefing, all pitfalls had an average of 3.25 or higher on both categories, showing that to some extent, both the design and the execution of the debriefing influence all pitfalls. This result came as a surprise, since it was expected that the pitfalls - or at the very least some of them - were independent either from the design or the execution of the debriefing. Therefore, it will be interesting in the future to validate these results and understand the underlying reason for the above.

– Both the experts that filled the questionnaire, and the ones that did not, reported that they perceive debriefing as a complex event due to the multiple context-and game-related factors it depends on. Nevertheless, their comments gave insight on the relationships among pitfalls and context factors, which in the future can help to model debriefing by abstracting it, the same way a game abstracts a real-world system.

– The personal traits of the facilitators, such as their skills, experience, attitude, style, and overall personality, influence in multiple ways the effectiveness of debriefing. Researching further when, where, and how a facilitator influences debriefing is both important and fascinating, since it introduces new aspects from different scientific fields to the analysis, such as psychology, education, and management.

4   2nd Round of Interviews: Factors Influencing Games' Success

The second round of interviews was conducted in 2018 [1] with 19 experts of which 7 game designers, 6 project leaders, 4 participants, and 2 department managers. The primary tool for analysis was Q-methodology, where the results from the first four interviewees were used to build the q-sort statements, which the remaining 15 interviewees used. Results, showing in Table 1, revealed several factors that either boost or inhibit games' success.

5   3rd Round of Interviews: Defining Successful Debriefing

The third, and final, round of interviews was also conducted in 2018 with 21 game facilitation experts, which was mainly characterized by the contradicting answers in almost all questions. This result translates in a non-unified approach towards games in general and debriefing in particular. The complexity characterizing modern systems immediately excludes pure analytical methods as the absolute and only solution, as the

Table 1. Results from second round of interviews using the Q-methodology.

Factor	Impact	Comments
Presence of a game manager	+	A person that would attend all game-related procedures was found to be beneficial. These procedures involve choosing participants, make these participants available the day of the game, managing missing players, taking care of the space and the infrastructure for the gaming session, to name a few
Managerial guidance and involvement Structured and concrete results	+ +	The involvement of mid/high level managers made the participants feel that what they are doing during the game session matters and it is not just a game. While the limitation of analytical sciences have been pinpointed in this thesis, complete absence of it is also detrimental. Apart from the lack of robust scientific methods for evaluating certain results, the absence of quantifiable results was found to be diminishing the credibility of the game itself
Strict rules	+	Stricter rules were perceived by the interviewees as an insurance of higher validity of results
High variety of roles involved in game design	+	Involvement of stakeholder not just during the game but also during the design process was appreciated by the interviewees, especially from operational personnel
Simulator validated beforehand	+	Not properly validated software has created frustration among the stakeholders and negative opinion about the game overall
Structured debriefing	+	Particularly for games for decision making, an unstructured open discussion after the game was found to often distract from the goal of the game
High complexity of the game's scope	−	Due to time and budget restrictions, over-complex games should be avoided, in order for results to be obtained in an affordable and timely manner. Moreover, often complex environments tend to overwhelm the participants causing the opposite effect from the desired one
Unexpressed and/or conflicting stakeholders' interests	−	Unexpressed interests and expectations were found to severely increase the risk of unanswered research questions and unclear results
Time pressure	−	Time pressure was recognized as a factor that forces untested or not well tested simulators to be used in game session that often causes crashes in the software leading to negative appreciation on behalf of the participants and potentially invalid results

(continued)

Table 1. (*continued*)

Factor	Impact	Comments
Pressure from external actors	–	Some stakeholders might put pressure for obtaining results that fit their interests and agenda, which in turn can cause conflicts among all the stakeholders and potentially invalid results

probability for ludic fallacy [26] increases significantly. There-fore, these interviews aim to provide insights on how facilitation experts approach debriefing, hence tap into their tacit knowledge.

The questions these interviews intended to address were:

- Given the limitation of analytical methods to provide clear criteria for success of game sessions, how should success be defined?
- What is the level of knowledge of clients regarding their goal using games and how should they be prepared prior to the game session?
- How do facilitators adapt their approach to the game session based on the players' characteristics?

The first question yielded perhaps the most answers with regards to how experts define success. 21 interviews resulted in more than 10 different answers, confirming the lack of consistency in the field. Nevertheless, three answers were far more common than the others. Freedom and feeling safe to share your experience from the game was considered a factor of paramount importance by six experts. The second most frequent criteria for success was the degree to which players would actually implement in their work, what they have learned during the game. Finally, a factor acknowledged particularly from game designers, that could determine success, was the level of involvement of players and their desire to play the game again.

The first part of the second question was initially expected to be answered overwhelmingly positively, yet more often than not, clients want to build a game but without knowing the actual goals. In the second part of the question, in order for facilitators to manage the varying levels of awareness of clients, the former inform the latter about the possible, unpredictable results of open games, like games for decision making.

The third question relates back to theory, where it was introduced the idea of the interchanging roles that facilitators can, and should, take during a game [11]. The first step for facilitators is to identify any knowledge gap of the players with regards to the game they will participate in. Then, when the participants feel safe enough during the debriefing, the facilitator should capitalize that by taking the conversation into a deeper level. It should be noted that the interviewees acknowledged the influence of particular debriefing methods but none stood out as more effective or preferred.

6 Conclusion

This paper focused on game sessions in general with debriefing having the lion's share. Debriefing is considered to be the most important part of games [5], since its aim is to bridge the abstracted world of games with reality, and thus transfer the acquired knowledge in a real world setting. Nevertheless, debriefing was not the only subject examined; the best practices in conducting game sessions, through a series of interviews with debriefing experts and other game stakeholders, were presented. The results were quite insightful, yet they also indicated several contradictions among experts.

In more detail, a factor that appeared in all three interviews was the participants feeling of safety to play and subsequently express themselves in the debriefing. Safety does not only relate to the emotional safety of an environment, where participants feel that they will not be judged. Safety as a concept also refers to a game environment that is a valid representation of the system under study, thus the participants can contribute the maximum of their capabilities. Moreover, such an environment, enhanced by a structured and appropriate guidance from the facilitator and perhaps a manager, and free from any time or external pressure, was found to be the key to success; a success that was also deemed, intuitively in retrospect, to be heavily depended on the applicability of the game insights and results.

References

1. Angeletti, R.: Managing knowledge in the era of serious games and simulations: an exploratory study on the elicitation of serious games' requirements for the generation and reuse of knowledge. Ph.D. thesis, Delft University of Technology, Delft, The Netherlands (2018)
2. Balci, O.: Verification, validation, and testing. In: Banks, J. (ed.) Handbook of Simulation, chap. 10, pp. 335–393. Wiley, New York (1998)
3. Balci, O.: Verification, validation, and certification of modeling and simulation applications. In: Chick, S., S′anchez, P.J., Ferrin, D., Morrice, D.J. (eds.) Proceedings of the 35th Conference on Winter Simulation, pp. 150–158. IEEE Press, New Orleans (2003)
4. Casti, J.L.: On system complexity: Identification, measurement, and management. In: Casti, J., Karlqvist, A. (eds.) Complexity, Language, and Life: Mathematical Approaches. Biomathematics, vol 16, chap. 6, pp. 146–173. Springer, Berlin, Germany
5. Crookall, D.: Serious games, debriefing, and simulation/gaming as a discipline. Simul. Gaming 41(6), 898–920 (2010). https://doi.org/10.1177/1046878110390784
6. Greenberg, S., Buxton, B.: Usability evaluation considered harmful (some of the time). In: Proceedings of the SIGCHI Conference on Human Factors in Computing Systems, pp. 111–120. ACM (2008). https://doi.org/10.1145/1357054.1357074
7. van den Hoogen, J.: The gaming of systemic innovations: innovating in the railway sector using gaming simulations. Ph.D. thesis, Delft University of Technology (2019)
8. ISO/IEC-9241-11: Ergonomics of human-system interaction. Part 11: Usability: Definitions and Concepts (2018). https://www.iso.org/standard/63500.html
9. Klabbers, J.H.G.: The Magic Circle: Principles of Gaming & Simulation, 3rd edn. Sense Publishers, Rotterdam (2009)

10. Kortmann, R., Sehic, E.: The railway bridge game usability, usefulness, and potential usage for railways management. In: Proceedings of the International Simulation and Gaming Association (ISAGA) (2010)
11. Kriz, W.C.: A systemic-constructivist approach to the facilitation and debriefing of simulations and games. Simul. Gaming **41**(5), 663–680 (2010). https://doi.org/10.1177/1046878108319867
12. van Lankveld, G., Sehic, E., Lo, J.C., Meijer, S.A.: Assessing gaming simulation validity for training traffic controllers. Simul. Gaming **48**(2), 219–235 (2017). https://doi.org/10.1177/1046878116683578
13. Law, A.M., Kelton, W.D.: Simulation Modeling and Analysis, 3rd edn. McGraw-Hill, NewYork (1991)
14. Lenth, R.V.: Some practical guidelines for effective sample size determination. Am. Stat. **55**(3), 187–193 (2001). https://doi.org/10.1198/000313001317098149
15. Lincoln, Y.S., Guba, E.G.: Naturalistic Inquiry. SAGE Publications Inc., New York (1985)
16. Meijer, S.: The power of sponges: comparing high-tech and low-tech gaming for innovation. Simul. Gaming **46**(5), 512–535 (2015). https://doi.org/10.1177/1046878115594520
17. Peters, V., Vissers, G., Heijne, G.: The validity of games. Simulat. Gaming **29**(1), 20–30 (1998). https://doi.org/10.1177/1046878198291003
18. Raser, J.R.: Simulation and Society: An Exploration of Scientific Gaming'. Allyn and Bacon, Boston (1969)
19. Roungas, B., Bekius, F., Meijer, S., Verbraeck, A.: Improving the decision-making qualities of gaming simulations. J. Simul. (2019, under review)
20. Roungas, B., de Wijse, M., Meijer, S., Verbraeck, A.: Pitfalls for debriefing games and simulations: theory and practice. In: Naweed, A., Wardaszko, M., Leigh, E., Meijer, S. (eds.) ISAGA/SimTecT -2016. LNCS, vol. 10711, pp. 101–115. Springer, Cham (2018). https://doi.org/10.1007/978-3-319-78795-4_8
21. Roungas, B., Meijer, S.A., Verbraeck, A.: A framework for optimizing simulation model validation & verification. Int. J. Adv. Syst. Measur. **11**(1& 2) (2018)
22. Roungas, B., Meijer, S.A., Verbraeck, A.: Harnessing Web 3.0 and R to mitigate simulation validation restrictions. In: International Conference on Simulation and Modeling Methodologies, Technologies and Applications. Porto, Portugal (2018)
23. Sargent, R.G.: Verifying and validating simulation models. In: Charnes, J.M., Morrice, D.J., Brunner, D.T., Swain, J.J. (eds.) Proceedings of the 28th Conference on Winter Simulation, pp. 55–64. IEEE Computer Society, Coronado (1996). https://doi.org/10.1145/256562.256572

Educational Escape Room – Challenges and Obstacles

Michał Mijal[✉], Martyna Cieśla, and Monika Gromadzka

University of Warsaw, Warsaw, Poland
{mijal,mciesla}@wz.uw.edu.pl,
monika.gromadzka@uw.edu.pl

Abstract. The purpose of this paper is to outline the designing and testing process of an educational escape room prepared by a team of international scientists participating in a research project. Its scope was to design the science-based escape room that could be used as an educational tool and support the dissemination of knowledge on the healthy lifestyle and healthy eating habits among the general population. Since games, in general, are one of the most engaging media, it was safe to assume that creating the escape room would involve participants in a way inaccessible to other teaching methods.

The project team led by the Technion University and comprised of researchers from the University of Helsinki, the University of Reading, and the University of Warsaw joined by EUFIC, developed a structured approach to the escape room design and step by step resolved issues emerging during the process. Underway we encountered several challenges that made us question some of the assumptions we had made before the procedure commenced.

Our main concerns were primarily the interculturality (or language dependence) of the escape room (five countries took part in the project) and its high difficulty level. As it turned out the former did not pose any design problems while the latter – unexpectedly – behaved counterintuitively: most players taking part in our tests managed to solve all the puzzles in less than a half of the pre-planned time and the record time was less than its quarter. This phenomenon was a result of a rather 'safe' approach to the puzzle design since we were more focused on knowledge dissemination.

Although the entertainment value proved to be a clear asset of our escape room, it is yet to be decided whether it, in fact, supports the learning process or is just a simple distraction and offers nothing new to the table of modern teaching methods. The next step of the project is to refine the existing escape room design and venture further into the realm of educational escape rooms to try out new approaches and decide what type of content is best suited for use in such educational projects.

Keywords: Games in education · Escape room · Game design · Interculturality

© Springer Nature Switzerland AG 2021
M. Wardaszko et al. (Eds.): ISAGA 2019, LNCS 11988, pp. 84–98, 2021.
https://doi.org/10.1007/978-3-030-72132-9_8

1 Introduction

The beginnings of game application in the educational process reach back to – supposedly – ancient China [1] and then to the post-Frederick the Great era in 19th century Prussia [2] but it was not until the WWII when they slowly gained acceptance among the decision makers as a useful tool in practicing specific skills and competences [3–5] Since then the spread of games into mainstream education has been slow but sure. Over the years it became apparent that a modern professional training not using this engaging and versatile tool has limited usability. Moreover while nowadays games in professional training hardly surprise anybody, the same does not necessarily apply to the traditional educational process in primary or secondary schools. Games (not sports) find their way into schools in a significantly slower manner [6–8]. And yet more and more teachers use games or gamification to the benefit of the students and their teaching process [7, 8]. Because games themselves have their limitations but when combined with an extended use in the form of gamification – elements of games used outside of the game context – it becomes clear that mostly the creativity of the teacher is the limiting factor in game applications.

2 Adult Education and Games

Educational games have been a valued method in adult education for many years. They belong to the so-called active methods of work and, unlike lectures, shows, stories and analogies, they require much commitment from the participant, while limiting the role and contribution of the trainer. What is essential, however, games are most often associated with these methods, which primarily support the development of skills and attitudes using previous or creating new experiences. In addition, it is possible to relate certain content to practice and often use theoretical tips and information to solve specific, practical problems. It is therefore a method that fits into the already canonical principles of adult learning developed in the 1980s by Malcolm Knowles [9].

Zombie Attack is a game aimed mainly at adults and older teenagers, therefore, creating mysteries and assumptions of the whole game we tried to use the achievements of andragogy. Due to the editorial requirements of the article, we are not able to quote all the assumptions, concepts and theories that constituted the theoretical foundation of our conceptual work. However, considering the nature of our project, andragogic knowledge has become a significant factor influencing the creation, selection and character of mysteries. Apart from considering the differences in learning between children and adults [10, 11] or elements of emotional and social adult learning [12, 13] as a central concept we adopted Jacek Mezirow's Transformative learning.

The subject of this concept is an adult human-specific learning process leading to a profound change in the way in which he perceives and interprets himself and the world and changes the surrounding reality [14]. The main categories are: frame of reference, habits of mind and point of view.

The frame of reference is a construction built on assumptions and expectations, through which we filter our sensual experience. It has three dimensions: cognitive, emotional and motivational. It selectively shapes and defines our perceptions, cognition, feelings and motivations by creating certain predispositions to our intentions, expectations and goals. It provides context for giving meaning [15] (p. 16). The frame of reference is created throughout life by adding, subtracting, and modifying individual "bricks" (associations, notions, emotions, values, etc.), and its aim is to enable us to interpret new experiences. Of course, what is the content of someone's frame of reference depends to a large extent on what direction the interpretation of their experiences and the surrounding world will take. This means that a person experiences something, that is, receives raw data from outside or inside, which he or she then tries to interpret. How a person reads an event depends to a large extent on what is within the frame of reference. The assumptions and predictions creating the reference framework can be more or less aware of what is visible during the work (e.g. coaching process) on one's own values or beliefs. In the frame of reference two dimensions can be distinguished: habits of mind and points of view [16 after: 14].

Habits of mind are certain ways of acting, thinking and feeling, which are conditioned by cultural, social, educational, economic, political or psychological codes. It is they that largely determine our values, beliefs, ways of learning, self-experience, etc., and that are the basis for our actions, thoughts and feelings, which are determined by cultural, social, educational, economic, political or psychological codes. According to Mezirow, they influence how people react in a new unknown situation, whether we like to stay and work in a group or whether we prefer individual work and political views (more than a party it is about a tendency to conservative or liberal views). After Krystyna Pleskot-Makulska I will recall the words of Mezirow, who believes that habits of mind work like filters through which experiences and information "flow".

Point of view is a collection of meaning schemes, interpretations, in which specific knowledge and content appear, especially of a given belief, attitude, etc., and in which the person's beliefs, attitudes, etc., can be seen. (e.g. conservative views are habits of mind, but opposing abortion is a point of view). This means that in relation to habits of mind they are more detailed ways of perceiving, they are also more conscious and less durable. We can say that, if we change our minds during the discussion under the influence of someone else's arguments that convince us, we will take the opposite point of view. You can also change your point of view, also under the influence of your own failures or successes.

Coming back to the issue of learning, learning is the process of using the individual's meanings to direct one's own thinking, action or feeling of what a person is currently experiencing, referring to the words of the creator of this concept [16] (p. 11). So, when someone experiences something new, he or she uses already known meanings (from his or her frame of reference). But sometimes these meanings are not enough. Then learning can result in the creation of a new framework, the strengthening of the old one, or its transformation. This means that in addition to transformative learning, there can also be formative learning when the frame is not transformed. This is the type of learning that most often occurs in children. Adults, on the other hand, are more predisposed to transformative learning due to their ability to self-reflect and critical thinking (of course, most processes are still formative).

Transformational learning occurs, when the existing frames are problematic, causing some kind of tension, not enough room for perspective for new experiences. If a person treats such a situation critically and with reflection, there may be a process of reframing which, in short, consists of three stages: a critical reflection on oneself: one's own beliefs and actions; discourse and action (undertaking or omission). The whole process takes place in the form of 10 phases, which are usually (not always!) arranged in the following order.

Reframing (change of frame)

- Activation: a disorientation dilemma arises - the feeling that the existing frame of reference does not bring the desired effects, becomes problematic for us;
- self-diagnosis, which may be accompanied by various states and emotions, e.g.: a sense of shame or guilt, anger, fear, surprise, disbelief;
- critical evaluation of one's own assumptions - in the process of subjective reframing or critical evaluation of other people's assumptions - in the process of objective reframing (i.e. thinking about the basis on which we/they base our/their beliefs, values, etc.);
- observation, that other people also experience a state of dissatisfaction and they change;
- discovering the possibility of playing new roles, entering into new relationships and taking new actions;
- planning the course of action;
- acquiring the knowledge and skills necessary to carry out the plan;
- trying to take on new roles;
- building confidence and competence in new roles and relationships;
- re-integration, integration of one's own life, considering the conditions dictated by the new frame of reference [17, 18] (p. 94).

The reframing itself can be sudden or gradual, objective or subjective, and can finally involve a change of point of view or habits of mind.

Finally, it is worth mentioning that the frame is also influenced by where and with whom we are, i.e. cultural canons or secondary socialisation. The groups to which we belong can very strongly influence the formation of our frame of reference, and the fewer content diverging from our frame of reference (more hermetic group), the less chance for transformative learning. Which in itself is not bad, because the frame of reference gives a sense of security, a belief in the "understanding" of the world and others. However, the problem is when the frame of reference is very narrow, and the points of view and habits of mind may harm others or affect some area of our lives in a negative way.

The concept of transformational learning can be an inspiration for those, who conduct educational activities very strongly associated with reframing (e.g. anti-discrimination workshops, training to replace aggression or work with one's own emotions). It is also possible, what we have just tried to use in our project, to create conditions for a disinformation dilemma and self-diagnosis process and to provide reliable information enabling a critical analysis of one's own assumptions.

It is worth emphasizing that the primary goal of our project was not to create an educational escape room, but to try out whether it is a good communication tool. So, we were wondering if the escape room can be useful for transferring reliable information, well-established in research. Accordingly, one of our goals was to check whether some deeper reflection or a small change in people's eating habits could be the consequence of participating in our escape room.

We assumed that the escape room could be the beginning of the process of transforming the frame of reference. It means that the disorienting dilemma can occur throughout "being in" escape room and solving puzzles. The experience of participating in the escape room may be more or less contradictory to our previous beliefs about healthy eating, and therefore the disorienting dilemma can appear, because, as we have already mentioned, it happens when we have the sense that our frame of reference may not be right for some reason.

Since all the phases of the process of reframing do not have to be arranged in the same order, we had assumed that the use of the escape room can also help in one of the next stages during which individuals notice that others also see the differences between what they believed or were convinced to and what they are learning now. Thus, we chose the escape room as a communication tool because it:

- gives a chance to act on and "being in" a new perspective,
- provides an opportunity for critical thinking,
- provides an opportunity to relate to others going through the same experience which can start transformation for some of them.

Important assumptions we made at the stage of creating the mysteries were also connected with the statements of Wiesław Łukaszewski, which concern the issue of memory and the process of remembering. According to him, we remember clear and concrete stimuli (the action of contrast); content that makes sense for us, is understandable and communicated to us in the language and using words we know; information that will be communicated to us in such a way that we will be convinced of their usefulness and possibility of using them in our own lives [19].

Finally, we would also like to mention one principle related to adult learning, which has been a challenge for us from the very beginning. Namely, in the developmental psychology of adults and adult education there is a conviction that adults learn, but also motivate to act by focusing on a certain effect. As it turned out later, this issue aroused our concern, because the constitutive feature of the escape room is the pressure of time. The participants have a certain number of minutes to get out of the room/rooms. This means that on the one hand time is a motivator to solve the task, on the other hand it can have a demotivating effect when focusing on the content of mysteries and remembering important content, from the point of view of the educational process.

3   Escape Room – The Basics

Escape room is a team adventure game performed in real-life conditions in which players are locked in a room and need to discover clues and hints, solve puzzles, and complete tasks within one hour in order to win. There is one main objective: to escape or find a hidden mystery object – an artefact. The teams consist of two to ten players aged above thirteen or eighteen depending on the theme of the escape game.

The first documented activity similar to present-day escape rooms is a single room created by the SCRAP company in Kyoto in 2007. It was named The Real Escape

Game. Five years later, at the turn of 2012, there was a sharp increase in the number of escape rooms first in Asia, then in Europe, Australia, Canada, and the United States of America. The country notwithstanding, escape game creators combine elements of live-action role playing games, point-and-click computer games including virtual escape games, treasure hunt games, haunted houses and interactive theatre, adventure game shows and movies, and themed entertainment industry in the escape room design [20].

Although every escape room has its individual character in terms of both storyline and décor, they all share similar types of puzzles and challenges. According to Scott Nicholson, the most common puzzle types are finding objects hidden in the room, team communication, counting, and noticing something "obviously" hidden in the room. Other popular puzzles are solved by substituting symbols with a key, out-of-the-box thinking, assembling of a jigsaw puzzle, or solving mathematical equations or riddles. Finally, hand-eye coordination challenges, traditional word puzzles, mazes, and puzzles involving senses: touch, smell, and taste, are the least common.

Escape room experience is structured in accordance with the plot of the game and the type of puzzles. There are three basic forms of puzzle organisation: open, sequential, and path-based – they are presented in the Fig. 1 below, where circles represent puzzles and the rectangles stand for either meta-puzzle or the victory.

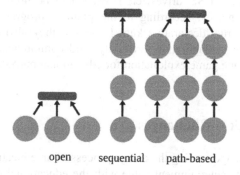

open   sequential   path-based

Fig. 1. Basic forms of puzzle organization [21] (p. 9.).

Each form of puzzle organisation is interrelated with the plot of the game and its level of difficulty. Escape room organised according to the open method consists of only two main plot points: entrance and escape, however, the gameplay is more difficult due to lack of particular order of the puzzles. The sequential method of puzzle organisation allows the players to immerse into the story of the game because the puzzles must be solved in the exact sequence, which renders the escape room easier to escape. The most multidimensional method of puzzle organisation is path-based since it combines attributes of both forms: open and sequential. It enables the players to fully participate in a complex story simultaneously retaining the random choice of paths which remain intrinsically chronological [21].

4 Escape Room in Education

Escape room was created as a game whose objective was purely ludic, entertainment. The first designers did not identify the educational potential of escape games. Nowadays however, over ten years since the first escape room had been launched, this potential begins to be recognized and exploited, be it by commercial and non-commercial institutions. In 2016 on the 5th international Games and Learning Alliance conference the EscapED project was presented. Its goal was simple:

> to conceptualize interactive experiences and aid other educational facilitators in creating their own, live-action games for the purposes of education and positive behaviour change in higher or further education settings [22] (p. 147).

The researchers designed and tested a prototype escape game whose objective was to increase soft skills of University staff, such as communication, leadership, and teamwork. The players assumed roles of sappers and hostages and were supposed to disarm a bomb [22].

Breakout EDU is another example of escape room's educational potential exploitation. Although it is not a location-bound escape game but a mobile kit, it serves its purpose. Facilitators receive a collection of escape room parts (locks, boxes, cards, UV torch with UV pen, USB drives, etc.) which can be used to design over two hundred fifty escape games, according to the planned program. During the game players not only construct declarative knowledge but they also develop the four C skills: critical thinking, collaboration, creativity, and communication [23]. The most recent example of escape game exploitation for educational purposes is Zombie Attack escape room design.

5 Zombie Attack – Challenges

One of the main challenges during the design process of an educational escape room is to carefully balance its entertainment value with the educational one. Tilting towards the latter makes for a good teaching tool but not very engaging or exciting, while tilting towards the former brings fun to the players but at the expense of a limited usability in the classroom or in other educational contexts. And while the theory behind the game design has been well described in various ways over the past few decades [24, 25], there is less literature providing any useful insights into the design of educational games [26]. And close to none on educational escape rooms – most of the literature in this topic are case studies [27–29] Which makes it even more difficult to determine ex ante what a right mix of fun and knowledge would be.

During our first run at the educational escape room design we adopted trial-and-error approach but some assumptions had to be made. First, we wanted the escape room to fit the market average in terms of playing time – 60 min seemed to be the right choice allowing for both: application of some engaging puzzles and knowledge dissemination at the same time. Second, everything should be thematic and somehow linked to the healthy food. This assumption allowed us to not lose out of our sight the main goal – educating. Third, we preferred rather educating than checking the knowledge. But in order to test the educational value of our escape room we had to measure the knowledge ex ante and ex post. Which led us to an extensive questionnaire, conducted before and (with some changes) after the game. Not an explicit assumption but rather an underlying thread in most of our efforts was also to create an escape room that is rather easy-to-build. We hesitated whether to go on 'full-mode' and design something spectacular or limit ourselves to props and interiors possible to recreate in most environments. The last aspect of design was rather the result of the multinationality of our team and parallel testing – all the project partners participated in tests and the first batch of props and puzzles was shipped by our project leader – Technion University. All partners contributed to the design but the manufacturing was 'centralized' and taken over by our project leader. And since the shipping of bigger props is troublesome we limited ourselves to the puzzles fitting into two oversized boxes.

The puzzles themselves were 'classical' in style – some padlocks with keys and padlocks with codes, texts with hidden messages, texts with colour codes, some calculations and some red herrings The design of our escape room was sequential in style, forcing players to walk a predetermined path and solve the puzzles in a required order. This was a conscious choice since the open design style requires from both designers and participants more experience and is more sensitive to unexpected behaviours of the participants.

An additional challenge was created by language dependence of some of the puzzles. Some partners decided to conduct the testing procedure using the English version while others (including the University of Warsaw) did a full localisation of the props. In most cases it didn't affect the gameplay but – as it out turned during tests – it influenced the total time needed for walking through the escape room. On top of the language dependence there was another crucial issue – on of the puzzles (referring to the food pyramid) had to be adjusted because in every country there is a slightly different food pyramid and the suggestions on the national level as to how much of each of the food types should be eaten vary.

In order to provide at least a partial comparability of the test results the project leader prepared the extensive manual for all partners, describing the props, the puzzles, possible outcomes and – most importantly – specific procedures for most common occurrences (how and when to give hints to the players etc.).

6   Zombie Attack – The Tests

Zombie Attack consisted of 9 puzzles solved in a predetermined order. They covered tasks like filling in the blanks, decipher a simple colour code, calculations of nutritional value of some dishes and protein daily intake value, substitution code, going through a text in order to find some information and watching a movie with a hidden message.

The game was tested in five countries: Belgium, England, Finland, Israel, and Poland, on over 250 players over the course of three months between September and November 2018. The participants' ages ranged from 18 to 61 years of age. They were mostly women, university students and university staff. The players were divided into teams of two to eight people. The estimated time of the game did not exceed one hour.

However, most teams solved all puzzles in less than thirty minutes. That is why many tests lasted only around fifty minutes, with ten minutes prior to the game for introduction and rules, and ten minutes after the game devoted to debriefing and final remarks. The players were not allowed to leave the room during the game, use their personal items, or interact with the research team observing the game save to ask for a hint.

To the tests we applied a mixed qualitative-quantitative approach and since there was no control group there were no experiments as such – rather an exploratory research focusing on testing of the abovementioned assumptions.

A key feature of the Zombie Attack escape room tests were extensive questionnaires which were filled by the players in before and after the game. The questionnaire comprised over forty questions divided into five categories: demographics and general questions, escape games, knowledge about nutrition, awareness about nutrition, and motivation to learn about nutrition. Additionally, thirty three randomly chosen players were interviewed in a semi-structured interview procedure. The questions referred to the players' opinion on the Zombie Attack experience and its educational value, changes in eating behaviour, and knowledge on healthy eating and food consumption.

7   Tests Results

Since the research material covers several different aspects of the eating habits and the escape room itself and due to the article volume limitations we had to present just a fraction of the results referring to the most prevalent issues raised by the participants.

The surveys conducted pre- and post- test in all countries suggest that – in spite of the sample not being representative – we achieved the educational impact on the participants. Across many dimensions, the majority of the players indicated an increased knowledge and awareness of the issues raised in the escape room. Although from the methodological standpoint we cannot extend the results on the general population, so far none of our initial assumptions were disproved. But while the quantitative data will be enriched by the tests that will be conducted with a more rigorous approach the qualitative data is already worth citing because in spite of a rather open structure of the interviews most participants agreed as to both: educational and entertainment value of our escape room. Over 250 participants completed pre- and post-test surveys which consisted of 49 and 36 questions respectively, 8 out of whom tested the participants' knowledge on nutrition. The Table 1 below presents their answers.

Table 1. Knowledge about nutrition.

Question	PRE	POST	CHANGE
1. How many calories are there in 1 g of protein?	37%	72%	35 p.p
2. What nutrients form the basis of energy calculation of food products?	81%	91%	10 p.p
3. How many grams of protein are recommended for a person to consume per day?	29%	45%	16 p.p

(continued)

Table 1. (*continued*)

Question	PRE	POST	CHANGE
4. What are essential amino acids?	56%	71%	15 p.p
5. What are complete proteins?	62%	71%	9 p.p
6. What are complementary proteins?	33%	51%	18 p.p
7. How much of the human body is protein?	36%	39%	3 p.p
8. What are the functionalities of proteins in our bodies?	55%	64%	9 p.p

% of responders who chose the correct answer

It is evident that the number of correct answers to each question increased after the game, which proves the educational effectiveness of the Zombie Attack escape game. The largest change was observed in the number of correct answers to the first question with 35 p.p. The puzzle linked to this question compels the players to read a short text about calories in essential nutrients and deduce a code to the padlock. What is more, there was only a 3 p.p. difference between the percentage of correct answers to the 7th question. The answer to this question did not constitute a part of a puzzle but was presented on posters in the escape room. On this basis it is safe to assume that the players' engagement and incorporation of information into the puzzles are crucial to the learning process in the escape room.

Apart from pre- and post-test surveys, 34 participants had been interviewed. The interviews were open and consisted of nine general questions. Most of the participants had been already eco-aware before playing the escape room, which can result in biased answers, but players commented on that themselves and used some of their knowledge during the play. The majority of them recognised the significance of raising awareness and sharing knowledge about healthy nutrition:

> *You should continue to improve the game because more learning methods are needed. If the topic is healthy nutrition, it is a very good topic, because the whole population should learn more about those things. There are a lot of beliefs and myths about nutrition and people don't know the truth.*

It is of utmost importance and value that adults of various nationalities consider the Games of Food project meaningful and purposeful. The participants not only expressed their appreciation for the cause but they also acknowledged the innovative learning method we used:

> *I think that an educational escape room is an interesting idea. It is worth going in this direction. New escape rooms should be something more than just entertainment. They should teach, just like here. I see this great potential, especially, that healthy eating is important.*

Another participant recognised the educational value of the Zombie Attack escape game, although they do not consider it a method suitable for every learner:

> *I believe that you can learn in the escape room for sure. I, for myself, learn slowly and I need to think deeply and so on. But this escape room would be a great place to solidify my knowledge. But I also think that there are a lot of people who learn faster than me and they remembered much more.*

It is worth mentioning that entering an escape room involves exposition to an abundance of information – regarding both learning materials and the game itself. The players need to organise their thoughts and actions, focus, and remain calm. Since the Zombie Attack escape experience is still in the testing stage, we are striving to find the golden ratio between education and entertainment.

The escape room served as a reference point for participants' own eating habits. During the game they learn about food pyramid, macro-nutrients and their energy value, protein energy calculation, protein daily value, essential amino acids, complete protein food, complementary protein sources, protein in the human body, and environmental aspects of protein consumption. The puzzles may inspire the players to reflect upon their eating habits and introduce positive changes:

> I think that, as I said before, I introduced some changes. The game was really an impulse to eat more healthily. And I had tried it before, and before. And the game reminded me why it's important and why it's worth it.

The players undoubtedly recognise the impact of the Zombie Attack experience on their knowledge and awareness as well as their motivation to make a difference. They were also eager to suggest adjustments which may increase the effectiveness of our escape room, such as including more video materials, fake puzzles, more puzzles loosely related to the healthy eating topic, rearranging reading-based puzzles so that they compel players to read the text in its entirety, and introducing more puzzles containing practical everyday easy-to-remember knowledge regarding healthy nutrition.

Despite the positive remarks, the participants also pointed out in detail elements and features of the Zombie Attack escape game experience which may negatively influence its educational effectiveness. Most players, both inexperienced and those who had previously participated in an escape game, concluded that the difficulty level of the puzzles and the escape room itself was moderate:

> The degree of difficulty could be slightly raised. The solutions were quite visible, I would rather read the whole text, but it wasn't necessary, because you could just spot the colourful letters and numbers.

This statement is particularly important: concerned that the game would be too difficult, we designed it too simple. More worryingly, being easy our escape game is not engaging enough. As the participant noticed, the reading-based puzzles should compel the players to familiarise themselves with the entirety of the text instead of just search for clues.

Secondly, the time factor proved to be an ambiguous challenge since the participants' opinions were divided. A number of participants stated that an hour is a sufficient amount of time to both win the game and thoroughly read learning materials, however, others disagree. They found it difficult to manage the time during the game because they did not know how many puzzles they had already solved and how many had been still incomplete:

> The matter of time is something negative because you don't really read, you don't learn as much as you could in this time. If the escape room had no time limitations, it would be possible to calmly read instead of searching for the key.

One of the participants suggested a solution:

I would like to know throughout the game what percentage of the puzzles remain to be solved so that I could assess it visually. We, the players, don't really know if there is a surprise there or not. And this awareness, or this ignorance of the scores of other teams wouldn't influence us. If we had known that we had completed most puzzles in 15 min, we would have had still 45 min to read the materials.

The challenge concerning game time is unexpected and insurmountable since the time restriction is an essential part of an escape game experience. It may, however, constitute a threat to the learning effectiveness. Our research on this matter has so far been inconclusive. We are yet to explore it and assess which solution would serve both the educational and the entertainment purpose of the escape room.

Finally, the players were mainly focused on solving puzzles as quickly as possible and on entertainment, not on the educational elements of the game. There are two immediate consequences of this approach: they do not read materials thoroughly and they do not concentrate on learning, as one of the participants stated:

Our team was really task-oriented. So, I think that we didn't read all the little books. We didn't read the last one for example, we just searched for the keywords. This notwithstanding, we remembered the most important things. Even if you scan through, you solidify this knowledge.

This participant paid attention to an issue which was unnoticed by many others – it does not matter whether the players rush through the puzzles or not, they are bound to learn, become more aware. The results of our tests indicate that there is a significant difference, even if the participants remain oblivious to it. Naturally all of the above-mentioned observations are based on participants' verbal declarations and require further investigation. The most common threads in the interviews were:

About entertainment:

- The difficulty level of the puzzles was considered to be moderate by the majority of the players.
- The use of multimedia (one of the puzzles involved playing of a movie on the tablet) enriched the experience significantly.
- The time pressure distracted from the immersion into the theme.
- All of the participants declared the fun factor as the dominating during the play.
- About education:
- The participants pointed out the usefulness of the data on sweet drinks and beverages.
- Escape room served a reference point for participants' assessment of their own eating habits.
- Majority of the players learned (and remembered that knowledge) about the types of proteins.
- Participants became more cautious about meat consumption.
- Most of the participants were already eco-aware before playing the escape room which can result in biased answers – players commented on that themselves and used some of their knowledge during the play.

About education:

- The participants pointed out the usefulness of the data on sweet drinks and beverages.
- Escape room served a reference point for participants' assessment of their own eating habits.
- Majority of the players learned (and remembered that knowledge) about the types of proteins.
- Participants became more cautious about meat consumption.
- Most of the participants were already eco-aware before playing the escape room which can result in biased answers – players commented on that themselves and used some of their knowledge during the play.

8 Conclusions

Based on tests conducted so far a few main directions of escape room development has been determined:

- The difficulty level needs to be increased. This will incorporate also the development of some variants of the same scape room allowing us to address different target groups with the similar puzzles. One of the ideas currently in development is to create the version for primary schools and another one for adults.
- The addition of puzzles spanning several tasks should contribute positively to the overall experience. After some initial tests of some additional puzzles this direction looks definitely promising. Preliminary results indicate a very positive reception.
- The entertainment goal has been achieved fully. However the educational value is still to be decided. In order to fully investigate the educational aspect of our escape room we will be working on the development of a more methodologically sound framework.
- Once the project team has gained some experience a less sequential and more path-based approach can be adopted. The development of another escape room (this time on obesity issues) is already underway and one of the main focuses of the design team is to make the escape room more path-based because it accommodates larger groups of players.
- Based on the knowledge created during the first year run another tool will be created – a card game in the year 2019 and possibly a board game in the year 2020. The first functioning prototype of the card game on food pyramid has already been developed and this path looks very promising in terms of supporting the main focus of the project – the escape rooms. The business model is still being negotiated but the card game supports very well the educational aspect of the project and enables the participants to stay in touch with the tool for longer time which usually translates well into the learning effects. The board game is still in early stages of development and it will be centred around food waste and waste management.

The results of our test run look promising in terms of the development of a tool that can be both useful and attractive for the participants. There is still a long road ahead of our project team before the escape room will be up-and-ready but the first tests confirmed the majority of the initial assumptions and the idea will be developed in the next phases of the project. The plan for the years to come covers not only the development of the escape rooms themselves but also a sustainable model for further advancement and enhancement of the games applied to various areas of food sciences.

References

1. Chen, Z.-Y.: Shao Yong's (1011-77) "Great Chant on Observing 'Weiqi'": an archetype of neo-confucian poetry. J. Am. Orient. Soc. **12**(2), 199–221 (2006)
2. Curry, J., Featherstone, D.: Paddy Griffith 1947–2010. Simul. Gaming **42**(1), 5–8 (2011). https://doi.org/10.1177/1046878110386103
3. Faria, A.J.: Business simulation games: current usage levels—an update. Simul. Gaming **29**(3), 295–308 (1998). https://doi.org/10.1177/1046878198293002
4. Zoroja, J.: Usage of business simulation games in Croatia: perceived obstacles. Manag. Glob. Trans. **11**(4), 409–420 (2013)
5. Liao, Y.-W., Huang, Y.-M,, Wang, Y.-S.: Factors affecting students' continued usage intention toward business simulation games: an empirical study. J. Educ. Comput. Res. **53**(2), 260–283 (2015). https://doi.org/10.1177/0735633115598751
6. Dishon, G.: Games of character: team sports, games, and character development in Victorian public schools, 1850–1900. Paedagogica Historica: Int. J. Hist. Educ. **53**(4), 364–380 (2017). https://doi.org/10.1080/00309230.2016.1270339
7. Forouzan, C., Abdolhassan, F.: Efficiency of Educational Games on Mathematics Learning of Students at Second Grade of Primary School. Tarih Kültür ve Sanat Araştırmaları Dergisi **6**(1), 232–240 (2017). https://doi.org/10.7596/taksad.v6i1.738
8. Øygardslia, K.: 'But This Isn't School': exploring tensions in the intersection between school and leisure activities in classroom game design. Learn. Media Technol. **43**(1), 85–100 (2018)
9. Holton Elwood, F., Knowles, M., Swanson, R.: Edukacja dorosłych. Wydawnictwo Naukowe PWN (2009)
10. Appelt, K.: Środkowy okres dorosłości. Jak rozpoznać potencjał dojrzałych dorosłych? In: Brzezińska A.I. (ed.) Psychologiczne portrety człowieka. Praktyczna psychologia rozwojowa, Gdańsk (2005)
11. Brzezińska, A., Wiliński, P.: Wspomaganie rozwoju człowieka dorosłego. Edukacja Dorosłych. **3**. 17–33 (1995)
12. Illeris, K.: Trzy wymiary uczenia się, Wrocław (2006)
13. Bandura, A.: Teoria społecznego uczenia się, Warszawa (2007)
14. Pleskot-Makulska, K.: Teoria uczenia się transformatywnego autorstwa Jack'a Mezirowa. Rocznik Andragogiczny. **2007**, 81–96 (2007)
15. Mezirow J.: Learning to think like an adult. Core concepts of transformation theory. In: Mezirow, J., Asscociates (eds.) Learning as Transformation. Critical Perspectives on a Theory in Progress, San Francisco (2000)
16. Mezirow, J.: Transformative dimensions of adult learning, San Francisco (1991)
17. Mezirow, J.: An overview on transformative learning. In: Illeris, K. (ed.) Contemporary Theories of Learning. Learning theorists... in their Own Words. Routledge Taylor & Francis Group, London and New York (2017)
18. Borrego, C., Fernandez, C., Blanes, I., Robles, S.: Room escape at class: escape games activities to facilitate the motivation and learning in computer science. J. Technol. Sci. Educ. **7**(2), 162–171 (2017)

19. Łukaszewski, W.: Wielkie pytania psychologii, Gdańsk (2011)
20. Nicholson, S.: Peeking behind the locked door: a survey of escape room facilities. https://scottnicholson.com/pubs/erfacwhite.pdf. Accessed 04 Apr 2019
21. Nicholson, S.: The state of escape: escape room design and facilities. https://scottnicholson.com/pubs/stateofescape.pdf. Accessed 04 Apr 2019
22. Clarke, S., Arnab, S., Keegan, H., Morini, L., Wood, O.: EscapED: adapting live-action, interactive games to support higher education teaching and learning practices. In: Bottino, R., Jeuring, J., Veltkamp, R.C. (eds.) GALA 2016. LNCS, vol. 10056, pp. 144–153. Springer, Cham (2016). https://doi.org/10.1007/978-3-319-50182-6_13
23. What is Breakout EDU? https://breakoutedu.com/. Accessed 04 Apr 2019
24. Schell, J.: The Art of Game design. CRC Press, Boca Raton (2008)
25. Koster, R.: A Theory of Fun for Game Design. Paraglyph Press, Scottsdale (2013)
26. Niman, N.B.: The Gamification of Higher Education Developing a Game-Based Business Strategy in a Disrupted Marketplace. Palgrave MacMillan, New York (2014)
27. Borrego, C.I., Fernández, C., Blanes, I., Robles, S.: Room escape at class: escape games activities to facilitate the motivation and learning in computer science. J. Technol. Sci. Educ. 7, 162 (2017). https://doi.org/10.3926/jotse.247
28. Eukel, H.N., Frenzel, J.E., Cernusca, D.: Educational Gaming for pharmacy students - design and evaluation of a diabetes-themed escape room. Am. J. Pharm. Educ. 81(7), 1–5 (2017)
29. Kinio, A.E., Dufresne, L., Brandys, T., Jetty, P.: Break out of the classroom: the use of escape rooms as an alternative teaching strategy in surgical education. J. Surg. Educ. 76(1), 134–139 (2019). https://doi.org/10.1016/j.jsurg.2018.06.030

Simulation Gaming Design
and Implementation

Simulated Construction of State's Intersubjective Reality in Virtual Games: An Emerging Tool of Social Power?

Svetlana Lobastova(✉) ⓘ

The University of Economics, Prague (VŠE), Prague, Czech Republic
lobs00@vse.cz

Abstract. The first decade of the 21st century was marked as the new era of public diplomacy and visual culture. Contemporary international relation systems exist in a hyperreal mode. Social interaction processes on the international global level proceed in virtualized hyperreal spaces. In an emergent modality of globalized international society each state aspires to expand its influence by the virtue of non-coercive methods utilization. Soft power, in this connection, that may be distributed by a state or non-state actor as the efficient form of social power. The hyperreal force may be intentionally distributed within the international system via popular mass media resources and online platforms. Consequently, online gaming platforms and appropriate construction of hyperreal space in gaming intercommunication may serve an efficient means of social power. However, gaming hyperreality space has not been considered an entire soft power tool yet. This paper focuses the key comprehension of modern power concept and proposes an innovative perspective of social force that may be represented by gaming virtual reality construction.

Keywords: Virtual games · Hyperreality · Social power · Social interactions · Virtual culture

1 The Subject Description

Nowadays, humanity development is to a deep extent influenced by data transmission processes and rapidly unfolding networking industry. Advanced global networking technologies and widespread broadcast media electronical devises and make possible the high-velocity interactive dialogue among people all over the world. The information transfer via social networking systems allows people to cooperate into intercommunities according to their areas of interest. Virtual games are dynamically gaining popularity over time and represent the category of popular mass media resources among young players of international global society [1]. Virtual games have become not only a significant part of postmodern popular culture [2], but also one of the top-selling products on the international market, that reflects a solid understanding of entertainment business [3].

The streaming popularity of virtual games has grown exponentially [4] due to globalization processes and rapid technological development. Currently, there are

M. Wardaszko et al. (Eds.): ISAGA 2019, LNCS 11988, pp. 101–108, 2021.
https://doi.org/10.1007/978-3-030-72132-9_9

being held the debates on the existing diversity of gaming simulations [5–7] and their influence on individual's consciousness [8–10]. There have been made attempts to identify the impact of audio-visual information content on the emotional aspects of individual's psychological dimension [11], also from scientific point of view [12, 13]. Otherwise, the precise influential impact of video gaming act on individual's psychological dimension and their perception of gaming reality has not been explored from scientific perspective to a sufficient extent yet.

A significant number of popular virtual games take place in a simulated illusory projection of virtualized intersubjective space which corresponds to an objective really of a real state. Appropriately, gamers' perception of a particular state's reality can be influenced by the gaming experience. The hyperreal reality of virtual game represents a simulated virtual construction designed by infographic systems, audio materials content and may include the elements of political symbolism and nationstate's attributes. The distribution of purposely constructed gaming virtual reality on the international market with instigated gaming experiences may have a significant impact on state's tourism industry development and economic advancement.

The ability of international actor to produce a high-quality virtual game is considered one of the underlying criteria of actor's economic and political success [14]. However, the utilization of hyperreality phenomenon has not been considered a substantive soft power instruments in the international context yet. This paper seeks to remedy this problem by analyzing the power concept and investigating hyperreality phenomenon. The aim of this research project is to propose an innovative perspective of social power that may be represented by gaming hyperreality and be further utilized on the international global level to increase power capacities and promote cultural ideas and social values.

2 The Modernized Idea of Social Power

Each state and non-state actor has the ability and aspiration to achieve the highest possible position and greater influence within the social hierarchy of the international global system. Furthermore, each actor has a privilege to create its personal strategy to achieve the highest possible position within the global system by the most efficacious possible way. In this connection, the actor can reach its power transition and move forward the international hierarchy by means of hard power and soft power instruments combination. Alternatively, the actor may devise.

or design its own individual mechanism, which would consist of these two diversities of prevalent forces. The competent ability of the international actors to compound the precise force machinery by disposing the petit capacities of each mode of power may afford the possession of effective apparatus for coercion or persuasion achievement of any particular issue, for instance, to attract potential partners or persuade contenders on the international stage.

The understanding of power notion in social and political sciences has been continually changing. In spite of the fact that hard power constitutes predominantly a prevalent type of force through the history of international relations discourse, an increasing attention nowadays is dedicated to the role of soft power. In 1990 there was proposed the concept of soft power by an American political scientist Joseph Nye. According to Joseph Nye, the state's power might be introduced by concepts of Soft and Hard Power. He argues that the cultural values of a state and its ideology can be considered as a peculiar diversity of a state's force [15]. From Joseph Nye's perspective, the main factors of soft power possess the availability to influence inclinations and preferences of remaining actors in the international relation system. It should be considered that in modern globalized world soft power has predominantly superior importance in comparison with hard power, which is assembled by economic and military power [16]. The soft power term was introduced by Joseph Nye in his book Bound to Lead: The Changing Nature of American Power and represents the ability to shape and influence preferences of actors in international relations through appeal and attraction [17]. Hard power is traditionally represented by various material means, such as military capacity, diversity of actor's economy and the level of its technological development. Soft power is represented by a set of cultural aspects and social values. It should be considered as cultural values and political ideology that are distributed within international system via mass media resources. This kind of force aims to attract, whether hard power strives to coerce. This contributes to the amplification of instrumentality and capacities of state's both hard and soft power.

It's important to emphasize, that the concept of power corresponds to resilience and capability of an actor to distribute its influence and to establish relations of obedience and predominance, consequently, actor's ability to ascertain the hierarchical structure of power distribution and to retain the dominant position within this structure. The United States of America hegemonically for a considerable time are regarded to be the soft power center of global culture [18]. Hollywood in cooperation with Ministry of Foreign Affairs of The United States of America and some public institutions have been implementing the global propagation of American culture and produced ideology by psychological means as a part of foreign policy strategy of the US via TV channels in foreign countries.

Virtual games represent the category of popular social media platform on the international level. This kind of social entertainment can be considered not only the popular mass media platform, but also a mediator between game producer and representatives of gaming society that dynamically gains the popularity with the lapse of time. Especially, if we take into consideration popularity of Cybersports that has still been constantly growing with geometric progression since the late the late 2000s and has already became a part of post-modern international pop culture and is officially recognized sport in 22 states all over the world and obviously have a potential to become Olympic sports in the immediate future. What is more, virtual games are not only significant part of modern pop-culture phenomenon, but also a solid product that reflects understanding of coetaneous entertainment business issues. Despite of the fact that due to dynamically streaming globalization processes and rapid technological development virtual games were not considered as one of contemporary soft power instruments so far. Even though one of the main criteria rating the economic and political successfulness of a state at the beginning of the twenty first century is the ability of the state to produce qualitative computer games.

The gaming industry has been rapidly developed from a niche segment to the global mainstream industry. Furthermore, international political and economic structures nowadays exist in a hyperreality form, which is stored by technical equipment and distributed via social media, respectively, the valuation of information. At the present time, such advanced democratic capitalist countries as North America, Japan and Western European countries can be considered as the most successful computer game producers on the world market. Each virtual game is a marketing product that is generated in purpose to satisfy the demand of virtual sensory information consumption in postmodern society. So, why not consider virtual games as a modern soft power tool that could be effectively implemented and utilized by a state as an instrument for achieving its strategic political and economic goals in a globalized world?

3   Virtual Games and Hyperreal Space

Hyperreality phenomenon affects all spheres of human life: social, political, economic and spiritual spheres. The idea of fictionalization processes of virtualized intersubjective hyperreality as a simulation of objective reality model was initially represented in works of a French philosopher and sociologist Jean Baudrillard. In the book *Simulacra and Simulation* [19] Baudrillard argues, that hyperreality phenomenon should be understood as the simulated illusion of reality and simulation models which gradually replaces objective reality [20].

In advanced technologically developed postmodern societies a reality simulation has already become a significant part of peoples' life. The great number of young representatives of post-modern cultures spend a significant part of their conscious day in a hyperreality spaces, that has progressively replacing their conscientious existence the objective reality. Moreover, the global social information networking interaction system is considered a central stage where the basic social transformations are enacted. Working with the idea about fictionalization, respectively simulation model of reality, [19] claims that objective reality is nowadays replaced by virtualized hyperreality.

Virtual gaming is young phenomenon that mankind faces. Otherwise, it already represents a significant element of global mass culture that influences the individual's perception of surrounding reality spaces [21]. Game studies has been established as a new approach among other social science disciplines since 2000 [22] and is devoted to studies of playing act and its impact on players' psychological aspects. This field of social studies incorporates various competences of several scientific disciplines: sociology, psychology, cultural studies, and gaming design. Game studies as a scientific discipline also focuses investigation of narateegaming interaction act [4]. In addition, game studies as an autonomous discipline incorporates sub-fields of social studies and is devoted to investigation of gaming act phenomenon, including repercussions of virtual games and their impact on the socio-cultural dimension of gaming communities.

Hyperreality of each virtual gaming space is constructed by infographic system of symbols and audio support materials [23]. During the gaming act game's consciousness is immersed into hyperreal space and their psyche enters a phase of vulnerability. So, the time that player spends within virtual gaming hyperspace corresponds the extent he is influenced by imaginary constructed virtual reality. Furthermore, it can be assumed, that in some cases the human behavior within the authentic reality space may be predetermined by the hyperreality representations constructed in virtual gaming. These aspects of gaming experience in virtual reality may be utilized by various actors on order to achieve their goals on domestic or international level.

In this case, it's important to notice, that each virtual game represents purpose-fully designed projection of hyperreality and has its algorithmically designed structure. Raster images performed by miscellaneous techniques of symbolization represent computer graphics as the visual organization of audio-symbolic systems. The virtual-ized intersubjective hyperreality, in this connection, is constructed by interconnected blocks of gaming spaces that are integrated into a simulation model of virtual reality spaces. In this way, virtualized intersubjective hyperreality exists as a graphic form of visual design. Game designers also have a privilege to place the player's mind into the simulated model of certain space-time structure and into a certain social context or particular reality of a certain state. The simulated illusory projection of intersubjective hyperreality that was purposefully constructed in order to influence the psycho-emotional dimension of peoples' consciousness with consequent alteration of their behavior strategy within objective reality and is transmitted via multichannel digital technologies and digital devices could be obviously understood as an effective social power tool.

Moreover, the virtual gaming design that has a structural composition may also be embed in diverse forms of emotional simulation and, as a result, evoke a particular mode of individual's behavior reaction. While the narratee-gaming interaction act, the narratee's consciousness is entirely immersed into hyperreality simultaneous narration. That could possibly serve an appropriate instant for individual's consciousness to be programmed for commission of certain behavior strategy acts. However, the history already knows some incidents of affective human–computer interaction with tragic impact on human behavior in a real world. After a person's consciousness existed in hyperreality that was constructed in a virtual game for some time, player's behavior strategy within a real-world space was identical to the previous gaming experience. The occurrence of such incidents may be observed internationally. The reasoning about this kind of incidents allows to continue the argument, that hyperreality of virtual game can influence an individual's psycho-emotional dimension to such a degree and program the player's mind for committing behavior strategy models. In addition, the hyperre-ality space that is constructed in virtual gaming spaces could perform the efficiently functioning power instrument, serve an information warfare tool and be considered a governing culture of postmodern society.

4 Gaming Modality of Social Power

If we consider virtual gaming one of the most popular mass-media platforms that persist into hyperreal spaces, then it may be argued that individual's self-perception and self-identification may also be influenced by gaming processes. The individual's per-ception of his motherland as well as his provision of a foreign state may be constructed by gaming hyperrealities. The essence of historical events that serve a constituent part of social basis construct and part of nation-building nowadays can hardly be regarded as objective. Representations of momentous events and historical developments are hypothecated into the intellection of young representatives in postmodern societies while gaming experiences, apart from other media surveillance.

Somers [24] argues that the narrative approach is a means for making common sense of social world and social identities. The permanent gaming experience, that takes a significant part of young player's conscious day, may articulate social values and influence an individual's identity formation. Gaming experience, that is insensibly constructed and contains representations of historic event acts, influences the players' perception of world fundamental principles. So, gaming representation of historical events and players' way of thinking may be formed under the influence of gaming virtual experiences.

It should be mentioned, that one of the most popular virtual games category is precisely represented by games with representations of historical act settings. The narrative and storyline of such games both take place in reconstructed historical context. For example, the game *Assassin's Creed* series, *Crusader Kings 2* represent simulated medieval Western European politics. The game *Empire Total War* simulates gaming experience during Napoleon war. Vietnam war is represented in a popular PC game *Far Cry 5: Hours of Darkness 2018*. The correlation between gaming experience and nation-identity formation process may be validated by the experience of the popular game Wolfenstein II. The game had initially contained representational fragments of the WWII events and Adolf Hitler's image. The game had been subjected to significant changes of a game plot and main characters modifications. A number of popular games have already been censored by governments, due to portraying national images as a national security threat. That serves a confirmation of the possible tremendous impact of gaming experience on players' perception of a foreign state's image. This reinforces the assumption, that virtual game as a popular mass-media platform and hyperreal construction of reality may cause a significant influence on a person's perception either of native land or a foreign state abroad. The opportunity of virtual gaming popularization with historical context in coherence with a state's market strategy may lead to the possible modification of a certain perception of historical events among young players internationally.

A number of popular virtual games with their game-setting take place into hyperrealities that correspond to an objective reality of a real states. For example, series of games *Assassins* refer to this category. Similarly, there are represented the simulated realities of New-York city and Paris in games *BioShock* and *BioShock Infinite*. The New-York city image is also represented in a game The Division. This allows to make an assumption, that the distribution of virtual game that promotes an appropriate image of state's objective reality and is deliberately distributed within a certain geographic territory may serve an effective social power force. Besides, there are some popular games, such as *Far Cry 5* or *BioShock Infinite*, which contain representations of national symbolism such as flags and religious motives.

It's important to mention, that representations of national symbolism play a significant role in constructing mass consciousness and nation-building processes. National symbolic system serves a tool of social regulations establishment and may pre-determine a common system of social values and non-verbal pattern of social behavior within a particular society structure. Besides, national symbolic system creates collective ethnicity, articulates a common historical context and generic strategy of social social behavior and serves an instrument for social construction basis. So, representations of national symbolism in gaming reality spaces may play a meaningful role in nation-building process and mass consciousness manipulation.

5 The Subject Perspective

Humanity faces a virtual gaming phenomenon last two decades. The impact of gaming experience on gamer's psychological aspects and dimensions of social behavior is not properly studied from scientific perspective yet. The research subject will focus on investigation of hyperreality phenomenon as an innovative mode of social force in the international context. The research will focus the appropriate means of virtual reality construction with utilization of state's intersubjective reality images and national symbolism elements within hyperreal world spaces. Primarily, it will focus the influential impact infographic systems as a gaming content promoted in popular virtual games and its potential affection of respondent's perception of a certain foreign state before and after the gaming experience. Furthermore, there will be made an attempt to identify the technique of gaming hyperreality construction that may serve an efficient tool of social power and may be utilized by government to promote their interests internationally.

To fulfill the goal there will be envisaged the combination of qualitative and quantitative research methods. The first section of the research will focus on the content analysis of chosen popular virtual games. This part of the research will represent the categorized results of gaming video documents analysis and communication artifacts. There also will be represented results of infographic systems and textual constituents of game screenplay analysis in chosen games. The following section of the research will be devoted to the investigation of a virtual gaming experience on respondents of international gaming community that will be indicated randomly. According to the classification od collected visual and textual data information there will be proposed the game-setting structure with nation-symbolism elements that can be effectively utilized by a state as a social power tool.

On the basis of conducted research and the analysis of game-content materials there will be represented an innovative perspective on gaming experience influence on young representatives of post-modern society. The research results will also indicate the impact of gaming experience on players' perception of simulated reality of a certain state abroad. There will be made an assumption relative to the feasibility of possible utilization of virtual game as an efficient power instrument. Furthermore, there will be proposed the model of gaming-design with hyperreality construction that could allow to implement a social power via virtual gaming experience.

References

1. Anthropy, A.: Rise of the Video Game Zinesters: How Freaks, Normal, Amateurs, Artists, Dreamers, Drop-Outs, Queers, Housewives and People Like You are Taking Back an Art Form. Seven Stories Press, New York (2012)

2. Steinkuehler, C.: Why game (culture) studies now? Games Cult. **1**(1), 97–102 (2006)
3. Kerr, A.: The Business and Culture of Digital Games: Gamework and Gameplay. Sage, London (2006)
4. Wolf, M., Bernard, P.: The Routledge Companion to Video Game Studies. Routledge, London (2014)
5. Kriz, W.C.: Types of gaming simulation applications. Simul. Gaming **48**(1), 3–7 (2017)
6. Clapper, T.: The way forward for Simulation & Gaming (S&G). Simul. Gaming **47**(1), 3–6 (2016)
7. Klabbers, J.: The Magic Circle: Principles of Gaming and Simulation. Sense Publishers, Rotterdam (2009)
8. Harviainen, J.T.: A hermeneutical approach to role-playing analysis. Int. J. Role-Play. **1**(1), 66–78 (2009)
9. Rodríguez-Aflecht, G., Hannula-Sormunen, M., McMullen, J., Jaakkola, T., Lehtinen, E.: Voluntary vs compulsory playing contexts: motivational, cognitive, and game experience effects. Simul. Gaming **48**(1), 36–55 (2016)
10. Pink, S.: The Future of Visual Anthropology: Engaging the Senses. Routledge, Abingdon (2006)
11. Anderson, C.A., et al.: Violent Video Game Effects on Children and Adolescents: Theory, Research and Public Policy. Oxford University Press, Oxford (2010)
12. Ferguson, C., et al.: Violent video games and aggression: causal relationship or by product of family violence and intrinsic violence motivation? Crim. Just. Behav. **35**(3), 311–332 (2008)
13. Hanjalic, A.: Extracting moods from pictures and sounds: towards truly personalized TV. IEEE Signal Process. Mag. **23**(2), 90–100 (2006)
14. Kline, S., et al.: Digital Play: The Interaction of Technology, Culture and Marketing. McGill-Queen's University Press, Montréal (2003)
15. Nye, J.S.: Bound to Lead. The Changing Nature of American Power. Joseph S. Nye write, and He xiaodong, pp. 24–25. Yi Wen Publishing Military, Beijing (1992). Gai yuyun translate
16. Nye, J.S.: Limits of American power. Political Science Quarterly, pp. 545–541, Library Core Research (2005)
17. Nye, J.S.: Bound To Lead: The Changing Nature of American Power. Basic Books, New York (1991)
18. Allison, A.: The Attractions of the J-Wave for American Youth. Soft Power Superpowers: Cultural and National Assets of Japan and the United States, pp. 106–107, M.E Sharpe, New York (2008)
19. Baudrillard, J.: Simulacra and Simulation. The Body, In Theory: Histories of Cultural Materialism. University of Michigan Press. 14th Printing ed, pp. 21–54 (1981)
20. Baudrillard, J.: Simulacra & Simulation. University of Michigan Press, The Precession of Simulacra (1994)
21. McAllister, K.S.: Gamework: Language, Power, and Computer Game Culture. University of Alabama Press, Tuscaloosa (2004)
22. Mäyrä, F.: An Introduction to Game Studies: Games in Culture. Sage Publications, Thousand Oaks (2008)
23. Salen, K., Zimmerman, E.: Rules of Play: Game Design Fundamentals. MIT Press, Cambridge (2003)
24. Somers, M.: The narrative constitution of identity: a relational and network approach. Theory Soc. **23**(5), 605–649 (1994)

A Review of Game-Based Research for English Language Learning in S&G Interdiscipline Journal

Panicha Nitisakunwut[✉] and Songsri Soranastaporn

Mahidol University, Salaya, Nakhon Pathom, Thailand
panicha.nit@mahidol.edu, songsri.sor@mahidol.ac.th

Abstract. Many experimental studies on game-based learning have resulted in constructive learners' learning outcomes, especially simulation and gaming for English language learning. However, there has been disagreement on the outcome of game-based learning. This leads to the necessity to conduct a systematic review on simulation and gaming studies to provide comprehensive analysis regarding to their effectiveness and implementation. This article carries out a review of literature research in terms of identifying research evidence about the positive impacts of games for language as a means to address the best practices and guidance for the implementation of game-based for language education. This article reviews and describes relevant simulation and game-based learning (GBL) studies published in S&G Interdiscipline journals from 2000 to 2019. Set keywords "gam*" related to simulation and gaming or game-based learning", and language related words for example "literacy", "ESL", "EFL", "listening", speaking", "writing" were used to search for articles on the database. 561 studies were found. Only 14 studies met the set inclusion criteria. The findings suggest that simulation-based gaming and debriefing would be beneficial for English language teaching, especially composition and literacy classrooms even though these studies are subject to limitations.

Keywords: Simulation · Gaming · Game-based learning · Game-based English language learning · English learning and teaching

1 Introduction

For the last two decades, educational research has been involved in the use of digital games for learning. This could indicate that educational researchers and practitioners show an increasing interest in the potential of games and providing new teaching technique to see how games influence students' learning outcomes. Many educational research studies have conducted in various learning domains such as language, business, mathematics, statistics, computer science, biology, and psychology [1, 2].

Some studied exploiting games in classroom revealed constructive effect on students' motivation, new knowledge, and skills acquisition [3, 4]; while other studies did not show the concrete evidence on students' high academic achievements or even psychological development [2].

© Springer Nature Switzerland AG 2021
M. Wardaszko et al. (Eds.): ISAGA 2019, LNCS 11988, pp. 109–114, 2021.
https://doi.org/10.1007/978-3-030-72132-9_10

Though researchers have conducted literature review research to defragment and systematically review research studies regarding to playing digital games in various educational contexts in an attempt to provide understanding the effects of games and propose guidance about best practices to use games in learning [1–3, 5], only few literature review research have been done on digital game-based language learning practices [6–9]. Most of the previous literature review analyzed the research on digital game-based learning purposing on various educational aspects rather than focusing on one domain-specific area.

Simulation & Gaming Interdiscipline Journal has delivered a delightful opportunity over four decades to explore simulation-based gaming. This article reviews the research articles regarding to simulation and gaming for English language teaching and learning within this journal between 2000 and 2019. The following questions are raised:

1. What game genres were used to support the learning and teaching of language in selected studies?
2. What language skills were focused in the selected studies?
3. What evidence on learners learning outcomes was illustrated in the selected studies?
4. What research methods were employed to examine the learning and teaching of languages in the selected studies?

2   Previous Literature Reviews

Educational games, usually refers to as serious games, are designed based on pedagogy with the intended purpose of promoting education [10]. They can sometimes exploit using electronic means to help, especially in the field of foreign language education that has now been influenced by the trend of using of technology and digital tools to support language learning [6]. One of the best ways to apply games and simulations in the classroom is exploiting games as learning tools or instructional materials. For instance, Yükseltürk, Altıok, and Başer, [11] integrated game-based learning activities with Kinect technology for first-year university students who enrolled in the foreign language course in Turkey. The games were developed and blended into the course which aimed to enable students to develop four English skills. While the students played games in groups, they are expected to acquire skill and knowledge in daily conversation, self-introduction, writing about everyday subjects, and other compulsory matters. And the results showed that experimental groups developed positive attitude toward learning English after using digital games. Saliés [12] combined gaming and simulation in an English for Academic Purposes class for international students. The simulation for the writing class, namely GUN CONTROL, in which aims to provide the student's tool to write an argument essays on the gun control controversy. She reported that the integrative simulation improved the students' knowledge of the topic and type of language and structure. Cook, Gremo, and Morgan [13] used Tabletop gaming through role-play system for literature class. The students in small groups play with the four game characters: warrior, ranger, mage, and healer. They work in the group to control characters throughout gameplay which resulted in collaboration. The findings also ac-counted for acquiring narrative experience and making decision. These examples show that when digital games were used as learning tools, they usually come with the effective results.

Deubel [14] stated that digital game-based learning has the potential to engage and motivate students and offer custom learning experiences while promoting long-term memory and providing practical experience. Role-playing, simulation, and adventure games are suggested as non-violent games for education to facilitate planning and problem-solving, and they also appeal to the development of more than one skill.

3   Method

3.1   Setting Inclusion and Exclusion Criteria

Once a clear intended research purposes and questions have been decided, defining inclusive criteria can be made to enact the standard of the quality of research. At this stage, inclusion and exclusion criteria will be developed in order to search for required game-based language learning articles to be studied and to restrict the scoping area of searching results. Field [15] stated that inclusion criteria can be developed based on the research question being addressed. To be included in this review and to answer the research question, the article paper should meet the following requirements:

(a) game-based language learning articles should be dated during the period of 2000–2019 published in Simulation & Gaming Interdiscipline Journal,
(b) game-based language learning articles should be research studies with dependent variables measured English language learning and should report learning outcomes,
(c) game-based language learning articles should target on implementing games for tertiary or undergraduate education, and
(d) game-based language learning articles should be published in English.

In other words, articles were excluded if they were not published within the designated time period. Other types of publications, such as book reviews, editorials, commentaries, literature reviews were also excluded.

3.2   Searching for and Identifying Potentially Relevant Studies

After setting what types of studies included in the analysis, searching for all relevant studies should be taken into account. At this stage, search terms play important roles. Set of keywords was created and used in database searches of Simulation & Gaming Interdiscipline Journal. This study employed two main sets: (a) the term (gam*) covering 'game', 'games', 'gaming', 'serious game', 'educational game', 'game-based learning', 'digital game-based learning', 'video game', 'computer game', 'gamification', 'MMOG', 'MMORG'; as well as (b) language learning and teaching related words including (language), (literacy), (English), (listening), (speaking), (reading), (writing), (vocabulary), (grammar) and (pronunciation).

3.3 Coding Scheme

After gathering the research articles from Simulation & Gaming Interdiscipline Journal database, the process of coding information began. As the research purposes of this study are to examine games genres, language skills, learners' learning outcomes, and research methods employed, the coding scheme is developed to classify and identify common features of the prospective retrieved studies. Cooper's [16] coding procedure, including the codebook construction, coder-training, discussion and negotiation on variation, and estimating reliability will be applied. Consequently, it might comprise of four groups of categories: 1) games genres (including availability, mobility, and interactivity), 2) language skills focus, 3) learners learning outcomes (including language acquisition, knowledge learning, higher-order thinking or competence) 4) research methodology (including type, duration of intervention setting). Then content analysis was employed.

4   Results and Discussion

4.1   Game Genres

Not surprisingly, game genres were not varied. Among 14 studies, most studies in Simulation & Gaming Interdiscipline Journal were simulation games (12 studies) and only two were roleplaying games. Correspondingly, most of simulation games were developed by the researchers themselves and they were not mobility. It should be noted that the genre of games encompasses a range of simulation and role-playing games. It might be result from the name and concept of the journal in which the research studies were published.

4.2   Language Skills Focus

The distribution of the target language skills being studied in Simulation & Gaming Interdiscipline Journal for over two decades focused on composition or writing skill. 7 studies have shown that their target language employed simulation-based gaming so as to enhance writing skills for undergraduate students in ESL and EFL classes. Coleman [17] used SIM COPTER simulation-based game for freshman ESL students who enrolled in composition course at a state university to help them learn the element of rhetorical for an essay writing and the students discovered that this activity serves as a useful exercise. In addition, speaking, listening and vocabulary were skills focused in this journal. One of the studies exploited role-play situations which adapted from the television American series *Friends* to help the university students in Romanian learn how to do apology speech acts [18]. The advantages of doing this role-plays were replication on native speakers and occurrence of natural conditions.

4.3   Learners' Learning Outcomes

The learning outcomes of simulation and gaming are an important focus of this review. Most studies suggested students' positive learning outcomes toward the use of simulations and roleplaying games. Regarding to language acquisition, most studies provided evidence for writing, speaking, listening, and vocabulary respectively including higher-order thinking of communicative competence. When looking at the specific language skills. Most studies apply simulations for composition courses. For example, Moder, Seig, and Elzen [19] used a thematically linked set of semester-long simulations in an English for academic purposes composition course and their study also showed the effectiveness of simulations. The teaching plan was a part of curriculum development and the target audiences were undergraduate international and American students enrolled in English composition courses. The results have indicated that simulations provided a powerful framework for the EAP composition curriculum and the students were able to overcome problems of unfamiliarity, low interesting, and plagiarism.

4.4   Research Methodology

The finding regarding methodology indicates that most studies employed qualitative method when doing the experiment. It can be noted that most of the studies used simulations as tools for language teaching and learning with small amount of students; this could be the most appropriate method. This method was small in scale but it enabled the researcher to examine the study in depth and report the findings with thick descriptions.

5   Conclusion

A review study of fourteen articles published in Simulation & Gaming Interdiscipline Journal from 2000 to 2019 was conducted, and the major findings can be summarized as follows: (1) simulations were the most common game genres among game-based learning studied and they were custom-built by the researchers; (2) most of game-based studied focused on composition skill and communicative competence was a subsequent; (3) the majority studies indicated positive learning outcomes related to acquired skills; and (4) most of the studies employed qualitative method to examine the educational use of simulation-based gaming and role-playing.

This current review does not claim to be solely comprehensive but summarized the research on game-based in Simulation & Gaming Interdiscipline Journal on the search term used and the time period of the review. It is therefore suggested that more comprehensive reviews that examine a greater number of papers be conducted to search for more topics of research interest or trend with in a wide variety of publications related to the field of education.

References

1. Boyle, E.A., et al.: An update to the systematic literature review of empirical evidence of the impacts and outcomes of computer games and serious games. Comput. Educ. **94**, 178–192 (2016). https://doi.org/10.1016/j.compedu.2015.11.003

2. Qian, M., Clark, K.R.: Game-based learning and 21st century skills: a review of recent research. Comput. Hum. Behav. **63**, 50–58 (2016). https://doi.org/10.1016/j.chb.2016.05.023

3. Connolly, T.M., Boyle, E.A., MacArthur, E., Hainey, T., Boyle, J.M.: A systematic literature review of empirical evidence on computer games and serious games. Comput. Educ. **59**(2), 661–686 (2012). https://doi.org/10.1016/j.compedu.2012.03.004

4. Van Eck, R.N.: Digital Game-Based Learning: Still Restless. After All These Years. EDUCAUSE Review **50**(6), 13–28 (2015)

5. Hwang, G.-J., Wu, P.-H.: Advancements and trends in digital game-based learning research: a review of publications in selected journals from 2001 to 2010. Br. J. Educ. Technol. **43**(1), E6–E10 (2012). https://doi.org/10.1111/j.1467-8535.2011.01242.x

6. Peterson, M.: Computerized games and simulations in computer-assisted language learning: a meta-analysis of research. Simul. Gaming **41**(1), 72–93 (2010). https://doi.org/10.1177/1046878109355684

7. Hung, H.-T., Yang, J.C., Hwang, G.-J., Chu, H.-C., Wang, C.-C.: A scoping review of research on digital game-based language learning. Comput. Educ. **126**, 89–104 (2018). https://doi.org/10.1016/j.compedu.2018.07.001

8. Chen, M.H., Tseng, W.T., Hsiao, T.Y.: The effectiveness of digital game-based vocabulary learning: a framework-based view of meta-analysis. Br. J. Edu. Technol. **49**(1), 69–77 (2018). https://doi.org/10.1111/bjet.12526

9. Tsai, Y.-L., Tsai, C.-C.: Digital game-based second-language vocabulary learning and conditions of research designs: a meta-analysis study. Comput. Educ. **125**, 345–357 (2018). https://doi.org/10.1016/j.compedu.2018.06.020

10. Zyda, M.: From visual simulation to virtual reality to games. Computer **28**(9), 25–32 (2005). https://doi.org/10.1109/MC.2005.297

11. Yükseltürk, E., Altıok, S., Başer, Z.: Using game-based learning with Kinect technology in foreign language education course. J. Educ. Technol. Soc. **21**(3), 159–173 (2018)

12. Saliés, T.G.: Simulation/Gaming in the EAP writing class: benefits and drawbacks. Simul. Gaming **33**(3), 316 (2002)

13. Cook, M.P., Gremo, M., Morgan, R.: We're just playing: the influence of a modified tabletop role-playing game on ELA students' in-class reading. Simul. Gaming **48**(2), 199–218 (2017). https://doi.org/10.1177/1046878116684570

14. Deubel, H.: The time course of presaccadic attention shifts. Psychol. Res. **72**, 630–640 (2008)

15. Field, A.: Meta-analysis. In: Millsap, R.E., Maydeu-Olivares, A. (eds.) The SAGE Handbook of Quantitative Methods in Psychology, pp. 404–422. SAGE Publications Ltd., London (2009). https://doi.org/10.4135/9780857020994.n18

16. Cooper, H.: Research Systhesis and Meta-Analysis: A Step-by-Step Approach, vol. 2. Sage Publications, Thousand Oaks (2015)

17. Coleman, D.W.: On foot in SIM City: using SIM copter as the basis for an ESL writing assignment. Simul. Gaming. **33**(2), 217–230 (2002). https://doi.org/10.1177/1046878102332010

18. Demeter, G.: Role-plays as a data collection method for research on apology speech acts. Simul. Gaming **38**(1), 83–90 (2007). https://doi.org/10.1177/1046878106297880

19. Moder, C.L., Seig, M.T.D., Van Den Elzen, B.: Cimarron valley: a simulation-based EAP composition curriculum. Simul. Gaming **33**(3), 284–298 (2002). https://doi.org/10.1177/104687810203300304

Accuracy in Business Simulations

Mihail Motzev[1]([⊠]) and Ophelia Pamukchieva[2]

[1] Walla Walla University, College Place, Washington, USA
mihail.motzev@wallawalla.edu
[2] University of National and World Economy, Sofia, Bulgaria

Abstract. The present paper provides some insights into accuracy in simulations and the opportunities to increase it in a very cost-effective way using Statistical Learning Networks. Learning is minimal if the simulation model is not accurate and the predictions made by students are not close enough to the real-life business. The results so far show significant achievements in minimizing the prediction errors, shortening the design time, and reducing the cost and the efforts in simulation models development.

Keywords: Accuracy · Business simulations · Deep learning · Statistical Learning Networks · Multi-layered nets of active neurons

1 Introduction

In business training and education, a properly designed simulation game would closely follow the assumptions and rules of the theoretical models. In the model-based games, especially, if the game does not accurately represent a real system, then the knowledge that the students receive about real-life business would be questionable. Consequently, if the game model is not accurate and the predictions made by students are not close enough to the real-life business case, then learning will be minimal.

Increasing simulation accuracy provides many benefits. This makes it possible to improve the decisions that students make during model-based business games. It is plain to see that the learning is minimal if the simulation model is not accurate and the predictions made by students are not close enough to the real-life business.

Ever increasing model accuracy helps researchers analyze problems more precisely, which leads to deeper and better understanding. Simulations with higher accuracy simply produce better predictions and support managers in making better decisions that are much closer to the real-life business case. For example, in [1] (pp. 317–318) the increasing of the model accuracy in forecasting equation, i.e. reducing its relative Mean Squared Error (MSE) from 7.5% to 2.44%, practically means that the prediction interval at 99% level of significance has been reduced from 45% (MSE relative to the mean) to 14.64% (MSE relative to the mean), that is 3.07 times! Certainly, every decision maker would like to have such narrow prediction interval when making decisions.

This paper discusses the problem of accuracy in business simulations and provides some insights into how to address it in a cost-effective way using Statistical Learning Networks in the form of Multi-Layered Networks of Active Neurons. It presents results from international research done in Europe, Australia, and the United States.

© Springer Nature Switzerland AG 2021
M. Wardaszko et al. (Eds.): ISAGA 2019, LNCS 11988, pp. 115–126, 2021.
https://doi.org/10.1007/978-3-030-72132-9_11

2 Techniques and Measures of Simulation Accuracy

2.1 How to Measure the Accuracy in Simulations

Risk and uncertainty are central to forecasting and prediction in simulations and it is generally considered good practice to indicate the degree of uncertainty attached to each forecast. Reducing uncertainty requires that a prediction should be sufficiently accurate for its purpose and be relied upon by the decision maker who will use it. There is no such thing as absolute accuracy and raising the level of accuracy increases cost but does not necessarily increase the value of information. It is important that the degree of accuracy should be clearly stated in the beginning of each particular forecasting process. This will enable users to plan for possible errors and will provide a basis for comparing alternative forecasts.

To judge the quality of models merely by formal criteria like the closeness of fit of a model and a true system, based on one data set is doubtful. Instead, it is necessary to have a purposeful judgment of the quality of model adaptation based on the suitability of the model to solve a predefined task. In spite of user experience, sometimes the choice of the model is too subjective – to make it more objective is a primary goal in many contemporary studies like [1–3] and others.

It is important to evaluate accuracy using genuine data. It is not correct to look at how well a model fits the historical data – the accuracy of predictions can only be determined by considering how well a model performs on new data that were not used when fitting the model. When choosing models, it is common to use a portion of the available data for fitting, and use the rest of the data for model validation. These testing data should be used to measure how well the model is likely to predict on new data.

In addition to the reasons mentioned above, a few more points should be noted:

- A model, which fits the data well does not necessarily forecast well.
- A *"perfect"* fit with zero prediction error can always be obtained by using a model with large enough number of parameters (as shown on Fig. 1).
- *Overfitting* a model to data is as bad as failing to identify the systematic pattern in these data.

As mentioned above, in most cases, it is not possible to select an optimal model from many possible models without some extra information. This process is referred to as *out-of-sample forecasting*. In [2] and [3] the term *external information* is used, referring to Godel's *external complement* [4]. In general, it is known as *cross-validation* or *rotation estimation* [5].

Cross-validation is a model validation technique for assessing how the results of a statistical analysis will generalize to an independent data set. It is mainly used in studies where the goal is prediction, and we want to estimate how accurately a predictive model will perform in practice. In a prediction problem, a model is usually given a dataset of known data on which training is run (*training dataset*), and a dataset of unknown data (or first seen data) against which the model is tested (*testing or validating dataset*).

There are many important measures for judging accuracy of a fitted model. Each of these measures has some unique properties, different from others and it is better to consider more than one performance criteria.

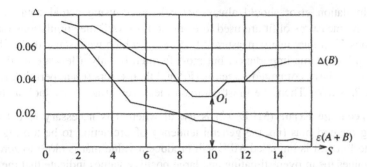

Fig.1. Variation in error ε(A + B) and error measure of an external complement Δ(B) for a regression equation of increasing complexity S; O1 is the model optimal complexity (Source [2], p.11)

2.2 Measures of Accuracy

Simulations are not perfect, as mentioned in previous sections, and actual results usually differ from predicted values. Predictions of outcomes are rarely precise and the researcher can only endeavor to make the inevitable errors as small as possible. The difference between the actual value and the predicted value for the corresponding period is referred to as the *forecast (prediction or simulation) error.* By default, the error (1) is defined using the value of the outcome minus the value of the forecast:

$$e_t = Y_t - F_t \tag{1}$$

where e_t is the forecast error at period **t** (*t = {1, 2, 3…N}*);

- Y_t is the actual value at period **t** and
- N is the prediction interval (or the size of the data set);
- F_t is the forecast for period **t**.

Each simulation represents the real-life business variable with some *accuracy,* related to the particular size of the forecast error. It is good to know some general facts, for example, the fact that forecast accuracy decreases as *time horizon* increases, i.e. short range forecasts usually contend with fewer uncertainties than longer-range forecasts, and thus they tend to be more accurate.

However, it is more important to know the degree of each particular forecast accuracy. There are different techniques to quantify the degree of accuracy. In most cases, the prediction is compared with an outcome at a single time-point and a summary of forecast errors is constructed over a collection of such time-points.

The simulation error should always be calculated using actual data as a base. Traditionally, measures of fit are used to evaluate how well the simulations match the actual values. There are many measures of accuracy, which we discuss in details in [1]. All of them have some importance, but most frequently only a few are used.

Suppose we have computed forecasts (F_t) and their errors (e_t) at period t, for a data set $t = \{1, 2, 3...N\}$. Then, the most common measures of accuracy look as follows:

Mean Percentage Error (MPE) (2) is useful when it is necessary to determine a forecasting method bias (i.e. the general tendency of prediction to be too high or too low). If the forecast is unbiased MPE will produce a value that is close to zero. Large negative values mean overestimating and large positive values indicate that the method is consistently underestimating. A disadvantage of this measure is that it is undefined whenever a single actual value is zero. In terms of its computation, it is an average percentage error:

$$MPE(\%) = \frac{1}{N} \sum_{t=1}^{N} \left(\frac{e_t}{y_t} \right) * 100 \tag{2}$$

MPE shows the direction of errors which occurred and the opposite signed errors affect each other and cancel out. It is desirable that for a good prediction with a minimum bias the obtained MPE should be as close to zero as possible.

Mean Absolute Percentage Error (MAPE) (3) puts errors in perspective. It is useful when the size of the forecast variable is important in evaluating. It provides an indication of how large the forecast errors are in comparison to the actual values. It is also useful to compare the accuracy of different techniques on same or different data.

$$MPE(\%) = \frac{1}{N} \sum_{t=1}^{N} \left(\frac{|e_t|}{y_t} \right) * 100 \tag{3}$$

MAPE represents the percentage of average absolute error and is independent of the scale of measurement, but it is affected by data transformations. It does not show the direction of error and does not panelize extreme deviations. For a good prediction, the obtained MAPE should be as small as possible.

Mean squared error (MSE) (4) is the average of the squares of the errors, i.e. the differences between the actual value and the forecast at period t:

$$MSE = \sum_{t=1}^{N} e_t^2 / (N - 1) \tag{4}$$

The MSE is the second moment (about the origin) of the error, and thus incorporates both the variance of the estimator and its bias. For an unbiased estimator, the MSE is the variance of the estimator. Like the variance, MSE has the same units of measurement as the square of the quantity being estimated. It is also sensitive to the change of scale and data transformations. Because of all these properties, researchers use the MSE square root most of the time.

Root Mean Squared Error (RMSE) (5) is the square root of calculated MSE. In an analogy to the standard deviation, taking the square root of MSE yields the root-mean-square error (RMSE), which has the same units as the quantity being estimated:

$$RMSE = \sqrt{MSE} \tag{5}$$

Unlike MSE, RMSE measures the forecast error in the same units as the original series and it has easy and clear business interpretation. It is a measure of average squared deviation of forecasted values and since the opposite signed errors do not offset one another, RMSE gives an overall idea of the error occurring during forecasting.

Most importantly, RMSE (like MSE) panelizes extreme errors (it squares each) oc curring while forecasting. It emphasizes the fact that the total forecast error is in fact much affected by large individual errors, i.e. the large errors are much more expensive than the small errors.

The RMSE serves to aggregate the magnitudes of the errors in predictions for various times into a single measure of predictive power. Thus, it is a good measure of accuracy, but only to compare forecasting errors of different models for a particular variable and not between variables, as it is scale-dependent.

Coefficient of variation of the RMSE, CV(RMSE) (6) is defined as the RMSE normalized to the mean of the observed values $\bar{y}$:

$$CV(RMSE) = RMSE/\bar{y} \tag{6}$$

It is the same concept as the coefficient of variation (CV) except that RMSE replaces the standard deviation. The CV is useful because the standard deviation of data must always be understood in the context of the mean of the data. In contrast, the actual value of the CV is independent of the unit in which the measurement has been taken, so it is a dimensionless number. For comparison between data sets with different units or widely different means, we should use the CV instead of the standard deviation. The smaller the CV(RMSE) value, the better the simulation.

Which metrics should be used depends on the particular case and its specific goals. As mentioned already, it is better to consider more than one performance criteria. This will help to obtain a reasonable knowledge about the amount, magnitude and direction of the overall simulation error. For this reason, experienced researchers usually use more than one measure for judgment and MPE, MAPE, RMSE and CV(RMSE) are a very good choice. The main benefit of this group is that it provides good information about the bias and the precision of the simulation. In addition, since CV(RMSE) panelizes extreme errors and MAPE does not, a researcher's goal should be to obtain close enough values for both criteria (more details we discuss in [1] pp. 67–94).

2.3   Simulations Evaluation

To determine the value of a simulation we need to measure it against some baseline, or minimally accurate reference forecast. There are many types of predictions that, while producing impressive-looking skill scores, are nonetheless naïve. For example, a persistence (naïve) forecast can still rival even those of the most sophisticated models. Two of the most important factors used to evaluate a simulation in real life are its **Cost** and **Accuracy**. Additional factors include the availability of historical data, computational power and software, time to gather and analyze the data, forecast horizon and others. The example in Fig. 2. Shows how cost and accuracy increase with sophis tication and charts this against the corresponding cost of forecasting errors, given some general assumptions. The most sophisticated technique that can be economically justi fied is one that falls in the region where the sum of the two costs is minimal.

The variety of measures of the simulation accuracy have different properties and could be used for different purpose. Though each case is particular and has its specific goals, there are some general rules of using the measures of accuracy:

- To measure simulation usefulness or its reliability, most frequently, researchers use RMSE and MPE.
- To compare the accuracy of two different techniques, the most common measures are MAPE and the RMSE normalized value CV (RMSE).
- There are some important points that need clarification as well, in terms of the specific properties of the simulation technique used, like the validity of the technique assumptions and significance of the model parameter estimations.
- Lastly, it is also important if the simulation technique is simple to use and easy to understand for decision makers.

It should be also noted that despite the fact that simulations are based on models, the use of good and accurate models does not guarantee a good decision. Nonqualified users cannot comprehend the rules for using the model, or may incorrectly apply it and misinterpret the results. In addition, no single technique/model works in every situation and selecting the most appropriate (cost-effective) one among many similar models is a never ending task in business simulations.

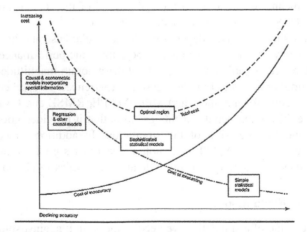

Fig. 2. Cost of forecasting versus cost of inaccuracy for a medium-range forecast, given data availability (Source: John C. Chambers, Satinder K. Mullick, Donald D. Smith, How to Choose the Right Forecasting Technique, Harvard Business Review, July, 1971)

3   Improving Simulation Accuracy

3.1   Deep Learning Artificial Neural Networks

"One of the great things about deep learning is that users can essentially just feed data to a neural network, or some other type of learning model, and the model eventually delivers an answer or recommendation. The user doesn't have to understand how or why the model delivers its results; it just does. But some enterprises are finding that the black box nature of some deep learning models – where their functionality isn't seen or understood by the user – isn't quite good enough when it comes to their most important business decisions. A lack of transparency into how deep learning models work is keeping some businesses from embracing them fully…" [6].

Some of the most successful deep learning methods involve Artificial Neural Networks (ANNs), where a Deep Neural Network (DNN) is defined to be an ANN with multiple hidden layers of units between the input and output layers. In general, DNNs attempt to model high-level abstractions in data by using model architectures composed of multiple non-linear transformations.

The main advantages of DNNs are that they make it possible to build faster and more accurate simulation models, but at the same time DNNs are difficult to develop and hard to understand. The difficulties with ease of development and use stem mainly from the extensive data preparation required to get good results from a neural network model. The results are difficult to understand because a DNN is a complex nonlinear model that does not produce rules.

Technically, a DNN is an ANN with multiple hidden layers of units between the input and output layers (Fig. 3). The neural network-based deep learning models, by default, contain a great number of layers, since they rely more on optimal model selection and optimization through model tuning. Usually, ANNs and the deep learning techniques are considered as some of the most capable tools for solving very complex problems. They are data-driven and self-adaptive in nature, i.e. there is no need to specify a particular model form or to make any a priori assumption about the statistical distribution of the data. Perhaps their greatest advantage is the ability to be used as an arbitrary function approximation mechanism that "learns" from observed data. According to Hornik et al. [7] ANNs are universal function approximators and can deal with situations where the input data are erroneous, incomplete, or fuzzy.

However, to have an extremely robust ANN (DNN or other type ANN) the model, cost function, and learning algorithm must be appropriately selected. Many issues can arise with ANNs if they are naively trained. The most common issues are overfitting and computation time, due to increased model and algorithmic complexity, which usually results in significant computational resource and time requirements. Other important questions, such as: How can secondary data series be inferred for the network generating process?; How should data be segmented for network training?; How many input nodes for the ANN are appropriate, i.e. what is the order of the model?, etc., should also be considered. Last but not least, questions concerning the ANNs architecture such as "How many hidden nodes are appropriate?" or "Which is the best activation function in any given instance?" must be addressed as well.

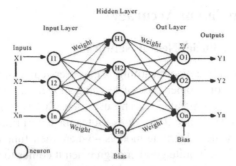

Fig. 3. General example of multilayer feed-forward ANN (Source: https://python3.codes/neuralnetwork-python-part-1-sigmoid-function-gradient-descent-backpropagation/)

4 Statistical Learning Networks

Statistical Learning Networks (SLNs) can fix the common problems of DNNs discussed above. In [8] we presented a highly automated procedure for developing SLNs in the form of Multi-Layered Networks of Active Neurons (MLNAN) for business simlations using the Group Method of Data Handling (Fig. 4).

In this paper, we discuss the problem of accuracy in business simulations and model- based business games and we will concentrate on how to address it with the help of SLNs. Statistical learning theory deals with the problem of finding a predictive function based on data. Typically, as shown in [9, 10], it is a framework for machine learning drawing from the fields of statistics and functional analysis.

The *Group Method of Data Handling (GMDH)* [2] is one of the most successful methods in SLNs. GMDH is an inductive approach to model building based on self-organization principles, known also as "Polynomial Neural Networks". In GMDH algorithms, models are generated adaptively from input data in the form of an ANN of active neurons in a repetitive generation of populations of competing partial models of growing complexity. A limited number is selected from generation to generation by cross-validation, until an optimal complex model is finalized.

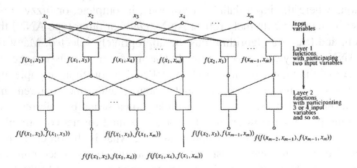

Fig. 4. GMDH iterative procedure – an example of multilayered active neuron neural network (Source: [2] p. 8)

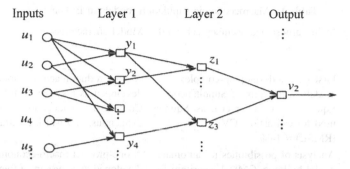

Fig. 5. General scheme of GMDH self-organizing modeling algorithm (Source: [2] p. 33)

This modeling approach grows a tree-like network out of data of input and output variables in a pair-wise combination and competitive selection from a single neuron to a final output – a model without predefined characteristics (Fig. 5). Here, neither the number of neurons and the number of layers in the network, nor the actual behavior of each created neuron is predefined. The modeling is self-organizing because the number of neurons, the number of layers, and the actual behavior of each created neuron are identified during the learning process from layer to layer.

SLNs, such as MLNAN, help to address most of the problems in Deep Learning. For example, ANNs cannot explain results and this is their biggest drawback in a business decision support context. In situations where explaining rules may be critical, such as denying loan applications, general ANNs are not a good choice. Müller and Lemke [11] provide comparisons and point out that in distinction to ANNs, the results of GMDH algorithms are explicit mathematical models, that are generated in a relatively short time on the basis of even small samples. Another problem is that deep learning and neural network algorithms can be prone to overfitting. Following Beer [12], only the external criteria, calculated on new, independent information can produce the minimum of the model error. GMDH algorithms for MLNAN address this problem with the cross-validation technique. In summary, algorithms like MLNAN combine in a powerful way the best features of ANNs and statistical techniques.

In [13] we presented a framework for developing MLNANs and discussed in details its advantages and the benefits of using it for business simulations in training and eduation. In the current paper, we will concentrate on the opportunities that the MLNANs provide for increasing the simulation accuracy and the results achieved.

5 Applications, Conclusions and Future Research

SLNs techniques such as MLNAN, help researchers by making business simulations and model-based business games development more cost-effective. The results obtained show that they are able to develop reliably even complex models with better overall error rates and at very low cost, compared to most of the current methods.

Table 1. Macroeconomic simulation models in Bulgaria.

Model name and year of design	Main purpose and accuracy achieved	Model characteristics
SIMUR 0 - 1977	First step in developing complex models in the form of Simultaneous Equations (SE). Indirect Least Squares used for estimation. CV (RMSE) = 14%	A one-product macro-economic model developed as a system of five SE. Contains five endogenous, one exogenous, and five lag variables
SIMUR I - 1981	Analysis of possibilities for automated model building. GMDH algorithm for MLNAN used. CV(RMSE) = 2.7%	A one-product macro-economic model developed as a system of five SE. Contains the same set of variables
SIMUR II - 1985	Design and verification of a program system for simulation experiments with SE. Analysis of validation criteria for accuracy evaluation of SE. GMDH algorithm for MLNAN used CV(RMSE) = 2.0%	Aggregated macroeconomic model in the form of 12 interdepending SE. Contains 12 endogenous, 5 exogenous and 26 lag variables with time lag of up to 3 years
SIMUR III - 1987	Improving the MLNAN for synthesis of SE with many equations. Simulation of main macroeconomic variables Average CV(RMSE) < 1%	Macroeconomic simulation model. Contains 39 SE and 39 endogenous, 7 exogenous and 82 lag variables with a time lag of up to 5 years

So far, SLNs like MLNAN have been successfully applied in many areas, including business simulations. When developing the working prototype of MLNAN [14], we used it to build a series of increasingly complex simulation models as linear systems of simultaneous equations (SE) of the national economy with a very high level of accuracy (Table 1). Other successful applications in predictive modeling with similar SLNs were made in Germany [3], the United States [15] and other countries. The comparisons of the results from different simulations and models, which we did in [1], show almost insignificant differences in their predictions and a very high level of accuracy.

Another area of SLN applications is in model-based simulation games for business training and education. The game "National Economy", developed initially using the model SIMUR 0, was improved significantly after applying SLN. With the same data and set of variables, the model SIMUR I was built using the MLNAN algorithm. The new model had much better accuracy (about five times smaller CV(RMSE) as shown in Table 1), providing a more reliable base for simulations and what-if analysis.

Later on, the SLNs were used in the "NEW PRODUCT" business game development [16]. This integrated, role-playing, model-based simulation game was designed for the purposes of business training and education. The latest versions of the game cover all major stages in the process of new product planning and development, production and operations management, as well as sales and marketing, and it could be used not only as an educational tool for teaching business, but it may also be carried out for real-life business training in different areas.

Table 2. Sales predictions accuracy using different models

Best model	Second best	Third best
MLNAN:	*Triple Exponential*	*Multiple Autoregression*
MASE: 0.0414	MASE = 0.0627	MASE = 0.0908
MPE = 1.42%	MPE = −0.57%	MPE = 2.03%
MAPE = 1.42%	MAPE = 1.76%	MAPE = 2.58%
CV(RMSE) = 1.56%	CV(RMSE) = 2.45%	CV(RMSE) = 3.17%

Just recently, the proposed in [13] framework for developing MLNANs was used in Business Forecasting and Predictive Analytics class at the Walla Walla University School of Business. For three years in a row (2017–2019), we developed many predictive models using more or less complex techniques. In summary, the predictions done with the MLNAN produced the smallest errors (see Table 2).

The benefits of utilizing SLNs in business simulations are substantial. SLNs such as MLNAN provide opportunities in both shortening the design time and reducing the cost and efforts in model building, as well as developing reliably even complex models with high level of accuracy [17].

Unfortunately, the future cannot always be predicted based on history. Data fitting limits somewhat the value of such techniques and decision makers have to decide the overall importance of the simulation outputs. However, the SLNs such as MLNAN provide processed data that are needed in the business context and the extracted information is useful to business decision making, which creates value or predict market behavior in a way, which provides a competitive advantage.

List of Acronyms Used:
ANNs - Artificial Neural Networks
DNNs - Deep Neural Networks
CV(RMSE) - Coefficient of variation of RMSEs
MASE - Mean Absolute Scaled Error
GMDH - Group Method of Data Handling
MSE - Mean Squared Error
MAPE - Mean Absolute Percentage Error
MPE - Mean Percentage Error
MLNAN - Multi-Layered Networks of Active Neurons
SE - Simultaneous equations
SLNs - Statistical Learning Networks
RMSE - Root Mean Squared Error

References

1. Motzev, M.: Business Forecasting – A Contemporary Decision Making Approach, 1st edn. Eudaimonia Productions Ltd. (2016)
2. Madala, H., Ivakhnenko, A.G.: Inductive Learning Algorithms for Complex Systems Modelling, 1st edn. CRC Press Inc., Boca Raton (1994)

3. Mueller, J.A., Lemke, F.: Self-organizing Data Mining: An Intelligent Approach to Extract Knowledge from Data, 1st edn. Trafford Publishing, Canada (2003)
4. Gödel, K.: Über formal unentscheidbare Sätze der Principia Mathematica und verwandter Systeme. I. Monatshefte für Mathematik und Physik **38**, 73–98 (1931)
5. Stone, M.: An asymptotic equivalence of choice of model by cross-validation and Akaike's criterion. J. R. Stat. Soc. **39**, 44–47 (1977)
6. Burns, Ed.: Deep learning models hampered by black box functionality. TechTarget, Advanced Analytics. (2017). http://searchbusinessanalytics.techtarget.com/feature/Deep-learning- models-hampered-by-black-box-functionality?utm_content=control&utm_medium=EM& asrc=EM_ERU _82565194&utm_campaign=20170914_ERU%20Transmission%20for%20 09/14/2017%20(User Universe:%202429004)&utm_source=ERU&src=5669449
7. Hornik, K., Stinchcombe, M., White, H.: Multilayer feed-forward networks are universal approximators. Neural Netw. **2**, 359–366 (1989)
8. Motzev, M.: Statistical learning networks in simulations for business training and education. In: Developments in Business Simulation and Experiential Learning: vol. 45, Proceedings of the Annual ABSEL Conference, Seattle (2018)
9. Hastie, T., Tibshirani, R., Friedman, J.: The Elements of Statistical Learning: Data Mining, Inference, and Prediction. Springer, New York (2017). https://doi.org/10.1007/978-0-387-84858-7
10. Mohri, M., Rostamizadeh, A., Talwalkar, A.: Foundations of Machine Learning. The MIT Press, Cambridge (2012)
11. Müller, J-A., Lemke, F.: Self-organizing modelling and decision support in economics. In: Proceedings of the IMACS Symposium on Systems Analysis and Simulation, pp. 135–138. Gordon and Breach Publisher (1995)
12. Beer, S.: Cybernetics and Management, p. 280. English University Press, London (1959)
13. Motzev, M.: A framework for developing multi-layered networks of active neurons for simulation experiments and model-based business games using self-organizing data mining with the group method of data handling. In: Lukosch, H.K., Bekebrede, G., Kortmann, R. (eds.) ISAGA 2017. LNCS, vol. 10825, pp. 191–199. Springer, Cham (2018). https://doi.org/10.1007/978-3-319-91902-7_19
14. Motzev,M., Marchev, A.: Multi-stage selection algorithms in simulation. In: XII IMACS World Congress Proceedings, vol. 4, pp. 533–535, Paris (1988)
15. Klein, L., Müller, J.-A., Ivakhnenko, A.G.: Modeling of the economics of the USA by self-organization of the system of equations. Sov. Autom. Control **13**(1), 1–8 (1980)
16. Motzev, M.: New product – an integrated simulation game in business education. In: Bonds & Bridges. Proceedings of the World Conference of the ISAGA, pp. 63–75 (2012)
17. Motzev, M., Lemke, F.: Self-organizing data mining techniques in model based simula tion games for business training and education. Vanguard Sci. Instrum. Man age. **11** (2015)

Group-Based Learning and Group Composition on the Provision of Public Goods: Incorporating Agent-Based Simulation and Gaming

Shuang Chang[✉] and Hiroshi Deguchi

Tokyo Institute of Technology, Yokohama, Japan
chang@cs.dis.titech.ac.jp

Abstract. Collective contribution to public goods is becoming important in modern social welfare and the understanding of its underlying mechanisms is critical to cultivate the contribution. Under the context of public service contribution and collaboration, group-based learning on improving the ability of using tools to contribute online contents and to conduct collective activities is important, yet its impact is still unclear. This work incorporates agent-based simulation and gaming to investigate the impact of group-based learning on cooperation in heterogeneous groups where individuals differ in their ability to contribute. We unfold public goods game to agent-based models incorporating a group-based learning mechanism to explore the individuals' collaborative decision in addition to the influence from either the environment or from their past experience. A corresponding gaming session is designed and played to triangulate the simulation results, and has the potential to improve further simulation models. Simulation results suggest that small groups with competent individuals are prone to contribute more. Group-based learning is more effective in the context of contributions associated with a high cost whilst its influence is overwhelmed by other factors, such as a high responsive rate to the past experience, in those easy-to-operate contributions.

Keywords: Agent-based simulation · Public goods game · Group-based learning

1 Introduction

Collective contribution to public goods are becoming important in modern social welfare [2]. Citizens' engagement and collaboration in public affairs is encouraged and leveraged to tackle a broad range of public problems. For instance, the local government of Osaka City launched the Japanese version of FixMyStreet (FMSJ) services aiming to prompt the formation of local groups with offline activities, and provide more transparent public services [15]. Although the potentials of such collaborative services to achieve the designated objectives are well recognized, the contribution rate is still relatively low. Therefore, understanding the underlying cooperation mechanisms is critical to cultivate the contribution [1].

© Springer Nature Switzerland AG 2021
M. Wardaszko et al. (Eds.): ISAGA 2019, LNCS 11988, pp. 127–138, 2021.
https://doi.org/10.1007/978-3-030-72132-9_12

The mechanisms of promoting cooperation and collective behaviors in public goods context have been extensively explored by both lab and field experiments [12]. Public goods game is one of such tools capturing the social dilemma between collective benefits and individual interests, and particularly suitable to examine pro-social behaviors within groups [4]. Several set-up factors have been examined and found influential, such as communication [3], group-size [5], etc.; mechanisms such as punishment and learning have been studied to explore the ways to prompt cooperative behaviors [7, 8, 12]; further, the emergence of contribution social norms has been investigated in not only homogeneous but also heterogeneous populations with varying endowment and preferences [19]; and also effects of social norms on individuals with varying strategies have been discussed extensively by institutional analyses from an evolutionary theory perspective [17, 18].

Abundant empirical evidences have demonstrated that individuals' decision to cooperate is subject to their social preferences and beliefs of other players' decisions [11]. As being "conditional cooperators", without any institutional design to prompt cooperation, the emergence of free-riding and fragile of cooperation can be explained by people's propensity to observe and follow others' behaviors [10]. Alternatively, when the environmental information is not available to players, observed substantial cooperation was also explained by simple reinforcement mechanisms in theoretical and simulation works [14], such as learning from self's past. Especially under the context of public service contribution and collaboration, apart from these two learning mechanisms, offline group-based learning on how to improve the ability of using advanced technology for online content contribution and activity is also important. Yet their influence on individuals' contribution to public goods is still unclear.

Therefore, this work aims to investigate the impact of this group-learning on cooperation in heterogeneous groups where individuals differ in their ability to contribute. This work also offers an alternative method by combining simulation and human experiments in exploring the cooperation behaviors. We unfold public goods game to agent-based models incorporating a group-based learning mechanism in addition to the learning process from either the environment or from their past experience to explore the individuals' collaborative decision. A corresponding game is designed and experimented to triangulate the simulation results and to improve the agent-based model design.

The remaining sections of this paper are organized as follows: agent-based models are proposed in Sect. 2 with a detailed explanation; simulation and gaming details are discussed in Sect. 3 and 4 respectively; conclusion with some future work discussion is presented in the last section.

1.1 Public Goods Game

We briefly review the public goods game in this section as follows. The payoff C_i of player i out of n players playing the public goods game is updated as follows,

$$C_i = y - g_i + \alpha \sum_{i=1}^{n} g_i \tag{1}$$

where the initial endowment is denoted by y, the points each player wants to contribute to public goods by $g_i \leq y$, marginal return rate by α and the gain of each player by $\alpha \sum_{i=1}^{n} g_i$.

2 Agent-Based Modeling

Individuals are modeled as autonomous agents. Each agent belongs to one and only one group composed of 5 to 10 agents [13]. We assume bounded rational agents [20] who do not have full knowledge of the game structure and will learn from the environment or from their past experiences, rather than rational agents interested in only maximizing their payoff. This assumption follows the empirical evidences that individuals are not always purely utility-maximizing actors, and social norms exert substantial impacts on their behaviors [21].

2.1 Agent

Individual set is defined as $D = \{1, 2, ..., n\}$, where $n \in N$ is the number of individuals. The heterogeneity of individuals is defined in terms of the different ability to contribute [19]. Each individual determines a strategy from a discrete strategy space $A = \{0, 1\}$ where 0 indicates no contribution, and 1 indicates full contribution.

Group set is defined as $G = \{1, 2, ..., k\}$, where $k \in N$ is the number of groups. Each group is defined by a set of individuals denoted by H_i, total number of individuals by $N_i(t) \in N$ and number of contributors by $NC_l(t) \in N$.

The payoff for individual $i \in D$ taking strategy $s \in A$ at iteration t is defined as follows,

$$C_{i,s}(t+1) = y_i - G_i(t+1) + \alpha \sum_{i=1}^{n} g_i \qquad (2)$$

where y_i is the intial endowment, g_i is the endowment contributed at each iteration, $\alpha = \sum_{\forall i, s=1} g_i / (n y_i)$ is the constant marginal return ranging between 0 and 1, and $G_i(t)$ is individuals' total contribution including the endowment and effort consumed. It is calculated as follows,

$$G_i(t+1) = (1 - \eta)g_i + \eta E_i(t+1) \qquad (3)$$

where $E_i(t)$ is the effort consumed by each contribution, which will be adapted through learning within groups at each iteration. η is used to adjust the proportion of effort involved.

Basically, we let agents learn from either the environment or from their past experience when making a decision.

Learning from the Past Experience. Agent will adjust their decisions depending on their response to the past experi-ence only. The probability of contribution, denoted by $P_{i,1}(t+1)$ is updated based on a directional learning schem [14]. $P_{i,0}(t+1) = 1 - P_{i,1}(t+1)$ and the responsive rate is termed by δ.

$$P_{i,1}(t+1) = \begin{cases} P_{i,1}(t) + \delta & \text{Condition 1} \\ P_{i,1}(t) - \delta & \text{Condition 2} \end{cases} \tag{4}$$

Condition 1: if $C_i(t) > C_i(t-1)$ and $g_i(t) > g_i(t-1)$, or if $C_i(t) < C_i(t-1)$ and $g_i(t) < g_i(t-1)$; if $P_{i,1}(t+1) \geq 1$, then $P_{i,1}(t+1) = 1$.
Condition 2: if $C_i(t) > C_i(t-1)$ and $g_i(t) < g_i(t-1)$, or if $C_i(t) < C_i(t-1)$ and $g_i(t) > g_i(t-1)$; if $P_{i,1}(t+1) \leq 0$, then $P_{i,1}(t+1) = 0$.
Otherwise: if neither of the above two conditions are satisfied, $P_{i,1}(t+1) = P_{i,1}(t) + \delta, P_{i,1}(t) - \delta \text{ or } P_{i,1}(t)$ with same probability.

Learn from the Environment. Agents will adjust their decisions depending on others' contributions, not limited to their own group but of all players. This design captures the online content contribution scenario that individuals may learn offline from their local community, but the public goods are available online to all individuals. The probability of choosing strategy s at iteration t for individual i is defined as follows based on social learning dynamics [6].

$$P_{i,s}(t+1) = P_{i,s}(t) + \beta P_{i,s}(t) \frac{C_{i,s}(t+1) - W(t)}{W(t)} \tag{5}$$

where $W(t) = \sum_{\forall i \in D} C_{i,s}(t)/n$ is the average endowment contributed by each individuals, through which the influence from other individuals' behaviors is imposed, and $\beta \in (0,1)$ is defined to adjust its proportion.

Group-Based Learning. In addition to the learning processes to update strategies, we define group-based learning as improving the ability to contribute, in terms of consumed effort $E_i(t)$, within each group until all members' abilities converge to the same level. $E_i(t)$ of individual $i \in H_l$, $i \in D$ and $l \in G$ is updated as follows,

$$E_i(t+1) = E_i(t)(1 - \gamma(E_i(t) - V_E^l(t+1))\lambda) \tag{6}$$

$$V_E^l(t+1) = \sum_{\forall j \in H_l} E_j(t)/N_l \tag{7}$$

$$\lambda = NC_l(t)/N_l \tag{8}$$

$V_E^l(t)$ indicates the average effort level of individuals within group l, in other words, the average ability of engaging in contribution within the same group. Here we assume individuals within the same group will not directly interact with each other, but be influenced by the status of the group indirectly. λ is a parameter considering the influences of the number of contributors. The value of γ, which is used to adjust the influence of group-based learning, is a constant positive real number ranging between 0 and 1.

3   Simulation

We have 500 heterogeneous individuals and 100 groups with varying group size at the initial step. The heterogeneity of individuals is represented in terms of their initial endowment y_i and effort $E_i(t)$. We run the simulation for 20 times and the average values of strategy selection are plotted for macro-level analysis.

Table 1. Parameter setting

y_i	η	δ
{20, [20, 40]}	{0, 0.5, 0.8}	{0.01, 0.1, 0.5, 0.9}

3.1   Parameter Setting

Parameters are set as shown in Table 1 [8, 19]. $E_i(t)$ is set initially as a random number ranging in [0.25 y_i, 0.75 y_i], β as 0.5, and γ as 0.2. Initially, individuals will choose each strategy randomly and evenly. We let $g_i = 20$ if contribute, $g_i = 0$ otherwise.

3.2   Learn from Past Experience

In this subsection, we examine the influence of this group-based learning when only learning from self's past experience is considered. Figure 1 plots the average contribution rate under a combined impact of responsive rate ($\delta \in \{0.01, 0.1, 0.5, 0.9\}$), marginal return rate ($0 < \alpha < 1$ in Fig. 1(a) and $\alpha = 2$ in Fig. 1(b)) and ability improvement ($\eta \in \{0, 0.8\}$).

The value of η indicates the percentage of effort involved in each contribution, and of a higher value may decrease the total endowment given to the collective goods. The simulation results with the basic setting ($\eta = 0$) are consisting with the discussions in [14]. Responses to people's past experience and marginal return rate influence the contribution behaviors: the higher the responsive rate when the return rate is lower than 1, the higher the contribution rate. But if the cost of each contribution is of the concern, the improving ability, i.e. a decreasing cost of contribution, may prompt cooperation when $\delta < 0.5$ though not significantly. In contrast, the responses to self's past experience may overwhelm the influence of this ability improvement when $\delta \geq 0.5$.

Further, we examine the influence of group properties, i.e. group composition and group size, on the contribution rate indicated by bubble size in Fig. 2(a) and (b) respectively; x-axis represents group size and y-axis represents average effort of a group. Figure 2(b) shows that when the responsive rate to past experience is low, agents from small groups composing by competent individuals may contribute more compared to those from larger groups or groups without competent agents.

3.3   Learn from the Environment

The impact of this group-based learning is more significant in the case of environmental learning as shown in Fig. 3 and Fig. 4. When the majority is becoming free-

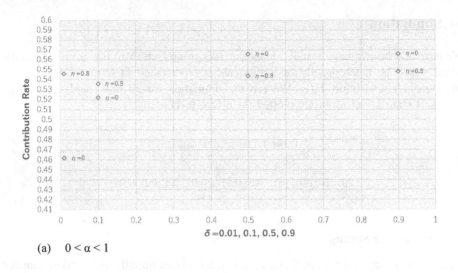

(a) $0 < \alpha < 1$

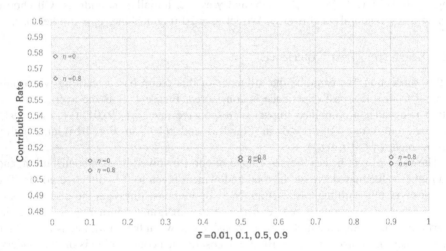

(b) $\alpha = 2$

Fig. 1. Learn from past experience.

riders, most of the remaining contributors are from smaller groups with a higher ability, as shown in Fig. 3(b). Additionally, Fig. 4 shows that for contributions which may require more effort to conduct, the ability improvement is more significant in improving the contribution rate, especially at the initial few stages.

Besides, free-riding is dominant in all situations, which is compliance with the results from empirical studies. Further, with a higher ability, i.e., $y_i \in [20, 40]$, individuals are having a higher contribution rate regardless of the value η as shown in Fig. 4.

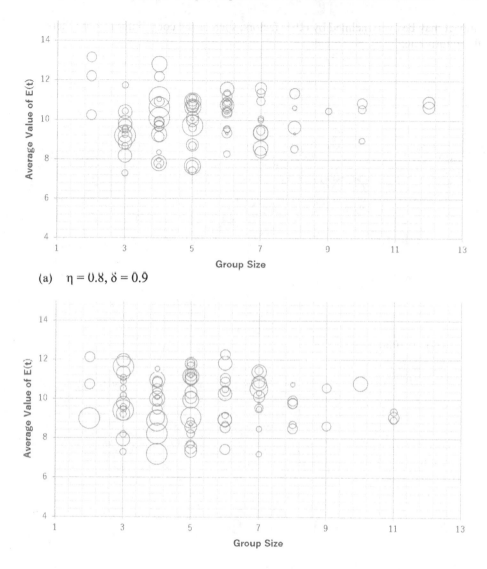

(a) $\eta = 0.8, \delta = 0.9$

(b) $\eta = 0.8, \delta = 0.01$

Fig. 2. Learn from past experience – group composition.

The results may have some policy implications for prompting public service collaboration. From the perspective of technology usage, an easy-to-operate system may prompt more online public service contributions. For systems involved with more complex operations, the contribution may be limited to individuals skilled in dealing with digital technologies. From the perspective of group-based learning, learning within small groups or from competent individuals may improve the situation, but the impact may be overwhelmed by other factors, such as the contribution from others, and the return rate.

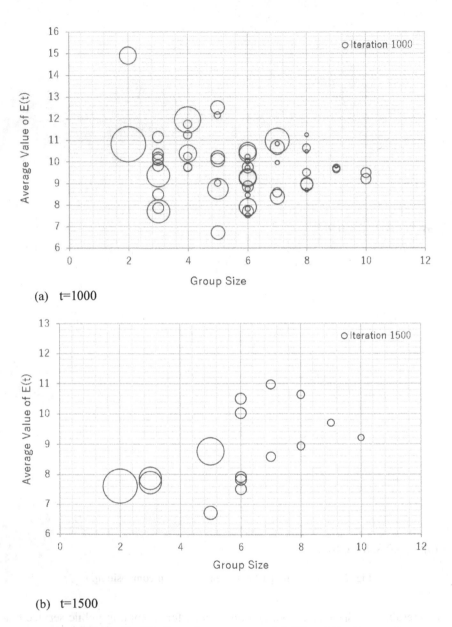

(a)　t=1000

(b)　t=1500

Fig. 3. Contribution rate across groups at different iteration.

For the Osaka City FMSJ services, although mass media promotion helped attract the public attention and encouraged the usage, the effect didn't last too long. Since

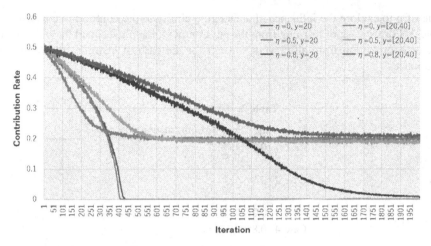

Fig. 4. Learn from the environment.

people are prone to learn and to use new practices under the influence of people who are similar or salient to them [21], it might be helpful to target particular types of individuals to amplify their influence on behavior shifts. In addition, instead of changing the pay-off structure, policy initiatives should focus on fostering the formation of new social norms and leverage the impact to cooperative behaviors. Yet how do different social contexts, or institutions, influence the social norms among heterogeneous individuals remains challenging and unclear [16].

4 Gaming

We also design a game played by human players in compatible with the simulation models. It follows the basic public good game structure with additional components, and initial settings are compliant with the agent-based simulation introduced in Sect. 3.

4.1 Design and Procedures

Each group consists of 4 to 5 players, who are undergraduate and postgraduate students. Each player had an initial 20 tokens and was asked to decide how many they wish to contribute to the common pool along 20 decision rounds. Any integer number smaller than 20 was allowed. In addition to the basic public good game, the players were also aware of the changing effort at each iteration, which is termed as the associated cost of each contribution. This cost will be adapted through iterations (Eqs. 6–8) automatically and acknowledged by the players.

We programed and conducted the game with the experiment software z-Tree [9]. The players were well informed with game instructions, group size and payoff structure before the game, and with associated cost and their own earning during the game at each iteration. They were not allowed to discuss with each other during the game. Besides, we design four cases varying in the available information to players and the value of η to explore the influence of a changing ability to the contribution, as given in Table 2. For the case of learning from the environment, the players had the information of total contribution from all players, but not for the case of learning from their past experience.

Table 2. Game setting.

	η	Provided information
Case 1	0.2	$\sum_{i=1}^{n} g_i, C_i, E_i$
Case 2	0.8	$\sum_{i=1}^{n} g_i, C_i, E_i$
Case 3	0.2	C_i, E_i
Case 4	0.8	C_i, E_i

4.2   Results Analyses

We plot the average contribution rate of 4 repeated sessions along 20 iterations for each case respectively in Fig. 5. The results indicate a decline of contribution in all cases except case 2. When the players are able to learn from the environment by knowing the total contribution from others, some cooperation emerges at the first few rounds and goes stable afterwards. In contrast, when the players can only learn from their past experience without knowing others' contribution, the decline is inevitable and the group-learning only smooths the decline process.

The players were interviewed after the gaming session on their motivations behind the actions. Some of them suggested that the cost is not their major concern when the value is not changing significantly and other factors may become critical. It is in compliance with the simulation results that for contributions associated with a higher cost, group-based learning may help prompt the contribution under certain circumstances, but not for those with a lower cost. A more rigorous assessment, such as statistical analysis, on the impact of group composition and personal ability on the cooperation behaviors is necessary, but due to the limited number of samples, we left it for future works.

Further, the adapting ability is termed as the associated cost of each contribution different for each player. In other words, the learning process is designed as a passive-learning scheme in the sense that players can only realize the improving ability, but not improve it spontaneously. More sophisticated game is required to elicit players' proactive learning behaviors and to evaluate their impact on the cooperation behaviors.

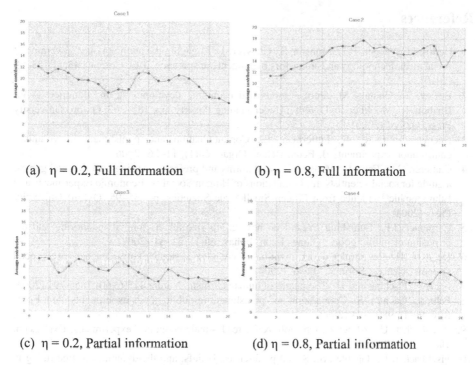

(a) η = 0.2, Full information   (b) η = 0.8, Full information

(c) η = 0.2, Partial information   (d) η = 0.8, Partial information

Fig. 5. Contribute rate of four cases.

5 Conclusion and Future Works

In this work, we examined the influence of group-based learning and group composition on individuals' behaviors towards contributing to public services by incorporating agent-based simulation and gaming. The simulation results suggest that small
groups composed with competent individuals are prone to contribute more; group
learning is more effective in the context of high-cost contributions yet its influence is
overwhelmed by other factors in low-cost contributions, such as a high responsive rate
to the past experience, a high marginal return rate, and a larger initial endowment.
A gaming session is designed to triangulate the simulation results. The results are
compliance with the simulation results to certain extent, but more sophisticated games
are necessary for a rigorous validation, and to inform the design of simulation models.
Also, it would be interesting if we incorporate computational autonomous agents in the
gaming session to investigate complex mechanisms.

Acknowledgment. This research was supported by Foundation for the Fusion of Science and
Technology (FOST), Japan.

References

1. Bertot, J.C., Jaeger, P.T., Munson, S., Glaisyer, T.: Engaging the public in open government: social media technology and policy for government transparency. IEEE Comput. **43**(11), 53–59 (2010)
2. Besley, T., Ghatak, M.: Public goods and economic development. In: Banerjee, A.V., Bnabou, R., Mookherjee, D. (eds.) Understanding Poverty, pp. 185–302. Oxford University Press, Oxford (2006)
3. Bochet, O., Page, T., Putterman, L.: Communication and punishment in voluntary contribution experiments. J. Econ. Behav. Organ. **60**(1), 11–26 (2006)
4. Camerer, C.F., Fehr, E.: Measuring social norms and preferences using experimental games: a guide for social scientists. In: Foundations of Human Sociality: Economic Experiments and Ethnographic Evidence from Fifteen Small-Scale Societies, pp. 55–95. Oxford University Press (2004)
5. Carpenter, J.P.: Punishing free-riders: how group size affects mutual monitoring and the provision of public goods. Games Econ. Behav. **60**(1), 31–51 (2007)
6. Deguchi, H.: Economics as an agent-based complex system - Toward agent-based social systems sciences. Springer, Japan (2004)
7. Fehr, E., Fischbacher, U.: The nature of human altruism. Nature **425**(6960):785– 791 (2003)
8. Fehr, E., Gächter, S.: Cooperation and punishment in public goods experiments. Am. Econ. Rev. **90**(4), 980–994 (2000)
9. Fischbacher, U.: z-tree: Zurich toolbox for ready-made economic experiments. Exp. Econ. **10**(2), 171–178 (2007)
10. Fischbacher, U., Gächter, S.: Social preferences, beliefs, and the dynamics of free riding in public goods experiments. Am, Econ, Rev, **100**(1), 541–556 (2010)
11. Gächter, S.: Conditional cooperation: Behavioral regularities from the lab and the field and their policy implications. In: Frey, B.S., Stutzer, A. (eds.) Economics and Psychology: A promising New Cross-Disciplinary field, CESifo Seminar Series, pp. 19–50. MIT Press, Cambridge (2007)
12. Gachter, S., Herrmann, B.: Reciprocity, culture and human cooperation: previous insights and a new cross-cultural experiment. Philos. Trans. R. Soc. Lond. B: Biol. Sci. **364**(1518), 791–806 (2009)
13. Lave, J., Wenger, E.: Situated Learning: Legitimate Peripheral Participation. Cambridge University Press, Cambridge (1991)
14. Nax, H.H., Perc, M.: Directional learning and the provisioning of public goods. Sci. Rep. **8** (8010), 1–6 (2015)
15. Osaka City, ICT Project. ICT Project Report on FixMyStreetJapan Trial (2015). https://www.city.osaka.lg.jp/shimin/cmsfiles/contents/0000261/261221/shiken-unyou-report.pdf
16. Ostrom, E.: A behavioral approach to the rational choice theory of collective action: presidential address, American political science association, 1997. Am. Polit. Sci. Rev. **92**(1), 122 (1998)
17. Ostrom, E.: Collective action and the evolution of social norms. J. Econ. Perspect. **14**(3), 137–158 (2000)
18. Ostrom, E.: Understanding Institutional Diversity. Princeton University Press, Princeton (2005)
19. Reuben, E., Riedl, A.: Enforcement of contribution norms in public good games with heterogeneous populations. Games Econ. Behav. **77**(1), 122–137 (2013)
20. Simon, H.A.: A behavioral model of rational choice. Q. J. Econ. **69**(1), 99–118 (1955)
21. World Bank 2015 World Development Report 2015: Mind, Society, and Behavior World Bank Washington, DCs

Can the Veil of Ignorance Create Consensus?

A Qualitative Analysis Using the Siting for a Contaminated Waste Landfill Game

Miki Yokoyama[1(✉)], Susumu Ohnuma[1], and Yukio Hirose[2]

[1] Hokkaido University, N10 W7, Kita-ku, Sapporo 0600810, Japan
myokoyama@lynx.let.hokudai.ac.jp
[2] Kansai University, Takatsuki, Osaka, Japan

Abstract. This study aims to demonstrate the significance of the discussion under the "veil of ignorance" in building consensus about the Not In My Back Yard (NIMBY) issue. The Siting for a Contaminated Waste Landfill Game simulating conflicts related to the site selection of a contaminated waste landfill created by the accident at Fukushima nuclear power plant was developed with the veil of ignorance implemented as the prevailing social structure. The game involves two types of players: mayors, who are aware of the interests of their regions but can only engage in discussion; and citizens, who are unaware of the specific concerns of their regions (i.e., under the veil of ignorance) but are tasked with engaging in discussions and making the final decision. The transformations in the ideas of the players were examined through this game relating to building consensus. Ten games were conducted, and no unfair decisions were discerned under the veil of ignorance. A qualitative analysis of the open-ended questions revealed that a) the participants focused on fair viewpoints and avoided obsessions with regional interests after the discussion, and b) the diversity of actors and the multiple value dimensions were consistently emphasized before and after the discussion. Hence, this study succeeded in demonstrating that by participating in discussions under the veil of ignorance, the participants were able to form a shared recognition of the multiple-decision process, which the involvement of a diversity of actors and values was crucial for the formation of a consensus on the NIMBY issue.

Keywords: Veil of ignorance · NIMBY issue · Consensus building · Contaminated waste caused by Fukushima nuclear power plant

1 Introduction

This study explores ways in which consensus in NIMBY (Not In My Back Yard) conflicts may be promoted using the Siting for a Contaminated Waste Landfill Game. NIMBY describes the phenomenon that even people who recognize the general social need for a facility do not want it to be constructed near their homes. NIMBY connotes that people living in a wider area, particularly in large cities, benefit from a facility while the inhabitants who reside in proximity to the facility assume its risks and burdens. In other words, NIMBY issues are dominated by the inequitable distribution

© Springer Nature Switzerland AG 2021
M. Wardaszko et al. (Eds.): ISAGA 2019, LNCS 11988, pp. 139–152, 2021.
https://doi.org/10.1007/978-3-030-72132-9_13

of biased risks. Hence, consensus building becomes difficult when people are confronted with such a problem. This study addresses the issue of designated waste caused by the incident at the Fukushima nuclear power plant as a typical NIMBY problem. Contaminated waste has been collected but it has not yet been disposed of. Even today, designated waste has been left in residential areas, farmlands, and on the roadside in some areas. The site for a facility for the long-term management of the designated waste must be determined to handle this waste safely and to avoid the risks associated with radioactive materials. Hirose (2015) developed the Siting for a Contaminated Waste Landfill Game simulating this situation. The game centers on the site selection of a contaminated waste landfill and employs the concept of the veil of ignorance, which will be explained in the following section [1]. Yokoyama et al. (2017) exhibited the effectiveness of the veil of ignorance in fair decision making using this game [2]. However, it is not yet clear whether subjective recognition of the situation was modified and whether the participants' contexts were altered by the discussions under the veil of ignorance. Therefore, this study examines the changes observed in the subjective representation of participants before and after discussions held under the veil of ignorance. In the process, it focuses on participants' perceptions of whether stakeholders can reach a consensus on their own, and whether they recognize the necessity of the involvement of citizens. The qualitative analysis conducted by this study underscores the effectiveness of discussions under the veil of ignorance. The manner in which the relevant actors should be engaged in the process of building consensus for NIMBY issues is also explored.

2 The Siting for a Contaminated Waste Landfill Game Incorporating the Veil of Ignorance

2.1 NIMBY Issues and the Possibility of Building Consensus Through the Veil of Ignorance

The disposal of designated waste is a typical NIMBY issue. In such a case, an inequitable situation results when people across a large area benefit from a facility while inhabitants living near the site bear the distribution of the burden and risks associated with the facility [3]. Although the facility benefits the public as a whole, it is almost impossible for residents to agree on a location for the site because no one wants such a facility near their home. This impasse results in the failure to achieve the public benefit. In such a situation, the verdict may be deferred to a disinterested third party. In reality, however, local inhabitants regard such verdict as forced and refuse to accept them. They may also sometimes become incentivized to incite strong opposition movements. Alternatively, consensus becomes impossible if only stakeholders with particular interests discuss the issue because no one wants to take on the risks. Hence, arguments based on conflicting interests arise. Thus, public engagement involving stakeholder dialogs and the participation of citizens is essential to consensus building under uncertainty, framing the goal of comprehending the broad values desirable for the public [4, 5]. The scope for obtaining public engagement is accorded by simulation and gaming content [6]. For example, Ohnuma and Kitakaji (2015) developed a game that simulated the conflicts concerning the site selection for wind power plants as a NIMBY concern. Through this game, the process of consensus and negotiate discrete values through stakeholder dialogs can be observed [7]. However, the difficulty in NIMBY issues vests in the building of an agreement on the site for a facility for designated wastes because no inhabitant has discharged such unwanted matter. Furthermore, such designated waste causes much fear and stigma similar to the other nuclear issues. Accordingly, discussions for choosing a site reach a deadlock as long as the victims are determined beforehand.

To overcome such stalemates, it was proposed that a consent about the decision-making process should be obtained in advance in a context within which everyone can potentially be a concerned party, without actually ascertaining their own particular interests. In this uncertain situation, everyone will be required to consent to a method of decision making that focuses on the interests of society as a whole, rather than on their own advantages. Such a decision-making process would be regarded as fair and would lead to public acceptance. This idea is derived from Rawls' notion of the veil of ignorance [8].

According to Rawls, people act by default on the basis of their own interests, ranks, and contexts. However, if they are placed in a situation where they do not know their present or future position, they assume the worst case and choose the best option for such circumstances (the maximin principle). Also, if people are unaware about the specific concerns of the parties, they are likely to evaluate not only their own self-interest but also various publicly desirable values. Rawls' definition of the veil of ignorance, the maximin principle, and the evaluation of values is considered vital for the fair distribution of resources. This study extends this principle to procedural fairness. A situation in which the concerned parties operate behind the veil of ignorance is created: they must make their assessments based on general considerations without specifically knowing how their choices would influence each party. In other words, they work in a context in which everyone becomes involved as a potential concerned party but remains ignorant about their own advantages and the gains of others. It is presumed that in such situations people will avoid resulting in undecided, which is undesirable for the whole public. In addition, it is assumed that people are concerned about the location of the site and will avoid irresponsible speech and behavior.

If this is so, then who should wear the veil of ignorance and join the discussions pertaining to NIMBY issues? Who should be involved in the decision-making process, in what role, and how are points to consider for consensus building in such matters? It should be noted that the roles of participants vary depending on the stage of the decision-making process, particularly with regard to the major stakeholders and citizens. For example, when narrowing down candidate sites to form a consensus, Renn and his colleagues [9] proposed "cooperative discourse", with a three-stage decision-making process involving stakeholders of the multiple location candidates, experts who would evaluate the locations, and citizen representatives from the entire region. The three-stage decision process functions in a specific manner at each step: the first step accords stakeholders the role of discussing and extending relevant claims; experts play a role in proposing how to evaluate the claims in the second step; and citizens evaluate the claims in the third step.

However, Renn et al. (1993) reported the failure of the application of the three-stage decision-making process [10]. In one case, an interview was first held on the issues concerning the interested parties; next, a citizen's meeting was conducted; and finally, the candidate site was decided. However, the residents surrounding the chosen area rejected the selection. The concerned parties were not clearly defined before the process of the selection of the candidate site. Rather, the concerned parties responsible for locating the facility were revealed as the process advanced. This lesson suggests the need for the postulation of a decision-making process in which everyone potentially involved as a concerned party agrees in advance to vest the evaluation to citizens who do not know their own or others' interests and who do not know where to locate the facility: thus, participants agree to being placed behind the veil of ignorance. Those under the veil of ignorance are expected to arrive at their judgment from the perspective of public benefit.

Also, the stakeholders may not have understood the roles of each participant in each process in advance. Further, the roles participants were expected to play could have been insufficiently defined. These factors could be cited as other reasons for the failure of the abovementioned previous study. Thus, the stepwise decision-making process that incorporated different roles of the participants at each stage was effective but not perfect. The final decisions stemming from a process cannot be accepted if the decision-making method is not fully accepted beforehand.

This research endeavor thus proposes a decision-making method to address the weaknesses of previous studies: first, only stakeholders who understand their own benefits participate in the discussions and experience the difficulty of consensus building; next, participants under the veil of ignorance have a discussion and make a decision. This study employed a game simulating this decision-making process for a NIMBY issue and examined whether decision making incorporating the veil of ignorance is effective, and whether participants regard this decision-making process as fair and accept the final decision, even if it is personally disadvantageous for them.

2.2   A Previous Study Using the Siting for a Contaminated Waste Landfill Game

Numerous games have been devised to better understand conflict resolution [6, 7, 11]. The Siting for a Contaminated Waste Landfill Game simulates a situation concerning designated waste from the Fukushima nuclear power plant accident. The game requires players to choose the location of a facility for the long-term management of the designated waste. The game adopts the veil of ignorance as its given social structure; hence, every player can become a potential concerned party (i.e., every region can potentially be a candidate site). The players are classified into two types: the delegates of a region (mayors) who understand the specific interests (i.e., the stakeholders), and citizens who are unaware of their own benefits and concerns and of the benefits and concerns of their regions, thus who operate behind the veil of ignorance. The game encompasses two decision stages. In the first stage, the mayors convene a discussion and express their claims with regard to the criteria for the site selection. In the second stage, citizens evaluate these claims and evaluate the criteria. The candidate site is determined in accordance with the values appraised by the citizens. All players are then asked whether the decision is acceptable to them. However, unfair decisions even by citizens unaware of their interests were observed (e.g., pushing against some city) in some games of the previous study, and the mayors did not accept the decisions. These outcomes implied that the veil of ignorance did not work [2]. Therefore, the rules were modified. A practice phase was conducted before the two-stage decision process. In this phase all the players were stakeholders who were aware of their own interests. Naturally, no consensus occurred. After this failure, the researchers introduced the two-stage decision making as the actual phase. In this round, the participants who took on the role of citizens did not make unfair decisions; instead, they concentrated on the relative importance of the criteria for the site, and even mayors of the regions that were ultimately selected as candidate sites accepted the verdict of the citizen's group. The questionnaire survey administered after the game confirmed that many participants considered the discussion by citizens under the veil of ignorance to be just and accepted the decisions resulting from the exchange of ideas. Further, many participants understood the necessity of public participation in the final decision. However, the transformative process of the participants' subjective recognition before and after the consensus building discussions held for the NIMBY issue under the veil of ignorance remains uncertain. Thus, the present study focuses on the changes that were observed in the perceptions of the participants.

2.3   The Purpose of This Study

This study aims to investigate the modifications in the subjective perceptions of participants in consensus building discussions conducted on a NIMBY issue under the veil of ignorance. The manner in which participants perceived stakeholder discussions and decisions under the veil of ignorance and how they changed their attitudes in the consensus building process during the two phases of meetings were examined. A questionnaire survey was administered after each phase to ascertain the subjective perceptions of the players. The obtained responses were classified and were subsequently mapped as representations of the opinions of participants. The participant perceptions before and after the administration of each questionnaire were compared. Finally, the changes in the participant representations were described from the perspective of the fairness of the decision-making, the recognition of the need for the participation of citizens placed under the veil of ignorance.

3   Method

3.1   An Overview of the Siting for a Contaminated Waste Landfill Game

Each player lives one of six cities in X prefecture: A-, B-, C-, D-, E-, or F-city. While designated wastes have been temporarily stored in various areas of X prefecture, selecting the location for a long-term management facility will bring the safer handling of the waste and will mitigate the risks associated with radioactive material. Scores are set for regional features to provide cues for decision making about where to locate the candidate site. The scores reflect criteria provided by scientific knowledge, and higher scores indicate diminished aptness of a location. However, since each city has specific regional features, a candidate site must be selected by weighing the significance of these characteristics.

This game encompasses a practice phase and an actual phase. In the practice phase, all players participate in the role of stake-holding mayors representing their particular regional concerns. It is assumed that this phase allows participants to experience the difficulties of arriving at an agreement of only stakeholders are engaged in discussions. The actual phase is executed a week after the practice phase, and at this juncture, the players are randomly assigned roles as mayors or citizens. The mayors act in their own regional interests and argue that their distinct regional features make their regions unsuitable as sites. The citizens listen to the contentions made by the mayors but do not hear the arguments offered by the mayors of their own cities. Afterward, each citizen can ask one question to the mayors. After the questions and answers are accomplished, all the citizens discuss and determine the ranking of regional features, unaware of the specific concerns of their own cities. The region assigned the lowest score by the citizens becomes the candidate site.

3.2   Regional Features and Method of Calculation

The six regional features used in the game were among those that mattered in reality. They were thus familiar and easy for the participants to apprehend. Each regional feature was accorded a reference point between 1 and 5 to reflect the feasibility of locating a long-term designated waste management facility in its presence. These reference points were assigned using criteria from the actual screening method proposed by the government. The reference points were simplified, and their evaluation methods differed according to the particular features. The scores assigned in this game for the regional features are evenly distributed among the cities (Table 1). It must be noted that different regional features and matrices of reference scores were used in the practice and actual phases.

Table 1. An example of a matrix of regional features.

Regional features unsuitable for site selection	A city	B city	C city	D city	E city	F city
Active fault	5	1	3	3	1	5
Groundwater vein	1	3	5	1	5	3
Debris flow	3	5	1	5	3	1
Hospital	4	1	2	2	1	4
Rare plants and animals	2	4	1	4	2	1
Farm land	1	2	4	1	4	2

The higher score signifies greater unsuitability of the location

The players ranked the regional features in order of importance for the location with higher rankings reflecting lesser suitability of the site. Table 2 shows the weighting given to the rankings in the actual phase. The city with the lowest score calculated through the weighting of the reference points for each city became the candidate site.

Table 2. Rank and weighting

Rank	Weighting
1	×6
2	×5
3	×4
4	×3
5	×2
6	×1

3.3 The Flow of the Game

All players functioned as mayors in the practice phase. First, the players knew the regional features of their communities and scored them by selecting a card. Prior to the mayors' meeting a time was arranged for the consideration of why features assigned high numerical scores would make a location unsuitable for the facility. For 20 min in the first half of the meeting, the participants discussed the methodology of selecting the candidate site. In the latter half, they debated the issues for 10 min and selected a candidate site in accordance with the procedures outlined earlier.

The actual phase was executed one week after the practice phase. The participants were randomly assigned roles as mayors or citizens. They were instructed that a high numerical score for a feature given on a card indicated that the attribute made the location unsuitable for the facility and that they should consider the reasons why particular characteristics would exclude a candidate site. The mayors then were divided into two unit and group discussions were held. The mayors argued in each group dialog outlined their reasons why certain regional features rendered a site unsuitable for the facility. Meanwhile, the players designated citizens simply listened to the contentions. Each citizen representing a city could ask one question to a single mayor only after the mayor had presented arguments. At this stage, the cities were divided into two groups to prevent the citizens from knowing the features of their own cities. For example, when the mayors of group X (A-, B-, and C-city) conducted their group discussion, the citizens belonging to the group X cities could not listen to them. Instead, they listened to the mayors of the group Y (D-, E-, and F-cities). Figure 1 illustrates this format.

After the mayors' argumentations were accomplished, the full group of citizens discussed and ranked the six regional features. The facilitators computed the final decision after the citizens' meeting, using the ranking and weighting assigned by the citizens. The candidate site was then selected through this calculation, and the outcomes were reported to the mayors and citizens. Finally, a debriefing session was held.

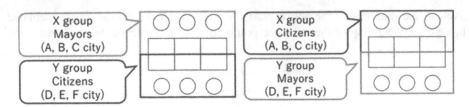

Fig. 1. The format of the mayors' meeting in the actual phase

3.4 The Implementation of the Game

Ten games were conducted with university students in November 2017 and July 2018. A total of 134 students participated, with 12–14 individuals engaged in each game. The actual phase was conducted one week after the practice phase for all ten games.

3.5 Questionnaire After Each Phase

Participants completed two questionnaires: one after the practice phase, and the other after the actual phase. The following inquiries were made in each questionnaire: "Do you think a decision could be reached only through a discussion by the mayors? Why do you think so? Do you think impartial third parties are required?" and "Do you think the participation of citizens is necessary for the final decision making about the site of the facility? Why do you think so?" As may be noted, two of the questions were open-ended.

4 Results

4.1 General Results

17 out of 20 groups reached a consensus in the practice phase with regard to the city selected for the site. This result was at variance from the previous study in which stake-holders failed to reach an agreement [2]. Two patterns were observed in the three groups that did not reach a consensus: two groups nearly achieved agreement but failed due to the lack of time; and the third group could not attain an accord because every member expressed different claims and the players could not compromise, propose alternative ideas, or make constructive suggestions.

Consensus was accomplished in all ten games at the citizen's meeting in the actual phase, and no remarks were made against the other cities.

4.2 Change in Subjective Perceptions After the Practice and Actual Phases

The two open-ended questions to compare the participant perceptions just after the practice and actual phases were qualitatively analyzed.

Evaluation of the Manner in Which the Discussions Were Conducted and an Appraisal of the Decision-Making Authority. First, the participants' thoughts about whether only mayoral discussions could suffice and result in a decision and whether impartial third parties were required were examined. Responses were classified using the KJ method [12, 13], a qualitative analysis technique that maps similar categories closer to each other and discrete categories further apart. Figure 2 depicts the distribution of opinions in the practice phase, and Fig. 3 portrays the outcomes of the qualitative analysis accomplished for the actual phase. The responses were categorized from (A) to (M), as shown in Figs. 2 and 3 The horizontal axis represents the opinions on the question asking whether or not the mayors could reach a consensus on their own. The right side of the horizontal axis signifies the belief that the mayors cannot reach consensus on their own, while the left side of the horizontal axis symbolizes the conviction that the mayors can reach a consensus on their own. The vertical axis embodies the involvement of other actors. The upper part of the axis corresponds to the belief that third parties, citizens, and experts should be involved. Notably, the origin point, where the vertical axis and the horizontal axis intersect, is moved to the left, evincing that only a few participants believed that mayors could achieve agreement on their own, and the majority did not agree with this idea.

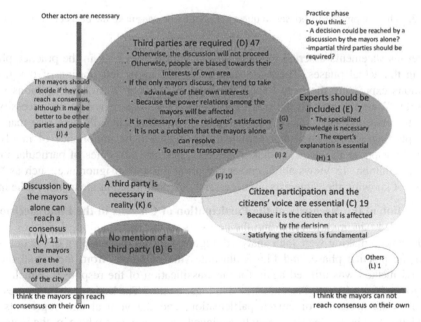

Fig. 2. The mapping of responses to questions about who can make the decision (practice phase)

Eleven statements in the practice phase (Fig. 2) described that mayors could reach consensus on their own. These were mapped at the bottom left of the illustration. However, this number was reduced to 3 in the actual phase (Fig. 3). In contrast,

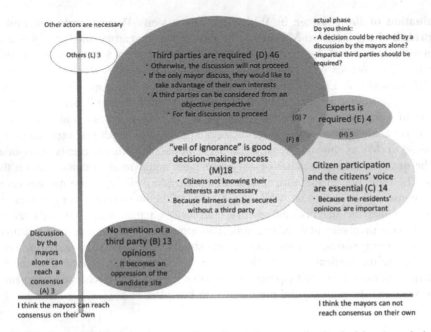

Fig. 3. The mapping of responses to questions about who can make the decision (actual phase)

numerous statements asserted the necessity of third parties both in the practice phase and in the actual phases. These are mapped on the upper left portion of the graph. Opinions expressing the need for citizens' voices, such as "residents' opinions were important", are mapped on the right. Participants' opinions regarding the necessity of experts versus citizens' voices, e.g., "experts should be included" were also mapped. This plotting demonstrated that participants recognized the importance of involving multiple actors in the decision-making process, not just advocates of particular interests. In addition, 18 views about citizens wearing the veil of ignorance, such as "citizens not knowing their interests are necessary" are positioned in the center of the map.

Evaluation of the Necessity of the Participation of Citizens in the Final Decision.
Responses to the inquiry regarding the necessity of the participation of citizens in the final decision making were then analyzed. Figure 4 shows the mapping of the opinions from the practice phase, and Fig. 5 illustrates the outcomes from the actual phase. The KJ method was utilized again for the classification of the responses, which were categorized from (A) to (T) as illustrated in Figs. 4 and 5 The horizontal axis represents belief in the necessity of citizen participation, and the vertical axis represents the conviction that better decisions may be achieved for society as a whole by the inclusion of varied actors. The left part of the horizontal axis signifies the opinion that the participation of citizens is necessary, while the right denotes the estimation that the involvement of citizens is unnecessary. The top of the vertical axis epitomizes the notion that better decisions result from the contemplation of diverse opinions and values by involving many actors through public participation.

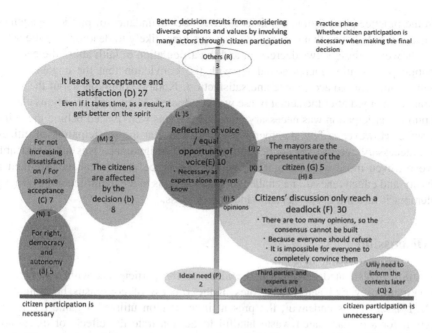

Fig. 4. The mapping of the responses to questions about the necessity for public participation (practice phase)

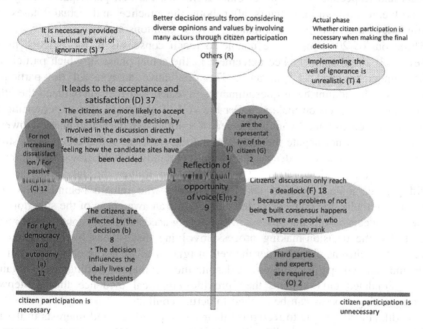

Fig. 5. The mapping of the responses to questions about the necessity for public participation (actual phase)

In the practice phase, some opinions asserted the redundancy of public engagement because it was believed that citizens' discussions were likely to deadlock. In the actual phase, however, these views decreased, and the articulation of faith about the necessity of public participation increased, along with the conviction that the engagement of citizens would lead to acceptance and satisfaction. Notably, opinions about the veil of ignorance emerged after the actual phase was conducted. Many such assertions claimed that public participation was necessary provided citizens were placed behind the veil of ignorance. However, a few statements also asserted that the participation of citizens was unnecessary because the application of the veil of ignorance was not practicable. However, even those who thought the veil of ignorance was unrealistic admitted its necessity and effectiveness. The challenge, thus, pertains to the identification of ways to implement it into the actual decision-making process.

5 Discussion

This study investigated changes in the ideas of the participants with regard to the involvement of varied actors and roles in the process of consensus building for a NIMBY issue. In its endeavor, the present investigation utilized a game on the site selection for a contaminated waste landfill to demonstrate the effects of discussions held under the veil of ignorance. The results indicate that participants were likely to strive for a fair perspective after the actual phase, avoiding obsession with regional interests and respecting the views of other residents. Further, participants recognized the involvement of various actors after both the practice and actual phases and acknowledged the value of contemplating diverse opinions and values.

Three out of 20 groups were unable to reach consensus in the practice phase. However, all 20 groups achieved agreement in the actual phase in which participants worked under the veil of ignorance. The qualitative analysis of the participant responses on the administered questionnaires revealed that they recognized the effectiveness of public decision-making under the veil of ignorance after experiencing the success of consensus building under the veil of ignorance in the actual phase. However, this outcome does not negate the decision-making rights of stakeholders with strong regional interests. A stakeholder meeting should certainly be held; however, the results of that discussion should not denote the final decision. Rather, the stakeholder meeting should precede a final decision taken by citizens who remain behind the veil of ignorance. Actually, the game accorded participants an awareness of the superiority of the two-step decision-making process in promoting acceptable decisions. These results suggest that the decision-making process involving discussions by both interested parties and by citizens placed under the veil of ignorance are not in opposition but are, rather, mutually compatible. Moreover, despite the fact that the findings were obtained from a simulated environment, they provide empirical evidence that a stepwise decision-making process can be applied to actual conflicts.

It is difficult for people to recognize their roles, positions, and interests in the real world, which makes it more difficult to build consensus. However, participants are aware of playing a role in gaming; the simulated environment of gaming can thus strip away the unacknowledged roles from our actual lives. The veil of ignorance may be applied by making those playing the role of citizens unaware of their own specific interests and positions but aware of being involved as concerned parties. Participants can liberate themselves from preconceptions and make fair judgments when they enact their roles free of particular positions and interests.

However, this study admits to certain limitations. Participants could reach a consensus because they did not completely assume the mayoral role. Indeed, some participants noted that it would be more difficult to achieve agreement in the mayoral discussions if real decision making was involved. The introduction to the role of the mayors should be modified in a manner that the players enacting the role feel they are burdened with regional interests as representatives. In addition, participants may not experience the gravity of the disadvantages and risks associated with their residential areas becoming the site for the facility. Conversely, participants may have been able to reach consensus because the necessity for the facility was so heavily emphasized. The rules and instructions, as well as the matrix of the game, must be refined so that participants can feel a strong and specific "sense of loss" in conjunction with stigma if they are to accept their region becoming the site for the disposal of designated waste contaminated by radioactive substances.

Despite these limitations, this study was able to demonstrate that the experience of discussing an issue under the veil of ignorance made participants recognize public participation to be a better means of achieving a fair decision. A criticism may be made that it is unrealistic to conceive of a situation in which citizens are unaware of their own attributes. However, it is possible to conceptualize a condition in which any area can be a candidate site before the inspection begins and none of the people know whether their residential area is a candidate site unless the detailed inspection is performed. This scenario may be regarded as incorporating the veil of ignorance in reality. In that sense, the application of the veil of ignorance may be practicable in the real world, although the game must be further fine-tuned. In sum, a possible stepwise public decision-making process involving diverse actors behind the veil of ignorance has been addressed in this paper.

Acknowledgments. This study was supported by the Foundation for the Fusion of Science and Technology, and Graduate Grant Program of Graduate School of Letters, Hokkaido University, Japan. The authors would like to thank MARUZEN-YUSHODO Co., Ltd. for the English language editing.

References

1. Hirose, Y.: Development of risk communication game promoting the consensus of siting designated waste. In: The Annual Conference of Japan Association of Simulation and Gaming 2016 Autumn, pp. 16–17 (2015)
2. Yokoyama, M., Ohnuma, S., Hirose, Y.: Can the veil of ignorance promote a consensus?: game of the "siting for landfill disposal of waste". Stud. Simul. Gaming **26**, 21–32 (2017)
3. Kago, Y.: Siting problems of hatred facilities - environmental risk and fairness. Reitaku University Economic Society Series, Chiba (2009)
4. Harashina, S.: Development of environmental planning and policy research: Consensus building for a sustainable society. Iwanami Shoten, Tokyo (2007)

5. Pidgeon, N.F., Demski, C.C., Butler, C., Parkhill, K., Spence, A.: Creating a national citizen engagement process for energy policy. Proc. Natl. Acad. Sci. U.S.A. **111**, 13606–13613 (2014)
6. Kaneda, T.: Simulation and Gaming of Social Design. Kyoritsu Publishing, Tokyo (2005)
7. Ohnuma, S., Kitakaji, Y.: Social dilemma as a device for recognition of a shared goal: development of "consensus building of wind farm game". Simul. Gaming **25**(2), 107–113 (2015)
8. Rawls, J.: A theory of Justice: Revised edition, 1st edn. Harvard University Press, Cambridge (1999)
9. Renn, O., Blättel-Mink, B., Kastenholz, H.: Discursive methods in environmental decision making. Bus. Strategy Environ. **6**(4), 218–231 (1997)
10. Renn, O., Webler, T., Rakel, H., Dienel, P., Johnson, B.: Public participation in decision making: a three-step procedure. Policy Sci. **26**(3), 189–241 (1993)
11. Obata, N.: Environmental Conflict Experiment Game: Environment Creation from Confrontation to Symbiosis. Gihodo Publishing, Tokyo (1992)
12. Kawakita, J.: A way of thinking: developing creativity. Chuoukoronsha, Tokyo (1967)
13. Plain, C.: Build an affinity for KJ method. Qual. Progr. **40**(3), 88 (2007)

The Development of the 3D Role-Playing Game on PC with an Assistive System for Deuteranopia

Paiboon Kiattikomol[✉], Ratchadawan Nimnual[✉],
and Pavarisa Sittisanguansak

King Mongkut's University of Technology Thonburi, Bangkhuntien,
Bangkok 10150, Thailand
ratchadawan.nim@mail.kmutt.ac.th

Abstract. The purposes of the study were 1) to design and develop the 3D role-playing game on PC with an assistive system for green vision impaired people, 2) to assess the quality of the game created by the experts, and 3) to evaluate the satisfaction of the samples towards the game. This game was qualitatively evaluated by three experts in gaming development through a purposive sampling. Thirty participants were recruited via accidental sampling method to evaluate a satisfaction towards the game. The quality evaluation results was found to be at a satisfactory level (mean = 3.90/SD = 0.12). The participants rated their satisfaction towards the game at the very satisfactory level (mean = 3.64/SD = 0.05). It can be summarized that the 3D role-playing game on PC with an assistive system for green vision impaired people is appropriate to be used for the visually impaired. The assistive system can also be applied to further develop games for the vision-impaired people. and relaxing users, which can be compared to being on a vacation.

Keywords: 3D role-playing game · Assistive system · Deuteranopia

1 Introduction

Despite a myriad of game development in the past, the patters and illustrations of the development have been limited by the insufficient qualities and variations of computer properties and operating systems. Due to the advanced technology, the current computer systems have been effectively developed. Moreover, programs have been created and improved to serve the game development and reinforce its effectiveness. This results in developing game patterns and compositions more perfectly and surreally. The programs can develop games in both 2D and 3D forms, which are more surreal and appealing than those in the past. Players are more entertained and enjoyable. This phenomenon consequently attracts organizations and developers to create and develop games. As a result, gaming business and marketing is growing in a fast pace. This makes gaming development captivating and become a demanding job.

Prior literature has been demonstrated that games with an assistive system for visually impaired people are scarcely available even though the game development has

© Springer Nature Switzerland AG 2021
M. Wardaszko et al. (Eds.): ISAGA 2019, LNCS 11988, pp. 153–159, 2021.
https://doi.org/10.1007/978-3-030-72132-9_14

been conventionally practiced. The games are also unable to sufficiently generate satisfaction and gaming comprehension among the vision impaired players. Opportunities in experiencing gaming variations and entertainment are also hindered. With this, the current study aimed to address this issue [1].

According to the, scholars have sought to identify causations among the visually impaired players. The results manifest that colors represented in games are unparalleled with what the players see, thereby misunderstanding the game systems through coloring illustration. The players are, moreover, visually fatigued by the inappropriate coloring. This could be considered as a principle problem as it impeded satisfaction and enjoyment of the players and needed to be solved. This could be done by modifying the coloring representation in the assistive system for the visually impaired to be clearer and more accurate, matching with their color properties. This is to help the players understand the game system and become less susceptible to visual fatigue. However, there are a various type of the visually impaired people, which have different visual and coloring perceptions. The sampling recruitment is, moreover, confided to a limited number of the visually impaired. The current study, hence, aimed to develop the assertive system in a game for the visually impaired people. The findings are expected to be beneficially used to implement the future visual assistive system.

To address the issue, the present research developed a role-playing game in a horror and fighting category. The game per se was in 3D and first-person on PC with a visual assistive system for deuteranopia. Unreal Engine 4 software was utilized in this study because of its novelty and effectiveness. The graphical outcomes were in satisfactorily acceptable level. Importantly, the developed system could offer a color displaying mode for people with deuteranopia. The developed game was qualitatively assessed by experts in gaming development. One of the experts had deuteranopia. This is to be ascertained that the visual assistive system is practical, reliable, and adaptable to future studies [2–6].

2   Material and Method

In designing and developing the 3D role-playing on PC with an assistive system for deuteranopia, related literature and informational data were sought and reviewed before applying to the gaming development. The procedures are as follows.

1) Studying how to use Unreal Engine 4 program
   Unreal Engine 4 offers a render system which generates a graphical performance at an optimal level. The program, moreover, provides a mode for the visually impaired which colors and textures can be adjusted. Due to highly graphical rendering and performance, expert consultation, literature and website search, this program is, hence, suitable for developing a game in this study (Fig. 1).
2) The visually impaired study
   Since the current study aimed to develop a 3D role-playing game on PC with an assistive system for deuteranopia, conditions and symptoms, as well as sighting characteristics, of the vision impaired must be correctly reviewed. This is to be applied to the gaming development and color selection, which can influence

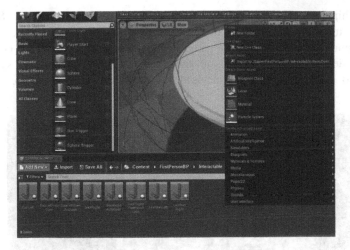

Fig 1. Import Animation for Unreal Engine 4

visually impaired players. The data were mainly collected through internet search and interviews with the visually impaired. This is to obtain further knowledge and understanding between the developers and the players. However, consulting experts for more accurate information should be done along with the processes (Fig. 2).

Fig. 2. The Example of fighting scene

3) The game system planning and designing

As people with deuteranopia are unable to normally see the green and red, the developed game was designed to emphasize on green and red color representation through danger and safety signs. Moreover, players who have no visual problems could enjoy the game. The 3D haunting and fighting role-playing game in first-person angle was created. In the game, a circular line around a character indicates an approaching threat, represented through a change of the circle color. Sign illustration, furthermore, serves as object indication throughout the game. When the game genre had been decided, a game story was created to frame the concept and internal designs before mapping out the game system. A preliminary system necessary for the whole game was devised in the process (Figs. 3 and 4).

Fig. 3. Shown the interface inside game

Fig. 4. Shown the game system planning and designing

3   The Result

When each gaming aspect was considered, it was found that all of them were at a good level. The highest rate was on the assistive system (mean = 4.33/SD = 0.58), the user interaction system (mean = 4.00/0.33), and the scene and scenic objects (mean = 3.92/SD = 0.29), respectively (See Tables 1 and 2).

Table 1. Shown average, standard deviation, and quality level of the 3D role-playing game on PC with an assistive system for deuteranopia

Evaluation questions	Mean	S.D.	Quality level
Game system			
Character control system			
• A vision of a character makes me feel sick, such as dizzy	4.33	0.58	Good
• The character control is smooth	4.33	0.58	Good
• The interaction between a character and objects in scenes is appropriate	4.33	0.58	Good
• The character can be easily controlled by a keyboard and a mouse	4.00	0.00	Good
• The shooting and reload systems are appropriate	3.67	0.58	Good
Overall	**4.13**	**0.26**	Good
Obstacles in the game			
• The difficult level of Artificial Intelligence is appropriate	3.33	0.58	Moderate
• Enemy's characteristics is suitable for the game	3.33	0.58	Moderate
• The difficulty level of the game puzzle	3.33	0.58	Moderate
Overall	**3.33**	**0.00**	**Moderate**
Overall for each aspect	**3.83**	**0.20**	Good

4 Discussion

The participants were, moreover, very satisfied with them. This may be the font colors used in the game were vivid and clear. For instance, the subtitles were in a suitable position. The Typeface was appropriately used, which did not interfere or impede the game. Respecting the scenes and scenic objects and the characters, the experts rated them at a good level. The participants were very satisfied with these aspects. This may be the scenic visions were well-designed and beautiful. The objects were well-organized. These can subsequently make them surreal and stimulate gaming participation. For example, furniture was perfectly and realistically arranged in its place. Lights and surrounding in the game promoted enjoyment while playing. The characters were fascinatingly and appropriately designed. For instance, movements and expressions were performed naturally, which further trigger players to be more enjoyable. The sound effects and audios were rated at a good level by the experts. The participants were very satisfied with the sound systems. This may be because the gaming system was interesting. The playing regulations were simple. Players were also facilitated through hints and guiding signs. These provisions and systems could help alleviate boredom and trigger desirable feelings while playing. With respect to the assistive system for the visually impaired, it was evaluated to be at a good level by the experts. It may be because this supportive system was practical and applicable. This reason was reflected from the expert with deuteranopia, who was able to use this system effectively. The color modifying system could appropriately adjust colors. The modification

Table 2. Shown manifests that the overall of the game was rated at the good level (mean = 3.90/SD = 0.12).

Evaluation question	Mean	S.D.	Quality level
• The assistive system for the visually im-paired	4.33	0.58	Good
• The user interaction system	4.00	0.33	Good
• Scenes and scenic objects	3.92	0.29	Good
• The program structure	3.89	0.39	Good
• The story	3.83	0.41	Good
• The characters	3.83	0.41	Good
• The game system	3.83	0.20	Good
• The sound effects and game audios	3.81	0.22	Good
• The fonts	3.63	0.25	Good
Overall	**3.90**	**0.12**	**Good**

could consequently make the coloring vision in the game viewed by the visually impaired like that of the normal people.

5 Conclusion

The results from the evaluation of three experts on the design and development of the 3D role-playing game on PC with an assistive system for deuteranopia revealed that the qualitative assessment was at an acceptable level. Every aspect of the game was rated at a good level (mean = 3.90/SD = 0.12). With respect to the participants' gaming satisfaction, they were very satisfied with the game (mean = 3.64/SD = 0.05).

For the general gaming compositions and the user interaction system, they were rated at a good level by the experts. Regarding the samples' satisfaction, they were moderately satisfied. This is because the signs representation and communication, and rules and regulations were clear and easy to understand. For example, signs and colors were well-designed and selected. Moreover, the rules and how to play were explained in simple and comprehensible language. This could help prevent confusion upon playing.

References

1. Jefferson, L., Harvey, R.: An interface to support color blind computer users. In: ACM SIGCHI, pp. 1535–1538 (2007)
2. Huang, J.B., Wu, S.Y., Chen, C.S.: Enhancing color representation for the color vision impaired. In: Workshop on Computer Vision Applications for the Visually Impaired, in conjunction with ECCV 2008, October 2008
3. Wakita, K., Shimamura, K.: Smart color: disambiguation framework for the colorblind. In: ACM ASSETS, pp. 158–165 (2005)

4. Jefferson, L., Harvey, R.: Accommodating color blind computer users. In: ACM SIGAC CESS, pp. 40–47 (2006)
5. Huang, J.B., Tseng, Y.C., Wu, S.I., Wang, S.J.: Information preserving color transformation for protanopia and deuteranopia. IEEE Signal Process. Lett. **14**(10), 711–714 (2007)
6. AlFalah, S.F., Harrison, D.K., Charissis, V., Evans, D.: An investigation of a healthcare management system with the use of multimodal interaction and 3D simulation: A technical note. J. Enterp. Inf. Manage. **26**, 183–197 (2013)

The Trust Game: The Influence of Trust on Collaboration in the Light of Technological Innovations

Anique Kuijpers[1(✉)], Heide Lukosch[2], and Alexander Verbraeck[1]

[1] Faculty of Technology Policy and Management, Delft University
of Technology, Jaffalaan 5, 2628 BX Delft, The Netherlands
a.g.j.kuijpers@tudelft.nl
[2] HIT Lab NZ, University of Canterbury,
Private Bag 4800, Christchurch 8140, New Zealand

Abstract. Adopting innovations is key for organizations to compete in a complex system, such as the transportation system. In a complex system where social (e.g. organizations) and technical (e.g. information systems) interact with each other, collaboration can be challenging. One of the barriers identified that hampers collaboration is trust. To understand the influence of trust on collaboration, enabled by technological innovations, simulation games in our perspective are a suitable method for our study. First, we introduce the results of a literature study that was carried out to identify related work regarding trust and simulation games. Subsequently, a case from the transport sector is defined to serve as a basis for the trust game. To conclude, we illustrate our simulation gaming approach and discuss the first initial results of a playtest session with the Trust Game.

Keywords: Trust · Collaboration · Technological innovations · Simulation games · The Trust Game

1 Introduction

Understood as competitive advantage, socio-technical innovations are becoming more and more interwoven within and between organizations [1]. The implementation of an innovation usually has large impacts on any organization. In a complex system where social (e.g. organizations) and technical (e.g. inter-organizational information) systems interact with each other [2], the adoption of innovations can lead to changes in business structures. While socio-technological innovations provide advantages for organizations, they can also increase the complexity of the system, i.e. technological innovations often transcend organizational boundaries [3]. The implementation of an innovation is a risky undertaking, yet could lead to a competitive advantage. Organizations are facing the dilemma as to use an innovation for competition yet at the same time needing the collaboration with actors that could be competitors. Different to traditional, simple technical innovations, the implementation of socio-technical innovations in complex systems requires actors to collaborate in an innovation network.

In our study, we work with the example of the innovation truck platooning that is currently tested in the Netherlands. We use this case to illustrate the challenges that are

© Springer Nature Switzerland AG 2021
M. Wardaszko et al. (Eds.): ISAGA 2019, LNCS 11988, pp. 160–169, 2021.
https://doi.org/10.1007/978-3-030-72132-9_15

related to the implementation of a socio-technical innovation within a complex system such as the system of transportation and mobility. The concept of truck platooning can be described as trucks that drive closely together, supported by communicating technologies [4]. Truck platooning provides advantages for the transportation sector, as it allows truck operators to react on future truck driver shortages and reduce fuel consumption. Its contribution can be seen in an increased safety on the road and the decrease of carbon emission. To be able to platoon, different organizations need to collaborate. Truck operators need to share travel speeds, departure times and destinations [5]. The sharing of this information means a huge difference to traditional ways of working together in a supply chain, where information sharing is scarce, and seen as possible threat to competitive advantage. To take advantage of the positive effects of truck platooning, collaboration within the transportation system becomes vital. On the other hand, we see that in complex systems, collaboration can be challenging and is hampered by a lack of trust. The importance of trust in the transportation sector is slowly becoming emergent, however, is not self-evident.

The transportation domain is a sector where simulations and games represent accepted instruments of decision-support [6], training, and exploration [7, 8]. Games can be used to investigate individual choices of actors. They enable both actors and researchers to explore possible actions as well as observing the consequences of actions and decisions in different scenarios. Transportation is a complex, dynamic system, and games are able to represent this socio-technical system [9] and make it explorable.

The aim of this paper is to show a simulation gaming approach to translate the concept of trust and to increase the awareness of the influence of trust on collaboration when using technological innovations. By using a simulation gaming approach, we will a) qualitatively conceptualize the concept of trust in socio-technical systems, based on the transportation related case of truck platooning, and b) create awareness on the role of trust amongst actors within the transportation domain.

The remainder of this paper is structured as follows. First, the importance of trust in complex socio-technical systems is introduced together with the case study of truck platooning. Subsequently, we discuss and analyze previous simulation gaming studies on trust to identify the knowledge gap we address, and to locate our study in the light of related work. The theory and design of the Trust Game are discussed in Sect. 3, following by the first initial results. Following from these results we discuss the limitations of certain game mechanics, e.g. strategy cards and the balance of the game environment, as well as the role of researchers as players in the game. We conclude with a discussion and a future outlook based on the first initial results of game play session with the Trust Game.

2 Trust, Innovation and Complex Systems

Adoption of innovations can provide advantages for organizations, such as increased efficiency. However, it can also increase the complexity, as innovations can have a certain impact on the structure of an organization. Thus, the role of trust with regard to complex, socio-technical systems is an ambivalent one. On the one hand, trust can reduce complexity for organizations [10, 11], can decrease transactions costs and limit uncertainties regarding innovations [12]. For example, truck operators have an expectancy that other actors will be reliable and behave in a good-faith effort when collabo rating. By this expectancy truck operators can partially predict how others will behave and this can reduce complexity as well as the negotiation time, i.e. not every detail needs to be discussed. One the other hand, a certain level of risk is involved when trusting an organization [10, 14]. Risk in this context is related to the other party [15]. Organizations might need to collaborate and share sensitive information with competitors. Competitors might act opportunistically and misuse information; trust in the actor is then misplaced.

The ambivalence of the concept of trust can also be illustrated by its relationship to distinct elements of a system. According to McKnight et al. [13], trust can for example be characterized on two levels, which are trust in people and trust in technology. Following this dichotomy, trust in people can be described as the expectation in the behavior of other individuals, groups or organizations. Trust in technology can be defined as the expectation that an IT artifact will operate as intended. Another approach describes trust as an actor's expectancy [14, 15], meaning that one actor has certain expectations towards the actions of another actor. Trust can be built in case these expectations are confirmed. Not every relationship requires the same amount of trust [14]. Trust is a dynamic phenomenon and is not necessarily reciprocal, i.e. organization A can trust organization B, not necessarily meaning that B needs to trust organization A. Additionally, trust is context dependent [16, 17] and occurs in environments where risks and uncertainties exist.

In summary, we will apply following definition of trust in socio-technical systems: trust is an expectation of an organization that fulfills its obligations, behave in a predictable manner, and will act and negotiate fairly [18]. In our study, we focus on the influence of trust when organizations collaborate by the means of technological innovations. One of the technological innovations that is currently tested in the transportation sector is truck platooning. Truck platooning, as already mentioned, can be described as multiple trucks that drive with a fixed inter vehicle distance via communication technology. Truck platooning promises to come with advantages with regard to CO_2 emission, congestion, and travel times [4]. In order to form and drive in a platoon, organizations, such as truck operators, need to collaborate.

To illustrate the process of platooning, we will briefly describe a possible scenario, in which truck operator A needs to transport valuable goods from Rotterdam to Duisburg. Via a service provider, truck operator A checks whether other organizations need to go into this direction too. As it turns out, organization B and C also need to go to Duisburg. To form a platoon, all actors would need to collaborate, and trust each other. Questions that arise are for example whether organization A trusts organization B and C, whether all organizations provide the correct information to each other, and whether all organizations will show up on time in order to platoon. As aforementioned, the importance of trust in the transportation system is not self-evident. It is based on a number of factors that could influence the level of trust between the parties, such as earlier experiences with each other. To show the importance of trust on collaboration when transportation experts are using technological innovation, simulation games are chosen as method.

2.1   Simulation Games on Trust

Simulation gaming is a powerful research tool that can make complexity of systems more understandable for actors as well as for researchers [19, 20]. Simulation games allow us to establish a safe environment where we can experiment, e.g. with low trust and high trust environments when actors need to collaborate by means of technological innovations. Moreover, simulation games are an appropriate tool to study a social, dynamic phenomenon in a complex system [20]. They enable us to represent a phenomenon like trust in an interactive and more understandable manner for (transportation) experts.

The concept of trust has already been addressed by different types of simulation games. Table 1 illustrates a brief overview of related simulation games that address the concept of trust. As one can see from the table, most of these studies use the prisoner's dilemma as the basis of their games. The prisoner's dilemma allows scholars to study the decision making on whether or not to collaborate. As argued in these studies, trust can be of influence when deciding to collaborate. However, in our perspective, the influence of trust on the interaction patterns when collaborating by means of technological innovations is not studied yet. Nonetheless, from these studies certain mechanisms can be derived that are interesting to create a trusted-distrusted environment. For instance, as shown by Meijer et al. [21], non-visible transactions and a reward system for cheating can already create a distrusted environment or an environment where trust can be decreased.

Table 1. Overview of simulation games that address trust

Study	Goal of the simulation game	Theory/Concepts	Game mechanisms
Berg et al. (1995)*	*The investment game.* To study trust and reciprocity in an investment setting	Prisoner's dilemma	Non-cooperative environment, anonymity
Meijer et al. (2006)	*Trust and Tracing game.* Learn about the influence of social structures on transaction in a trade network	Netchains, governance mechanism, value creation, social structure	Cheating behavior is rewarded, non-visible transactions, Misaligned information, Reputation
Ebner & Winkler (2008)	*PASTA WARS.* Players can experience the key obstacles while cooperating	Four way prisoner's dilemma	Role descriptions, No communication between participants, Single player strategy
Oertig (2010)	*Knowledge sharing simulation game.* Players can experience the fragility of trust when sharing knowledge in a global virtual team	Prisoner's dilemma	Non-cooperative game, Company description, Conflicting goals, Reward system

*Note: Multiple simulation games are grounded on this study (see for an overview Johnson & Mislin, 2011)

Nevertheless, the translation of an ambivalent concept as trust into a simulation or a simulation game can be challenging, and is context depended. As shown, trust can occur in different interactions and is not necessarily reciprocal. In our study, we only focus on inter-organizational trust, i.e. an organization's expectancy that another organization behaves in a reliable and in good-faith effort during collaboration.

3   The Trust Game: A Simulation Gaming Approach

3.1   Design Considerations of the Trust Game

To create awareness among practitioners from the transportation and logistics domain on the role of trust regarding collaboration and innovation, we adopt the Triadic Game Design philosophy of Harteveld [22]. This approach is based on the balancing of three worlds; reality, meaning and play. The 'real' system, in this case the transport system, and the case of truck platooning, is represented in the world of reality. The purpose, or meaning, of the game, is defined as creating awareness for the role of trust in such complex system, and when collaboration has to be established based on a socio-technical innovation (in this case, truck platooning). The aspect of play is focused on the game world, such as the game mechanics and elements.

Developing a simulation game where the concept of trust is central, we started from the reality aspect. As aforementioned, we focus our research on the transportation sector. To create a deeper understanding of the characteristics of the transportation sector, we first conducted a system analysis. Derived from scientific and grey literature, information streams, business processes and actors in the systems could be identified. Based on the business process modelling approach, the actors and their processes are visualized through swimming lanes. Our analysis shows that business processes are highly interdependent and aligning processes and decisions can be challenging. Based on the system analysis, we can decide which roles in the game should be represented. As truck platooning serves as the technological innovation where we can study the role of trust on collaboration, we also looked into this innovation in particular. Truck platooning is not yet implemented in reality. To let transportation experts experience the influence of trust while truck platooning, we defined a future scenario where truck platooning is implemented as transport mode for the distribution of goods via the road. The purpose of this game is not only to study the role of trust on collaboration but also to create awareness among practitioners.

In its current state, the Trust Game is a physical game (Fig. 1). From a meaning and play perspective, a physical game allows us to study trust by observing the communication and discussion of the players. Certain game mechanics are used, such as strategy cards, shielding of the resources and assets of the players. The game material relates to the real system and creates an environment where trust can be explored.

The Trust Game is part of a game session consisting of an introduction to the new socio-technical innovation of truck platooning, the game play itself, and a debriefing phase. It is a round-based game, where goods from Rotterdam to different hinterland locations (i.e. Bremen, Hannover, and Frankfurt am Main) need to be transported. The overall goal of the game is to match trucks to form a platoon in order to transport goods

Fig. 1. Prototype of the Trust Game

from Rotterdam to the hinterland locations. As a result of the system analysis, we defined four roles of -small to medium sized-truck operators to be played by one player respectively. Each of the four players receives information of the company, e.g. a description of the company, the particular company assets, individual goals, and the experiences reputation of other player's roles. Especially the latter is to create a situation where relations to trusted as well as distrusted parties are already established. In that sense, the game starts from a predefined situation that supports the research aim. In the game a differentiation in truck types and positions, i.e. lead and follow trucks, is made. At the beginning of the game, each of the players receives his/her own amount of follow and lead trucks. Lead trucks earn a higher income, while the revenue for the follow trucks decreases with their position in the platoon. The last truck earns the least amount of money. Trucks can be used throughout the whole game, but only within the limitations of the given number for each truck type. Thus, players face the dilemma of choosing between costs and revenue, and have to evaluate the most beneficial situation between lead and follow trucks throughout the whole network. During each round, more than one platoon can be formed by the players. Players receive their own personal goal, i.e. distribute the goods from origin to destination with the highest profit possible. To be successful in the game as a player, you need to transport all the goods by means of a platoon and have the highest profit. One facilitator accompanies the game play. The function of the facilitator is to manage the time and resources, and to observe the players' actions and decisions for the debriefing phase.

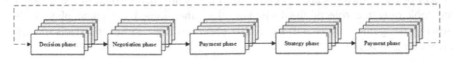

Fig. 2. Game sequence of the Trust Game

The Trust Game consists of 5 phases, each with its own processes, as illustrated in Fig. 2. A game round starts with the Decision phase. During this phase, players can check to which city they need to transport goods to. Additionally, players need to decide whether they want to be a lead truck or follow truck to the specific locations and players need to select one of their strategies that they want to play. The strategy cards in the game represent issues such as truck driver shortages, takeover of truck drivers, or changing the platoon spot. The information that is represented on the strategy cards is based on scientific and grey literature, thus strongly relating to the reality aspect of the game. Secondly, players engage with each other in the Negotiation phase. To form a platoon there needs to be a lead truck, i.e. a truck with a certified truck driver, and follower trucks, i.e. trucks that have uncertified truck drivers. To arrange the order of a platoon, players in the game need to negotiate and make an agreement. Next follows the Payment phase. During this phase, players get paid according to their spot in a platoon. The player who is a lead truck receives more compared to a player who is a follower truck. The fourth phase in a game round is the Strategy phase. During this phase, players can play their strategy card. On these cards the actions are described including their possible consequences for other players. After all strategy cards are played, and all consequences are administered, the round concludes with the fifth and final phase, the Payment phase. Based on the action cards played, players need to pay other players a certain amount as stated on the respective strategy card.

3.2   Set Up of the Game Play Sessions

The Trust Game has been played during a session with six game design and transportation experts to validate the design of the game with regard to its playability and relation to the concept of trust. The experts were invited to a game play session consisting of two games, both focused on truck platooning as innovation. While the first game focuses on the challenges of a technical innovation itself, the Trust Game aims at exploring and creating awareness for the role of trust in such innovation process in particular. The participants first received a brief introduction on the technology of truck platooning, after which the first game was played for about one hour. After a short break, the Trust Game was introduced. After the game play, which took about one and a half hours and consisted of three rounds with sub-steps as described above, a debriefing was held on the game experience, and on aspects that could be improved in the light of the meaning of the game. The first round of the game was played as a tutorial round, to learn about the game play. After three rounds, the player with the largest amount of money was announced as winner of the game. The debriefing after the game play was prepared with questions on the mechanics in the game related to the concept of trust. Two researchers involved in this study participated in the game play. One took over the role of the facilitator, the other joined the game play, without knowing the game beforehand. Both also observed the actions and decisions of all players, and took notes.

3.3   Initial Results of the Playtest

While during the design of the game, we encountered that capturing trust as a concept in a game is challenging, the qualitative analysis of both game play and debriefing revealed that the players were able to identify trustworthy and untrustworthy situations, and what mechanics lead to higher or lower trust. The Trust Game aims to study the influence of trust on collaboration by using technological innovations. Following from the feedback of the playtest session, the assessment whether or not to collaborate in the negotiation phase could be more addressed in the game. The players identified that the strategy cards and the information (i.e. reputation of other players) they received had an impact whether or not they trusted another player during negotiations. However, the strategy cards created in some circumstances a locked-in situation that influenced negotiations. For example, information was given about preferred parties to collaborate with, and others not to work with. As some players followed this information very strictly, others were excluded from certain negotiations, without having any action available to change this situation. To overcome this issue a narrative, trade-offs and consequences of a decision could be provided. By stipulating a more complex environment for decision-making, the collaborative assessment during the negotiation phase could be more substantiate to players.

From the game play session, we see that a game with a low trusted can get demanding, especially for players who are locked in a less preferable situation. During game play this was also expressed by the players as somehow frustrating experience. On the other hand, we could observe that the game was able to evoke strong situations that can be used in a debriefing phase. For less frustrating game play and for studying the influence of trust in an innovation process, an updated version of the game will represent a more balanced trust environment. For instance, the first three rounds can be a low trusted environment whereas the last two rounds can be a high trusted environment. The transitions between the low trusted environment and high trusted environment can be established by positive and negative strategy cards. This will enable us to even better identify trust mechanisms that play a role in collaboration supported by technological innovation.

4 Conclusion and Future Research

The concept of trust is a hard to capture in a simulation game because of its stratification. As shown in this paper, various simulation games have been designed that represent trust as an (central) element. Most of these games use the prisoner's dilemma game approach that is grounded on rational decision making. However, trust is not only based on rational decision making as it can emerge at different stages and is influenced by emotional, cognitive and behavioral elements [14]. In our perspective, a simulation gaming approach that is based on the TGD philosophy allows us to explore and create awareness for the role of trust in a complex, socio-technical system. Additionally, it allows us to study the influence of trust, as a whole, on the interaction patterns in an innovation process.

The first results of the Trust Game showed that a low trusted environment could be created, in which it is difficult to establish collaboration. The playtest session gave us valuable insights how trust can be addressed in a simulation game and how the different game mechanics should be balanced. One of the limitations of the playtest session was that the researchers of this study took over the role of the facilitator in the game play as well as the role of one of the players in the game. For instance, the facilitator and researcher as player could influence the game play. Yet, as the Trust Game is still under development, we took over these roles with the purpose to being able to directly observe the game mechanics and playability of the game. In future sessions, researchers will not take over in-game roles anymore, but observe what happens during game play. Yet, the role of facilitator can still be of value for research, as this role provides control over the quasi-experimental situation of the game play.

In the future development of the game, we will adjust the Trust Game based on the feedback that we received from the playtest session. In its current state, trust is qualitatively measured by observations and a debriefing. In future work we will design quantitative measurement mechanisms based on trust characteristics, such as fulfillment of obligations, reliability and opportunistic behavior. Subsequently, game experiments will be designed grounded on a conceptual model of trust in a complex, socio-technical system. According to the results of the various experiments that will be conducted with transport experts, the conceptual model of trust will be adjusted.

The final aim of the research, of which this study represents a vital corner stone, is to create a better understanding of trust in a socio-technical system in the context of trust on collaboration in an innovation process.

Acknowledgement. This research, as part of the Trans-SONIC project (Transport Self Organization through Network Integration and Collaboration), is funded by NWO, the Netherlands organisation for Scientific Research.

References

1. Thatcher, J.B., Mcknight, D.H., Baker, E.W., Erg, R., Roberts, N.H.: The role of trust in postadoption IT exploration: an empirical examination of knowledge management systems. IEEE Trans. Eng. Manage. **58**(1), 56–70 (2011)
2. de Bruijn, H., Herder, P.M.: System and actor perspectives on sociotechnical systems. IEEE Trans. Syst. Man Cybern. Part A Syst. Hum. **39**(5), 981–992 (2009)
3. Koppenjan, J., Groenewegen, J.: Institutional design for complex technological systems. Int. J. Technol. Policy Manage. **5**(3), 240 (2005)
4. Alam, A., Besselink, B., Turri, V., Martensson, J., Johansson, K.H.: Heavy-duty vehicle platooning for sustainable freight transportation: a cooperative method to enhance safety and efficiency. IEEE Control. Syst. **35**(6), 34–56 (2015)
5. Bhoopalam, A.K., Agatz, N., Zuidwijk, R.: Planning of truck platoons: a literature review and directions for future research. Transp. Res. Part B: Methodol. **107**, 212–228 (2018)
6. Duke, R.D., Geurts, J.: Policy Games for Strategic Management. Rozenberg Publishers, Amsterdam (2004)
7. Lukosch, H., Kurapati, S., Groen, D., Verbraeck, A.: Microgames for situated learning: a case study in interdependent planning. Simul. Gaming **47**(3), 346–367 (2016)
8. Mayer, I.S., et al.: The research and evaluation of serious games: toward a comprehensive methodology. Br. J. Educ. Technol. **45**(3), 502–527 (2014)
9. Klabbers, J.H.G.: A framework for artifact assessment and theory testing. Simul. Gaming **37**(2), 155–173 (2006)
10. Bachmann, R.: Trust, power and control in trans-organizational relations. Organ. Stud. **22**(2), 337–365 (2001)
11. Luhmann, N.: Trust and Power, 1st edn. Polity Press, Cambridge (1979)

12. Nooteboom, B.: Micro-foundations for Innovation Policy. Amsterdam University Press, Amsterdam (2008)
13. Mcknight, D.H., Carter, M., Thatcher, J.B., Clay, P.F.: Trust in a specific technology. ACM Trans. Manage. Inf. Syst. **2**(2), 1–25 (2011)
14. Lewis, J.D., Weigert, A.: Trust as a social reality. Soc. Forces **63**(4), 967–985 (1985)
15. Mayer, R.C., Davis, J.H., Schoorman, F.D.: An integrative model of organizational trust. Acad. Manag. Rev. **20**(3), 709–734 (1995)
16. Hattori, R.A., Lapidus, T.: Collaboration, trust and innovative change. J. Chang. Manag. **4**(2), 97–104 (2004)
17. Tan, Y., Thoen, W.: Towards a generic model of trust for electronic commerce. Int. J. Electron. Commer. **5**(2), 61–74 (2000)
18. Zaheer, A., McEvily, B., Perrone, V.: Does trust matter? Exploring the effects of interorganizational and interpersonal trust on performance. Organ. Sci. **9**(2), 141–159 (1998)
19. Kriz, W.C.: Creating effective learning environments and learning organizations through gaming simulation design. Simul. Gaming **34**(4), 495–511 (2003)
20. Lukosch, H.K., Bekebrede, G., Kurapati, S., Lukosch, S.G.: A scientific foundation of simulation games for the analysis and design of complex systems. Simul Gaming **49**(3), 279–314 (2018)
21. Meijer, S., Hofstede, G.J., Beers, G., Omta, S.W.F.: Trust and tracing game: learning about transactions and embeddedness in a trade network. Prod. Plann. Control **17**(6), 569–583 (2006)
22. Harteveld, C.: Triadic Game Design: Balancing Reality, Meaning and Play, 1st edn. Springer, London (2011). https://doi.org/10.1007/978-1-84996-157-8

The Funnel of Game Design - Proposing a New Way to Address a Problem Definition Using the IDEAS Approach

Maria Freese[1(✉)] and Heide K. Lukosch[2]

[1] Faculty of Technology, Policy and Management, Delft University of
Technology, Jaffalaan 5, 2628 BX Delft, The Netherlands
M.Freese@tudelft.nl
[2] HIT Lab NZ, University of Canterbury, Private Bag 4800, Christchurch 8140,
New Zealand
heide.lukosch@canterbury.ac.nz

Abstract. New technologies, complex problems, interconnectedness between different actors: All these are challenges of our today's society and characteristics of complex systems. Simulation games are a suited approach to analyse complex systems. The process of designing and developing those games for complex systems follows certain steps. One of such steps is the definition of the underlying problem. Deriving a concrete problem statement under consideration of the changing complexity of today's society is crucial for the validation of a simulation game. Therefore, the following paper will introduce IDEAS, an approach to derive a specific problem statement as one part of the simulation game design process. In general, IDEAS consists of four steps: interviews, discussion rounds with experts, moscow analysis and gamestorm. The approach itself as well as a case study, where this approach has been used, will be presented. Finally, we discuss the advantages and disadvantages of the approach and give recommendation for future work.

Keywords: Simulation games · Game design · Problem statement · Validation · Biotechnology · T-TRIPP · MachiaCELLi

1 Introduction

Much has been written about the design and development of simulation games: There are a number of traditional (e.g. [1–3]), but also some modern (e.g. [4, 5]) approaches towards the design of simulation games. Some of them (e.g. [5]) focus on a problem definition as a first step of the design of a simulation game. Defining a concrete problem statement is not always easy to realize due to the nature of complex systems. Complex systems are characterized by different actors with different goals and priorities, interdependencies and collaborations under uncertainties [6]. A number of subsystems of today's society (e.g. transportation, security, biotechnology) show those characteristics. Complexity is not a new topic at all, but it becomes more and more important due to increasing dynamics, more interconnectedness and complex, uncertain problems. As [1] has stated, games are a suited approach to analyse complex systems

© Springer Nature Switzerland AG 2021
M. Wardaszko et al. (Eds.): ISAGA 2019, LNCS 11988, pp. 170–180, 2021.
https://doi.org/10.1007/978-3-030-72132-9_16

and problems. Yet, it is vital to consider the changing complexity of today's society. By reflecting on this aspect and to support the design process of simulation games for complex systems, the following paper will discuss how we can narrow down the analysis of the problem statement to guarantee a valid instrument. Therefore, the paper is structured as follows: First, we give an overview on existing design approaches for simulation games and their understanding of complexity. This is followed by a description of the new IDEAS approach we propose in this paper - an approach to derive a specific problem statement. The approach itself as well as a case study, where this approach has been used, will be presented after this. Finally, we discuss the advantages and disadvantages of the approach and give suggestions for future work.

2 State of the Art: From the Past to the Present

We conducted a literature review to analyse the current state of the art in terms of the design of simulation games. The results are shown in Table 1. We focused on these approaches because they are well-known and often cited ones (e.g. in [7, 8]).

Table 1. Comparison of traditional and modern game design approaches due to complexity.

	Examples	Complexity
Traditional approaches	[1] **Duke (1974)** 5 phases of game design	Societal complexity ("This situation has grown more urgent because the problems of today are more complex", [1, p. 24])
	[2] **Duke & Geurts (2004)** 5 Phases (process for the design and use of policy exercises)	Focus on policy gaming, cognitive complexity, socio-political complexity, normative complexity
	[3] **Klabbers (2006)** Actors, Rules, Resources	Algorithmic complexity, organizational complexity, organized complexity
Modern approaches	[9] **Hunicke, LeBlanc, Zubek (2004)** Mechanics, Dynamics, Aesthetics	"Interaction between subsystems creates complex dynamic, unpredictable behavior, interdependencies must be considered" [9, p. 1]
	[10] **Amory (2007)** Different components of the games and how they interact internally with each other	"Development and analyses of complicated designs, facilitate the understanding of complex situations" [10, p. 53]
	[11] **Sicart (2008)** Core, primary, secondary game mechanics	"Complexity requires a precise terminology, concept of primary (core) mechanics and secondary (core) mechanics" [11]

(continued)

Table 1. *(continued)*

Examples	Complexity
[12] **Westera, Nadolski, Hummel & Wopereis (2008)** Conceptual, technical and practical level of game development	Complexity at conceptual, technical and practical levels "uncertainty of the system" [12, p. 3]
[13] **Winn, 2007** Design, Play, Experience	Complex mechanics and user interface features
[4] **Harteveld (2011)** Reality, Meaning, Play	Complexity as one part of the reality
[5] **Kurapati (2017)** Defining the research problem, Requirements, Prototype, Validation and testing	Simulation games as a research instrument, complexity due to size of systems, "diversity, dynamism, social component, distributed nature, uncertainty, and vulnerability to disruptions" [5, p. ix]
[14] **Walk, Görlich & Barrett (2017)** Design, Dynamics, Experience	Always too much complexity

Table 1 shows how complexity is defined in each of the approaches. We analysed these approaches to show that the IDEAS approach is based on these acknowledge concepts, yet taking into account the specific characteristics of today's increased complexity of systems and society.

All analysed approaches have one similarity. They all consider complexity, but in different ways: They all have a different understanding of complexity (see also [15–20]), clustering different levels of complexity and focusing on either an individual, group or institutional level. Thus, there is no common understanding of complexity in scientific literature. At the same time, we see complexity of modern societies steadily increasing, becoming more important and challenging to actors, and to the tools they can use. That means that the understanding of a complex system will change due an increasing number of social challenges, e.g. more and more involved actors, interdependencies, uncertainties, (im)balance between cooperation as well as competition and technological challenges, e.g. fast developments and no up to date regulations. Questions arise such as whether we are still able to cope with the complexity in systems, which are characterized by today's challenges [7]. Another point that we identified on the base of the literature review is the fact of not having a clear description of how one can generate a concrete problem statement. Some of the approaches presented in Table 1 consider the derivation of a problem statement as an important step in the design of a simulation game (e.g. [5]), but due to different understandings of what a problem statement is about (e.g. Does research problem really mean the same as game objective and purpose of the game) and different weights on the relevance of this topic, it is not possible to compare those approaches with each other or even find a consensus.

All in all, in identifying challenges and problems to deal with, one is also confronted with increasing complexity. The reasons for problems to occur are not straight forward anymore, yet show the same growing amount of interdependencies and uncertainties as other aspects of complex systems. Yet, a clear problem definition is important for the validity of a simulation game. When a simulation game is based on a vague or even wrong problem description, a valid research instrument cannot be guaranteed anymore. This analysis lead us to following research question:

How can we guarantee a valid problem statement as one main part of the simulation game design process for complex systems?

To answer this, we developed the IDEAS game design approach, which will be explained in further detail in the next section.

3 The IDEAS Game Design

IDEAS is a four step-based approach to concretize the problem statement as part of the simulation game design process and to face the challenges mentioned in Sects. 1 and 2. The four steps of IDEAS to face those challenges are:

1. Challenge: complex topic, uncertain problem

   - Interviews

2. Challenge: different actors

   - Discussion rounds with Experts

3. Challenge: different prioritizations

   - MoSCoW-Analysis

4. Challenge: different understandings

   - GameStorm.

As a first step, we recommend to conduct open or semi-structured interviews with related game design project partners or related experts (depending on the general structure of your project). Open or semi-structured interviews as method of qualitative research are valuable when little is known about a topic, and further details need to be explored [21]. The aim of those interviews within the IDEAS approach is to identify current challenges (the problem is still very open at this stage) regarding the complex topic you are working on with people who are both familiar with the problem, and with the idea of your game approach. This step is meant to start up the problem definition with trusted parties. As it can be seen in Fig. 1, the interviews symbolize the wide, circular top of the funnel.

In a second step, it is important to analyse the interviews and discuss the analysed results with experts working in the domain of your project. This step adds a perspective to your problem analysis from an expert view that is not familiar with your project itself. Here, you can already derive some (general) problem statements based on the discussion rounds.

The third step includes the use of the MoSCoW-analysis [22]. The MoSCoW-analysis is one approach to think about more concrete requirements and to classify problem statements into four categories:

1. **M**ust-Haves (must be addressed in the game for it to succeed)
2. **S**hould (should be in the game, but not crucial)
3. **C**ould (could be in the game, but could do very well without)
4. **W**on't (what we purposefully do not include in the game).

On the base of all three steps you already should be able to generate (a) very concrete problem statement(s). In terms of the design of a simulation game for complex systems, we also want to recommend a so-called gamestorm with experts and your project partners as the last step of the design process. The aim of such a participatory game design session is to really understand what the content of the concrete problem statement is and how you can transfer it to a simulation game for complex systems.

In addition to this, feedback loops are important. Therefore, you should compare the outcome of the different levels with the outcome of the previous levels and if necessary, adjust your analysis. An overview of all steps can be found in Fig. 1.

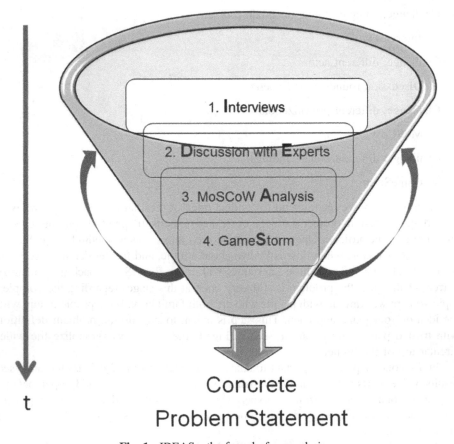

Fig. 1. IDEAS - the funnel of game design.

4 Case Study T-TRIPP

The IDEAS approach has been applied and tested within the T-TRIPP (Tools for Translation of Risk Research into Policies and Practices) project. The general aim of T-TRIPP is to contribute to a translation between policy and science to guarantee the safe development of new and innovative technologies in the domain of biotechnology. Those rapid technological developments are getting more complex and therefore pressure current regulatory frameworks [23]. Furthermore, different actors, like scientists, risk assessors and policy-makers, must be involved in the search for solutions to face those challenges. Innovative methods are needed to bring these actors together and to meet the challenge of modernizing the regulatory framework of biotechnology. One of these methods is the approach of simulation games. To identify the main problem in this complex and uncertain domain that should be addressed by the game, the IDEAS approach has been used.

1. Semi-structured Interviews
First, we conducted semi-structured interviews and asked project partners in the field of biotechnology to identify current challenges in the biotechnology domain. We clustered their answers to the following six categories:

- Acceptance of biotechnological practices
- Trade-off between risks and benefits
- Translation between policy-maker and scientists
- Responsibility allocation
- Addressing the public
- Others (slow regulations, unexpected results).

An overview of the first step of the IDEAS approach in our study as well as the used material and applied set-ups can be found in Table 2.

Table 2. IDEAS approach for the T-TRIPP project – interviews.

IDEAS approach	Materials	Example
1. Interviews (open, semi-structured)	Interview guideline, questionnaires, sticky notes, flipcharts	

2. Discussion with Experts

Second, together with experts in the biotechnology domain we derived some problem statements based on the interview results. For the design of a simulation game it is not realistic to consider all the different problem statements. Therefore, we had to prioritize those (see Table 3).

Table 3. IDEAS approach for the T-TRIPP project – discussion rounds with experts.

IDEAS approach	Materials	Example
2. Discussion rounds with Experts	Structured guideline, good time management	

3. MoSCoW Analysis

The prioritization of the current challenges in the biotechnology domain was based on the MoSCoW [22] approach that distinguishes four categories: Must Haves (fundamental requirements), Should Haves (Important requirements), Could Haves

Table 4. IDEAS approach for the T-TRIPP project – MoSCoW-Analysis.

IDEAS approach	Materials	Example
3. MoSCoW-Analysis [22]	A prepared flipchart for the MoSCoW-Analysis, sticky notes	

(Negotiable requirements) and Won't Haves (Non-value adding requirements). In our case, the results have shown that the focus of the simulation game should be focused on regulatory issues. The problem description was narrowed down to the challenge of deep uncertainty in the biotechnological field on technology progress and matching regulations (new technologies do not fit with current regulations, current regulations are not good enough, too strict, too much paperwork, too old) (see Table 4).

4. GameStorm

The idea beyond conducting participatory gamestorm sessions as fourth step in developing a simulation game for the biotechnology domain was to concretize and really understand the problem. Therefore, we conducted a gamestorm session with experts from the field using the Triadic Game Design Approach [4]. This approach consists of the analysis of the reality, meaning and play aspect of a game. In our case, the focus was on the reality and meaning aspect, less on the role of play. The play aspect was added by professional game designers by adopting the concept of an entertainment game to the problem (see Table 5).

Table 5. IDEAS approach for the T-TRIPP project – GameStorm.

IDEAS approach	Materials	Example
		Gaming Sheet: Meaning
4. GameStorm	Good time management, also work a bit with time pressure, gaming sheets	What do the players take home after the game play?
		When do we consider the game to be successful?
		Where, when and how will the game be played? By whom?

Based on the IDEAS approach, we were not only able to identify a concrete problem for the design and development of a simulation game for the complex system of biotechnology. We also used the structured game design process and the collected material from it as input for a playable simulation game prototype for the domain. This game is called MachiaCELLi. In this competitive game, four to six players engage in one game session. The task of each player is to engineer and to validate an artificial cell. Engineering and validation steps follow each other up during the game. Each round, a player takes over a different role, e.g. of a project manager, a scientist, or a regulator. With this role-taking element, the players experience different perspectives on the engineering phase in biotechnology.

5 Discussion and Conclusions

The present paper showed that most of the existing simulation game design approaches represent only a limited understanding of today's societies' complexity, and the complexity of systems and their complex problems and challenges. Yet, in our opinion and based on our experiences with game design for complex systems during the last 10 years, of which the T-TRIPP project is only one example, we argue that a new level of system complexity calls for new game design approaches such as the IDEAS approach. The multi-levelled approach with its rich combination of methods, allowing for a participatory game design approach, enables game designers to develop a simulation game based on a concrete problem statement to guarantee a valid instrument.

To address both topics, the four step-based IDEAS approach has been developed and already successfully been used within the T-TRIPP project. As part of this discussion, we will discuss the advantages and disadvantages of the new developed funnel of game design.

First, some of the game design approaches mentioned in Table 1 consider the phase of clarifying a problem as at least one of the first steps of the design process of a simulation game (e.g. [1, 5]). In addition to this, IDEAS offers a structured step-by-step approach to identify and understand a concrete problem statement to guarantee a valid instrument. If a simulation game is based on a vague or even wrong problem description, this can lead to a non-valid (research) instrument and can also influence your results negatively (see also [24]). We also recommend an iterative procedure. This means that intermediary results in the game design process should be compared with previous ones. This is especially important to identify and relate different perspectives on the complex problem and system to each other, to better understand the problem itself as well as its complex nature.

Second, the involvement of actors and project members leads to more acceptance and trust in the simulation game. In our cases, most actors were not familiar with simulation games. Therefore, we decided to integrate them as early as possible in the design process of MachiaCELLi. Future work will show how experts beyond our own study will respond to the game.

The resources needed for the IDEAS approach have been pointed out as one criticism. This approach seems to be recommendable as part of a bigger research project. For smaller gaming design/development companies, it might be a bit challenging in terms of time and financial resources. Furthermore, the integration of perspectives from different actors is another challenge that must be considered.

However, the IDEAS approach is also transferrable to other complex sub-systems of today's society.

Acknowledgement. This work has received funding from the Technology Foundation of NWO, the Netherlands Organisation for Scientific Research.

References

1. Duke, R.D.: Toward a general theory of gaming. Simul. Games **5**(2), 131–146 (1974)
2. Duke, R.D., Geurts, J.: Policy Games for Strategic Management. Rozenberg Publishers, Amsterdam (2004)
3. Klabbers, J.H.G.: The Magic Circle: Principles of Gaming & Simulation. Sense Publishers, Rotterdam (2006)
4. Harteveld, C.: Triadic Game Design. Springer, London (2011). https://doi.org/10.1007/978-1-84996-157-8
5. Kurapati, S.: Situation awareness for socio technical systems: a simulation gaming study in intermodal transport operations. Doctoral thesis. TRAIL Research School, Delft, The Netherlands (2017)
6. De Bruijn, H., Herder, P.M.: System and actor perspectives on sociotechnical systems. IEEE Trans. Syst. Man Cybern. Part A Syst. Hum. **39**(5), 981–992 (2009)
7. Lukosch, H.K., Bekebrede, G., Kurapati, S., Lukosch, S.G.: A scientific foundation of simulation games for the analysis and design of complex systems. Simul. Gaming **49**(3), 279–314 (2018)
8. Wardaszko, M.: Complexity in simulation gaming. In: Developments in Business Simulation and Experiential learning: Proceedings of the Annual Absel Conference (2010)
9. Hunicke, R., LeBlanc, M., Zubek, R.: MDA: a formal approach to game design and game research. In: Game Developers Conference (2004)
10. Amory, A.: Game object model version II: a theoretical framework for educational game development. Educ. Tech. Res. Dev. **55**(1), 51–77 (2007)
11. Sicart, M.: Defining game mechanics. Int. J. Comput. Game Res. **8**(2) (2008)
12. Westera, W., Nadolski, R., Hummel, H.G.K., Wopereis, I.: Serious games for higher education: a framework for reducing design complexity. J. Comput. Assist. Learn. **24**(5), 420–432 (2008)
13. Winn, B.: Design, play, and experience: a framework for the design of serious games for learning. In: Handbook of Research on Effective Electronic Gaming in Education, pp. 1010–1024 (2007)
14. Walk, W., Görlich, D., Barrett, M.: Design, dynamics, experience (DDE): an advancement of the MDA framework for game design. In: Korn, O., Lee, N. (eds.) Game Dynamics, pp. 27–45. Springer, Cham (2017). https://doi.org/10.1007/978-3-319-53088-8_3
15. Capra, F.: The Web of Life: A New Scientific Understanding of Living Systems. Anchor Books, New York (1997)
16. Maturana, H.R., Varela, F.J.: Problems in the neurophysiology of cognition. In: Maturana, H.R., Varela, F.J. (eds.) Autopoiesis and Cognition, vol. 42, pp. 41–47. Springer, Dordrecht (1980). https://doi.org/10.1007/978-94-009-8947-4_5
17. Ridolfi, G., Mooij, E., Corpino, S.: Complex-systems design methodology for systems-engineering collaborative environment. In: Cogan, B. (ed.) Systems Engineering-Practice and Theory, pp. 39–70. InTechOpen, London (2012)
18. Thrift, N.: The place of complexity. Theory Cult. Soc. **16**(3), 31–69 (1999)
19. Waldrop, M.M.: Complexity: The Emerging Science at the Edge of Order and Chaos. Viking, London (1992)
20. Walby, S.: Complexity theory, systems theory, and multiple intersecting social inequalities. Philos. Soc. Sci. **37**(4), 449–470 (2007)
21. Wilson, C.: Chapter 2 - Semi-structured interviews. In: Wilson, C. (ed). Interview Techniques for UX Practitioners. A User-Centered Design Method, pp. 23–41. Morgan Kaufmann, Amsterdam (2014)

22. Clegg, D., Barker, R.: Case Method Fast-Track: A RAD Approach. Addison-Wesley, Boston (1994)
23. Hogervorst, P.A.M., van den Akker, H.C.M., Glandorf, D.C.M., Klaassen, P., van der Vlugt, C.J.B., Westra, J.: Assessment of human health and environmental risks of new developments in modern biotechnology – Policy report RIVM-2018-0089. https://www.rivm.nl/bibliotheek/rapporten/2018-0089.pdf. Accessed 20 May 2019
24. Harteveld, C., Guimarães, R., Mayer, I.S., Bidarra, R.: Balancing play, meaning and reality: the design philosophy of LEVEE PATROLLER. Simul. Gaming 41(3), 316–340 (2010)

Little Things Mean a Lot in Simulations

Richard Teach[1]([✉]), James Szot[2], and Larry Chasteen[2]

[1] Georgia Institute of Technology, Atlanta, USA
richard.teach@scheller.gatech.edu
[2] University of Texas Dallas, Richardson, USA
jimszot@UTDallas.edu, Chasteen@utdallas.edu

Abstract. All teachers using business simulations are concerned about what students learn when they participate in these games. Their questions are often: Is the business game I am using designed to teach the concepts I want it to? Are the teams balanced in terms of ability? Is the room designed correctly for little group discussions? There may also be other, simpler, and more controllable conditions to worry about that some would call, "the little things". For example, Does the gender of the participant influence performance? Do teams with international students perform differently? Do teams that "share the load" perform differently than teams that do not try to "share the load?" Do teams that select their own leaders perform better than teams with designated leaders? Did teams that became good friends do better than teams that did not become good friends? This paper discusses exploratory research about the impact of some of these "little things". This research has found that many of these "little things" have highly significant influences upon performance and should be considered when using a business simulation for experiential learning.

The authors found few differences between Males and Females nor between International students and US students enrolled in US institutions. In addition, most of the measured learning skills were highly related to the set of "little things" that often are even not considered important when planning to use a business simulation as a experiential teaching methodology.

Keywords: Business simulation · Learning · Multi university study

1 Introduction

This study is an ongoing multi-university project into student learning using business simulations. As of this writing, 15 faculty at 13 US universities ask their students to participate in a post-simulation survey to evaluate their learning experience using various strategic management and project management simulation games. The data collection is ongoing, and it is providing extensive information about the learning that occurs while students participate in business simulations.

Related to this research, at the ABSEL 2018 Conference, Teach [1] discussed the difficulty of measuring learning; Chasteen, Teach and Szot [12] discussed student impressions of difficulty vs realism; Teach and Szot [3] described the survey and presented preliminary findings; and Nugent [4] explored the impact of reflective

© Springer Nature Switzerland AG 2021
M. Wardaszko et al. (Eds.): ISAGA 2019, LNCS 11988, pp. 181–193, 2021.
https://doi.org/10.1007/978-3-030-72132-9_17

observation questions after each round of a simulation. The effect of debriefing was further explored using this data at ISAGA 2018, Teach and Szot, [5].

This paper discusses relationships found between self-assessed participant learning skills and self-reported opinions about a set of often consider incidental issues when planning to use a business simulation as an experiential learning activity in a classroom.

2 The Survey

Measuring the learning claimed by business simulation participants and their perceptions of the experience is an on-going element of this research methodology.

The survey uses an 8-point Likert-like scale to measure self-reported learning from "I did not improve this skill in this area at all" to "my skill in this area was greatly increased" and a 6-point Likert-like scale from "disagree strongly" to "agree strongly" to measure student beliefs and opinions about the simulation. Teach and Szot, [3]. Table 1 lists the 16 learning skills evaluated and Table 2 lists the questions involving demographics, behaviors, beliefs, and opinions about "the little things".

Table 1. The learning skills set. The ability to…

1	Set goals (see Pray T & Gold S [6])
2	Make competitive decisions (see Edman, J [7])
3	Differentiate important information from unimportant information (see Casimir, R [8])
4	Work well in teams see (see Hall, J [9])
5	Do marginal analysis (see Cannon et al, [10])
6	Work under uncertainty (see Fekula, M [11])
7	Forecast outcomes such as cash flows, units of ending inventory, unit demand, etc. see (Dickson, J [12])
8	Analyze reports and financial results (see Gosen, G & Washbush, J [13])
9	Create budgets (see Roge, J & Linn, G [14])
10	Understand the interactions among two or more decision variables (see Goosen, K [15])
11	Analyze quality control measurements (see Watson, C & Chasteen, S [16])
12	Anticipate competitive reactions to our firm's decisions (see Clark B & Montgomery, D [17])
13	Assess risk (see Butler, P & McEvoy, G [18])
14	Consider possible competitors' decisions when making my firm's competitive decisions (see Palia, A & Ryck, J [19])
15	Be innovative (see Summers, G [20])
16	Be creative (see Wheatley et al, [21])

The data for this research were obtained from an extensive web-based survey that included a feature that allowed the student to leave the survey and return later to continue. We measured the time-on-task to complete this survey comparing the time and date when each student started and completed the survey. Most completed it in one sitting. The median time taken to complete the survey was 9.9 min and 80% completed the task within 15 min. Nevertheless, because of the "stop and continue later" feature, a few students took more than 24 h.

In addition to the 15 behavior, belief, and opinion questions (variables A through O in Table 2). These 15 behavior, belief, and opinion questions were mostly derived from the authors experiences in using business simulation in university classrooms since 1962, and there are very few research papers published that detail the effects of these behaviors, beliefs or opinions. The survey also collected demographic and ranking data and used open-ended questions to capture the name of the simulation used in the student's class and the country where they graduated from high school. Questions P, Q and R. represent demographic characteristics and the final position of the participating students' teams. There are references listed for the items in which the authors found relevant published works.

Table 2. The questions involving demographics, behaviors, beliefs, and opinions; the "little things".

A. Our team shared the work as even as possible
B. We selected our own leader
C. Only a few team members did all the work
D. Those who put in the most effort learned the most (See Carbonaro, W., 2005 [22]
E. The simulation's team experience will result in being a better employee
F. Our team quickly became good friends (see Wolfe, J & Box, TM 1988 [23])
G. At the end of the simulation, our team were not friends
H. We had difficulty coordinating our efforts
I. I felt well prepared when I started the simulation
J. The simulation was unrealistic
K. The effort was well worth it
L. The simulation took entirely too much effort
M. The simulation represented the "real world" (see Norris, DR 1986, [24])
N. I spent more time on the simulation than I did on any other course
O. Gender: male or female (see Jenson, J., & de Castell, 2010 [25])
P. Team rank. last, next to last, middle of the pack, second place, we won (see Wellington, W & Faria, AJ, 1992 [26])
Q. Country of high school graduation The high school's country location was used to distinguish International students from US students. (see Krain, M & Lantis, J, 2006 [27])

For this study, variables A through O were rescaled from the 6-point Likert-like scale to a 2-point (agree-disagree) scale due to insufficient data to support analysis using the 6-point scale.

3 Methodology

The survey was developed using Qualtrics survey generator and hosted on a Qualtrics web server. Supporting faculty provided the anonymous participation link to their students following completion of the simulation activity in their course and encouraged students to participate in the survey. Data was exported from Qualtrics and imported into SPSS for the analysis.

The survey was approved by the Georgia Tech IRB, which required each student to be aware that he or she had the option of not participating in the survey or stopping the survey process whenever the participant decided to quit. Those who decided not to participate at the start did not generate a data record. However, once a person began the survey, they generated a data record. The first question in the survey asked if the respondent wished to participate or not, and if the person selected "No", the responded exited the survey but left a mostly blank data record. The survey was also approved by the IRB at The University of Texas at Dallas.

The second question asked if the respondent was a student or a faculty member previewing the survey. Sometimes an instructor completed the survey, but this second question allowed us to excluded instructor data records from analysis.

After reviewing the data set, we decided to exclude all respondents' data if they spent less than 4 min answering the questions. The responses from this set of students were mostly a jumble of generally incoherent values. In addition, we scanned the data looking for patterned responses such as 25252525 or 666666 and eliminated these data records as well. The number of surveys examined and excluded for various reasons is shown in Table 3.

Table 3. The number of surveys processed.

Action	Count
Total responses received	688
Exclude students deciding not to participate after starting the survey	109
Exclude respondents spending less than 4 min on the survey	94
Exclude faculty members responding while reviewing the survey	15
Exclude students not responding to the 16 learning skills questions	38
Exclude students with patterned responses	196
Exclude students not responding to the little thing questions	10
Available for analysis	226
Attended high school in United States	192
Attended high school outside United States	34

Analysis of variance of the means was used to identify significant correlations between the learning skill responses and the little things. Using $p < 0.10$ as the test for significance, we show the p-values for the statistically significant correlations in Tables 4 through 6. Normally, $p < 0.05$ is the sacred value for showing significance; however, we believe relationships with $p < 0.10$ are meaningful for this analysis. Why? Recall that a *p*-value is the probability that the null hypothesis may be correct. This is referred to as "significance". Although significant or not significant is a binary outcome, significance cannot be considered as true or false. We believe the selection of a *p*-value should be the function of a loss table and it should never be a hard and fast value. Where the cost is high, such as the cost of a person's life, most would want a very low *p*-value related to failure of a surgical procedure. On the other hand, if the problem regarded how satisfying the taste of ice cream is, most would likely agree a much higher *p*-value is reasonable because the cost of failure is lower.

4 Results

The three tables labeled 4A through 4C, use the rows for learning skills and the columns for the behaviors, beliefs and opinions (little things) and the row intersections contain the significance of the interaction between each learning skill and each little thing question for "*p*" < 0.10. Blank cells indicate "*p*" > − 0.10.

Table 4. ANOVA significance of learning skills vs. Little things showing "*p*" < 0.10

Learning skill (The ability to...)	A. Shared work evenly	B. Selected own leader	C. Few members did all the work	D. Most effort learned most	E. Better employee from experience	F. Became good friends	G. Not friends at the end
1. Set goals	0.058			<0.0005	<0.0005	0.013	
2. Make competitive decisions				<0.0005	<0.0005	0.010	
3. Differentiate important information				0.001	<0.0005	0.003	0.058
4. Work well in teams	0.004		0.002	0.011	<0.0005	0.001	0.019
5. Do marginal analysis				<0.005	<0.0005	0.025	
6. Work under uncertainty	0.037		0.008		0.003		
7. Forecast outcomes		0.017		<0.0005	<0.0005	0.009	0.058
8. Analyze reports and financial results		0.037		<0.0005	0.001	0.045	0.019
9. Create budgets				0.064	0.006		
10. Understand decision variable interactions					<0.0005	0.062	

(continued)

Table 4. (*continued*)

Learning skill (The ability to...)	A. Shared work evenly	B. Selected own leader	C. Few members did all the work	D. Most effort learned most	E. Better employee from experience	F. Became good friends	G. Not friends at the end
11. Analyze quality control measurements		0.068		0.0105	<0.0005	0.088	
12. Anticipate competitive reactions to our decisions				<0.0005	<0.0005	0.001	
13. Assess risk					<0.0005	< 0.0005	0.003
14. Consider possible competitors' decisions when making own decisions		0.009		<0.0005	<0.0005	0.032	0.095
15. Be innovative				<0.0005	<0.0005	0.005	
16. Be creative						0.059	

Table 5. ANOVA significance of learning skills vs. Little things with "*p*" < 0.10

Learning skill (The ability to...)	H. Difficulty coordinating efforts	I. Well-prepared at start	J. Felt simulation was unrealistic	K. Felt simulation took too much time	L. Effort was well worth it	M. Took too much effort	N. Sim represented real world
1. Set goals		0.006	< 0.0005	0.015	<0.0005		0.014
2. Make competitive decisions		0.019	0.002	0.008	<0.0005		
3. Differentiate important information		0.005	< 0.0005	0.015	<0.0005	0.019	0.086
4. Work well in teams	0.009		0.004	0.087	<0.0005	0.021	0.011
5. Do marginal analysis		0.085	0.05	0.005	<0.0005	0.003	0.09
6. Work under uncertainty			0.066		<0.0005	0.041	
7. Forecast outcomes	0.022			0.047	<0.0005	0.034	
	0.011		0.045	0.054	<0.0005	0.045	

(*continued*)

Table 5. (*continued*)

Learning skill (The ability to...)	H. Difficulty coordinating efforts	I. Well-prepared at start	J. Felt simulation was unrealistic	K. Felt simulation took too much time	L. Effort was well worth it	M. Took too much effort	N. Sim represented real world
8. Analyze reports and financial results							
9. Create budgets			0.009		<0.0005	0.006	0.001
10. Understand decision variable interactions	0.010	0.075	0.015	0.056	<0.0005	0.083	0.051
11. Analyze quality control measurements	0.068	<0.0005	0.004	0.083	<0.0005	0.081	0.008
12. Anticipate competitive reactions to our decisions		<0.0005		0.073	<0.0005	0.077	
13. Assess risk		<0.0005	0.036		0.001		
14. Consider possible competitors' decisions when making own decisions	0.009	<0.0005	0.002	0.054	0.083	0.057	
15. Be innovative	0.068		0.004	0.083	<0.0005	0.088	0.001
16. Be creative				0.073	<0.0005	0.071	

Table 6. ANOVA significance of learning skills vs. Little things showing "p" < 0.10

Learning Skill (The ability to...)	O. Spent more time om simulation	P. Male vs. Female	Q. Team rank at end	R. US vs. International
1. Set goals	0.015		0.089	
2. Make competitive decisions	0.008		0.087	
3. Differentiate important information	0.015	0.020	0.063	
4. Work well in teams	0.087		0.078	
5. Do marginal analysis	0.005	0.034	0.002	
6. Work under uncertainty				
7. Forecast outcomes	0.047		0.083	
8. Analyze reports and financial results	0.054	0.015		
9. Create budgets				

(*continued*)

Table 6. (*continued*)

Learning Skill (The ability to...)	O. Spent more time om simulation	P. Male vs. Female	Q. Team rank at end	R. US vs. International
10. Understand decision variable interactions	0.056		0.024	
11. Analyze quality control measurements				0.028
12. Anticipate competitive reactions to our decisions	0.072		0.088	
13. Assess risk			0.077	
14. Consider possible competitors' decisions when making own decisions		0.004	0.033	
15. Be innovative				
16. Be creative				0.056

5 Discussion

Tables 4, 5 and 6 show many of the little things have significant covariation with the learning skills while others are far less important. In discussing these findings, the authors will hypothesize some possible rationale for the strong interactions.

5.1 Sharing Work Evenly

Little thing question A, "We shared the work as evenly as possible" is highly related to three learning skills: the ability to set goals, the ability to work well in teams, and the ability to learn how to work under uncertainty. Nevertheless, "sharing the work" was not closely related with the other aspects of learning that we measured. It suggests that these three skills are difficult without team interaction and the others can be developed individually.

5.2 Selected Our Leader

Little thing question B, "We selected our own leader" strongly co-varied with the ability to forecast outcomes, the ability to analyze results, the ability to analyze quality control measurements, and the consideration of possible competitors' decisions when making our firm's decisions. This covariance may be because these skills require high levels of trust among the team members and trust must be earned. When the team selects its own leader, that act demonstrates a high level of trust. Teams that are not allowed to select, or are unable to select, their own leader do not have a built-in expression of trust to the leader.

5.3   Few Team Members Did All the Work

Little thing question C, "only a few team members did all the work", closely matches Question A, "we shared the work". Although these questions purport to measure the same thing from the opposite perspective, only the abilities to work well in teams and work under uncertainty correlated strongly, the ability to set goals did not.

5.4   Most Effort Learned the Most and Becoming a Better Employee

Little thing question D, "those who put in the most effort learned the most" is an acceptance that hard work pays off. This belief highly co-varies for most skills with little thing question E, "the simulation's team experience will result in being a better employee". This "better job" belief co-varies with the ability to understand the inter-actions among two or more decision variables and the ability to assess risk". This suggests students believe these two learned skills will be important when they enter the work force. And the simulation supports these two skills.

5.5   Team Friendship

The last two little things shown in Table 4, "our team quickly became good friends" and "at the end, we were not friends", are almost opposite sides of the same issue; however, both may be true. These answers strongly co-vary with most of the learning shills. This demonstrates the importance of creating a teaming environment in a sim-ulation that goes well beyond the simulation itself. It may be impossible to control, but some of the teachers or game administrators may be able to influence this by incor-porating team-building activities into the curriculum before the start of the simulation.

5.6   Difficulty Coordinating Efforts

The little thing question, "We had difficulty coordinating our efforts" co-varied with learning skills that require group learning and less on skills that can be learned by working alone. It is most highly related to the skill of "Work well in teams", ": understanding decision variable interactions". In all likely-hood, this item is the fre-quent topic of team interactions during team meetings. Other issues like "Analyzing reports and financial results", Considering possible competitor's decisions", and "Forecasting" are often the major discussion in team meetings.

5.7   Prepared at the Start

Many skills that can typically be learned alone or prior to beginning a simulation, either in prior coursework or by strong preparation. The most important skill (not included in the list) is "Learning how to learn". This "Learning how to learn" is essential when a student undertakes participation in a simulation. Preparation was essential with several of the little things question, "I felt well prepared when I started the simulation", highly relates to one-fourth of the learned skills. These four learned skills all have "p" values less than 0.0005. These questions were "Analyzing Quality Control measures",

"Anticipating competitive reactions", "Assessing risks", and "Considering possible competitors decision" Three additional questions had very low "p" values. The ability to "Differentiate between important and unimportant information" had a "p" value of 0.005, "The ability to set goals" had a "p" value of 0.006 and "The ability to make competitive decisions" had a "p" value of 0.019.

5.8   Realism

The little thing questions, "The simulation was unrealistic" and "The simulation represented the 'real world'" are essentially opposites of one another. This is shown by the degree of commonality of the responses to the entire set of learning skills co-variations shown by the responses to most of the learning skills questions. The unrealistic question had only two out of the sixteen learning skills had "p" values of 0.10 or higher in its relationship to the realism question.

5.9   Duration and Effort

"The simulation took entirely too much time" and "the simulation took entirely too much effort" were designed to measure different aspects; however, the response patterns to the duration question were similar to the effort question. Three learning skill questions had "p" vales equal to or greater than 0.1000. They were; "The ability to work under uncertainty", "The ability to create budgets", and "Assessing risk".

"The effort was well worth it" strongly co-varied with fifteen of the sixteen learning skills. "Considering possible competitors' decisions" had the high "p" value which was only 0.083. These findings support to old adage that "Hard work pays o0ff in the long run.

5.10   Simulation Represented the Real World

The belief that the simulation represented the working environment was very important. The differences between those who considered that the simulation represented the working environment was extremely important when it came to the learning skills of; "Being innovative", "Creating budgets", "Analyzing quality control measurements", "Working well in teams", and "Setting goals". It tended to be unimportant to; "Making competitive decisions", "Working under uncertainty", "Forecasting", "Analyzing reports", "Anticipating competitive reaction,: "Assessing risks", nor "Considering possible competitors' decision".

5.11   Team Spent More Time on the Simulation Than any Other Course

The responses for "I spent more time on the simulation than I did on any other courses" significantly co-varied with a little more than half of the learning shills. Those who agreed this this statement reported they gained greater skills at "Marginal analysis", "Making competitive decisions", "The ability to set goals", and "Differentiating between important and unimportant information", and "Making more accurate forecasts". These five skills had "p" vales less than 0.05. The four shills of "Analyzing reports and financial results", Understanding decision variable interactions", Antici-pating competitive reaction", and the ability to "Work well in teams" all had "p" vales between 0.054 and 0.087.

5.12 Gender

Gender differences indicated few significant co-variation with skills acquisition. There were four exceptions. "The most significant differences were the skills of "Considering possible competitors' decisions", with a "p" value of 0.004, "Analyzing reports", with a "p" of 0.015, "Differentiating important information from unimportant information", with a "p" value of 0.020, and lastly "The ability to analyze reports and financial results". Which had a "p" value of 0.034. All other learning skills had "p" vales that were equal to or greater than 0.100 0.

5.13 Team Rank at the Completion of the Simulation

Overall team performance on the simulation as measured by its ranking at the end of the completion co-varied with "p" values under 0.10 with 11 of the 16 learning skills. Mastering these, 11 skills determine the competitiveness or success of the teams. The authors have no explanation for why team rankings were not more related to the final team ranking. They may indeed be related, but if so, the relationships have "p" values of 0.100 or greater.

5.14 The Differences Between International Students and US Students

International students were defined as students who had been graduated from a high school located outside of the United States. The country at which a student was graduated from high school had almost no significant differences with the acquisition of skills. There were two exceptions; "Analyzing quality control measures" had a "p" value of 0.028 and "Being creative" differed between international students and US students with a "p" value of 0.056. The response to the "being creative" question may be a culture difference between the US students and international students, but why the difference in "analyzing quality control measures" was significant remains a mystery to the authors.

6 Conclusions

Learning is a multifaceted process. Many of the things associated with the amount of learning that takes place when individuals are participating in business simulations are, at least partially, under the control of the simulation administrator or teacher. He or she has the capability of enhancing the degree of learning that takes place when students participate in business simulations.

The male-female mix and the number of international students are not under the teachers' control; however, our study indicates those issues are not particularly important to the set of learning skills by participating in a business simulation.

As these are preliminary results of our study, we make no overall conclusions. However, we can claim that many more interactions exist among the different groups of students when they experience a business simulation than we previously thought. We plan to examine some of these other interactions in the future and encourage other faculty to ask their students to participate in the survey.

Table 7. Contributing faculty

Professor	University
Dr. Eric Kinnamon	Alabama A&M
Dr. Raghu Kurthakoti	Arcadia University
Dr. Stuart Graham	Georgia Institute of Technology
Dr. Kathleen Gruben	Georgia Southern University
Dr. Steven Gold	Rochester Institute of Technology
Dr. Can Usley	Rutgers University
Dr. Michael Nugent	SUNY Stony Brook
Dr. Al Lovvorn	The Citadel
Dr. Frances Fabian	University of Memphis
Dr. Mick Fekula	University of South Carolina at Aiken
Dr. Shawn Carraher	University of Texas at Dallas
Dr. Blaine Lawlor	University of West Florida
Dr. Mihail Motzev	Walla Walla University

Acknowledgements. This publication was the result of a multi-university study of the learning that takes place while students participate in a business simulation in US universities. The authors gratefully acknowledge the professors and universities listed in Table 7 for their assistance in forwarding the electronic surveys to their students.

References

1. Teach, R.: Why is learning so difficult to measure when "playing" simulations. Dev. Bus. Simul. Exp. Learn. **45**, 55–63 (2018)
2. Chasteen, L., Szot, J., Teach, R.: Simulations for strategy courses: difficulty vs. realism. Dev. Bus. Simul. Exp. Learn. **45**, 64–68 (2018)
3. Teach, R., Szot, J.: How students "play" business simulations and what they learn: the preliminary report. Dev. Bus. Simul. Exp. Learn. **45**, 89–96 (2018)
4. Nugent, M.: Business simulation performance after competing a reflective observation module. Dev. Bus. Simul. Exp. Learn. **45**, 31–41 (2018)
5. Teach, R., Szot, J.: What business simulations teach: The effect of debriefing. In: ISAGA 2019 Proceedings (2018b). Publication pending
6. Pray, T., Gold, S.: Goal setting and performance evaluating with different starting positions – the modeling. Dev. Bus. Simul. Exp. Learn. **14**, 169–174 (1987)
7. Edman, J.: A Comparison between solutions and decisions in a business game. Dev. Bus. Simul. Exp. Learn. **32**, 110–116 (2005)

8. Casimir, R.: Teaching about information with management games. Dev. Bus. Simul. Exp. Learn. **27**, 42–48 (2000)
9. Hall, J.: Designing the training challenge. Dev. Bus. Simul. Exp. Learn. **39**, 1–5 (2012)
10. Cannon, H., Cannon, J., Schwaiger, M.: Simulating customer lifetime value: implications for game design and student performance. Dev. Bus. Simul. Exp. Learn. **32**, 54–64 (2005)
11. Fekula, M.: Information and uncertainty as strange bedfellows: a model and experiential exercises. Dev. Bus. Simul. Exp. Learn. **21**, 133–136 (1994)
12. Dickson, J.: Correlation of measures of forecasting accuracy and profit. Dev. Bus. Simul. Exp. Learn. **44**, 183–188 (2017)
13. Gosen, J., Washbush, J.: Analyzing and thinking while playing a simulation. Dev. Bus. Simul. Exp. Learn. **32**, 141–143 (2005)
14. Roge, J., Linn, G.: Performance evaluation: the effect on the propensity to create budgetary slack. Dev. Bus. Simul. Exp. Learn. **26**, 146–152 (1995)
15. Goosen, K.: Reducing the complexity of interactive variable modeling in business simulations through interpolation. Dev. Bus. Simul. Exp. Learn. **20**, 56–61 (1993)
16. Watson, C., Chasteen, S.: Concepts of internal estimation and quality control charts via computer simulated sampling. Dev. Bus. Simul. Exp. Learn. **19**, 180–183 (1992)
17. Clark, B., Montgomery, D.: Perceiving competitive reactions: the value of accuracy (and paranoia). Mark. Lett. **7**(March), 115–129 (1996)
18. Butler, P., McEvoy, G.: A model for developing student skills and assessing MBA programs outcomes through outdoor training. Dev. Bus. Simul. Exp. Learn. **17**, 25–29 (1990)
19. Palia, A., Ryck, J.: Assessing competitor strategic business units with the competitor analysis package. Dev. Bus. Simul. Exp. Learn. **42**, 52–68 (2015)
20. Summers, G.: Analyzing manager's judgments and decisions with an educational business simulation. Dev. Bus. Simul. Exp. Learn. **26**, 58–64 (1999)
21. Wheatley, W., Platt, R., Peach, E.: Utilizing the cosmopolitan/local marginal constructs to measure students' propensity for creativity. Dev. Bus. Simul. Exp. Learn. **22**, 232–233 (1995)
22. Carbonaro, W.: Tracking, students' effort, and academic achievement. Sociol. Educ. **78**(1), 27–49 (2005)
23. Wolfe, J., Box, T.M.: Team cohesion effects on business game performance. Simul. Gaming **19**(1), 82–98 (1988)
24. Norris, D.R.: External validity of business games. Simul. Gaming **17**(4), 447–459 (1986)
25. Jenson, J., de Castell, S.: Gender, simulation, and gaming: research review and redirections. Simul. Gaming **41**(1), 51–71 (2010)
26. Wellington, W., Faria, A.J.: An examination of the effect of team cohesion, player attitude, and performance expectations on simulation performance results. Dev. Bus. Simul. Exp. Exerc. **19**, 184–189 (1992)
27. Krain, M., Lantis, J.: Building knowledge? Evaluating the effectiveness of the global problems summit simulation. Int. Stud. Perspect. **7**(4), 395–407 (2006)

Impact of Competition in Energy Market on Promotion of Renewables: An Agent-Based Model Approach

Arashi Ogihara[1]([⊠]), Kengo Suzuki[2], and Keita Nakai[1]

[1] Department of Risk Engineering, University of Tsukuba, 1-1-1 Tenno-dai,
Tsukuba, Ibaraki 305-8573, Japan
s1820575@s.tsukuba.ac.jp
[2] Division of Engineering Mechanics and Energy, Faculty of Engineering,
Information and Systems, University of Tsukuba, 1-1-1 Tenno-dai, Tsukuba,
Ibaraki 305-8573, Japan

Abstract. This study developed the agent-based model (ABM) in which agents play the multiplayer game "Energy Transition" instead of human players. The theme of "Energy Transition" is the energy transition from fossil fuels to renewables in a deregulated energy market. The purpose of this study is to clarify the impact of price competition on the promotion of renewables in the energy market. Two types of contrastive agents are designed for the model. One is a competitive agent who is aggressive in expanding the market share to make profits. The other is a non-competitive agent who is more eager to invest in renewables for long-term profits than to compete with others for short-term profits. Two types of simulations are performed. In the simulation-1, the total number of agents is fixed and the ratio of two types of agents is changed. In the simulation-2, the ratio of two types of agents is fixed, and the aggressiveness of competitive agents is changed. The results show that the total usage of renewable energy and total profit in the market become smaller as the number of competitive agents increases. Further, more aggressive agents make the competition stronger and largely decrease the usage of renewables.

Keywords: Agent-based simulation · Energy transition · Renewables · Fossil fuels

1 Introduction

About 88% of Japan's primary energy is supplied by fossil fuels, such as coal, oil, and natural gas [1]. However, these fossil fuels are exhaustible resource; for example, minable years of crude oil is estimated to be 50.2 years [2]. Further, the CO2 emissions from the fossil fuels causes the global warming. Additionally, with the rapid growth of developing countries, the worldwide energy demand is increasing. It is also predicted that the price of fossil fuels will be higher in the future [3].

Much attention has been paid to renewables, such as solar power and wind power, as an alternative energy sources for fossil fuels in terms of stable energy supply and global warming. Renewables does not emit CO_2 during power generation and can be

© Springer Nature Switzerland AG 2021
M. Wardaszko et al. (Eds.): ISAGA 2019, LNCS 11988, pp. 194–209, 2021.
https://doi.org/10.1007/978-3-030-72132-9_18

permanently used. Therefore, the energy transition from fossil fuels to renewables plays the key role in constructing a sustainable energy system.

However, the cost for renewables is higher than that for fossil fuels. In Japan, the cost for solar power generation is 29.4 JPY/kWh while that for gas-fired and coal-fired power generations are 13.7 and, 12.3 JPY/kWh, respectively [4]. Further, the output of renewables such as solar and wind power fluctuate over time because of daily and seasonal changes in solar irradiation and wind condition. To level these output fluctuations, further investments in grid flexibility, such as backup power sources, grid extensions, and energy storages, are required. Then, further reductions in the cost for renewables, including the cost for grid flexibility, is required to make the renewables cost competitive with fossil fuels and to continuously install renewable energy in Japan.

Investments in research and development (R&D) play an important role for such cost reductions. Since the price of fossil fuels is expected to be higher in the future, the reduction in the cost for alternative energy appear to be beneficial for energy companies. However, in order to survive in competitive energy market in these days, reduction in retail price may be given a priority over investments for the future. In other words, there is a dilemma between the long-term and short-term benefit: investments in renewables and price competition in the market. To realize the energy transition under such a state, policy makers must design rules of the market such that the managers of the companies can emphasize the future benefits from the investments in renewables.

There are some previous studies investigating an optimal pathway to switch from fossil fuels to renewables [5]. These studies assume that all market players have complete information such as future fossil fuel price and effect of R&D investments, and that they reasonably act to maximize their total profit over long-term. However, in the real market, each player sequentially makes decisions without such information under the competition with other companies. Under such a situation it is difficult to realize the optimal pathway because the behavior of the market is affected by the dynamic interactions between the decisions of players and market status.

This study develops an agent-based model (ABM) which represents energy supply businesses in a competitive market to clarify how the dynamic interactions between the decisions of players and market status affect the energy transition from fossil fuels to renewables. First, we designed a computer game played by multiple players. The role of players is a manager of an energy company in a competitive market, and they sequentially make decisions with limited information. By using a game model instead of an optimization model, the interactions between the decision of players and the market status can be represented. Then, we developed the ABM in which computer agents play the game instead of human players. By using the ABM, we investigate how the share of competitive and non-competitive agents and aggressiveness of competitive agents in a market affects the promotion of renewables.

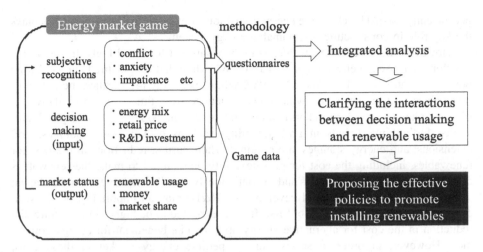

Fig. 1. Conceptual diagram of the game "Energy Transition"

2 Methodology

2.1 Concept of Game

The multi-player computer game "Energy Transition" models the energy business in a competitive market.

The role of players is managers of energy companies. The purpose of players is to earn money as much as possible until the end of game. Players have a duty to satisfy final energy demand of their customers. Their work is to produce final energy from fossil fuels or renewables and sell the final energy to their customers. It is assumed that there is only one type of fossil fuel, renewables resource, and final energy. The unit production cost for final energy from fossil fuels is exogenously given, and that from renewables is endogenously reduced by the investments in renewable technologies. Figure 1 shows the conceptual diagram of the game.

2.2 Model of Game

Figure 2 shows the relationship among the variables in "Energy Transition" focusing on a single player. Each square represents a variable: black is an operational variable input by a player, white is an endogenous variable determined within the model, and gray is a predetermined parameter. The amount of increase in the agent i's money in the term t is expressed by Eq. (1).

$$\Delta V(i,t) = D(i,t-1) \times p_s(i,t) - Er(i,t) \times p_r(i,t-1) - \{D(i,t-1) - E_r(i,t)\} \times p_f(t-1) - I(i,t) \tag{1}$$

The first term of Eq. (1) is an income, and the second term to the fourth terms represents expenses. $D(i,t)$ is the amount of customers (hereinafter referred to demand) of

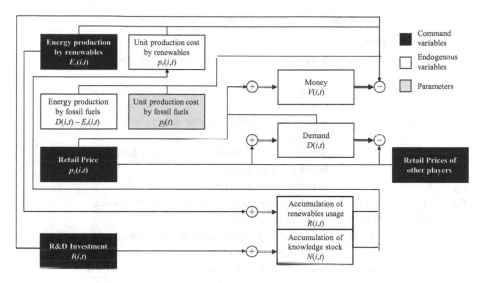

Fig. 2. Relationships among variables in "Energy Transition" focusing on a player

player i period t, $p_S(i, t)$ is retail price of final energy by player i term t. The second term represents expenses by producing final energy from renewables, $E_r(i, t)$ is the amount of energy production from renewables by player i in term t, and $p_r(i, t)$ is unit production cost for final energy from renewables by player i in term t. The third term represents expenses by producing final energy from fossil fuels: $(D(i, t) - E_r(i, t))$ is the amount of energy production from fossil fuels by player i in term t, and $p_f(t)$ is unit production cost for final energy from fossil fuels at term t. $p_f(t)$ is given exogenously. The fourth term, $I(i, t)$, is R&D investments in renewables by player i in term t.

The total energy demand in the market is constant, but the demand of each player changes as the result of competition. The change in the demand of player i in the term t is represented by the following expression (2).

$$\Delta D(i, t) = \alpha\{\mu(t - 1) - p_s(i, t)\} \tag{2}$$

$$\mu(t) = \sum_{\neq i} \{D(i, t) \times p_s(i, t)\} / \sum_i D(i, t) \tag{3}$$

where α (>0) is a parameter representing the sensitivity of the demand against retail price. $\mu(t)$ is the average retail price of the market in term t. Equation (2) represents that demand moves from players with relatively higher retail prices to these with relatively lower prices. Because sharp changes in retail price are not realistic, the maximum value of changes in retail prices, m, is set as follows.

$$p_s(i, t - 1) - m \leq p_s(i, t) \leq p_s(i, t - 1) + m \tag{4}$$

The unit production cost for final energy from renewables, $p_r(i, t)$, is reduced by the usage of renewables and R&D investments. This relationship is represented by the typical two factor learning curve

Table 1. Parameter list in "energy transition".

	Value	Unit	Description
α	0.5	[E]/ [G/E]	Sensitivity of the demand against retail price
β	0.07	[-]	Sensitivity of production cost from renewables against R&D investments
γ	0.125	[-]	Sensitivity of production cost from renewables against renewables usage
ε	0.75	[-]	Sensitivity of knowledge stock against R&D investments
V_0	20	[G]	Initial value of money
D_0	5	[E]	Initial value of demand
P_{r0}	16	[G/E]	Initial value of production cost from renewables
P_{s0}	10	[G/E]	Initial value of retail price
R_0	4	[E]	Initial value of accumulated amount of renewable
N_0	4	[K]	Initial value of knowledge stock
m	1	[G]	Maximum value of changes in retail prices in a term

[G]: unit of money, [E]: unit of energy, [K]: unit of knowledge

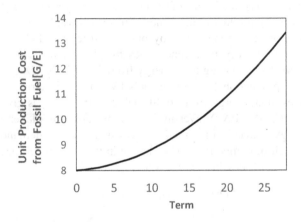

Fig. 3. Change of unit production cost for final energy from fossil fuels (p_f)

$$pr(i,t) = p_{r0}\{N(i,t)/N_0\}^{-\beta}/\{R(i,t)/R_0\}^{-\gamma} \tag{5}$$

where p_{r0} is the initial value of $p_r(i, t)$, $N(i, t)$ is knowledge stock about renewables of player i in term t, and $R(i, t)$ is accumulated amount of renewables usage by player i in term t. N_0 and R_0 represent initial values of N and R. $\beta(>0)$ and $\gamma(>0)$ are sensitivities of production cost from renewables against R&D investments and renewables usage. The amount of increase in the knowledge stock by R&D is expressed as follows.

$$\Delta N(i,t) = I(i,t)^{\varepsilon} \tag{6}$$

$\varepsilon \ (0 \leq \varepsilon \leq 1)$ is a parameter representing the sensitivity of knowledge stock against the R&D investments. As far as ε is less than 1, if you make the same amount of R&D investments, the amount of increase in knowledge stock is larger when you divide it into several periods rather than intensively invest in the first period [7]. This represents that long-term continued investments can efficiently proceed a research rather than short-term intensive investments. The accumulation of renewables usage R increases according to the following Eq. (7).

$$\Delta R(i,t) = E_r(i,t) \tag{7}$$

Table 1 and Fig. 3 are the summaries of parameters and variables in the game.

2.3 Strategies of Agents

This study designed two types of agent with different strategies that assumed to be typical in real energy markets. One is the normal-agent with non-competitive strategy (hereinafter referred to N-agent), and the other is the competitive agent (hereinafter referred to C-agent). At the beginning of a game, both the agents supply all energy by fossil fuel. When the unit production cost for final energy from renewables (p_r) is reduced to some extent, they switch a part of energy source from fossil fuels to renewables. For market competition, the C-agents actively expand the market share by reducing retail price until they acquire the largest share in the market. On the other hand, the N-agents are not interested in expanding the market share while they also reduce retail prices when the C-agents try to exploit their own customers. For investments, both agents invest in R&D from the beginning of the game. Table 2 shows the differences in the strategies of the two types of agents.

The processes of decision makings by the two types of agents are divided into the following four steps.

(1) Determine the default value of energy production by renewables (E_r) and R&D investments (I) based on the ratio of unit production cost by fossil fuel to that by renewables, p_f/p_r. If this ratio is lower than 1, that means that fossil fuels is cheaper than renewables. When the ratio is lower than a certain level, all final energy is produced from fossil fuels, and R&D investments are continued. When the ratio exceeds a certain level but below one, a part of energy source is switched to renewables, and R&D investments are gradually decreased. When the rate is larger than one, i.e. the renewables is cheaper than fossil fuels, all final energy is produced by renewables, and R&D investments drop to zero.

(2) Check if the demand of each agent is enough from the viewpoint of their strategies. If the agents regard the current market share insufficient, they reduce their retail price. Otherwise, the retail price is kept unchanged from the previous term.

Table 2. Comparison of strategies between C-agent and NC-agent of before and after production cost from renewables is cheaper than that from fossil fuels.

Condition	Variables	Strategy	
Before ($p_f < p_r$)	E_r, E_f	Supply all energy by fossil fuel Switch the energy source from fossil fuels to renewables. When the unit production cost for final energy from renewable (pr) is lower than that of fossil fuels	
	ps	Basically, the retail price is kept unchanged Lower the retail price when his demand is lower than the certain level	Reduce retail price until acquiring the largest share in the market
	I	Invest in R&D as far as money is available	
After ($p_f > p_r$)	E_r, Ef	Produce all final energy from renewables	
	ps	Rise retail price than the unit production cost for final energy from renewable	Reduce retail price until acquiring the largest share in the market
	I	R&D investments is zero	

(3) Compare the current retail price with the threshold price. If the current price is lower than threshold, the current price is raised to the same value as the threshold. The threshold price of the N-agents is equal to the unit production cost while that of the C-agent is lower than the unit production cost. In other words, the retail price of the C-agents can be lower than the unit production cost to some extent while that of N-agents cannot.

(4) Adjust the value of energy production by renewables, R&D investments, and retail price to avoid bankrupt. In this game, money cannot be lower than 0. There are three types of options to increase the income in next term: (i) raise retail price, (ii) switch a part of energy source from renewables to fossil fuels, and (iii) decrease R&D investments. The priorities among these options are different among the agent type; the priority for the C-agents is (i) > (ii) > (iii) while that for the NC-agents is (iii) > (ii) > (i).

The schematic flowcharts of decision makings by agents are shown in Fig. 4. The parameters of the NC-agent were determined by fitting to the optimal behavior of Energy Transition [6]. In addition, the parameters of the C-agent were determined considering the characteristics of the C-agent based on the parameters of the NC-agent.

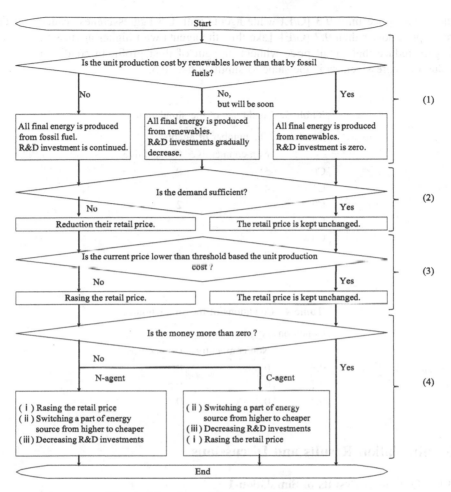

Fig. 4. Flowchart of decision making of agents

Table 3 shows the conditions of simulation-1 performed in this study. The purpose of simulation-1 is to investigate the impact of the ratio of non-competitive and competitive agents on the promotion of renewables and the market profit. Therefore, we set the total number of agents in the market to 5, and change the ratio of N- and C- agents as shown in the Table 3. In condition C0, there is 5 N-agents and no C-agents.

In condition C1, there are 4 N-agents and 1 C-agent. In the same manner, we set the six conditions of simulation as shown in Table 3.

Table 4 shows the conditions of simulation-2 performed in this study. The purpose of simulation-2 is to investigate the impact of aggressiveness of C-agents on the promotion of renewables and the profit in the market. In this study, the aggressiveness of agents is defined as the lower limit of retail price allowed by them, and is given as the relative value against the average retail price of the market. For example, when the average retail price of market is 10.0 [G/E], agents with 0.7 aggressiveness can reduce their retail price until 9.3 [G/E] while agents with 0.3 aggressiveness cannot set the retail price lower than 9.7 [G/E]. Like this, the agents with higher aggressiveness can largely reduce their retail price without thought of their profit. In condition 2-2, the value of aggressiveness is the same as simulation-1, 0.5.

Table 3. Conditions of the simulation-1.

Condition	The number of agents	
	Non-competitive	Competitive
C0	5	0
C1	4	1
C2	3	2
C3	2	3
C4	1	4
C5	0	5

Table 4. Conditions of the simulation-2.

Condition	Aggressiveness	
	Non-competitive	Competitive
0.3	0	0.3
0.5	0	0.5
0.7	0	0.7

3   Simulation Results and Discussions

3.1   Outline of Results of Simulation-1

Table 5 shows the amount of money and the total renewables usage per agent at the end of the simulation-1 for each condition. The money of the N-agents becomes larger as the market share of N-agents increases; their final money is 78 [G] when there is no C-agent (condition C0). On the other hand, the money of the C-agents at the end of the game is 59 [G] in the condition C1, but if the share of C-agent is further increased, the final money becomes lower than 10 [G]. Basically, the total renewables usage by both types of agents increases as the ratio of N-agents increases.

Table 5. Money and the accumulated amount of renewable usage at the end of simulation-1 for each agent.

Condition	Money [G]		Renewables [E]	
	N	C	N	C
The optimal pathway	79		71	
C0	78	–	72	–
C1	53	59	57	129
C2	40	1	48	45
C3	24	6	31	28
C4	2	3	6	18
C5	–	1	–	10

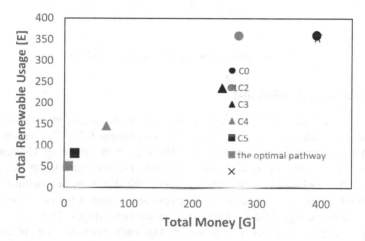

Fig. 5. Total money and renewable usage at the end of simulation-1

Figure 5 shows the relationship between the total amount of money and renewables usage in each condition: the sum of these values in five agents at the end of simulation. The numbers in legends indicate the number of C-agent, e.g. "C4" has 1 N-agent and 4 C-agents. The result of condition C0 almost the same as the value of the optimal pathway. In the condition C1, the total amount of money decrease compared with that of C0, but the accumulated amount of renewables usage is almost the same. From condition C1 to condition C5, both the total amount of money and the accumulated amount of renewables usage decrease. In condition C5, the sum of the money and that of the accumulated amount of renewables usage is the smallest among all conditions; 6 [G], 50 [E]. Thus, the total amount of money and renewables usage in the market tends to decrease as the market share of C-agent increases.

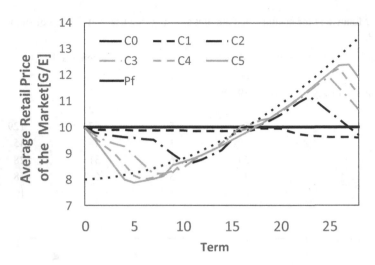

Fig. 6. Average retail prices in each condition

3.2   Dynamics of Simulation-1

Figure 6 shows changes in the average retail prices in the market in each condition. In the conditions with two or more C-agents (conditions C2–C5), the retail prices immediately decrease as the game starts. The higher the share of C-agents in the market, the higher the level of decrease. After that, the average retail prices gradually increase as the fossil fuel price increases. On the other hand, in the conditions with no more than one C-agent, the average retail prices are constant at the earlier stages of the games and does not significantly change even in the latter stages. These results suggest that the price competitions occur at the earlier stage only when the share of competitive agent is larger than a certain level.

Figure 7(a) and (b) show the changes in the money of N- and C-agents. For both agents, the money increases just after the opening of game but begin to decrease sooner or later. The higher the share of C-agents in the market, the larger and faster the reductions in money. The money of C-agents reaches to zero and does not recover thereafter while that of N-agents begin to increase again in the later part of simulations.

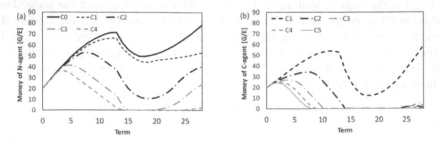

Fig. 7. Changes in money of (a) N-agents (b) C-agents

The decrease in the money in earlier stage appears to be caused by the price competitions: the cost for energy production from renewables and R&D investments cannot be passed on retail prices. The recovers in money of N-agents in the later part of simulation is caused by the cost reduction of renewables: the renewables become competitive against fossil fuels as the result of continuous investments.

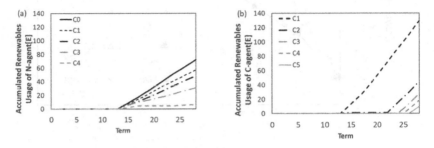

Fig. 8. Changes in accumulated renewables usage of (a) N-agents (b) C-agents

Figure 8(a) and (b) show the changes in accumulated renewables usage of each agent. The timing at which N-agents start energy production from renewables is terms 13 in all conditions while the amount of renewables usage per term, indicated by the slopes of the lines, negatively correlates with the number of C-agents. The timing at which C-agents start energy production from renewables is the different from N-agents except for C1. That is because there are not enough saving money when transition from fossil fuels to renewables.

These results suggest the difference between relatively cooperative results, such as conditions C0–C1, and the relatively competitive results, such as conditions C2–C5. In the competitive conditions, the amount of renewables usage by both agents are relatively small because the N-agents have smaller market share and the C-agents begin to use renewables from later terms. These are caused by the price competitions in the earlier stages of the game. In the cooperative games, on the other hand, both the N- and C-agents uses the larger amounts of renewables. Because the retail prices do not decrease in the earlier stages, both agents afford to invest in renewables, and can also make a profit in the process of energy transition.

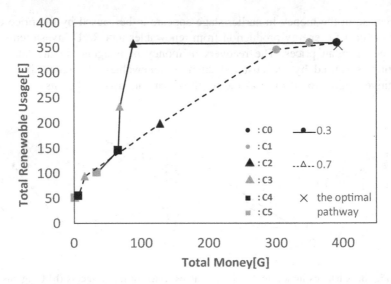

Fig. 9. Total money and renewable usage at the end of simulation-2

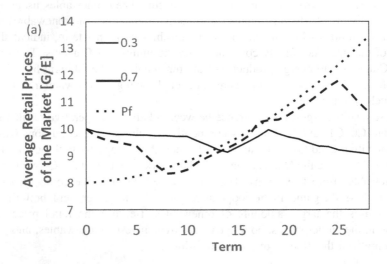

Fig. 10. Average retail prices in each condition of simulation-2

3.3 Outline of Results of Simulation-2

Figure 9 shows the relationship between the total amount of money and renewables usage for the different values of aggressiveness for C-agents. The result of condition 0.5 is excluded because it is the same as simulation-1. Regardless of the level of aggressiveness, the total money and renewables usage decrease as the ratio of C-agents increases. The total money significantly decreases from condition C1 to condition C2 regardless of aggressiveness. However, the total amount of renewable usage hardly

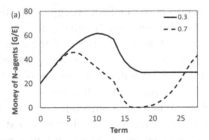 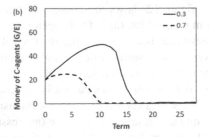

Fig. 11. Changes in total money of five agents in simulation-2

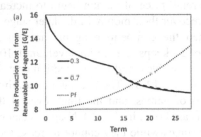 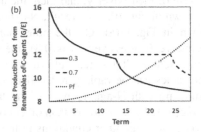

Fig. 12. Changes of unit production cost for final energy from renewables in simulation-2 (a) N-agents (b) C-agents

changes from the C0 to C2 in the condition 0.3 while it largely changes from the C0 to C2 in the condition 0.7. In conditions C4 and C5 where the share of C-agents is high, the total amount of money and renewables usage are very small regardless of the aggressiveness. In conditions C2 and C3 where the share of both agents is close, the total amount of renewables usage differs greatly depending on the aggressiveness. Therefore, we focus on condition C2 (3 N-agents and 2 C-agents) and investigate that there is a large difference in the total amount of renewables usage.

Figure 10 shows the changes in the average retail price of the market for different values of aggressiveness. When the aggressiveness is 0.7, the average retail price decreases from the initial value at the earlier stage of a game, and then, gradually increases as the cost for fossil fuel (p_f) increases. On the other hand, when the aggressiveness is 0.3, the average retail price does not largely change through the game. At the end of the game, the average retail price is 11.6 [G/E] when aggressiveness is 0.7 while the price is 9.1 [G/E] when the aggressiveness is 0.3.

Figure 11 shows the changes in money of each agent under the same conditions. Regardless of the aggressiveness, both types of agents increase their money at the earlier stages while begin to lose their profit from 5 to 15 terms. At the later stage of games, N-agents recover their money while C-agents cannot get money again. Focusing on the N-agents, when aggressiveness is 0.3, the money keeps around 30 [G] from term 15 to the end. However, when aggressiveness is 0.7, the money once drops to zero, and then, recover to 40 [G].

Figure 12 shows the changes in unit production costs for final energy production from renewables: (a) is for N-agents and (b) is for C-agents. For N-agents, the cost for renewables becomes cheaper than fossil fuels in 18th term regardless of the aggressiveness of C-agents. For C-agents, when aggressiveness is 0.3, the cost for renewables becomes cheaper than fossil fuels at 17th term. However, when aggressiveness is 0.7, the cost for renewables cannot be cheaper than fossil fuels until 24th term.

These results suggest the mechanism below. When the competitive agents (C-agents) are relatively aggressive (aggressiveness is 0.7), retail prices significantly drop in the earlier stages, and it makes C-agents difficult to get profit. As a result, they need to stop investing in renewables, and the production cost for renewables stop reducing as shown in Fig. 12(b). In the later part of game, C-agents stop competing with N-agents because of their poverty, and then, the average retail price of market begin to increase as shown in Fig. 10. As a result, N-agents can recover their money in the later stage as shown in Fig. 11(a). On the other hand, when the competitive agents are not so aggressive (aggressiveness is 0.3), the retail price keeps the initial level until 10th terms. As a result, C-agents afford to invest in renewables, and the production cost for renewables can be rapidly reduced as shown in Fig. 12(b). Then, C-agents continue competing with N-agents even in the later part of games, and the final level of the average retail price is lower than other conditions as shown in Fig. 10. N-agents can get larger profit than other conditions in the earlier stages while they cannot increase their money in the later stage as a result of relatively low average market prices as shown in Fig. 11. By such a mechanism, the aggressiveness of agents prevents the promotion of renewables while it does not decrease the total profit of market.

4 Conclusion

In this study, we developed the agent-based model (ABM) to investigate how the competitions in the market affect the promotion of renewables. Two types of contrastive agents, competitive and non-competitive agents, are designed. The simulation-1 were performed in six conditions with different shares of these two types of agents. The results suggest that the energy transition from fossil fuels to renewables can be realized with relatively high profits as far as the share of competitive agents is relatively low while the transition is delayed and makes less profits as the competitive agents increase. In simulation-2, the impact of aggressiveness of competitive agents was examined. The results suggest that the relatively aggressive competitive agents prevent the promotion of renewables because the strong competition decreases the profits of energy business and shrink the investments in renewables. In conclusion, the reduction in the ratio of competitive companies and the mitigation of their aggressiveness appear to be effective to promote renewable energy.

Some limitations exist in this study. The algorithm of agents in this study is formally determined. Therefore, agents have no learning process from their own past actions or other agents' actions and do not update decision-making algorithms. Furthermore, there are only two types of agents that are considered to be typical in the market. In the future work, we will design the agents whose behaviors are like actual human players. For the purpose, the characteristics of agents will be modified based on the gaming experiments by human players. Furthermore, we will incorporate the conditions representing energy policies to the ABM model and examine the effectiveness of these policies to mitigate the competitions in the market.

Acknowledgements. The authors are grateful for financial support by the Foundation for the Fusion of Science and Technology (FOST).

References

1. Ministry of Economy, Trade and Industry (METI) Agency for Natural Resources and Energy: Energy supply and demand results 2018. METI website. http://www.enecho.meti.go.jp/statistics/total_energy/pdf/stte_025.pdf. Accessed 29 Mar 2019
2. British Petroleum: BP Statistical Review of World Energy (2018). BP website. https://www.bp.com/en/global/corporate/energy-economics.html. Accessed 29 Mar 2019
3. International Energy Agency: World Energy Outlook 2016. IEA, Paris (2016)
4. METI Agency for Natural Resources and Energy: Report on verification of power generation costs to the long-term energy supply and demand forecast subcommittee (2015). http://www.enecho.meti.go.jp/committee/council/basic_policy_subcommittee/mitoshi/cost_wg/006/pdf/006_05.pdf. Accessed 29 Mar 2019
5. Tsur, Y., Zemel, M.: Optimal transition to backstop substitutes for nonrenewable resources. J. Econ. Dyn. Control **27**, 551–572 (2003)
6. Suzuki, K., Nakai, K., Ogihara, A.: Design of simulation and gaming to promote the energy transition from fossil fuels to renewables. In: Hamada, R., Soranastaporn, S., Kanegae, H., Dumrongrojwatthana, P., Chaisanit, S., Rizzi, P., Dumblekar, V. (eds.) Neo-Simulation and Gaming Toward Active Learning. TSS, vol. 18, pp. 201–210. Springer, Singapore (2019). https://doi.org/10.1007/978-981-13-8039-6_19
7. Gupta, S.D.: Dynamics of switching from polluting resources to green technologies. Int. J. Energy Econ. Policy **5**(4), 1109–1124 (2015)

The Perception of Business Wargaming Practices Among Strategic and Competitive Intelligence Professionals

Adam Kowalik[✉] [iD]

SWPS University, Warsaw, Poland
akowalik@swps.edu.pl

Abstract. The main aim of this research was to investigate the perception of business wargaming practices. The survey was run with the members of a leading professional association. According to the survey results the primary function of business wargames is improving decision-making. Business wargames are typically conducted less than once a year, they are conducted no matter of overall economic situation and are conducted proactively rather than reactively. Methods used to conduct business wargames are typically qualitative. Managers of various levels attend business wargames more often than staff. Business wargames are typically handled internally and this effort is lead by units dealing with strategy & analysis or market & competitive intelligence. Critical success factors related to running business wargames shared by the respondents are also presented.

Keywords: Business wargame · Strategy simulation · Competitive intelligence

1 Introduction

1.1 Strategic, Market, Competitive Intelligence

Achieving a lasting market success is not an easy task for companies. Market leaders such as Wal-Mart, Apple or GM constantly watch the market, competitors and customers to adjust business strategies. The role of Strategic, Market, Competitive Intelligence (SMCI) is of utmost importance in this process. The lack or SMCI may lead to market failures – Polaroid, Kodak or Nokia were market leaders in the past but they failed. Many factors contributed to these failures but improper use of SMCI seems to be the crucial one. These companies were probably not able to detect the threats and opportunities in their environments and respond to them early enough.

SMCI has originated in the US and has gradually evolved into a separate discipline: from the Fugger News, Rothschild pigeons, through D&B agencies, to the first SMCI teams in Motorola or Kellog. There are professional associations like Strategic and Competitive Intelligence Professionals (SCIP) with thousands of members globally.

Intelligence is as an information that has been analyzed and processed so that it is useful to decision-makers when making strategic and tactical decisions. Above all, it is a methodical assessment of future events. Companies use SMCI to improve the competitive position and win in the market. Narrowly, SMCI is an intelligence about

© Springer Nature Switzerland AG 2021
M. Wardaszko et al. (Eds.): ISAGA 2019, LNCS 11988, pp. 210–220, 2021.
https://doi.org/10.1007/978-3-030-72132-9_19

competitors. Broader view is that SMCI is an intelligence that allows the company to be more competitive. SMCI must not be confused with industrial espionage which is illegal. SMCI activities should reflect ethical standards like the ones promoted by SCIP in the Code of Ethics.

Business requirements for SMCI can be strategic, operational or tactical. Strategic ones refer to understanding where the value is migrating, operational ones refer to evaluating the key investments or changes in the context of business strategy and tactical ones refer to supporting the process of winning market transactions against major competitors. SMCI activities are carried out in the course of traditional intelligence cycle which comprises the following steps: requirements, scoping, planning, collection, processing, analysis, reporting, dissemination. In practical terms those activities do not follow sequentially, but they intersect [1]. Intelligence deliverables shall meet the six criteria of the FAROUT model [2] and be: future oriented, accurate, resource efficient, objective, useful, timely.

The critical element in the cycle is the analysis which leads to discovering new knowledge from collected information. The ability to see the disruptions and interpret them is the critical element of SMCI [3]. Analysis is not aimed at telling the future or anticipating the "black swan" events [4] since it is impossible. It should be aimed at assessing the most likely courses of action. During the analysis the questions being answered include: "what?", "so what?", "now what?" [2]. The taxonomy of structured intelligence analysis techniques comprises dozens of items, including structured brainstorming, what if analysis, devil's advocacy, red team analysis, scenarios [5]. There are also analytical methods specific for business such as PESTEL, Porter 5 Forces, Ansoff Matrix, strategic groups. Using those various methods should lead to developing possible competitors' strategic moves, possible competitors' reactions to those moves, possible competitors' reactions to industry changes and competitors' reactions to changes in the wider environment [6].

To initiate the SMCI program the decision-makers should provide relevant input to scope it correctly. The scoping ends up with formulating the Key Intelligence Topics (KITs). Running top class SMCI operations requires taking actions in six dimensions: scope, process, deliverables, tools, organization, culture [7]. Professional SMCI operations generate value added - companies which run SMCI activities claim their investments pay of [8].

1.2   Business Wargaming as an Intelligence Co-creation Method

Intelligence co-creation is as a joint effort of both intelligence producers and consumers aimed at developing insights to support decision-making on strategic moves. It assumes involving decision-makers in the intelligence analysis and drawing conclusions together with the SMCI team. Such methods allow to generate high-value intelligence, assess strategic situation from different perspectives, provoke unconventional thinking, engage people across the firm, obtain human intelligence. They have the potential to produce excellent results but are difficult in execution since they require both profound technical and social skills.

Applying the intelligence co-creation methods is one of the measures to address the challenges the SMCI teams face today such as aligning KITs to strategic priorities, communicating competitive data and insights to stakeholders, using informal networks to capture human intelligence [9]. Co-creation fulfills such important axioms of intelligence analysts as aggressive thinking, avoiding mirror imaging, intelligence dissemination, proactive collection [10]. Co-creation methods reduce the risk of human thinking errors such as the tendency of failing to see things that should be seen, the tendency of perceiving what we expect to see and the tendency of rapid opinion forming and adhering to it [5]. Co-creation also allows to use elements of critical thinking which include: clear purpose, precise question, clear assumptions, point of view, relevant information, concepts to express thinking, inferences or interpretations, implications or consequences [11]. Such methods are part of a new paradigm for analysts and should be used routinely to cure the flaws in intelligence analysis [12].

Wargaming derives from the military sector and can be defined as "a warfare model or simulation whose operation does not involve the activities of actual military forces, and whose sequence of events affects and is, in turn, affected by the decisions made by players representing the opposing sides" [13] or as "an attempt to get a jump on the future" [14]. In business context wargaming can be defined as "competitive time-based simulation in which participants 'playing' on teams develop and present competing strategies" [15]. Since there are some reservations with the use of "war" and "game" terms in business world wargaming is also being referred to as "strategy simulation".

Wargaming assumes a rivalry between companies, although cooperation-oriented measures like coopetition are acceptable. Already in 1984 it was argued that the economic and social transformations required companies to take a new approach to market struggle, i.e. to adopt their strategies to reflect the combative nature of market competition [16]. This assumption has not changed over time - business wargames are sometimes being referred to as "cognitive warfare" [17].

Business wargaming assumes that if a company wants to win against its competitors it needs to think the way they do. The ultimate goal is to discover the most likely actions of the competitors and develop plans to outsmart them. Wargame is a serious, realistic game and is not oriented for entertainment by any means. Business wargaming uses only real data on companies and markets. Wargaming shall not be confused nor associated with gamification which is oriented for increasing the engagement and motivation of people. There are various types of wargaming events: workshop, inductive/deductive game, scenario planning, alternative futures, etc. [18]. The advanced form of wargaming is a multi-level simulation which links the strategic, operational and tactical levels [19].

The value-added from such simulations is the creation of a situation which allows the host company to analyze the situation from different perspectives by temporarily entering the shoes of competitors (according to the Sun Tzu's proverb "To know your enemy you must become your enemy"). This different perspective allows to discover new things. Wargaming can be perceived as one of the methods to generate foresight for companies. Some authors [20] claim it is possible because wargames have participative and dynamic nature and allow companies to deal with cognitive errors, challenge status quo, identify weak signals and re-focus activities. Wargaming is probably the most powerful project the SMCI team may run. SMCI teams which engage in wargaming assess their operations as very effective and more strategic [21].

1.3   The Practice of Business Wargaming

Business wargame is an interactive simulation attended by the company's leadership. The executives are split into teams representing the competitors. Those teams develop the most likely business actions and reactions of competitors in an iterative manner, usually in 3–4 rounds. The proposed actions are then assessed by other teams representing clients, regulators, shareholders, etc. The content of each round derives from the goals of simulation. The simulation concludes with recommendations of strategic actions for the management board of a host company.

Wargaming can be applied to test the strategy, prepare crisis response, develop foresight, manage change, educate and recruit, develop early warnings [22]. It is the right solution when a company faces an important decision such as launching new product, entering new market, merger or is concerned about the uncertainty of the environment like changing technologies, regulations, social trends, economic situation, customer habits.

Business wargaming is a unique way to analyze the future market situation. Having such knowledge before making a key decision and engaging significant resources is invaluable. This is possible thanks to a structured, rigorous analysis of the most likely moves and counter-measures of competitors and stakeholders in the mid-term horizon.

2   Survey Description

The survey aimed at investigating the perception of business wargames practices in companies. The aim of the survey was also to identify and describe the relationships between the use of wargaming and intelligence co-creation and improving competitive position of companies. The later aim is not covered in this article.

The draft survey was designed by the author and was consulted with 2 dozens of individuals familiar with wargaming. All collected comments were analyzed and some of them implemented.

The target audience was the members of SCIP association who are SMCI practitioners. The survey was primarily targeted at individuals who deal with or dealt with business wargames. While probably not all the SCIP members had direct experience with business wargaming, most of them were probably familiar with this concept which made them relatively good target group for this survey.

The survey contained some explanations of terms to set a common denominator. Business wargaming was explained as "a simulation of possible future actions of various market stakeholders; it aims at developing the winning moves of the home company given the real market situation and data; this method is also being called 'red hat analysis', 'red team analysis'". Intelligence co-creation was explained as "a joint and highly interactive effort of intelligence team and company's leadership that is oriented for developing valuable insights to drive the actions of the company."

The survey was sent to 12566 emails from SCIP database. The responses were collected anonymously via Survey Monkey from 7th IV till 12 V 2017. 227 responses were collected but not all of them comprised answers to all the questions. The responses must not be treated as representative sample and therefore the survey results cannot be generalized.

The primary industry focus of respondent's company was manufacturing (25 responses); pharmaceuticals, health sciences, health care (24); information, communications, entertainment (18); financial services, insurance, banking (14); professional services (13). The primary geographical focus of respondent's company was North America (64 responses), multiple geographies (62), Europe (13), Asia (4), South America (4), Africa (1) and Australia (1). The total yearly revenue of respondent's company in all business units was as the following: $0–100M - 34 responses; $100–500M – 16; $500M–1B - 14; $1B–$10B - 37; $10B or above - 25. 117 respondents indicated they were in various roles in business wargaming such as designing, conducting, managing, coordinating, participating, advising, deciding, analyzing. 99 respondents declared no practical experience with business wargames.

3 Survey Results

53 respondents indicated that strategic level wargames are conducted less than once a year, 49 respondents indicated that operational level wargames are conducted less than once a year and 43 respondents indicated that tactical level wargames are conducted less than once a year. Summary of those responses follows below (Fig. 1).

Q2: How often are business wargames conducted?	Less than once a year	Once a year	Several times a year	Do not know / Difficult to answer / Not applicable	Total
Strategic level wargames(focused on major changes in doing business: example- launching a new product)	53	28	30	56	167
Operational level wargames (focused on improving business operations: example - closing one of the factories)	49	23	24	71	167
Tactical level wargames (focused on winning market transactions: example - pricing the customized service	43	23	34	67	167

Fig. 1. Summary of responses to Question 2.

Business wargames are typically conducted no matter of overall economic situation according to 81 respondents, mainly during overall economic downturn according to 18 respondents and mainly during overall economic prosperity according to 7 respondents.

47 respondents indicated business wargames are used sometimes reactively and sometimes proactively. 46 respondents indicated wargames are used mostly proactively (it is done to position a company given the anticipated shifts) while 23 respondents indicated they are used mostly reactively (it is done in response to something that has already occurred).

The primary function of business wargames - according to 96 respondents - was to drive, facilitate, improve decision-making. Other functions were assessed as follows: enhance learning and development (12 responses), facilitate team-working and net-working (7), other (14).

Methods typically used to conduct business wargames were mostly qualitative (group-work and discussion) according to 71 respondents. 47 respondents indicated both qualitative and quantitative methods. Mostly quantitative (computer-based sim-ulation) methods were indicated by 4 respondents.

As far as the participation in business wargames per seniority of participants and per frequency of participation is concerned 51 respondents indicated middle level leadership often participates in business wargames and 32 respondents indicated senior level leadership always attends business wargames. Summary of those responses fol-lows below (Fig. 2).

Q7: Who and how often typically participates in business wargames?	Always	Often	Sometimes	Rarely	Never	Do not know / Difficult to answer / Not applicable	Total
Senior level leadership (i.e. board members)	32	28	26	18	20	38	162
Middle level leadership (i.e. directors)	32	51	26	11	12	31	163
Lower level leadership (i.e. managers)	25	37	34	17	19	31	163
Staff (i.e. associates, specialists)	15	31	27	28	25	36	162

Fig. 2. Summary of responses to Question 7.

When handling business wargames typically most of the work is done internally according to 60 respondents, 44 respondents stated some work was done internally and some by consultants and 17 mentioned most of the work was done by consultants.

The leading role in making business wargames happen belongs to the following functional units: strategy & analysis (51 responses), market & competitive intelligence (39), respective business unit (10), other (10), marketing (7), business development (5), sales (5), talent management (2).

The respondents had an opportunity to share their views on critical success factors in exploiting the full potential of business wargames by answering an open text question. All received responses were subjectively grouped into various categories and slightly edited for better clarity by the author.

- Sponsor:
  - topic is defined and important,
  - buy in from management,
  - willingness to see the issue and change;
- Participants:
  - strategic-level participants with market knowledge are required,
  - having the right people from various functions to participate,
  - cross-section of backgrounds and skills on each team,
  - use senior managers as the judging panel,
  - bring people with an external perspective,
  - people need to be emotionally and intellectually engaged;
- Organization:
  - fit into the planning cycle,
  - routinely doing wargames to stay on top,
  - doesn't take up too much time,
  - allow time to participate,
  - decent venue (large enough, non-distracting, ability to cater);
- Design:
  - making sure it is aligned with the problem to be solved,
  - design to develop in-depth understanding of the competitors,
  - allow for experiencing possible future moves of the competitors,
  - design to develop tangible outputs / insights,
  - allow for co-creation of the game;
- Preparation:
  - early involvement and preparation of participants,
  - motivate people to participate actively,
  - defining expectations up front,
  - briefing book with relevant knowledge,
  - make sure participants do the pre-work;
- Conducting a wargame:
  - personnel skilled and experienced in running wargames,
  - providing clear framework and instructions,
  - get contributions from everyone, particularly opposing views,
  - monitoring of break-out sessions to ensure groups are on track,
  - help people asking the right questions,
  - avoiding groupthink, politics;
- Output:
  - analytical capability to summarize findings and learnings,
  - the insights need to be framed in an actionable way,
  - ability to understand lessons learned and adjust strategy,
  - follow-up on recommendations,
  - transparency with group members after game is played.

4 Discussion of Results

The primary function of wargaming according to 74% of respondents is driving, facilitating and improving decision-making. These results coincide with the descriptions of a number of business wargames carried out by business consultants [17] from which it is clear that wargaming primarily supports decision-making on strategic company moves. Functions such as enhancing learning and development or facilitating team-working and networking should therefore be treated as secondary ones, especially that using business games for leadership development is considered as difficult [23].

Business wargames are typically conducted no matter of overall economic situation and this answer was predominating (76%). Only 7% of respondents indicated that wargames are usually carried out during economic prosperity which may suggest that if the economic situation is good the willingness of companies to think how to win with competition will be lower. In turn, 17% of answers indicating that wargames are mainly organized during economic downturn may indicate that companies understand that this is more a tool for predicting and preventing a crisis rather than reacting to it. A similar understanding of business wargame also resonates in the answers to Question 4 "What is the balance between using business wargaming proactively and reactively?" because only 20% of respondents indicated that business wargames are conducted mostly reactively.

Methods used to conduct business wargames are typically qualitative (group-work and discussion) which was indicated by 58% of respondents. This shows that in most cases, business wargame is conducted without the use of mathematical models which process decisions of teams into specific results such as market share, company value, revenues. The use of a computer model would require a number of assumptions and limitations, which would narrow the possible competitor moves and therefore distort the essence of business wargaming. The underestimation of the difficulty of creating a real business model for business wargaming was mentioned as early as in 1958 [24]. Decades later - despite the impressive development of the software - there is still no such flexible algorithm that would allow uncompromisingly taking into account the entire range of possible moves of competitors.

The leadership of various levels would be more typical participant of a business wargame rather than the staff. In addition, the most frequent answer to this question was that middle level leadership often participated in wargames. Wargaming is mainly targeted at leadership. Senior executives are invited too, but typically the simulation is attended just by the representatives of management board. Lower level managers are less likely to participate in the simulation due to insufficient business and industry experience.

Business wargames are mostly conducted less than once a year and that does not differ much for various types of wargames, be it strategic, operational or tactical ones. In particular 48% respondents indicated that strategic level wargames are conducted less than once a year. Interestingly, the response rate for "Do not know/Difficult to answer/Not applicable" answer is higher for the operational and tactical level wargames rather than for strategic wargames which may suggest that strategic business wargames are more common.

Business wargames are typically handled internally according to 50% of respondents. 36% of respondents claim that this is a joint effort of employees and consultants. It's not easy to decide who should run a business wargame. On the one hand wargame concerns sensitive issues for the company which reduces the tendency to engage consultants despite the possibility of signing a non-disclosure-agreement with them. On the other hand the experience in preparing, running and summarizing wargames speaks for the involvement of consultants.

The leading role in making business wargames happen is on the side of strategy & analysis (40% of responses) or market & competitive intelligence (30% of responses) units. Other units play marginal role. The fact that the wargames are conducted mostly by those two units does not mean they are the only beneficiaries of such efforts. They are project coordinators and they process the results to be consumed by the management board. It would be striking if these two units were not organizing or at least participating in wargaming. It is puzzling that talent management gained only less than 2% of responses because this unit often supports business wargame by providing adequate resources, recruiting participants, conducting internal communication, giving feedback to participants, etc. Such a low percentage may stem from the fact that the respondents did not associate "talent management" with "human resources".

The respondents indicated impressive number of critical success factors related to running business wargames. The factors mentioned by the respondents concerned the sponsor, participants, organization, design, preparation, conduct and output of business wargame. It is difficult to find significant gaps or flaws in those responses which suggests the respondents were well-versed in the topic. The list of these factors is a set of practical tips for professionals who consider running wargames in their companies. These factors can be referred to the 7 tests of effective wargame [25] according to which wargaming should be realistic, empowering, accessible, enjoyable, inexpensive, simple and transparent. In the respondents' answers only the enjoyable and inexpensive issues were not raised. This suggests that respondents recognize business wargame as a serious strategic initiative and not an opportunity to have fun. Respondents also do not mention low cost as a critical factor because probably they realize that wargaming is associated with certain costs – at least in the form of time of participants.

5   Limitations and Suggestions

The research is not free from defects. Three examples of disadvantages and limitations include the following: very small number of responses to the survey despite addressing it to the group of professionals associated in the leading global industry organization; uneven distribution of companies from various industries and countries which was inherited from the structure of the members of the industry organization to which the survey was sent; lack of knowledge about whether responding to the survey the respondents took into account all their professional experience or just from the company in which they worked at the moment of completing the survey.

Although the results of the survey provide answers to a number of questions, they simultaneously reveal new areas of interest such as:

- determining the actual scale of business wargaming,
- developing a flexible and realistic computer model to run the simulation,
- investigating industry specifics in the use of business wargames,
- identifying the topics which are most often "played" during wargames,
- the use of business wargames in an open and closed convention,
- the extent to which mental models allow the participants to change the perspective.

References

1. Wheaton, K.J.: The New Intelligence Process, 21 March 2012. https://sourcesandmethods. blogspot.com/2012/03/part-12-new-intelligence-process-second.html. Accessed 18 May 2019
2. Fleisher, C.S., Bensoussan, B.E.: Strategic and Competitive Analysis: Methods and Techniques for Analyzing Business Competition. Prentice Hall, Upper Saddle River (2003)
3. Fuld, L.M.: The Secret Language of Competitive Intelligence. How to See Through and Stay Ahead of Business Disruptions, Distortions, Rumors, and Smoke Screens. DogEar Publishing, Indianapolis (2010)
4. Taleb, N.N.: The Black Swan the Impact of the Highly Improbable. Random House, New York (2007)
5. Heuer, R.J.: Psychology of Intelligence Analysis. Center for the Study of Intelligence, Central Intelligence Agency, Washington, D.C. (2010)
6. Porter, M.E.: Competitive Strategy: Techniques for Analyzing Industries and Competitors. Free Press, New York (1980)
7. Hedin, H., Hirvensalo, I., Vaarnas, M.: The Handbook of Market Intelligence: Global Best Practice in Turning Market Data into Actionable Insights. Wiley, Hoboken (2011)
8. GIA: The State of Market Intelligence in 2013, June 2013. https://www.m-brain.com/wp-content/uploads/2015/04/10848.pdf
9. Frost & Sullivan: Market Research and Competitive Intelligence Priorities Survey Results. Business (2011). https://www.slideshare.net/FrostandSullivan/growth-team-membership-2011-market-research-and-competitive-intelligence-priorities-survey-results
10. Watanabe, F.: Fifteen Axioms for Intelligence Analysts (1997). https://www.dtic.mil/docs/citations/ADA525713
11. Moore, D.T.: Critical thinking and intelligence analysis (2007). https://purl.access.gpo.gov/GPO/LPS93921
12. Cooper, J.R.: Curing analytic pathologies: pathways to improved intelligence analysis (2006). https://www.fas.org/irp/cia/product/curing.pdf
13. Perla, P.: The Art of Wargaming: A Guide for Professionals and Hobbyists. Naval Institute Press, Annapolis (1990)
14. Dunnigan, J.F.: Wargames Handbook: How to Play and Design Commercial and Professional Wargames. Writers Club, San Jose (2010)
15. May, M., Smith, T.: Wargaming for business, non-profit, and government strategy development (chap. 29). In: Cruz-Cunha, M.M. (ed.): Handbook of Research on Serious Games as Educational, Business and Research Tools (2012)
16. Barrie, J.: Business Wargames. Abacus, Tunbridge Wells (1984)
17. Herman, M., Frost, M., Kurz, R.: Wargaming for Leaders: Strategic Decision Making from the Battlefield to the Boardroom, 1st edn. McGraw-Hill Education, New York (2008)

18. Burns, S., Della Volpe, D., Babb, R., Miller, N., Muir, G.: War Gamers' Handbook: A Guide for Professional War Gamers. Naval War College (U.S.) & War Gaming Department (2013)
19. Perla, P., Markowitz, M.: Wargaming Strategic Linkage (2009). https://www.dtic.mil/docs/citations/ADA494300
20. Schwarz, J.: Business wargaming: developing foresight within a strategic simulation. Technol. Anal. Strat. Manag. **21**(3), 291–305 (2009). https://doi.org/10.1080/09537320902750590
21. Fletcher/CSI: Effective Competitive Intelligence Units, January 2014. https://fletchercsi.com/wp-content/uploads/2016/08/FletcherCSI_Effective_CI_Survey_Results_2014.pdf
22. Oriesek, D.F., Schwarz, J.O.: Business Wargaming: Securing Corporate Value. Gower, Hampshire (2008)
23. Lopes, M.C., Fialho, F.A.P., Cunha, C.J.C.A., Niveiros, S.I.: Business games for leadership development: a systematic review. Simul. Gaming **44**(4), 523–543 (2013)
24. Andlinger, G.R.: Looking ahead. Harv. Bus. Rev. **36**(4), 147–160 (1958)
25. Gilad, B.: Business War Games: How Large, Small, and New Companies Can Vastly Improve Their Strategies and Outmaneuver the Competition. Career Press, Franklin Lakes (2009)

Managing Competing Values in Sustainable Urban Tourism: A Simulation-Gaming Approach

Jessika Weber-Sabil[1(✉)], Lidija Lalicic[2], Thomas P. Buijtenweg[1],
Kevin Hutchinson[1], Carlos Santos[1], Frans Melissen[1], Ko Koens[1],
and Igor Mayer[1]

[1] Breda University of Applied Sciences, Breda, The Netherlands
{weber.j,buijtenweg.t}@buas.nl
[2] MODUL University Vienna, Vienna, Austria
Lidija.Lalicic@modul.ac.at

Abstract. Tourism is an important economic sector that has a significant impact on sustainability indicators, such as GHG emissions and cohesion. Local policy makers are increasingly challenged to manage the urban tourism system at large. As part of a EU funded project, the authors have conceptualized sustainable urban tourism as the 'management of competing values' represented in a conceptual model of ecology, visitability, livability, equity, economic growth and smart citizenship. A simulation game was designed and implemented to improve social learning about these competing values. The game was played in six European cities, with around 15 local policy-makers and stakeholders in each session. The players indicated a high level of satisfaction with the game and social learning. In order to understand to what extent the game is able to validate and communicate the competing values model, the start and end states of the tourism values of the cities, as logged in the game's dashboard, were analyzed in a comparative manner. The analysis shows significant differences in how cities manage sustainable tourism, with marked differences in ecology and smart citizenship. The differences in tourism issues and policy making styles demonstrate the value of a simulation approach to support future planning processes.

Keywords: Stakeholder collaboration · Tourism planning · Sustainability · Policy making · Serious gaming

1 Introduction

1.1 Managing Sustainable Urban Tourism

Statistics show that the direct and total contribution of travel and tourism to the global economy mounts up to 8.27 trillion US dollars worldwide [1]. This is delivered by a sheer 1.32 billion international arrivals worldwide, which is expected to grow further with 4–5% annually. At the same time, tourism – mainly (air) travel and luxury consumption – has significant impact on all sustainability indicators, from CO_2 emissions and biodiversity to neighborhood cohesion [2]. Research has indicated that between 2009 and 2013, tourism's global carbon footprint has increased from 3.9 to

© Springer Nature Switzerland AG 2021
M. Wardaszko et al. (Eds.): ISAGA 2019, LNCS 11988, pp. 221–234, 2021.
https://doi.org/10.1007/978-3-030-72132-9_20

4.5 GtCO2, accounting for about 8% of global greenhouse gas emissions [3]. Whereas these numbers give an indication of the sustainability impact of tourism on a global scale, the daily impact of tourism is mainly felt in and around a touristic *hot spot*, which is often (in) a city [4]. Tourism not only contributes significantly to the local economy, with employment as an important socio-economic indicator, but also has detrimental effects, such as the degradation of the local natural environment, real estate prices and gentrification, nuisance and commodification. It is well known that cities like Barcelona, Venice and Amsterdam are increasingly suffering from the pressures that a constantly growing number of visitors put on the urban infrastructure, a modern day phenomenon addressed as *visitor pressure* and *overtourism* [5]. As a result, residents in popular tourist destinations are starting to speak up against the erosion of values, such as *authenticity*, *livability* and *cohesion* in their city [6]. In short, sustainable tourism is a very multifaceted concept where *hard sustainability* indicators (greenhouse gas emissions, biodiversity), and softer sustainability definitions such as liveability and preservation of cultural heritage need to be taken into account.

Local policy makers are increasingly challenged to manage the urban tourism system at large; the daily impact that tourism has on the city and its residents, on the natural environment as well as on targets defined in the Paris climate agreement [7]. This is a challenging endeavor, because tourism has become intricately linked to nearly all other aspects of the urban system, its economy, mobility, housing, culture, security and so on. Academics and practitioners have therefore argued for an *integrated approach* to sustainable urban tourism; where tourism becomes an integral part of longer term municipal policy making and city planning [6, 8, 9]. This is easier said than done. It requires a proper understanding of the many sustainability issues, the contributing factors and the possible interventions to address them. This should be done evidence- based, which requires data and knowledge, as well as sharing among cities what works and what doesn't. It also requires a good deal of cooperation among the different sectoral policy makers in a municipality and with the many stakeholders: tourist operators, project developers, nature conservationists and environmental groups, residents, etc. However, municipalities tend to be compartmentalized, and sectoral policy makers do not necessarily speak the same language. Participatory processes with stakeholders need to be designed and managed well. But where stakes are high, tensions easily flare up around issues such as the admission of cruise ships or Airbnb. (Municipal) tourist destination management organizations often have a coordinating and mediating role [10], but are often not very influential when it comes to municipal sectoral policies. Technological developments, such as with social media, artificial intelligence (AI) and big data, are constantly changing the tourism system itself, as can be witnessed in the staggering rise of the sharing/platform economy and the effect it has on tourist accommodation (Airbnb) and transportation (Uber, Bike sharing). Technological innovations can also be part of the solution such as with green energy, electrification of transport, crowd management, camera surveillance and tourist information apps [11]. The management of such emerging technologies can bring a whole new dimension to the complexity of sustainable tourism.

In short, more expertise and better tools are needed to support the management of sustainable urban tourism. The objective of the EU funded project was to develop and try out such innovative tools, among others by using simulation gaming (SG) [12]. In this paper, we present the design of the simulation-game approach, how it was used in six (anonymized) European cities and discuss the first insights from the play sessions.

2 Theory and Concepts

Integrated policy making requires *social learning* among policy-makers, residents and stakeholders, in our case about how to make *value tradeoffs* in sustainable urban tourism. It also helps if European municipalities can learn from each other, about their strategies, instruments, best practices and failures. To facilitate this social learning about sustainable urban tourism in and among European cities, the authors used a gaming-simulation approach. We define the key concepts in this approach, below.

Simulation-gaming *or* **serious gaming (SG)** make use of the technologies of games and the principles of play to achieve objectives that are valued not for their intrinsic value—i.e., merely for the sake of entertainment—but for the extrinsic value achieved by the consequences, such as the fact that engagement and feedback in play is a good condition for learning and change [14]. The game presented below aims to promote stakeholder engagement, deepen the understanding about the complexity of sustainable urban tourism and to explore integrated strategies to manage sustainable tourism.

Social Learning. Social learning has been conceptualized and studied relatively well for instance for natural resources management. According to Reed et al. [13] for social learning, a process must: "(1) demonstrate that a change in understanding has taken place in the individuals involved; (2) demonstrate that this change goes beyond the individual and becomes situated within wider social units or communities of practice (CoP); and (3) occur through social interactions and processes between actors within a social network." Instrumentally, theories of social learning have been connected to CoP arranged in online platforms, living labs and methods such as simulation-gaming (SG).

Managing Competing Values. The game-based, social learning approach is based on the conceptual model of 'managing competing values in sustainable urban tourism'. Although associated by name, our model has little or no relationship with the well-known organizational effectiveness model [15]. The model is based on the triple bottom-line *(people-planet-profit, or economy ecology equity)* added with a triplet for tourism (*livability, visitability and smart citizenship*) [16–19]. Figure 1 gives an impression of the model, with explanation of the terms.

1. *Natural viability (Ecology)*: the ability of the natural system, locally and globally, to support the needs and wishes of current and future generations;
2. *Economic wealth (Economy)* the balance between direct and indirect economic costs and benefits for a sector or the system as a whole;
3. *Equity:* is the extent to which benefits and disadvantages are shared equitably to ensure a fair distribution of quality of life between different stakeholders.;
4. *Liveability:* the extent to which residents and other local stakeholders that make regular use of the city (e.g. commuters, local business owners) experience the city as a place for living and working;

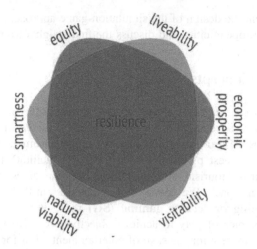

Fig. 1. Managing competing values in sustainable urban tourism

5. *Visitability*: the extent to which those visiting the city (tourists, both day visitors and overnight stay visitors), as well as local stakeholders experience the city as a place for visiting (both for leisure and working);
6. *Smart citizenship*: The extent to which the city's governance structures, physical structures and digital structures provide opportunities for stakeholders to get involved in decision-making to come to a long-term vision and efficient short and mid-term decision-making.

The essence of the model can best be captured through the metaphor of a water bed; pushing on one side of the bed (model), is likely to shake the other sides of the bed (model). Following this metaphor, policy makers would be wise to anticipate and legitimate the rocking and shaking of the bed (model), or perhaps even better try to find a balance among changes in the values which eventually results in a resilient tourism city planning. The main challenge for policy makers in tourism is to balance out the values that are tensional, not only between CO_2 emissions and economic growth, but also between 'being hospitable to visitors and maintain livability for residents', to make sure that the 'benefits and burdens of tourism are shared in a fair manner'.

3 Materials and Methods

3.1 The Sustainable Urban Tourism Game

The *sustainable urban tourism simulation game* is a multiplayer, computer supported strategy game that communicates the complexity of managing sustainable tourism in urban areas. The development and use of the game was accompanied by other research activities, such as interviews in the cities, desk research, a systems dynamics model and 'media apps', in several work packages. The simulation game was developed in 2018 by a design team, in which some of the authors participated. An impression of the game can be viewed at [12]. Part of the agreement with the cities, is that experiences and insights from the game sessions are reported in an anonymized fashion. The cities have therefore been relabeled as city A-F. The game was tested in City A (results not reported here), soon followed by game sessions in all six partner cities, with City A again as *finale*. All sessions took place between January and March 2019, and were moderated by the same team.

The six cities vary between around 130.000 to 800.000 inhabitants, and are situated in North-western (2), Northern (2), Southern (1) and Eastern-central (1) Europe. The cities are quite different in terms of city infrastructure (old town, business district, modes of public transport etc.), hot spot tourist attractions (culture, skiing resort, mountains, cruises or beach etc.), number and type of visitors (party, backpackers, business, family etc.), level and type of tourism pressure (low to high) and so on. The game therefore needed to be able to fit different city characteristics and different sustainability challenges to play with. How this was achieved is described below.

Fig. 2. Game board with 3D miniatures representing tourism and city infrastructure

Design and Management of the Game

The game takes about 3–5 h to play, and can accommodate 10 to 20 players, divided over five stakeholder roles. The game is played in several rounds (three to six) depending on how fast players are progressing. The game is moderated by one or two persons who are familiar with the topic, have experience with this game and know how to insert player decisions into a software tool that calculates the consequences of the players' decisions. The game is primarily designed for professionals (to be) with an affinity to the topic of sustainable tourism. Players may include (but are not limited to) municipal policy makers, tourism industry stakeholders, local environmental or resident groups, academics, consultants or students in relevant areas.

The game is played on 1.5 × 1.5 m game board that consists of a modular set of hexagon shaped tiles, printed with abstract representations of common areas in European cities (see Fig. 2): old town, city center, residential areas, business district, harbor, nature area, etc. The flexible hexagon tiles allow for a variety of game-city set ups to

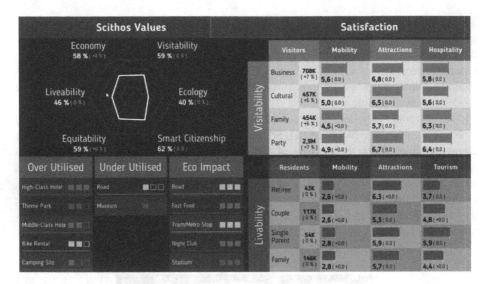

Fig. 3. Game dashboard representing the competing values model on the left upper corner.

play with. The game kit furthermore comes with a large number of 3D printed objects that symbolize city infrastructure, such as hotels in different categories, theme parks, transportation categories etc. The game simulates residents' and visitors' preferences using these facilities. This mechanic allows the players to market the city to a specific target group, e.g., less party visitors, and more families or business travelers, when they feel one value is over or under represented. Each team has a set of policy cards, which fit the player role: 'Increase [high class] hotels in the city' or 'Make [type] buildings [CO2 neutral]'. In order to pursue those actions, stakeholders have to negotiate with other teams to get their support, often by getting certain resources. During the game, players can select and put up infrastructure and policy propositions for a vote. This, for instance, allows tourism infrastructure development, or the regulation of certain facilities (e.g. Airbnb), which eventually has an influence on the satisfaction of visitors and residents, and therefore on the overall system of competing values. After each round, the players explain to each other, what they have implemented, why and what they expect to change in the system.

The decisions of the players – infrastructure and policies – are inserted by the game moderators into a software model, so that the consequences can be calculated and displayed on the dashboard. This brings the game to a new state, the start of a another play round or debriefing. The changes and current state of the city is visualized in a dashboard which is projected on a large screen for all players to see (see Fig. 3). The competing values model (Fig. 1) forms the core of the dashboard.

3.2 Game Quality

In all sessions, a pre- and post-survey with closed and open questions was distributed. Intermediate and post-game reflective discussions were conducted as well. Although a detailed analysis of the survey is not subject of this paper, some indications of the quality and benefits of the game for tourism planning are presented. By and large, the player satisfaction with the game was rather high. Players indicated that the game was useful (m = 4.2, st.d: 0.72 on a 5-Point-Likert scale with 5 as the highest, n = 5), interesting and motivating (m = 4.5, st.d: 0.57) and represented the challenges in tourism planning accurately (m = 4.1, st.d: 0.64). The players indicated that the game promotes collaboration on urban tourism planning between stakeholders (m = 4.5, st.d: 0.64). The observations and answers to open questions reveal that participants enjoyed playing the game and appreciated the interaction with other players. Some mentioned that this game could work well to change politicians view on sustainable tourism. Because a game allows players to make mistakes or act in an inconsistent way, players indicated that they learned from these moments and now understood the complexity of tourism planning better. The sustained debate and enthusiasm for tourism planning in the game and debriefings coupled with a likeness to recommend the game to others, also hinted at the potential for wider learning within the broader stakeholder community. The conclusion, is that the game met basic requirements of engagement, appreciation and learning, and that this gives sufficient grounds for improvements and further dissemination in their cities.

3.3   Research Question and Approach

The main question in the remainder of this paper, is to what extent the game is able to validate and communicate the competing values model, as described above. To answer this question, the begin and end states of the tourism values in the six cities, as logged in the game's dashboard, are analyzed in a comparative fashion.

4   Findings

4.1   City Strategies

In the following, a comparison of the start and end states of the six anonymized cities A-F, enriched with observations and analysis of the player's decision is provided in order to make an informed decision of the suitability of the serious game to validate and communicate the competing value model for sustainable tourism planning.

City A is a medium sized city in North-western Europe that experiences a high level of pressures from visitors. In real life, the city is quite active in developing sustainable tourism strategies and instruments. Players in the session are active stakeholders in real life, who were highly engaged, picked up the game-play quickly and discussed a lot. Players were most concerned with the *livability* in the model city. They prepared and implemented policies to enhance residents and visitors mutual acceptance. Negative effects such as pollution were remediated by policies like recycling systems. The strategy of the players was to make visitors feel welcome and satisfied when visiting the city e.g. by improving quality and quantity of tourism attractions (e.g. museums, theme parks) and simultaneously increasing safety and security in the city, decreasing the social impact of tourist shops, night clubs, fast food and clearly demarking entertainment facilities in the city. Overall, this led to a significant increase for *equity* and *ecology* values at the end of the game. Another strategy was to eliminate the negative impact of the sharing/platform economy (such as Airbnb) and optimize the city infrastructure. This increased *visitability* and *livability* within the city (see Fig. 4).

City B is a relatively large city in Eastern-central Europe where economic growth, employment also from tourism is high on the agenda. Compared to Northern-European cities, the policy making style is less consensual and stakeholder oriented. This may have been the reason, why it proved more difficult to recruit real stakeholders and decision-makers for the game. The shortage of stakeholders as players was therefore filled with students in tourism. Players focused very much on their own interests and strategies, seemed less visionary and collaborative. In the first round, they concentrated on designing a *car-free city* without catering for alternative infrastructure for residents and visitors. This caused the satisfaction level for residents and visitors to drop. The player group managed to increase the value for *ecology* for instance by plastic prevention, improved garbage collection and low emission modes of transportation. Nevertheless, *livability* and *visitability* only slightly improved as some of the introduced measures had opposing effects (see Fig. 5).

City C is a relatively small city in North-western Europe. It has a tourist hot spot just outside the city, known to give peak visitor pressures at certain times in the year. Overall the city does not suffer much from overtourism. The city has an active local environmental policy in the making, but the integration of tourism can still be improved. In daily life, the players are actively involved in tourism in the city. During the game, the players were dedicated and engaged, however it took a while before they discovered the benefits of working together with all stakeholders. From the first round onwards, players focused on measures with regard to sustainable transportation, such as low emission public transport, restriction of private transport and lowering public transport prices. This continued over the four rounds with the development of transportation infrastructure (e.g. tram stops, bike rental). Other measures focused on ecology, such as reduction of waste, food spill and energy consumption of hotels and tourist facilities. This resulted in a high *ecology* value of 0.57 at the end of the game. The economy benefitted from marketing the city to cultural tourists and the improvements of hotel and restaurant quality. Residents however were not so much consulted in their tourism development plans, such as building a theme park outside the city. This explains a lower value for *smart citizenship* of 0.4 by the end of the game (see Fig. 6).

City D is relatively small city in Northern Europe. The city has an authentic charm that attracts visitors, but plenty of them also come to it as a port of entrée for business affairs or for traveling into the surrounding natural areas. To experience its beauty, or to go hiking or skiing. From the start of the game, the players worked very much as a collective and came up with creative, future oriented solutions from which everyone could benefit. As in real life, the model city still has not reached its full carrying capacity and the players focused on a tourism growth strategy balancing *visitability* and *livability* (see Fig. 9). *Visitability* was increased to 0.6 for instance by improving hospitality and tourist attractions, decreasing the social impact of visitors and reducing transport prices. In the second part of the game, the players increased the livability score to 0.49 by improving transportation modes, recycling systems, and attractions (see Fig. 7).

City E is quite a large city in Southern Europe, that attracts plenty of visitors of different types, all year round. Although visitor pressure is already significant, there are concerns that this may further rise and overstretch capacity. One of the discussions is how to prevent tourism to go wrong, as in other hot spot cities. The session tended to be hectic, almost chaotic. With many real stakeholders as players discussing very lively with many references to real life. Hence, the pace of the game-play was relatively slow. Players were occupied with many values such as *equity* (fair distribution of costs and benefits) and the balance between *economic growth* and *ecological impact*. Although the players followed a strategy of tourism growth, they tried to ensure *liveability* through measures of security, and discounts for residents. At the same time, they increased the *ecology value* of tourism planning by measures of low emission transport infrastructure, anti-pollution measures (see Fig. 8).

City F is a fairly large city in Northern Europe that in real life among others targets 'curious visitors'. Players in this session very much enjoyed the game. The players were very deliberative, weighted alternatives and tried to understand how each decision impacted the city. In comparison to other cities, they seemed more inclined to take residents opinions into account. Players were very much aware of the ecological impact of tourism, and livability whereas economy growth seemed less dominant. Player-stakeholders developed the city center into a car-free zone and introduced electric public transport. Eventually, they decided to increase the livability of the city (e.g. marketing tourist attractions to residents, residents discounts, decrease ecological impact of transportation and hotel facilities) while maintaining a high level for the other values (see Fig. 9).

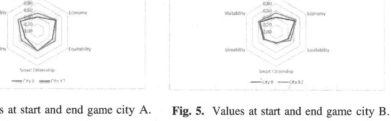

Fig. 4. Values at start and end game city A.   **Fig. 5.** Values at start and end game city B.

Fig. 6. Values at start and end game city C.   **Fig. 7.** Values at start and end game city D.

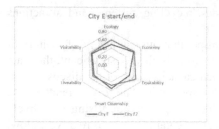

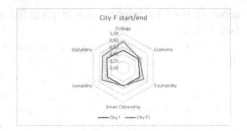

Fig. 8. Values at start and end game city E.   **Fig. 9.** Values at start and end game city F.

4.2   Comparative Strategies

Figure 10 (a) shows the starting values for the six cities, compared to Fig. 10 (b) representing the end state of the values. The start values were defined in collaboration with the city representative and on-site as well as desktop research. Figure 10 (a) shows that the start values for *liveability*, *visitability*, *ecology*, *economy*, and *equity* are not so far apart. There is slightly greater variation for *smart citizenship* though. Where City B rated itself a 0.33, all other cities ranged between 0.4 to 0.57 which might be due to political structures in which citizens are not actively involved in yet. The Nordic cities (City D and City F) by contrast, show a high level of citizen involvement in tourism policy making processes.

Fig. 10. Values for the six cities at the start (a) and end (b) of the game

Figure 11 gives a comparison of the value changes between start and end of the game for each city. The figure shows that the Northern European cities managed to achieve a significantly larger change towards *ecology* (average score of 0.7, 0.23 for city D and 0.25 for city F.) than the other cities. Issues around green energy and preservation of nature played out stronger in these model cities. City F. had a deliberate strategy to attract a certain type of visitors (*visitability*) without compromising on *ecology*. A focus on *economic growth* seems to have played out stronger in city C, and a limitation of economic growth for the benefit of *equity* (fairness) in city A and E.

One of the most pronounced observations is that *smart citizenship* either does not change very much, or it decreases (e.g. for city E). The reason, we suspect, is twofold.

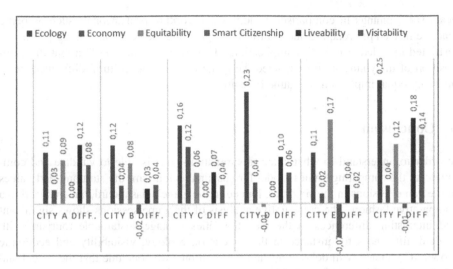

Fig. 11. Calculated differences of the end game compared to the start game values for each city

First of all, players were genuinely not very responsive to the interests of residents. In the debriefings, the cities acknowledged that they had largely ignored, or not involved the residents and that via the game they became more aware of it. Second, and this is an issue of game design and model validity, the *smart citizenship* value seems not clearly defined enough, and tends to have overlap with *equity*. This reduces the validity of the model, and the game.

Independently of the outcome of the play session, simulation gaming as a tool has hardly been introduced in tourism decision making and planning processes [20]. The idea to introduce simulation gaming into the tourism planning process resulted in the call to develop alternative and innovative methods to cater for stakeholder participation as these processes became multi-objective and spatially-oriented which were hard to facilitate and manage with conventional methods [21]. Tourism planning as a multi-faceted processes, requires player engagement and breaking down historically developed barriers between stakeholders. Simulation gaming allows for game participants to operate, explore and experiment in a safe and collaborative environment [20], which has proven to be successful in other research fields like maritime spatial [22] or urban planning games [23].

4.3 Limitations

The comparability of the game outcome might be limited due to the variation of the composition of the player group from city B. Although we have tried to aim for a homogenous group of professional tourism policy makers from transportation, city marketing, hospitality representatives and city attraction managers, players of city B consisted of a somewhat different player group. Perhaps due to indifferent political structure the majority of players were students as opposed the working professionals. Playing with students might have caused a different output as student decision making bears shortcomings in comparison to long-term working professionals such as being reactive instead pf proactive due to limited insights into the decision making process or restricted knowledge in policy implications. However, it is not verified that the composition of the young group impacted the game outcome, as cultural differences have probably equal impact on the game outcome.

5   Conclusion

In order to understand to what extent a simulation-game is able to validate and communicate the competing values model for sustainable tourism, the start and end values of the game sessions in the six cities, logged in the game's dashboard, are analyzed in a comparative fashion. The comparative analysis of the game sessions shows significant and interesting differences in the way the cities manage sustainable tourism, with marked differences for instance in their focus on ecology, visitability and economic growth. Combined with debriefings and observations, we conclude that the model and the game are able to reflect differences in policy making styles, real life issues and strategies in the various cities.

While the game was initially aimed at tourism policy experts, we made the experience that it works best for newly formed coalitions and people with entry knowledge of the field. The game has potential to be integrated in different as a tool in tourism policy making. The game might be a useful tool in the initial phase of strategic tourism planning and development process to support perspective taking, to define the area of stakeholder influence and to evaluate the policy impact on the system. The strength of the game lies in the aspect to allow local and national decision makers to engage in a new form of collaborative and social learning by the means of role-playing, simulation gaming and system thinking [20].

Nevertheless, we found room for improvement in the design of the *competing values model* and the game, especially with regard to the value defined as *smart citizenship*. We believe that the results of the six sessions demonstrate that an improved version of the game, combined with wide scale availability of the game, can become an effective instrument to enhance social learning in and among cities about the important topic of sustainable urban tourism.

Acknowledgements. The SCITHOS project was funded by ERANET, under the JPI Urban Europe joint programming initiative. Execution of the project is managed by NWO, the Netherlands and its partner organizations in the respective countries. The project is co-funded by CELTH, the Tourism Research Center of Breda University of Applied Sciences, and coordinated by the BUas Academy for Hospitality and Facility Management. Other partners in the SCITHOS project are: Western Norway Research University (Norway), Worldline (Spain), MODUL University (Vienna) and six (anonymized) municipalities in Europe. The authors wish to acknowledge the contribution of BUas colleagues Jeroen Klijs, and Eke Eijgelaar, as well as Play the City, Amsterdam for their involvement in the design process of the game.

References

1. Global travel and tourism industry - Statistics & Facts—Statista. https://www.statista. com/topics/962/global-tourism/. Accessed 29 Mar 2019
2. Hall, C.M.: The Routledge Handbook of Tourism and Sustainability. Routledge, Abingdon (2018)
3. Lenzen, M., Sun, Y.-Y., Faturay, F., Ting, Y.-P., Geschke, A., Malik, A.: The carbon footprint of global tourism. Nat. Clim. Change **8**, 522–528 (2018). https://doi.org/10.1038/ s41558-018-0141-x
4. Bock, K.: The changing nature of city tourism and its possible implications for the future of cities. Eur. J. Futures Res. **3**(1), 1–8 (2015). https://doi.org/10.1007/s40309-015-0078-5
5. Ramaswami, A., et al.: A social-ecological-infrastructural systems framework for interdisciplinary study of sustainable city systems. J. Ind. Ecol. **16**, 801–813 (2012). https://doi.org/ 10.1111/j.1530-9290.2012.00566.x
6. Koens, K., Postma, A., Papp, B.: Is overtourism overused? Understanding the impact of tourism in a city context. Sustainability **10**, 4384 (2018). https://doi.org/10.3390/ su10124384
7. Scott, D., Hall, C.M., Gössling, S.: A report on the Paris climate change agreement and its implications for tourism: why we will always have Paris. J. Sustain. Tour. **24**, 933–948 (2016). https://doi.org/10.1080/09669582.2016.1187623
8. McKercher, B., Wang, D., Park, E.: Social impacts as a function of place change. Ann. Tour. Res. **50**, 52–66 (2015). https://doi.org/10.1016/J.ANNALS.2014.11.002
9. Mata, J.: Intelligence and innovation for city tourism sustainability. In: Fayos-Solà, E., Cooper, C. (eds.) The Future of Tourism, pp. 213–232. Springer, Cham (2019). https://doi. org/10.1007/978-3-319-89941-1_11
10. Timur, S., Getz, D.: Sustainable tourism development: how do destination stakeholders perceive sustainable urban tourism? Sustain. Dev. **17**, 220–232 (2009). https://doi.org/10. 1002/sd.384
11. Romero Dexeus, C.: The deepening effects of the digital revolution. In: Fayos-Solà, E., Cooper, C. (eds.) The Future of Tourism, pp. 43–69. Springer, Cham (2019). https://doi.org/ 10.1007/978-3-319-89941-1_3
12. SCITHOS – Smart City Hospitality. https://scithos.eu/. Accessed 5 Apr 2019
13. Reed, M.S., et al.: The importance of social learning in restoring the multifunctionality of rivers and floodplains. Ecol. Soc. **15**, 10 (2010). What is social learning? Response to Pahl-Wostl. 2006
14. Mayer, I.S.: Playful Organisations & Learning Systems. NHTV Breda University of Applied Science. Breda/The Hague, The Netherlands (2016). ISBN 978-90-825477-0-2
15. Quinn, R.E., Rohrbaugh, J.: A spatial model of effectiveness criteria: towards a competing values approach to organizational analysis. Manag. Sci. **29**, 363–377 (1983). https://doi.org/ 10.1287/mnsc.29.3.363
16. Camagni, R., Capello, R., Nijkamp, P.: Towards sustainable city policy: an economy-environment technology nexus. Ecol. Econ. **24**, 103–118 (1998)
17. Choi, H.C., Sirakaya, E.: Sustainability indicators for managing community tourism. Tour. Manag. **27**, 1274–1289 (2006). https://doi.org/10.1016/j.tourman.2005.05.018
18. Ko, T.G.: Development of a tourism sustainability assessment procedure: a conceptual approach. Tour. Manag. **26**, 431–445 (2005)
19. Hunter, C., Shaw, J.: The ecological footprint as a key indicator of sustainable tourism. Tour. Manag. **28**, 46–57 (2007)

234 J. Weber-Sabil et al.

20. Lalicic, L., Weber-Sabil, J.: Stakeholder engagement in sustainable tourism planning through serious gaming. Tour. Geogr. (2019, in press). Special Issue on Research Methods
21. McCabe, S., Sharples, M., Foster, C.: Stakeholder engagement in the design of scenarios of technology-enhanced tourism services. Tour. Manag. Persp. **4**, 36–44 (2012). https://doi.org/10.1016/J.TMP.2012.04.007
22. Keijser, X., et al.: Stakeholder engagement in maritime spatial planning: the efficacy of a serious game approach. Water (Switzerland) **10**(6), 1–16 (2018). https://doi.org/10.3390/w10060724
23. Poplin, A.: Games and serious games in urban planning: study cases. In: Murgante, B., Gervasi, O., Iglesias, A., Taniar, D., Apduhan, B.O. (eds.) ICCSA 2011. LNCS, vol. 6783, pp. 1–14. Springer, Heidelberg (2011). https://doi.org/10.1007/978-3-642-21887-3_1

Simulation Games as a Framework to Conduct Scientific Experiments – The Example of Prospect Theory Research

Małgorzata Ćwil[(✉)]

Kozminski University, 57/59 Jagiellonska Street, 03-301 Warsaw, Poland
mcwil@kozminski.edu.pl

Abstract. The main aim of this article is to examine the possibility of using simulation games as a framework to conduct scientific experiments. The main advantage of this solution is the fact that a researcher can provide the conditions that are as similar to real-life situations as possible while at the same time having control over the environment and control variables. This way of carrying out experiments aims at maximizing the ecological validity of the study. In the described research simulation game is used as a framework to verify the main hypothesis from prospect theory – one of the most prominent behavioral economic theories concerning the way people make decisions in situations involving risk. The results of the conducted experiment are described and conclusions for the future research are drawn.

Keywords: Simulation game · Experiment · Prospect theory

1 Introduction

Controlled experiments constitute a fundamental part of the scientific practice and are used in numerous scientific disciplines – social sciences, medicine, engineering and many more. The main aim of scientific experiments is to verify the hypothesis in controlled conditions. In laboratory research a person that is being tested often is asked to make some choices, however they do not influence his real life. This is one of the main drawbacks of controlled experiments which results in low ecological validity of research, meaning that it would be hard or even impossible to generalize the findings to a real life setting. In this article the author hypothesizes that this can be at least partially overcome by using simulation games as a framework for scientific experiments. In a simulation game we can analyze the process of making decisions that influence the player situation within a game. In this article a research is conducted on the basis of prospect theory using simulation game as a framework.

2 Scientific Experiments

Experiment is one of the most popular methods of conducting scientific research and forms a fundamental part of the scientific practice that aims to increase our knowledge about the world [1]. In an experiment an independent variable (the cause) is

© Springer Nature Switzerland AG 2021
M. Wardaszko et al. (Eds.): ISAGA 2019, LNCS 11988, pp. 235–246, 2021.
https://doi.org/10.1007/978-3-030-72132-9_21

manipulated while the dependent variable (the outcome) is measured [2]. In its simplest form an experiment aims to predict the outcome by introducing a change of the pre-conditions. In this process any extraneous variables are controlled, meaning that they stay at constant level to prevent external factors from affecting the results. The aim of the experiment is to scientifically test a stated hypothesis.

2.1 History

One of the first experiments that was conducted in a similar way to modern times was in 18th century by James Lind [3]. This Scottish doctor run clinical trials on potential remedies for scurvy in 1747. James Lind selected 12 men from the ship, all suffering from scurvy, with similar effects to reduce extraneous variation and divided them into six pairs. Each of the pairs got different supplements to their basic diet for two weeks and it led to the conclusions that citrus fruits can be used to cure scurvy.

At the end of 19th century a theory of statistical inference was developed by Charles Peirce in "Illustrations of the Logic of Science" [4] and from that time is widely used in scientific experiments. Nowadays researchers conduct a wide range of different types of experiment where the most important ones are described in the next part of the article.

2.2 Types of Experiments

There are a few different classifications of scientific experiments but the most important one from the point of view of this research is the one taking into consideration conditions in which an experiment takes place. We can distinguish laboratory (controlled) experiments, field experiments and natural experiments [2].

Natural experiments are conducted in everyday environment of the participants while the experimenter has no control over the independent variable as it occurs naturally in real life. In comparison, during field experiments the researcher has influence on and actually manipulates the independent variable. The experiment still takes place in a real-life setting, so it is impossible to really control extraneous variables.

The level of control in laboratory experiments is the highest. They are conducted in a well-controlled environment – it does not have to be a laboratory - where accurate measurements are possible. The researcher decides where the experiment takes place, at what time, with which participants, in what circumstances etc. This kind of experiments undoubtedly has many important strengths, for example the possibility to replicate a research. Controlled experiments are carried out using a standardized procedure so that other researchers can conduct similar ones. However, the artificiality of the setting may produce unnatural behavior that does not reflect real life. This problem is known as low ecological validity [5, 6] and means that it would be impossible to generalize the findings to a real life setting.

The main research question in this article is whether we can use simulation games to minimize the low ecological validity of experiments, especially the ones concerning prospect theory. The decisions that a player makes within a game does influence his situation in the game, so the decisions should be more natural and more similar to real-life ones in comparison to the results of many laboratory psychological experiments that does not affect decision-maker's life at all.

3 Prospect Theory

The experiments within this research have been conducted on the basis of prospect theory. This is one of the most prominent behavioral economic theories concerning the way people make decisions in situations involving risk [7, 8]. This behavioral, normative theory was created by Daniel Kahneman and Amos Tversky in 1979 which describes how do people really behave rather than says what leads to optimal decisions.

The prospect theory shows how people decide between alternatives that involve risk and uncertainty, in situations where they know what the probability of different outcomes is. It states that people make decisions based on the potential value of losses and gains rather than the final outcome and that people evaluate these losses and gains using heuristics.

Furthermore people behave differently in the case of possible loses and gains. Humans in general are loss-averse and dislike losses more than they like the equivalent gains and as a result the value function in prospect theory is steeper for losses (Fig. 1). They are also willing to take risks to avoid a loss.

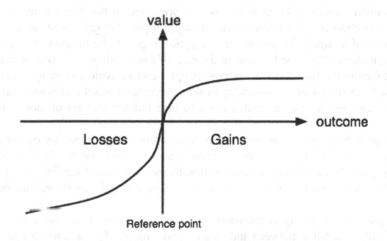

Fig. 1. The value function according to prospect theory.

The interplay of overweighting of small probabilities and concavity-convexity of the value function leads to the so-called fourfold pattern of risk attitudes (Table 1). People are risk-averse when gains have moderate probabilities or losses have small probabilities and at the same time they are risk-seeking when losses have moderate probabilities or gains have small probabilities [9].

Table 1. The fourfold pattern of risk attitudes – examples of decisions.

Example	Gains	Losses
High probability (certainty effect)	A: 100% chance to obtain $9,500 B: 95% chance to win $10,000 Behavior: Fear of disappointment, risk aversion Choice: A	A: 100% chance to lose $9,500 B: 95% chance to lose $10,000 Behavior: Hope to avoid loss, risk seeking Choice: B
Low probability (possibility effect)	A: 100% chance to obtain $500 B: 5% chance to win $10,000 Behavior: Hope of a large gain, risk seeking Choice: B	A: 100% chance to lose $500 B: 5% chance to lose $10,000 Behavior: Fear of a large loss, risk aversion Choice: A

In all of the pairs of choices presented in the Table 1, each of the choices have the same expected value – on average the expected gains or losses are the same. The choices differ, however, in terms of risk. As presented in the Table 1 people have a tendency to choose risky options in the situation of possible gains when there is a low probability of a huge gain, but the certain option seems to be unsatisfactorily low for decision makers. The same happens in the case of losses when there is a chance (even small) to avoid the loss. On the contrary, people tend to avoid risk in the situation of gains when there is a small probability of not getting the reward and in the situation of losses when there is even a small chance to lose but the amount of money is comparatively high.

The probability distortion stems from the fact that people generally do not look at the value of probability uniformly between 0 and 1. Lower probability is said to be over-weighted (people are over concerned with the outcome of the probability) while high probability is under-weighted (people are not concerned enough with the outcome of the probability).

An another interesting phenomenon concerning making decisions in risky situations, is the difference between individuals and groups. Teams tend to make more extreme choices than the individuals, meaning that in all of the situation they usually choose more risky option [10–12]. It applies to gain and loss situations, with both – low or high probability of obtaining certain results. This tendency is known as a group polarization effect and was first defined in 1970s [12, 13].

4 Experiment Design

The objective of this paper is to verify the prospect theory hypothesis in decisions made within simulation games. In traditional psychological experiments concerning decision making process researchers show to participants two different options from which they need to choose only one. The problem is that the choices usually does not affect their lives. The majority of experiments testing the prospect theory hypotheses were conducted in artificial situations. This means that the test subjects could not win or lose a given amount of money.

Simulation games create a great opportunity to test the prospect theory hypothesis in situations where research subjects can win or lose a defined amount of money within the simulation game. There is a possibility to make an experiment, which outcomes will influence the player performance. In this way, the decisions made should be more important for decision makers.

In this research three different hypothesis were tested:

H1: In gain situations, when there is a high probability of winning, people tend to avoid taking risk.

H2: In gain situations, when there is a little probability of winning, people have a tendency to take risk.

H3: In loss situations, when there is a high probability of losing money, people have a tendency to take risk.

The hypotheses were tested by analysing the decisions made by single players and teams while playing Marketplace business simulation game. In each of the situations research subjects had to choose one from the two options, where one choice was risky and the other was not. All of the situations were closely linked to the narrated story of the simulation game and had exactly the same expected value. The results of the study show whether we can confirm prospect theory hypotheses on the basis of decisions made within simulation games.

A simulation game attempts to copy various activities from real life in the form of a game for various purposes such as training, analysis, or prediction [14]. Business simulation concentrates on aspects related to managing a company, such as: marketing, human resources management or finance and accounting.

In the designed experiment the Marketplace simulation game was used. It is a business simulation created by Innovative Learning Solutions Inc and regularly used during management courses in one of the main business universities in Poland. In this simulation game students play in teams and their main task is to launch a new product (computers) to the market and manage the entire product life cycle - from introduction through growth to maturity. Students form teams of 3–6 players. Each of the players has its own area of responsibility (ex. marketing and product design, Fig. 2) but the team needs to formulate the strategy together and manage the company.

The game consists of six to eight decision rounds, each of them representing one quarter of a year in the real life. Students make decisions simultaneously during each of the rounds. After the decision have been submitted by all teams, choices are processed and feedback is displayed. In the scenario of the game there is a possibility to add some

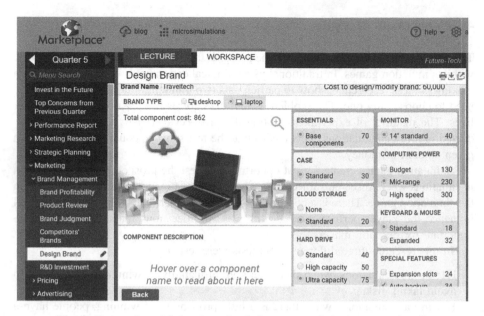

Fig. 2. Screen from Marketplace simulation game – designing a new brand.

extra decisions with risk and uncertainty. The decisions concerning gains are usually connected with some of the rewards that virtual companies get or some different investor options. In the case of losses – companies get some penalties or fines that need to be paid for.

Examples of decision situations involving risk added to Marketplace simulation game scenario in the described experiment:

Situation no. 1: gains, high probability of winning
There are two investors interested in financing your company. You have to choose between the following options:

A: One of the investors is a huge, stable company of international renown. They will finance you with an amount of $3,800,000. This investment option is certain due to the investor's reputation.

B: The other investor is a small, aggressive hedge fund. They are prepared to offer you an investment of $4,000,000. This investment option is however burdened by risk. There is a 5% chance, that the investor's money transfer will not go through.

Situation no. 2: gains, little probability of winning
Your advertisement has received an award in a local media event. You can either choose to cash out (30,000$) or to have this advertisement sent to a major international advertisement competition in Cannes (main prize: 300,000$). It is estimated that there is a 10% chance that you will win the competition in Cannes.

A: 30.000$ with 100%
B: 300.000$ with 10%

Situation no 3: gains, little probability of winning
Congratulations! You have received an award from local MoneySaver magazine for the best product for Costcutter target group! You can choose to take the prize ($10,000) or invest this money in a bet that in 2017 Leicester will win the Champions League ($200,000 with 5% chance).

A: $10,000 with 100%
B: $200,000 with 5%

Situation no 4: gains, little probability of winning
Your superior sales system has been noticed by a national investment fund targeting start-up companies with a potentially good future. You can either receive a grant from the fund immediately ($20,000) or apply for funding from EU ($200,000 with 10% chance).

A: $20,000 with 100%
B: $200,000 with 10%

Situation no 5: losses, high probability of loosing
You have been sued for your advertisement "GOD DAMN IT 2". Your rivals claim that this ad is deceptive and does not represent the truth. You have the following options:

A: Settle out of court. That way you are certain to pay an amount of $90,000.
B: Go to court and fight the suit. There is a 10% chance that the judge may decide you have been unrightfully sued, but if he/she judges you guilty, your company will have to pay indemnities in the amount of $100,000.

Situation no 6: losses, high probability of losing
Due to the lack of decisions and delays in CE marking certification process your company has not been allowed to sell its computers in the UK on the planned date. Your company has also been fined for not conforming to all the norms specified by the EU for electronical equipment to be sold within the Common Market. You have the following options:

A: You can either go to trial with the European Commission. That way you can avoid paying the penalty (10% probability) but in case you lose (90% probability) your company will have to pay $100,000.
B: You can decide to settle with the EC and pay $90.000.

Situation no 7: losses, high probability of loosing
The lack of decisions caused the delays in obtaining the permission for factory construction. You can be fined by the construction site inspector. There are two possible options:

A: You pay the penalty of $90,000.
B: You try to bribe the inspector. There is 90% chance that the penalty will be higher ($100,000) and 10% probability that you will escape from paying the fine.

Each of the players was asked to make a certain choice. First of all, the players made choices individually and then – in teams. Each team consisted of people managing one of the virtual companies. If a team chose certain option – the money was immediately transferred to or from the account in the simulation game. If the team chose risky option – they learned the final results of their decisions shortly after making a choice. The researcher used the easiest way to provide proper probability of winning or losing money. She had a box with small pieces of papers on which there was one of the numbers written from 1 to 100. If a risky option was chosen - for example 10% chances of winning money – a person or a team drew a number from the box where 1 to 10 meant that they are winning the money.

The choices that will be analyzed in the experiment are personal ones as well as group ones. First of all, each of the players had to define their individual choices and only then, the whole teams was asked to choose one of the options. The control variables that were taken into consideration in the research include: current position within the game, cash balance, role in the team (CEO or other) and gender of the decision maker.

5 Results

In the experiment a total number of 207 people were included, accordingly: 38 to verify the first hypothesis (gain situation, a high probability of winning, risk-avoidance), 120 to verify the second one (gain situation, a little probability of winning, risk-seeking) and 49 for the last hypothesis (loss situation, a high probability of losing, risk-seeking) (Table 2).

Table 2. Number of people included in the experiment.

H1	N	38
H2	N	120
H3	N	49

H1: In gain situations, when there is a high probability of winning, people tend to avoid taking risk.

Table 3. Results of the experiment (hypothesis 1).

	N	%
No risk	33	86,8
Risk	5	13,2

The first hypothesis assumes that in situations when people have an opportunity to gain money and there is a high probability of winning it, they tend to avoid risk. This hypothesis was verified using Marketplace simulation and the results are presented in the Table 3. The vast majority of people (33 out of 38) did not want to take a risk in the gain situation when there is a high probability of winning. This is in accordance with previous laboratory research [9].

H2: In gain situations, when there is a little probability of winning, people have a tendency to take risk.

Table 4. Results of the experiment (hypothesis 2).

	N	%
No risk	21	17,5
Risk	99	82,5

The second hypothesis states that in gain situations with low probability of winning money, people tend to take risk. According to the results presented in the Table 4 more than 80% of respondents chose the risky option.

H3: In loss situations, when there is a high probability of losing money, people have a tendency to take risk.

Table 5. Results of the experiment (hypothesis 3).

	N	%
No risk	13	26,5
Risk	36	73,5

The third hypothesis concerns loss situations with high probability of losing money. According to prospect theory in this kind of situations people have a tendency to take risks. The results of the experiment are in accordance with this theory – almost 3 out of 4 players took risk in this kind of situations (Table 5).

To sum up this part of the research, the results obtained from the experiment conducted using simulation game are in line with prospect theory findings (Fig. 3). In gain situations, when there is a high probability of winning, most of the people chose non-risky option. On the contrary, in gain situations, when there is a little probability of winning and in loss situations, when there is a high probability of losing money the majority of people decided to take risk.

During the experiment, there was a chance to observe the choices made by single players as well as the teams. The results of personal and team choices are compared in the Table 6.

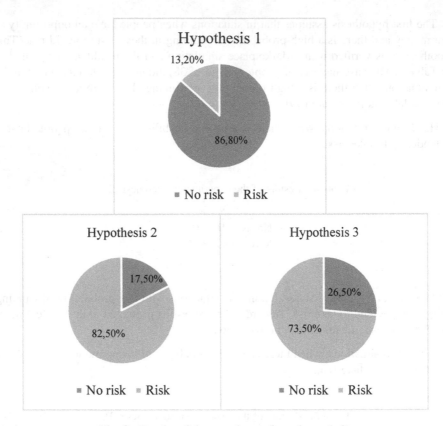

Fig. 3. Results of the experiment (hypotheses 1–3).

Table 6. Personal versus group decisions.

		Personal decisions	Group decisions
H1	No risk	86,8%	84,2%
	Risk	13,2%	15,8%
H2	No risk	17,5%	10,8%
	Risk	82,5%	89,2%
H3	No risk	26,5%	18,4%
	Risk	73,5%	81,6%

As it can be observed in the Table 6, groups more often choose a risky option in comparison to individual decisions. This trend can be observed in all of the situations – gains or losses, high or low probability of gain or loss. It is similar to what has already been described by the researcher running controlled laboratory experiments [10–12]. This is known as a group polarization effect - a tendency of a group to make decisions that are more extreme than the initial inclination of its members.

The impact of controlled variables was also verified. Surprisingly, such factors as gender or position in the team did not affect the acceptance of risk. No matter in which situation a person was – gain or loses, high or low probability of obtaining certain results – his/her gender did not influence his/her choices. While verifying each of the hypothesis the similar percentages of men and women chose the risky option (Table 7). This dependence was confirmed using Chi-square test.

Table 7. Contingency table presenting the correlation between gender and choosing risky options.

			Women	Men	All
H1	No risk	N	18	15	33
		% from gender	100,0%	75,0%	86,8%
	Risk	N	0	5	5
		% from gender	0,0%	25,0%	13,2%
H2	No risk	N	14	7	21
		% from gender	22,6%	12,1%	17,5%
	Risk	N	48	51	99
		% from gender	77,4%	87,9%	82,5%
H3	No risk	N	5	8	13
		% from gender	25,0%	27,6%	26,5%
	Risk	N	15	21	36
		% from gender	75,0%	72,4%	73,5%

6 Discussion

The results of the conducted experiment show that simulation games can be used as a framework to carry out scientific experiments. There are some unquestionable advantages of this solution. First of all, the environment that is in the simulation game represents real-life conditions and decisions that are made within the simulation are similar to the ones undertaken in the real world. The players can see the results of their choices immediately – the money shortly after making a decision is transferred to or from their account. The decision that they make and its result has an impact on their scores in business simulation game. This environment have the most important advantages of laboratory experiments and at the same time limits its drawbacks. Secondly, this risky choice is just one from the series of decisions that players make within the game which is more similar to the situations that we have in the real world.

The results of the experiment stand in line with the results of other experiments, confirming that in some of the situation people prefer to take risk and, in some others, – to avoid it. Moreover, Marketplace simulation game provides an environment that makes it easy to compare the decisions made by individuals and teams.

7   Limitations of the Study and Future Research

The idea of using simulation games as a framework to conduct scientific experiments should be tested more widely – with different theories. However, the results of experiments give positive feedback towards using simulation games as such a framework, especially while conducting research concerning decision making process.

During the study three main hypothesis were verified, and additionally – group decisions were compared to individual ones. In the future the fourth hypothesis from prospect theory can be tested. This is the one in which people are in possible loss situation, where there is a low probability of losing money (but the quantity is quite high). People should show the fear of loss in this situation and be risk-averse.

Moreover, the possibility to use simulation games as a framework to conduct scientific experiments should definitely be verified using other traditional experiments to compare its results to classical laboratory ones.

References

1. Soldatova, L.N., King, R.D.: An ontology of scientific experiments. J. R. Soc. Interf. **3**(11), 795–803 (2006)
2. Shaughnessy, J.J., Zechmeister, E.B., Zechmeister, J.S.: Research methods in psychology. McGraw-Hill, New York (2000)
3. Dunn, P.M.: James Lind (1716–94) of Edinburgh and the treatment of scurvy. Arch. Dis. Child.-Fetal Neonatal Ed. **76**(1), F64–F65 (1997)
4. Peirce, C.S.: Illustrations of the Logic of Science. Open Court, Chicago (2014)
5. Encyclopaedia Britannica, Inc.: EncyclopaediaBritannica. Encyclopaedia Britannica, Incorporated (1969)
6. Brewer, M.: Research design and issues of validity. In: Reis, H., Judd, C. (eds.) Handbook of Research Methods in Social and Personality Psychology. Cambridge University Press, Cambridge (2000)
7. Kahneman, D., Tversky, A.: Prospect theory: an analysis of decision under risk. In: Handbook of the Fundamentals of Financial Decision Making: Part I, pp. 99–127 (2013)
8. Kahneman, D., Egan, P.: Thinking, Fast and Slow, vol. 1. Farrar, Straus and Giroux, New York (2011)
9. Kahneman, D.: Thinking. Fast and Slow, Macmillan, New York (2011)
10. Stoner, J.A.: Risky and cautious shifts in group decisions: the influence of widely held values. J. Exp. Soc. Psychol. **4**(4), 442–459 (1968)
11. Stoner, J.A.F.: A comparison of individual and group decisions involving risk. Doctoral dissertation, Massachusetts Institute of Technology (1961)
12. Myers, D.G., Lamm, H.: The group polarization phenomenon. Psychol. Bull. **83**(4), 602 (1976)
13. McCauley, C.R.: Extremity shifts, risk shifts and attitude shifts after group discussion. Eur. J. Soc. Psychol. **2**(4), 417–436 (1972)
14. Jones, K.: Simulations: A Handbook for Teachers and Trainers. Routledge, Abingdon (2013)

Study on Occurrence Mechanism of Quality Scandal in Enterprises by "Sontaku", "Air" and "Water" Theory Using Business Game

Hiroyasu Seita[1(✉)] and Setsuya Kurahashi[2(✉)]

[1] Faculty of System and Information Engineering, Department of Risk Engineering, University of Tsukuba, Tsukuba, Japan
s1830138@u.tsukuba.ac.jp
[2] Graduate School of Business Sciences, University of Tsukuba, Tsukuba, Japan
kurahashi.setsuya.gf@u.tsukuba.ac.jp

Abstract. The quality assurance falsification continues in a part of Japanese companies that have been sweeping the world with its top priority on customer first principles and quality first principles. In these cases of misrepresentation, as seen in the Akafuku case of the food fraud, there are cases in which the conjecture to a specific target worked. Until now, each company has been absolutely quality based on quality first principle, why is it so fragile and crumbling why?

In this research, we use a business game based on the framework of the Giddens's theory of structuring to show that "quality" is absolutely made with "sontaku" and "air" theory, which can be said as unique culture of Japan as Mr. Shichihei Yamamoto says, and furthermore that it is collapsed due to real problems.

Keywords: Serious games · Simulation · Corporate fraud

1 Introduction

1.1 Consciousness of Problem-Organizational Culture and Corporate Scandal of Quality First Principle of Japanese Companies

In production activities, the ZD movement has become one of the major codes of conduct for quality control in Japan as well as QC activities. In recent years, It is said that production activities and service industries in the Japanese manufacturing industry have also been emphasized and have a significant contribution. On the other hand, it has also been pointed out that the word "zero defect" is the cause of an increase in management costs due to quality deviation, and hence high cost constitution. In the research conducted by [1], cost is emphasized by analyzing the problem-solving behavior of process engineers who play a central role in determining quality and production cost in the first line of production. It is revealed that quality is overwhelmingly emphasized in comparison with cost even at the production site.

M. Wardaszko et al. (Eds.): ISAGA 2019, LNCS 11988, pp. 247–258, 2021.
https://doi.org/10.1007/978-3-030-72132-9_22

However, in recent years, why is the case of quality scandal occurring one after another in leading manufacturers in Japan?

2 Research Background

2.1 Mechanism of Falsification

A United States organized crime researcher [2] systematizes the mechanism of occurrence as "The Fraud Triangle" as follows.

1. "Pressure" - Psychological pressure, such as having to meet excessive desires for delivery and productivity.
2. "Opportunity" - Vulnerable organizational environment that cannot prevent fraud
3. "Justification" - "Justification" is reasoning to convince the cheating that you have done for selfish reasons such as "for a short time" or "not rational"..

These are common to many fraud cases, but they are only qualitative. It is important in the specific cause investigation and measures to quantitatively measure how large each factor leads to the actual misrepresentation, but its quantification has not been studied.

In addition, according to [3], organizational scandals are brought about by the collapse of defense in depth that is soft defense such as rules and procedures, training, administration and qualifications and hard defense such as engineering safety facilities, equipment, alarm and nondestructive inspection. Breakdown of defense in depth is because that potential factors are triggered by insecurity by organizational factors such as determination of management's awareness, budget allocation, personnel assignment, planning, communication, management, etc., or worker factors such as excessive time, Lack of labor, inadequate equipment, lack of training. It is reported that the damage will be brought out to the outside.

Reason's theory is easy to detect what can be linked to concrete measures, but does not take into consideration the development process of the interaction between individuals, organizations and society, and time-series structure.

2.2 Giddens's Theory of Structuring; the Mechanism of the Development of Organizational Culture by the Recursion of Individuals and Organizations, Society

Giddens [4] explained the problems of socio-cultural theory such as functionalism and hermitism based on dualism in the theory of structuring. The theory of structuring states that while social structures are created by individual actions, at the same time such social structures are themselves created by individual actions. Social structure recursively described the relationship between personal actions and social structure as having such dual character.

However, although it provides a basic framework that can express the development process of individuals, organizations, and social interactions and structures well (Fig. 1).

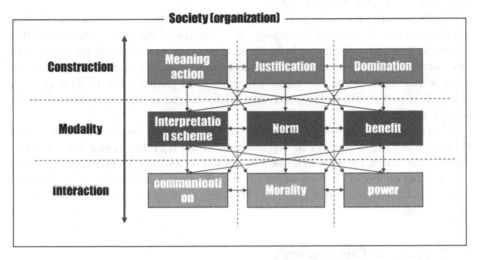

Fig. 1. Interactions, modalities, and structures according to the theory of structuring in Giddens.

Majima [5] developed A. Giddens's theory of organization into organizational scandals, and structural changes due to time series interaction with [6], micro and macro links (interactions with individuals and society) Applied to the organizational scandals. As a result, he modeled how the organizational culture to be created between individuals, organizations, and society would be distorted and developed into an organizational scandal. By applying the Giddens framework to the problem of corporate scandal, the process of representation can be successfully depicted with the interaction of individuals, organizations and society with time-series changes. However, identification of specific causes and quantification of their effects have not been achieved, and the ability to provide specific measures is not enough. In addition, it has not been able to take into account Japan's unique social climate issues such as "Sontak", self-approval, which is behavior to infer what you want your partner to do, and act by yourself even if you are not told.

2.3   The Occurrence of Quality Scandals Due to "Sontaku" and Yamamoto's "Air" and "Water" Theory

According to [Yamamoto. 83], "air", atmosphere in English, is a situation not to be able to say "no" in which everyone feels in conversations and discussions in real society, while everyone recognizes that it is not acceptable and should be denied.

This "air" is based on fictitious beliefs that are not based on grounds or facts. And this atmosphere is often accompanied by slogans and idols that symbolize it. This slogan or idol's obedience acts as a power or judgment standard, greatly affecting the decisions of things. This function is called "Sontaku" in Japanese and is one of the causes of corporate scandals in Japan.

If this is compared with quality, it is a conviction that "the quality is absolute (quality first principle), and the company cannot survive if the quality gets worse" that dominates Japanese companies. In Japanese companies, passing defective products to customers is a bad thing and it is considered taboo, and excessive consideration is given to customers and despite being sufficiently good products, it is likely to be a big defect. It is over-costed to the quality that is absolutized as "the possibility of losing credibility".

However, these curseds will eventually be relativized and lose their absolute power if losses due to some actual delivery date or cost are regarded as problems. We call them "water", same meaning to throw a cold water on the idea. Furthermore, when this chaotic state continues, it is considered more important than the quality to keep the delivery date, which is a real problem, eventually, leading to a fraud to maintain the delivery date.

3   Purpose of This Research

3.1   Verification of the Mechanism of Corporate Scandal of the Cheating in Quality Judgment by "Sontaku" "Air" and "Water" Theory Using Business Game

Therefore, in this research, we try to show, using the business game, the quality first principle that has been absolutized by "Sontaku" to the customer has led to the corporate scandal, with Cressie's the fraud triangle theory, Giddens and Majima's the structure theory of organizational culture, and Yamamoto's "air" and "water" theory.

4   Business Game Development

4.1   Business Game Specifications

In this game, as a remedial application process when a quality defect occurs, the game determines a remedial method based on a determined company rule. The scenario shown in the game manual like following (Figs. 2 and 3).

1) You are the Quality Department Representative. You are responsible for product shipping decisions.
2) The products currently being produced are products expected to become the next major product, but if the quality is not stable and the shipping deadlines is

approaching. So It is necessary to determine the possibility of shipping taking into consideration the situation of the customer.

3) We have set up special remedies for this product that is not stable in quality.
4) There are two types of remedies, customer remedies and in-house remedies, and it is required to use properly depending on the degree of quality defect.

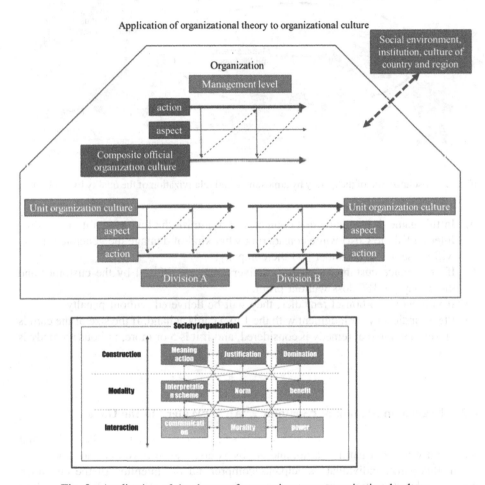

Fig. 2. Application of the theory of structuring to an organizational culture.

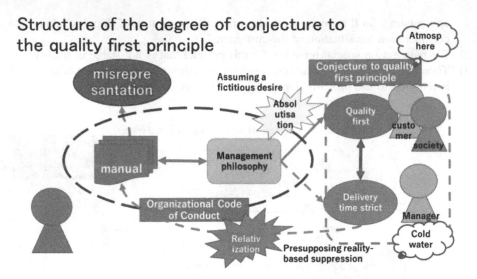

Fig. 3. Absolutization of the quality by atmosphere and relativization of the quality by cold water.

5) In this game, it is a game that competes to minimize the loss of quality cost (IFC; Internal Failure Cost) while considering what kind of damage the generated defect will cause to the customer and the company.

6) If you choice customer remedies, delivery may be refused by the customer and there may got IFC loss without profit.

7) If you choice in-housel remedies, they will be delivered without penalty.

8) Please indicate your judgment with the 1 to 9 cards at hand. If the size of the card is closer to 9, internal remedy is considered, and if it is 5 or more, in-house remedy is judged.

4.2   Evaluation Method of "Sontaku", "Air", "Water" in the Game

In Japan's high context society, a "Sontak", self-approval, which is behavior to infer what you want your partner to do, and act by yourself even if you are not told.

In this game, individual participants comprehend the intention of the customer, choose high-risk customer remedy, ignoring the outcome of the game. But it is to be a in-house remedy. Therefore, the "Sontaku" to the customer in this game is the act of expecting the profit by gaining the customer's credit by not shipping the defective product to the customer. At the same time, shipping even a few defective items is an exaggerated fear of bringing about a crisis for the company.

"Water" in this context refers to realistic problems such as "delivery time", "guidelines for relief", "supervisor's orders" and the like. Express the size of "Sontaku" as the difference between the judgment result originally requested by the game rule (It is expected from the rules of the game to be 9).

Therefore, as an evaluation method of the degree of "Sontaku", when the degree of "Sontaku" is S, reasonable expectations predicted from game rules is R (= 9), and the group judgment value is G, it can be expressed by the following equation.

$$S = R - G$$

5   Experimental Result

The composition of the game participants was 10 people including one graduate teacher, 8 men and 2 women, and the age is from late 20's to late 50's. From the answers of the questions prepared in advance, they were divided into "A group of honest thinking" and "B team of rational thinking", and debriefing is performed after the game was over. Table 1, 2 and 3 shows Judgment factors and corresponding group judgments for each question, and rational judgment results requested from the game. In addition, the judgment results of individuals and groups are shown in Fig. 4, 5, 6 and 7.

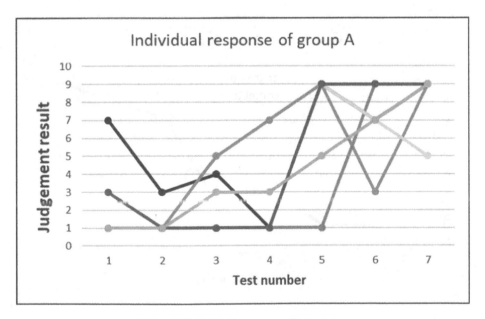

Fig. 4. Individual response of group A.

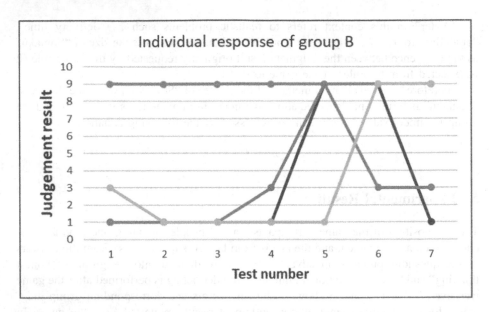

Fig. 5. Individual response of group B.

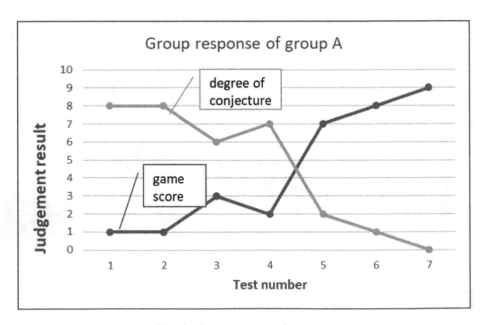

Fig. 6. Group response of group A.

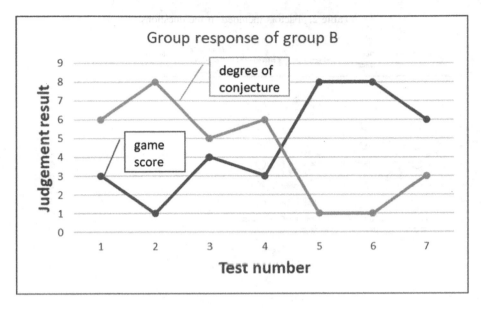

Fig. 7. Group response of group B.

Table 1. Questions of each scenario.

Cenario settings
Q1 There is a light defect in the item which is not in the customer requirement standard in the product. The delivery date is tomorrow.
Q2 We decided to deliver to company B, which is just fine because the product performance is at the upper limit of specifications.
Q3 Quality standards within the IFC target tend to deviate within the limits of measurement error. Customers have a high safety factor and no problem.
Q4 Although it was NG in the measuring instrument in the process, it became OK if it measured again.
Q5 It exceeds standards but does not affect customer quality. It is said that the customer side is not a problem because it is an urgent requirement. Also, if you keep the delivery date, you can get gold coins by raising customer credit.
Q6 It was clearly out of spec, but it was ordered to be rescued by the president's decision because it involved a large business talk.
Q7 The product has an appearance defect that is not a customer requirement item. There seems to be no problem in product performance and application. It will be delayed if we do not deliver by tomorrow.

Table 2. Factors included in the questions.

	Specification target item	Out of standard	Delivery date	Performance	Transfer to another company	Customer acceptance	Incentive	power
Q1	×	△	×	○				
Q2	○	○		○	○			
Q3	○	○		○				
Q4	○	○						
Q5	○	×	×	○		○	○	
Q6	○	×		×				○
Q7	×	△	×	○				

○ : Standard object
× : Not subject to standard

○ : Within the standard
△ : Mild
× : Severe

× : Delivery time will be late

○ : No customer impact
× : Affect customers

Table 3. Judgement results.

	A	B	Judgment result of group A	Judgment result of group B	Judgment result by game rule	
Q1	1	3	customer's remedy	customer's remedy	in-house remedy	×
Q2	1	1	customer's remedy	customer's remedy	in-house remedy	×
Q3	3	4	customer's remedy	customer's remedy	in-house remedy	×
Q4	2	3	customer's remedy	customer's remedy	in-house remedy	×
Q5	7	8	in-house remedy	in-house remedy	customer's remedy	×
Q6	8	8	in-house remedy	in-house remedy	in-house remedy	○
Q7	9	6	in-house remedy	in-house remedy	in-house remedy	○

6 Discussion

Looking at the group judgments (see Table 3), questions 1 to 4 also select customer remedies for items that should be in-house remedies from the request of the game. Those that fall under the specification item or anything suspicious are considered costly customer remedies.

In question 5, the game rules should not be approved by the person in charge from the rules of the game, so it should be a customer remedy, but it is judged as an in-house remedy because the customer's consent is obtained regardless of that. It seems that a strong peer pressure is working. In fact, even in the subsequent debriefings, there were comments that "because the customer is good."

In Question 6, although it is an obvious failure, it is an in-house remedy. This is considered to be the result of the large power of approval of the president and the request for guidelines fulfilling the function of "water".

In Question 7, it is not a requirement item, and it is an in-house remedy due to the effect of "water" such as delayed delivery date.

In question 6, all of A's sincere groups, chose internal remedies6, while B's rational groups were divided into customer remedies and in-housel remedy. We want to emphasize that, in the post-game debriefing, one of the B group's participants said that "We certainly chose in-house remedy, but leave it in writing that this is the president's order, in case it becomes a problem later. "These actions are considered to be a manifestation of fairness as well as for self-reliance.

7 Conclusion

In this study, we modeled the mechanism of the generation of the corporate scandals, like a fraudulent misrepresentation in Japan, using a theory from to Cressie, to Giddens, to Majima, and Yamamoto's dissertation" air" and "water" discourse.

The process of corporate scandals is as follows.

When a problem occurs in a company, excessive morality is generated from the corporate philosophy which is the organizational code and the "Sontaku" to customers. These norms and morals create peer pressure and show a tendency to choose excessive measures. However, actual problems such as delivery date and profit become the action of "water" and bring about deviation from the norm. While it repeats, organizational norms are transformed and lead to corporate scandals.

Based on this, as expected, the participants of the game initially selected an altruistic customer response that would have been disadvantageous to the player, but as expected, realistic problems such as delivery time and loss would eventually occur, then they gradually come to choose the correspondence that would be in favor of the player own.

From the above, it can be said that this game reproduced the scandal occurrence process.

8 Future Issues

Furthermore, we would like to clarify the influence of each factor leading to the quality scandal by observing the behavior when using many such "water" elements.

In addition, since many participants and long game runs are difficult, we will use agent simulation to study whether individual behavior changes organizational norms and leads to social norms.

References

1. Seita, H.: Study on Quality Deviation of the Manufacturing Site in Selected Behavior by Process Engineer's Problem Solving Method, Master thesis Graduate School of Business Sciences University of Tsukuba (2016) (2018)
2. Cressey, D.R.: Other People's Money, p. 30. Patterson Smith, Montclair (1973)
3. Reason, J.: Human Error. Cambridge University Press, New York (1990)
4. Giddens, A.: New Rules of Sociological Method: A Positive Critique of Interpretative Sociologies, 2nd edn. Hutchinson, London (1976) (1993)
5. Majima, T.: Organizational scandal-analysis by organizational culture theory, Bunshindo (2007)
6. Barley, S.R.: Technology as an occasion for structuring: evidence from observations of CT scanners and the social order of radiology department. Adm. Sci. Q. 31, 78–108 (1986)

Interpersonal Competitiveness in a Cohesive Team: Insights from a Business Simulation Game

Vinod Dumblekar[1]([envelope]) and Upinder Dhar[2]

[1] Mantis, New Delhi 110025, India
games@mantis.co.in
[2] Shri Vaishnav Vidyapeeth Vishwavidyalaya, Indore 453111, India
upinderdhar@gmail.com

Abstract. Interpersonal competitiveness is the trait of an individual that affects her behaviour and performance with respect to others in similar situations. Cohesion is the characteristic of a team that facilitates the collaborative work of its members and affects their members' and team performance. To understand the nature of relationship of individual behaviour in competitive and cohesive conditions, an instrument of statements describing such behaviour was administered on 330 management graduate students at the end of their day-long business simulation game. Intrinsic motivation was the key attribute in the individual's interpersonal competitiveness. Goal orientation was the key attribute in team cohesion, and was facilitated by discussion and assessment without prejudice or pain in an environment with focus on alignment of interests and actions. The game served as a platform with conditions and experiences that provided necessary stimuli for their competitive and cohesive behaviour. Implications of this study for further research and application are discussed.

Keywords: Goal orientation · Interpersonal competitiveness · Intrinsic motivation · Open communication · Measured aggression · Mutual understanding · Proactivity · Team cohesion

1 Introduction

Individual competitiveness as a person's tendency to choose a competitive environment for entry, such as a career or games, to pursue her goals [1]. A competitive individual likes to act before others in her workplace and social groups act. She seems to edge out others in her desire to seize the opportunities and to earn the rewards before others do. She likes to battle, and may ignore her colleagues, when in competitive action. She is probably a lone fighter who succeeds due to her gutsy behaviour and inclination to attend to problems before others do. She wants to win, even if alone and under adverse circumstances. She is the reason for entrepreneurial confidence and behaviour, and may be the team's troubleshooter in crises.

Cohesion is the force that bound a team together and affected team performance in areas such as pooling skills, producing knowledge, and encouraging creativity [2]. It was a temporal phenomenon that could be best understood and measured at the team

M. Wardaszko et al. (Eds.): ISAGA 2019, LNCS 11988, pp. 259–272, 2021.
https://doi.org/10.1007/978-3-030-72132-9_23

level in terms of task and social indicators. The cohesive team has members who want to be together in the team. They like each other's company because they can depend on each other, in case of need. They make quick decisions because the members understand each other, may seldom disagree with each other, or may have cultural rituals or procedural methods to attend to interpersonal conflict. Their members seek consensus, even to attend to crisis. They do not defy the conventions because everyone conforms to the group norms.

The personality of the competitive individual vastly different from the culture of her cohesive team, especially in terms of their respective values, needs, motivations, and decision making processes. Her behaviour may be abrasive to others, and may cause friction and misunderstanding because of her apparently selfish desire to solve problems before others do. The cohesive team may not allow its members to act faster or be competitive because they value consensus more than competitive behaviour. How would her competitiveness affect the cohesive team? Are the competitive individual and the cohesive team mutually exclusive constructs? The performance of a sports team worsened during the playing season despite high social cohesion [3]. Would this team have benefitted with less groupthink and more competitive members? How can the competitive individual co-exist in her cohesive team?

1.1 Review of Literature

Interpersonal Competitiveness. Competitive consumer behaviour expresses itself in the interest of the fans in watching sports, in purchasers participating in and out-beating others in such sports, and in purchases to show superiority to others. Competitiveness in USA could be seen in the illustrative behaviour of firms in business, lawyers who fought the legal system, and managers who strived for promotions [4]. Within organisations, competitiveness was seen in the reactions of employees to performance ranking feedback; they responded by working harder and sometimes, unethically. While some competitive employees responded to enhance their status, others attempted to cheat or sabotage the work of their colleagues [5]. Game players perceived their competitors to be aggressive, after the conclusion of the game, proving that aggression was a perception produced by the competitive game experience [6].

Using the critical incident technique and thematic content analysis, 1,064 critical professional incidents were codified and studied that led to the identification of three types of competitive strategies on the basis of the behaviour of every professional in her situation and environment [7]. Destructive, short-term and long-term competitive strategies were characterised by actions such as group conflict, solving immediate problems, and brand development, respectively. Observing that competitive motivation may mean either to excel others' performance or to improve personal performance, two scales were combined to produce the competitive attitude scale [8]. The data from 1,011 adolescent school students produced two factors of the scale in adolescent competitive attitudes, viz., hyper-competitive attitude (HCA) and development-competitive attitude (DCA). HCA correlated positively with bullying and negatively with prosociality, while DCA correlated positively with prosociality.

Team Cohesion. One of the earliest descriptions from research defined as group cohesiveness as attraction between its members [9]. Such attraction reduced dissonance and disagreement among members, and that team performance was subjectively perceived and affected by contextual factors. As an interpersonal context, task cohesion in teams, interdependence, psychological safety, and group potency jointly affected the engagement of the members with implications for team learning and perceived team effectiveness [10]. Strong network ties between neighbourhood members enhanced their cohesion [11]. Perceived cohesion was found to be stronger in small groups, and the sense of belonging was a stronger predictor of cohesion than feelings of morale. However, the relationship between team cohesion and team performance was uncertain due to problems in conceptualisation and operational definitions, measures and assessments of constructs and variables used in such studies [12].

Teamwork was significantly correlated to the team cohesion attributes of attraction to the team, valued roles, and unity of purpose [13]. The self-efficacy of the team members correlated positively with the social aspect of cohesion, and was predicted by valued roles and unity of purpose. Therefore, teams with strong shared beliefs about their ability were more likely to succeed, and that members with valued roles were more likely to do well. Team cohesion and climate were some of the emerging states of intrateam efforts, which emerged from preparatory processes such as planning and strategy, action processes that included communication, collaborations, and coordination, and interactions such as interpersonal support and conflict between team members [14]. Cohesion among soldiers was an outcome of social integration and personal bonding. The reduction of psychological distress and sleep disorders of nearly 2,000 soldiers over a 10-week period was found to be related to not only improvements in their resilience but also the development of their military unit cohesion [15]. Thus, cohesion had a beneficial effect on the soldiers and could affect their performance.

1.2 Objective of This Study

A study of the relationship between the variables and their respective attributes would be valuable because the results could be generalized and extended for further research in interpersonal competitiveness and team cohesion and for better management practices. From the findings, guidelines could be developed to use the competitiveness of individuals to build and enhance the cohesiveness of teams, and vice versa. Therefore, the objective of this study was to examine the relationships between the variables, interpersonal competitiveness and team cohesion, and their respective attributes. Interpersonal competitiveness and team cohesion had been studied as constructs with stimulating conditions [16, 17]. The interpersonal competitiveness scale had five factors, viz., measured aggression, proactivity, intrinsic motivation, winning orientation, and verbal aggression. The team cohesion scale had three factors, viz., goal orientation, open communication, and mutual understanding. These factors would be the variables for this study.

2   Method

2.1   The Instrument and Its Variables

The study instrument was comprised of scales representing interpersonal competitiveness and team cohesion, and used a 5-point Likert scale that ranged from 1 (strongly disagree) to 5 (strongly agree). The Interpersonal Competitiveness scale had an internal reliability of $r = .77$ and was composed of five factors and 18 items. Data had been collected from a sample of 391 post-graduate management students from three management schools after they had played a management simulation game in a business context [16]. However, only three factors, viz., measured aggression (with six items, e.g., 'I like competition'), proactivity (with five items, all reverse scored, e.g., 'I try to avoid arguments'), and intrinsic motivation (with four items, all reverse scored, e.g., 'I try to avoid competing with others') were used in this study. The remaining two factors of the scale were not used because they were represented by only three statements.

The Business Simulation Game Team Cohesion scale had an internal reliability of $r = .89$ and was composed of 19 items [17]. Data was collected from a sample of 356 post-graduate management students of a management school after they had played a management simulation game in a business context. It had three factors, viz., goal orientation (with eight items, e.g., 'our members had positive attitudes toward the ultimate goal'), open communication (with eight items, e.g., 'we were eager to create awareness and share information within the team'), and mutual understanding (with three items, e.g., 'our team members had similar work values'). Both scales had been developed against similar playing conditions in separate business simulation games.

Aggression. Two types of aggression were identified and distinguished [18]. Hostile aggression was an impulsive and retaliatory act that was provoked by negative emotions like anger and ridicule with the evil intention to cause harm to others. In contrast, instrumental aggression was a planned effort to accomplish a goal such as profit. Aggression may sometimes be the result of the aggressor's perceived threat to her self-esteem, but not every act of aggression was violent in intent. Interactions between groups could be more aggressive than in interpersonal interactions, perhaps due to the courage and confidence evolved from the group cohesiveness [19]. Aggression was negatively correlated with the Big Five personality traits of agreeableness and conscientiousness, and positively correlated with neuroticism [20], suggesting that the aggressive person was more likely to be self-centered and have little or no concern for others or social norms. In this study, aggression was deemed to be both an attitude and the behaviour of an individual to overcome others in games, sports, and other interpersonal interactions, without any intention of the aggressor to harm her opponent.

Proactivity. Three motivational states, viz., can do, reason to, and energized to were the triggers of proactivity [21]. Thus, proactivity was defined as an emotionally charged state that made things happen, anticipated and prevented problems, and seized opportunities. It was affected by psychological differences such as personality and values, and external conditions such as leadership and organisational culture. Proactive employees were acceptable only to receptive leaders but may fail under extraverted leaders, because their proactive behaviours would be 'zero-sum'. A study of 57 store leaders and 374 employees showed employee proactivity to be a composite of three variables, viz., taking charge, voice, and upward influence [22].

Intrinsic Motivation. To categorise motives as either extrinsic or intrinsic was not easy. As such constructs and their variables could not be assessed easily for their construct validity, measurement reliability, and experimental control, a multi-faceted model of intrinsic motivation (IM) with 16 scales of basic desires (also called universal reinforcements) was developed with indicators such as acceptance, curiosity, order, power, romance, and status [23]. These needs were universally common to the human species, focused on end purposes, and would explain and drive individual behaviour towards goals. As it was difficult to conceptualise IM as a construct and to distinguish it from extrinsic motivation in terms of outcomes, an integrated and computational approach was proposed to IM using collative variables to describe stimulus elements of IM in terms of properties such as ambiguity, change, complexity, novelty, and uncertainty [24]. IM was the experience of challenge, excitement, enjoyment, pleasure, or satisfaction expected by an individual from an activity, without being influenced by any benefit expected from the activity.

Goal Orientation. The significance of goal orientation lies in its ability to influence performance and satisfaction with results, self-efficacy, and motivation [25]. The nature of the goal also affected the behaviour of the individuals. Individuals with a performance goal orientation could complete their tasks better and earlier than those with a learning goal orientation. Individuals with a performance goal orientation chose easy tasks to work with, while those with learning goal orientation were not affected by the difficulty of their tasks. Individuals with a performance goal orientation preferred consistent tasks, while those with learning goal orientation seemed to be motivated by the inherent challenge and difficulty of inconsistent tasks. Goal orientation was a perspective of human motivation, and was studied either as a state or a trait [26]. Orientations such as mastery versus performance, approach versus avoidance, and extrinsic, and identified difficulties and weaknesses in their definitions, elements, and measurement were then evaluated and compared. Goal orientation was then proposed to be a schema of and combination of two facets, viz., a purpose that responded to stimuli and a script that produced and directed action. Finally, it became a composite of frameworks for filtering information, constructing and appraising the nature of the situation, creating meaning, and guiding action. Thus, it clarified and determined the reasons for an individual's actions to accomplish something of value, because it was either task oriented (focused to complete a task) or ego oriented (focused on relative superiority).

Open Communication. A rigorous study of over 2,000 employees in three organisations led to the conclusion that organisational identification (a 5-item construct similar to cohesion because it measured pride in, ties to, and belongingness to the company) was affected by the company's external prestige in better known companies [27]. However, cohesion in less prestigious companies was affected by openness, trust and participation as features of their communication climate. Therefore, open communication within the organisation was instrumental for the development of its cohesion, and that the nature of the communication climate (an open process that included trust) was more important than the content of the communication to produce cohesion. Team members with different levels of communicative behaviour produced relationship conflict due to interpersonal misunderstanding and mis-matched emotions. A study of 145 work teams in 63 Korean firms showed that high levels of open communication could reduce such relationship conflict, whereas low levels could enhance status conflict [28]. Open communication persuaded team members to change their interpersonal attitudes and behaviour, and thus, enhanced mutual understanding of each other's motives.

Mutual Understanding. This factor represented statements that focused on joint action of team members and their common values and concern for each other's safety and well-being. The member's reason to assist others in her team is based on her prosocial attitudes that would explain and guide her actions. Previous research had indicated that task conflict encouraged constructive discussion leading to better cognitive understanding of the problems and better decisions within the teams [29]. Prosocial behaviours such as *anonymous, altruistic, compliant, dire, emotional,* and *public behaviours* promoted understanding between team members because they encouraged collaboration, innovation, diversity, and fair and polite behaviour within the community [30]. The agreeableness trait, prosociality and empathic self-efficacy beliefs predicted each other across two periods four years apart in a study of 340 young adults [31].

2.2 The Participants

Students of the two-year Post Graduate Diploma in Management (PGDM) in a management school in New Delhi, India, participated in the study. They were 22–24 years old, and were graduates in commerce, science, engineering, and similar disciplines in India and abroad.

2.3 The Procedure

The students played IceBreaker, a day-long business simulation game conducted and facilitated by the first author, who had developed it in 2003. At the beginning, they were randomly cast in teams of 4–5 students each, but care was taken to maintain gender parity across teams. Ten such teams comprised a simulated market of products, producers, customers, dealers, utilities, and labour. Each team was then placed in charge of a separate business firm, each identical to the others. The teams received manuals, instructions and guidelines. They managed their respective firms for two calendar periods of three months each, during which they produced goods according to their capacity and customer demand, and offered them for sale by quoting prices and through dealers. They paid for advertisements and promotions, and incurred a variety of costs. At the end of each period, they received statements describing the financial status of their respective firms. During the game, the facilitator released documents, gave instructions, discussed common problems, and analysed business and competitive conditions, prospects, and business results.

Icebreaker created a learning experience in a competitive environment for the students. It exposed them to management and business operations, conditions, expressions, processes, decisions, and financial perspectives. They assumed roles within their teams who competed against other teams. Each team got information about its and the other teams' financial performance in the market. Their conversations contained enquiries, clarifications, debates, and decisions, all of which led to excited interactions and emotional bonding within the teams. Thus, the game generated both competitiveness and cohesion, and therefore, was appropriate for this study. The game players completed the study instrument at the end of the game.

3 Results

Although the instrument was administered to 330 students in 80 teams, only 309 responses were found to be complete and correct, and therefore, processed for this study. The respondent data was processed using SPSS 21.0. The interpersonal competitiveness and team cohesion variables showed acceptable internal reliability (Cronbach α) of .79 and .87, respectively. Except for mutual understanding (.58), all other attributes showed satisfactory reliability between .73 and .80. The correlations between the variables, interpersonal competitiveness and team cohesion, and their respective attributes are shown in Table 1.

Table 1. Descriptive Statistics and Correlations between Variables and their Attributes

n = 309	Mean	Std. Deviation	MA	PRO	IM	GO	OC	MU	IC	TC
Measured Aggression (MA)	22.81	3.73	0.79							
Proactivity (PRO)	17.21	3.64	.04	0.75						
Intrinsic Motivation (IM)	16.61	2.52	.41**	.32**	0.80					
Goal Orientation (GO)	32.81	3.85	.10	.02	.17**	.73				
Open Communication (OC)	33.09	3.54	.07	.06	.12*	.68**	.78			
Mutual Understanding (MU)	12.22	1.54	.10	.02	.06	.51**	.59**	.58		
Interpersonal Competitiveness (IC)	62.24	8.80	.65**	.68**	.80**	.13*	.12*	.08	.79	
Team Cohesion (TC)	78.11	7.80	.11	.04	.14*	.85**	.88**	.84**	.13*	.87

**. Correlation is significant at the 0.01 level (2-tailed). *. Correlation is significant at the 0.05 level (2-tailed).
Figures along the diagonal represent the internal reliability of the variables and the attributes

The attributes and variables were positively and significantly correlated with each other in 12 instances at $p < .01$ and in five instances at $p < .05$. Intrinsic motivation correlated strongly with measured aggression (.41), proactivity (.32), goal orientation

(.17), and open communication (.12). Additionally, goal orientation correlated strongly with open communication (.68) and mutual understanding (.51), and open communication correlated positively and significantly with mutual understanding (.59). Finally, the two variables, interpersonal competitiveness and team cohesion, correlated positively and significantly with their own attributes ($r = .65 -.88, p < .01$), and with each other ($r = .13, p < .05$) and with three attributes of the other variable ($r = .12 -.14, p < .05$).

The inter-attribute and inter-variable regression results are shown in Table 2. The independent attributes predicted all other attributes in 12 instances, positively and significantly. Intrinsic motivation separately predicted measured aggression ($r = .41, p < .01$) and proactivity ($r = .37, p < .01$). Measured aggression ($r = .39, p < .01$), proactivity ($r = .26, p < .01$) and goal orientation ($r = .17, p < .01$) collectively predicted intrinsic motivation. Intrinsic motivation ($r = .07, p < .05$), open communication ($r = .62, p < .01$), and mutual understanding ($r = .16, p < .01$) collectively predicted goal orientation. Goal orientation ($r = .46, p < .01$) and mutual understanding ($r = .29, p < .01$) collectively predicted open communication. Goal orientation ($r = .22, p < .01$) and open communication ($r = .53, p < .01$) collectively predicted mutual understanding. Finally, the two variables, interpersonal competitiveness and team cohesion, predicted each other ($r = .13$ and .09, $p < .05$).

Table 2. Regression Coefficients between Variables and their Attributes

Dependent variable, below	Constant	MA	PRO	IM	GO	OC	MU	IC	TC
Measured Aggression (MA)	2.12			$.41^{**}$					
Proactivity (PRO)	1.93			$.37^{**}$					
Intrinsic Motivation (IM)	1.07	$.39^{**}$	$.26^{**}$		$.17^{**}$				
Goal Orientation (GO)	0.61			$.07^{*}$		$.62^{**}$	$.16^{**}$		
Open Communication (OC)	1.07				$.46^{**}$		$.29^{**}$		
Mutual Understanding (MU)	0.98				$.22^{**}$	$.53^{**}$			
Interpersonal Competitiveness (IC)	3.27				$.13^{*}$				
Team Cohesion (TC)	3.74			0.09*					

**. Correlation is significant at the 0.01 level (2-tailed). *. Correlation is significant at the 0.05 level (2-tailed).

4   Discussion

The study examined the relationships between the variables, interpersonal competitiveness and team cohesion, and their respective attributes. The significant correlations of the variables with their respective attributes (Table 1) and their satisfactory internal reliability established the validity of the factor analysis process which produced the attributes as factors of the variables in earlier studies. This conclusion confirmed the adequacy of the statements in the instrument used in the study.

Generally, the attributes of interpersonal competitiveness and team cohesion correlated respectively with the attributes of its respective variable. Intrinsic motivation and goal orientation were the most pervasive independent attributes, and they affected each other, six other attributes, and both variables, positively. Open communication was the strongest predictor, and it predicted goal orientation ($r = .62$, $p < .01$) and mutual understanding ($r = .53$, $p < .01$) along with other attributes.

Goal orientation had the smallest constant (.61) which stood out against the largest constant (2.12) of measured aggression in the regression results (Table 2). The small size suggested that it may remain low in a cohesive team while measured aggression may be high in a competitive team. Goal orientation is not likely to grow without the combined effects of intrinsic motivation, open communication and mutual understanding. On the contrary, measured aggression is likely to be high in a competitive team, and may grow with the effect of intrinsic motivation, only.

Aggression correlated positively and significantly with and was predicted by intrinsic motivation, only. It is a behaviour that may be triggered by feelings of power and competence, and could be measured by the competitive reaction time required to complete a task [32]. One's aggressive behaviour may be higher against an opponent who had lost before, suggesting that the aggressor's motivation was driven by the confidence that she would win and that her opponent would lose again. A general aggression model comprising of inputs (person and situation), routes (affect, cognition, and arousal), and outcomes (decision processes, and impulsive and thoughtful actions) could describe a variety of motivations and factors instrumental in the development of aggression [32]. Cognitions such as attitudes, ideas, and perceptions, emotions such as anger and shame, personality traits such as Machiavellianism and narcissism, hormones such as testosterone and oxytocin, and environmental factors such as rumours, violent media and the availability of weapons as drivers and environments made aggression happen [33].

Proactivity correlated positively and significantly with and was predicted by intrinsic motivation, only. Employees' positions in their hierarchy affected their proactivity [34]. Office ranks shaped the perceptions of the employees, and concluded that proactive efforts produced adaptive efforts which, in turn, generated proactive efforts. Thus, individuals who were motivated by empowerment were more likely to become proactive within their organisations. A study of the Big 5 model of personality traits in a sample of 1,447 staff-supervisor pairs showed that proactivity was associated positively with openness to experience but negatively with agreeableness and extraversion [35]. Age and organisational roles affected the needs, contexts and goal orientations of individuals, but did not reduce their eagerness and tendency to change their environment, despite difficult conditions. Older employees were just as proactive as younger employees but differently [36]. Older individuals' proactivity was focused on mentoring and citizenship behaviours, while younger individuals were more concerned about their careers and education.

Intrinsic motivation correlated positively and significantly with and was predicted collectively by measured aggression, proactivity, and goal orientation. Intrinsic motivation (IM) was the 'desire and willingness to engage in an activity for the pleasure inherent in the activity' [37]. They proposed a tripartite model of three IM factors, viz., IM to know, IM to accomplish, and IM to experience stimulation, with unique antecedents and consequences. They could be predicted by personality characteristics of curiosity, achievement orientation, and sensation orientation, respectively, which in turn, could predict the affective states of knowledge, accomplishment and stimulation, respectively. When more time was spent in the IM activity, it enlarged the experience of the affective states. Using the Academic Motivation Scale in a study of 1,118 students in two separate studies, IM was found to be more concerned with the engagement, efforts and experience in working for or reaching an achievement [38].

Goal orientation correlated positively and significantly with and was predicted collectively by open communication, mutual understanding, and intrinsic motivation. Engaging employees in conversation, motivating them with challenging tasks, and empowering them would help to unify their interests towards the common goal. The values of individuals (e.g. using skills, self-esteem, and seeking recognition) and organisational values (e.g. customer concern, innovation, quality, and integrity) should be integrated and aligned before the organisation embarks on change management initiative [39]. In a study of 276 university students, goal orientation and perceived competence were found to predict their intrinsic motivation [40]. From a longitudinal study of 245 university students across 12 weeks of research, researchers found that high levels of learning goal orientation (LGO) correlated with higher goals and superior performance [41]. Students' mastery goal orientation (MGO) was their ability to learn and understand better and faster. A study of 1,680 Austrian school students showed that the freedom to shape and choose learning content, instructions and methods, exposure to learning experiences with emphasis on curiosity and engagement, assessment without embarrassment, and recognition of their learning success could enhance their MGO [42].

Open communication correlated positively and significantly with and was predicted collectively by goal orientation and mutual understanding. Communication was a deep and complex activity that conveyed meaning between people and improved interaction between them, and therefore, was an important element of any organisation [43]. To be effective, it had to produce trust, build understanding, and generate more and better outputs. This would be possible only if it would conform to measures such as timely, clear, accurate, pertinent, credible, responsible, concise, and sincere. On the basis of insights from five attitude-behaviour theories, communication was found to create cognitive dissonance and change human behaviour (cognitive behaviour theory) [44]. It could generate attitudes, perceptions, and judgements (social judgement theory), produce attitudinal change (heuristic-systematic model), and predict attitude and behaviour depending on willingness and ability (elaboration likelihood model) and on the basis of social norms (theory of planned behaviour). Therefore, communication was both a persuasive process and a useful instrument for change and performance in social groups.

Mutual understanding correlated positively and significantly with and was predicted collectively by goal orientation and open communication. The avoidance and control of interpersonal conflict facilitated mutual understanding which was best achieved by balancing the concerns for self with concerns for others. When team members adopted one of these five conflict management styles, viz., integrating, obliging, dominating, avoiding, and compromising, the team was able to focus on the problem goal [45]. Prosocial behaviours such as informing, comforting, sharing and helping actions could reduce others' pains and put them at ease, with empathic concern, sympathy, and sacrifice being the most visible signs [46]. Compassion was an individual's empathetic understanding of others' problems leading her to respond, at first emotionally, and later, with assistance that would bond her with them [47].

4.1 Conclusion

It can be concluded that intrinsic motivation was the key attribute in the individual's interpersonal competitiveness. It was driven by her curiosity and desire to accomplish a goal, and was responsible for the development of her aggressive and proactive personality. Aggression was driven by perceptions of relative power, and is a product of attitudes, emotions, traits, and the environment. Her proactive behaviour was driven by the perceived freedom to act in her role as provided by the environment. Goal orientation was the key attribute in team cohesion, and was facilitated by discussion and assessment without prejudice or pain in an environment with focus on alignment of interests and actions. Open communication produced clarity, reduced conflict, and built trust and consensus. It created an environment of mutual understanding in the team where its members informed and persuaded each other under conditions of empathy, concern and compassion. For teams to make change happen, some of the most important stages were to understand the urgency of the problem (proactivity), to build a shared commitment (team cohesion), to convey the vision (open communication), and to create short term wins (measured aggression) [48]. If such change efforts were not meticulously managed, the loss of momentum may affect the morale of employees.

Implications for Further Research. The study discovered the nature of interactions between two mutually exclusive constructs, interpersonal competitiveness and team cohesion (Tables 1 and 2). It was based on a sample of adult management students where their key intrinsic motivations were to learn management practices and to win as a team in the game. It may be extended to samples of managers in large organisations (where cohesion may be more desired than employee competitiveness) and in entrepreneurial firms (where employee competitiveness may be more needed than cohesion) to determine the effect of the relative attributes and the variables in the two contexts. Because of the transactionary nature of the employees' relationship with their organisations, their extrinsic motivation (in the form of remuneration and promotions) may be more effective than their intrinsic motivation. The findings of such new research findings may enable business organisations to hire and deploy their employees with appropriate traits.

An organisational crisis is a challenge for a cohesive team which may not be able to respond quickly because some members may not be competitive. Cohesion may result in a concurrence-seeking tendency of teams called groupthink where the members' desire for consensus causes defective decisions and poor outcomes because of their reluctance to seek and appraise alternatives [49]. Competitive individuals are outliers in their teams and may feel uncomfortable in teams with a strong groupthink culture.

Therefore, a model is needed to guide leaders to identify, develop, advise, and empower competitive team members and to blend them into the cohesive environment.

Recommendations for Action. This study has validated the scales for interpersonal competitiveness and team cohesion. Business organisations may use these scales to assess their employees for these variables and their respective attributes, and thereafter, deploy them for appropriate tasks.

How does one control competitive behaviour which may be in defiance of team culture? Employees' deviant behaviour could be reduced by empowering them which would enhance their trust with others, without diluting their initiative or responsibility, and encourage them in their in-role performance [50].

The findings offer new insights about the nature and interactions between the attributes. Team leaders may seek to develop their members' intrinsic motivation because of its predictive effect on their aggression and proactivity. Similarly, open communication would enhance goal orientation and mutual understanding, and goal orientation would facilitate open communication. Thus, the two scales with their variables and attributes are useful tools for organisational change and managerial development.

References

1. Bönte, W., Lombardo, S., Urbig, D.: Economics meets psychology: experimental and self-reported measures of individual competitiveness. Pers. Individ. Differ. **116**, 179–185 (2017)
2. Salas, E., Grossman, R., Hughes, A.M., Coultas, C.W.: Measuring team cohesion: observations from the science. Hum. Factors **57**(3), 365–374 (2015)
3. Rovio, E., Eskola, J., Kozub, S.A., Duda, J.L., Lintunen, T.: Can high group cohesion be harmful? A case study of a junior ice-hockey team. Small Group Res. **40**(4), 421–435 (2009)
4. Mowen, J.C.: Exploring the trait of competitiveness and its consumer behaviour consequences. J. Consum. Psychol. **14**(1–2), 52–63 (2004)
5. Charness, G., Villeval, M.-C.: The dark side of competition for status. Manag. Sci. **60**(1), 38–55 (2014)
6. Balas, B., Thomas, L.E.: Competition makes observers remember faces as more aggressive. J. Exp. Psychol. **144**(4), 711–716 (2015)
7. Klyueva, O.A.: Competitiveness of personality as a psychological phenomenon: the content of the construct and its typology. Psychol. Russ.: State Art **9**(2), 151–166 (2016)
8. Menesini, E., Tassi, F., Nocentini, A.: The competitive attitude scale (CAS): a multidimensional measure of competitiveness in adolescence. J. Psychol. Clin. Psychiatry **9**(3), 240–244 (2018)
9. Lott, A.J., Lott, B.E.: Group cohesiveness as interpersonal attraction: a review of relationships with antecedent and consequent variables. Psychol. Bull. **64**(4), 259–309 (1965)
10. den Bossche, P.V., Gijselaers, W.H., Segers, M., Kirschner, P.A.: Social and cognitive factors driving teamwork in collaborative learning environments: team learning beliefs and behaviors. Small Group Res. **37**(5), 490–521 (2006)
11. Hipp, J.R., Perrin, A.: Nested loyalties: local networks' effects on neighbourhood and community cohesion. Urban Stud. **43**(13), 2503–2523 (2006)

12. Casey-Campell, M., Martens, M.L.: Sticking it all together: a critical assessment of the group cohesion–performance literature. Int. J. Manag. Rev. **11**(2), 223–246 (2009)
13. Marcos, F.M.L., Miguel, P.A.S., Oliva, D.S., Calvo, T.: Interactive effects of team cohesion on perceived efficacy in semi-professional sport. J. Sports Sci. Med. **9**, 320–325 (2010)
14. Rico, R., Alcover de la Hera, C. M., Tabernero, C.: Work team effectiveness, a review of research from the last decade (1999–2009). Psychol. Spain **15**(1), 57–79 (2001)
15. Williams, J., Brown, J.M., Bray, R.M., Goodell, E.M.A., Olmsted, K.R., Adler, A.B.: Unit cohesion, resilience, and mental health of soldiers in basic combat training. Mil. Psychol. **28** (4), 241–250 (2016)
16. Dumblekar, V.: Interpersonal competitiveness – a study of simulation game participants' behaviour. In: Paper Presented at 40th Annual Conference of International Simulation and Gaming Association, Singapore, June–July 2009
17. Dumblekar, V., Dhar, U.: Development and standardization of business simulation game team cohesion scale. AIMS J. Manag. **3**(1), 1–22 (2017)
18. Anderson, C.A., Bushman, B.J.: Human aggression. Ann. Rev. Psychol. **53**, 27–51 (2002)
19. Meier, B.P., Hinsz, V.B.: A comparison of human aggression committed by groups and individuals: an interindividual–intergroup discontinuity. J. Exp. Soc. Psychol. **40**, 551–559 (2003)
20. Ang, R.P., Ng, A.-K., Wong, S.S., Lee, B.-O., Oei, T.P.S., Leng, V.: Relationship between Big Five traits and aggression: a comparison between undergraduates from Australia and Singapore. J. Psychol. Chin. Soc. **5**(2), 291–305 (2004)
21. Parker, S.K., Bindl, U.K., Strauss, K.: Making things happen: a model of proactive motivation. J. Manag. **36**, 827–856 (2010)
22. Grant, A.M., Gino, F., Hofmann, D.A.: Reversing the extraverted leadership advantage: the role of employee proactivity. Acad. Manag. J. **54**(3), 528–550 (2011)
23. Reiss, S., Havercamp, S.M.: Toward a comprehensive assessment of fundamental motivation: factor structure of the Reiss Profile. Psychol. Assess. **10**, 97–106 (1998)
24. Oudeyer, P.-Y., Kaplan, F.: How can we define intrinsic motivation? In: Schlesinger, M., Berthouze, L., Balkenius, C. (eds.): Modeling Cognitive Development in Robotic Systems: Proceedings of the Eighth International Conference on Epigenetic Robotics. Lund University Cognitive Studies, vol. 139, pp. 93–101. Lund, Sweden (2008)
25. Steele-Johnson, D., Beauregard, R.S., Hoover, P.B., Schmidt, A.M.: Goal orientation and task demand effects on motivation, affect, and performance. J. Appl. Psychol. **85**(5), 724–738 (2000)
26. Kaplan, A., Maehr, M.L.: The contributions and prospects of goal orientation theory. Educ. Psychol. Rev. **19**, 141–184 (2007)
27. Smidts, A., Pruyn, A.T.H., van Riel, C.D.M.: The impact of employee communication and perceived external prestige on organizational identification. Acad. Manag. J. **44**(5), 1051–1062 (2001)
28. Chun, S.J., Choi, J.N.: Members' needs, intragroup conflict, and group performance. J. Appl. Psychol. **99**(3), 437–450 (2014)
29. Simons, T.L., Peterson, R.S.: Task conflict and relationship conflict in top management teams: the pivotal role of intragroup trust. J. Appl. Psychol. **85**(1), 102–111 (2000)
30. Carlo, G., Randall, B.A.: The development of a measure of prosocial behaviors for late adolescents. J. Youth Adolesc. **31**(1), 31–44 (2002)
31. Caprara, G.V., Alessandri, G., Eisenberg, N.: Prosociality: the contribution of traits, values, and self-efficacy beliefs. J. Pers. Soc. Psychol. **102**(6), 1289–1303 (2012)
32. Muller, D., Bushman, B.J., Subra, B., Ceaux, W.: Are people more aggressive when they are worse off or better off than others? Soc. Psychol. Pers. Sci. **3**(6), 754–759 (2012)

33. Warburton, W.A., Anderson, C.A.: Social psychology of aggression. In: Berkowitz, L. (ed.): International Encyclopedia of the Social Behavioral Sciences, 2nd edn., pp. 373–380 (2015)
34. Berg, J.M., Wrzesniewski, A., Dutton, J.E.: Perceiving and responding to challenges in job crafting at different ranks: When proactivity requires adaptivity. J. Organ. Behav. **31**, 158–186 (2010)
35. Neal, A., Yeo, G., Koy, A., Xiao, T.: Predicting the form and direction of work role performance from the Big 5 model of personality traits. J. Organ. Behav. **33**(2), 175–192 (2012)
36. Zacher, H., Kooij, D.T.A.M.: Aging and proactivity (chap. 10). In. Parker, S.K., Bindl, U.K. (eds.): Proactivity at Work: Making Things Happen in Organizations, pp. 258–294. Routledge, New York (2017)
37. Carbonneau, N., Vallerand, R.J., Lafrenière, M.-A.K.: Toward a tripartite model of intrinsic motivation. J. Pers. **80**(5), 1147–1178 (2012)
38. Litalien, D., Morin, A.J.S., Gagné, M., Vallerand, R.J., Losier, G.F., Ryan, R.M.: Evidence of a continuum structure of academic self-determination: a two-study test using a bifactor-ESEM representation of academic motivation. Contemp. Educ. Psychol. **51**, 67–82 (2017)
39. Sullivan, W., Sullivan, R., Buffton, B.: Aligning individual and organisational values to support change. J. Change Manag. **2**(3), 247–254 (2001)
40. Núñez, J.L., Martín-Albo, J., Paredes, A., Rodríguez, O., Chipana, N.: The mediating role of perceived competence: testing a motivational sequence in university students. Universitas Psychologica **10**(3), 669–680 (2011)
41. Taing, M.U., Smith, T., Singla, N., Johnson, R.E., Chang, C.-H.: The relationship between learning goal orientation, goal setting, and performance: a longitudinal study. J. Appl. Soc. Psychol. **43**, 1668–1675 (2013)
42. Lüftenegger, M., van de Schoot, R., Schober, B., Finsterwald, M., Spiel, C.: Promotion of students' mastery goal orientations: does TARGET work? Educ. Psychol.: Int. J. Exp. Educ. Psychol. **34**(4), 451–469 (2014)
43. Almonaitienė, J., Žukauskas, D.: Managerial communication and related variables in a food retail chain. Soc. Sci. **2**(88), 24–36 (2015)
44. Teng, S., Khong, K.W., Goh, W.W.: Persuasive communication: a study of major attitude-behavior theories in a social media context. J. Internet Commer. **14**(1), 42–64 (2015)
45. Aritzeta, A., Ayestaran, S., Swailes, S.: Team role preference and conflict management styles. Int. J. Conflict Manag. **16**(2), 157–182 (2005)
46. Jensen, K.: Prosociality. Curr. Biol. **26**, 748–752 (2016)
47. Brill, M., Nahmani, N.: The presence of compassion in therapy. Clin. Soc. Work J. **45**(1), 10–21 (2016)
48. Kotter, J.P.: Leading change. Why transformation efforts fail. Harvard Bus. Rev. **86**, 92–107 (2007)
49. Janis, I.: Groupthink. In: Griffin, E. (ed.) A First Look at Communication Theory, pp. 235–246. McGrawHill, New York (1991)
50. Kim, M., Beehr, T.A.: Self-efficacy and psychological ownership mediate the effects of empowering leadership on both good and bad employee behaviours. J. Leadersh. Organ. Stud. **24**(4), 466–478 (2016)

Simulation Games for Current Challenges

Review of Haptic and Computerized (Simulation) Games on Climate Change

Andreas Gerber[1(✉)], Markus Ulrich[2], and Patrick Wäger[1]

[1] Empa, Technology and Society Laboratory, Lerchenfeldstr. 5,
9014 St. Gallen, Switzerland
andreas.gerber@empa.ch
[2] UCS Ulrich Creative Simulations GmbH, Pfingstweidstr. 31,
8005 Zurich, Switzerland

Abstract. Climate change imposes tremendous, complex challenges on humanity. Thoughtfully designed games can support solving them. This article presents a review of climate games and thereby updates the review conducted by Reckien and Eisenack in 2011. It provides an overview of published climate games and reveals the development of the field over the last years. A total of 119 climate games were found whereof 52 were already part of the review of 2011. The broad variety of discovered games indicates a lively community and different settings where such tools are being applied. A substantial number of games addressed topics such as international climate conferences, global impacts of global decisions, and effects of individual decisions on their local environment. Other topics, however, were largely absent. They included - amongst others - the connection between climate change and health, and games that bride local and global levels. Furthermore, the game types "video games" and "alternate reality games" were not applied frequently. Both, the absent topics and the scarcely used game types open up possibilities to develop the field. Forty-six per cent of the games listed by Reckien and Eisenack seem to have disappeared and could not be found for this review, an observation that may need further attention.

Keywords: Climate change · Game · Review · Simulation game · Greenhouse gases · Global warming · Paris agreement · Transition · Climate mitigation · Education · Awareness rising · Political action · Creating impact

1 Introduction

Climate change imposes tremendous and complex challenges on humanity. Such challenges include the warming of the earth system and its impacts on human and natural systems on different spatial and temporal levels [1]. The Intergovernmental Panel on Climate Change indicates that immediate and drastic mitigation efforts are

Electronic supplementary material The online version of this chapter (https://doi.org/10.1007/978-3-030-72132-9_24) contains supplementary material, which is available to authorized users.

M. Wardaszko et al. (Eds.): ISAGA 2019, LNCS 11988, pp. 275–289, 2021.
https://doi.org/10.1007/978-3-030-72132-9_24

needed to achieving the 1.5 °C warming target of the Paris Agreement [2], which would imply a fundamental societal transformation [3].

Wrong but common mental models about climate related dynamics are one of several aspects that make it difficult to deal with climate change issues (e.g., [4, 5]). Because such mental models do not result from poor training in science or an unfamiliarity with climate science, Sterman et al. [6] advise against simply presenting people with more information about climate change. Instead, they propose methods of interactive learning where people experience how complex systems behave and how they can be managed.

Games in general and simulation games in particular are well suited for dealing with complex and interrelated problems, and such tools could be beneficially applied in the context of environmental problems and sustainable development [7]. Reckien and Eisenack [8] emphasize the potential of games to translate scientific results into a language that is understood by the public. Ulrich [9] has identified three major potentials for simulation games to contribute to a sustainable world: embracing time (i.e. making large time spans accessible to first-hand experience), approaching large audiences, and generating real impact. In the context of climate change, games could – amongst others – "help to develop confidence and ownership and reduce the fear of the unknown" [10] (p. 27) or enable participants "to experience the benefits of change as well as our ability to be successful" [11] (p. 43). In this context, we apply the term "climate game" for games that explicitly address climate change and/or related topics (e.g. mitigation or adaptation).

The objective of this article is to provide an overview of the development of climate games over the last decades. Accordingly, the paper presents a review of climate games and analyzes specific characteristics of the games such as release year, type, topic and further aspects. The article draws on the previous works of [7] who presented a first overview of simulation games about environmental issues and of Reckien and Eisenack [8] who presented a review of climate games. The application of the same selection criteria as Reckien and Eisenack [8] allowed for tracking and comparing the development of climate games over almost a decade.[1]

The following section of this article, "definitions and methods", introduces the methodological approach in terms of the search process, selection criteria and analysis. The "results" section presents an overview of the games in general, as well as the analysis of selected game characteristics, before the article concludes with the section "discussion and conclusion" that contextualizes the results achieved. A central part of this article is the appendix that lists the games analyzed.

2 Definitions and Method

For this review about climate games, the terms "climate game", "climate change game" and "climate related games" were used interchangeably. This reflects the situation in practice, where such games are mostly developed to illustrate one or several aspects

---

[1] The study from Reckien and Eisenack was conducted in 2011, and published in 2013.

related to climate change. As in the review of Reckien and Eisenack [8], games were searched with the two key words "climate" and "game" in English, and "Klima" and "Spiel" in German[2]. To cover a broad variety of games, the following resources were used for the search: the Internet[3], app platforms for mobile phones, the journal "Simulation & Gaming", SAGSAGA-newsletter[4] and personalized communication in the authors' network. The search was conducted from May 2018 until February 2019.

Like the review of Reckien and Eisenack [8], this study focused on "sophisticated" climate games, which meant that the following selection criteria were applied:

- Climate change is an integral aspect of the story line;
- The application shows typical characteristics of a game (e.g. having a goal and offer the player the possibility for interaction);
- The model according to Duke and Geurts [10] (p. 256) is not oversimplified (e.g. simple quizzes were excluded from the review).

As a consequence, applications that were pure simulators or very simple in content were excluded from the review. This also applied to applications without clear focus on climate change, e.g. by exclusively addressing topics such as energy or disaster risk reduction.

For games that matched the selection criteria above, an ad hoc analysis about specific game characteristics was performed. The characteristics included:

- Release year: For most games, it was possible to find out explicitly the release year. In some cases, indirect information had to be used, such as the earliest mentioning in the Internet.
- Type: Considered types were role-play, simulation, online game, video game, board game and other (e.g. alternate reality games).
- Scale: Considered scales were global, several countries, one country, organization/city/community, individual/household, and other (e.g. fictional planet).
- Topic: The topics that games covered were classified into mitigation, politics, impacts/adaptation, energy issues, investment, carbon footprint, insurance, deforestation, disaster risk reduction (DRR), technological change, physics, life quality, and health.
- Language: English or/and German.
- Organization type of the game developers: Private, governmental, non-governmental and academic organizations.

The next section reports on the outcomes of the analysis in the form of descriptive statistics. The data used can be found in Table S1 "Game Characteristics" in the Supplementary Materials.

---

[2] German was included to allow comparing our results with the Reckien & Eisenack review.

[3] Google was used as the main search engine. Interesting platforms were, amongst others: www.boardgamegeek.com, www.climateinteractive.org, www.games4sustainability.org, and www.bpb.de.

[4] SAGSAGA: the Swiss Austrian German Simulation and Gaming Association.

3   Results

This review identified 119 relevant games. This is a notable increase compared to the 5, and 52 climate-related (simulation) games reported by Ulrich [7], and Reckien and Eisenack [8], respectively. Figure 1 provides the number of games released since 1983. Until 1994, only few games have been released. 1995 was the first year for which more than 1 game per year was found. From 2003 onwards, the number of games released started to increase clearly. In the period 2007–2018, an average of 8 games have been released per year. The annual fluctuations include two peaks in 2009 and 2016 that may reflect the topic's attention because of climate conferences, but essentially seem to be random.

For the period from 1983 to 2010, 60 climate games have been found, in contrast to Reckien and Eisenack [8], who found 50 games for the same period. The difference may be explained by the slightly broader search criteria applied for this review. Twenty-four games listed by Eisenack [8] could not be found anymore. In some cases, traces in the Internet indicate their (prior) existence, and enough information could be gathered to include them in the in-depth analysis presented in the following section. In other cases, however, no traces were found and the games had to be excluded from the in-depth analysis. Furthermore, some games of the 2013 review did not comply with the selection criteria mentioned above. Thus, 24 of the 119 games had to be excluded, leaving 95 games for the in-depth analysis presented below. Examples for excluded games are "Love Letters to the Future", or the "Game Framework for CO2 issue" [12] that did not meet the criteria to be considered a game. A list with the games included in the analysis, and the corresponding links can be found in the appendix. The appendix further lists the games that were part in the review of Reckien and Eisenack [8], however, had to be excluded for the current study, together with the reason for exclusion.

3.1   Formal Aspects: Type of Developers and Language

This review distinguishes four types of game developers: academic (universities, research institutions), private (business, consultancy), governmental (authorities), and non-governmental (NGOs). In some cases, institutions from different categories were involved in the development of the same game. These games were assigned to the category that had the most prominent role in its development and application. Private organizations played the most important role in developing climate games (about half of all games), followed by academic institutions, providing one fourth of all games. The remaining parts have been developed by governmental and non-governmental organizations (Fig. 2).

Out of the 95 analyzed games, 70 games were available in English only, 16 games in German only, and 9 in both languages. Some games were available in additional languages, such as French or Japanese.

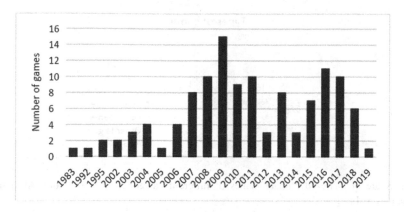

Fig. 1. Number of "sophisticated" climate games released from 1983 to February 2019.

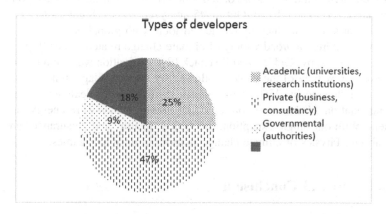

Fig. 2. Share of analyzed climate games by developer categories, n = 95.

3.2   Content-Related Aspects: Game Types, Scale and Climate Issues

The review classified the games in six types (Fig. 3). Many games combined aspects of several types. In such cases, games were classified according to their most dominant type. Role-play games are most prominent, followed by online-games, board games, and simulations. Interestingly, the types "video games" and "augmented reality games" were not common.

Climate change is a global phenomenon, and yet, it is linked to decisions taken on levels down to single individuals. Climate change thus covers a wide range of scales, which are addressed in this review: global, several countries, one country, organization/city/community, individual/household, and other (e.g. fictional planet). "Global", for example, means that players engage in a global issue such as international climate negotiations. Similarly, "one country" means, that players played actors such as ministers that run one country.

The overwhelming part of the analyzed games deals either with global aspects of climate change (38%, Fig. 4), or with local issues of climate change

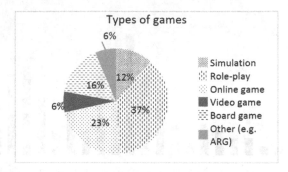

Fig. 3. Share of analyzed climate games of different categories, n = 95. Note: ARG means "augmented reality game".

(organization/city/community 20%, or individual/household, 22%). Scales on country level are rarely addressed (13%). Out of 95 analyzed games, 8 games (8%) explicitly covered several scales and thereby connected local with global issues.

The games address a broad variety of climate change related issues (Fig. 5, similar categories as applied by Reckien and Eisenack [8]). Mitigation was the most prominent topic, addressed by 69% of the games, followed by impacts/adaptation (38%). Climate politics was addressed by 25% of the games, which mostly dealt with international climate negotiations. Other common topics in climate games were energy issues, and investment. With one single exception, the topics "health" and "insurance" are almost entirely absent. Physics of climate change is topic in only five games.

4   Discussion and Conclusion

The objective of this article was to provide an overview of the development of climate games over the last decades. In a review, 119 relevant games were identified of which 95 were analyzed in more detail. While climate games started to be an issue in 1983, the number of released climate games really took off between 2002 and 2009 and remained on a high level since then. The broad variety of published games indicates a lively community and different settings and topics for which such tools are being applied.

The comparison of the results with the review of Reckien and Eisenack [8] showed the development of climate games since 2011. It is obvious that the number of published games has increased considerably since then. However, 24 games (46%) of the games listed in the 2013 review could not be found anymore. In some cases, traces on the Internet, such as entries in game databases, or references in other publications, point to the earlier existence of these games. In other cases, not even traces were found. The disappearance of 24 of 52 games within only 6–9 years is startling. Possible reasons for this could be that these games are outdated, were designed for one-time events, or had a very short lifespan for other reasons. This issue might be worth considering in future studies.

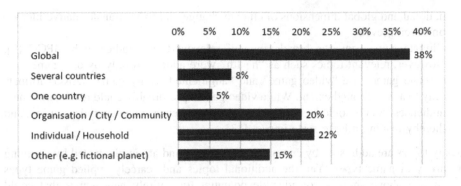

Fig. 4. Scale of issues considered in the selected games. Multiple categories may apply to a single game.

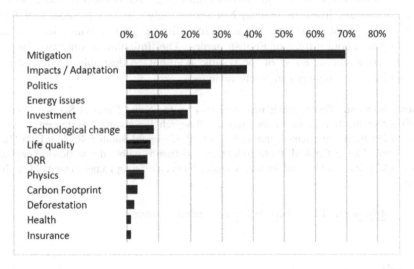

Fig. 5. Issues addressed in the selected games. Multiple categories may apply to a single game. Note: DRR means "disaster risk reduction."

This review analyzed game type, scope and thematic focus of a subset of 95 of the current climate games. In line with the findings of Reckien and Eisenack [8], it has been found that a substantial number of games focuses on one of the following topics: international climate conferences, impacts of global decisions, or effects of individual decisions on their local environment. The most common game types applied were role-play, board games, simulations and online games. Other possible game types and potential topics, however, were largely absent. Amongst others, those topics and game types include the following:

- IPCC [2] urges for a quick phase-out of all greenhouse gas emissions by 2050 to limit global warming to 1.5 °C, implying a fundamental societal transformation. Nevertheless, very few games explicitly connect the individual or local level to the national and global dimensions of climate change and foster transformative literacy on several levels.

- Climate games cover a broad range of relevant topics indicated by IPCC [2]. However, relevant topics such as "health" were addressed only by one game.
- Climate games use "video game" and "augmented reality game" (ARG) formats only to a very limited extent. While video games presumably could reach out to new audiences, ARGs could be used to reach large audiences in an everyday setting, and thereby making a large-scale impact [13].

Many topics are addressed by current climate games and are implemented by applying a variety of game types. Yet, the additional topics and scarcely applied game types mentioned above show a considerable potential for entirely new games that could develop the field and contribute to mitigate and adapt to climate change, as identified by Ulrich [9].

The limitation to German and English excluded a large number of games available in other languages from the review. Not surprisingly, the results show that English clearly is the most important language for climate games, with German games accounting for about a third of English games. The limitation to only two languages limits the comprehensiveness of the results. It might be desirable to include games available in other languages in future reviews.

Acknowledgement. This research was supported by the Swiss National Science Foundation (SNSF) within the framework of the National Research Programme "Sustainable Economy: resource-friendly, future-oriented, innovative" (NRP 73) (grant number 407340_172402). The authors would like to thank all those colleagues and friends within the worldwide network of ISAGA, SAGSAGA and beyond for their valuable hints on existing games in the field of climate change.

Conflicts of Interest. The authors declare no conflict of interest.

Appendix

List of 95 more sophisticated games used for detailed analysis.

Name	Link
2° und es wird immer heißer	https://dpsg.de/fileadmin/daten/dokumente/Internationale_Gerechtigkeit/planspiel_klima.pdf
2050 Pathways (former my 2050)	https://www.gov.uk/guidance/2050-pathways-analysis
Age of energy	https://www.cityzen-smartcity.eu
Before the storm	https://climatecentre.org/resources-games/games/3/before-the-storm

(continued)

(*continued*)

Name	Link
Beyond Paris	https://www.planpolitik.de/wp-content/uploads/2018/04/planpolitik-Planspieluebersicht-2018-DE-2.pdf
Broken cities	https://www.playistheantidote.com/games/broken-cities/
Cantor's World	https://fieldsofview.in/projects/cantors-world/
Carbon copy politics	https://boardgamegeek.com/boardgame/186039/carbon-copy-politics
Carbon Warfare	https://www.virtuosgames.com/en/carbon-warfare
CEO2	https://www.allianz.com/en/press/news/commitment/environment/news-2010-05-27.html
Clim Way	https://climcity.cap-sciences.net/
Climate Action Game	https://cafod.org.uk/Education/Secondary-and-youth-resources/Climate-Action-Game
Climate Bathtube Simulator	https://www.cakex.org/tools/climate-bathtub-simulation
Climate Challenge (1)	https://www.bbc.co.uk/sn/hottopics/climatechange/climate_challenge/
Climate Challenge (2)	https://www.theperspectivitychallenge.org/
Climate Change Showdown	https://www.bcsea.org/learn/resources-for-educators/climate-change-showdown/contest
Climate Defense	https://www.gamesforchange.org/game/climate-defense/
Climate Diplomat	https://www.iucnael.org/en/documents/656-hart-climate-diplomat-negotation/file
Climate Engineering-Planspiel	https://www.spp-climate-engineering.de/ce-planspiel.html
Climate Game (1)	https://boardgamegeek.com/boardgame/67996/climate-game/credits
Climate Game (?)	https://games4sustainability.org/gamepedia/climate-game/
Climate Game- Save Earth while having fun	https://play.google.com/store/apps/details?id=com.teraception.climatechange
Climate Health Impact	https://playgen.com/play/climate-health-impact/
Climate Oasis	https://boardgamegeek.com/boardgame/249405/climate-oasis
Climate Poker	https://boardgamegeek.com/boardgame/57422/climate-poker
Climate Quest	https://play.google.com/store/apps/details?id=com.EarthGames.ClimateQuest
Climate-Change Policy Exercise	https://pure.iiasa.ac.at/id/eprint/4937/

(*continued*)

(*continued*)

Name	Link
Co2	https://boardgamegeek.com/boardgame/72225/co
CO2peration	https://www.earthspeople.co.uk/projects
Connect2climate	https://www.zmqdev.org/connect-2-climate/
Cool it!	https://thepolarhub.org/database/
Cooling down	https://boardgamegeek.com/boardgame/168555/cooling-down
D3 Planspiel	https://www.umweltbundesamt.de/en/publikationen/entwicklung-eines-quantitativen-modells-2
d'Aquino and Bah [14]	Land Policies for Climate Change Adaptation in West Africa: A Multilevel Companion Modeling Approach
Das 3D-Planspiel	https://www.umweltbundesamt.de/publikationen/entwicklung-eines-quantitativen-modells-2
Die Klimaschutzbasis	https://www.umweltschulen.de/net/nocozwo.html
Earth Remembers	https://twitter.com/earthremembers?lang=de
Earthers	https://diary.earthers.studio/2016/10/29/theEarthersPitch.html#
Ecoego	https://www.marukin-ad.co.jp/ecoego/ecoego.html
Electrocity	https://www.electrocity.co.nz/
Enercities	https://www.enercities.eu/
Energetingen	https://www.energetingen.de/
Energie 21	https://boardgamegeek.com/boardgame/16519/energie-21
Energie für die Zukunft	www.eu-planspiele.de
Energie, Klimaschutz und Verbraucher	https://www.ilearning-company.de/
Energy transition game	https://energytransition.socialsimulations.org/en/
Energy Wars: Green revolution	https://play.google.com/store/apps/details?id=com.gz.EnergyWars
Europas Klima wandeln!	https://www.bpb.de/lernen/formate/planspiele/65586/planspiele-detailseite?planspiel_id=166
Fate of the world	https://www.soothsayergames.com/
Flood Resilience Game	https://floodresilience.socialsimulations.org/
Future Delta 2.0	https://futuredelta2.ca/
Gender and Climate Game	https://www.climatecentre.org/resources-games/games/9/gender-and-climate-game

(*continued*)

(continued)

Name	Link
Globalisierung und Global Governance	https://www.planpolitik.de/de/pdf/planspiel_globalisierung.pdf
Go2Zero	https://www.cityzen-smartcity.eu
Greenhouse Emissions Reduction Role-Play Exercise	https://www.climate.gov/teaching/resources/greenhouse-emissions-reduction-role-play-exercise
Greenhouse gas game	https://www.climatecentre.org/resources-games/games/14/greenhouse-gas-game
Greenify	Lee, Ceyhan, Jordan-Cooley, and Sung [19]
Grönlands Gier	https://www.planet-schule.de/fileadmin/dam_media/wdr/klimawandel/pdf/AB5_Planspiel_Klimakonferenz.pdf
Imagine Earth	https://www.imagineearth.info/
Increasing Climate Change Resilience of Urban Poor Communities in Asia-Pacific	https://www.ipa-netzwerk.de/portfolio/simulation-game-increasing-climate-change-resilience-of-urban-poor-communities-in-asia-pacific
Interactive Energy and Climate Simulation	https://tropicsu.org/interactive-energy-and-climate-simulation-game/
Invest in the future	https://www.climatecentre.org/resources-games/games/7/invest-in-the-future
Keep Cool	https://www.climate-game.net/keep-cool-brettspiel/
Keep Cool Online	https://www.climate-game.net/keep-cool-mobil-2/
Klimakonferenz - Internationale Klimapolitik	https://www.planpolitik.de/de/pdf/planspiel_klima.pdf
KRAFLA	https://www.umweltschulen.de/krafla/
Lebel, Sriyasak, Kallayanamitra, Duangsuwan, and Lebel [15]	Learning about climate-related risks: decisions of Northern Thailand fish farmers in a role-playing simulation game
Let's Negotiate! - Simulation of the Climate Change Conference	https://www.pacs.ovgu.de/fltf_media/Downloads/Berichte/Bericht+Planspiel+Oktober+2016.pdf
Losing the Lake	https://sensor.nevada.edu/nccp/Education/Losing%20the%20Lake/Default.aspx
Mobility	https://www.umweltspiele.eu/mobility.htm
Model United Nations with climate engineering	Matzner and Herrenbrück [20]
New Shores	https://newshores.socialsimulations.org/
Operation Climate Control	https://www.climateinteractive.org/policy-exercises-and-serious-games/19-climate-games-that-could-change-the-future/

(continued)

(continued)

Name	Link
Paying for Predictions	https://www.climatecentre.org/resources-games/games/2/paying-for-predictions
Peak Oil	https://boardgamegeek.com/boardgame/169215/peak-oil
Planspiel zur UN-Klimakonferenz COP21	https://www.kas.de/veranstaltungsberichte/detail/-/content/planspiel-zur-un-klimakonferenz-cop21
Polar Eclipse	https://www.polareclipsegame.com/
Simulation of International Climate Regime Formation	Kauneckis and Auer [18]
Sinking island	https://www.climatecentre.org/resources-games/games/19/sinking-island
Solar city	https://boardgamegeek.com/boardgame/248182/solar-city
Stabilization Wedges Game	https://cmi.princeton.edu/wedges/game
Stop Disasters!	https://www.stopdisastersgame.org/
Susclime	https://journals.sagepub.com/doi/abs/10.1177/1046878198292006
Sustainable Delta	https://www.deltares.nl/en/software/sustainable-delta-game/
The Adventures of Carbon Bond	Feldpausch-Parker, O'Byrne, Endres, and Peterson [17]
trico2lor	https://ucs.ch/ref/reftrico2lor.html
UrbanClimateArchitect	https://www.clisap.de/stadtklimaarchitekt/
V GAS	https://www.climateinteractive.org/policy-exercises-and-serious-games/19-climate-games-that-could-change-the-future/
Valkering, van der Brugge, Offermans, Haasnoot, and Vreugdenhil [16]	A Perspective-Based Simulation Game to Explore Future Pathways of a Water-Society System Under Climate Change
War game: clut and climate change	https://www.cnas.org/events/war-game-clout-and-climate-change
Was kostet die Welt: Gemeinsam gegen den Klimawandel?	https://www.hausrissen.org/zielgruppen/jugendbildung/41-nachhaltige-klima-und-energiepolitik.html
Winds of change	https://boardgamegeek.com/boardgame/23973/winds-change
World Climate	https://www.climateinteractive.org/programs/world-climate/
World Energy Simulator	https://www.climateinteractive.org/programs/world-energy/
World without Oil	https://writerguy.com/wwo/metacontact.htm
Worlds Future	https://systemssolutions.org/portfolio-items/the-worlds-future-game/

List of 24 more sophisticated games from the Reckien and Eisenack [8] article that were not used for the analysis.

Name	Reason for exclusion
A game framework a game framework for scenario generation for the co2 issue (Robinson & Ausubel, 1983)	a
Aqua-planing	b
CO2-Emissionshandel	b
CO2FX	b
CO2-the interactive negotiation	a
C-ROADS	a
Dynamic Climate Change Simulator	a
Early warning, early action	a
Energiekonferenz	h
Energy City (1)	b
Energy City (2)	b
Frischer Wind in Stahlhausen	b
Greenhouse gas simulator	a
Keep Cool in sunshine city	b
Klimakonferenz Lausitz	b
LogiCity	b
Love letters to the future	a
Planet Green Game	b
Plantville	b
Rizk	b
Strom für Europa!	b
Surfing Global Change: Negotiating Sustainable Solutions	a
The climate challenge	b
Weltklimagipfel	b

Remarks:
a means "the application did not meet the selection criteria for a sophisticated game",
b means "not enough information available".

Supplementary Materials: Table S1 "Game Characteristics".

References

1. IPCC: Summary for policymakers. In: Field, C.B., Barros, V.R., Dokken, D.J., Mach, K.J., Mastrandrea, M.D., White, L.L. (eds.) Climate Change 2014: Impacts, Adaptation, and Vulnerability. Part A: Global and Sectoral Aspects. Contribution of Working Group II to the Fifth Assessment Report of the Intergovernmental Panel on Climate Change. Cambridge University Press, Cambridge (2014)
2. IPCC: Summary for Policymakers. In: Masson-Delmotte, V., Zhai, P., Pörtner, H.-O., Roberts, D., Skea, J., Waterfield, T. (eds.) Global Warming of 1.5 °C. An IPCC Special Report on the impacts of global warming of 1.5 °C above pre-industrial levels and related global greenhouse gas emission pathways, in the context of strengthening the global response to the threat of climate change, sustainable development, and efforts to eradicate poverty Geneva. World Meteorological Organization, Switzerland (2018)
3. Schneidewind, U., Wiegandt, K., Welzer, H.: Die Große Transformation: Eine Einführung in die Kunst gesellschaftlichen Wandels: FISCHER E-Books (2018)
4. Moxnes, E., Saysel, A.K.: Misperceptions of global climate change: information policies. Clim. Change **93**(1), 15 (2008)
5. Sterman, J., Sweeney, L.B.: Cloudy skies: assessing public understanding of global warming. Syst. Dyn. Rev. **18**(2), 207–240 (2002)
6. Sterman, J., et al.: Climate interactive: the C-ROADS climate policy model. Syst. Dyn. Rev. **28**(3), 295–305 (2012)
7. Ulrich, M.: Games/simulations about environmental issues - existing tools and underlying concepts. Paper Presented at the 28th Annual Conference of the International Simulation and Gaming Association, Tilburg, The Netherlands (1997)
8. Reckien, D., Eisenack, K.: Climate change gaming on board and screen: a review. Simul. Gaming **44**(2–3), 253–271 (2013)
9. Ulrich, M.: Gaming, the language to shape a sustainable future - a journey from 1974 to 2054. In: Duke, R., Kritz, W.C. (eds.) Back to the Future of Gaming. wbv Bertelsmann Verlag, Germany (2014)
10. Duke, R., Geurts, J.: Policy Games for Strategic Management. Pathways into the Unknown. Dutch University Press, Amsterdam (2004)
11. Wenzler, I.: The role of simulation games in transformational change. In: Kritz, W.C. (ed.) Planspiele fur die Organisalionsenfwicklung ed Berlin: WVB (2008)
12. Robinson, J., Ausubel, J.H.: A game framework for scenario generation for the Co2 issue. Simul. Games **14**(3), 317–344 (1983)
13. McGonigal, J.: Reality Is Broken: Why Games Make Us Better and How They Can Change the World. The Penguin Press, New York (2011)
14. d'Aquino, P., Bah, A.: Land policies for climate change adaptation in West Africa: a multilevel companion modeling approach. Simul. Gaming **44**(2–3), 391–408 (2013)
15. Lebel, P., Sriyasak, P., Kallayanamitra, C., Duangsuwan, C., Lebel, L.: Learning about climate-related risks: decisions of Northern Thailand fish farmers in a role-playing simulation game. Reg. Environ. Change **16**(5), 1481–1494 (2015). https://doi.org/10.1007/s10113-015-0880-4
16. Valkering, P., van der Brugge, R., Offermans, A., Haasnoot, M., Vreugdenhil, H.: A perspective-based simulation game to explore future pathways of a water-society system under climate change. Simul. Gaming **44**(2–3), 366–390 (2013)
17. Feldpausch-Parker, A.M., O'Byrne, M., Endres, D., Peterson, T.R.: The adventures of carbon bond: using a melodramatic game to explain CCS as a mitigation strategy for climate change. Greenhouse Gases: Sci. Technol. **3**(1), 21–29 (2013)

18. Kauneckis, D.L., Auer, M.R.: A simulation of international climate regime formation. Simul. Gaming **44**(2–3), 302–327 (2013)
19. Lee, J.J., Ceyhan, P., Jordan-Cooley, W., Sung, W.: GREENIFY: a real-world action game for climate change education. Simul. Gaming **44**(2–3), 349–365 (2013)
20. Matzner, N., Herrenbrück, R.: Simulating a climate engineering crisis: climate politics simulated by students in model United Nations. Simul. Gaming **48**(2), 268–290 (2017)

Food-Web Modeling in the Maritime Spatial Planning Challenge Simulation Platform: Results from the Baltic Sea Region

Magali Goncalves[1]([✉]), Jeroen Steenbeek[2], Maciej Tomczak[3],
Giovanni Romagnoni[4], Rikka Puntilla[5], Ville Karvinen[5],
Carlos Santos[1], Xander Keijser[6], Lodewijk Abspoel[6],
Harald Warmelink[1], and Igor Mayer[1]

[1] Breda University of Applied Sciences, Mgr. Hopmansstraat 1,
4817 JT Breda, The Netherlands
goncalves.m@buas.nl
[2] Ecopath International Initiative, Barcelona, Spain
[3] Stockholm University, Stockholm, Sweden
[4] University of Oslo, Oslo, Norway
[5] Finnish Environment Institute (SYKE), Helsinki, Finland
[6] Ministry of Infrastructure and Water Management,
The Hague, The Netherlands

Abstract. The MSP Challenge Simulation Platform helps planners and stakeholders understand and manage the complexity of Maritime Spatial Planning (MSP). In the interactive simulation different data layers covering an entire sea region can be viewed to make an assessment of the current status. Planners can create scenarios for future uses of the marine space, over a period of several decades. The different plans for energy, shipping and the marine environment are then simulated and the effects are visualized in indicators and heat maps. To support in the implementation of the EU MSP Directive principles of evidence-based and ecosystem-based MSP, the authors created a link between the MSP Challenge and the food web modelling approach Ecopath with Ecosim (EwE). For each regional edition of the MSP Challenge, such as the North Sea or the Baltic Sea, a food-web model for the sea basin needs to be integrated. In this paper, the authors explain the integration of EwE into the MSP Challenge and evaluate the behavior of the food web model for the Baltic Sea from historic data, a baseline scenario and in shipping and offshore energy scenarios developed by planners from the region in a game session. The conclusion is that the current integration of the Baltic Sea food-web model into the platform gives ecologically realistic feedback and that this makes the players more aware of the effects of their plans on the entire ecosystem.

Keywords: Marine spatial planning · Ecosystems · Food-web modelling · Ecopath with Ecosim · Baltic Sea

© Springer Nature Switzerland AG 2021
M. Wardaszko et al. (Eds.): ISAGA 2019, LNCS 11988, pp. 290–305, 2021.
https://doi.org/10.1007/978-3-030-72132-9_25

1 Introduction

The EU Maritime Spatial Planning (MSP) Directive (2014/89/EU) [1] lays down obligations for the EU Member States to establish a 'maritime planning process', resulting in a 'maritime spatial plan, or plans' (Art 9.) by 2021. MSP is defined as 'a process by which the relevant Member State's authorities analyze and organize human activities in marine areas to achieve ecological, economic and social objectives.' Some of the guiding principles of the MSP directive are: *evidence-based, ecosystem-based, integrated, transboundary and stakeholder oriented* [1].

An important constraint to the ambitions of maritime sectors and countries is the health status of marine ecosystems. Globally, marine and coastal ecosystems are under enormous pressure [2, 3]. The cumulative effects of human uses on marine ecosystems is not yet fully known. Different international treaties and agreements, such as the *Convention on Biological Diversity* (CBD, 1992), including the *Aichi targets* [4], and the *United Nations' Sustainable Development Goals*, specifically the SDG 14, call upon nations and stakeholders to 'conserve and sustainably use the oceans, seas and marine resources for sustainable development' [5].

MSP is therefore in dire need of innovative approaches and effective *Planning Support Systems* (PSS) by which sectoral planners and stakeholders can assess the current ecological status of marine areas, like the North Sea or the Baltic Sea, but can also jointly explore the future consequences of planning decisions on the marine environment [6]. In the last few years, several PSS for ecosystem based MSP have been developed, each one having specific strengths and limitations [7–10]. However, few of these tools can be qualified as 'integrated' in the sense that they link with simulation models for a wider range of maritime sectors, such as energy (offshore wind farming, energy grid) or shipping. Furthermore, these PSS tend to be specialized and scientific, making them useful for desk analysis but less so for interaction by and with stakeholders, for instance in stakeholder engagement or transboundary co-design sessions.

In the seminal book '*Gaming: the future's language*', Duke [11] argues that a simulation game or serious game (SG) is an excellent communication and learning tool for planning and decision-making. Through play, planners and stakeholders experientially understand the dynamic interrelations among various subsystems, the interdependencies among the actors and the consequences of actions well into the future. SG thus become connected to a communicative and learning style of planning and planning support [12–14].

The MSP Challenge brand of board games and digital games, was developed to explore these ideas further in the context of ecosystem-based maritime spatial planning [15]. The MSP Challenge Simulation Platform (from now on referred to as MSP Challenge) integrates real geographic and marine data provided by many proprietary institutions (e.g. Helcom, Emodnet, IMO) with science based simulation models for shipping, energy and ecology [16, 17].

The simulation-platform allows anyone – experts as well as non-experts - to *playfully* operate it for scenario development, and/or for multi-player game sessions. This can have multiple purposes such as scenario exploration, co-design, validation or policy oriented learning.

Currently the MSP Challenge hosts three editions created for independent areas, namely the Clyde Marine Region in Scotland and the complete Baltic Sea and North Sea basins. Because it is built in highly modular fashion, it can host any sea basin in the world. Since its launch in 2018, the platform has been used in dozens of playful sessions in various settings; educational as well as for stakeholder consultation, and scenario exploration.

To accommodate the principle of ecosystem-based MSP in the simulation game, the authors created a link between the game and an ecosystem modelling software - Eco- path with Ecosim (EwE) [18]. Working with local experts, pre-existing EwE models of the North Sea, Baltic Sea and Clyde Marine Region were adapted to be used in the MSP Challenge. While the North Sea and Clyde models have been described in detail (Steen- beek et al., accepted), in this paper, first we explain how it was possible to link EwE with the MSP Challenge, and then evaluate the behavior of the food web model for the Baltic Sea, based on historic data.

2   Integration of Ecopath into the Simulation Platform

2.1   Ecosystem Modelling

Ecosystem modelling is one of the methodologies used to understand ecological dynamics, including species interactions, the impacts of environmental change such as rising temperatures, and anthropogenic stressors such as habitat destruction and variations in fishing intensity, etc. [19].

EwE is a free modeling software suite that enables the representation of ecological systems as a food web in terms of biomass, and predation links between functional groups [20–23]. A functional group can be representative of one specie, a group of species or a sub-group of a specie (for instance juveniles/adults) that have functional and ecological similarities [19].

In EwE, ecosystem dynamics can be simulated over time to explore impacts of fishing and environmental disturbances as well as for exploring optimal fishing policies [24]. These dynamics can then be reproduced over a spatial temporal map grid to allow exploration of alternative spatial management scenarios such as marine protected areas [19, 24, 25].

2.2   MSP Challenge with Ecopath Link (MEL)

To be able to represent the potential environmental effects of the planned scenarios on marine waters we developed an integration tool that connects the MSP Challenge backend system to the EwE food-web modelling software. We named the tool MEL (MSP Challenge with EwE Link).

MEL is a customizable tool that supports transferring data from/to any sea basin edition of the MSP Challenge and the corresponding EwE food-web model specifically designed for that sea region. In a nutshell, MEL calculates pressure layers for the sea basin based on the existing human activities in the sea basin at the start of the game, and for each time step of the simulation (1 month), it updates these layers to take into account any planned activities that were meanwhile implemented in the game.

The pressures layers are raster-based information, where each cell represents an area of the sea basin with values ranging from 0 (no pressure) to 1 (maximum pressure). The pressure values are calculated using cumulative values from all human activities, depending on the coverage area and relative weights defined previously in an activity/pressure matrix provided as Annex 1 (see Fig. 1). The size (width and height) of the raster image defines the resolution of the output, depending thus on the represented region, the food-web model requirements, and desired performance of the system.

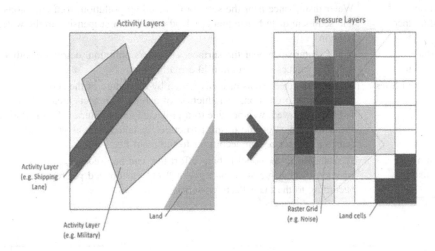

Fig. 1. Scheme of pressure calculations in MEL in [26]

MEL feeds the data from the pressure layers to the corresponding EwE model.

Although the systems are able to cope with any number of pressure layers, we determined that a good balance and representation can be achieved by six types of pressures, namely those represented in Table 1.

In the spatial module of EwE (Ecospace), species are distributed to their preferred habitats and environmental conditions (e.g., conditions of salinity, temperatures, depth, etc.). While adapting the model for the MSP Challenge, experts also define how each specie is likely to respond to each pressure, based on scientific literature or expert knowledge. In this fashion, the so-called habitat capacity model calculates the distribution of marine species, not only due to the environmental preferences, but also in reaction to the pressures created by human activities, such as shipping and construction of offshore windfarms.

Via MEL the EwE model receives heat maps of the relative pressures in the ecosystem and provides results in the form of heat maps and key performance indicators (KPIs) (Fig. 2).

Table 1. Pressure layers to drive the ecosystem model adapted from [26]

Title	Description
Artificial substrate	Man-made alterations of the sea floor, infrastructures, which provide shelter and habitat to specific species Various species benefit from the shelter and surface area that artificial substrate provides, while other species are known to avoid manmade structures
Noise	Low-frequency noise caused by human activities that impacts specific ecological functional groups in a positive or negative way. Noise also accounts for vibrations caused by operating heavy machinery Most species will tend to relocate away from noisy activities
Bottom disturbance	Water disturbance near the sea floor, including pollution from emissions and sediment disturbance that can lead to solids in suspension in the water column
Surface disturbance	Water disturbance near the surface, considers pollution, detritus or other multiple sources of disruption like marine litter
Protected Sites	Marine Protected Areas or areas which by the nature of the activities offer some sort of protection, or reduction of fishing. It reflects areas where no fishing is allowed, weather due to a protected area (Natura 2000 or Marine Protected Areas) or due to infrastructures installed such as wind parks. (customized per region according to the main fleets present)
Fishing intensity	A scalar for EwE model fishing effort that can be used to reduce or intensify fishing pressure for a given fleet. (customized per region according to the main fleets present)

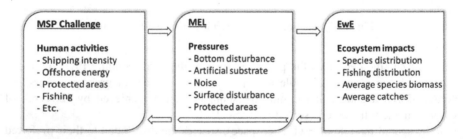

Fig. 2. Scheme of the data flow between the MSP Challenge and EwE via MEL

For each edition of the game (North Sea, Clyde Marine Region, Baltic Sea) a food-web model and corresponding Ecospace module need to be built or adapted. Guidelines and requirements for a EwE model to be implemented in MSP Challenge were defined to guide future work in different regions [27]. In essence, the EwE model should be representative of the region, it should include the main iconic and commercial species, and represent relevant trophic levels and fishing fleets [27]. It should be able to mimic historic time series based on actual data in the past, and show plausible future base line scenarios [27, 28].

2.3   Adapting the Baltic Sea Model to Use in MSP Challenge

The Baltic Sea has great spatial variation in temperature, salinity, oxygen and other environmental factors [29] which by turn makes it heterogeneous in terms of species distribution. Consequently, a single and unified EwE model for the whole Baltic Sea does not exist.

Therefore, it was thought best to start from an available EwE model for the Baltic Proper (southern-middle Baltic Sea) developed by Tomczak et al. [30]. We subsequently extended this model to also include the Bothnian Sea (located just north of the Baltic Proper) because the species composition in the Bothnian Sea are similar enough to the Baltic Proper [31]. The Baltic Proper and the Bothnian Sea cover together approximately 2/3 of the Baltic Sea area.

Since the pressure layers information does not depend on the EwE model, MEL calculates them for the whole Baltic Sea Region, but the impact on the marine ecosystem can thus far only be calculated and visualized for the Baltic Proper and Bothnian Sea.

Future work can lead us to improve MEL and enabling it to connect to several EwE models to be able to cover different ecological areas, and still have an unified ecological simulation for one MSP Challenge edition (see also the conclusion section below), since it is a very complex modelling task to create a single model for such heterogeneous regions.

In order to reduce computing time in the game, and accommodate to the playful use of the system, the level of detail of the EwE model needed to be reduced, for instance by grouping species together. Working with marine ecologists from the area, we grouped some functional groups of the Baltic Proper model and added others in order to also capture the dynamics of the Bothnian Sea. The extended Baltic Proper and Bothnian Sea model feature thus a total of 22 functional groups (Annex 2). The main commercial species were represented by groups of cod, herring and sprat, that account for 95% of the total catches in the region [32]. The top predators of this model are the 'seals' group representing the grey seals an iconic specie in the Baltic.

The fishing fleets and catches also needed to be redefined to better represent the fishing dynamics of the Baltic Proper and Bothnian Sea. We considered three main fishing fleets: demersal trawls, gillnets and pelagic trawls [32].

Then a series of iterative modeling cycles were performed, to balance this extended model and reach equilibrium between all the species, adjusting the diets, growth rates and other biological parameters [23, 27].

The Baltic Proper model was not originally implemented in Ecospace, but to be able to connect the model to MSP Challenge we had to implement the extended model in Ecospace. In order to be able to simulate the species distribution we needed to provide the model with data regarding the species preferences to environmental factors such as salinity, oxygen content, and depth, just to name a few, as well as spatial data of the same environmental factors [19].

Although the Baltic Sea experiences great variance of environmental factors like salinity and temperature, both spatially and in time, for MSP Challenge purposes these are static in time, so while these factors will determine the initial species distribution, during the simulation, only the pressures derived by planned human activities are updated.

Ecospace uses raster grids which size can be defined by the modeler, taking into account that a very detailed grid will compromise computing time and a too coarse grid may not grasp well the dynamics in the ecosystem (for instance if there are MPAs with a smaller area than the grid size). Taking that into consideration we adopted a grid of 15*15 km which provide a good balance between the factors mentioned above.

3 Findings

3.1 Calibration

After balancing the Baltic Proper and Bothnian Sea model we fitted the model to time series. Figure 3 shows how the model predictions compare with actual data collected over the years 1974–2006. We conclude that for some of the functional groups the estimates from the model matches the trends, especially for the fish groups, while for the groups with less data in the time series are satisfactory. Less satisfactory are the estimates of catches of Herring ('CJuv.Herring' and 'CAd.Herring' in Fig. 3) that are clearly over- estimated. Note that only the species for which we have times series are shown in Fig. 3 and that the species that are fished have two data sets: one with B for biomass and the other one with C for catches (regarding fisheries) as first letter. The sum of squares, a statistical measure of goodness of fit of the predictions of the model comparing to times series data, is showed in each graph at the top right.

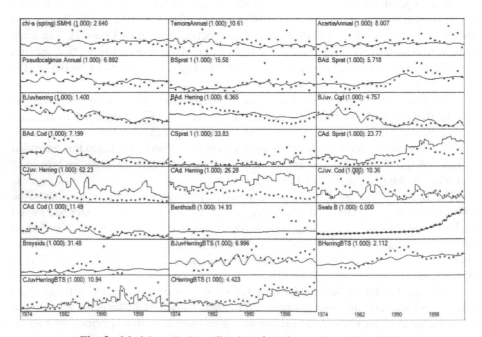

Fig. 3. Model predictions (lines) against time series values (dots).

Figure 4 shows the evolution overview of the species' biomass over a period of 50 years. During the first 25 years the modelling software enters into a self-balancing period to accommodate the predator-prey dynamics of the species and moving towards a stable state. This is taken into account when connecting the game to the model, the model will run an initial spin-off period of 30 years before starting communication with MEL to minimize model fluctuations' influence in the game's results.

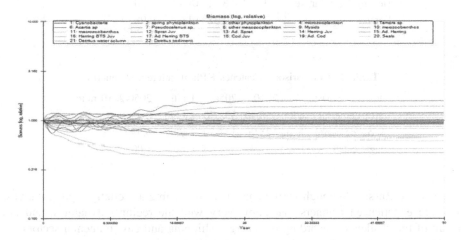

Fig. 4. Relative biomass simulation in time (50 years)

The species response to the different pressures considered in the game were defined with base on several studies and expert knowledge. Tests were carried together with local experts to make sure that the results provided in the game were the ones expected in the simulation conditions and the model was adjusted when needed.

3.2 Baseline Scenarios

The model was tested 'in game' to make sure that *i)* MEL is communicating well with both the MSP Challenge and the EwE model; *ii)* the implementation of the linkage was correctly done, and *iii)* the model provides ecologically realistic results in response to the plans implemented in the platform.

For testing purposes, we ran a MSP Challenge simulation without implementing any further plans or activities and documented the results for comparison against any future scenarios implemented. The results show that the biomass and catches values are stable in the region (Tables 2 and 3), except from a slight decrease of the seals biomass.

3.3 In-Game Scenarios

In this section we present indicative results of a first hands-on play session with the Baltic Sea Edition. The daylong session took place mid-February 2019 in Hamburg, with 14 participants from 7 countries: Germany, Poland, Estonia, Latvia, Finland,

Table 2. Comparison of ecology KPIs in reference scenario

Species (biomass)	2010	2050	Units	2050/2010 ratio
Benthos	27.75	27.76	t/km^2	1.00
Seals	370.40	336.90	g/km^2	0.91
Cod	578.50	575.60	kg/km^2	0.99
Herring Baltic proper	11.43	11.33	t/km^2	0.99
Herring Bothnian sea	3.52	3.51	t/km^2	1.00
Sprat	7.55	7.38	t/km^2	0.98

Table 3. Comparison of catches KPIs in reference scenario

Catches (biomass)	2010	2050	Units	2050/2010 ratio
Active demersal catch	356.40	353.80	kg/km^2	0.99
Passive demersal catch	125.90	124.50	kg/km^2	0.99
Pelagic catch	2.99	2.95	t/km^2	1.00

Sweden and Russia. Although participants were not acting as country representatives, they are experienced planners that know very well the region's dynamics, and are aware of the challenges regarding the energy, shipping and environmental sectors.

The game session generated a wealth of data, far beyond what can be presented here. We limit ourselves to the main plans with regard to shipping and energy and the combined effects this had on the ecology in the game.

In a nutshell the planners did the following: they optimized shipping routes, but the most noticeable change happened when the participants approved the removal of one of the major shipping lanes from the east of Gotland, to be replaced with no-shipping zones (Fig. 5). The intention was to decrease the pressure from heavy shipping on the ecosystem. While trying to achieve national and regional energy targets, they implemented offshore windfarms (Fig. 6). A few Marine Protected Areas (MPAs) were planned in German, Swedish, Russian and Latvian Exclusive Economic Zones (EEZ) with shipping protection measures implemented in the most Northern parts of the Swedish areas to the south of Gotland.

The effects can clearly be seen on the species distribution returned by the ecosystem model. The most obvious effects seen was in the distribution of seals. Seals avoid areas were the shipping intensity is high because they are sensitive to noise. After displacing the shipping lane on the East of Gotland, the seals distribution readjusted and they start to re-occupy the area (Fig. 7). Similar effects can be seen in the fish populations at a smaller scale, since they are sensitive to noise but less than Seals. The offshore wind farms are also influencing the distribution of species but at a smaller scale. This is due to residual noise from the wind farms while in an exploitation phase. This can be seen on the north of Gotland in the Swedish EEZ (Fig. 7). No significant effects can be observed from the MPAs implemented during the play session. This may be due to the fact that the MPAs were not large enough to be accounted for by the ecosystem model since the grid size is 15*15 km.

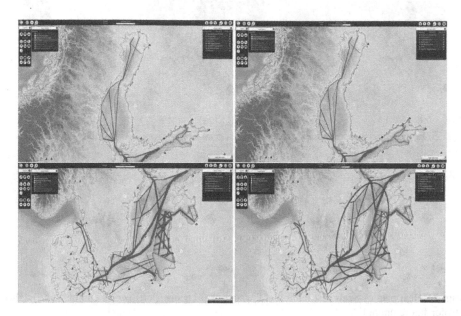

Fig. 5. Shipping scenario at start of game (left) *versus* end of game (right). The blue lines represent shipping lanes. (Color figure online)

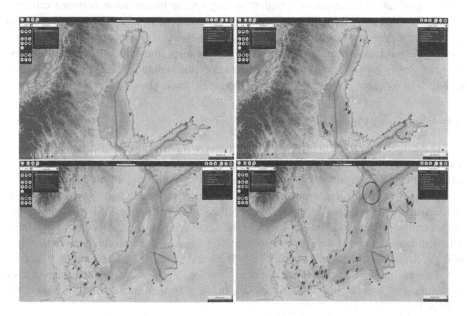

Fig. 6. Energy scenario at start of game (left) *versus* end of game (right). Dark orange polygons with green lightning bolts represent wind farms. (Color figure online)

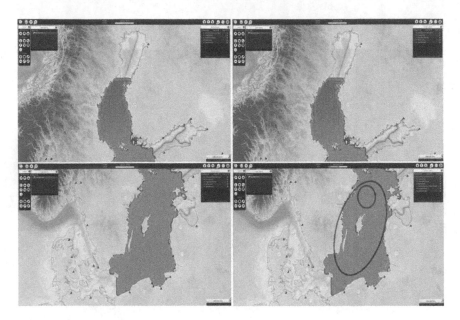

Fig. 7. Heat map of Seals distribution at the start of the game (left) *versus* end of game (right). (Color figure online)

Discussions and evaluations of these results with the players show that the simulation significantly enlarged their understanding on the interrelation between ecology, shipping and energy. Participants became more aware of how noise impacts different species in different ways, and that different phases of a project can have divergent effects. A good example are the offshore wind farms, they do not imply the same pressure on the ecosystem during the construction phase than in the exploitation phase, resulting in different impacts on the species during each phase.

3.4   Game and Player Experience

The players informally provided us their impressions about the MSP Challenge game, and informed us the different areas where they fell this will improve their work, not only for planning purposes, but also for stakeholder engagement and education.

As MSP experts, the players were able to recognise the tensions and issues of the Baltic Region represented in the simulation data represented by MSP Challenge, and the reactions of the modelling software were deem realistic by the ecologists present. This validates the use of the game for education purposes. Playing the game, the player will get acquainted with inter-sectorial conflicts and synergies and grasp the effects of the different human activities in different species. To understand the inter-species dynamics the user would have to engage a step further and browse through the Wikipedia.

We are formally performing an evaluation over the MSP Challenge digital version in the player experience similarly to the evaluation we performed to the board game which results can be seen in [33]. Unfortunately the results from the MSP Challenge Simulation Platform are not yet available.

4 Conclusion

The main conclusions of our case study with the integration of EwE into the MSP Challenge simulation platform in the Baltic are the following:

A complete EwE model for the whole Baltic Sea region does not yet exist. Given its very diverse environmental characteristics modelling the whole area in a single model is a very complex task and not feasible with the available resources. Still, we were able to extend the existing Baltic Proper model to North including the Bothnian Sea, which was only possible due to the similarities of the two areas, the data availability, and the contribution of regional experts.

However, since the current EwE model does not yet cover the entire Baltic Sea, and in order to represent the whole region, we are considering expanding the integration tool MEL to be able to link a single MSP Challenge to several separate EwE models, which would take the performance requirements of the platform to a new level, but would increase the versatility of the system greatly.

The extended EwE model (which covers 2/3 of the Baltic Sea) was validated against historical data, and integrated through MEL into the MSP Challenge Simulation Platform. Besides internal testing the platform was extensively used in a day long game session where 14 experts from the Baltic region with multiple backgrounds (including ecology) found that the model behavior makes sense ecologically speaking.

Overall, the game provides insights into plausible effects of human activities on species distribution and average biomass. Therefore the platform is becoming a good training and decision support tool and can also help future players of the MSP Challenge Baltic Sea Edition to understand how unique and valuable the ecosystem of that region is.

Acknowledgements. MSP Challenge Simulation Platform was developed by Breda University of Applied Sciences co-funded through the NorthSEE project (2016 2019), (Interreg North Sea Region program of the EU-RDF), the Baltic LINes project (2016–2019), (Interreg Baltic Sea Region program of the EU-RDF); The Scottish Government, Marine Scotland and the Scottish Coastal Forum through SIMCelt (2015–2018), (EU Directorate General for Maritime Affairs and Fisheries). The design and development of MEL was funded by the Ministry of Infrastructure and Water Management/Rijkswaterstaat, the Nether lands.

Annex 1

Human Activities/Pressures Matrix (e.g. Baltic Sea Edition)

Pressures

Activities	Artificial substrate	Noise	Bottom disturbance	Surface disturbance	Protected Sites (Fishing fleets)		
					Active demersal	Passive demersal	Pelagic
Shellfish farms	0,3	0	0	0,2	0	0	0
Finfish farms	0,3	0	0	0,2	0	0	0
Dredging sites areas	0	0,8	1	0	0	0	0
Dredging de posit sites	0	0	0,8	0	0	0	0
Sand and gravel extraction	0	0,8	1		0	0	0
Cables	0	0	0	0	0	0	0
Cables (construction phase)	0	0,3	0,2	0	0	0	0
Oil Gas Plat forms	0,5	0,3	0,5	0,5	0	0	1
Ports	0,8	1	0	0	0	0	1
Pipelines	0,2	0	0,2	0	0	0	0
Pipelines (construction phase)	0	0,3	0,5	0	1	0	0
Total ship ping intensity	0	1	0	1	1	1	1
Wind farms	0,3	0,2	0	0,2	1	1	1
Wind farms (construction phase)	0	1	0,8	0,5	1	1	1
Military Areas	0	0,2	0	0,2	0	0	0
Fisheries closure	0	0	0	0	1	1	1
Cod fisheries	0	0	0	0	1	1	0
Closure MPA	No protection against fishing			0		0	0
	Active demersal fleet				1	0	0
	Passive demersal fleet				0	1	1
	Pelagic fleet				0	0	1

Annex 2

Functional Groups in the Baltic Proper and Bothnian Sea Food-Web Model

Group name	Biomass in habitat area (t/km^2)
Cyanobacteria	3.4
Spring phytoplankton	2.8
Other phytoplankton	4.8
Microzooplankton	3.1
Temora sp	1.9
Acartia sp	1.35
Pseudocalanus sp.	4.39
Other mesozooplankton	4
Mysids (estimated)	5.3
Meiozoobenthos	4.8
Macrozoobenthos	27.3
Sprat Juvenile	0.347
Sprat Adult	4.086
Herring juvenile	11.592
Herring adult	6.302
Herring BTS juvenile	1.153
Herring BTS adult	2.346
Cod juvenile	0.544
Cod adult	0.502
Seals	0.0006
Detritus water column	3256
Detritus sediment	4651

References

1. European Union Directive 2014/89/EU of the European Parliment and of the Council of 23 July 2014 establishing a framework for maritime spatial planning. Off. J. Eur. Union 2014, pp. 135–145 (2014)
2. Tamis, J.E., et al.: Toward a harmonized approach for environmental assessment of human activities in the marine environment. Integr. Environ. Assess. Manage. **12**, 632–642 (2016)
3. Kannen, A.: Challenges for marine spatial planning in the context of multiple sea uses, policy arenas and actors based on experiences from the German North sea. Reg. Environ. Change **14**(6), 2139–2150 (2012)
4. United Nations. https://www.cbd.int/sp/targets. Accessed 02 Apr 2019
5. United Nations Transforming our world: the 2030 Agenda for Sustainable Development. Gen. Assem. 70 Sess. 16301, 1–35 (2015)

6. Jean, S., et al.: Serious games as planning support systems: learning from playing maritime spatial planning challenge 2050. Water **10**, 1786 (2018)
7. HELCOM Baltic Sea Impact Index and its use in Maritime Spatial Planning (2018)
8. Symphony: a tool for ecosystem-based marine spatial planning|European MSP Platform. https://www.msp-platform.eu/practices/symphony-tool-ecosystem-based-marine-spatial-planning. Accessed 01 Apr 2019
9. Menegon, S., Sarretta, A., Depellegrin, D., Farella, G., Venier, C., Barbanti, A.: Tools4MSP: an open source software package to support maritime spatial planning. Peer J. Comput. Sci. **4**, e165 (2018)
10. Pınarbaşı, K., Galparsoro, I., Borja, Á., Stelzenmüller, V., Ehler, C.N., Gimpel, A.: Decision support tools in marine spatial planning: Present applications, gaps and future perspectives. Mar. Policy **83**, 83–91 (2017)
11. Duke, R.D.: Gaming: The Future's Language, 1st edn. Sage Publications, New York. (1974). ISBN: 0-470-22405-3
12. Healey, P.: The communicative turn in planning theory and its implications for spatial strategy formations. Environ. Plan. B Plan. Des. **23**, 217–234 (1996)
13. Muro, M., Jeffrey, P.: A critical review of the theory and application of social learning in participatory natural resource management processes. J. Environ. Plan. Manage. **51**, 325–344 (2008)
14. Mayer, I.S.: Playful Organisations & Learning Systems. NHTV Breda University of Applied Science, Breda/The Hague, The Netherlands. (2016). ISBN 978-90-825477-0-2
15. MSP Challenge. www.mspchallenge.info. Accessed 12 Apr 2019
16. Abspoel, L., Mayer, I., Keijser, X., Warmelink, H., Fairgrieve, R., Ripken, M., Abramic, A., Kannen, A., Cormier, R., Kidd, S.: Communicating Maritime Spatial Planning: the MSP Challenge approach. Mar. Policy (2019)
17. Mayer, I.S., et al.: Integrated, ecosystem-based marine spatial planning: design and results of a game-based quasi-experiment. Ocean Coast. Manage. **82**, 7–26 (2013)
18. Ecopath with Ecosim – Ecopath with Ecosim food web modeling approach. https://ecopath.org. Accessed 12 Apr 2019
19. Christensen, V., Coll, M., Steenbeek, J., Buszowski, J., Chagaris, D., Walters, C.J.: Representing variable habitat quality in a spatial food web model. Ecosystems **17**, 1397–1412 (2014)
20. Polovina, J.J.: Model of a coral reef ecosystem. Coral Reefs **3**, 23–27 (1984)
21. Christensen, V., Pauly, D.: ECOPATH II - a software for balancing steady-state ecosystem models and calculating network characteristics. Ecol. Model. **61**(3–4), 169–185 (1992)
22. Walters, C., Christensen, V., Pauly, D.: Structuring dynamic models of exploited ecosystems from trophic mass-balance assessments. Rev. Fish Biol. Fish. **7**, 139–172 (1997)
23. Christensen, V., et al.: Best practice in Ecopath with Ecosim food-web models for ecosystem-based management. Ecol. Model. **331**, 173–184 (2016)
24. Christensen, V., Walters, C.J.: Ecopath with Ecosim: Methods, capabilities and limitations. Ecol. Model. **172**, 109–139 (2004)
25. Steenbeek, J., et al.: Bridging the gap between ecosystem modeling tools and geographic information systems: driving a food web model with external spatial-temporal data. Ecol. Model. **263**, 139–151 (2013)
26. Santos, C., Gonçalves, M.: MSP Challenge 2050 - Ecopath link Design Document (2016)
27. Steenbeek, J.: 2017 EwE tools for MSP – EwE model guidelines for MSP gameplay (2017)
28. Steenbeek, J., et al.: Ecology for all: combining ecosystem modelling and serious gaming to aid transnational management of marine space. Ecol. Soc. **25**(2), 1–24 (2020). (Approved Spec. issue)

29. Reusch, T.B.H., et al.: The Baltic Sea as a time machine for the future coastal ocean. Sci. Adv. **4**(5), p.eaar8195 (2018)
30. Tomczak, M.T., Niiranen, S., Hjerne, O., Blenckner, T.: Ecosystem flow dynamics in the Baltic proper-using a multi-trophic dataset as a basis for food-web modelling. Ecol. Model. **230**, 123–147 (2012)
31. Kuosa, H., et al.: A retrospective view of the development of the Gulf of Bothnia ecosystem. J. Mar. Syst. **167**, 78–92 (2017)
32. ICES WGBFAS Report 2016 Report of the Baltic Fisheries Assessment Working Group (WGBFAS). Management, pp. 17–26 (2016)
33. Keijser, X., et al.: Stakeholder engagement in maritime spatial planning: the efficacy of a serious game approach. Water (Switz.) **10**, 1–6 (2018)

Unpacking and Overconfidence in a Production Management Game

Mieko Nakamura[✉]

Ryutsu Keizai University, Ryugasaki 3018555, Ibaraki, Japan
mnakamura@rku.ac.jp

Abstract. People often make judgements irrationally. For example, people tend to underestimate the completion time of tasks and be overly confident in their estimations. Previous research shows that unpacking tasks into a series of required steps reduced the underestimation of completion times. The purpose of this research was to examine the phenomenon of overconfidence in simulation and gaming situations and study the relationship between unpacking and overconfidence. For this research, a production management game, the "OPT SCHEDULING GAME," was used. Two different questionnaires were distributed before game run to examine whether some informative questions improved the quality of estimations by participants; the results for this were affirmative. A post-game questionnaire assessed the attitudes of participants regarding their understanding of the process, result prediction, etc. The results of this questionnaire showed that their attitudes remained the same whether they were provided with informative questions or not before game run. This was consistent with the results of previous research that showed unpacking did not improve the overall quality of performance on a task, even though unpacking does improve the quality of estimations on the time needed to complete that task. One reason would be those who have an incorrect understanding of the situation tend to be overconfident and convincing and those who have a correct understanding of the situation tend to be less confident and silent. If we could assist those with an incorrect understanding and a sense of overconfidence to become good listeners and support those with a correct understanding and a feeling of uncertainty to become more open and outspoken, then the effect of overconfidence would be reduced. If simulation and gaming can assist people to learn from each other, people can make better judgements as a team.

Keywords: Estimation of the completion time · Overconfidence · Production management · Simulation and gaming · Unpacking

1 Introduction

1.1 General Review

Individually, people often make irrational judgments [1]. According to Tversky and Kahneman [1], there are three main heuristics employed in making judgements under uncertainty: representativeness, availability, and anchoring. Representativeness leads to the illusion of validity, i.e., unwarranted confidence. People are confident with their

M. Wardaszko et al. (Eds.): ISAGA 2019, LNCS 11988, pp. 306–319, 2021.
https://doi.org/10.1007/978-3-030-72132-9_26

prediction depending on the degree of representativeness. Availability includes imaginability. If people can easily imagine more good than bad points, they will overestimate a positive alternative and underestimate a negative one. Anchoring indicates the phenomenon where different starting points yield different estimates, which are biased toward the initial values. Kahneman and Tversky [2] say, "The factors which enhance confidence, for example, consistency and extremity, are often negatively correlated with predictive accuracy" and "people are prone to experience much confidence in highly fallible judgement" (p. 249).

We are hopeful that we can learn from mistakes. After making mistakes, we review what went wrong, consider how we can improve, and prepare for the next opportunity. Through our own or someone else's experiences, we can learn lessons, develop ourselves, and make better decisions. Simulation & gaming (S&G) is one powerful method to learn through experiences in a simulated situation.

The topic of this study is unpacking and overconfidence. Since I am concerned with designing a game related to this topic, I will examine how unpacking and overconfidence happen in S&G situations. Based on this research, I intend to narrow down factors that are essential to designing a game aimed at teaching unpacking and warning against overconfidence. The goal of this research is to obtain data and extract factors that will be useful in the design of an appropriate game.

1.2 Unpacking

Unpacking a task is "to consider each of the subcomponents of the task" (Kruger and Evans [3], p. 588). Kruger and Evans [3] reported several experiment results on the phenomena that unpacking improves the quality of judgment. For example, when participants were asked to predict the time required for preparing a special meal, they tended to underestimate the completion time. However, when participants were given a list of each of the steps that need to be completed such as slicing fruit, putting filling in celery, boiling shrimp, etc., and asked to indicate the order in which they planned to complete each task, they predicted the completion time appropriately. That is, unpacking reduced underestimation. However, unpacking did not contribute to performance improvement. There was no difference between actual completion times in the packed and unpacked conditions, despite indications that unpacking does help one more accurately estimate how much time is needed. In other words, the time needed to complete the task does not change whether one correctly estimates the time that will be needed or not.

1.3 Overconfidence

The most commonly studied type of overconfidence is overestimation, in which people overestimate their actual ability, performance, or level of control [4]. Fabricius and Buttgen [4] dealt with another type of overconfidence, "overprecision, which refers to people's unrealistically positive self-assessment of their accuracy in estimations" (p. 2) and reported that "overconfidence is high when little task-specific knowledge is available, which increases the likelihood of making incorrect decisions when faced with low knowledge" (p. 1). They performed a cluster analysis for their exploratory research and identified four clusters from the combination of knowledge and comparative optimism levels: 1) high knowledge and very high comparative optimism; 2) slightly-above-average knowledge and very low comparative optimism; 3) below-average knowledge and low comparative optimism; and 4) low knowledge and high comparative optimism. The percentages for each cluster were 19%, 32%, 6%, and 43%, respectively. Clusters 1 and 4 showed overconfidence about their estimation. In total, 62% of participants showed overconfidence. Fabricius and Buttgen [4] noted that "overconfidence is strongest for people with low task-specific knowledge" and "people who are comparatively optimistic about their future prospects are more likely to be overconfident when little knowledge is available" (p. 9). Fabricius and Buttgen suggested that people may try to hide their lack of knowledge by indicating high levels of confidence in their estimates. This may be the case for 70% of those with overconfidence, but not for the other 30%, suggesting that individual differences in overconfidence must be taken into account.

Buehler, Griffin, and Ross [5] examined the process of producing overconfidence and concluded, "People tend to generate their predictions by considering the unique features of the task at hand and constructing a scenario of their future progress on that task" and "the act of scenario construction may lead people to exaggerate the likelihood of the scenario taking place" (p. 8). They also said, "The scenario thinking approach threatens the accurate estimation of completion times because there are many ways for the future to unfold that are not as planned" (p. 9). People believe in what they predict simply because they have not come up with other provable results.

Those who are overconfident about their inaccurate estimations are likely overly satisfied with their abilities, afraid of showing their weaknesses, or have tunnel vision regarding their future. In either case, the result is unwarranted confidence in their inaccurate estimation. People who are overconfident are often unable to learn from their mistakes and are likely to repeat them.

1.4   Purpose of This Research

The purpose of this research is to identify the trends of participant estimations in the context of S&G. With the benefit of this research, it would be possible to design a game in the future where participants can experience the importance of unpacking by avoiding the pitfalls of overconfidence. For this research, a production management game, the "OPT SCHEDULING GAME" was used. Two different pre-game questionnaires were prepared to examine whether informative questions improved the quality of participants' estimations. A post-game questionnaire assessed the attitudes of participants regarding their understanding of the process, result predicting, etc.

The purpose of this research is to examine the phenomenon of overconfidence in simulation and gaming situations and study the relationship between unpacking and overconfidence.

2 Method

2.1 An OPT SCHEDULING GAME

In this research, I prepared a questionnaire prior and subsequent to a game. I will explain the content of the game here and explain the content of the questionnaires below. The game was designed by Legg [6] and based on a concept outlined in *The Goal*, a book by Eliyahu M. Goldratt [7]. It was designed to simulate a mechanism of optimized production technology that he termed the "OPT SCHEDULING GAME." This research used a Japanese version of this game [8].

In an OPT SCHEDULING GAME, participants work in teams of about ten people. The goal of the game is to make as high of a profit as possible by producing airplanes with A4 plain paper. Individual members have eight tasks, as shown in Table 1.

Table 1. Eight tasks and contents

Task	Content
Mark out	Draw two straight lines with a pencil and a scale on a sheet of A4 paper to trisect the long side of the paper
Cut	Cut a sheet of paper with a pair of scissors into three pieces along the two straight lines
Fold wings	Fold a strip and make a pair of wings
Write on the wings	Write "OPT" on each of the two wings
Fold fuselages	Fold a strip and make a fuselage
Write on the fuselages	Write the name of a company "RYUTSU KEIZAI UNIVERSITY" and three words, "TRY," "OUT," and "OPT," on each side of the fuselage
Combine wings with fuselages	Combine a pair of wings with a fuselage into the shape of an airplane by stapling the two parts
Transport materials	Transport materials between members who are allocated different tasks at different places. The materials include A4 plain paper, strips of paper, and the work-in-progress

The total running time of this game is 900 s. The bottleneck of the process is found in the "write on the fuselages" step, which takes about 30 s to finish. In terms of the cost, the initial cost is ¥200,000 and the cost of a sheet of A4 plain paper is ¥3,000. In terms of the profit, one airplane profits ¥20,000, a pair of wings profits ¥5,000, and one fuselage profits ¥10,000. To recoup the initial cost, at least 10 airplanes need to be produced. Making a profit is numerically possible since producing 10 airplanes takes 300 s, which is much less than the running time of 900 s.

2.2 Participants and Procedures

Participants were those who registered in a "project management" course for the first semester in the first grade. The course consisted of a once-a-week class for 15 weeks.

Two groups of students registered for the course, and the size of the class was around 50 for Group 1 and 45 for Group 2. The age of the participants ranged from 18 to 21. The ratio of males to females was 89 to 9. During the semester, students experienced several types of S&G on subjects including communication, information-sharing, leadership, social dilemmas, and team building before participating in an OPT SCHEDULING GAME. The game was run for two class meetings in a row, with session 1 occurring at the end of June and session 2 in the beginning of July in 2018. The number of attendees for the two consecutive weeks are shown in Table 2.

Table 2. The number of participants in two consecutive sessions

	Session 1	Session 2
Group 1 (5 teams)	50 participants	54 participants
Group 2 (4 teams)	44 participants	44 participants

Session 1 was dedicated to preparation: understanding the rules and procedures of the game, organizing teams, making plans, allocating tasks to each member, and having a rehearsal with the whole group. The teams were organized mainly by the students themselves. They were instructed to form teams of 10 in Group 1 and 11 in Group 2. When the team size was too big or small, the facilitator mediated a transfer between groups. Five teams were organized for Group 1 and four teams were organized for Group 2.

Session 2 was dedicated to the game itself: checking the plans and executing them. Some students were absent for the first session but attended the second session. Others attended session 1 but were absent from session 2. At the beginning of session 2, I asked each team to check whether all members were present and rearranged the teams such that they were approximately the same size. As a result, all teams except Team C, which consisted of ten members, had eleven members and most teams had a few new members with little knowledge of the game or its procedures. The first topic for all teams in session 2 was to review what was discussed and agreed on in session 1 and to confirm or reconsider their previous plans within the team. This helped new members understand the team's plan and refreshed old members' memory.

2.3 Questionnaires

Prior and subsequent to the game run, questionnaires were distributed. The details of the questionnaires are as follows.

Questionnaires Prior to the Game Run

In session 2, prior to the game run, two different types of questionnaires were distributed. In Group 1, question items were intended to remind team members of the initial costs and minimum number of airplanes required to recoup the initial cost. In addition, questions about the most difficult task were prepared to make them think about the critical path of this production process. Contrarily, in Group 2, no informative questions were prepared. Their enthusiasm for their tasks was asked instead. In both groups, people were asked to estimate the net profit gain of their team.

Questionnaire for Group 1

(1) Do you realize that the initial cost is ¥200,000?
(2) Do you realize the minimum number of airplanes required to recoup the initial cost?
(3) Which task do you think is the hardest? Please choose one from the following alternatives.

> Mark out, Cut, Fold wings, Write on the wings, Fold fuselages,
> Write on the fuselages, Combine wings and fuselages, Transport

(4) Please estimate the net profit gain (sales minus costs) of your team.

Participants answered questions (1) and (2) by choosing among four options: "Yes, I do," "Now I realize," "Neither yes nor no," and "I have no idea." Participants answered question (3) by choosing among eight options. Question (4) called for a free description.

Questionnaire for Group 2

(1) Please estimate the net profit gain (sales minus costs) of your team.
(2) Please tell us of your enthusiasm for this work.

Participants answered questions (1) and (2) by providing a free description.

Questionnaires Subsequent to the Game Run
At the end of session 2, subsequent to the game run, the same debriefing sheet was distributed to both Groups 1 and 2. Question items asked about the degree of understanding and satisfaction.

Debriefing Sheet for Both Groups 1 and 2

(1) Please tell us your feedback of this game run in two lines.
(2) How much did you understand the whole process of producing the airplane?
(3) How well did you understand the plan of your team?
(4) Did you predict your team would end up with this result?
(5) How much are you satisfied with the result of this game?
(6) What do you think should have been done better?
(7) If you were to participate in the same game again, what would you like to do?
(8) If you were to apply what you have learned from this game, what would it be?

Participants answered questions (2), (3), (4), and (5) on a 6-point scale ranging from 1 (never) to 6 (fully). Questions (1), (6), (7), and (8) called for free description. In this research, the quantitative data were analyzed to identify differences in the attitudes of Groups 1 and 2.

2.4 Hypothesis

In Group 1, participants were asked about the initial cost and the minimum number of airplanes to recoup the initial cost. These informative questions would make participants more cautious when they estimate the net profit gain. Therefore, the average of the estimated net profit gain of Group 1 will be lower than that of Group 2. In addition, the estimated net profit gain by Group 1 will be more on-target than the one by Group 2.

3 Results

3.1 The Profits of Each Team

Table 3 shows the results from Groups 1 and 2, respectively. In Group 1, Teams A and C generated a surplus and Teams B, D, and E ended in the red. In Group 2, Teams G, H, and I generated a surplus and Team F ended in the red. Overall, the performance of Group 2 was better than that of Group 1.

Table 3. Group 1 and Group 2 profits

Group 1		Group 2	
Team A	¥84,000	Team F	− ¥346,000
Team B	− ¥801,000	Team G	¥86,000
Team C	¥70,000	Team H	¥29,000
Team D	− ¥469,000	Team I	¥132,000
Team E	− ¥247,000		

3.2 Answers to the Questionnaire Prior to the Game Run

Table 4 shows the frequency distribution of answers to questions (1) and (2) in Group 1. Concerning the question about the initial cost, 38 out of 54 realized the initial cost. After being asked about it, 10 participants answered that they had just realized it. Concerning the question about the minimum number of airplanes required to recoup the initial cost, 24 out of 54 had realized it. After being asked about it, 20 answered that they had just realized it.

Table 4. Frequency distribution of answers to questions (1) and (2) in Group 1

	Realize	Just now	Neither	No idea	Total
(1) The initial cost	38	10	2	4	54
(2) The minimum number of airplanes required to recoup the initial cost	24	20	7	3	54

Table 5 shows the frequency distribution of answers to the question about the hardest task. Writing on the fuselages, the bottleneck in an OPT SCHEDULING GAME, was chosen by 25 participants. Transporting was chosen by 13 participants. In Group 1, around half of the participants correctly understood the critical part of the production process.

Table 5. Frequency distribution of answers to question (3)

	Group 1
Write on the fuselages	25
Transport	13
Mark out	5
Cut	4
Combine wings and a fuselage	4
Write on the wings	3
Fold fuselages	0
Fold wings	0
Total	54

Looking deeper, the frequency distribution of answers to questions (1) to (3) in Group 1 are shown in Tables 6, 7 and 8.

Table 6. Answers to the question about the initial cost in Group 1

	Realize	Just now	Neither	No idea	Total
Team A	11	0	0	0	11
Team B	6	4	0	1	11
Team C	8	1	1	0	10
Team D	5	3	1	2	11
Team E	8	2	0	1	11

Table 7. Answers to the question about the required number of airplanes in Group 1

	Realize	Just now	Neither	No idea	Total
Team A	10	1	0	0	11
Team B	4	6	1	0	11
Team C	3	6	1	0	10
Team D	3	1	5	2	11
Team E	4	6	0	1	11

Table 8. Answers to the question about the hardest task in Group 1

	Write on the fuselages	Transport	Others	Total
Team A	5	2	4	11
Team B	5	2	4	11
Team C	7	3	0	10
Team D	3	3	5	11
Team E	5	3	3	11

Table 9 shows the estimated net profit gain by individual participants in Groups 1 and 2. The lowest range, from ¥0 through ¥100,000, was chosen by the largest number of participants in both Groups 1 and 2. In Group 1, the lowest range was chosen by 27 out of 52, and in Group 2, it was chosen by 16 out of 44. The second range, from ¥100,001 through ¥200,000, was chosen by 12 participants in Group 1, which was the second largest number of participants in Group 1. The third range, from ¥200,001 through ¥300,000, was chosen by 11 participants in Group 2, which was the second largest number of participants in Group 2. The midpoints of estimation were ¥100,000 in Group 1 and ¥290,000 in Group 2. As a whole, the estimated amount of profit was lower in Group 1. The differences between Groups 1 and 2 were due to the content of the questionnaire: Informative questions were asked of Group 1 and not Group 2.

Table 9. The estimated net profit gain by individual participants in Groups 1 and 2

	Group 1	Group 2
¥0–¥100,000	27	16
¥100,001–¥200,000	12	4
¥200,001–¥300,000	5	11
¥300,001–¥400,000	2	4
¥400,001–¥500,000	1	3
¥500,001–¥1,000,000	0	2
¥1,000,001–¥10,000,000	3	3
¥10,000,001–¥5,000,000,000	2	1
NA	2	0
Total	54	44

Figure 1 shows the relative proportion of each category in the two groups. About 75% of the participants in Group 1 and 45% in Group 2 estimated less than ¥200,000. By answering questions about the initial cost and the minimum number of airplanes to recoup the initial cost, participants in Group 1 may have become cautious about estimating the profit. This is consistent with the hypothesis.

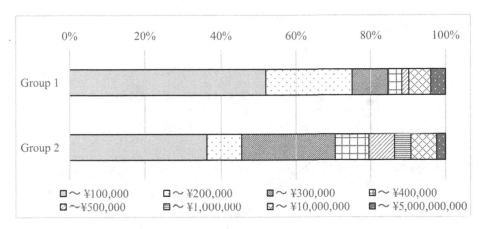

Fig. 1. Relative proportion of the estimated amount of profit

In Fig. 1, about 10% of the participants estimated a profit of more than ¥1,000,000 in Groups 1 and 2. By dividing the total running time by the time required for the bottleneck (900 s divided by 30 s), 30 a maximum of airplanes can be produced, which would bring the profit to ¥600,000. Subtracting the initial cost of ¥200,000 results in a profit of ¥400,000. Therefore, the profit cannot exceed ¥400,000 by most definitions. It is surprising that there were some who estimated more than ¥1,000,000. Those who made such an estimation made unwarranted assumptions and estimated without paying attention to the given conditions. The top three estimations were ¥5,000,000,000 in Team F of Group 2 and ¥1,000,000,000 and ¥30,000,000 in Team B of Group 1. These three extreme outliers were excluded from the team's average in Table 10 and Fig. 2.

Table 10. Team's average of individual estimations and team's actual result

Group 1	Team's average	Actual result	Group 2	Team's average	Actual result
Team A	¥80,727	¥84,000	Team F	¥730,000	−¥346,000
Team B	¥1,412,222	− ¥801,000	Team G	¥313,909	¥86,000
Team C	¥122,700	¥70,000	Team H	¥117,273	Y29,000
Team D	¥211,111	− ¥469,000	Team I	¥273,636	¥132,000
Team E	¥116,909	− ¥247,000			

Table 10 shows the average of individual estimations of the net profit gain for each team and the team's actual result in the game run. Teams with an especially high average of individual estimation, Teams B and F, ended in the red as a result of their game run. Figure 2 shows a scatter diagram of Table 10. The determination coefficient is 0.604 and the correlation coefficient is −0.777. There was a strong negative correlation between the average of individual estimations and a team's result. The higher the average of individual estimations, the lower the team's actual result.

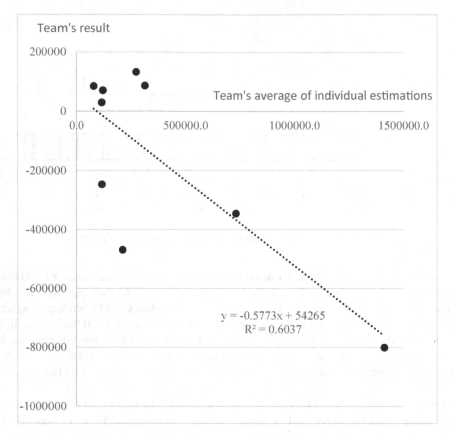

Fig. 2. A scatter diagram with team's average of individual estimations and team's result

3.3   Answers to the Questionnaire Subsequent to the Game Run

Tables 11 and 12 show the frequency distribution of answers to questions (2) to (5) in Groups 1 and 2, respectively. Participants answered on a 6-point scale from 1 (never) to 6 (fully). The average score of more than 3.5 indicates a tendency toward positive direction. Both in Tables 11 and 12, the average scores on questions (2) and (3) were more than 4.0. This means that the responses of participants were positive in understanding the process and the strategy. The average scores on questions (4) and (5) in Tables 11 and 12 were a little less than 3.5. This means that the responses of participants were slightly negative in the prediction of the result and the satisfaction of the result. Comparing the four pairs of averages between Groups 1 and 2, t-scores were not significant at a level of 0.05. This means that the participants' attitudes after the game run were not different between the two groups on average, whereas their estimation about net profit gains was different before the game run.

Table 11. Frequency distribution of answers to questions (2) to (5) in Group 1 (N = 48)

	1	2	3	4	5	6	Average
(2) Understanding the process	2	6	5	16	11	8	4.08
(3) Understanding the strategy	1	4	6	19	9	9	4.21
(4) Predicting the result	11	8	7	11	6	5	3.17
(5) Satisfaction of result	6	11	11	7	9	4	3.29

Table 12. Frequency distribution of answers to questions (2) to (5) in Group 2 (N = 38)

	1	2	3	4	5	6	Average
(2) Understanding the process	2	5	2	15	9	5	4.26
(3) Understanding the stratcgy	1	3	5	16	8	5	4.30
(4) Predicting the result	9	6	5	9	6	3	3.00
(5) Satisfaction of result	3	8	10	6	8	3	3.46

Overall, participants in Group 1 were better than those in Group 2 at predicting the net profit gain before the game run but were worse than those in Group 2 at producing the actual net profit gain during the game run. There was no difference between the attitudes of the two groups after the game run.

4 Discussion

In Table 10 and Fig. 2, we can see that Teams B and F ended up with devastating consequences. We excluded the top three extremely high estimations when we calculated the average scores in Table 10 and Fig. 2. Even if we included the top three estimations in the calculation, it did not affect the dominant trend of the results, since all top three estimations were in Teams B and F. The reason these two teams achieved poor results could be explained by the heuristic of anchoring. The existence of an extraordinarily high score of estimation may have a strong influence on the other members in the same team and their judgement as a team could be biased toward an inappropriate direction.

There were two more teams who ended in the red: Teams D and E. These teams did not have any extreme members. The average of individual estimations in Table 10 shows that both Teams D and E were ordinary. What was wrong with these two teams? Let us look at the frequency distribution of answers to prior questions (1) to (3) in Tables 6, 7 and 8. Among five teams, Team B showed a heavy deficit because of anchoring. Among the rest, Teams A and C succeeded in making profits, whereas Teams D and E did not. Comparing Teams D and E with Teams A and C in Tables 6, 7 and 8, we can see that the levels of understanding in Teams D and E were low. In Tables 6, 7 and 8, almost all members of Team A understood the initial cost and the required number of airplanes to recoup the initial cost. In Table 8, most members of Team C correctly chose "write on the fuselages" as the hardest task. Altogether, we can conclude that Teams D and E understood the situation poorly. However, there were a certain number of members in Teams D and E who understood the situation in an accurate way. What happened to them? Did they fail in convincing teammates, or did they just keep quiet? We do not know what happened or how it happened. What we know is that those who understand the situation in an accurate way should communicate and convince others, or those who understand the situation poorly should remain quiet and listen to the opinions of other members. How can we make this happen with S&G?

How can people share their knowledge with others and/or persuade them to arrive at better solutions as a team? This aspect of the research holds importance for Japanese participants at the university level. Suppose people work as a team in S&G and only a few members understand the situation adequately or possess the information essential to reaching a goal. It is very common for Japanese students who have essential information to refrain from speaking out, an abstention that contributes to a team's failure to find a solution. Therefore, it is worthwhile to effectively design a game to experience and emphasize the importance of sharing information and listening to the opinions of others on the team.

One of the primary goals of S&G is to assist participants in transferring constructive experiences learned from S&G to real-world situations. In this research, I conducted an analysis of questionnaires and explored the possibility of designing a game to encourage participants to recognize the importance of unpacking and avoiding overconfidence. When people are overconfident about their estimation, they typically do not pay attention to the importance of unpacking and continue to make off-target estimations.

In conclusion, when we design a game related to unpacking and overconfidence, we must take into consideration the following: Unpacking will contribute to reducing inaccurate estimations, but accuracy of estimation will not automatically lead to a positive result in the actual game run. Those who have an erroneous understanding of the situation tend to be overconfident and outspoken. We need to assist them in becoming better listeners. Those who have an accurate understanding of the situation tend to be less confident and silent. We need to support them to be more outspoken. Actualizing such goals will be lengthy, but it is worthwhile to try with the appropriate game.

References

1. Tversky, A., Kahneman, D.: Judgment under uncertainty: heuristics and biases. Science, New Series **185**(4157), 1124–1131 (1974)
2. Kahneman, D., Tversky, A.: On the psychology of prediction. Psychol. Rev. **80**(4), 237–251 (1973)
3. Kruger, J., Evans, M.: If you don't want to be late, enumerate: unpacking reduces the planning fallacy. J. Exp. Psychol. **40**, 586–598 (2004)
4. Fabricius, G., Buttgen, M.: The influence of knowledge on overconfidence: consequences for management and project planning. Int. J. Bus. Manage. **8**(11), 1–2 (2013)

5. Buehler, R., Griffin, D., Ross, M.: It's about time: optimistic predictions in work and love. Eur. Rev. Soc. Psychol. **6**(1), 1–32 (1995). Republished on line 04 March 2011. https://doi.org/10.1080/14792779343000112. Accessed 21 Mar 2019
6. Legg, L.: Planes or bust: an OPT scheduling game. In: Armstrong, R., Percival, F., Saunders, D. (eds.) The Simulation and Gaming Yearbook Volume 2: Interactive Learning, pp. 209–219. Kogan Page, London (1994)
7. Goldratt, E.M., Fox, R.E.: The Goal: A Process of Ongoing Improvement Third Revised Edition. North River Press, Great Barrington (2004)
8. Nakamura, M.: Japanese translation of Legg's "Planes or bust: an OPT scheduling game." J. Ryutsu Keizai Univ. **31**(1), 57–65 (1996)

Authentic Learning in Entrepreneurship Education

Luiz Antonio Titton[1](✉) and Michal Jakubowski[2](✉)

[1] Universidade de Sao Paulo, São Paulo, Brazil
`titton@usp.br`
[2] Kozminski University, Warsaw, Poland
`mjakubowski@kozminski.edu.pl`

Abstract. Entrepreneurship Education has characteristics of engagement and motivation differentiated from ordinary education because it is something that refers directly to the ultimate goal of university education. Students tend to be more likely to devote themselves when the form of teaching is highly related to future professional activity. In this context, Authentic Learning stands as an additional element for the science of simulations & games. A platform is presented to demonstrate how this junction occurred in order to adapt to current models of use of internet-based media such as social networks and learn-doing. The proposal was successfully implemented and its participation in innovation ecosystems and in the universities has grown and studies on its efficiency are in the beginning.

Keywords: Entrepreneurial competencies · Authentic learning

1 Entrepreneurship Education

Entrepreneurship education (EE) is proliferating faster than ever. The field has reached maturity in USA based on a chronology study on this topic from 1876 to 1999 [1]. The first entrepreneurship class in 1947 is in the context of the need for employment and today entrepreneurship programs are spread in all universities in that country. Other countries followed the same path, considering this field essential for economy development, such as Germany where EE was also developed using simulation and gaming (S&G) with considerable results for education and S&G science [2]. From the Theory of Planned Behavior, "people's attitudes towards education are positively influenced by entrepreneurial education" that can lead to the willing to be an entrepreneur (narrow definition) or to be entrepreneurial (wide definition) [3].

However, emerging countries such as Brazil are still at the beginning of this saga, the first entrepreneurship program started only on 2007. After two years, 1% of the universities adopted the program not only because of scarce education resources but for the large territory issues, long distances and lack of government engagement.

The need for an approach with distance learning capabilities and low cost is not only specific for that country but a global need due to the current trend to distance learning courses adoption.

M. Wardaszko et al. (Eds.): ISAGA 2019, LNCS 11988, pp. 320–327, 2021.
https://doi.org/10.1007/978-3-030-72132-9_27

In Brazil, 2 million students start university every year and about 50% leave the courses before completing the studies. One of the main causes is that they don't see employability after university. In fact, one million students complete university every year and will compete with 14 million unemployed also looking for a good job. Becoming an entrepreneur is not an opportunity, it is a need.

Global Entrepreneurship Monitor showed that United States entrepreneurship index (0.15) is not far from Brazil (0.11). Noticeable is both are considerably lower than Poland, as example, presenting 0.42 – in a range from −1 to 1 and all are higher than Japan (last position) with −0.95. The GEM Entrepreneurship Spirit Index consider entrepreneurial awareness, opportunity perception, and entrepreneurial self-efficacy. Clustering countries according to economic development stages demonstrates the dominance of entrepreneurial spirit among efficiency-driven economies [4].

Another way to compare entrepreneurship among countries is the Improvement-Driven Opportunity/Necessity Motive relative position. While in USA most new business start from opportunity (5th position) and ends for new opportunities, in Brazil new business starts from necessity (45th position) and ends for entrepreneurship unpreparedness. At the second country, 10% of all university students are in business schools and less than 1% starts a new business along or just after ending studies. Also, in the whole country, 60% of new business ends before 5 years foundation.

The objective on this paper is to accomplish the methodological step defined in Design Science Research that clearly indicates the need to present to peers and specialists the main idea as part of the design process to produce the artefact.

2 Startups and Startup Ecosystems

While entrepreneurship programs aim to develop individuals, the history of Silicon Valley and some startup definitions suggest business world gives less value to personal skills by emphasizing successful companies with great profitability in a short time. Blank [5] stated that it is "a temporary organization in search of a scalable, repeatable, profitable business model". Even when individuals area considered, they are components of a company, Ries [6] defined startup as "a human institution designed to create a new product or service under conditions of extreme uncertainty.".

If we consider that Education is related to prepare people to success in real world, the economic success can be found in Silicon Valley where these authors based their research and where their methods for startups development is used. The same social and business complexity found in Sillicon Valley is found all over the world where there are innovative clusters and startups together. The definition for startup ecosystem is not yet clear in literature, an operational description of its characteristics that.

"startup ecosystem operates in the environment of a specific region. It involves actors that can act as stakeholders, such as entrepreneurs, investors, and other groups of people who have some self-interest in the ecosystem. They collaborate with supporting organizations, such as funding agencies, governments, and educational institutions. They establish organizations to create an infrastructure in which a common network that could support and build startups on a smaller scale is set up, as well as to increase domestic product development and the creation of new jobs in the country on a larger scale." [7].

Entrepreneurship education is not considered as part of the startup ecosystem. Instead of these skills, talent is valued as part of individual skills related to the business core. However, the only way to have people really prepared to entrepreneurship is by education since these skills are not developed alone. Important factors play roles in ecosystem growth such as the interactions among stakeholders, available skills and talents in a region, however entrepreneurship skills are developed on-the-job instead of an educational structure. This is not bad at all, because successful companies are born and developed this way.

Education can also be understood as behavior change by new connections and knowledge. This fits well with entrepreneurship as a soft skill that is developed in startup ecosystems along the development of each new company.

A proposed definition for a startup ecosystem centered on individuals is a complex system where people with a collection of specific skills develop a business from an idea using stakeholders in the system and its relations and resources.

So, entrepreneurship education is not limited to management skills but uses them after beginning operating their startups. Also, entrepreneurs come from all fields of knowledge with different skills and entrepreneurship education should be driven to specific skills related to entrepreneur functions, not be driven to the facilities of existing educational structures, academics or regions. Entrepreneurship education objective is to prepare individuals to the known specific entrepreneurship skills, however not all business is scalable and repeatable enough to be considered startups nor all entrepreneurs are going to start a company. Intra-entrepreneurship is a new concept for desired employees that acts as if they were owners of the company. Their attitude and behavior are entrepreneur skills, but they feel good on being employees.

3 Entrepreneurship Competencies

It is reasonable to plan any education program knowing exactly the desired competencies. OCDE initiatives to increase entrepreneurship among its members considers that "one of the aims of developing competencies for entrepreneurship is to reduce the fear of failure through a combination of measures focused on awareness-raising, as well as providing knowledge and know-how that allow individuals to demonstrate resilience and persistence in the face of obstacles". However, not all students intend to have an own business[2] and for this reason, "emphasis is placed on helping people to consider the desirability and feasibility of starting a business or acting entrepreneurially as an employee - and to develop the ability to cope with failure" is the approach adopted [8].

Approaches that misunderstand management skills as entrepreneurship competencies should be reconsidered since the quantity of startups with business graduated founders are not uncommon. Table 1 presents a framework outlining some key entrepreneurial competencies and their relation to cognitive and non-cognitive competencies.

The more non-cognitive is the sub theme, more tacit are the developed competencies. In the same way, these competence learning are of the kind in which traditional didactic approaches reveals to be less effective than active learning.

4   Authentic Learning

Most educators consider learning-by-doing the most effective way to lean and students say they are motivated by solving real-world problems. However, experiments may be dangerous, difficult or expensive to conduct along classes. For this reason, simulations are frequently used when these issues overcome.

Simulations can be used in more motivational and engaging way by adding game elements, but their instructional strength is on executing debriefing sessions. Simulation and game are in the field of Game Science [9, 10].

In the other hand, entrepreneurship education using issues without direct connection to real problems are perceived as not as good as desired despite of the highest simulator quality, complexity, attachment to reality, and other issues. What students would like in a entrepreneurship simulation would be to have an authenticity with what they really want to do to make a better world by solving a real problem. This can be done by simulating the building of a business from an original self-creation.

"Authentic learning typically focuses on real-world, complex problems and their solutions, using role-playing exercises, problem-based activities, case studies, and participation in virtual communities of practice. The learning environments are inherently multidisciplinary. They are "not constructed in order to teach geometry or to teach philosophy." [9].

There are 10 design elements that defines a good practice authentic learning experience: real-world relevance, ill-defined problem, sustained investigation, multiple sources and perspectives, collaboration, reflection (metacognition), interdisciplinary perspective, integrated assessment, polished products and multiple interpretations and outcomes[9].

A game designed considering such issues is not a rule-based game with manageable knowledge problems. Instead, it is a free-form gaming with wicked problems. The activities and solutions found at each cycle can be uncertain and conflicted. This kind of game needs to be played in a social environment where debriefing is part of a common assessment done together to make each participant's result discussed to make it better.

This is exactly what happens in any start-up ecosystem. Pitch presentations are a routine for these wannabe entrepreneurs when the main idea, a problem, the proposed solution, how to implement the fitness between problem and solution, are shown to a peer audience and eventually mentors and instructors.

The authentic learning didactic approach for an entrepreneurship educational program is that one where the problem-solution fitness is developed by the student. (S)He starts from its own desire to solve a problem that is relevant to society and himself. Validates if it is a real problem in real world. Go beyond possible solutions to discover which is an acceptable and recognisable to support it economically, ethically, environmentally, socially and any other relevant issue.

An argument about this approach is that the idea itself maybe not enough for a new business or a start-up. It is not the problem due to Entrepreneurship Education is not directed only to produce start-ups, it is about enabling people to an entrepreneurship attitude, e.g., to be entrepreneurial or to be entrepreneur.

Table 1. Entrepreneurial competencies. Framework Adapted [3]

	Main theme	Sub themes	Interpretation used in this paper
Cognitive competencies	Knowledge	Mental models	Knowledge about how to get things done without resources, risk and probability models
		Declarative knowledge	Basics of entrepreneurship, value creation, idea generation, opportunities, accounting, finance, technology, marketing, risk, etc
		Self-insight	Knowledge of personal fit with being an entrepreneur/being entrepreneurial
	Skills	Marketing skills	Conducting market research, Assessing the marketplace, marketing products and services, persuasion, getting people excited about your ideas, dealing with customers, communicating a vision
		Resource skills	Creating a business plan, creating a financial plan, obtaining financing, securing access to resources
		Opportunity skills	Recognizing and acting on business opportunities and other kinds of opportunities, product/service/concept development skills
		Interpersonal skills	Leadership, motivating others, managing people, listening, resolving conflict, socializing
		Learning skills	Active learning, adapting to new situations, coping with uncertainty
		Strategic skills	Setting priorities (goal setting) and focusing on goals, defining a vision, developing a strategy, Identifying strategic partners
Non-cognitive competen cies	Attitudes	Entrepreneurial passion	"I want". Need for achievement
		Self-efficacy	"I can". Belief in one's ability to perform certain tasks successfully
		Entrepreneurial identity	"I am/I value". Deep beliefs, Role identity, Values
		Proactiveness	" I do". Action-oriented, Initiator, Proactive
		Uncertainty ambiguity tolerance	"I dare". Comfortable with uncertainty and ambiguity, Adaptable, Open to surprises
		Innovativeness	"I create". Novel thoughts/actions, Unpredictable, Radical change, Innovative, Visionary, Creative, Rule breaker
		Perseverance	"I overcome". Ability to overcome adverse circumstances

5   The Simulation Game

The saga of a new game design was analysed in depth by Klabbers addressing that Design Science Research is the scientific path in this field. In fact, presenting the result of the produced artefact is part of the design and justifies the present paper [10–12].

The Newis Cool platform is a simulation game in a context of a company ideation and building using real world parameters as well as internal ones to provide a closer fidelity to real world. The intended profile of the students participating in this platform is students from 15 to 24 years old, in special along their high school courses.

The Newis.Cool platform [13] is exposed ahead while answering to six questions. How and where is explicit and tacit knowing generated in the design (epistemology)? What is the purpose of the design (ontology)? What are the end goals of the design (teleology)? Causality in the design: Where are causes and effects – if any - configured in the design? Causality in the actual use: how are cause-effect chains and loops – if any - embedded? Causality for the evaluation: what are the theoretical models for attributing cause-effect? [10, 14].

The instructional objective of the platform is to combine the dream of professional achievement with the real business world; recognize the complex and integrative nature of entrepreneurship, whether in business or as part of a company; recognize the core competencies to develop your entrepreneurial attitude; deeply understand the challenges and methods for achieving success in your area; develop critical entrepreneurial reasoning in your area of knowledge; acquire time management habits for performing tasks and for personal life; gain an understanding of the business complexity of your business area; main entrepreneurial skills. The purpose of the design is to have an interface that is close to the daily use of the electronic devices by students. For this reason, a private social network was created working just like the most used (Facebook®, Linkedin®). It is not public and only students and members of real start-up ecosystems can access it from direct invitation from the system manager. Anyone can publish events, general tips about entrepreneurship and startups, students' achievements, short task movies produced by students such as pitches, self-presentations and product tests. There is also a ranking where a classification of engagement and achievement levels are shown for all. This interface design is the main game element as includes badges and points in a authentic way since they comes from real problem-solution development representing each participant or team ranking. The design includes the option to work alone or in teams because each student has flexibility do select and engage others into the virtual startup-up as is part of the job. They are encouraged to have 3 members with roles as leader, finance and technology (CEO, CFO, CTO).

Participants execute weekly missions in different areas that include not only tasks directly related to the competencies listed on Table 1 as well as others about patents, how to open a company, legal aspects, and others about how to build a company. The main idea is to demand at least 4 h job week, but participant can decide to do a better job and spend more time on any task. Explicit knowledge comes from content presented in written and video way whenever possible. This enable participants to use their smartphone to get this content anywhere.

There are 5 levels of development and a specific goal: Ideation (the goal is to present a pitch assessed by 3 to 5 ecosystem mentors), Seed (the goal is to get investment for a real business, or virtual coins or crowdfunding from the private social network), Operation (prove that can operate the business either using internal business simulator or a real one), Growth (prove that can make the business expand operations in a sustainable way using internal business simulator or in real world) and Maturation (means that the business is good enough to migrate from virtual space to real world or get a second investment round).

The platform has internally 3 highly parameterized simulators: the commerce and industry simulator is in use for the last 15 years in use at high school (around 20 thousand students), the second is a logistic simulator (10 years old simulator) and the third is a service business simulator (2 years old). Their complexity is above the normal expected level for a business simulation. This platform enables parameters to be filled by participants directly from real world data. First results from the simulators becomes more realist as data is validated from their own research and filled in the system. The tacit knowledge comes from this job on validating data from real world while research and learn explicit meaning for each didactic content.

The effects of learning explicitly what to look for about validating each step to develop an idea to make it feasible generates tacit knowledge about concepts learned explicitly. As an example, the relation about cost and profit derives from sales price. It is really not easy to teach how to stablish a price for a product or service because it is not only a number, it is about value, its perception on solving a problem, how much a problem is relevant, and a long list of social and economic issues. Knowledge is learned explicitly from presented content and tacitly from the experiential tasks.

Some tasks sound real enough to be misunderstood as a concrete action. The price is validated by asking people from the market segment about what price would pay for a product/service. The participant asks as if it is a real product/service for an audience advised it is a research. In real life it would be done by a specialized company but in many real start-ups in Syllicon Valley that is the way it happens to validate price level. The relation between causes and effects are faced in real world and using internal simulators however that is not when the learning happens.

There are 2 debriefing models in course. The first uses peer blind review. Some tasks generate movies or short texts saved in the system. This material is assessed by at least 2 peers and eventually by a tutor. Each of them receives a rubric guide about what to be assessed. They answer by writing what to do to make it better so the participant can increase quality. The participant applies a rank for reviewers from 1 to 5 and this rank is converted to virtual coins. The virtual coins can be used inside the system to "buy" mentor sessions, invest on other companies' ideas, as examples. The use of rubrics to assess others tasks creates knowledge for the reviewer as well as enables to have different cultures opinions about the task [15, 16].

The second debriefing happens each 4 to 6 weeks when each participant records a 5 min video presenting the whole development done up to then. There is a chance that the reviewers determine that it was not a good quality job and the last module should be done again. Other possibility is that the participant decides not to go ahead. Any of these situations is welcome because a full explanation is required. Rubrics includes issues like the quality of data included in the system such as market size, price level or feasibility to implement the solution. The participant understands by previous repeated tasks that it is better to do it again than to continue and eventually invest on a weak idea. All earnings along the weeks are not lost, maybe s(he) starts it with more virtual coins. The platform is available as a Complementary Curricula Activities Platform since 2019, January. As this paper is being produced one hundred students started using the platform and first results are coming now.

References

1. Katz, J.A.: The chronology and intellectual trajectory of American entrepreneurship education 1876–1999. J. Bus. Ventur. **18**(2), 283–300 (2003). https://doi.org/10.1016/S0883-9026(02)00098-8
2. Kriz, W.C., Auchter, E.: 10 Years of evaluation research into gaming simulation for German entrepreneurship and a new study on its long-term effects. Simul. Gaming **47**(2), 179–205 (2016). https://doi.org/10.1177/1046878116633972
3. Lackeus, M.: Entrepreneurship in Education - What, Why, When, How (2015). OECD Working Paper
4. Herman C.: Global Report 2017/18 (2018). https://www.gemconsortium.org/report/50012. OECD Working Paper
5. Blank, S., Dorf, B.: The Startup Owner's Manual: The Step-by-Step Guide for Building a Great Company (BookBaby, ed.) (2012)
6. Ries, E.: The Lean Startup: How Today's Entrepreneurs Use Continuous Innovation to Create Radically Successful Businesses. Crown Books (2011)
7. Tripathi, N., Seppänen, P., Boominathan, G., Oivo, M., Liukkunen, K.: Insights into startup ecosystems through exploration of multi-vocal literature. Inf. Softw. Technol. **2019**(105), 56–77 (2018). https://doi.org/10.1016/j.infsof.2018.08.005
8. OECD: Developing entrepreneurship competencies. In: OECD Minist Conference Small Medium Enterp, 3–8 February 2018. oe.cd/SMEs. OECD Working Paper
9. Lombardi, B.M.M., Oblinger, D.G.: authentic learning for the 21st century : an overview. Educ. Learn. Initiat. **1**(2007), 1–12 (2007). https://doi.org/10.1016/j.nuclphysa.2007.07.005
10. Klabbers, G.: On the architecture of game. Science (2018). https://doi.org/10.1177/1046878118762534
11. Hevner, A.R.: A three cycle view of design science research. Scand. J. Inf. Syst. **19**(2), 1–6 (2007) http://aisel.aisnet.org/sjis/vol19/iss2/4
12. March, S.T., Smith, G.F,: Design and natural science research on information technology. Decis. Support Syst. **15**, 251–266 (1995). https://doi.org/10.1016/0167-9236(94)00041-2
13. Titton, L.A.: Newis.Cool. https://newis.cool (2019). Accessed 30 Mar 2019
14. Blasi, L., Alfonso, B.: Increasing the transfer of simulation technology from R&D into school settings: an approach to evaluation from overarching vision to individual artifact in education. Simul. Gaming **37**(2), 245–267 (2006). https://doi.org/10.1177/1046878105284449
15. Ribeiro, L.A., Neto, J.D., Titton, L.A., da Silva, M.F.: Self-, peer- and professor assessment using rubrics in accounting. In: Proceedings of 13th CONTECSI International Conference Information System Technology Manage, vol. **13**, pp. 1682–1697 (2016). https://doi.org/10.5748/9788599693124-13contecsi/ps-3891
16. Titton, L.A., Oliveira Neto, J.D.: A Model for Cross-Cultural Experiential Learning Based on Business Game, May 2014. https://doi.org/10.5748/9788599693100-11contecsi/ps-704

Learning from a Business Simulation Game:
A Factor-Analytic Study

Vinod Dumblekar[1(✉)] and Upinder Dhar[2]

[1] Mantis, New Delhi 110025, India
games@mantis.co.in
[2] Shri Vaishnav Vidyapeeth Vishwavidyalaya, Indore 453111, India

Abstract. Learning is an active self-directed experience of the individual that changes her thinking and behaviour. A simulation game offers multifaceted learning experience to its players because it produces critical thinking skills and knowledge from their interactions with others and from their reflections of their actions and outcomes. To understand what business issues could be learned in a simulation, a 20-item instrument was developed and statistically tested on post-graduate management students in a business simulation game. The analysis of their responses showed that the game provided them with deep understanding of business goals, competitiveness and collaboration, and awareness of business and selling skills. This game covered the critical subjects of the business management course. The relevance of the findings for research and application have been discussed.

Keywords: Business goal orientation · Business skills · Collaborative action · Competitiveness · Experiential learning · Sales function · Simulation game

1 Introduction

Learning is the process that changes the perspectives and abilities of the individual to think and behave differently from before. The learning experience creates and changes her knowledge through the adaptation and continuous transformation of that experience, and therefore, it occupies a central role in her learning process [1]. Her learning would be an active and self-directed process, and would be the result of her interactions between the objective and subjective perceptions of her experience. It would be an opportunity to become more aware and productive than before, and therefore, she became invaluable to herself, her community, and her organisation.

Her learning process may be a deliberate activity such as a training programme where she would be a participant. It may also be an experience such as her recapitulation and reflection of an event where she may have been either an observer or participant. Her cognition and emotions would facilitate her learning through stages of her experience, viz., *concrete experience, abstract conceptualization, reflective observation,* and *active experimentation* in sequence beginning with her exposure to an event that would lead to her understanding [1]. Students played croquet to understand its material factors, patterns of human behaviour, individual differences, and game structure on the basis of Kolb's experience states [2]. First, the *concrete experience* of

M. Wardaszko et al. (Eds.): ISAGA 2019, LNCS 11988, pp. 328–340, 2021.
https://doi.org/10.1007/978-3-030-72132-9_28

the game shaped their *abstract* and *reflective experience*; later, they built models based on their gaming experience (*active experimentation*); finally, they extended and applied their theoretical perspectives to understand the practices in international relations, conceptually.

Learners' motivation may be affected by progress expectancy (that learning efforts would result in learning progress) and valence (that learning outcomes would be valuable) [3]. They found that conscientious individuals (i.e. committed, disciplined, and hardworking) would have a stronger motivation to learn because they would perceive that their efforts lead to performance that was both useful and valued.

Experiences, both good and bad, lead to powerful learning for the individual. Trainee soldiers performed far better when they became more aware of their failures and successes, every day [4]. Failures were remembered more than successes, and provoked enquiry, new thinking and awareness, while successes did not do so. Individuals were keen to explore more reasons for their failures than for success. Therefore, they found it easier to discuss faults and mistakes after failures than after a success. Those whose behaviour changed after an experience were more likely to be aware of and be able to explain the reasons for the events, whether failure or success. They were also more likely to accept responsibility for their actions, and were more confident to accept difficult tasks.

1.1 Simulations and Games

A simulation was an interactive teaching method and a powerful learning environment that produced critical thinking skills and encouraged the discovery and construction of knowledge [5]. It may be a structured game where the participants' attention is engaged in attempts to win. Educational objectives, specific roles, background information, rules of procedure, and a debriefing for discussion, reflection, and drawing conclusions were the major design elements of any simulation. A simulation depicts the behaviour of problems or issues within a system, entity, phenomenon, or process for study. A simulation could be any one or a mix of a role play, a game played with cards and other icons, on a board or in the open (field), or on a computer [6]. The typical game had interactions such as cooperation, competition, collusion, or conflict. The simulation could be likened to a caricature that simplified and reduced a larger system to a manageable smaller size, and then, used the game rules to manipulate and represent it to convey features, goals, constraints and other elements of the game [7].

The game could be perceived as an interactive environment of rules, competition, challenge, complexity, and constraints, and showed that students learnt when there was no peer pressure under competition, and concluded that competitiveness did not induce learning [8]. Students without pressure due to competition asked questions, read instructions, and exhibited more curiosity, while students under pressure due to competition limited themselves to surface learning. They surmised that competitions distracted the students from learning objectives.

A game architecture has three interconnected elements, viz., actors, rules, and resources, which create explicit and tacit contexts and problems [9]. The actors engage in analysis, planning, and making decisions. The rules guide the actors by setting the boundaries of play, including procedures for action and performance measurement. The signs and symbols are the resources that facilitate the actors' actions and help them track their progress in the game. Together, these elements build the players' experience through awareness, articulation, and activity. From studies of other game researchers, Games were multifaceted, interdisciplinary, and non-disciplinary activities that engaged the players in solving problems [10]. Therefore, learning from games was best understood when analysed from different perspectives of humanities, social sciences, and design studies.

Both soft and hard skills could be learnt in business simulation games [11]. Team building, communication, inter-personal skills, negotiation, creativity, and collaboration were deemed soft skills, while hard skills included product knowledge, sales, decision-making skills, innovation and others relevant to managing business. A business was a complex interactive system of owners, managers and other employees, suppliers, customers, and government interacting under a variety of organisational and industry norms and other practices. Its external environment was under pressure from its competitors, technology effects, social conventions, regulations, national economics, and political changes. A business simulation game offered a learning experience to assist its players to understand such complex systems [12]. It was effective because the game play simplified the context, roles, and interactions for the players to reduce and bring ideas together (chunking), sequenced them, and coordinated the tasks in the game.

1.2 Objective of This Study

The business simulation game was an experiential learning exercise whose participants could learn business practices because of its interactive, exploratory, and inter-disciplinary environment. The objective of this research was to analyse the nature of learning produced and felt by the participants from their experiences in a business simulation game. The learning from a business simulation game would augment and enhance the knowledge and understanding of game designers and users for the production of effective business simulation games and the use of such games, appropriately.

2   Method

2.1   The Game Players

The students were participating in the induction program of their two-year post-graduate course at the management school, New Delhi, India. This program was a four-day platform for their studies to follow, and the one-day simulation game was expected to form the foundation offering experiential exposure to and understanding of business and management issues. The students had graduate degrees in disciplines such as commerce, business administration, humanities, economics, engineering, science, and psychology. Most students were about 22 years of age and had no career experience. About 25% of the students were females.

2.2   The Business Simulation Game

The participants played *IceBreaker*, a competitive role-play enterprise business simulation game developed and conducted by the first author in 2003. Every student received a 30-page manual with instructions, descriptions of key terms, and explanations of key processes in the game, and used a pen, paper, and an electronic calculator. The game was played across one day and represented two stages of business activity. Before the game began, they were allocated to teams of 4–5 members each, with each team having a similar proportion of males and females. During the game, they received other game documents describing business situations and seeking their decisions. The team results were in the form of financial statements, and each team received reports unique to its decisions. The roles for each team member were explained by the first author as the game facilitator, who also guided them about business and management issues and how to take decisions.

To facilitate their learning, the students interacted enthusiastically with each other in the team, engaged in debate, asked questions, read manuals and other game documents, and studied a variety of business data. Towards the end of the game, each team appraised its members' actions, decisions and business results, and described the nature and process of its learning in a quick vocal presentation. This was a critical debriefing process that enabled the participants to recall, reflect, consolidate and convert their play experiences into learning in the form of awareness of issues and decision rules [13].

2.3 The Instrument

A list of words and expressions that described learning and related action verbs such as *understand, awareness, do, act, conclude, perception, discover, analyse, measure, compute, integrate, mix, use,* and *found* was made. It was enlarged with business and management vocabulary like *selling, product, conflict, goal, data, competition, resource,* and *cash.* These words were then used to produce 28 statements. Then, long sentences were shortened, and difficult and confusing words were substituted with shorter and simpler words. Sentences with similar meaning were recast or avoided. The list was then scrutinised by three subject experts, whose suggestions for two changes were accepted and incorporated in the list. 'I learned how to influence sales', 'I recognised the presence of competition in the markets', and 'I discovered the purpose and use of cash in business' were some of the statements used in the instrument. The final instrument for learning had only 20 statements as it was administered along with another instrument of identical length for a study on *team cohesion* [14]. As was stated in that study, a longer instrument was avoided as it 'may not have received fair responses from the participants at the end of a rigorous game'. It was administered after the team's presentations at the end of the game.

3   Results

Complete and correctly filled copies of the instrument were received from 356 participants, although 369 copies were distributed and received from them. In the analysis of corrected item-total correlation data, item #1 showed a low value of .16, and was therefore, dropped from any further use in this study. The remaining 19 items were then subjected to exploratory factor analysis under principal component analysis with varimax rotation using SPSS 21.0. Table 1 shows the five factors and their respective

Table 1. Learning from a business simulation game: statements, factors and loadings

Statements and *factors* (N = 356)	Business goal orientation	Collaborative Action	Competitiveness	Business Skills	Sales function
Business goal orientation					
19. I was able to contribute, effectively, to the overall objective of the team	.74				
8. I became aware of the relationship between prices, customers, and sales	.62				
14. I was able to measure and direct organisational resources for achieving our goals	.60				
2. I learned how to influence sales	.53				
20. I now have a better appreciation of the business goals of an organisation	.53				
Collaborative action					
17. I concluded that the best decisions came from discussions and common consent		.75			
10. I found ways to resolve conflict with other members in the team		.64			
3. I found that working with others is more effective than working alone		.63			
11. We changed our thinking in tune with new information and events		.43			
18. I learnt from announcements, manual guidelines, and business data to take decisions		.39			
Competitiveness					
4. I recognized the presence of competition in the markets			.62		
13. I acquired a better view of the business of the organisation.			.60		
12. I now understand that purchase behaviour is a response to marketing efforts			.47		
9. It is important to link together organisational resources, decisions, and business goals			.38		
Business skills					
16. I discovered the purpose and use of cash in business				.67	
7. I acquired confidence in the speedy application of basic arithmetic skills				.65	
6. It will help me understand business events as reported in newspapers, TV and other media				.54	
15. I could see that data must be measured, understood and interpreted before use				.49	
Sales function					
5. I understood how sales was influenced by product features					.79
Eigenvalues	4.48	1.38	1.30	1.15	1.03
Per cent of variance explained	12.78	11.12	9.39	8.86	7.00

Extraction Method: Principal Component Analysis. a. Rotation converged in 20 iterations. Rotation Method: Varimax with Kaiser Normalization.

statements and loadings. Each factor had an eigenvalue exceeding one, and cumulatively, the extraction explained 49% percent of the variance.

The rotation converged in nine iterations. At a significance of .000, the Kaiser-Meyer-Olkin measure of sampling adequacy of .85 was above the recommended value of .6, confirming the adequacy of the sample size and the correlations between the statements as variables. Bartlett's test of sphericity was highly significant $(\chi^2 (171) = 1132.60, p < .001)$. The high value of Cronbach α of .81 confirmed the reliability of the instrument.

The factor names represented the words and expressions in their respective statements and their respective loadings. In decreasing order of their eigenvalues, these factors were named *business goal orientation, collaborative action, competitiveness, business skills,* and *sales function.*

The factors were positively correlated with each other (Table 2). Four factors, *business goal orientation, collaborative action, competitiveness,* and *business skills* were highly and significantly correlated to each other $(r = .39$ to $.48, p < .01)$. However, the correlation of *sales function* with the other four factors was not as strong $(r = .13$ to $.25, p < .01$ and $p < .05)$.

Table 2. Learning from a business simulation game: Interfactor correlations

	M	SD	Business Goal Orientation	Collaborative Action	Competitiveness	Business Skills	Sales Function
Business Goal Orientation	20.31	2.33	.68				
Collaborative Action	20.98	2.30	.43**	.63			
Competitiveness	16.81	1.76	.48**	.39**	.54		
Business Skills	16.52	1.87	.43**	.40**	.41**	.55	
Sales Function	3.67	0.86	.15**	.17**	.25**	.13*	

**. Correlation is significant at the 0.01 level (2-tailed). *. Correlation is significant at the 0.05 level (2-tailed).
Figures on the upper diagonal represent internal consistency of the factor in the first column

All regression results were positively predictive with moderate significance (Table 3). The analysis showed that *business goal orientation, collaborative action,* and *business skills* predicted three other factors each, *competitiveness* predicted all the other four factors, and *sales function* predicted only *competitiveness* (.08***). The *sales function* factor was predicted only by one factor, *competitiveness,* with the highest effect (.48***), while all other factors were predicted by three factors each.

Table 3. Learning from a business simulation game: interfactor regressions

Dependent Variable / factor	Constant / slope	Business goal orientation	Collaborative action	Competitiveness	Business skills	Sales function
Business goal orientation	0.89			0.29***	0.31***	0.21***
Collaborative action	1.53	0.25***			0.18**	0.21***
Competitiveness	1.31	0.29***	0.15**		0.19***	.08**
Business skills	1.34	0.23***	0.22***	0.23***		
Sales function	1.64			0.48***		

. Correlation is significant at the 0.01 level (2-tailed). *. Correlation is significant at the 0.001 level (2-tailed).

An analysis of the dyads of factors affecting each other identified the stronger factor in every dyadic relationship. Out of the seven dyads, *competitiveness* predicted *sales function* (.48***) far stronger than *sales function* could predict *competitiveness* (.08**). Of the remainder, viz., *collaborative action-business goal orientation* (.29*** and .25***), *competitiveness-business goal orientation* (.31*** and .29***), *business skills -business goal orientation* (.21*** and .23***), *competitiveness-collaborative action* (.18** and .15**), *business skills-collaborative action* (.21*** and .22***), and *business skills-competitiveness* (.19*** and .23***), the gap between the effects of each dyad was small.

The *sales function* had the highest constant (1.64) suggesting its relatively higher pre-existence, as compared to the lowest constant for *business goal orientation* (.89). The students acquired more understanding from the function, without the influence of other factors, than from the other four learning factors in the game.

4 Discussion

The factor analysis showed *learning from a business simulation game* to be a composite of five factors. The first four factors had high correlation with each other, and predicted each other, significantly. *Competitiveness* was the most versatile factor with the capability to predict all other factors. These results compared with past research findings from the literature review of simulation games that game participants acquired knowledge and gained conceptual clarity through action-directed and problem-centered learning [15]. They developed their social, emotional, and collaborative skills, built collaborations and relationships with their colleagues, interacted with team members, and managed conflicts constructively. The nature of these factors and their relationships and affects are first examined below, and later, their contributions to the study are discussed.

4.1 Business Goal Orientation

Performance is an outcome variable because results due to work orientation need some time to happen. For example, the performance of 268 airline employees materialized only after 4–8 months after the training which laid the foundation for their orientation [16]. Therefore, goal orientation may not produce instant results which may be due to personality characteristics, work issues (process and leadership), and external situations like tools and technology.

The achievement goal orientation was determined by the nature and content of the goal and its proximity from its actors and their resources. The goal orientation of 524 trainees in their study affected their self-regulatory processes of monitoring (thoughts and behaviours), evaluation (comparison to performance standards), and reactions (emotions and cognitive attention) [17]. The nature of the goal was determined in terms of its frame of intensity, difficulty, and specificity. The goal content had learning (competence and task mastery) orientations and performance orientations (with respect to others' ability). Goal proximity could produce challenge, anxiety, frustration and failure because the distance of the goal from the actions would enlarge the difficulty to achieve the goal.

The goal was the purpose or reason that drove achievement-related behaviour. Motivation was an action-based process that affected the self and created motivational systems [18]. Although performance driven goals and mastery were both affected by competence, performance driven goals may hurt the learning of students in their classrooms.

The nature of goal orientation could affect team behaviour to respond to changing goals. While a learning orientation pursued knowledge and challenges with persistence to understand and overcome the problem, individuals in a performance orientation sought to outperform others in a competitive situation, but with little attention to or focus on learning [19]. Alone, performance orientation took time to produce any performance, while too much learning orientation may lose sight of performance, and produce little or none of it. Individuals with high levels of both learning orientation and performance orientation may be too confused in action, and produce no results.

According to the goal setting theory, a clearly understood and challenging goal may attract more attention and produce better performance than one that is vague, abstract, and easy to achieve [20]. The individual's potential to accomplish a goal depends upon her ability, situational resources, commitment to its achievement, and receipt of valid, adequate and timely feedback to motivate her and help her learn and change in her journey to the goal.

Achievement goal theory or goal orientation explains an individual's motivation, her response to challenge, her resilience, and the depth of her engagement with work. It links her emotions, thoughts, behaviour, and experience to produce goals and outcomes such as to acquire competence, to outperform others, to learn and to act, but in ways and conditions that have been difficult to recognise, measure or understand [21].

4.2 Collaborative Action

Individuals come together to share interests, concerns, problems, and knowledge with each other. Collaborative action within amorphous and fluid groups in an organisations tends to focus on sharing information, not solving problems or on interdependent tasks, and operate under facilitative, not directive, leadership environments [22]. Thus, members of such communities of practice interact with each other and evolve to become formal teams with clear goals, purposeful leaders, visible cultural practices, and regulated processes. Driven by and shaped by these collaborative actions, they become more aware, productive, and useful to others and themselves. However, their satisfaction would depend on their empowerment and the extent of the concern of leadership for teamwork and cooperation in the groups.

Collaboration created opportunities because it was about working together [23]. He explained how teachers could share pedagogy, practices, and experiences to understand the meaning of their work, to conduct experiments, and to deliver and complete a variety of educational projects. An outline of the collaborative theory identified two strands of collaborative behaviour from the shared experiences of 100 graduate students in a study [24].The *Individual First* behaviours were represented by the interactions of a team member with and influence over her colleagues, viz., *turn-taking, observing and doing,* and *status seeking.* The *Team First* behaviours were represented by the team's interactions with its members, viz., *group cohesion, influencing others,* and *organizing work,* and appeared to be managerial and leadership oriented. Thus, collaboration was a blend of shared aspirations, objectives, roles, and actions of the individual and her interacting partners.

Learning how to collaborate is rooted in actions such as discussions, getting consent, and resolving conflict through interactions with others. Two types of in-game collaborations could be attributed to the scripted and emergent roles of the players [25]. The *complementarity* type was seen in the actions of its players, while in the *information sharing* type, data was collected and processed to develop clarity between the players. Solving problems jointly was the most visible collaboration activity.

4.3 Competitiveness

A hypercompetitive individual may use unethical practices, may be dogmatic, unsympathetic and uncooperative, and may show Machiavellianism traits of ruthlessness, impatience and irritability [26]. Alternatively, in the personal development model of competitiveness, the individual is keen to improve herself, enjoy and seek mastery of her actions, processes and tasks, to help others, and to behave ethically. Thus, competitive individuals may differ in terms of their ethical and altruistic behaviours.

Four factors of competitiveness were extracted and explained from 11 subscales of competitiveness and a confirmatory factor analysis of 37 items [27]. *General competitiveness* represented the person's assessment of her enjoyment of competitiveness and belief in herself as a competitive individual, including a desire to win in her chosen contexts. *Pervasive competitiveness* represented her competitive desire to outperform and excel over others. *Dominant competitiveness* was her need to be the best with respect to others and show superiority over them. *Personal enhancement competitiveness* was her intention to compete to become more competent or achieve more than before.

Competitive players in team sports acquired and developed skills to execute key moves and to overcome the actions of their opponents [28]. Although competitive, they interacted and coordinated, adaptively and cooperatively, with their co-players to win. Perceiving competitiveness to be as a personality trait, a behaviour, and a dynamic state, the researchers proposed that the competitive process encouraged and produced creativity, innovation, learning, and performance.

Although men and women had similar capabilities, women were likely to avoid competitive situations such as negotiation, unlike men. Eight studies showed that women preferred smaller competitions, irrespective of domains, as compared to men, due to contextual factors dictated by socially acceptable gender norms [29]. Thus, women may frequent smaller rather than larger social groups due to their perceived level of comfort.

A study of 339 under-graduate students pursuing entry into medical courses found that their enjoyment of competition correlated positively with their physical health and self-efficacy [30]. Their competitiveness was studied as a trait, not as a learned behaviour, and it indicated their desire to succeed in interpersonal conditions. The researchers concluded that good physical health produced not only good grades and satisfactory learning outcomes, but also enjoyable competitive and learning environments.

4.4   Business Skills

The entrepreneur's communicated vision, self-efficacy, and goals directly affected the growth of her firm. Conversely, her passion for work, tenacity, and new resource skills affected such growth, indirectly [31]. Thus, her effective business skill was not any single attribute, but would be a composite of her traits, skills, and motivations. Her strategic foresight, her conviction to get things done and accomplish tasks, and her fierce commitment to her goals would enable her to succeed in and grow her business firm. As a factor of production, skills played a key role in the management of the firm and helped it to grow. A skill was 'the ability to execute specified tasks' and stated that skills were classified on the basis of such tasks [32].

A study of 287 under-graduates of textile and apparel courses found that their intercultural, networking, and financial skills predicted their entrepreneurial knowledge and skills [33]. These business skills comprised the course and helped them acquire the entrepreneurial confidence necessary to start and manage a small business and to develop a global perspective. A skill was an evolution and the product of repeated practice that ended in superior performance. The skills of the FIDE chess players were acquired over years of play, and were recognised in terms of their competition results and against the relative strengths of their opponents [34]. Using the basis of the power law of practice (an example of the learning curve on performance), each player developed such cognitive skills at her own pace.

An extensive review of literature showed that skill variety comprising of knowledge and skills predicted and produced entrepreneurship [35]. Typically, along with industry-specific knowledge such as languages, mathematics, and technical, the skills were comprised of management and business skills such as decision making, research, analytical, negotiation, production, financial and marketing skills. Often, this skill variety was due to work-related task experience in a business environment, and may be found in individuals with low appetite for risk, an inclination to create and innovate, and an eagerness to absorb new experiences.

4.5   Sales Function

A competency was a behavioural characteristic of the individual that enabled her to achieve her goal. A content analysis and interviews of marketing managers in South Africa showed that marketing competency included oral and written communication, interpersonal and persuasion skill, service marketing ability, technological and computing skill, and global perspectives [36].

A study of 461 sales representatives showed that they spent their time on customer acquisition (searching for and finding leads), customer retention (relationship management and cross-selling), and other activities (accounting, training, etc.) [37]. Their efforts were focused on the customer who, in the ultimate analysis, was the key to the firm's success in terms of revenues, sustenance, and survival.

4.6   Conclusions, Implications for Further Research, and Recommendations for Action

This study produced five factors of learning from a business simulation game, viz., *business goal orientation, collaborative action, competitiveness, business skills,* and *sales function.* The game participants became aware of the business goals of their firms, and learnt to hone their analytical skills and to make resource, business and marketing decisions with focus on their goals. They learnt to collaborate with their team members and to perceive the presence of competition from the other teams. Thus, they acquired multiple views of the business of the firm from their learning experience in the game. The game was found suitable for teaching and learning activities in a business management course, countering other findings and apprehensions of suitability barriers [6].

Individuals with Machiavellian tendencies may endanger the organisation and its stakeholders, and the members of the teams they belong to. The study of the relationship of Machiavellian behaviour with the other learning factors, viz., *business goal orientation, collaborative action,* and *business skills* may generate new and useful knowledge. Such findings may have serious implications for a manager's recruitment and placement in the organisation [26].

Does a player's creativity and innovation affect her learning from simulations and games? Does playing in simulations and games enhance her creativity and innovation [28]? As creativity, innovation, simulations and games are critical thinking exercises, we need research to find the answers to these questions because they may offer profound insights in learning and development behaviours.

Collaborations use informational, social and personal resources of team members who invest in their colleagues to produce value, jointly. Although the time spent in collaborative work had increased during the last two decades, value from collaborations had emerged from barely 3–5% of the participants [38]. The value in collaborative action is vastly unexploited. Organisations must restructure roles, work and processes, appropriately, to produce more efficient teamwork and collaborations from interactive arrangements.

Game designers must create multi-faceted learning experiences that have elements such as business objectives, resources, and products for sale in their business simulation [9, 10]. Their participants must interact frequently with others to produce knowledge from data analysis, make decisions, and collaborate with others in a team under changing environmental and competitive conditions.

Individuals with *general competitiveness, pervasive competitiveness* and *dominant competitiveness* traits are suitable for competitive business roles such as business development and sales [27]. Those with *personal enhancement competitiveness* may be better suited for exploratory roles such as business research development and customer interaction roles. Business simulation games could be used to measure and identify their players in terms of the competitive traits, and then, fit them to roles, appropriately.

References

1. Kolb, D.A.: Experiential Learning: Experience as the Source of Learning and Development. Prentice Hall, Englewood Cliffs (1984)
2. Duffy, S.P.: Teaching with a mallet: conveying an understanding of systemic perspectives on international relations intuitively - croquet as experiential learning. Int. Stud. Perspect. **2**, 384–400 (2001)
3. Colquitt, J.A., Simmering, M.J.: Conscientiousness, goal orientation, and motivation to learn during the learning process: a longitudinal study. J. Appl. Psychol. **83**(4), 654–665 (1998)
4. Ellis, S., Davidi, I.: After-event reviews: drawing lessons from successful and failed experience. J. Appl. Psychol. **90**(5), 871–957 (2005)
5. Lantis, J.S.: Simulations and experiential learning in the international relations classroom. Int. Negot. **3**, 39–57 (1998)
6. Lean, J., Moizer, J., Towler, M., Abbey, C.: Simulations and games: use and barriers in higher education. Act. Learn. High. Educ. **7**(3), 227–242 (2006)
7. McCall, J.: Video games as participatory public history. In: David, M.D. (ed.) A Companion to Public History, pp. 405–418. Wiley, Hoboken (2018)
8. Chen, C.-H., Liu, J.-H., Shou, W.-C.: How competition in a game-based science learning environment influences students' learning achievement, flow experience, and learning behavioral patterns. Educ. Technol. Soc. **21**(2), 164–176 (2018)
9. Klabbers, J.H.: On the architecture of game science. Simul. Gaming **49**(3), 207–245 (2018)
10. Stenros, J., Kultima, A.: On the expanding ludosphere. Simul. Gaming **49**(3), 338–355 (2018)
11. Blažič, A.J., Novak, F.: Challenges of business simulation games - a new approach of teaching business. In: Gradinarova, B. (ed.) E-Learning - Instructional Design, Organizational Strategy and Management, pp. 227–250 (2015). https://doi.org/10.5772/61242
12. Wardaszko, M.: Interdisciplinary approach to complexity in simulation game design and implementation. Simul. Gaming **49**(3), 263–278 (2018)
13. Crookall, D.: Serious games, debriefing, simulation/gaming as a discipline. Simul. Gaming **41**(6), 898–920 (2010)
14. Dumblekar, V., Dhar, U.: Business simulation game team cohesion scale. AIMS J. Manage. **3**(1), 2–2 (2017)
15. Vlachopoulos, D., Makri, A.: The effect of games and simulations on higher education: a systematic literature review. Int. J. Educ. Technol. High. Educ. **14**(1), 1–33 (2017). https://doi.org/10.1186/s41239-017-0062-1
16. Helmreich, R.L., Sawin, L.L., Carsrud, A.L.: The honeymoon effect in job performance: temporal increases in the predictive power of achievement motivation. J. Appl. Psychol. **71**(2), 185–188 (1978)
17. Kozlowski, S.W.J., Bel, B.S.: Disentangling achievement orientation and goal setting: effects on self-regulatory processes. J. Appl. Psychol. **91**(4), 900–916 (2006)
18. Maehr, M.L., Zusho, A.: Achievement goal theory: the past, present and future. In: Wentzel, K.R., Wigfield, A. (eds.) Educational Psychology Handbook Series: Handbook of Motivation at School, pp.77–104. Routledge, New York (2009)
19. Porter, C.O.L.H., Webb, J.W., Gogus, C.I.: When goal orientations collide: effects of learning and performance orientation on team adaptability in response to workload imbalance. J. Appl. Psychol. **95**(5), 935–943 (2010)
20. Latham, G.P., Seijts, G.H.: Distinguished scholar invited essay: similarities and differences among performance, behavioral, and learning goals. J. Leadersh. Organ. Stud. **23**(3), 225–233 (2016)

21. Senko, C.: Achievement goal theory: a story of early promises, eventual discords, and future possibilities. In: Wentzel, K., Miele, D. (eds.) Handbook of Motivation at School, vol. 2, pp. 75–95. Routledge, New York (2016)

22. Kirkman, B.L., Mathieu, J.E., Cordery, J.E., Rosen, B., Kukenberger, M.: Managing a new collaborative entity in business organizations: understanding organizational communities of practice effectiveness. J. Appl. Psychol. 96(6), 1234–1245 (2011)

23. Kaplan, A.: Editor's introduction: collaboration as opportunity. Schools: Stud. Educ. 11(2), 173–179 (2014)

24. Colbry, S., Hurwitz, M., Adair, R.: Collaboration theory. J. Leadersh. Educ. 13(14), 63–75 (2014)

25. Hämäläinen, R.H., Niilo-Rämä, M., Lainema, T., Oksanen, K.: How to raise different game collaboration activities: the association between game mechanics, players' roles and collaboration processes. Simul. Gaming 49(1), 50–71 (2018)

26. Mudrack, P.E., Bloodgood, J.M., Turnley, W.H.: Some ethical implications of individual competitiveness. J. Bus. Ethics 108(3), 347–359 (2012)

27. Newby, J.L., Klein, R.G.: Competitiveness reconceptualized: psychometric development of the competitiveness orientation measure as a unified measure of trait competitiveness. Psychol. Rec. 64(4), 879–895 (2014)

28. Passos, P., Araújo, D., Davids, K.: Competitiveness and the process of co-adaptation in team sport performance. Front. Psychol. 7(1562), 1–5 (2016)

29. Hanek, K.J., Garcia, S.M., Tor, A.: Gender and competitive preferences: the role of competition size. J. Appl. Psychol. 101(8), 1122–1133 (2016)

30. Henning, M.A., Krägeloh, C.U., Booth, R., Hill, E.M., Chen, J., Webster, C.: An exploratory study of the relationships among physical health, competitiveness, stress, motivation, and grade attainment: pre-medical and health science students. Asia Pac. Scholar 3(3), 5–16 (2018)

31. Baum, J.R., Locke, E.A.: The relationship of entrepreneurial traits, skill, and motivation to subsequent venture growth. J. Appl. Psychol. 89(4), 587–598 (2004)

32. Murti, A.B., Bino, P.G.D.: Determinants of skill shortages in Indian firms: an exploration. Indian J. Ind. Relat. 49(3), 439–455 (2014)

33. Hodges, N., Watchravesringkan, K., Yurchisin, J., Hegland, J., Karpova, E., Marcketti, S., Yan, R.-N.: Assessing curriculum designed to foster students' entrepreneurial knowledge and small business skills from a global perspective. Family Consum. Sci. Res. J. 43(4), 313–327 (2015)

34. Howard, R.W.: Development of chess skill from domain entry to near asymptote. Am. J. Psychol. 131(3), 323–345 (2018)

35. Krieger, A., Block, J., Stuetzer, M.: Skill variety in entrepreneurship: a literature review and research directions. Int. Rev. Entrepreneurship 16(1), 29–62 (2018)

36. Melaia, S., Abratt, R., Bick, G.: Competencies of marketing managers in South Africa. J. Market. Theory Pract. 16(3), 233–246 (2008)

37. Sabnis, G., Chatterjee, S.C., Grewal, R., Lilien, G.L.: The sales lead black hole: on sales follow-up of marketing leads. J. Market. 77(1), 52–67 (2013)

38. Cross, R., Rebele, R., Grant, A.: Collaborative overload. Harvard Bus. Rev. 94(1), 74–79 (2016)

Gamification and Gaming Cultures

Resolving Migrant Issues in Thailand Using the Framework of 'Simulation Game – Project PAL'

Ryoju Hamada[1(✉)], Nanako Iwasa[2], Tomomi Kaneko[3], and Masahiro Hiji[4]

[1] National Institute of Technology, Asahikawa College,
Asahikawa 0718142, Hokkaido, Japan
hamada@edu.asahikawa-nct.ac.jp
[2] Hokkaido University, Sapporo 0600801, Hokkaido, Japan
[3] Hokkaido University of Science, Junior College, Sapporo 0060817,
Hokkaido, Japan
[4] Tohoku University, Sendai 9808577, Miyagi, Japan

Abstract. The authors researched to make new gaming by using the 'Project PAL' framework to let students learn migrant or refugee issue in Thailand. Many people are staying in Thailand for many reasons, we have to find a way to co- live, but students have few opportunities to consider this kind of story as their problem. The PAL gaming has the power to recognize such social issues and to consider proactively. The authors compiled two versions of the game to find a solution of migrant/refugee both from Cambodia and Myanmar. By comparing the results of questionnaires conducted before and after the gaming, those games worked well, that tells us 'Learning by Gaming' is effective. Throughout the process, the authors grew up senior project students to create, to conduct, and to analyze the migrant or refugee problem both in Japanese University and Thai University. Most of them accepted the experience positively. This fact shows us the possibility that 'Learn by developing and facilitating gaming' provides an excellent opportunity of learning.

Keywords: Migrant · Refugee · Gaming · Student Teacher · Learning by teaching · Learning by developing · Project PAL

1 Introduction

1.1 Co-living Issue in Thailand

Globalization is accelerating, especially in Indo-China countries. While the population of Thailand (66 million) is decreasing because of its aged society, many foreigners (4 to 5 million) have mostly come to work and live here [1]. According to the Asahi Shimbun Plus [2], Thai industries have relied on foreigners for labor. Foreign nationalities and populations are estimated at about 3.0 million from Myanmar, 1.0 from Cambodia, and 0.6 from Laos. They comprise nearly 10% of the total Thai population, but there is a lack of understanding altogether. Even though they are in

M. Wardaszko et al. (Eds.): ISAGA 2019, LNCS 11988, pp. 343–357, 2021.
https://doi.org/10.1007/978-3-030-72132-9_29

Thailand, their existence is almost forgotten or discriminated against by Thai people. We cannot dismiss that these people are generally suffering because of poverty and disease, and illegal activity is commonly accepted. If we do not take any action, it will be a serious issue which can make countries' relationships unstable. Therefore, Thai people have to learn how to address such a problem. There are many NGOs or volunteer groups that support foreign workers. However, their work is not known well in Bangkok since it is difficult to recognize this as 'our issue'.

1.2   Recent History of Cambodia and Thailand

Let us summarize the reason many Cambodian people exist in Thailand. The Kingdom of Cambodia is a country located in the immediate east of Thailand. Most of its citizens are Khmer people. The population is 16 million, and more than 90% are Buddhist. Its origin can be traced at around the third century in Chinese literature, and the Kingdom of Khmer was established in the ninth century. However, its national history is filled with invasion from other countries; Mongolia, France, and Thailand were significant enemies. During World War II, Cambodia was the colony of France. After World War II, the Kingdom of Cambodia was reigned by King Norodom Sihanouk, but its base was unstable. In 1970, while Sihanouk was visiting the Soviet Union and China, Prime Minister Lon Nol caused a military coup, but its favorable governance to the United States caused invasion by North Vietnam's commitment, and finally, Cambodia was governed by an extreme left-wing party Khmer Rouge, led by Pol Pot, and it practiced genocide from 1975 to 1979. Pol Pot's ideology is primitive communism strongly influenced by Mao Zedong's Cultural Revolution. The damage caused by Khmer Rouge was remarkable. According to Kierman, 1.7 million citizens were killed [3]. In such circumstances, many people abandoned their hometowns, became refugees, and escaped to other countries.

In 1978, Vietnam sent troops to beat Khmer Rouge and occupied Cambodia until 1989. The United Nations took over tasks to rebuild a democratic order. In 1993, Cambodia had a general election. As the death of Pol Pot was confirmed in 1998, the whole country was reunited. In 2017, the GDP of Cambodia was ranked as 108th (22,158 USMD), while Thailand was 25th (455,303 USMD) [4]. In 2018, the GDP per capita was 1,485 USD in Cambodia and 7,084 USD in Thailand [5].

While Cambodia suffered countless tragedies, Thailand is the only country which supported the United States and capitalism in the Indo-China Peninsula, thus possessing an economy significantly higher than its neighboring countries. Furthermore, in the recent decade, the labor shortage issue has become severe in Thailand because of its aging society [4]. This is also the reason many Cambodian people have come to Thailand.

The authors must also point out that there is a discriminative sense of superiority among Thai people, who have considered that there are many illegal migrants. Whether these migrants are legal or illegal, Cambodians in Thailand work in bad environments for low wages. Their healthcare and education are also not enough. Many NGOs and volunteers are working to resolve these issues; however, their funds and enthusiasm are unstable. If such a situation continues, it will drop into a negative circle – 'poverty generates poverty in the next generation'. Although Thai and Khmer people are neighbors, they know too little about each other. Understanding each other, considering the future together, building a consensus to raise migrants' QOL with benefits to Thai people, and eliminating discriminative ideas are required. The authors' research purpose is to contribute to approach such goals.

1.3 Recent History Between Myanmar and Thailand

Many Myanmar people also exist in Thailand for many reasons. Thailand and Myanmar are separated by a 2,004-km border and were bitter enemies in the middle ages and imperial era. Today Thailand is one of the largest investors and trading partners of Myanmar. Nevertheless, relations between Thailand and Myanmar have been characterized by suspicions, mutual criticisms, and border troubles. In the past, Thailand's leaders had put some pressure on Myanmar to democratize and free Aung San Suu Kyi, and now Thailand, like every country in Asia, is leaping into Myanmar to get a piece of the action as Myanmar opens up and becomes more democratic [6]. For decades, Myanmar migrants have crossed the border to work in Thailand, and only in the 2000s did Thailand launch a long-term policy aiming to recruit formal migrants and legalize migrant workers holding temporary work permits. However, no extension would be permitted after 2012. That year, the number of registered Myanmar migrants stood at 1,186,805 Myanmar migrants, with 619,644 comprising regular skilled and unskilled workers and another 567,161 migrants consisting of irregular unskilled workers in various labor-intensive industries, agriculture, trading, and services [7].

Thailand has been affected by events in neighboring Myanmar, which saw unprecedented political developments in 2011 and 2012. Negotiations between the government of Myanmar and ethnic armed groups have resulted in a series of ceasefire agreements that have brought relative calm to South-Eastern Myanmar. The cessation of hostilities is significant for Myanmar refugees in Thailand: the vast majority of those registered and living in the Thai camps originate from areas in Myanmar where ceasefires have been announced. While peace is fragile, it has increased the prospects for voluntary returns to Myanmar [6]. Today 97,021 refugees are living in nine refugee camps in Thailand (as of February 2019). Most refugees are ethnic minorities from Myanmar, mainly Karen and Karenni, who live in nine fields in four provinces along the Thai– Myanmar border. Refugees in Thailand have been fleeing conflict and crossing Myanmar's eastern border jungles for the safety of Thailand for nearly 30 years [8]

2 Purpose of Research

2.1 Making a Game to Learn About Migrants' or Refugees' Issues

In this paper, the authors designed a useful learning tool to recognize, consider, and determine a path for a society in Thailand in which Cambodians or Burmese and Thai live peacefully. The authors labelled the game the 'PAL-BASEd Migrator Game' (P-BMG), which stands for PAL' that was developed by Iwasa, and with 'BASE' from author

Hamada, Kaneko, and Hiji's brand. This is the collaborative research of two projects that involve business and ethnics. The authors are certain that gaming can guide learners to be interested in and take on the social issues within Thailand, Cambodia, and Myanmar. The study includes several specialized fields: social responsibility, economics, legislation, and human rights concerned with the sufficiency to work in harmony.

2.2 Learning by Developing and Facilitating Game to Resolve the Issues

Migrants' or refugees' problems are wide and heavy. If society tries to resolve such an issue, based on the people's understanding and consensus, someone must facilitate the program. The facilitator has to understand the problem more than any participant, be ready to answer any questions, and guide the game participants correctly. Therefore, while developing the game, the authors also trained the students not only to manage the game but also to facilitate discussions on the resolution of the issue. The authors had a lot of opportunities to develop many games in collaboration with the students. The student players loved their student teacher. The authors attempt to strengthen the knowledge of student teachers by allowing them to make the games. This research, beyond 'learning by gaming', promotes 'learning by developing and facilitating the solution'.

3 Research Methodology

The authors and their senior project students develop two games (Cambodian and Burmese) to learn about issues and culture. After careful validation between the authors and the students, the latter compete to make the games. The students facilitate the gaming lecture for other students. Before and after the games, the authors and students conduct questionnaires to organize their discoveries.

3.1 Framework

To create the P-BMG, the authors used the framework of 'Simulation Game, Project PAL' (hereafter the PAL game) [10–12], and that has five game stages;

Stage 1: Individual Images (drawing symbols in a workshop),
Stage 2: Group Images (drawing group images colleting the individual images in Stage 1),
Stage 3: Learning (for solutions by learning the six GMs: Game Materials),
Stage 4: Planning (establishing a global company and making the company logo and its missions by using the group images and stories in Stage 2, and drawing action image of projects for the solutions), and
Stage 5: Presentations for sharing the solutions images and Debriefings.

Iwasa introduces the PAL game frame using 'Project PAL: Ainumosir' [11] (hereafter 'PAL: Ainu') for students to make a new tailored PAL game for Thai issues, and the PAL six game materials (GMs), which relate to geography, history, economy, issues, culture etc. Originally, Iwasa developed 'Project PAL' for resolving the social issues of indigenous people by designing their future well-being and visions in indigenous communities. She adapted to the Ainu ? that is, the indigenous people of Japan ? in 'PAL: Ainu'. The authors plan to make this original PAL game adapted to Thailand and swap the compliments from Ainumosir to Cambodian migrant/refugee issues. To understand and to respect the framework, they established the Settlement Association (SA). By following the PAL frame game, the learners understand the game gradually and finally define the role of the SA. Figure 1 shows the game flow using the PAL five game stages.

Fig.1. Five stages of P-BMG.

3.2 Learning Goals

Learning Goals of Students. By playing P-BMG, the learners can recognize why such social problems exist and why it is necessary to resolve them. When someone makes actions to resolve the issue, they can easily remember the story and cooperate. They consider that it is their duty, not someone else's, to solve this issue. The authors also expect some of the participants will work through further studying on this issue by any means.

Learning Goals of Senior Project Students. By co-developing the P-BMG, the authors intend to let the senior project students teach the game to other students. Repeating such experiences both in Japan and in Thailand, the authors try to raise their skills as professional facilitators at the end of the senior project ('learn by teaching'). Their ultimate image of a 'professional' is a person with a multitude of high skills set to resolve the migrants or refugee co-living issue. However, such a skill set is too difficult, complicated, and difficult for an individual to acquire. Therefore, the authors defined ancillary learning goals to make a game that is easy to play, includes enough information to build a new policy, and is able to describe the concepts of SA. The authors

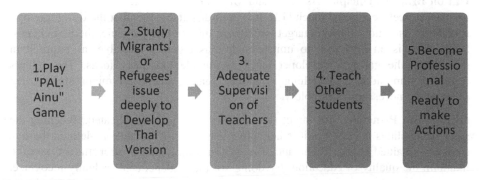

Fig. 2. P-BMG: Student's learning by developing and teaching.

have had numerous opportunities to let the ordinal student become a student teacher. In this research, the authors extend our idea from 'learning by teaching' to 'learning by developing and teaching' to encourage human resources to resolve big issues in society by playing the game. Figure 2 shows the authors' wishes for senior project students.

3.3   Game Trial

Author Hamada was serving as a faculty member at Sirindhorn International Institute of Technology (SIIT), Thammasat University, Thailand, then. To understand the framework of the gaming, Hamada invited Iwasa to Thailand in September 2018 and asked her to facilitate the 'PAL: Ainu' game for ten senior project students. They previously had no knowledge on the Ainu in Japan, but by playing the game, they learned that such an issue exists in Japan and that there is a need to consider how to co-live peacefully. After playing the game, Iwasa conducted a debriefing and explained the structure of the game while focusing on how they would develop their versions.

3.4   Selecting Two Neighboring Countries; Cambodia and Myanmar

The authors decided to divide the ten senior project students into two groups and made two games at once. Thailand is bordered from Myanmar, Malaysia, Cambodia, and Laos. Between Malaysia and Thailand, there is a political issue called the 'Deep South Problem', which came from conflicts between Buddhists and Muslims. Therefore, the authors considered Malaysia too tricky to gamify. The relationship between Laos and Thailand is generally fine, and the language used in Laos (Passa-Lao) is quite similar to the Thai language (Passa-Thai), so the authors thought that this is not an urgent issue. Consequently, the authors decided to make games to teach the students by using cases of Cambodian, Burmese migrants or refugees living in Thailand.

3.5   Rules for Game Development

The authors made the P-BMG with the simplest ideas and rules. The authors also followed the BASE game's developing principles, as defined earlier [12].

Cut-off Branch Principle. As Teach and Murff argued, simplicity is best, and there is no need to seek reality too much [13]. It is an indisputable fact that the developer of a specified topic knows about a target issue more than ordinary people, the participants. Since there is an obsession to imitate reality as much as possible, as required in developing the game, a developer tends to include too many ideas. The authors refrained from adding everything to imitate reality, dismissed minor stories, and selected the necessary rules boldly.

Gradualism Principle. Our target story is very long and complicated. Teaching the story using slides is easy, but it is not active learning. So the authors defined the five steps as explained in Fig. 2. The authors never rush the senior project students so as to maintain the quality of education. By doing so, the students can gradually recognize, analyze, and visualize the path to solve the issue, consider the other team's idea to improve their concept, and finally be able take action.

3.6   Contents of P-BMG

The P-BMG respects the PAL game method and procedures, requiring only paper and colored pens. The game is designed to not only feel fun but also give the players opportunities to learn about the issues between Thailand and Cambodia. This game is not intended to be played by a single player; everyone in the group must come up with creative solutions and use their imagination to solve these conflicts. Players can use the provided tools to follow the game stage process (Fig. 1). The core materials are for explaining the rules of the game and used to give players an idea on the culture, history, and social issues of Cambodia and Thailand. The game material also explained the conflict to be resolved by the players.

Game Leaflet. The P-BMG respects the 'Project PAL' game materials and uses the five materials from 'PAL': (1) game story and rules (the role of the players and what they need to do to come up with a solution to solve the conflict and background), (2) map and history (to learn about the target areas), (3) social issues (to determine the conflicts between Thailand and Cambodia), (4) cultural keywords (from two countries to Thailand), and (5) cultural information (e.g. art, music, photos, etc.).

Our purpose is to develop a person who can make actions; however, the presentation is easy to forget, and the gaming materials are collected to protect the operational idea. Thus, the authors have to retain something to study the issue. The authors ordered each team to compile a 30to 40-page book, which the authors will hand out to the players. The book tells the players all about the important background and history of Cambodia and Thailand, with a timeline of important events, maps, a detailed description of their livelihood, tips for common understanding, and literature information.

Student Teachers' Knowledge. As discussed above, the gaming materials are minimized. Our goal for the participants is for them to recognize the issue and be able to cooperate when the situation further occurs. However, for the student developer and student teacher, this experience entails more detailed know-how to solve the problem. To facilitate students who do not know anything about the migration issue, the trainer must study the problem and must be able to answer any questions. The student teacher's studying period is much longer than that of the participants. In our case, the author Hamada had ten senior students who developed games, and all of them became student teachers. They visited a library and rented books on history, culture, ethnics, poverty, the activities of NGOs, and so on, and they studied the literature deeply. Then, they compiled the core teaching materials and leaflets and were able to answer most of the participants' questions, a step to increase their studying.

3.7   How to Play the P-BMG

The authors operate the P-BMG in three works and three presentations:

1. The instructor operates the 'before' questionnaire and introduces the student teacher.

2. He/she explains the outline of the game and the participants' duty: to live with Cambodian migrants with the least conflicts, which is required for the settlement association (SA).
3. Each participant receives core materials. Within 10 min, they draw an 'icon' of the SA on A4 paper.
4. The participants explain their ideas to their teammates and share their ideas in the group within 10 min.
5. The group combines the players' 'icons' and optimizes a 'company logo' with a hand-drawn A3 image, including a suitable name for the SA, within 10 min.
6. They each present their SA's name and 'company logo' to other groups within 5 min.
7. Including the ideas of other groups, they summarize the 'concept' (Fig. 3 and Fig. 4) of the SA and write down their concept in a piece of A2 paper within 20 min. They have to define five new keywords.
8. Each group presents their keywords and 'concept' to other groups within 5 min.
9. The student teacher summarizes the stories, and the instructor debriefs the whole session.
10. The instructor operates the 'after' questionnaire and provides a final debriefing.

Fig. 3. Example of 'concept'.

Fig. 4. Presentation of a 'concept'.

4   Results

4.1   Outline of Experiment

Ten senior project students developed the draft of the two games at the end of November 2018. They formed two teams. One team facilitated the other team to play their game. Throughout such an exercise, they repaired the discovered flaws, improved the quality of the game, and finalized the game. With confidence, the authors planned to present the game both in Japanese University and Thai University.

4.2   Experiment at Hokkaido University

Eight student teachers travelled to Japan. Before travelling, author Hamada provided tips on how to be professional, including how to dress (tie, jacket, belt, and so on), how to greet businesspeople, how to exchange business cards, and how to take care of the Japanese participants. In Sapporo, author Iwasa took the role of the instructor, and others guided 14 participants (Fig. 5). Given the time limitation, the author could not conduct the questionnaires; however, the author received comments from the students. They can be categorized into 'new learning' and 'joy'.

Fig. 5. Session at Hokkaido University conducted by Iwasa and student teachers

"This game provided more information so that we can understand the co-living problem between Thailand and Myanmar or Cambodia and gave a chance for us to find the solution from our opinion."

"I enjoyed introducing [myself], making a logo, and solving issues of Thailand–Myanmar disputes. We cannot solve all problems faced by Myanmar or Cambodia at once, but it is essential to understand the fact that there is a solution to such issues. We played games and tried to solve some problems like poverty, starvation, as well as unemployment. Working in a group was easy. It did not feel like we were addressing issues while playing games; however, we were trying to solve [Myanmar's] or [Cambodia's] related co-living problems from our point of view. I loved being part of this workshop. Thank you so much."

4.3   Experiment at SIIT

In Thailand, the author conducted two more sessions for SIIT students. The number of participants was 35. They were mostly second-year undergraduate students in the Management Technology program.

Questionnaire. After two questions on identification, the authors asked six questions to be answered by playing the game, as shown in Tables 1 and 2. The participants were required to answer the questions by following a commonly used five-point scale:

1. Strongly No
2. No
3. Neutral
4. Yes
5. Strongly Yes

Result. For the Cambodia version, 13 students answered both the 'before' and 'after' questionnaires correctly. Table 1 shows the result. For the Myanmar version, 16 participants answered correctly. In both cases, it is obvious that the game provided an excellent opportunity to learn about the refugee/migrant issue in Thailand. The P-BMG is sufficient in increasing understanding on the history of the two countries, determining the current status of migrants/refugees, and training students to find a practical solution for an actual social problem. Therefore, we can consider that the learning goals of the players can be achieved using this game.

Table 1. P-BMG's major performances of Cambodia version (n = 13).

Question	Before		After		A/B	t-stat	P(T ≤ t) two-tail
	Average	Variance	Average	Variance	Average		
3. Do you know there are many migrants or refugees from Cambodia and Myanmar in the territory of Thailand?	3.308	1.397	4.462	0.436	134.9%	−3.426	0.005*
4. Do you know what kind of conflicts exist between those two countries?	3.000	1.167	4.385	0.423	146.2%	−5.740	0.000***
5. Do you know about migrants' or refugees' common lifestyle of people who live in Thailand?	3.000	0.500	4.615	0.423	153.8%	−6.697	0.000***
6. Do you know what the legal statuses of the migrant are or refugee around the border?	3.077	0.410	4.462	0.436	145.0%	−5.740	0.000***
7. Do you know what main migrants or refugee's career are?	3.308	0.564	4.692	0.231	141.9%	−6.501	0.000***
8. Do you have idea to improve those migrants or refugee's quality of life?	3.077	0.410	4.462	0.603	145.0%	-9.859	0.000***
9. Do you have practical idea to co-live with refugees without discrimination?	3.077	0.410	4.538	0.269	147.5%	−7.982	0.000***
Average	3.083	0.735	4.451	0.398	144.5%	–	–

Note: n = 13; *significant at < 0.01, **significant at < 0.005, ***significant at < 0.001

Table 2. P-BMG's major performances of Myanmar version (n = 16).

Question	Before		After		A/B	t-stat	P(T ≤ t) two-tail
	Average	Variance	Average	Variance	Average		
3. Do you know there are many migrants or refugees from Cambodia and Myanmar in the territory of Thailand?	3.375	1.238	4.333	0.381	128.4%	−3.240	0.006*
4. Do you know what kind of conflicts exist between those two countries?	2.438	0.663	4.063	0.329	166.7%	−5.665	0.000***
5. Do you know about migrants' or refugees' common lifestyle of people who live in Thailand?	2.938	0.596	4.000	0.400	136.2%	-4.000	0.001**
6. Do you know what the legal statuses of the migrant are or refugee around the border?	2.813	0.696	4.000	0.400	142.2%	−4.842	0.000***
7. Do you know what main migrants or refugee's career are?	2.688	0.896	3.875	0.650	144.2%	−5.694	0.000***
8. Do you have idea to improve those migrants or refugee's quality of life?	2.750	0.867	4.125	0.517	150.0%	−3.780	0.002**
9. Do you have practical idea to co-live with refugees without discrimination?	3.063	0.863	4.313	0.229	140.8%	−4.226	0.000***
Average	2.866	0.831	4.101	0.415	144.1%	–	–

Note: n = 16; *significant at < 0.01, **significant at < 0.005, ***significant at < 0.001

Satisfaction. To determine the impact and impression of the game as a learning method, the authors attached some questions in the 'after' questionnaire and confirmed that this method is comfortable for the students. The results are in Table 3. Focusing on definite answers, the results show that more than 90% of the participants enjoyed the game. More than 75% of the students wished to play again if there was another opportunity. Therefore, we can conclude that 'learning by gaming' was highly appreciated in SIIT.

Table 3. Satisfaction rate of participants (n = 29).

Question/answer score	Strongly Yes	Yes	Neutral	No	Strongly No	Total
	5	4	3	2	1	
11. Did you enjoy your game?	15	12	2	0	0	29
	51.72%	41.38%	6.90%	0.00%	0.00%	100.00%
12. Do you want to play again?	10	12	6	1	0	29
	34.48%	41.38%	20.69%	3.45%	0.00%	100.00%

Student Teachers' Learnings. The P-BMG provides a chance to recognize hidden issues for ordinary students and also offers a great opportunity for the student teachers. They developed and facilitated the game both in Japan and in Thailand. The authors conducted the questionnaire and were not required to identify the names of the participants to avoid bias. Eight in ten student teachers answered the questionnaire. Table 4 shows the result.

Table 4. Student teachers' feelings on the project after a year (n = 9).

Question/answer Score	Strongly Yes	Yes	Neutral	Strongly No	No	Total
	5	4	3	2	1	
1. Do you think you learned migrants/refugee issue in our Project?	5	4	0	0	0	9
	55.56%	44.44%	0.00%	0.00%	0.00%	100.00%
2. Do you think your game developing skill increased?	6	3	0	0	0	9
	66.67%	33.33%	0.00%	0.00%	0.00%	100.00%
3. Do you think your game facilitation skill increased?	5	3	1	0	0	9
	55.56%	33.33%	11.11%	0.00%	0.00%	100.00%
4. Do you think the project was useful experience?	5	3	1	0	0	9
	55.56%	33.33%	11.11%	0.00%	0.00%	100.00%
5. Do you think you have grown up compare with beginning?	6	3	0	0	0	9
	66.67%	33.33%	0.00%	0.00%	0.00%	100.00%
6. Did you enjoy the project?	6	3	0	0	0	9
	66.67%	33.33%	0.00%	0.00%	0.00%	100.00%

Knowledge on the migrant/refugee issue (Q1) and skills to develop (Q2) and facilitate the game (Q3) have significantly increased. They feel they have grown up (Q5), had fun (Q6), and facilitated the process while earning positive experiences (Q4). Wthin our student teachers, the author can say that our learning goal has been achieved.

5 Limitations and Further Research

In this section, the authors state the current limitation of the research and the possibility to extend the research from perspectives of the PAL project and BASE project.

5.1 To Improve the Work

PAL has several existing games on ethnic issues, and this research increased the variety of such games. BASE has stayed in the business game category and never had this kind of gaming. Therefore, it was a completely new trial that brought us the possibility to spread our know-how to a common social issue. However, the current game lacks a sense of business, especially for the sustainability of SA, social capital, or entrepreneurs. From such a viewpoint, BASE can contribute more to providing reality to the game based on the PAL project. However, a merit of the PAL game is its simplicity. If the authors create more stories that are missing in the current version, it is against the cut-off branch principle and makes the game more complex. Seeking the improved image while maintaining the current versions' good points is a big issue for the authors.

5.2 To Spread the Idea with Others

Our scope of research is limited. The authors discussed only the Cambodian and Myanmar issues in Thailand even though this kind of conflict exists all over the world. However, to resolve all issues, the authors' power is limited. The authors must pay the maximum attention to share their ideas positively and strongly.

5.3 To Prove 'Learning by Developing and Facilitating Game'

Physical game is impossible to create without co-operators. In our research, ten senior project students studied hard and grew up to the authors' partner. Moreover, the authors let them conduct the game. The authors have confidence that this way is good learning opportunity for students. However, only nine students' answer is not enough to say this is universal theory. To make sure combination of making and facilitating is effective way to learn, we need to continue this research for coming several generations.

6 Conclusion

The authors made two games called the P-BMG to contribute to the students' knowledge on co-living with migrants/refugees from neighboring countries. The authors also trained 'student teachers' to gain enough knowledge and facilitation skills to become social entrepreneurs. By doing so, the authors confirmed that gaming is a suitable learning method, so 'learning by gaming' is truly possible. The authors succeed in cultivating ten students to work globally with a sense of gaming. The authors proved that 'learning by making and teaching games' is effective within the students in this year. Co-living is worldwide issue and to grow up leaders is urgent. Our duty is too large to handle only by the authors' team. Therefore, continuing this research with new members is required and welcomed.

Acknowledgements. This research was partially funded by Technology Transfer SIG, JASAG (Japan Association of Simulation and Gaming). The authors express highest appreciation to one-year work of ten 'Student Teachers' by indicating their names as follows.

Thanasit Bunyaritpaisit
Supatat Iamchangpun
Pakdipoom Rattanopas
Warathep Sornnoei
Apivit Laohirantakool
Jirayu Ratanayatikul
Peerapong Akaharasetthakan
Palatwong Prempho
Chatchal Somjit
Sarisa Panya

References

1. International Organization for Migration Thailand, Labour Migration. https://thailand.iom. int/labour-migration. Accessed 31 Mar 2019
2. Yagisawa, K.: Is Current Thai a future Japan? Asahi-Shinbun Plus, 2018/11/09. https:// globe.asahi.com/article/11902425. Accessed 31 Mar 2019. (in Japanese)
3. Kiernan, B.: A world upside down. In: DePaul, K. (ed.) Children of Cambodia's Killing Fields: Memoirs by Survivors, vol. 16. Yale University Press (1999). https://doi.org/10. 1007/s12126-009-9027-6
4. World Development Indicators database 2019, World Bank (2019). https://databank. worldbank.org/data/download/GDP.pdf. Accessed 23 Mar 2019
5. International Monetary Fund, IMF Data Mapper (2018). https://www.imf.org/external/ datamapper/. Accessed 23 Mar 2019
6. Hays, J.: Myanmar's relations with Thailand and Southeast Asia, vol. 7 (2014).http:// factsanddetails.com/southeast-asia/Myanmar/sub5_5f/entry-3113.html. Accessed 31 Mar 2019
7. Chantavanich, S., Vungsiriphisal, P.: Myanmar migrants to thailand: economic analysis and implications to myanmar development in economic reforms in Myanmar: pathways and prospects. In: Lim, H., Yamada, Y. (eds.) BRC Research Report No.10, Bangkok Research Center, IDE-JETRO, Bangkok, Thailand (2012). https://www.ide.go.jp/library/English/ Publish/Download/Brc/pdf/10_06.pdf. Accessed 31 Mar 2019
8. UNHCR's work is humanitarian, social and non-political. Its Statute and Subsequent UN resolutions mandate the agency to provide international protection and seek durable solutions for refugees and other people of concern (2019). https://www.unhcr.or.th/en. Accessed 31 Mar 2019

9. Iwasa, N., Kila, G. M., Oliveira, C.: Simulation Game. Project PAL: Hawaii, ESD Campus Asia (2015). Faculty of Education, Hokkaido University (See also SimTecT 2016. Australasian Simulation Congress 2016, Melbourne Convention & Exhibition Centre. Melbourne, Victoria, Australia) (2016)

10. Iwasa, N.: Urespa, Simulation Game. Project PAL: Ainumosir, ESD Campus Asia Pacific 2016, Faculty of Education, Hokkaido University, Urespa Club, Urespa Ainu Cultural Club. Sapporo University, Japan (2016)

11. Iwasa, N., Mataira. P.J.: Simulation game. Project PAL: iKoru: place-based active learning - empowering indigenous youth through entrepreneurship. In: 49th ISAGA Conference Proceedings (ISAGA2018), pp. 717–721 (2018)

12. Hamada, R., Yokouchi, T., Kaneko, T., Hiji, M.: Development of the BASE life planning game to teach students the balance between money and happiness. Developments in business simulation and experiential learning. In: Proceedings of the Annual ABSEL Conference, vol. 46, pp. 18–24 (2019)

13. Teach, R.D., Murff, E.: Are the business simulations we play too complex? Developments in business simulation and experiential learning. In: Proceedings of the Annual ABSEL Conference, vol. 35, pp. 205–211 (2014)

Gamification Design Strategies - Summary of Research Project

Michał Jakubowski[✉] iD

Kozminski University, Jagiellonska 57, 03-301 Warsaw, Poland
mjakubowski@kozminski.edu.pl

Abstract. In the paper Author will describe outcomes of his interviews with focus on how certain game elements are chosen and compiled into working gamification systems. Most popular elements which can be found in current gamified platforms and literature reviews are leaderboards, points, badges and levels. It seems that designers are using it over and over again as it would be the only possibility when one thinks about boosting engagement. What is the reason that designers won't take advantage of other combinations of game design elements? How they are guiding the creative process of game design construction in gamification design process? Following paper will try to deliver answers basing on data gathered during the research.

Keywords: Gamification · Design · Game design · Frameworks

1 Introduction

Following article will summarize research project about the strategical perspective of gamification system design in the area of employee engagement. The target group of the research was 15 experienced gamification designers with at least 2 finished and implemented projects in the past. Basing on cross-analysis of multiple case study that will gather the design perspective of corporate gamification systems the expected result will be a set of best working design guidelines in corporate area. Guidelines will be corrected by the end-user perspective and will state open perspectives for future development.

Hamari positions gamification in the field of hedonistic-utilitarian information systems [1]. Within such systems, each interaction that takes place is by definition seen as an awakening pleasant feeling. Birth of that systems can be connected to the mutual interest of software developers (software like office application) and video games developers. Software developers appreciated the effectiveness of modeling engaging user experience in games. Game developers on the other hand use knowledge about building the correct architecture of information and deliver features according to recipients expectations [2].

One of the reasons why gamification is treated as a negative phenomenon is too shallow design perspective that uses constantly the same game mechanics [3]. Current state of art of gamification research in enterprise area is con-firming that revelations [4–7]. Unfortunately, none of the reviewed research papers takes account designer

M. Wardaszko et al. (Eds.): ISAGA 2019, LNCS 11988, pp. 358–362, 2021.
https://doi.org/10.1007/978-3-030-72132-9_30

perspective nor knowledge or skill of their gamification designs. The way of how next iterations of gamification systems will be created have crucial meaning not only for that area but also for the quality of its influence inside organizations.

2 Project Description

Scientific problem of that project is the design strategies of gamification systems. Basing on cross-analysis of multiple case study that will gather the design perspective of gamification systems the expected result will be a set of best working design guidelines. Guidelines will be corrected by the end-user perspective and will state open perspectives for future development. The initial study will involve a thorough examination of circumstances for building well-functioning gamification system for employee engagement improvement and management. Results will come from the literature review of research domains and gamification design guidelines described by respondents.

Main findings from the literature review were positioned around two works. Raftopoulos [8] analyzed what are the effective approaches to enterprise gamification and what can be potential tools that assist such gamification. Having scope on the corporate environment doesn't mean it can't be related to learning. One of the enterprise activities where employees are gamified is in-house learning (about the company, product, skills). An outcome of her study presented a framework based on more than 300 gamification artifacts and their design.

Second work by Morschheuser [9] again tries to set a framework for proper gamification design. With the use of design science authors conceptualized and then build artifact of the gamification design process. Based on literature review, desk research and most important – in-depth interviews with gamification designers, they prepared a comprehensive method of gamification.

Both sources have a rather limited view of what are the game elements that should be used in gamification systems. Raftopoulus mentions key mechanics and core gameplay groups as design elements, but there are no guidelines on how to connect elements of those groups into working and engaging system that will answer the problem. Second work brings ideation toolbox which is a guide of best practices about combining game elements in gamification design.

3 Methodology

Research methodology in the following project is positioned in interpretative-symbolic paradigm [10]. Qualitative methods can be sufficient to explain a phenomenon that appears in reality. The research will be constructed upon a grounded theory which assumes that research area can be understood best by engaged in actors [11]. Research hypothesis will emerge during the collection of research evidence. There is also an assumption that some elements or areas, that were not stated at first, will appear somewhere during the research and will have important meaning for research problem.

That methodology results from a relatively fresh area which is gamification. Because of its characteristic of long-term influence on implementing subjects [12] and a small number of long-enough implementations, state of art of gamification in employee engagement management is still open for new findings. Qualitative methods that explore research area have better application in the following project than explanative ones. As for now - broadest knowledge of the research area still lies in the hands of practitioners and using their experience this research project will deliver new and structured information.

Research method will be an exploratory case study [13] in the form of group case analysis. A juxtaposition of a couple of cases will help with a deeper understanding of the research problem. To strengthen qualitative results I will use questionnaire method with employees who took part in gamification activities. That group perspective will help with the supplement of knowledge and experience of the designer by adding conclusions which they could overlook.

The research was structured as design science research. Gasparski [14] distinguish design science subdisciplines like design phenomenology (background, taxonomy, technology); design praxeology (analysis of design activities and organization) and design philosophy (axiology, epistemology, and pedagogy of design). Here Author will analyze how the design is processed, so the praxeology of that action is in the main focus of the research. When it comes to design methodology then it will be covered different types of design activities and its analysis, description of design tasks and procedures which Gasparski titles as a pragmatic design methodology.

Research group:

- 15 gamification designers

Research tools:

- IDI script,
- Observation diary,
- Data from designers (design documents, guidelines, frameworks)

IDI script was divided into three parts: questions about gamification, questions about design, and questions about game design. Then each chapter of the interview was covered with a couple of question starting from general topics and finishing with specific ones. Each of the interviews has followed the same script, but the characteristics of IDI allowed Author to sometimes ask additional questions if something emerged during the talk.

4   Results

The outcome of this research project was to present multiple case study of gamification design strategies and gather best practices in one framework that can be a guide for other designers. The following paper will cover the latter with a focus on the creative process of gathering game design elements. It was the first idea of the Author to research what are the real purposes of combining such elements and why is that so popular to use often similar elements (i.e. points, badges, leaderboards) when there is the much broader choice.

General analysis of the interviews was conducted with use of Johnny Saldana method that uses two cycles of coding [15]. Figure 1 covers categories and codes that emerged after the first cycle of analysis.

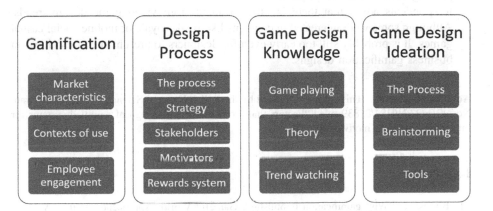

Fig. 1. Interview questions categories and codes.

Although some insights about design strategies should be presented as well. To make it more clear for the purpose of this paper it will be presented as list with short description of each element.

1. Project vs product approach. There are those two styles of thinking and working on gamification solutions. Project work assumes that each solution will be build up from scratch, with ground research of the problem and tailor-made mechanisms. It is more costly and time-consuming but the results are generally better. Product means that the company has some already existing gamification 'engine' which is prepared and modified accordingly to clients requirements.

2. Generic vs mature gamification. Generic gamification is the easiest way of using points, badges, and leaderboards as a layer on existing activities that gain new instruments to measure the performance of its peers. Mature gamification states to be more immersing, uses other – often experimental – elements for engaging user behavior.

3. The user is less important than some stakeholders. That is something that was observed in some interviews, designers were not interested in the user perspective on the first place. It was dictated by the business objectives of the project and end users were involved in the project only at the testing phase or in one case – not at all!

4. Rewards should fit user characteristics and needs. Different levels of employees in the organization have different needs and expectations about the prizes. Managers were more into using their gamification capital (like virtual currencies) for charity or knowledge enhancers (books, training). However, lower level employees love physical goods and rewards that can improve their status.

5. Heavy use of tools known in human-computer interactions design (user journey map, user stories, storyboards, personas). It can also lead to other connections with user experience design and the general image of how gamification blends with UX.
6. Brainstorming while playing games can deliver innovative mechanics. Most of the respondents stated that there is the positive influence on design process when playing video (or tabletop) games.
7. Respondents admit that there is little to adapt from video game design trends. Although some were interested in concepts like battle royale or mobile/social/casual games. It is probably still too early even for designers to present such fresh ideas in business gamification designs.

Acknowledgements. This work was funded by the Polish National Science Center under Grant No. 2016/23/N/HS4/03839 titled "Factors that promote specific design of gamified systems for managing employee motivation.".

References

1. Bogost, I.: "Why gamification is bullshit". Gameful World: Approaches, Issues, Applications. MIT Press (2014)
2. Cardador, M.T., Northcraft, G.B., Whicker, J.: A theory of work gamification: something old, something new, something borrowed, something cool? Hum. Resour. Manageme. Rev. **27**(2), 353–365 (2016)
3. Ferrara, J.: Playful Design: Creating Game Experiences in Everyday Interfaces. Rosenfeld Media (2012)
4. Gasparski, W.: Science of Designing. Elements of the Study of Designing (1988)
5. Glaser, B.G.: Basics of Grounded Theory Analysis: Emergence vs Forcing. Sociology press (1992)
6. Hamari, J., Koivisto, J.: Why do people use gamification services? Int. J. Inf. Manage. **35**, 4 (2015)
7. Hamari, J., Koivisto, J., Sarsa, H.: Does Gamification work?-a literature review of empirical studies on gamification. In: HICSS, vol. 14, no. 2014 (2014)
8. Herger, M.: Gamification in human resources. Enterprise Gamification, vol. 3 (2014)
9. Konecki, K.: A study of the qualitative research methodology. Grounded theory (2000)
10. Morschheuser, B., Werder, K., Hamari, J., Abe, J.: How to gamify? Development of a method for gamification. In: Proceedings of the 50th Annual Hawaii International Conference on System Sciences (HICSS), Hawaii, USA, 4–7 January 2017
11. Raftopoulos, M.: Towards gamification transparency: a conceptual framework for the development of responsible gamified enterprise systems. J. Gaming Virtual Worlds **6**(2), 159–178 (2014)
12. Rapp, A., et al.: Fictional game elements: critical perspectives on gamification design. In: Proceedings of the 2016 Annual Symposium on Computer-Human Interaction in Play Companion Extended Abstracts. ACM (2016)
13. Robson, K., et al.: Game on: engaging customers and employees through gamification. Bus. Horiz. **59**(1), 29–36 (2016)
14. Saldaña, J.: The Coding Manual for Qualitative Researchers. Sage (2015)
15. Yin, R.K.: Case Study Research and Applications: Design and Methods. Sage publications (2017)

Fostering Adaptive Organizations: Some Practical Lessons from Space Pirates

Derek W. Wade[✉]

Kumido Adaptive Strategies, Arlington Heights, IL 60005, USA
dwade@kumido.com

Abstract. Research in business leadership, team communication, and simulation/gaming each suggest models for improving performance outcomes by increasing organizational adaptivity and resilience to disruption. A case study of players in a commercial, massively-multiplayer online simulation (MMO) is presented through the lenses of these three theoretical domains. Analysis of the case study attempts to synthesize the theoretical models, and connect them to practical applications for facilitating organizational performance. Formational and interventional success factors are presented: organizational identity, flexible structure, congruence of leader espoused vs. practiced values, and active community management. Opportunities for further exploration of the relationship between theory and practice via this method are suggested.

Keywords: Community · Leadership · Macro-cognition · Simulation · Games · Play · MMO · Online games · Elite:Dangerous · Learning organization

1 Introduction

"The passion for destruction is a creative passion, too."
Mikhail Alexandrovich Bakunin, Russian anarchist and philosopher [3]

On January 11, 2017, community leader "Wickedlala" logged in to Discord, an online chat tool, to discover that her world had changed overnight. Her community, a worldwide group of several hundred independent players in the massively-multiplayer online video game *Elite:Dangerous,* was facing an imminent disaster. There was an emergent problem which threatened community morale. Solving the problem would require unity of purpose and action among workers with a variety of motivations. There could be no compromise on results. And all this had to be dealt with despite the fiercely independent values common to their culture. They had to learn, as a whole, and rapidly —or fail.

This scenario, although an online simulation set in a fictional 34th century, shares challenges with those of many 21st-century enterprises. The context for both can be viewed through several lenses which offer models for improving organizational performance by creating learning organizations. Viewed through the lens of business management, the problem is "VUCA"—volatility, uncertainty, complexity, and ambiguity [4]. One possible solution is to apply the self-organization and servant

M. Wardaszko et al. (Eds.): ISAGA 2019, LNCS 11988, pp. 363–377, 2021.
https://doi.org/10.1007/978-3-030-72132-9_31

leadership concepts typical of systems thinking and Agile methods [26, 27]. Viewed through the lens of cognitive science, group communication is the problem, and a solution is to improve the mental models shared by team members [9, 25]. The lens of gaming suggests that a key problem is risk, and a solution is the use of simulated worlds where risky scenarios can be explored safely [18]. Immersive entertainment games could even be a "tool for harnessing collective action" [19].

For facilitators of teams facing diverse problems, contexts, and organizations—who may be Wickedlala's real-world counterparts—these lenses can feel like largely theoretical domains from which it can be difficult to find practical applications. Facilitators can try to borrow specific interventions from real-world scenarios based in a specific domain and hope it will apply to their own. But such interventions are often either so tightly coupled to the domain or so broad that it is hard to see how they are relevant. Alternatively, they might try to synthesize across domains in order to craft bespoke interventions for their unique situation. But the depth and focus of each of these theoretical domains necessarily constrains their applicability.

While this is a paper about a gang of space pirates, for leaders who want high-performing adaptive teams is also a fable; a story with a moral. When we look at the story through the optics of all three of the above lenses we may glimpse something superior to either theory or practices from any one domain. We may see lessons that are both relevant across many domains and also easy to apply. Wickedlala's space pirates became a resilient learning community which adapted to overcome catastrophic change. Your organization can as well.

2   Adaptivity

2.1   The Privateers' Alliance

"Take command of your own starship in a cutthroat galaxy!"
Elite:Dangerous marketing copy [10]

Welcome to the 34th century and the massively-multiplayer online simulation (MMO) that is *Elite:Dangerous*. The play area spans more than 400 billion stars in the Milky Way, many with their own planetary systems and complex economies. In any given moment, about 8,000 very real humans are in the game, each indulging their own very real human motivations. Some explore unknown stars, trade goods for profit, upgrade their ships, or try to take over star systems. Some fight foes together or fight against each other. Despite this banquet of pre-defined in-game activities, one popular player choice is to push the constraints of the game itself to affect other players. This results in frequent examples of what the creators of *Elite:Dangerous*, UK-based studio Frontier Developments, market as "emergent content." Which is a polite phrase to mean that rules are made to be broken, anything you can imagine will probably happen, and things you'd never imagine can sometimes ruin your whole day.

While the majority of player-pilots work solo, many band together into factions—some with over 1,000 members—to share knowledge, cooperate toward larger goals, or just have company during long interstellar travels. Real friendships and rivalries form in-game even though the pilots may never learn each others' identities beyond their callsigns, player-chosen handles like ElvisKremmen, Roknori, CMDRJorlan, and Psykit.

The Privateers' Alliance faction ("P.A." for short) was founded by player Ph1Lt0r ("Phil") and his real-life wife Wickedlala as a club of about 15 friends. Initially the club had no purpose beyond playing *Elite:Dangerous* and broadcasting their gameplay on the internet streaming service Twitch. By November of 2017 P.A. had grown to over 150 members, but the faction's purpose remained less than clear to a potential new recruit. With a name like "Privateers' Alliance" and the slogan, "Where everyone plays together, and everyone plays their own way," the group appeared as chaotic as a band of 17th-century pirates on the Caribbean Sea. It was hard to tell if Phil and Wickedlala were running the Privateers' Alliance or if it was the other way around. As they explained in conversation with the author:

> *Phil:* We get a lot of Jack-of-All-Trades, people who want to trade and explore and do bounty hunting.
> *Wickedlala:* We've always followed the lead of the people in P.A. If there's something that they're interested in doing in the game, then we tend to support that.
> *Phil:* You can build a stronger community because instead of it being anchored around yourself, it's anchored around something that you all enjoy.

Every now and again, Frontier Developments—"FDev" to the players—would organize temporary events to stimulate more player interaction in-game. These were time/speed/distance challenges that rewarded individual players with in-game currency based on their individual performance. One month the best payouts might go to the top explorers for the greatest number of star systems visited. Another challenge might pay the combat pilots who did the most bounty-hunting that month. But in November 2016, FDev announced something different.

The Colonia Initiative seemed to be another time/speed/distance challenge. The rules required a pilot to use their starship to transport as much cargo as possible within a limited time, across a very long distance, to a particular destination (Fig. 1). But the Colonia Initiative went beyond challenging individual pilots; it was player faction against player faction, with a limited number of prizes for the winners. For those few factions that delivered more cargo than their competition, the reward was compelling. Winning factions would get to name a new planetary base—coveted real estate—in the unspoiled territory near the middle of the galaxy. Other than naming the base, winning conferred no permanent rights to the faction. Any player in the game could use the base. Individual players gained nothing beyond the pride of a job well done with the other members of their faction.

For a comparatively small, volunteer faction of Jack-of-All-Trades pirates, to attempt this challenge seemed a little like trying to get a herd of cats to solve the Moon landing. The only thing Ph1lt0r and Wickedlala could count on was the will of the individual faction members. Surprisingly, it seemed this might be enough. One unusual rule about the Colonia Initiative was a 10 item-per-starship limit on the amount of cargo that pilots could take on at the trip's origin. This rule, along with the long duration of the trip (16–34 hours in real life) gave the advantage to factions with more members. P.A.'s determination found a loophole: One pilot—the Loader—could take

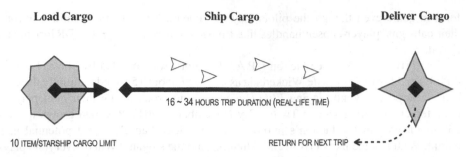

Load Cargo   **Ship Cargo**   **Deliver Cargo**

16 ~ 34 HOURS TRIP DURATION (REAL-LIFE TIME)

10 ITEM/STARSHIP CARGO LIMIT   RETURN FOR NEXT TRIP

Fig. 1. Workflow for the Colonia Challenge

on 10 items of cargo and then hand it off to another pilot—the Shipper—until the Shipper's starship was filled to capacity. The Shipper would begin the long journey to the destination while the Loader began filling a new Shipper. Players in other factions were often amazed that P.A. was transporting 400 items at a time while they were hauling 10 [22].

P.A. soon established standard operating procedures for this handoff. An internal announcement to Loaders on the P.A. website admonished that the Loading process "is no time to show off your Maverick skills. Shippers carry hours worth of labor. Please fly safe and use only a nose-to-nose delivery method during the Loading process" [6]. When a few P.A. members found an improved method, other members chafed at the variation and asked Ph1Lt0r to make them conform. Not taking the bait, Phil asked the players to demonstrate their methods to each other so everyone could learn which way was best. They did, the new method was faster, and the group adopted it. This sort of controlled chaos was typical for the Privateers' Alliance approach to the Colonia Challenge:

> "I've gotten to see your teamwork first hand. I've witnessed nothing short of a well oiled machine of humans working with minimal need for direct supervision. Bravo ladies and gents. We couldn't ask for a grittier bunch. [5]

2.2 The Colonia Challenge—Analysis

> "Everything should be made as simple as possible, but no simpler."
> *Attributed to Albert Einstein*

How can this story of the Privateers' Alliance vs. the Colonia Initiative relate to any real-world situation? *Elite:Dangerous* is just a game and, no matter how complex the real-world system on which a game is based, the game's own complexity is likely to be less. This is because in order for game development to be possible, developers must make design choices which tend to limit players to simpler actions with more predictable results than those found in real-world scenarios [15, 24].

In the real world, deterministic actions are less effective and outcomes less predictable. Technology is uncertain. People disagree. Moore's Law and globalization are increasing the impact of both. Where leaders find simple situations they can repeat lessons learned from the past and apply best practices. But as uncertainty and dis-agreement—or technical complexity and social complexity, if you prefer—increase toward "the edge of chaos," organizations must find solutions based on innovation, creativity, and diversity in approaches [28, 29]. Product development organizations face this kind of complexity simply as a consequence of being in business in the 21st century. Further, they face it not only within their own organization but at the interface to the world outside.

Consider technical and social complexity as two dimensions. Figure 2 compares the relative complexity impact of some factors found both within (circles) and outside (squares) of an organization's control. Examples are shown for both the P.A./Colonia Initiative scenario (solid shapes) and a real-world software product development scenario (outlined shapes).

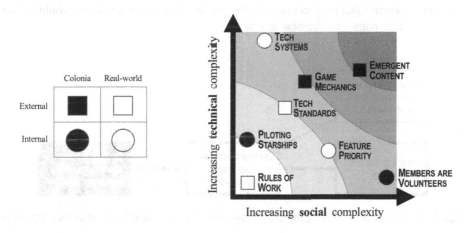

Fig. 2. Example complexity factors internal to and outside of the organization

Internally, development teams must know *technical systems* and their convoluted interconnections. The Privateers' Alliance pilots must be skilled in *piloting starships* and long-range navigation, each a difficult skill requiring many tens of hours of practice to reach proficiency. Members of development teams often have a single role to *pri-oritize the features* for a software product. Despite the presence of leadership roles in the Privateers' Alliance, *members are volunteers* with lives outside the game, and answer to no authority.

External to their organization, teams have to deal with emerging *technical stan-dards*, while pilots in P.A. are regularly surprised by changes to the *game mechanics*. Development teams can have issues with vendors and other teams but the *rules of work* tend to be stable. For space pirates, player creativity and the varying attitudes of other factions—sportsmanlike, or less so—cause much of the game's *"emergent content."*

For members of the Privateers' Alliance, the simulated challenge of the Colonia Initiative was comparable in complexity to real-life challenges. When product devel-opment organizations confront competitive markets, often what initially appears to be a deterministic problem—a small matter of shipping, for example—masks a more subtle, interconnected web of risks and opportunities. Even if it requires more resources, the simplest solution is frequently the most attractive choice. The risk of deviating from past lessons or best practices is perceived to be worse. To even consider alternate paths to success requires more discerning awareness and a willingness to embrace complexity. In high-VUCA situations, optimal strategies frequently require the whole organization to accept the continuous cost of finding better ways to coordinate.

Sometimes the deterministic solution is the proper one. Sometimes its worth the extra effort to question assumptions and think of optimizing the whole system. What matters is how one sees it.

From the perspective of Frontier Developments, the Colonia Initiative seemed straightforward. "You need to make the trip out there to have truly taken part in the expansion initiative," posted Zac Antonaci, FDev's Head of Communications [2]. The 10 item-per-starship limit would set a low cap on any individual player's throughput. This would ensure that the factions with the greatest number of members would be the ones with their names on the new territory.

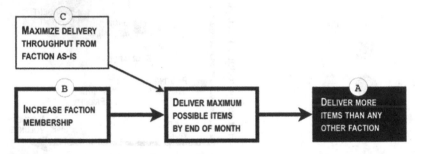

Fig. 3. Causal chain to winning the Colonia Initiative as envisioned by Frontier Developments

This is shown in Fig. 3 as a cause-effect diagram of the critical success factors leading to a faction win [14, 23]. Optimization (factor C) did not appear to be as critical a link in the causal chain to success (goal A) as faction membership size (factor B); the cost to coordinate handing off cargo between the Load and Ship phases of the journey seemed too high. Few players would be willing to spend their in-game time waiting for other players to be available, chasing down items dropped in the handoff, and repeatedly flying monotonous shuttle routes. Even the Loaders of the Privateers' Alliance agreed that Loading is not a glamorous activity:

> What we do isn't fancy work. What we do isn't even particularly enjoyable work. Maybe we don't get the glory of finally making a 22,000 light-year journey to Colonia. Some of us, can't even afford the ships necessary to make such a long distance journey. [5].

Nevertheless, they viewed the complicated business of Loading as critical to their success:

> We load because it must be done. This goal will not be accomplished without your work. We could have 50 more [long-distance pilots] waiting in the wing. But with no one willing to actually bring them cargo? We fail. [5]

While at first glance P.A.'s chances of success seemed to be constrained by their small faction size, rather than accepting this view at face value and hoping to eliminate the constraint with more headcount, P.A. instead identified the 10 item limit as a better improvement opportunity (factor C). They then worked to optimize an already greatly improved system (factors D, E). A model of this perspective is shown in Fig. 4.

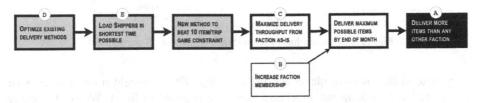

Fig. 4. Causal chain to winning the Colonia Initiative from the Privateers' Alliance perspective

This mirrors the systems-thinking principle of starting with what is, finding bottlenecks, and improving incrementally [1]. The members of P.A. were never instructed in these principles. As in the complex process of social change, they "made the road by walking" [13]. Many real-world organizations could benefit from trying this approach more often.

Success for P.A. depended on the ability of the organization *as a whole* to determine an effective model for their situation and a causal path to their desired outcome. Then the organization *as a whole* must walk this path in a complex, VUCA context where the act of walking the road could cause it to change at any moment.

3   Resilience

3.1   Destination Lockdown

"No plan of operations extends with certainty beyond the first encounter with the enemy's main strength." *Helmuth von Moltke the Elder* [21]

Things were going great. The Privateers' Alliance were bypassing the 10 item per ship limit, shipping and delivering cargo at record rates. Until the middle of the month when reports started coming in from the delivery point that no cargo could be offloaded.

A rival faction, seeing their present lead over others, had managed to halt *all* other factions' progress for the month. This rival faction hoped to win the Colonia Initiative that month through the use of a little-known, poorly understood game mechanic. By attacking non-player character (NPC) starships near the destination space station, they triggered the simulation to place the station into "Lockdown" status, where no cargo can be offloaded (Fig. 5).

This was a clever—and unforeseen—move. Lockdown brought the entire Colonia Initiative to a crashing halt. With Shippers unable to offload cargo, they were unable to return home to pick up new cargo. Loaders had nobody to load. Lockdown is not an

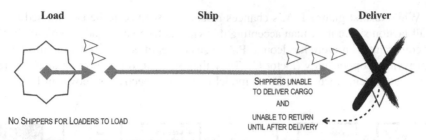

Fig. 5. Lockdown halts the entire workflow for all participants.

easy state to lift: massive player action (attacking NPCs) brought it on, and massive player action (attacking the attackers) would be required to lift it. Worse, the game simulation only flips between system states between every 3 days, so this situation was likely to persist for a significant portion of the month's challenge.

The Colonia Initiative appeared to be all but over for the month. As the news of Lockdown spread, the momentum of many factions began to dissipate. This was demoralizing for everyone playing—not just P.A—and while well within the possibilities afforded by the game, there were grumblings all around. "We run by the rule Don't Be a Jerk," said Ph1Lt0r, "and it's imperative that we keep that up, because there's a lot of jerky things that you can do in games. That's not the community that we are. While we aren't afraid to defend ourselves, we aren't going to do it in a way that's going to reduce the enjoyment of another person's time in the game."

Members of the Privateers' Alliance feared that even if the Lockdown was lifted, the elements of the "well oiled machine of humans" would have completely dispersed and lost focus. This wasn't just an attack on a transportation chain, this was an attack on the collective, focused will of the P.A. members. But the P.A. leaders worked to keep the members focused. They started broadcasting ("streaming") their own attempts to lift the Lockdown on Twitch. And all the while, they kept talking about the near future when Lockdown would be lifted. If everyone hung together, they suggested, this massive attack would be nothing but a hiccup.

> *Wickedlala:* I streamed on my own for quite a while to show them that I was making these runs. Not in a big, fancy ship doing the [high- speed] neutron jumps. I was jumping the slow way with a tiny ship, and I did that three times.
>
> *Phil:* We were streaming the latest [destination security] influence numbers and saying "yes, this a setback, but we have a force on the way, we can turn the tide." Every day you could see the improvement and we'd say "look how the influence is going up. If you're stuck there at Colonia, hang out and wait. We'll keep the wait to a minimum."

The P.A. pilots saw this and realized that even if the rules of the game had suddenly changed, the game itself was still on. Some pilots banded together in a subgroup, dubbed themselves the Colonia Defense Force, and headed to the destination system to help lift the Lockdown. Shippers blocked at the destination station landed on nearby planets and sat out to wait. But the members of P.A. weren't content to accept the situation. Some pilots wondered: What if, when Lockdown ended, they didn't have to build momentum again but instead had a whole stash of cargo ready to inject back into the transportation flow? This seemed impossible. There are no warehouses or storage facilities in *Elite:Dangerous*. The only place to store cargo is in the hold of a starship; cargo can only be stored in a starship with an active pilot; and a pilot can only fly one active starship per copy of the game they own. But just as they had when they optimized the Loading procedures, P.A. members questioned assumptions. Another group of pilots, in a bit of self-mockery, dubbed themselves the Hoarders and volunteered to do nothing more than store cargo at the origin station until Lockdown was lifted.

The Colonia Defense Force lifted the Lockdown in the first 3-day window. Thanks to the Hoarders, cargo started flowing immediately. As fast as the Shippers could offload, they returned back for loading. The experiment had worked: Lockdown was just a hiccup on the performance of P.A.'s delivery numbers. This was a big contrast to other factions which, by this time, had mostly given up and hoped to try again next month. When the final tallies came in at the end of the month, P.A.'s delivery numbers were the highest on the list.

The Privateers' Alliance had won their planetary base.

Now they just had to choose a name. It had been an intense challenge and, now that it was over, everyone needed a rest. Some of the Shippers said they never wanted to see a hyperspace jump ever again. The members kicked around a few ideas for the name of their new base and finally agreed that they wanted to honor ElvisKremmen, one of their most visible and effective Shippers. But the final name of the base reflected the hard work put in by everyone in P.A. who participated: "Kremmen's Respite."

3.2   Destination Lockdown—Analysis

"Like the man says, there's no problems, only solutions." *Tron* [17].

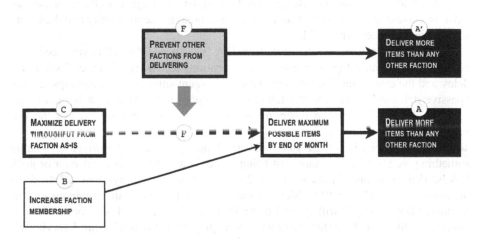

Fig. 6. An alternate path to success: Disrupt your competitors' path

The cause-effect diagram in Fig. 6 shows the importance of questioning assumptions and validating the mental models that an organization's members share about the reality of their situation [9, 16]. The tactic of disruption used by the rival faction (goal

A') reinforces the discussion from Sect. 2.2 that increased membership (factor B) was not the critical success factor that FDev had envisioned (goal A). The causal chain to success required maximizing delivery using whatever resources a faction had available to them (factor C). This chain was what the rival faction disrupted (factor F), halting progress in the Colonia Initiative for all player factions except P.A.

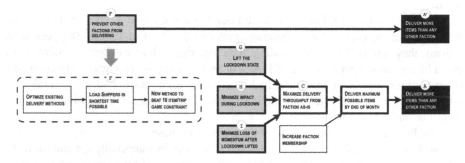

Fig. 7. Causal chain for the Privateers' Alliance during "Lockdown"

Unlike other factions, P.A.'s model (Fig. 7) afforded additional opportunities on the causal chain to success. Seeing the world in this way allowed P.A. members to realize that lifting the Lockdown state (factor G), minimizing the impact of downtime (factor H), and minimizing loss of momentum (factor I) were all different ways they could engage toward their goal. The rival faction did shift P.A.'s reality out from under them, though, and the required update to their shared mental model was part of the reason for the impact to P.A.'s morale. Being forced to adjust to not just a change *within* an existing context, but a *change of context* can be a threat to social identity and thus to an organization's effectiveness [7].

Real-world organizations can learn from P.A.'s resilience. Not all threats need to be countered with leadership interventions. Interventions are "active defenses," subject to delay and the cost of mobilizing them during emergent situations. It also helps to have "passive defenses" built in to the fabric of the organization. One such is the organization's identity; how the members of the organization see themselves. For the Privateers' Alliance, "where everyone plays together, but everyone plays their own way," adaptivity is woven into their values. Their identity is based on *belonging*—"doing something we all enjoy"—more than being centered around a specific person or goal. P.A.'s identity is also based on being *learners*. Wickedlala says that a lot of the members like to call her "P.A. Mom" because she helps remind the community of its identity. "Day to day I will go in [to the Discord chat] and if I see something disconcerting, like somebody talking down to new players, I'll remind them: Everybody's here to learn, and to teach too, but not to discourage."

A second passive defense is the flexibility of an organization's leadership structure. "Leadership should be less something a member can *be* and more something a member can *do*," says Ph1Lt0r. This philosophy manifests in P.A.'s avoidance of hierarchical structure. As P.A. grew, Phil and Wickedlala didn't want to deal with centralized control, an emphasis on giving/taking orders, and the time lag between orders and action. They wanted a structure more like a network, with an emphasis on achieving goals, decentralized control, and lateral communication. P.A.'s "Flight Leaders" are not bosses, but key contacts for loosely-connected member "tribes" of similar interests (e.g.: exploration/long distance flight, trading/local flight, or fighting/bounty hunting). Moving into or around tribes is "something a member can do" by opting in to as many as they like. The P.A. Board exists primarily to help keep network visible to itself and keep the networks connected.

An organization needs active defenses vs. emergent situations, also. A key to P.A.'s resilience during Lockdown was leaders visibly "walking their talk" to model the community values of *learning* and *persistence*. Wickedlala modeled learning via her Twitch broadcasts ("streams") as she shipped goods to Colonia:

> You have to be willing to be the example, if you're asking people to meet goals, you have to be in the trenches with them. Not all the time, but you have to be there and available, not telling them what to do, but doing it with them. They saw that I'm asking you to do this and I'm damn well going to do it too.

Simultaneously, Phil modeled persistence. "I took 2 days off work, I knew this was gonna be a huge morale hit," he said about his own Twitch streams in the Colonia Defense Force. Adapting to adjust to change, especially change forced by crisis, causes discomfort that many people prefer to avoid. Effective leaders like Phil and Wickedlala validate that discomfort by being in the same situation as their members—and then modeling the necessary values anyway. The results speak for themselves (Fig. 8).

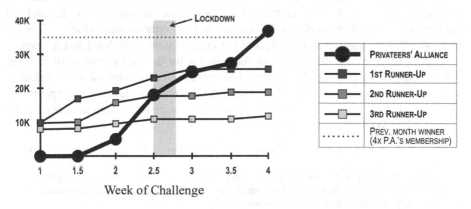

Fig. 8. Delivery performance: Privateers' Alliance vs. top competitors

The Privateers' Alliance demonstrated not just the best performance during their own month of participation in the Colonia Initiative, but the best performance by any player faction to take part in the Initiative. The closest runner-up to P.A.'s incredible performance was a faction with *over four times* P.A.'s membership. When this author sees this kind of performance, it usually means something else is happening besides simple economies of scale. P.A.'s network leadership model was able to repurpose on the fly. The Hoarders independently discovered the principle of Eli Goldratt's "buffer" as a way to smooth out uneven flows in a value delivery system [12]. And again, they gravitated to best logistical solution without formal training or theory. By approaching every challenge that came their way as a kind of game within the game, the Privateers' Alliance demonstrated an enviable resilience to chaos.

4 Conclusion

"One of the biases of an information-oriented age is the tendency to neglect the fact that, throughout history, the adaptive advantage has often gone to those who ventured upon their possibility with cries of exultant commitment." *The Ambiguity of Play* [30]

This case study of leadership and team communication within a playful game environment offers guidance for forming and nurturing learning communities. Not just for learning, but for gaining the "adaptive advantage" required to achieve challenging outcomes in complex domains. As Phil is reminded almost every time someone joins P. A., even if they don't know the term, members in an adaptive organization know they're part of one:

We're proud of what we've got. And members new or old alike have that pride when they join. They learn very quickly that this is something to be proud of, you're part of something great. And this isn't something that we tell them. This is something that they learn over time. There have been people who've come to me after being in a week where they're just blown away, they're like, "I've never been a part of a group like this, I'm so happy and proud to be here."

Learning communities are resilient. Not just adaptive within a context, but adaptive to changes of context. As ElvisKremmen said, "when the shit hits teh [sic] fan and that call goes out is when everyone bands together and not only counter whatever it is but enjoy working as a group should [8]. But learning communities don't just happen.

During her tenure at the American Association for the Advancement of Science, Lou Woodley was responsible for fostering professional networks for the scientific community to collaborate online. She warned that someone must fill an explicit role and regularly engage with community members to help keep them connected. [33] Someone like Wickedlala, for example:

People throw the word "community" around especially on Twitch, because it's a buzzword. But our community is not about me and Phil, or about [P.A. members] KZFusion, or about FaceHugr. It's about everybody. It's about coming together and working for common goals and helping each other out. And if somebody needs our help we try to put our own stuff aside and go and help somebody else. Because it's not about us.

People who foster adaptive organizations have an unusual skill-set. Their skills "are usually perceived as opposites and so… community managers hold these 'in tension', a bit like a cobweb. Community leaders may use different instances of a particular trait depending on specific circumstances, rather than being inclined to one or other end of the spectrum of a feature." [31, 32].

This case study is necessarily limited, but suggests further questions. The Colonia Initiative, and its reward, were within the game context of players of *Elite:Dangerous*. Individual participants in the challenge were therefore likely to be motivated by the faction reward. It would be instructive to examine similar gaming situations where individual goals and group goals are in conflict. While the causal chain to the Colonia Initiative goal was subtle, the goal itself (maximize delivered cargo) was explicit and unambiguous. Scenarios requiring minimum-maximum optimization, such as those with multiple ambiguous or conflicting goals, could offer greater applicability to real-world scenarios.

This author is particularly interested in the effect of group communication tools. The Privateers' Alliance relied almost solely on the text-and-voice chat system Discord. Discord has limited knowledge-management functions beyond text search within the chat history. By contrast, professional collaborative groups often make use some form of knowledge repository—e.g. a wiki, Sharepoint, a wall of sticky-notes—as a boundary object to explicitly construct and modify their shared mental models [11]. While this model of knowledge management suggests that Discord's limitations would reduce P.A.'s effectiveness, it is possible that they may actually have improved P.A. it by forcing explicit meta-communication among its members. Just sitting quietly in chat, a member can build critical "team-work" knowledge about which other members possess which skills and information [16, 20]. This question invites future experiments, using semantic analysis of player faction communications on Discord, to learn more about how they form and update shared mental models.

This case study has attempted to provide generally applicable yet practical guidance for those leaders seeking to foster adaptive organizations. For leaders confronting complexity, business leadership theory suggests agility; for those confronting communication issues, cognitive science suggests shared mental models; and for those confronting behavioral change in high-stakes scenarios, gaming suggests simulation. For leaders confronting all three challenges at once, this fable of space pirates offers a story and lessons of gaining the adaptive advantage from "cries of exultant commitment." Practitioners must remember: the members, not the leaders, are the heart of a learning community; a flexible leadership structure and a group identity rooted in learning can serve as passive defenses against disruption; espoused community values can be reinforced by leaders publicly modeling them; and pride in the community can fuel performance as well as—or in some cases, better than—compensation.

The adaptive advantage of play comes from "not only the skills that are a part of it but also the willful belief in acting out one's own capacity for the future." [30] If real-world organizations worked to reinforce this belief this as much as MMO games do, perhaps we would hear more statements about our workplaces, our schools, our neighborhood communities, and elsewhere that sound like how ElvisKremmen speaks of the Privateers' Alliance: "everyone knows how much i love this group, the people. Its the general attitude of everyone, *together we can accomplish so much.*"

References

1. Anderson, D.J.: Kanban: Successful Evolutionary Change for Your Technology Business. Blue Hole Press, Chicago (2010)
2. Antonaci, Z.: News: Colonia Expansion Initiative. https://forums.frontier.co.uk/threads/colonia-expansion-initiative-sign-up.311509/page-2#post-4836392. Accessed 20 Jan 2020
3. Bakunin, M.: The reaction in Germany. In: Bakunin on Anarchy, p. 68 (1842)

4. Bennett, N., Lemoine, G.J.: What a difference a word makes: understanding threats to performance in a VUCA world. Bus. Horiz. **57**, 311–317 (2014). 10/ggjvsr
5. BKidderz: Got a hold? We'll load it. https://www.privateersalliance.com/got-a-hold-well-load-it/. Accessed 20 Jan 2020
6. BKidderz: Mission: Colonia Expansion Initiative. https://www.privateersalliance.com/mission-colonia-expansion-initiative/. Accessed 20 Jan 2020
7. Branscombe, N., Ellemers, N., Spears, R., Doosje, E.: The context and content of social identity threat. Sepsis. 35–55 (1999)
8. ElvisKremmen: Private message in Privateers' Alliance Discord server (2018)
9. Fiore, S.M., Rosen, M.A., Smith-Jentsch, K.A., Salas, E., Letsky, M., Warner, N.: Toward an understanding of macrocognition in teams: predicting processes in complex collaborative contexts. Hum. Factors J. Hum. Factors Ergon. Soc. **52**, 203–224 (2010). 10/cxx29c
10. Frontier Developments: Elite Dangerous. https://www.frontier.co.uk/our-games/elite-dangerous. Accessed 20 Jan 2020
11. Fujimura, J.H.: Crafting science: Standardized packages, boundary objects, and "translation." (1992)
12. Goldratt, E.M.: What is this thing called theory of constraints and how should it be implemented? (1990)
13. Horton, M., Freire, P.: We Make the Road by Walking: Conversations on Education and Social Change. Temple University Press, Philadelphia (1990)
14. Ishikawa, K., Loftus, J.H.: Introduction to Quality Control. Chapman and Hall, London (1990)
15. Kriz, W.C.: Creating effective learning environments and learning organizations through gaming simulation design. Simul. Gaming **34**, 495–511 (2003). 10/dzw67f
16. Lim, B.-C., Klein, K.J.: Team mental models and team performance: a field study of the effects of team mental model similarity and accuracy. J. Organ. Behav. **27**, 403–418 (2006). 10/bqhjms
17. Lisberger, S.: Tron. Buena Vista Distribution (1982)
18. Lofgren, E., Fefferman, N.: The untapped potential of virtual game worlds to shed light on real world epidemics. Lancet Infect. Dis. **7**, 625–629 (2007). 10/d7dwmb
19. McGonigal, J.: This is not a game: immersive aesthetics and collective play. In: Melbourne DAC 2003 Streamingworlds Conference Proceedings. Citeseer (2003)
20. Mohammed, S., Ferzandi, L., Hamilton, K.: Metaphor no more: a 15-year review of the team mental model construct. J. Manag. **36**, 876–910 (2010). 10/d2dw2t
21. Moltke, H.G.: Moltke on the Art of War : Selected Writings. Presidion Press, New York (1996)
22. PA Colonia Reward. https://www.reddit.com/r/EliteDangerous/comments/5u6hmv/pa_colonia_reward/. Accessed 20 Jan 2020
23. Rockart, J.F.: Chief executives define their own data needs. Harvard Bus. Rev. **57**, 81–93 (1979)
24. Roungas, B., Bekius, F., Meijer, S.: The game between game theory and gaming simulations: design choices. Simul. Gaming (2019). 104687811982762, 10/ggjvsp
25. Salas, E., Sims, D.E., Burke, C.S.: Is there a big five in teamwork? Small Group Res. **36**, 555–599 (2005)
26. Schwaber, K.: Agile project management with Scrum. Microsoft Press (2004)
27. Senge, P.M.: The Fifth Discipline: The Art and Practice of the Learning Organization. Doubleday/Currency, New York (2006)
28. Snowden, D.: Multi-ontology sense making: a new simplicity in decision making. J. Innov. Health Inform. **13**, 45–53 (2005). https://doi.org/10.14236/jhi.v13i1.578
29. Stacey, R.D.: Strategic Management and Organisational Dynamics. Prentice Hall (2007)

30. Sutton-Smith, B.: The Ambiguity of Play. Harvard University Press, Cambridge (2009)
31. Wenger-Trayner, B.: Social learning leadership. https://wenger-trayner.com/all/social-learning-leadership/. Accessed 20 Jan 2020
32. Woodley, L.: Community Manager musings: A web of skills "held in tension", rather than a skills wheel? https://socialinsilico.wordpress.com/2017/06/26/community-manager-musings-a-web-of-skills-held-in-tension-rather-than-a-skills-wheel/. Accessed 20 Jan 2020
33. Woodley, L.: Personal conversation (2017)

Comparison of Experience of Using Business Games in University of Lodz and Kaunas University of Technology

Anna Pamula[1], Martynas Patasius[2], and Irena Patasiene[2(✉)]

[1] University of Lodz, Lodz, Poland
apamula@wzmail.uni.lodz.pl
[2] Kaunas University of Technology, Kaunas, Lithuania
{martynas.patasius,irena.patasiene}@ktu.lt

Abstract. Institutional collaboration allows teachers of universities to discuss more widely and deeply about experience, culture and traditions of using different teaching methods in education of similar study programs. Teachers of University of Lodz and Kaunas University of Technology (KTU) started collaborate around ten years ago. Common annual conferences, mobility of teachers according ERASMUS program allow teachers better to understand situation and good practices in neighbor University. Both universities have experience in using business games. University of Lodz pay attention in applying Business games and simulations for seeking better results in teaching management, ERP and decision making. Kaunas University of technology has positive results in helping students better understand business processes and usefulness of using ICT in business administration. Running the same Business Game "Hard Nut" in both universities has showed similarities and differences in the field of education both universities. The main result of collaboration is possibility of applying best practices of using business games.

Keywords: Business game · Simulation · Decision making

1 Simulation and Business Games in Teaching ERP, Decision Making and Business

The first business simulation, the exercise of Ligovo typewriter factory applied to train managers on how to handle production problems in 1932 is considered. More widely, they have started to appear in the business from the 1950s in the US.

The University of Washington applying business game developed by the consulting company in 1957 for one of the course was the first to start the era of business simulation at Higher Education [3]. According to the taxonomy of business games to classify and characterize the games different criteria can be applied including: activity, modality, interaction mode, and environment and application area [7]. The business games taxonomy proposed by Biggs [1] distinguishes following types: simulating whole enterprise or part of it, competitive and non-competitive, interactive or non-interactive games, individual or team, games to a specific industry or generally

© Springer Nature Switzerland AG 2021
M. Wardaszko et al. (Eds.): ISAGA 2019, LNCS 11988, pp. 378–386, 2021.
https://doi.org/10.1007/978-3-030-72132-9_32

business, based on a deterministic or stochastic model, games whose complexity is determined by the player's or model's decisions mathematical, games with different period time simulation.

Decision games are distinguished from other types of business simulation as their model is based on two elements: a player - the person or team taking decisions and a changing environment (internal or external) depending on players' choices.

The first business games (BG) were rather simple with a limited number of decisions making steps and considered variables and the results were hand scored. Since the rapid growth of ICT business games migrated to computer platforms increasing the complexity of the games [3].

The number of business games developed in different domains, including education, training, well-being, advertisement, cultural heritage, interpersonal communication, energy efficiency, or health care is growing each year. Simulation decision games are gaining popularity as an essential or additional teaching tool at all levels of formal education, concerning economics, management and entrepreneurship [12].

To support the business process companies widely implement information systems. The most often applied are ERP systems, as the support integrated core and supportive business process. Those systems are extremely complex, especially for new users. The business students are supposed to manage business processes and made optimal decisions; therefore, the simulation of the ERP environment and simulation of decision - making becomes essential in their education.

Simulating ERP system and teaching ERP skills at the university levels seems to be a prerequisite for modern business schools, but it requires a good knowledge of the functionality of the particular system as well as some technical support to manage the system environment. A few decades ago, some Higher Schools decided to implement and maintain education versions of ERP on premise, which required a lot of teacher's engagement and extra technical work. The class was usually run in traditional lab mode. As the learning venues are changing and increasing online ERP education is observed presenting an excellent learning potential [5]. New innovative teaching concepts appear to increase the effect of teaching the ERP skills like e-learning SAP UCC services or software platform "The ERP Challenge" developed by the University of Koblenz [10]. The proposed platform combines e-learning with ERP environment offering the possibility to track students learning progress. ERP systems are difficult from their nature, even if e learning platform is in use still requires the teacher support. The business schools put a lot of effort to support their students with the practical competencies highly appreciated by the employers, so the trend on applying simulation will be continued. There are many factors the lie behind the success of the particular simulation and business game, but one of the most important is to achieve a balance between the fun element, student engagement and the primary purpose of the game [7], which in case of business school is to best match the student's skills to the labor market. Taking into account student's mobility program, it must be noticed that some latest studies express differences in students attitudes towards simulation. D. M. Brown, A. Robson and I. Charity [2] indicated that Asian students perceive simulations as a less useful way to learn and claimed that according to their findings they prefer instructor-led structured input and ongoing intervention.

Development of BG has not only educational, but also social and cultural importance. M. Wardaszko notes that BG "lay grounds for a new form of culture" [11]. Importance of social dimension of BG is noted by J. H. G. Klabbers [6]. Success of use of BG also depends on game's complexity [8]. Complexity of BG should correspond to needs and preparation level of students. Analysis of BG use in various universities allows researchers better to understand how to use them effectively. Experience of universities of neighboring countries can help one to choose the suitable games (amount, kind, complexity etc.), evaluate necessary time.

2   University of Lodz Experience of in Teaching ERP and Decision Making Skills

From the establishment in 1996 the Faculty of Management put a lot of effort to support the students with high practical skills. Simulation and business games are applied for the course from the very beginning. This chapter considers only some courses run by the teacher form Department of Computer Science. The brief description and teaching experience from three types of simulation will be analyzed.

2.1   Decision Game

The first business simulation applied in the computer environment was a decision game devoted to the students of Master degree. The game was developed by Tomasz Głuszkowski, PhD, member of department of Computer Sciences. MS Excel engine was applied for calculation and simulation. The underlying game assumptions were:

- Each of the participants of the game manages a company that produces four types of products.
- At the beginning of the game, all companies (one player/team - one company) have the same value.
- Everyone has access to the same historical data of sales about all products in the previous 48 periods (months). Seasonal effect was applied.
- All players have the same production capacity and can buy raw materials from the same suppliers.
- The same rules for payments, loans, and inventory are applied for each player/team.
- Operational decisions were taken every playing period. Each month the decisions: how much to produce, how much to produce on stock, how to deal with material management are required from the players/teams.
- From the third period next decisions was required: if, if so, how much and for what price products shell be sell on the market (in these decisions it was helpful to know the forecasting and using the normal distribution to estimate the probability of sale and minimize the planned storage costs and gross margin losses. Those rules were than described in additional teaching materials [4].
- Tactical decisions: the game requires optimization of warehouse costs under certain uncertainty level, in some periods the production capacity is too small to be able to produce the number of products forecasted for sale in some months. Players had to

calculate when it was worthy to start production on stock. Additionally each product had a different storage cost, and production process. The market mechanism was applied. If all players/teams decide to produce for stock, prices are falling (the law of price elasticity works) - sometimes it is not profitable to store products. Therefore, before the game, the players should prepare tactics: what to do when they are ready for stock, so that it would be profitable to sell later.

- The course of the game required the exchange of files between the participants and the leader each period (players send files with decisions, the leader sends the output to the next stage of the game).

The task of the game was to maximize the value of the company within 12 simulated periods (months) that required a historical data analysis (done with separate tools outside of the game functionality).

The expected outcome was defined as: to give the students a chance to get skills that can help them to analyze data and support operational as well as tactical decisions in the company that is, to develop the ability to transform such data so that they can be used to support decisions.

The game was used in courses from 2000–2012. More than 1000 students were trained, the course rank was very high – more 4, 5 (based on voluntary students questioners provided by the Faculty of Management each semester). Now the author offers the game via the Internet to the business users with some extensions of macroeconomic aspects and strategic decisions. After the preparation of the game, the operating costs in each semester were low.

2.2   Managing the Company with ERP System

Another simulation applied at the Faculty of Management was an idea of integrated teaching (by teachers from different departments) with the support of ERP system. An agreement with IFS Application – the software company was arranged. It took the teaching group almost 2 years to prepare the whole (180 h) teaching materials. The group decided to create virtual Company named GreenPole that was established to design green areas and apply gardening services.

The processes were defined by the teachers with the support of business practitioner and applied in ERP systems with the support of IFS staff. The server was installed locally at the faculty building. The idea of the course was to show the students different views of the company and the way managerial decisions on different levels are made. The process of selecting the ERP system was outside of the course scope, but some part of its parametrization were applied in the lab while courses. The ERP technology, the database engine had no impact on the management of the GreenPole company and were not considered in the class.

The firm GreenPole was implemented in the ERP system in 2004, first course based on it were offered in 2006. The underlying assumptions were:

- Each of the participants had the same authority to access the data and the processes.
- The main process was to fulfill customer order from the inquiry to the payment.
- GreenPole company the design and develop of green areas. No additional CAD software was applied, predefined project from the stock were used.

- To plan the project additional software was used (MS Project) data were imported into the IFS application.
- Decision making required while the course were based on data collected in the system. Additional software (MS Excel) was used to analyze the data after exporting the result of data query from the IFS Application.
- Students were divided into group dealing with the similar projects.
- Each semester the groups were responsible to enter the data into the system.
- Students were responsible to manage the resources in IFS Application (hire the employees, buy materials).

The course was offered between 2006–2012 on the voluntary mode. Each semester it was very popular, so the limit of 40 students had to be applied. More than 200 projects were fully designed, applied and calculated. The program was ranked very high more than 4,5 almost each edition.

Around the program, the knowledge community was created at the Faculty of Management the University of Lodz. The respect for the knowledge of others, the tendency to broaden the base of own knowledge and the integration of knowledge around real processes and practical problems were involved and share to teachers and student due to this type of cooperation.

The teaching experience from this programs showed that running this type of business simulation consumes nearly three times as much teaching time as it does with traditional classes.

2.3   Simulating Business Processes with ERP

Since 2014 the Faculty of Management decided to offer the SAP.ERP courses. That required a special teacher qualifications and singing the agreements by the rector of the University of Lodz. The SAP UCC offers different types of software, databases and courses. The biggest problem in this solution is that the courses require periodical fee payment and it is difficult to find a financial support, as the fee is rather high for the public Higher School. In case of the faculty, the courses are applied for Logistics and Management students. The decision to apply SAP.ERP on Global Bike database was made as comes with very good teaching material offered by SAP UCC. The additional advantage of this solution is the access to the defined business processes in the ARIS platform.

From a few years of experience with running the course it can be observed that students are focused more of data integration and finishing the case studies than general understanding the integration between roles and processes but they highly appreciate the possibility to understand the idea of SAP.ERP, the idea of master data management and the acquisition of a minimum practice to work with this system.

In response to labor market demand and student expectations Faculty of Management offers the students different types of simulation for different course. The comparison of described applied cases is briefly compared in Table 1.

The experience coming from running different type of simulation shows that the best results (student engagement, skills, and students' course assessment) were observed while combination of method was applied. The important part coming from

Table 1. Comparison of IT Based Business Simulations Applied in 2000–2018 years.

Business Game	Domain/Period	Advantages	Disadvantages	Students outcome
Locally installed 4TG decision game	Logistics, supply, demand; Decision making/Year	On line results. Group competitions. Group decision making. Strong competition, results known after each period (12 months simulation)	Not considered macroeconomics influence Limited area of decision	The impact of the decision on the company profits and value
Locally implemented ERP IFS application	Project Management. HCM. Material Management./ 3 months	Integrated knowledge. Focus more on the "virtual company" then ERP itself Competition based on profit results of the company by the end of the course (3 months)	Huge work to prepare system to work, Strong support from supplier required Difficulties to simulate every day and periodical transactions ex. Accounting and Periods closing in accounting	The role of data integrity. Data exchange IS as a support of business processes and decision making in project management
SAP.ERP by SAP UCC	Cross-functional business processes Focus on logistic: SD, MM, WM /No limit	Focus on roles and data integrity in business processes Some transaction automatically performed by the hosting institution ex. Periods closing. Support	Individual work No competition No decision making	Business process, roles, data integrity Data export

the students remarks is the explanation of the result of each their work and decisions is highly appreciated. That means that simulation game offered in the course is important but teacher explanation of its impact offers additional value. Offering the ERP courses to students' shows the great results but is expensive in case of the time to prepare and cost if it is used as the hosted solution.

3 Experience of Using Business Games in Kaunas University of Technology

Kaunas University of technology started to use Business games in education only after 1990. The set of BG used at present time is shown in the Table 2.

Table 2. Comparison of IT Based Business Games and Simulations applied by Kaunas University of Technology in 1996–2018 years.

Business game	Field of activity	Number of variables	Description	Rate of using
Hard Nut	Enterprise model	29 basic variables controlled by a student. Number of users are no limited	Gathered data are open source DB	Regularly in different modules
ManSimSys	Simulation of operations	Modeling of production in sewing or furniture enterprises	The queues of production are observed and minimized by changing connection between equipment, operations	Regularly
ERP SimSys	Enterprise model	Modeling is done using MS Dynamics	Students are modeling one of five types of production enterprise	Regularly
EcoSim	Enterprise model	5 variables controlled by a student	Students understand market model	Regularly

School of Economic and business at Kaunas University of Technology regularly uses BG "Hard Nut", ManSimSys, EcoSim and ERP SimSys. BG EcoSim has been used in module of Microeconomics for 3 years in all bachelor study programs in the Faculty. Industrial Technology Management bachelor study program uses ERP SimSys and ManSimSys. Master students in module "Business process analytics" use ERP SimSys. Study programs of Economics, Marketing and Accounting use BG "Hard Nut" in module concerning ICT. Business administration (now Business and Entrepreneurship) study program has the most experience in use of BG.

4 Common Use of Business Games in Both Universities

During a visit of KTU teachers according to Erasmus mobility, students of University of Lodz had a possibility to play English version of Lithuanian BG "Hard Nut". A survey was performed to check if the opinions of students of both universities concerning business game differ. The results of the survey are shown in Fig. 1.

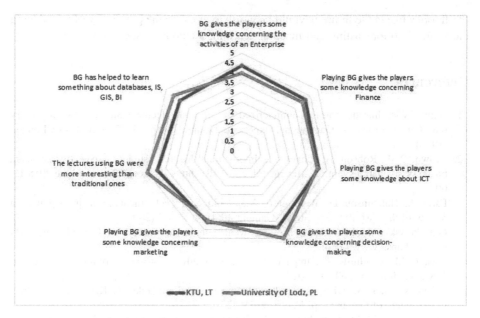

Fig. 1. Comparison of Opinion of Students both Universities applying BG "Hard Nut".

The survey has not shown any major differences between universities. Respondents of University of Lodz gave slightly more points to the propositions:

- "The lectures using BG were more interesting than traditional ones";
- "BG has helped to learn something about databases, IS, GIS, BI";
- "BG gives the players some knowledge concerning decision-making".

Other propositions were given more points by KTU students. It seems likely that the results are similar because the universities were in neighbouring countries having close cultural and economic ties, similar history, culture, social environment etc. More detailed analysis of the results of the survey can be found in proceedings of ALTA 2019 international conference [9].

Statistical analysis of results was not done, since the sample was not meant to be representative of population of all Lithuanian or Polish students, and it mostly coincided with population of students of those two universities who played the business game in the given year.

5   Conclusions

The evaluations of the students about using business game "Hard Nut" were mostly positive. However, it looks like at least some students might benefit from significant time being dedicated to the game and preparation for it. The cultural differences between universities of Poland and Lithuania did not seem to create significant problems.

It looks like in the future it would be worth to evaluate the possibility of introducing the students to forecasting and machine learning methods in such way.

References

1. Biggs, W.D.: Introduction to Computerized Business Management Simulations. In: Gentry (ed.) Guide to Business Gaming and Experiential Learning, pp. 23–35. Nichols/GP, London (1990)
2. Brown, D.M., Robson, A., Charity, I.: International Masters' student perspectives of team business simulations. Int. J. Manag. Educ. (2018). https://doi.org/10.1016/j.ijme.2018.11.004
3. Faria, A., Hutchinson, D., Wellington, W.J., Gold, S.: Developments in business gaming a review of the past 40 years. Simul. Gaming 40(4), 464–487 (2009)
4. Głuszkowski, T., Jabłońska, M.: Prognozowanie i analiza sprzedaży. Modele w Excelu. 4TG (2008). https://www.4tg.pl
5. Hwang, M., Cruthirds, K.: Impact of an ERP simulation game on online learning. Int. J. Manag. Educ. 15, 60–66 (2017)
6. Klabbers, J.H.G.: Social problem solving beyond method. In: Duke, R., Kriz, W. (eds.) Back to the Future of Gaming, pp. 12–29. WBV (2014)
7. Laamarti, F., Eid, M., El Saddik, A.: An overview of serious games. Int. J. Comput. Games Technol. 2014, 15 (2014) https://doi.org/10.1155/2014/358152. Article ID 358152
8. Patasiene, I., Rakickas, A., Skuncikiene, S., Patasius, M.: Increasing complexity of business simulations and games is expected in the future. In: Duke, R., Kriz, W. (eds.) Back to the Future of Gaming, pp. 228–241. WBV (2014)
9. Patasiene, I., Patasius, M., Pamula, A., Kregzdyte, R.: Teaching data analytics for business using business game. In: ALTA 2018 Conference: Advance Learning Technologies and Applications: Games for Education, pp. 13–18. Technologija (2018)
10. Schwadea, F., Schubert P.: The ERP challenge: an integrated e-learning platform for the teaching of practical ERP skills in universities. In: Conference on Enterprise Information Systems/International Conference on Project Management/Conference on Health and Social Care Information Systems and Technologies, CENTERIS/ProjMAN/HCist 2016, 5–7 October 2016 (2016). https://doi.org/10.1016/j.procs.2016.09.134
11. Wardaszko, M.: Global domination games. In: Duke, R., Kriz, W. (eds.) Back to the Future of Gaming, pp. 187–197. WBV (2014)
12. Wawrzeńczyk-Kulik, M.: Simulation game as a tool supporting the teaching process within the "Basics of entrepreneurship" subject. Zeszyty Naukowe WSEI seria EKONOMIA 6 (1/2013), 303–321 (2013)

Board Perspective on Simulation Gaming

Video Game Monetization Mechanisms in Triple A (AAA) Video Games

Martin Ivanov[1], Helmut Wittenzellner[1],
and Marcin Wardaszko[2]([⊠]) [iD]

[1] Hochschule der Medien, Nobelstraße 10, 70569 Stuttgart, Germany
{mi019,wittenzellner}@hdm-stuttgart.de
[2] Kozminski University, 57/59 Jagiellońska Street, 03-301 Warsaw, Poland
wardaszko@kozminski.edu.pl

Abstract. The process of video game monetization has existed ever since video games became a consumer product. It underwent multiple stages throughout the years until it reached a mature state in the economy of today. Monetization in video games is a highly relevant and controversial subject as it has caused a negative outcry in consumers. This is due to frequent exploitation on a moral and ethical level focused on identifying psychological weak points in consumers and using them to achieve a financial advantage. On the other hand, the revenue boost that has been provided with these advanced marketing strategies cannot be denied as they generate billions of USD for the major players on the video game market annually and contribute to the massive growth of the video game market of today. Furthermore, since the topic's complexity has only been increasing parallel to the economic importance of this marketing sub-process, it is becoming one of the most important segments of a video game's business model. The en masse implementation of various in-game currencies enabling consumers to purchase so-called "in-game unlockables" has begun. These currencies, such as credits, tokens or plain virtual money, are highly differentiated and usually unique per game, with the common denominator between them being the way of acquisition – by paying with actual money. Their implementation has generated undisputable increase in revenue for companies in the game industry as currently hundreds of millions of US dollars are being generated by purchases made with in- game currencies [1, 2].

Keywords: Monetization · Unlockables · Loot boxes · Game currencies ·
DLC · Marketing mechanisms

1 Business Model Definition

The business model of a company is the most basic, yet vital component of revenue creation and is the fundamental part of every company's "DNA". The business model is de facto the blueprint of how a specific company is intending to generate value, target its customers, distribute its products, plan and expend its resources, monitor its key performance indicators (KPIs) as well as manage all, if any, supplier connections. This basic strategy is highly dependent on the company's character – its size, offered

© Springer Nature Switzerland AG 2021
M. Wardaszko et al. (Eds.): ISAGA 2019, LNCS 11988, pp. 389–404, 2021.
https://doi.org/10.1007/978-3-030-72132-9_33

products and/or services coupled with the corresponding industry or sector the company is active in as well as customer target groups [3].

Business models are of varying complexity and detail. This is usually a consequence of the parent company's size and market orientation. However, it is also critical to mention that a multitude of business model types (BMTs) exist. The most distinctive trait of what actually every different type aims to achieve always correlates heavily with the revenue generation process (cf. Appendix, Table 3).

When compared to other industries on the market, the video game industry's business model often proves to be the most complicated. This is due to the fact that it cannot be identified as a single type as easily as other models. The construction, as well as customer targeting and revenue generation are spanning over different layers, often with additional companies (publishers and developers) resulting in a complex, yet efficient multi-facetted digital business model [4, 5].

2 Introduction to Video Game Monetization

We are all living in a vastly interconnected and digitalized society. Mankind is constantly pushing its limits in fields such as science and production, but also entertainment. Video games and their respective market share have vastly evolved in the past five decades – going through all the economic stages of a niche market up to a massive international multi-billion market giant. Representatives of this market include small to medium companies as well as huge enterprises known as triple A (AAA) producing companies. This is not the final maturity stage of the market as the demand for more is increasing annually. This has led to more gaming products being produced and distributed on all possible platforms – from computer and console to smartphone and tablet [6].

Game monetization has undergone a multi-layered evolution in the past decade (cf. Table 6). Initially, the whole concept of revenue generation was just focused on a basic fixed price in exchange for which the customer would acquire the given video game. However, due to a sensitive market fixed price milestone of around \$ 60/€ 60 that even today cannot be bypassed, developers and publishers needed an alternative for revenue optimization of their products [5]. The findings of an extended research performed in the UK regarding the complex price structure of video games have been summarized in Fig. 3 (cf. Appendix, Fig. 3) (Table 1).

The so-called "expansion" packs were the first major successful attempt that managed to increase the product lifecycle of video games as well as the generated revenue. The next evolutionary step of this process was the creation of DLC add-ons, which were based on the expansion packs, but were gradually more complex in nature. They were always distributed digitally, which allowed producers and publishers to bypass the physical stores. Other aspects of video game monetization include a subscription based revenue model where the consumer is expected to pay a monthly fee in order to retain access to the game servers [6]. Games can also be marketed as "free to play" – where the initial price point has been completely eliminated in favor of in-game purchases that can greatly enhance the gameplay experience and feeling [9].

Table 1. Overview of the evolution and marketing strategies of video game monetization [6, 7, 26, 30, 31]

Monetization type	Relevant specifications
Standard product price	Basic triple A (AAA) game price coined at $/€ 60
Expansions or expansion packs	Adds additional content on basis of the standard game for a fix price. Usually require the original game in order to be played. Exceptions of this rule are the so called "standalone expansion packs"
DLC add-ons or DLC packs	Digital additions to the basic game with prices depending of the DLC size. Can be clustered in two categories – cosmetic DLCs and gameplay DLCs [31]
In-game currencies	Virtual currencies that can usually only be acquired through purchasing with real world currency. Examples include: credits, silver, gold, bottle caps, etc. Needed in order for the player to access premium content inside the basic game
Loot boxes	Randomized standard and premium additional content. Customer does not know the substance of the loot box until its post-purchase opening. Bears heavy similarities to gambling and has been treated as such in some countries as of 2018. A plethora of academic researches have been already conducted on the topic and have proven a significant relationship between loot box use and problem gambling in thousands of participants [26, 30, 32, 34]
Subscription based revenues	Customer is expected to repeatedly pay in order to be able to continue using the developer's services primarily on a monthly basis. Usually applied in multiplayer-only games
Free-to-play products with microtransactions	Players can choose to purchase "packs" of content that gives them an upper hand against standard players. Usually found in multiplayer-only games

However, the evolution of microtransactions (a.k.a. monetization) has evolved even further, bypassing the major idea of the content adding DLC. So-called premium content is offered in most games on the market nowadays (albeit prevalent in free to play or products based on the freemium business model) and offer drastically reduced content packages for smaller and fixed prices. This content usually comes in one of two possible categories – gameplay relative content or cosmetic relative content. The cosmetic content has been proven to have next to no negative impacts on the game's enjoyment factor and the customer satisfaction as it usually offers different design of already existing features. Cosmetic add-ons focus on the user's personalization of the end product, aiming to create a personal connection with the customer.

In comparison gameplay relevant content usually provides gamers improved means of playing the game – such as weapons, equipment, gear, perks, abilities or knowledge as well as possible temporary boosts in comparison to the standard player [8].

3   Microtransactions and In-game Currencies

Microtransactions (MTX) are a type of in-game conducted purchases that aim to give the customer access to special or premium abilities, content or characters. The publisher usually decides what type of services fall into this category and for what price they may be acquired by the players. The purchases are always virtual and may be acquired with real world currency or their equivalent in the specific product's in- game currency. The price range of MTXs usually begins at $0.99, while not yet having a clearly defined upper limit [9].

Microtransactions have been around since the 1990s in the form of arcade machines and their life-per-coin rate. Players had to insert real life currency whenever they ran out of lives in order for their progress to be saved and they could continue playing. This basic principle started to be included in digital video games in the 2000s as the arcade video game market crumbled. It has been concluded that no more than 6% of a given game's audience actively engage in MTXs. Despite that the revenues generated by this type of services has been on the rise ever since it's en masse implementation.

According to the Touro University the revenue generation principle of micro-transactions has matured significantly and can be classified in four different archetypes to be found in apps and video games (cf. Fig. 1).

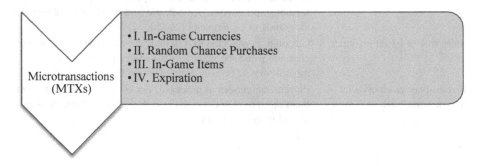

Fig. 1.   Types of Microtransactions [10].

In-game currencies are one of the most widespread forms of microtransactions. The exchange rate between these fake currencies and real-life money usually varies between different games. This amplifies the confusion effect, as the player is usually unaware of the real value of the content he purchases with this new currency. For example in the triple A (AAA) title "For Honor" published by Ubisoft in 2017 the in-game currency is named "steel". Small quantities of this currency are awarded after every completed match, but collectibles usually costs tens of thousands of Steel. Currently, the publisher offers 4 packs with in-game currencies: 5.000 Steel for 4.99€, 11.000 Steel for 9.99€, 65.000 Steel for 49.99€ and 150.00 Steel for 99.99€ [8]. Fortnite developed by Epic Games, also offers its own in-game currency called "V-Bucks". Currently three packs of V-Bucks are available – 1.000 for $9.99, 2.500 (+300 bonus) for $24.99 and 10.000 (+3.500 bonus) for $99.99 [12].

Microtransactions via in-game currency have proven to be so successful that even traditionally single player video game developer and publisher studios have started to implement them in their products. Such an example is Bethesda Game Studios and one of their most iconic products – Fallout 4 – through a post-release patch in 2017 [13].

The second and undisputedly most relevant and revenue efficient type of micro-transactions are the so-called "random chance purchases", most widely known as "loot boxes". They consist of a package with content that is unknown to the player until it has been purchased. The items included in such a package can be gameplay content, cosmetics content or both.

The third category identified by experts is the so-called "In-Game Items" category. This category encompasses mainly gameplay relevant "upgrades" attainable in exchange for real-life currency. The usual long-term drawback is the separation of the game community to "free" players and "premium" players, where the standard gamers are more numerous but in possession of weaker content. This phenomenon is usually found in free to play online games.

The last category "Expiration" is virtually the antipode of "In-game items". Being implemented mostly in single-player games players are offered to purchase items with a limited time duration that can speed up their progress. After the duration has expired the items need to be repurchased in order for the bonuses to be reactivated [13].

The implementation of some types of microtransactions can actually avoid the splitting of the game community while maintaining the positive effects of an increased budget. Example for this type of successes is the popular triple A (AAA) anime shooter Overwatch, developed and published by Activision Blizzard [14]. Billions of USD are being generated through microtransactions, but since the content that a player can acquire from this type of deal are limited to only cosmetic content – no strife has been created inside the player community [16].

3.1   Unlockables

The term unlockable content mainly refers to bonus content that is unavailable to the player at the start of the game. This content may include concept art, alternative skins or paint jobs (cosmetic content) or additional armament, cheat codes, characters, challenges or levels (gameplay content). A mixture of both is usually practiced in the game industry of today.

In their original context, unlockables are meant to be obtainable without the need to spend in-game or real life currency. However, game developer publishers and developers have started to implement different strategies aimed at boosting a product's revenue generation – some of which include an option to unlock such content for money instantly instead of waiting and spending time in-game [14].

3.2   Loot boxes

Loot boxes are currently considered the state of the art and by far the most financially effective form of microtransactions in the video game industry. These seamlessly harmless reward-mechanisms generate hundreds of millions of revenues every year for various video game companies and publishers. These increases in revenue have proven to pose a gambling health hazard on gamers. In another research led by a professor of behavioral addiction at the Nottingham Trent University, UK, the connection between gambling addiction and the loot box reward system was discussed and proven medically. The ultimate conclusion was that there is indeed such a strong connection [27].

Loot boxes essentially resemble baseball cards or any other collection-related blind content package. They can be acquired in two ways – either by spending real world money on them for instant access or by playing the core video game and acquiring the necessary amount of in-game currency needed for the purchase. The second, financially free option, usually takes moderate to long periods of time, depending on the video game. A loot box usually consists of multiple items – generated on a random basis and obtainable only after the box has been purchased and opened by the customer. The customer then gets these items, which belong to a specific item class based on the item's rarity and in-game effects. There is a chance for the customer to acquire a particularly powerful item this way as the algorithms behind the winning chances are not disclosed by video game publishers. The only exception to this rule is China where video game developers and publishers are forced by law to publish the numerical values and chances for players to receive items from specific categories and rarities [17, 18, 33].

Many publishers rely on different and often unique marketing strategies, however. Some of them include the usage of the so-called "power" loot boxes as they have proven to generate more sustainable economic revenue over the short and medium term. Due to their heavily negative impacts on the game community, implementing this marketing approach has proven to lead to many disastrous side effects on the medium and long term after the game has been launched. Additional examples, apart from the already described cases in Star Wars Battlefront II, FIFA and For Honor also include: Destiny 2 developed by Bungie and published by Activision, Evolve developed by Turtle Rock Studios and published by Take-Two Interactive Software, Call of Duty: WW II published by Activision, Rainbow Six: Siege published by Ubisoft as well as Forza Motorsport published by Microsoft Studios to name a few. A comprehensive comparison between the two major types of loot boxes has been included in Table 5 (cf. Appendix, Table 5).

4 Quantitative Research

Taking into account the main objective of this research paper and its relevance for the video game industry it was determined that a quantitative research was needed. This would allow for a better understanding of the main microtransaction consumer – the gamer's perception towards these advanced marketing practices. The research is based on a conducted study in the time period between 12.12.2018 and 13.01.2019. As this paper is more specific than the master thesis from which the survey is originally part of, only relevant segments of it will be extracted [19].

4.1 Gamer Survey

The survey consisted of 16 questions (cf. Appendix, Table 4) assigned to 4 logical sections – "Decisive section" (1 question), "Sociodemographic factors" (5 questions), "Gaming Industry" (10 questions), "Conclusion" (0 questions). In total there were 15 multiple choice and 1 open-answer question. The average duration of the survey was estimated to be around three-to-five minutes. The entirety of the academic survey was programmed, based and stored via Google Docs and Google. Recipients were addressed over a variety of Internet platforms and their forums such as Steam, Uplay, Origin, 9gag, Reddit, Facebook and Twitter as well as personally being informed about the survey and provided with a link in order to participate. The first logical bloc named "Decisive section" consisted of only 1 question – "Would you consider yourself a person that regularly plays video games, a.k.a. gamer?" – If the recipient would answer with the second option "No", the survey would then come to the last logical bloc "Conclusion" and the survey would be over.

4.2 Results

Based on the scope of this research paper only a fragment of the conducted survey will be analyzed even further. The relevant questions include: Q1, Q7, Q8, Q9, Q10, Q11 and Q13. The answers for the chosen questions are summarized in the Table 2 below.

4.3 Result Analysis

Over half of all participants play for a total time between 1 and 3 h a day – 164 (52.90%). Nearly one fourth of all recipients play for less than 1 h a day – 76 (24.52%). The group of highly-dynamic gamers made up almost one fifth of recipients. 59 or 19.03% of the people surveyed admitted to playing for more than 4 h a day, while 11 (3.55%) play video games for more than 7 h every day. The number of gamers aware of the term "microtransaction" proved to be completely prevalent with 276 or 89.03% of all gamers knowing what the term referred to. There still was a fraction of recipients that were not familiar with the terminology – 34 (10.97%). Such decisive feedback was expected and could be explained with the heavy microtransaction implementation in most, if not almost all, modern video games covered in the theoretical segment of this research paper. Slightly more participants were familiar with the term "loot box" – 277 or 89.35% acknowledged that they knew what was being described, while 33 or 10.65% did not. Over two thirds of participants admitted (209 or 67.42%) to have been involved into video game microtransactions at some time during their gaming experience. Below one third of gamers still have not conducted any form of microtransaction – 101 or 32.58%. The financial credibility and sustainability of microtransactions in most modern titles can be easily explained with the predominant number of people that have at least once in their gaming experience have gotten themselves involved with microtransactions in any form.

Results looked different when recipients were asked if they were involved in reoccurring in-game purchases on at least a monthly basis. Only a tiny fragment of recipients agreed – 21 or 6.77%. Over half of all participants answered with negatively

Table 2. Survey questions and answers.

Question number	Answer option in absolute and percent value	Answer option in absolute and percent value	Answer option in absolute and percent value	Answer option in absolute and percent value	Answer option in absolute and percent value
Q7, N = 310	Below 1 h, 76 (24.52%)	Between 1–3 h, 164 (52.90%)	Between 4–6 h, 59 (19.03%)	Above 7 h, 11 (3.55%)	–
Q8, N = 310	YES, 276 (89.03%)	NO, 34 (10.97%)	–	–	–
Q9, N = 310	YES, 277 (89.35%)	NO, 33 (10.65%)	–	–	–
Q10, N = 310	YES, 209 (67.42%)	NO, 101 (32.58%)	–	–	–
Q11, N = 310	YES, 21 (6.77%)	NO, 171 (55.16%)	I have, but no longer, 63 (20.32%)	I have never participated in in-game microtransactions, 55 (17.74%)	–
Q13, N = 310	Below $/€ 5, 97 (31.29%)	$/€ 6 - $/€15, 50 (16.13%)	$/€ 16 - $/€ 25, 16 (5.16%)	Above $/€ 25, 7 (2.26%)	I have not and I not see myself considering the purchase of microtransactions in the future, 140 (45.16%)

– 171 or 55.16%. More than a fifth – 63 or 20.32% admitted into being involved in such depth, but no longer. The remaining 55 or 17.74% participants declared that they have never participated in microtransactions. Nearly half of all recipients – 140 (45.16%) stated that they do not consider an eventual purchase of microtransactions in the future after being asked how they would be willing to spend on a monthly basis. Almost a third of recipients – 97 or 31.29% - agreed to allocated a budget equivalent to less than 5 $/€. 50 or 16.13% felt that they would spend between $/€ 6–$/€ 15, while 16 or 5.16% would be willing to increase their budget to $/€ 16–$/€ 25. Only a tiny fragment of recipients – 7 or 2.26% consider going over the 25 $/€ threshold for microtransactions on a monthly basis, which was also the highest formulated amount.

5 Hypotheses and Analysis

The conducted survey's recipient information was exported to excel (2010), further refined and imported to SPSS (Version 19) for a more detailed analysis. Different data was crosschecked and tested for a significant relationship via Pearson's Chi- Square test. Results with a Chi-Square coefficient of less than 0.05 were accepted, with a significance level of 95%. In the situations where significant relationships were present, the levels of association between the categories were measured via the value of Cramer's V. All tests were conducted in SPSS. This coefficient was deciphered according to a table provided by the University of Toronto, Canada [20].

Based on the chosen information and collected data the following hypotheses were formulated:

H1 - The majority participants' (over 50%) budget for microtransactions does not exceed $/€ 5

H2 - Gamers that spend more time playing video games daily are more likely to be involved in a video game microtransaction than gamers that play less on a daily basis

The validity of H1 can be judged when question 12 (How much would you be willing to, or have already, spend on in-game microtransactions on a monthly basis?) is analyzed. The percentage of recipients that reported to spend "Below $/€ 5" were 31.29%, while the total percent of recipients that have not and are not planning to involve themselves in an in-game microtransaction were 45.16%. When both values were summed as both categories of recipients rely on a monthly budget smaller than $/€ 5, it was concluded that 74.6% of recipients would spend under the $/€ 5 threshold, thus accepting the hypothesis.

In order to validate or reject H2 question 6 (How many hours a day do you spend playing video games on average?) and question 9 (Have you involved yourself in a video game microtransaction (have you ever made an in-game purchase, ex. Skin, loot box, goodies)) had to be statistically analyzed. Question 1, which was the logical barrier in the survey was not considered when numbering the questions.

Looking at the SPSS table (cf. Fig. 3) it is safe to conclude that there is a significant relationship between daily play time and knowledge regarding microtransactions, x^2 (3, N = 310), p = 0.000. Highly interesting is the fact that recipients tend to be more aware of microtransactions the more they play on a daily basis. 42.1% of people playing below 1 h are aware of the new marketing concept. The percentage rises to 72.6% for gamers between 1–3 h a day and again to 79.7% for gamers that play between 4–6 h daily, ultimately reaching 100% in gamers that play above 7 h on a daily basis. Therefore the conclusion that the more active the gamer is, on a daily basis, the more likely it is for him to engage in video game microtransactions, hereby accepting Hypothesis 2. The Cramer's V value calculated by SPPS is .329, which indicates a strong level of association between daily play time and potential involvement in in-game microtransactions (Fig. 2).

Q6 * Q9 Crosstabulation

			Q9 YES	Q9 NO	Total
Q6	Below 1 hour	Count	32	44	76
		Expected Count	51.2	24.8	76.0
		% within Q6	42.1%	57.9%	100.0%
	Between 1-3 hours	Count	119	45	164
		Expected Count	110.6	53.4	164.0
		% within Q6	72.6%	27.4%	100.0%
	Between 4-6 hours	Count	47	12	59
		Expected Count	39.8	19.2	59.0
		% within Q6	79.7%	20.3%	100.0%
	Above 7 hours	Count	11	0	11
		Expected Count	7.4	3.6	11.0
		% within Q6	100.0%	.0%	100.0%
Total		Count	209	101	310
		Expected Count	209.0	101.0	310.0
		% within Q6	67.4%	32.6%	100.0%

Chi-Square Tests

	Value	df	Asymp. Sig. (2-sided)
Pearson Chi-Square	33.486[a]	3	.000
Likelihood Ratio	35.546	3	.000
Linear-by-Linear Association	28.683	1	.000
N of Valid Cases	310		

a. 1 cells (12.5%) have expected count less than 5. The minimum expected count is 3.58.

Symmetric Measures

		Value	Approx. Sig.
Nominal by Nominal	Phi	.329	.000
	Cramer's V	.329	.000
N of Valid Cases		310	

Fig. 2. H2 - SPSS results.

6 Conclusion

The video game industry is without a doubt one of the most rapidly growing industries of today. Combining various forms of entertainment on multiple platforms and end-devices it has been achieving double digit growth on a global scale with minimum to none cannibalization between branches. Based on the unique existing formats and genres of video games everyone is a potential customer and target for huge enterprises and indie developers alike. A brand new array of "modernized" marketing tactics has seen en-masse implementation in a plethora of new triple A (AAA) productions. The most relevant of these methods include the introduction of title-specific in-game currency models as well as "loot box" packages containing a random array of items. The process of acquisition of these loot boxes or of separate acquisition of cosmetic and power goodies has been dubbed "microtransactions" by video game experts alike. These processes have proven incredibly effective and have stimulated massive revenue growth of many titles – even eclipsing the revenue created by the retail price of the title itself, in some cases. The core audience and consumers of video game products – gamers – have met these practices with mixed feelings, however. Based on the included research in this paper it has been concluded that there is a very high awareness regarding the concepts of microtransactions and loot boxes. It was also statistically proven that the majority of participants' (over 50%) budget for microtransactions does not exceed \$/€ 5 as well as that gamers that spend more time playing video games daily are more likely to be involved in a video game microtransaction than gamers that play less on a daily basis.

Appendix

Table 3. Business Model Types according to the primary revenue generation activity [20–22, 28, 29].

BMT	Description and examples	Examples
"Manufacturer"	Revenue is being generated through the production of complete products, often from raw resources. The products are usually distributed in two ways – either directly to the customer (business to customer, B2C) or through a specialized instance, a.k.a. "middleman" to the customer	Hilti, Bosch Power Tools, Milwaukee, DeWalt, Tesla
"Distributor"	Revenue is being generated through reselling of products. Usually between producers to specialized instances (industry "middlemen") or to the customers directly	Amazon, Avon
"Aggregator"	Perhaps one of the most recent variations of revenue generation – through the exploit of a niche market, where already existing competitors are being offered to customers under the brand of the initial company. Revenue is being generated additionally through commissions – charged over time or per successful order/purchase	Lieferando, Lieferheld, Pizza.de, Airbnb
"Retailer"	The following step of the "Distributor" BMT. Already acquired products (from distributors or manufactorers) being directly sold to the customers	Sennheiser, LifeLine Repairs

(continued)

Table 3. (*continued*)

BMT	Description and examples	Examples
"Franchise"	No new product is practically created or generated. The parent business model and/or brand are being used in return for revenue (often in the form of royalties)	Subway, Burger King, Starbucks
"Bricks-and-clicks"	Company is present both digitally and physically, allowing their customers the added flexibility to begin their customer decision journey (CDJ) online, but finish it offline – in a physical store	Saturn, Mediamarkt, Wallmart
"Nickel-and-dime"	The primary product is offered to the customers as the lowest profitable price possible. Additional revenue is being gathered through additional services	Ryanair, Wizzair
"Freemium"	Hugely popular BMT for companies offering digital services on the world wide web (WWW). Part of the end-product, stripped from multiple functions, is offered for free to the customers. Upgrading this basic service through additional functionalities or user specific preferences are the main source of revenue generation for the company	LinkedIn, Xing, Keyhole, Skype
"Subscription"	In the case of above average product or service cost, revenue could be acquired at lower, but steadier rates, through a long-term contract known as a subscription	Netflix, Spotify
"High Touch"	This BMT is usually exploited by companies offering services, rather than products. The key aspect here is human interaction between customer and a company appointed specialist	Porsche Consulting, McKinsey & Company,
"Low Touch"	Practically the antipode of the "High Touch" BMT. Business process optimization, digitalization and automation are key processes here. Manpower is seen as an unnecessary resources related to revenue generation and is constantly reduced	Mailchimp, Surveymonkey

Table 4. Survey questions and answers [19].

Survey questions	Question answers
1. Would you consider yourself a person that regularly plays video games, a.k.a. gamer?	Binary question – YES, NO (in case of NO – end of survey)
2. How old are you?	Categories: Below 18 18–22 23–27 28–32 Above 32
3. What is your gender	Male Female
4. Which is your geographical region of residence?	West Europe Central Europe and East Europe North America South America Asia-Pacific Africa & Middle East
5. Which is your current country of residence?	Free answer
6. What is your current employment status	Student – School, High School Student – University Unemployed Employed part-time Employed full-time Student – University employed part-time Student – University employed full-time
7. How many hours a day do you spend playing video games on average?	Below 1 Between 1–3 Between 4–6 Above 7
8. Are you familiar with the term "microtransaction"	Binary question – YES, NO
9. Are you familiar with the term "loot box"	Binary question – YES, NO
10. Have you involved yourself in a video game microtransaction (have you ever made an in-game purchase, ex. Skin, lootbox, goodies)	Binary question – YES, NO
11. Do you get involved in reoccurring in-game purchases (on average more than once every month)	YES NO I have, but no longer I have never participated in in-game microtransactions
12. Do you feel that the retail price for triple A (AAA) games on their launch date is justified (ex. 60 $/€ for a PC Title)	YES No, It should be more No, It should be less I am not sure

(continued)

Table 4. (*continued*)

Survey questions	Question answers
13. How much would you be willing to, or have already, spend on in-game microtransactions on a monthly basis?	I have not and I do not see myself considering the purchase of microtransactions in the future Below \$/€ 5 \$/€ 6–\$/€ 15 \$/€ 16–\$/€ 25 Above \$/€ 25
14. Do you feel in-game microtransactions and loot boxes have a negative impact on the video game industry?	Binary question – YES, NO
15. Do you feel in-game microtransactions and loot boxes have an addictive character (similar to the effects of gambling)?	Binary question – YES, NO
16. How likely are you to recommend microtransactions and/or loot boxes to a friend?	Scale 1 (lowest) – 5 (highest)

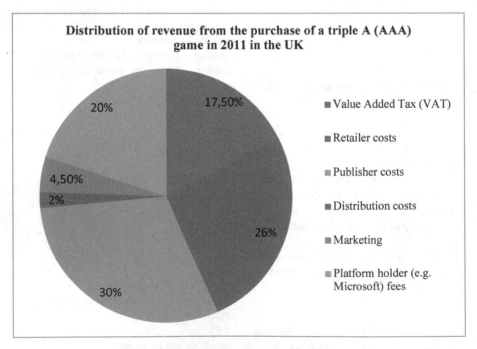

Fig. 3. Distribution of revenue from the purchase of a triple A (AAA) game in 2011 in the UK [24].

Table 5. Types and specifications of loot boxes [2, 17, 25]

Types and specifications of loot boxes	
Cosmetic loot boxes	Cosmetic loot boxes
Include only cosmetic type of content such as skins, outfits, voice commands and effects, alternative visualization of in-game elements	Include only cosmetic type of content such as skins, outfits, voice commands and effects, alternative visualization of in-game elements
Does not disrupt in-game balance between loot box-heavy users and standard users. The so-called "pay to win" effect is avoided	Does not disrupt in-game balance between loot box-heavy users and standard users. The so-called "pay to win" effect is avoided
No gameplay effect due to purely cosmetic and aesthetic nature	No gameplay effect due to purely cosmetic and aesthetic nature
No major player outcry has been targeted at cosmetic loot boxes	No major player outcry has been targeted at cosmetic loot boxes

References

1. Thubron, R.: Over half of Activision Blizzard's $7.16 billion yearly revenue came from microtransactions (2018). https://www.techspot.com/news/73230-over-half-activision-blizzard-716-billion-yearly-revenue.html. Accessed 15 Mar 2019
2. Lawrence, H.: Are Loot Boxes the Future of Mobile Game Monetization? (2018). https://gameanalytics.com/blog/loot-boxes-future.html. Accessed 15 Mar 2019
3. aha.io: What are some examples of a business model? (2018). https://www.aha.io/roadmapping/guide/product-strategy/what-are-some-examples-of-a-business-model. Accessed 15 Mar 2019
4. Chesbrough, H.: Business model innovation: it's not just about technology anymore. Strategy Leadersh. **35**(6), 12–17 (2007)
5. Rayna, T., Striukova, L.: 'Few to Many': change of business model paradigm in the video game industry Digiworld Econ. J. (94) (2014). 2nd Q. 2014
6. Cobb, C.: Video Game Monetization Strategies (2017). https://medium.com/@chris_cobb/video-game-monetization-strategies-715d78e80fa0. Accessed 15 Mar 2019
7. Davidovici-Nora, M.: Paid and free digital business models innovations in the video game industry. Digiworld Econ. J. (94), 83 (2014). 2nd Q. 2014
8. McKinney, J.: The Rise of Pay to Win in Video Games (2017). https://www.theodysseyonline.com/the-rise-of-pay-to-win-in-video-games. Accessed 15 Mar 2019
9. Agarwal, P.: Economics of Microtransactions in Video Games (2017). https://www.intelligenteconomist.com/economics-of-microtransactions/. Accessed 15 Mar 2019
10. Duverge, G.: Insert More Coins: The Psychology Behind Microtransactions (2016). https://www.tuw.edu/content/psychology/psychology-behind-microtransactions/
11. ubistore: For Honor DLC prices (2018). https://store.ubi.com/de/search?q=for%20honor%20steel. Accessed 15 Mar 2019
12. Microsoft: Fortnite – 1,000 V-Bucks (2018). https://www.microsoft.com/en-us/p/fortnite-1-000-v-bucks/c0f5ht9nv86p?activetab=pivot%3Aoverviewtab. Accessed 15 Mar 2019
13. Steamstore: Fallout 4 – Creation Club (2018). https://store.steampowered.com/app/598110/Fallout_4Creation_Club/. Accessed 15 Mar 2019
14. Tvtropes: Unlockable Content (2018). https://tvtropes.org/pmwiki/pmwiki.php/Main/UnlockableContent
15. Sarkar, S.: Overwatch is already a billion-dollar game (2017). https://www.polygon.com/2017/5/4/15551040/overwatch-revenue-billion-dollars-blizzard. Accessed 15 Mar 2019

16. Alexandra, H.: Activision Patents Matchmaking That Encourages Players To Buy Microtransactions (2017). https://kotaku.com/activision-patents-matchmaking-that-encoura ges-players-1819630937. Accessed 15 Mar 2019

17. Lum, P.: Video game loot boxes addictive and a form of "simulated gambling", Senate inquiry told (2018). https://www.theguardian.com/games/2018/aug/17/video-game-loot-boxes-addictive-and-a-form-of-simulated-gambling-senate-inquiry-told. Accessed 15 Mar 2019

18. Tang, T.: A Middle-Ground Approach: How China Regulates Loot Boxes and Gambling Features in Online Games (2018). https://www.mondaq.com/china/x/672860/Gaming/A +MiddleGround+Approach+How+China+Regulates+Loot+Boxes+and+Gambling+Features +in+Online+Games. Accessed 15 Mar 2019

19. Ivanov, M.: The evolution of the business model within the triple A (AAA) gaming industry. Master thesis. Fachbereich Druck und Medien, Studiengang Crossmedia Publishing & Management, Hochschule der Medien, Stuttgart (2019)

20. Utoronto: POL242 LAB MANUAL: EXERCISE 3A: Crosstabulation with Nominal Variables (n.y.). https://groups.chass.utoronto.ca/pol242/Labs/LM-3A/LM-3A_content.htm. Accessed 15 Mar 2019

21. Das, S.: What is a Business Model? Types of business Models (2018). https://www.feedough.com/what-is-a-business-model/. Accessed 15 Mar 2019

22. Investopedia: What are some examples of different types of business models in major industries? (2018). https://www.investopedia.com/ask/answers/042715/what-are-some-examples-different-types-business-models-major-industries.asp. Accessed 15 Mar 2019

23. Nicasio, F.: 12 Examples of Retail Stores That Will Inspire You to Run Your Business Better (2018). https://blog.vendhq.com/post/64901830513/retail-examples-to-inspire-you-to-run-a-better-business. Accessed 15 Mar 2019

24. Yin-Poole, W.: Where does my money go? (2011). https://www.eurogamer.net/articles/ 2011-01-10-where-does-my-money-go-article. Accessed 12 May 2019

25. Freeman, W.: Understanding 'Early Access' (and Why Games Like Fortnite Battle Royale Use it) (2018). https://www.askaboutgames.com/understanding-early-access-and-why-games-like-fortnite-battle-royale-use-it/. Accessed 11 May 2019

26. Zendle, D., Cairns, P.: Video game loot boxes are linked to problem gambling: results of a large-scale survey. PLoS One 13(11), e0206767 (2018). https://doi.org/10.1371/journal. pone.0206767. Accessed 12 May 2019

27. Mark, D.: Griffiths. Gaming Law Review, February 2018 ahead of print https://doi.org/10. 1089/glr2.2018.2216. Accessed 12 May 2019

28. Beynon-Davies, P.: Characterizing business models for digital business through patterns. Int. J. Electron. Commer. 22(1), 98–124 (2018)

29. Al-Debel, M.M., Avison, D.: Developing a unified framework of the business model concept. Eur. J. Inf. Syst. 19(3), 359–376 (2010)

30. King, D., Delfabbro, P., Griffiths, M.: Int. J. Ment. Health Addict. 8, 90 (2010)

31. Lizardi, R.: DLC: perpetual commodification of the video game. Democratic Communiqué 25(1) (2012). ISSN 1555-8967

32. King, D.L., Delfabbro, P.H.: Predatory monetization schemes in videogames (e.g. 'loot boxes' and internet gaming disorder). Addiction 113, 1967–1969 (2018)

33. Schwiddessen, S., Karius, P.: Watch your loot boxes! – recent developments and legal assessment in selected key jurisdictions from a gambling law perspective. Interact. Entertain. Law Rev. 1(1), 17–43 (2018)

34. Abbott, M., Binde, P., Clark, L., Hodgins, D., Johnson, M., Manitowabi, D., Quilty, L., Spångberg, J., Volberg, R., Walker, D., Williams, R.: Conceptual Framework of Harmful Gambling: An International Collaboration, 3rd edn., p. 4, 42–44. Gambling Research Exchange Ontario (GREO), Guelph (2018)

Learning with Location-Based Gaming

Jaakko Vuorio$^{(\boxtimes)}$ ⓘ and J. Tuomas Harviainen ⓘ

Tampere University, 33014 Tampere, Finland

Abstract. Along with popular location-based game Pokémon GO and advancements with mobile technology, location-based gaming has drawn interest in education. Schools may well pose a feasible context for the further mainstream use of location-based games aimed for educational purposes. We present conceptual work with location-based gaming in education and mobile learning literature together with in-use examples of location-based games to highlight the ongoing tendency in schools to adopt these games for pedagogic activities. Implications are provided for further research, practice and game design.

Keywords: Location-based games · Schools · Learning

1 Introduction

Location-based gaming shifted from its previously niche status to mainstream agenda as Pokémon GO (PGO) [1] was launched in 2016. This also increased the amount of research conducted on location-based games in general. Location-based gaming has drawn interest of scholars in its early years [2, 3], in the past decade [4, 5, [6], and exponentially in terms of publications and citations after PGO was introduced to the world [7–9]. In the past, mobile devices were seen as setting limitations for the gameplay [2], but these limitations have partly vanished with developments of smartphones and networks. The wide appeal of Pokémon GO (See Fig. 1) implicates past technological nuisances with location-based gaming have become bearable, although providing accuracy and reliability in these games still remain an issue [10]. We think the time, technology and research is ripe for opening up a discussion of location-based gaming in education.

The purpose of this paper is to initiate a discussion, though not for the first time, about the use of location-based gaming for education, especially in the context of basic education (from now on here, for the sake of consistency: school). As mobile devices have become ubiquitous in learning environments, using location-based games in school context with moderately young players can add an interesting path for research and practice. Smartphones have already changed the ways in which we learn and teach outdoors [12]. Likewise, there is nascent evidence of the movement of scaling location-based games to schools for educational activities. In the post Pokémon GO era, there are new affordances to be found for education, affordances which we provide here. Our research question is therefore: **what are the implications of using location-based games in schools?**

M. Wardaszko et al. (Eds.): ISAGA 2019, LNCS 11988, pp. 405–416, 2021.
https://doi.org/10.1007/978-3-030-72132-9_34

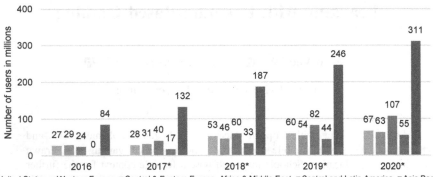

note: *estimation

Fig. 1. Number of active users of Pokémon Go worldwide 2016 – 2020, by region [11].

2 Location-Based Games

Until Pokémon GO, location-based games were mostly research demos without major significance or mainstream status [13]. They were often considered difficult to create, grow, and maintain over long periods of time [14]. Short-run examples such as Bot-Fighters [15], Songs of North [16] and Shadow Cities [17] were seen in the early years, but none of them gained a significant foothold or financial viability. Unlike other game types, location-based games are commonly played outside one's home. They are a subcategory of pervasive games [10] that uses real-life environments such as city streets, parks and indoor places for game play [18]. Pervasive games exist in the intersection of phenomena such as urban culture, mobile technology, reality fiction and arts thus combining varying contexts to produce new play experiences. Pervasive games blur and bend the traditional boundaries of game. Before mobile technology became the platform for arranging pervasive game experiences, many of the pervasive game genres were already established. These include *treasure hunts* and *assassination games, pervasive larp, alternate reality games* (ARG) and *urban adventure games* [19]. Many of these pervasive game genres are fundamentally based on location and environment of the player which then has influenced the more technology-enhanced location-based gaming of today.

Game events and play balance in location-based games are built around the physical location of the mobile device, which mostly relies on Assisted-Global Positioning System (A-GPS) [10]. More accurate and robust indoor positioning using for instance Bluetooth beacons, QR-codes or Wi-Fi still remains a challenge inside the industry [20]. Location-based mobile games such as Pokémon GO, Parallel Kingdom [21], and Ingress [22] use a virtual map as a basis for displaying, monitoring, and projecting the game reality. They use maps as portable game-boards that may transform everyday spatiality, performativity and practices, and can create emotional relationships to places [23, 24]. According to de Souza e Silva and Hjorth [25], these games force people to consider urban spaces as a game board, challenging traditional definitions of play and how we see city spaces as playful spaces. As noted by Leorke [26], location-based games enable strangers to play and interact with each other and transforms public spaces for shared playful areas. Location-based games enable people to coordinate in urban spaces and to create communities, being simultaneously formed in physical and digital spaces. This has been also described as hybrid reality [4]. We believe that this hybridization can be used for learning.

3 Mobile Game-Based Learning

From the learning perspective, location-based gaming may offer advantages. Mobile learning is characterized as the disentanglement of traditional obstacles, such as school buildings and schedules, from learning. Sharples, Taylor and Vavoula [27] define mobile learning as a situation where learners are constantly "on the move", changing their location across spaces where learning resources are seized from one context to another. Based on activity theory [28], and task model for mobile learning [29], an activity-based approach has been suggested for the mobile learning agenda by Naismith, Lonsdale, Vavoula and Sharples [30], and it has previously being applied in Avouris and Yiannoutsou's [31] review on the learning potential of location-based games. But unlike Naismith et al.'s approach to create categories for mobile learning pedagogies based on educational paradigms, Frohberg, Göth and Schwabe [32] see paradigmatic categorization ambivalent, since a single setting (in our case a location-based game) could be positioned to several educational paradigms, making such general categorization impractical. Frohberg, Göth and Schwabe [32], however, introduced a classification of mobile learning based on task model [29] including (1) context, (2) tools, (3) control, (4) communication, (5) subject and objective. Frohberg, Göth and Schwabe [32] presented that each category can be evaluated regarding specific mobile learning technology with a scale ranging from 1 to 5. In addition, context (See Fig. 2) is constitutive since instead of providing mere content to mobile device (independent context), it is seen less advanced and innovative approach compared to building for instance virtual reality for learning (physical context). The location of the learner (i.e. context) and its connection with learning activities is seen highly relevant in mobile learning [33].

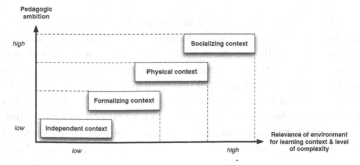

Fig. 2. Classification of mobile learning by the factor 'context' [32].

Formalizing context is described as typical classroom-like learning environment, where benefits are found mainly from learners being in the same environment, learning from each other. Physical context is about a place being relevant for learning (e.g. museum guides, location-based games). In a socializing context, in turn, learners share sustainable, interpersonal relationships, including past situations, emotions, friends and learning history covering the whole informal learning setting as well. This socializing context, however, lacks examples that would perfectly exist [32]. *Tools* refer to material, content or medium that is used to mediate the learning process. Tools can be categorized from (1) one-size-fits-all content delivery to (5) high-end content construction. *Control* reflects on the responsibility of the learning process ranging from (1) tight teacher control to (5) full learner control with varying advantages between modes. *Communication* includes social aspects that are fundamental in learning. Depending on the tool and learning activities, (1) learner can be isolated when it comes to communicating with other learners, or (5) in full reflective cooperation completing the learning task in a social group. For instance, location-based game *Savannah* [34] was developed to enable learner communication and social interaction with game and tasks. *Subjects* are learners that are considered as novice (1) or (5) experts from their previous knowledge on the given topic, and how the educational medium considers its users from their previous knowledge. Finally, *object* refers to the level of knowledge from (1) know to (5) synthesize and evaluate [32]. For educational activities used with location-based game, physical context comes by default, because the location and environment of the player is relevant for the game. If and when one adopts location-based game for learning activities, the level of complexity and pedagogic ambition should be considered as well. Active learning may provide a comprehensible approach to evaluate location-based games from learning activities perspective and how to design the actual learning activities with varying modes of ambition.

Games in general have been rigorously studied for decades from the learning perspective (e.g. [35]). According to Kiili [36], games as learning environments make it possible for learners to discover new rules and ideas rather than memorizing the material that others have presented. His model highlights the importance of providing players with feedback, clear goals and challenges that are matched to user's skill levels [36]. Educational games are an effective way to facilitate flow condition, engagement and immersion thus supporting learning that is eventually a rather complex process [37]. In 2012, Avouris and Yiannoutsou published a review of the learning potential of location-based games [31]. They investigated research conducted from location-based games that were typical so-called "first generation" location-based games. The research publications were from 2004 - 2010, and the majority of the games were played using Portable Digital Assistant (PDA) devices. Avouris and Yiannoutsou (ibid.) introduced a viable category of traditions for location-based games that we adopt here: the ludic, the pedagogic and the hybrid. In this system, ludic games are games that are mainly constructed for the enjoyment of the players (e.g. Pokémon GO), and hybrid games are those combining entertainment and learning such as games built for museums or cultural sites. The pedagogic tradition consists of games with explicit learning objectives, in a probably less developed field compared to the ludic or hybrid traditions [31]. These traditions however overlap, when thinking about learning, since ludic and hybrid traditions can and usually do possess learning dimension: these games broaden our understanding of our surroundings, and social interactions occur in these games. In addition, it is not always clear whether and if people recognize something as learning [30].

4   Location-Based Games in School

Vuorio, Okkonen and Viteli [38] investigated the affordances and usage of location-based game aimed mainly for educational purposes in Finnish comprehensive schools (n = 10) with 324 children age between 8 to 15 (Table 1). It found that a location-based game aimed for schools was scalable for multiple content domains and disciplines, and that teachers found new ways to use the game for educational purposes, even when they were not explicitly instructed for such use.

Table 1. Activities done with location-based game in schools (ibid.).

Subjects	Sports	Biol. & Geography	Miscellaneous	Mathematics	Arts	History	Chemistry	Religion
Activities	Push-ups Long-jump Dance Running Walking Orienteering X-jumps Hill run	Nature walk Animal recognition Plant recognition Forest quiz Nature arts Forest cottage visit Bird recognition	Christmas quiz Christmas carols Unicef-walk Team shout task Oldest teacher quiz	Percentage Recess math tasks Fractions Divisions Multiplications	Selfies Photo-graphing Filming a video Art history quiz	Centennial quiz Historical persons	Vitamin quiz Fire safety	Pilgrimage

The study also found that although sports was the most influential domain for the use of a location-based game, physical activation occurred across all domains, because all of the interactive quizzes and tasks regarded walking. Seasonal festivities and local community and culture also influenced the way in which teachers used the game with children (e.g. Christmas, centennial quiz). Furthermore, teachers constructed stand alone games that students could play during recesses by scanning QR-codes placed in the school's courtyard [38].

Schools can be a viable context for location-based games for many reasons. Here, we demonstrate that these games are probably being adopted increasingly, since they deliver many of the aforementioned benefits for enhancing learning and making daily school activities more enjoyable. Research is still however missing in this area, despite such tools foster learning in an authentic environment, delivering engagement and promote learning outside conventional formal learning environments [5]. We therefore present four key examples of location-based games with educational uses. They come from Finnish and Estonian context yet carry implications for the development and future of location-based educational gaming around the globe.

Here we present four case examples of already in-use location-based games in that are mostly in schools. First, in Fig. 3 there are two location-based games: Nomadi [39] and Action Track [40]. Both games are used with mobile devices yet creating content and monitoring requires an access to browser in laptop or desktop computer (i.e. Mac/PC).

Fig. 3. On the left Nomadi, copyright Citynomadi; on the right Action Track, copyright Team Action Zone, used with permission.

Both platforms have similarities in how they are being used. First, teacher place points of interest on virtual map layer and then adds content to those points using content creator in a dashboard view. Content can be text, hyperlinks, YouTube videos, pictures, quizzes, and so on. In addition, teacher can add tasks involving field data gathering by using smart phones camera. After GPS-points and content is being set, a typical way is to combine all GPS-points to create a consistent learning path or a track where one can find a starting area and a finish line. Advanced features are available such as automated alert in student's smartphone if leaving a specified gameplay area, chat-tool to support communication between teacher and student, and open repository of tasks, ready-to-use games (e.g. treasure hunt) and content. Indoor positioning is available by scanning QR-codes, a rather low tech solution yet probably convenient for schools. From dashboard view, teacher can monitor the real-time activity of students during the gameplay and all data and answers are recorded and can be accessed later from the dashboard. Both Nomadi and Action Track are highly scalable meaning teacher can virtually pick any subject domain and start creating engaging content. Both systems are also being used to discover cultural sites, for tourism and recreational purposes.

In Fig. 4 there are two location-based games Seppo [41] and Avastusrada [42].

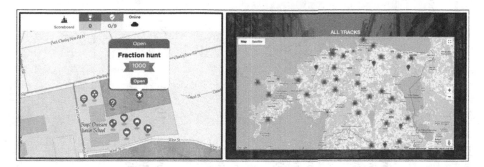

Fig. 4. On the left Seppo, copyright Seppo.io; on the right Avastusrada, copyright Tallinn University, used with permission.

Seppo is a location-based game aimed specifically for schools to gamify lesson plans and educational activities whereas Avastusrada was developed for environmental education, schools and for recreational activities. Seppo combines gamification, social learning, digital storytelling and physical movement via virtual map. Setting up game activities in Seppo is similar to previous examples with teacher led content creation, dashboard settings, shared content repositories and reporting tools. Avastusrada that is partly a research spin-off (See [43]) consists of tracks created by schools and other organizations covering all Estonia yet focused around the capital city Tallinn. Compared to other games, Avastusrada is an open game platform with virtual tours, quizzes and information linked to environmental education and historical sites aiming to gamify outdoor learning in general. Avastusrada is used with browser whereas Seppo can be played by using either smartphones browser or with an application.

To conclude our examples, we present to illustrate the ongoing development with location-based games in schools. We also highlight the notion these games do not yet possess an augmented reality component, which in many ways have influenced the widespread of Pokémon Go respectively.

In Table 2, we conclude provided location-based games possess relatively interesting approach to set up learning activities through the lens of mobile learning task model and classification. With moderate differences, these games in our understanding may well provide means from mere content delivery to content construction e.g. through data gathering with smartphone camera and through student led content and activity construction. It is therefore up to teachers how much they give away control from creating learning tracks solely on their own. In addition, as students can accomplish tracks on their own or typically in dyads or groups, these games could also support further communication through these game systems. Finally, there are no augmented reality components in these games (yet) in our understanding.

Table 2. Case examples listed by their preferences according to task model.

Location-based game	Mobile Learning Classification (Frohberg, Göth &Schwabe 2009; Taylor et al., 2006)						Tradition (Avouris & Yiannoutsou 2012)	AR enhancement
	Context	Tools	Control	Communication	Subject	Objective		
Nomadi	Physical (3)	Content delivery (1) to content construction (5)	Full teacher control (1) to mainly teacher control (3)	Lose couples (2) to communication within group (4)	Novice (1) to little previous knowledge (2)	Know (1) to analyze (4)	Hybrid	No
Action Track	Physical (3)	Content delivery (1) to content construction (5)	Full teacher control (1) to mainly teacher control (3)	Lose couples (2) to communication within group (4)	Novice (1) to little previous knowledge (2)	Know (1) to analyze (4)	Hybrid	No
Seppo	Physical (3)	Content delivery (1) to content construction (5)	Full teacher control (1) to mainly teacher control (3)	Lose couples (2) to communication within group (4)	Novice (1) to little previous knowledge (2)	Know (1) to analyze (4)	Pedagogic	No
Avastusrada	Physical (3)	Content delivery (1) to content construction (5)	Full teacher control (1) to mainly teacher control (3)	Lose couples (2) to communication within group (4)	Novice (1) to little previous knowledge (2)	Know (1) to analyze (4)	Hybrid	No

5   Discussion and Conclusion

Location-based games are a rising trend in schools, and present learning opportunities. The urban environment as a historical context of location-based games where these games have been developed and used at scale is a start. In addition, cities may plausibly be testbeds of location-based games and learning in the future, through a widespread of sensors and services, and through the social dimensions of these games, which invite people to shared play. Furthermore, after the initial success of Pokémon GO the overall interest towards location-based games has progressed. It has influenced research, development and users, as well as schools that may now be ready to adopt location-based games.

In this paper, we have highlighted that for education, location-based games should be considered through their context of use, which possessed relevancy and pedagogical value. Likewise, location-based games appear to be scalable for varying subject domains, and should be studied more for that purpose. These games seem to provide a viable and interesting approach for pedagogic ambitions as we have demonstrated from the mobile learning theory. Finally, we presented four examples of these games demonstrating that location-based games are attracting users from schools and educational society and these games have been starting to appear in Northern Europe. Hopefully, we'll learn there are other games as well out there.

First, there are implications for schools considering adopting location-based game. Game-based learning was found to be efficient way to consolidate engagement, flow, motivation and eventually learning. Play-based achievements are known to be efficient as learning tools [44], but it is important to note how physical presence and movement from one location to another affects that sense of achievement. Secondly, location-based games remove certain obstacles from learning activities such as time and place, especially since nowadays even the physical location of all players in a team is no longer a hindrance, as location based games can be played also from the home couch (e.g., The Walking Dead: Our World [45]). A teacher may monitor the progress of several students simultaneously, arrange stand-alone recess activities or gamify outdoor learning. In general, learning can be arranged in authentic environments. Thirdly, using location-based game enables the physical activation of students, with possible positive health and recreational outcomes for students. Finally, it seems location-based games can be efficiently used for any subject domain. Currently our examples showed these games are designed mainly for the teacher to monitor and construct activities yet we believe loosening up this control may plausibly add more value for learners. Location-based games should therefore foster active learning and learner-centric approaches and support deeper communication and group activities as well.

Several limitations nevertheless occur, since this is a conceptual indication of a much wider research agenda toward location-based games in schools and for learning. For example, the social motivation of PGO players is more relevant to gaming time than are health, immersion, or achievement-based motivation [46]. It would be negligent not to think that this social motivation would not occur in also the learning context in some sense.

In addition, we believe that studying whether learning takes place in the context of ludic, pedagogic, or hybrid traditions is a discussion that needs further work in the context of locational games. In all of our four examples, more ludic activities could have been provided, and the potential learning better grounded in game elements and game-based storytelling. Furthermore, to move away from the orchestrated and teacher-to-student learning activities that seem to be the common case in our game examples, it is apparent that location-based games, and how the activities in them are created, must stem from the learners themselves. A viable path is therefore to use the collaborative design of location-based games (e.g. [47]). We also think adding AR to these games would enrich the learning experience beyond as proved in PGO. To conclude, robust studies are needed from these games in order to examine their potential for learning, social interactions, motivation, flow conditions, health, engagement but also of their transformative and cultural dimensions for schools and education.

Acknowledgements. We sincerely thank all participating game companies and Tallinn University Centre for Educational Technology and Center for Ecology.

References

1. Niantic. Pokémon GO (2016)
2. Sotamaa, O.: All the world's a botfighter stage: notes on location-based multi-user gaming. In: Computer Games and Digital Cultures Conference Proceedings, pp. 35–44 (2002)
3. Benford, S., et al.: Coping with uncertainty in a location-based game. IEEE Pervasive Comput. **2**(3), 34–41 (2003)
4. de Souza e Silva, A.: Hybrid reality and location-based gaming: redefining mobility and game spaces in urban environments. Simul. Gaming **40**, 404–424 (2009)
5. Huizenga, J., Admiraal, W., Akkerman, S., ten Dam, G., Ten Dam, G.: Mobile game-based learning in secondary education: engagement, motivation and learning in a mobile city game. J. Comput. Assist. Learn. **25**(4), 332–344 (2009)
6. Clough, G.: Geolearners: location-based informal learning with mobile and social technologies. IEEE Trans. Learn. Technol. **3**(1), 33–44 (2010)
7. Althoff, T., White, R.W., Horvitz, E.: Influence of pokémon go on physical activity: study and implications. J. Med. Internet Res. **18**(12), 1–14 (2016)
8. Howe, K.B., Suharlim, C., Ueda, P., Howe, D., Kawachi, I., Rimm, E.B.: Gotta catch'em all! Pokémon GO and physical activity among young adults: difference in differences study. BMJ **355**, 1–4 (2016)
9. Alha, K., Koskinen, E., Paavilainen, J., Hamari, J.: Why do people play location-based augmented reality games: a study on Pokémon GO. Comput. Hum. Behav. **93**, 114–122 (2019)
10. Alavesa, P., et al.: Ludic markers for player-player observation in location-based mobile games. Simul. Gaming **49**(6), 700–717 (2018)
11. Lynch, M., Bank of America: Number of active users of Pokémon Go worldwide from 2016 to 2020, by region (in millions). In Statista - The Statistics Portal (2016). https://www.statista.com/statistics/665640/pokemon-go-global-android-apple-users/. Accessed 13 Mar 2019

12. Santos, P., Hernández-Leo, D., Blat, J.: To be or not to be in situ outdoors, and other implications for design and implementation, in geolocated mobile learning. Pervasive Mobile Comput. **14**, 17–30 (2014)
13. Paavilainen, J., Korhonen, H., Alha, K., Stenros, J., Koskinen, E., Mäyrä, F.: The Pokémon GO experience: a location-based augmented reality mobile game goes mainstream. In: Proceedings of the 2017 CHI Conference on Human Factors in Computing Systems, pp. 2493–2498. ACM (2017)
14. Neustaedter, C., Tang, A., Judge, T.K.: Creating scalable location-based games: lessons from Geocaching. Pers. Ubiquit. Comput. **17**(2), 335–349 (2013). https://doi.org/10.1007/s00779-011-0497-7
15. It's Alive. BotFighters (2001)
16. Lankoski, P., Heli, S., Nummela, J., Lahti, J., Mäyrä, F., Ermi, L.: Proceedings of the third Nordic Conference on Human-Computer Interaction - NordiCHI 2004. In the Third Nordic Conference, pp. 413–416 (2004)
17. Grey Area. Shadow Cities (2010)
18. Benford, S., Magerkurth, C., Ljungstrand, P.: Bridging the physical and digital in pervasive gaming. Commun. ACM **48**(3), 54 (2005)
19. Montola, M., Stenros, J., Waern, A.: Pervasive Games Theory and Design. Morgan Kaufmann, Burlington (2009)
20. Lymberopoulos, D., Liu, J., Yang, X., Choudhury, R.R., Handziski, V., Sen, S.: A realistic evaluation and comparison of indoor location technologies: experiences and lessons learned. In: Proceedings of the ACM/IEEE IPSN, April, pp. 178–189 (2015)
21. Parallel Kingdom (n.d.). https://www.parallelkingdom.com/
22. Niantic. Ingress (2013)
23. Lammes, S., Wilmott, C.: The map as playground: Location-based games as cartographical practices. Convergence **24**(6), 648–665 (2018)
24. Oleksy, T., Wnuk, A.: Catch them all and increase your place attachment! The role of location-based augmented reality games in changing people - place relations. Comput. Hum. Behav. **76**, 3–8 (2017)
25. De Souza, E., Silva, A., Hjorth, L.: Playful urban spaces a historical approach to mobile games. Simul. Gaming **40**(5), 602–625 (2009)
26. Leorke, D.: Location-Based Gaming: Play in Public Space. Palgrave Macmillan, London (2019)
27. Sharples, M., Taylor, J., Vavoula, G.: A theory of learning for the mobile age. In: Andrews, R., Haythornthwaite, C. (eds.) The Sage Handbook of Elearning Research, pp. 221–247. Sage, London (2007)
28. Engeström, Y.: Learning by Expanding: An Activity-Theoretical Approach to Developmental Research. Orienta-Konsulit Oy, Helsinki (1987)
29. Taylor, J., Sharples, M., Malley, C.O., Vavoula, G., Waycott, J.: Towards a task model for mobile learning: a dialectical approach. Int. J. Learn. Technol. **2**, 138–158 (2006)
30. Naismith, L., Lonsdale, P., Vavoula, G., Sharples, M.: Literature review in mobile technologies and learning. Educational Technology, vol. 11 (2004)
31. Avouris, N.M., Yiannoutsou, N.: A review of mobile location-based games for learning across physical and virtual spaces. J. UCS **18**(15), 2120–2142 (2012)
32. Frohberg, D., Göth, C., Schwabe, G.: Mobile Learning projects - a critical analysis of the state of the art. J. Comput. Assist. Learn. **25**(4), 307–331 (2009)
33. Fulantelli, G., Taibi, D., Arrigo, M.: A framework to support educational decision making in mobile learning. Comput. Hum. Behav. **47**, 50–59 (2015)
34. Facer, K., Joiner, R., Stanton, D., Reid, J., Hull, R., Kirk, D.S.: Savannah: mobile gaming and learning? J. Comput. Assist. Learn. **20**, 399–409 (2004)

35. Whitton, N.: Digital Games and Learning: Research and Theory. Routledge, New York (2014)
36. Kiili, K.: Digital game-based learning: Towards an experiential gaming model. Internet High. Educ. **8**(1), 13–24 (2005)
37. Hamari, J., Shernoff, D.J., Rowe, E., Coller, B., Asbell-Clarke, J., Edwards, T.: Challenging games help students learn: an empirical study on engagement, flow and immersion in game-based learning. Comput. Hum. Behav. **54**, 170–179 (2016)
38. Vuorio, J., Okkonen, J., Viteli, J.: User expectations and experiences in using location-based game in educational context. In: Väljataga, T., Laanpere, M. (eds.) Digital Turn in Schools—Research, Policy, Practice. LNET, pp. 17–35. Springer, Singapore (2019). https://doi.org/10.1007/978-981-13-7361-9_2
39. Nomadi. Citynomadi (n.d.). https://citynomadi.com/
40. Action Track. Team Action Zone (n.d.). https://www.taz.fi/
41. Seppo. Seppo.io (n.d.). https://seppo.io/
42. Avastusrada. Tallinn University (n.d.). https://avastusrada.ee/en
43. Väljataga, T., Moks, U., Tiits, A., Ley, T., Kangur, M., Terasmaa, J.: Designing learning experiences outside of classrooms with a location-based game Avastusrada. In: Lavoué, É., Drachsler, H., Verbert, K., Broisin, J., Pérez-Sanagustín, M. (eds.) EC-TEL 2017. LNCS, vol. 10474, pp. 614–617. Springer, Cham (2017). https://doi.org/10.1007/978-3-319-66610-5_75
44. van Roy, R., Deterding, S., Zaman, B.: Collecting Pokémon or receiving rewards? How people functionalise badges in gamified online learning environments in the wild. Int. J. Hum.-Comput. Stud. (2018, in press)
45. The Walking Dead: Our World. Next Games (2018). https://www.thewalkingdeadourworld.com/
46. Kaczmarek, L.D., Misiak, M., Behnke, M., Dziekan, M., Guzik, P.: The Pikachu effect: social and health gaming motivations lead to greater benefits of Pokémon GO use. Comput. Hum. Behav. **75**, 356–363 (2017)
47. Wake, J.D., Guribye, F., Wasson, B.: Learning through collaborative design of location-based games. Int. J. Comput.-Support. Collab. Learn. **13**(2), 167–187 (2018). https://doi.org/10.1007/s11412-018-9278-x

Methodological Challenges of Creating a Next-Generation Machine Learning-Based Game Engine for Generating Maps and Vehicle Behavior

Błażej Podgórski and Marcin Wardaszko

Kozminski University, Warsaw, Poland
{bpodgorski,wardaszko}@kozminski.edu.pl

Abstract. The article presents conceptual work in the area of technological challenges for the construction of a next-generation racing game engine. The team creating the game decided to implement the project based on the Unreal solution. The main innovation of the product is to be: realism of driving experience and the use of machine learning elements to improve work under the engine. In terms of realism, the team will make real measurements using race vehicle telemetry devices. The Machine Learning component is intended for two purposes as a map detailing element and for setting the parameters of physics of objects in the game. The paper aims to present the ideal project idea to the critical analysis and thus improve the concept.

Keywords: Vehicle physics · Game engine · Research methodology · Telemetry · Machine learning · Artificial intelligence · Unreal engine

1 Introduction

The game will use the Unreal engine is because it perfectly renders graphics and controls lighting, enables connection to contextual geometry derived from computer-aided engineering models (CAD) [1]. The Unreal environment is well documented, making it often the basis for creating new products.

Besides, older generations of the game engines compared to other products, for example, Quake, had more sophisticated graphics and were described as an easier environment for the game programmer [2]. Features such as spatial topology and time dynamics used during the ISAGA 2007 conference presentation also testify to the wide application of the engine [3]. The wide range of possibilities for using the Unreal engine is also evidenced by the use of it for the design of the Tesla museum in Belgrad [4]. All these elements mean that he is eagerly chosen to create games [5].

In order to create an engine concept, which is based on machine learning and A.I., it is necessary to verify technological capabilities. The goal of artificial intelligence (machine learning-based) module will be used to generate maps and vehicle behavior. Generating maps can be based on previously made graphic elements or photos. In addition, based on physical measurements and trajectories to generate the behavior of in-game vehicles. In 2013, the dynamic development of machine learning began, many

M. Wardaszko et al. (Eds.): ISAGA 2019, LNCS 11988, pp. 417–422, 2021.
https://doi.org/10.1007/978-3-030-72132-9_35

models were created such as: Convolutional Neural Networks (CNN) [6], Deep Belief Networks (DBN) [7], Recurrent Neural Networks (RNN) [7], Long Short Term Memory Networks (LSTM) [8], Gated Recurrent Unit Neural Networks (GRU) [9] and Generative Adversarial Networks (GAN) [10], Deep Convolutional Generative Adversarial Networks (DCGANs) [11].

2 Stage of Project Realization

In order to implement the project, it is necessary to overcome three technological challenges.

1) Developing the optimal methodology for engine prototype construction,
2) Verification of the concept of engine prototype construction
3) Developing a methodology for measuring and collecting data for the artificial intelligence prediction model.

2.1 Issue 1 "Development Of An Optimal Methodology For Engine Prototype Construction"

As part of the first stage, the key research problem will be the selection and development of the optimal method for constructing critical components of the universal engine prototype, such as light support, vertical noise, vertical detection, audio, motion, navigation, physics, rendering, wireframe, static grid. The goal is to achieve the most realistic reflection of the physics of vehicle behavior and to achieve advanced gameplay effects typical of AAA production. Due to the high costs of recording physical vehicle behavior and the need to prepare a wide map package, the gaming market is dominated by the largest producers, whose racing games series like Forza, Need For Speed are the endpoint for the quality of gameplay in this type of productions. At the same time, these manufacturers do not provide commercially available technologies.

The project assumes the elimination of the above barriers while taking into account the mitigation of the risk of continuous technological progress, which generates the need to develop a prototype that allows an affordable upgrade of the technological version and the use of flexible algorithmic models. In order to select the technology that meets the above requirements for the solution being developed, the Unreal engine technology was chosen, on which the prototype engine will be developed - having the advantage in the form of, among others, better rendering of Unreal Graphic Designers and lighting control than, e.g. comparable Vehicle Physics Pro engine available commercially on the market.

An important challenge for project team will be the use of, among others, employing the machine learning technology extended with artificial intelligence algorithms, for enabling a game physics model of vehicle behavior characterized by parameters far exceeding the solutions currently available on the market. An analysis of the solutions available on the market was carried out and current state of publications in the field, which showed the lack of any information regarding the use of this type of technology in the scope of A.I. application. Artificial intelligence technology will also be used, in the project, to generate maps (maps, charts, 3D courses) based on prepared parameters, elements and algorithm models that allow the final effect of being close to the comparison with model created by game designers and 3D graphic artist within the real conditions of use e.g. racing game maps are modeled.

The implementation of this task will begin with the analysis of the state of the art in the field of engine components (support of light, riser noise, detection of risers, audio, motion, navigation, physics, rendering, wireframe, static grid, etc.) and other compatible with the Unreal engine (written in C++ and other languages e.g. havok, PhysyX, Cuda) to confirm their use as part of the critical functionality of the planned project result. An analysis of available coding libraries will also be carried out, which will be aimed at performing the next two tasks, i.e., analyzing machine learning models and their adaptation. Next, the methodology of construction of selected components will be analyzed to meet the requirements of the project. The tram of C++ programmers, unreal graphic designer, and game designers will be responsible for analyzing the C++ components for the Unreal engine and will perform an analysis of their construction. At the same time, C++ programmers will analyze the adaptation of components to the project to detect possible (potential) problems at subsequent stages and to detect gaps in current tools. The task will also identify current practices in the field of technology used to develop models of vehicle behavior, generate isometric views and other functionalities for map design/gameplay levels, as well as trends in the design of popular and attractive players.

An analysis of ready-made libraries will also be carried out in terms of computational mechanisms in terms of requirements for building machine learning models in two areas: (1) the ability to predict the parameters of motor vehicle movement, (2) the ability to recognize and generate graphic objects for maps/levels. Due to the planned design of ML / AI models in Python, the following libraries have been identified that will be analyzed: TF-GAN, Numpy, Scipy, Scikit-learn, GAN, Thean, TensorFlow, Keras, PyTorch, Pandas, Matplotlib. Machine learning techniques such as: Convolutional Neural Networks (CNN) [6], Deep Belief Networks (DBN) [7], Recurrent Neural Networks (RNN) [7], Long Short Term Memory Networks (LSTM) [8], Gated Recurrent Unit Neural Networks (GRU) [10] and Generative Adversarial Networks (GAN) [10, 11].

2.2   Issue 2 "Verification of the Game Engine Prototype Design"

As part of the second issue, the key search problem will be organized under the model three main dimensions: (1) realism, (2) flexibility - the possibility of using numerical values of parameters, (3) dynamic implementation planning.

Due to the fact that each of the enclosing functions is in contradiction to the others, as part of the triggering action, methods for building the prototype must be developed that allows free adaptation of the game-based game to the receiver. The level of in-game vehicle response to preset vehicle model parameters will have a significant impact on the perception of the different players. Professional driver or player will have much different perception of such simulated car, and in the case of a casual gamer or driver of the impact of changes in these parameters will be less important from game feeling. Therefore, the necessary step is to prepare a solution (engine mechanic) that will expand the workshop of the developer and allow optimization and customization engine re-sponsiveness and fidelity. Formulas for which mathematically relevant algorithms containing data/transformations/parameters for vehicle behavior physics should be identified [12, 13]. Currently, no such solutions on the market have been identified.

2.3   Issue 3 "Developing a Methodology for Measuring and Collecting Data for the Artificial Intelligence Prediction Model"

The third challenge is methodological nature - the key to develop a validated measurement collecting methodology, in particular, to determine the range of parameters that will make up the density of data used in the artificial intelligence prediction model. It is assumed that the conditional validation level will be at least 80% compliance - which means that the prediction model will be able to generate at least 80% of the vehicle's behavior following actual driving conditions in the predetermined environment. Based on the planned actions, data will be collected during tests performed with live cars in different driving conditions. The scope of the implementation of artificial intelligence is twofold. The first level of implementation will be an analysis of the information that can be downloaded from cars telemetry. Identification and classification of data will be the next step, followed by the analysis of the typology and methodologies for creating models of the behavior of motor vehicles for different environmental conditions. Tests with selected models will be carried out in order to develop the telemetry analysis methodology planned for use in subsequent stages of the project. A comparative analysis will be developed consisting of compiling documentation regarding parameters that can be adapted to the needs of the project.

The next task will be to test three cars with front, rear and 4x4 drive, completed by mapping of the characteristics of the parameters of motor vehicles collected during the implementation of defined scenarios and readings from telemetry via a measuring computer. A professional driver will be responsible for making and cataloging basic vehicle maneuvers on the track. The identified key vehicle movement parameters for the game engine and artificial intelligence modules are: (1) suspension physics, through overload parameters, (2) tire physics, via pressure change, [12, 14] (3) brake behavior and performance, based on telemetry results in terms of brake pedal pressure, brake fluid pressure, and speed and distance, [15] (4) transmission ratio, transmission ratio measurement, acceleration and overloads (g parameter measurement), (5) engine parameters, such as water and oil temperature, acceleration, torque, [16] (6) adhesion parameters on a given surface, together with the slide parameters resulting from loss of grip, [17] (7) GPS position relative to track [18].

Tests will be carried out at intervals depending on the significance and characteristics of the parameters tested, if the analyzed parameter requires very high data density to develop a correct model, e.g., as in the case of brake pressure and disc response, the intervals will be carried out in millisecond distances. If the data will be less important, or their characteristics will indicate the lack of legitimacy of such a large set of information, such as in GPS data, the intervals will be within 60 s. The total estimated minimum number of all records for one car is 50,000 records, while the maximum is 100,000 records.

Then the measurements and telemetry readings will be compared with the parameters analyzed in the theoretical analysis. By entering all the available data into the artificial intelligence module, it will be checked whether the developed model shows predictive accuracy for vehicle physics at 80%. The data will be subjected to simulations until reaching the assumed level so that ultimately subsequent realistic simulations of vehicle behavior are generated based on machine learning [19, 20].

The second scope of artificial intelligence and machine learning implantation will cover the needs of the robotized map generator module. The best solution for this task seems to be GAN model [10, 21]. In this regard, the key will be to identify the ability of the technologies studied to recognize and generate graphic objects for maps, obtain high resolution [22] or texture synthesis [23].

3 Summary

In recent years we can observe quite fast development of both the Unreal engine and machine learning applications, which points to the importance and relevance of the topic. The methodological approach will be critical to the outcomes of the project. The initial steps require a strong rigor in the theoretical analysis and model selection, yet criteria for the selection need to be determined. The data generating and collecting process of the reference cars and standardized maneuvers create a completely different set of challenges. Validity, repeatability and data density will be a critical factor in the data collection process. The coding and classifying data is always the biggest challenge for machine learning and Artificial Intelligence training. All those layers of complexity is the biggest challenge in the successful completion of the project.

Acknowledgments. This research project is supported within the framework of the EU project entitled: GearShift - building the engine of the behavior of wheeled motor vehicles and map generation based on artificial intelligence algorithms implemented on the Unreal Engine platform - GAMEINN. POIR.01.02.00-00-0052/19.

References

1. Kelly, R., Skilton, R., Naish, J.: Real-time volumetric rendering of radiation fields using 3D textures. Fusion Eng. Des. **146**(Part A), 551–554 (2019) https://doi.org/10.1016/j.fusengdes. 2019.01.020
2. Lewis, M., Jacobson, J.: Game engines in scientific research. Commun. ACM **45**, 27–31 (2002)
3. Price, C.B.: Computer games as vehicles to learn physics: mechanics, oscillations and waves. In: Mayer, I., Mastik, H. (eds.) Organizing and Learning Through Gaming and Simulation: Proceedings of Isaga 2007, Eburon Delft (2008)
4. Vučković, V., Stanišić, A., Simić, N.: Computer simulation and VR model of the Tesla's Wardenclyffe laboratory. Digit. Appl. Archaeol. Cult. Heritage **7**, 42–50 (2017). https://doi. org/10.1016/j.daach.2017.11.001

5. Davison, T., Samavati, F., Jacob, C.: LifeBrush: painting, simulating, and visualizing dense biomolecular environments. Comput. Graph. **82**, 232–242 (2019). https://doi.org/10.1016/j.cag.2019.05.006
6. Goodfellow, I., Bengio, Y., Courville, A.: Deep Learning. MIT Press , Oxford (2016)
7. Graves, A., Mohamed, A., Hinton, G.: Speech recognition with deep recurrent neural networks. In: 2013 IEEE International Conference on Acoustics, Speech and Signal Processing, pp. 6645–6649 (2013)
8. Sainath, T.N., Vinyals, O., Senior, A., Sak, H.: Convolutional, long short-term memory, fully connected deep neural networks. In: 2015 IEEE International Conference on Acoustics, Speech and Signal Processing (ICASSP), pp. 4580–4584 (2015)
9. Chung, J., Gülçehre, C., Cho, K., Bengio Y.: Empirical evaluation of gated recurrent neural networks on sequence modeling. CoRR, abs/1412.3555 (2014)
10. Goodfellow, I., et al.: Generative adversarial nets. Advances in Neural Information Processing Systems (2014). arXiv:1406.2661v1 [stat.ML], 10 June 2014
11. Radford, A., Metz, L., Chintala, S.: Unsupervised Representation Learning With Deep Convolutional, pp. 1–16 (2016)
12. Pacejka, H.: Tire and Vehicle Dynamics. Butterworth-Heinemann, Oxford (2012)
13. Pauwelussen, J.: Essentials of Vehicle Dynamics. Butterworth-Heinemann, Oxford (2015)
14. Garatti, S., Bittanti, S.: Parameter estimation in the Pacejka's tyre model through the TS method. IFAC Proc. Vol. **42**, 1304–1309 (2009)
15. Langhof, N., Rabenstein, M., Rosenlöcher, J., Hackenschmidt, R., Krenkel, W., Rieg, F.: Full-ceramic brake systems for high performance friction applications. J. Eur. Ceram. Soc. **36**, 3823–3832 (2016)
16. Li, X., Zou, C., Qi, A.: Experimental study on the thermo-physical properties of car engine coolant (water/ethylene glycol mixture type) based SiC nanofluids. Int. Commun. Heat Mass Transfer **77**, 159–164 (2016)
17. Abe, M.: Vehicle Handling Dynamics. Butterworth-Heinemann, Oxford (2015)
18. Balkwill, J.: Performance Vehicle Dynamics. Butterworth-Heinemann, Oxford (2018)
19. Du, F., Zhang, J., Hu, J., Fei, R.: Discriminative multi-modal deep generative models. Knowl.-Based Syst. **173**, 74–82 (2019)
20. Glaser, J.I., Benjamin, A.S., Farhoodi, R., Kording, K.P.: The roles of supervised machine learning in systems neuroscience. Prog. Neurobiol. **175**, 126–137 (2019)
21. Borji, A.: Pros and cons of GAN evaluation measures. Comput. Vis. Image Underst. **179**, 41–65 (2019)
22. Ledig, C., et al.: Photo-Realistic Single Image Super-Resolution Using a Generative Adversarial Network, pp. 4681–4690 (2017) (n.d.)
23. Gatys, L.A., Ecker, A.S., Bethge, M.: Texture synthesis using convolutional neural networks. In: Cortes, C., Lawrence, N., Lee, D., Sugiyama, M., Garnett, R. (eds.) Advances in Neural Information Processing Systems. Curran Associates, Inc. (2015)

Agent-Based Simulation for Sustainable Management of Supply Chain and Natural Resources: Basic Model

Keiko Zaima[✉]

Kyoto Sangyo University, Motoyama, Kamigamo, Kita-ku 603-8555,
Kyoto, Japan
zaima@cc.kyoto-su.ac.jp

Abstract. The purpose of this study was to develop an agent-based model including both supply chain and resource management in order to investigate the effects of changing business rules and policy. In this paper, the basic model is suggested and the results from the simulation is provided. Two patterns were obtained from the simulations of the basic model. In the first pattern, resources are depleted rapidly and the economy is not sustained. In the second pattern, the resource reached a sustainable level, but society was not economically sustained. In both patterns, product waste occurred in the store, although at different levels. From these results, it is apparent that the basic model can accurately reproduce the situation in which a trade-off between the environment and the economy occurs. In this paper, two applications were discussed: scenario analysis and gaming simulation. Scenario analyses can be designed to illustrate some of the issues concerning food loss and waste in the supply chain and the relationship with waste and natural resource management. Gaming simulations can be designed for consumer education and business gaming using hybrid simulation.

Keywords: Agent-based modeling · Supply chain management · Resource management · Food loss and waste · Environmental policy

1 Introduction

The Earth is a materially closed system, as "In which no matter moves in and out of the system, although energy and information can move across the system's boundaries" [1]. The carrying capacity of the Earth is finite, and natural resources can be used sustainably if harvested at a rate that enables a continuation of harvesting at the same rate in the future. The sustainable management of natural resources is a significant issue. Human society benefits from natural resources, such as fish and fruit.

However, food loss and waste has increasingly become a serious issue in recent years. The Food and Agriculture Organization of the United Nations (FAO) defined food loss and waste as "the decrease of food in subsequent stages of the food supply chain intended for human consumption" [2]. The concept of food loss and waste includes instances where food is discarded because of a deterioration in quality, and in which food is discarded despite it still being suitable for consumption. Food loss and waste can occur during any process of the food supply chain: harvesting, processing,

© Springer Nature Switzerland AG 2021
M. Wardaszko et al. (Eds.): ISAGA 2019, LNCS 11988, pp. 423–440, 2021.
https://doi.org/10.1007/978-3-030-72132-9_36

distribution, and final consumption. According to the FAO, the amount of global food waste reaches approximately 1.3 billion tons annually, which means that about one third of the food produced for human consumption is discarded.

In Japan, the total amount of food wasted amounts to approximately 28.4 million tons, and food loss amounts 6.4 million tons. 20.1 million tons of the total food waste occurs during industrial processes such as harvesting, processing, manufacturing, distribution, and sales, and approximately one fifth of this industrial waste is via food loss. One factor that leads to food loss is Japanese business practices, such as penalties for lack of goods in stores and the "one third rule" which affects all processed food with an expiration date. The one third rule states that processed food cannot be shipped after one third of the period between the production date and the expiration date, and it is removed from the store shelf before the latter third of this period. The expiration date suggests the period during which the food is still of high quality.

Food loss and waste is not only a significant issue in itself but can also be related to an excess in the use of natural resources. However, consumers are not usually aware of either these issues or the problems concerning the entire food supply chain from harvesting to consumption.

The purpose of this study was to develop an agent-based model including both the supply chain and resource management in order to investigate possible changes to the rules concerning business and management. In this paper, the design of the basic model is demonstrated and results from the simulation are presented. It is suggested that the results of the simulation using the basic model can illustrate the current situation. In addition, two applications for scenario analysis and gaming simulation are discussed. The former application is for investigation of the issues of food loss and waste. The latter is concerned with consumer education and business gaming.

The remainder of this paper is organized as follows. Section 2 provides a review of agent-based modelling (ABM) for environmental issues. Section 3 explains the basic model for the analysis of a supply chain including the management of resources and products. Section 4 shows the results of the simulation of the basic model. Section 5 discusses the validity of the model and mentions the implications of the results of the simulation. Section 6 discusses the two applications of scenario analysis and gaming simulation. Finally, the conclusions and issues for further research are presented in Sect. 7.

2 Brief Review of ABM for Environmental Issues and Behavior

ABM is a computational method for studying systems that include interacting autonomous agents. Heckbert, Baynes, and Reeson [3] pointed out that ABM has two features: (1) interactions leading to emergent outcomes, and (2) the explicit representation of the dynamic behavior of heterogeneous agents. ABM enables the clarification of the dynamics that emerge from the interaction between agents with an individually internal model that make decisions autonomously. This study focused on multiple interactions between heterogeneous agents.

Existing research that is related to environmental issues using ABM is roughly classified into four categories [4]. The first category is related to the traditional issue of pollution control. For example, Kuscsik, Holvath, and Gmitra [5] analyzed the effects of a feedback mechanism in the decentralized control of a polluting plant using a cellular automaton type of ABM. The second category is concerned with the use and supply of land and resources. Matthews, Gilbert, Roach, Polhill, and Gotts [6] provided a review covering ABM studies on land use. In this category, reality is analyzed using realistic model design and the development of simulator based on empirical data and experimental results.

The third category is related to the diffusion of environmentally conscious behavior. For example, Mosler and Martens [7] analyzed the effects of an environmental campaign on the diffusion of environmentally conscious attitudes. Market models are included in this category. Janssen and Jager [8] and Zaima [9, 10] developed ABMs based on social psychology studies of environmental behavior, although the market models for this research were concerned with the trades of abstract goods as opposed to actual commodities. Schwoon [11] and Zhang, Geisler, and Garcia [12] provided ABM models for the trading of fuel cell vehicles. In these studies, agent-based models were designed based on empirical research and the analysis of specific products and services. Research that includes market models is known as "agent-based diffusion models", which describes the application of ABM to the diffusion of innovation. Kiesling, Gunther, Stummer, and Wakolbinger [13] also reviewed agent-based diffusion models. The fourth category is focused on addressing global environmental issues such as climate change. For example, Yamagata and Mizuta [14] analyzed international negotiations on the trading of emissions.

This study belongs to the third category. Although research in this category includes models of single markets, Zaima [15] modeled two related markets: a product market and the market for its parts. The former is a trade model between consumers and large firms that supply final goods, and the latter is a trade model between large firms and small and medium-sized firms. This study aims to construct a supply chain model, which include two markets with multiple agents: harvesting firms, processing firms, the store, and the consumers.

3 Basic Model

3.1 Society, Categories of Agents and Outlines of Settings

The model in this study considers a society that consists of the environment and five categories of agents: the harvesting firm, the processing firm, the store, the consumer and the authorities (see Fig. 1). The harvesting firm, the processing firm and the consumer are autonomous agents that have internal model and learning rules. The numbers of the harvesting firm, the processing firm, and the consumer are represented by N_h, N_f, and N_c, respectively. These are all assumed to be constants. In the basic model, there is only one store involved. All the products from all the processing firms are displayed in the store for the consumer. The number for the authority is also set at 1.

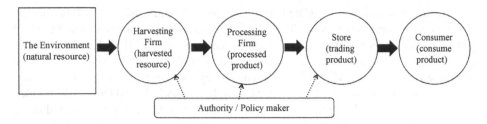

Fig. 1. A construction of the basic model.

The model includes two categories for the markets. One is the market for the product which the processing firm supplies and the consumer demands. The other is the market for the harvested resource which the harvesting firm supplies and the processing firm requires.

In this model, the product is assumed to be made from a specific harvested resource, and it is set as a processed food which has a specific expiration period. The natural resource is assumed to be a certain species that is harvested from the natural environment. This is set as a species of fish from which the processed food is made, in this case kamaboko or surimi.

In this model, resource loss, food loss, and food waste occurs during the processes carried out by the harvesting firm and the processing firm. Processed food loss occurs in the store. Although the fish resource recovers when it is harvested, the number declines via excess harvesting that is above the reproduction rate.

3.2 Natural Resource

The amount of initial resource is $R(0)$. This changes according to the amount harvested, and the amount of the resource at period t is $R(t)$ which is expressed using the Eq. (1), which describes the discrete time logistic function.

$$
\begin{aligned}
R(t) = &\left(R(t-1) - \sum V_{hi}(t-1)\right) \\
&+ r_p\left(R(t-1) - \sum V_{hi}(t-1)\right)\left\{1 - \left(R(t-1) - \sum V_{hi}(t-1)\right)/R_{max}\right\}
\end{aligned}
\tag{1}
$$

The reproduction rate of the resource is denoted r_p, which is assumed to be constant in the basic model. The total amounts of resource harvested by the i-th harvesting firm at t is $V_{hi}(t)$. The maximum amount of natural resource is expressed as R_{max}.

3.3 Authority for Sustainability

The authority examines the existing amount of the resource and determines the desirable volume $V_{sus}(t)$ as the sustainable level that can be harvested per harvesting firm. In the basic model, harvesting firms are not required to adhere to that amount, as the desirable value is not government regulation. The authority certifies the harvesting firm according to the application of this suggestion, and the volume taken by a certified firm should therefore be beneath the desirable level. The desirable level at period t is calculated using Eq. (2).

$$V_{sus}(t) = R(t)r_{sus}/N_h \tag{2}$$

In Eq. (2), r_{sus} is a parameter of the sustainable rate.

3.4 Harvesting Firm

The harvesting firm decides the volume of natural resource to be harvested during every period according to the demand $V_{Dhi}(t-1)$ of the processing firms during the previous period. The harvesting volume $V_{hi}(t)$ of the i-th harvesting firm at period t is expressed by Eq. (3).

$$V_{hi}(t) = V_{Dhi}(t-1) + V_{Random}(t) \tag{3}$$

In Eq. (3), $V_{Random}(t)$ is a random value with parameter V_{max} set as the maximum volume.

The harvesting firm decides whether it accepts the desirable amount set by the authority or not. When it adheres to the desirable amount, the harvesting firm is certified as sustainable.

The base price of the natural resource is P_{Rbase}. When the harvesting firm is certified by the authority, the firm adds a premium p_{sus}. The price $P_{Rhi}(t)$ of the i-th harvesting firm at period t is described by Eq. (4). A_h is a dummy variable of certification

$$P_{Rhi}(t) = P_{Rbase} + A_{hi}(t)p_{sus} \tag{4}$$

The amount of resource loss and waste $W_{Rhi}(t)$ of the i-th harvesting firm at period t is expressed by Eq. (5). In Eq. (4), $V_{Shi}(t)$ is the amount sold at period t.

$$W_{Rhi}(t) = V_{Dhi}(t) - V_{Shi}(t) \tag{5}$$

The harvesting firm follows the rule concerning certification, as shown in Table 1. When the firm decides to take certification, the harvesting volume should be under the desirable level.

Table 1. Rule candidates for the harvesting firm.

Rule number	Certification	Value
1	No	0
2	Yes	1
3	Random	1 or 0 at random

The profit $\Pi_{hi}(t)$ of the i-th harvesting firm at period t is expressed by Eq. (6). In Eq. (6), c_{WR} is the parameter for the unit cost required to treat resource waste, and c_A is a parameter of certification.

$$\Pi_{hi}(t) = P_{Rhi}(t)\, V_{Dhi}(t) - c_{WR}W_{Rhi}(t) - c_A A_{hi}(t) \tag{6}$$

At interval T of a specific period, the harvesting firm evaluates the average value of the aggregated profits from all rules and selects a new rule under reinforcement learning.

3.5   Processing Firm

The processing firm decides its eco-level, price, volume of product for sale, and volume of harvested resource used in the product. The processing firm follows a rule concerning decision-making for the eco-level of its environmental management and the price of the product. The eco-level means the extent of environmental management carried out by the firm. The higher the level, the higher the level of environmental management. This model assumes that the environmental management level of the firm matches the eco-level of the product. The firm sets the change variables for eco-level and price under the rule that was selected by the firm. The rule candidates are as in Table 2.

Table 2. Rule candidates for the processing firm.

Rule number	Change variable of price-level	Change variable of eco-level
1	0	0
2	0	1
3	0	−1
4	1	0
5	1	1
6	1	−1
7	−1	0
8	−1	1
9	−1	−1

The eco-level $E_{fj}(t)$ and price level $P_{fj}(t)$ of the j-th processing firm at period t are adjusted under its own selected rule. These variables are positive integers that do not exceed 10. The base price of the product is P_{Pbase}.

The processing firm decides the volume of product for sale in each period, considering the demand (sold volume) $V_{PDfj}(t-1)$, the shortage $S_{PDfj}(t-1)$, the product waste $W_{Pfj}(t-1)$ over the specific period determined by the store from the previous period, and the stock $I_{Pfj}(t-1)$ that is in the store during the present period. The product volume $V_{Pfj}(t)$ of the j-th processing firm at period t is expressed using Eq. (7).

$$V_{Pfj}(t) = v_0 V_{PDfj}(t-1) + v_1 S_{PDfj}(t-1) - v_2 I_{Pfj}(t) - v_3 W_{Pfj}(t-1) \tag{7}$$

The processing firm orders the resources harvested at period t, considering the production volume and the resource loss rate of the processing firm. The resource loss rate $L_{fj}(t)$ and ordered resource volume $V_{RDfj}(t)$ of the j-th processing firm at period t are expressed by Eqs. (8) and (9), respectively.

$$L_{fj}(t) = 0.1 + (10 - E_{fj}(t))/10 \tag{8}$$

$$V_{RDfj}(t) = (1 + L_{fj}(t)) V_{Pfj}(t) \tag{9}$$

The resource loss volume is written as in Eq. (10).

$$W_{Rfj}(t) = L_{fj}(t) V_{Pfj}(t) \tag{10}$$

The profit $\Pi_{fj}(t)$ of the j-th processing firm at period t is expressed by Eq. (11), in the case that the processing firm purchases the harvested resources from the i-th harvesting firm.

$$\begin{aligned}
\Pi_{hi}(t) = {} & (1-m)(P_{Pbase} + P_{fj}(t)) V_{PDfj}(t) - P_{Rhi}(t) \, V_{RDfj}(t) \\
& - (1-b) c_{WP} W_{Pfj}(t) - c_{WR} W_{Rfj}(t) - c_E d_{Efj}(t) - c_{PS} d_{Sfj}(t)
\end{aligned} \tag{11}$$

In Eq. (11), m is a margin parameter for the store, and t b is the sharing rate for treating product wastes in the store. $W_{Pfj}(t)$ is the product waste volume of the j-th processing firm that occurred in the store, and c_{WP} is a parameter of the unit cost for the treatment of product waste. As in Eq. (6), c_{WR} is a parameter concerned with the unit cost for treating resource waste. In Eq. (11), c_E is a parameter of the unit cost for improving environmental management by one level, and c_{PS} is the penalty cost imposed by the store. Variables $d_{Efj}(t)$ and $d_{Sfj}(t)$ are dummy variables that express the levelling-up of the eco-level and the existing shortage, respectively.

At interval T of a certain period, the processing firm evaluates the average value of the aggregated profits of all rules and selects a new rule via reinforcement learning.

3.6 Store

In this model, the number of stores is set at only 1. All products made by all of the processing firms are displayed. The product is removed from the shelf after a certain period T_w, as determined by the store. The product displayed on the shelf will be displayed during the next period if the product is not sold out beforehand. The freshness of the unsold product decreases with time.

The store acquires its margins from the sale of products and receives penalty payments from processing firms for product shortage. Although the store pays the cost of treating product waste, the processing firm is claimed a certain rate of payment calculated with regard to the volume of product wasted.

The profit $\Pi_S(t)$ of the store is expressed by Eq. (12). In Eq. (12), the first term is sales income, the second is penalty income, and the third is the treatment income of product waste.

$$\Pi_S(t) = \sum m \, P_{fj}(t) V_{PDfj}(t) + \sum c_{PS} d_{Sfj}(t) - \sum b \, c_{WP} W_{Pfj}(t) \qquad (12)$$

3.7 Consumer

The consumer follows the preference rule of a product, which determines the priority for selection: low price, freshness, and a high eco-level. The candidates for the rule of preference are given in Table 3, where the higher the priority variable, the higher the priority for selection.

Table 3. Rule candidates for the consumer

Rule number	Priority value		
	Low price	Freshness	High eco-level
1	3	2	1
2	3	1	2
3	2	3	1
4	2	1	3
5	1	3	2
6	1	2	3

The consumer searches and selects a product according to this rule. When the selected product is no longer available, the consumer cannot make a purchase and informs the store of the shortage. Consumers know the average values for price, freshness, and eco-level of the products displayed in the store. The consumer calculates the utility, considering the priority value of the chosen product and the difference between the purchased factor and the average value. The profit $\Pi_{ck}(t)$ of the k-th consumer at period t is expressed in Eq. (13). In Eq. (13), d_{ck} is a dummy variable concerning whether the consumer buys the product or not, uC is a unit utility, and $U_{ck}(t)$ is a priority variable shown in Table 3. $D_{ck}(t)$ is a calculated variable of the difference between its own level and the average.

$$\Pi_{ck}(t) = d_{ck} \, u_C \, U_{ck}(t) + D_{ck}(t) \qquad (13)$$

At interval T of a certain period, the consumer evaluates the average value of the aggregated profits of all the rules and selects a new rule under reinforcement learning.

3.8 End Condition

In this model, although the maximum period is set as T_{max}, the simulation ends if the value for the amount of natural resource reaches zero.

4 Simulation Results of the Basic Model

4.1 Parameters of the Simulation

The model was implemented in Java. The parameters used in the simulation are listed in Table 4. In the simulation of the basic model, it is assumed that firms do not seriously consider the volume of waste when determining the volume of production. It is also assumed that the costs of treating waste is low.

Table 4. Parameters

Parameter	Values of parameters
Number of agents	$N_h = 10$, $N_f = 20$, $N_c = 1000$
Initial resource, Maximum volume	$R(0) = 5000000$, Rmax = 5000000
Reproduction rate of the resource	$r_p = 0.04$
Rate of sustainable resource	$r_{sus} = 0.8$
Premium price of certified resource	$p_{sus} = 0.5$
Unit cost parameters	$c_A = 100$, $c_{WR} = 0.01$, $c_{WP} = 0.01$, $c_E = 500$, $c_{PS} = 0.5$
Parameters in production function	$v_0 = 1.0$, $v_1 = 1.5$, $v_2 = 0.5$, $v_3 = 0$,
Margin of the sales	$m = 0.3$
Sharing rate of treating product wastes	$b = 0.5$
Unit utility of the consumer	$u_c = 2.0$
Base price of resource and product	$P_{Rbase} = 3.0$, $P_{Pbase} = 10.0$
Period of removal from the shelf at store	$T_w = 3$
Interval of periods for learning	$T = 5$
Maximum simulation period	$T_{max} = 500$

4.2 Simulation Results: Two Patterns

The simulation was implemented 20 times. Two patterns were observed (see Fig. 2).

The first is a pattern in which resources were depleted early. The second is a pattern in which resources were sustained. The first pattern appeared 13 times out of 20 simulations, and the second pattern appeared 7 times. In simulation No. 1 of the first pattern, the resource decreased at the fastest rate, and in simulation No. 2, the resource decreased most slowly. In simulation No. 0 of the second pattern, the resource grew the fastest, and in simulation No. 19, the resource grew most slowly.

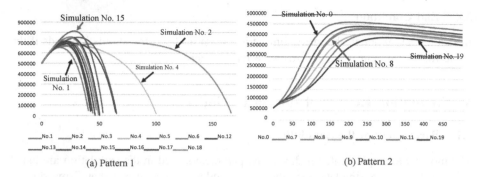

(a) Pattern 1   (b) Pattern 2

Fig. 2. Two patterns found in the simulation results for the basic model.

4.3   Simulation Results: Comparison of Two Typical Cases

Two cases are compared in the following: simulation No. 15 as a typical case of the first pattern, and simulation No. 8 as a typical pattern of the second pattern.

Figure 3 shows the time change in the aggregated profit of the processing firm in both cases. In pattern 1, Firm12 and Firm 16 gained profits rapidly, although the aggregated profit of the other firms was decreasing. In pattern 2, the aggregated profit of all the processing firms were decreasing.

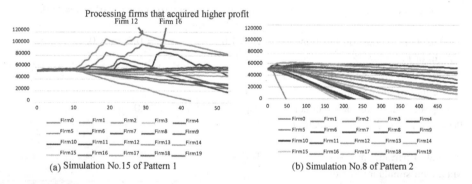

(a) Simulation No.15 of Pattern 1   (b) Simulation No.8 of Pattern 2

Fig. 3. Time change of the aggregated profit of the processing firm in both patterns.

Figure 4 shows the time change in the aggregated profit for the harvesting firm in both cases. In pattern 1, the aggregated profit of the harvesting firm increased gradually. In pattern 2, the aggregated profit of the harvesting firm decreased gradually.

Figure 5 compares the time change in averages of price and eco-levels of the product supplied during each period to the store by the processing firm for both cases. In pattern 1, although the average price level increased and reached the maximum level, it subsequently decreased to the lowest level gradually, while the average eco-level remained at a lower level and converged at the lowest level. In pattern 2, the average eco-level converged at the highest level, while the average price level converged at the lowest level.

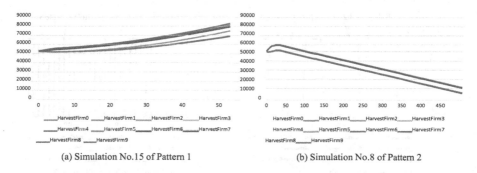

(a) Simulation No.15 of Pattern 1   (b) Simulation No.8 of Pattern 2

Fig. 4. Time change of the aggregated profit of the harvesting firm in both patterns.

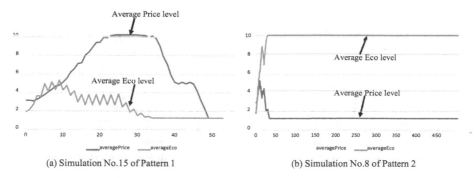

(a) Simulation No.15 of Pattern 1   (b) Simulation No.8 of Pattern 2

Fig. 5. Time changes of the average levels of the product in both patterns.

Figure 6 compares the time change for the rules selected by the processing firms. In simulation No. 15 of the first pattern, Rule 3 and Rule 7 were repeated after Rule 4 and Rule 6 were selected. Rule 3 is the rule in which the price is not changed and the eco-level is lowered. Rule 7 is the rule in which the price is lowered and the eco-level is not changed. In simulation No. 8 of the second pattern, Rule 2 and Rule 8 were repeated to the end period. Rule 2 is the rule in which the price is not changed and the eco-level is raised. Rule 8 is the rule in which the price is lowered and the eco-level is raised.

Figure 7 compares the time change of rules No. 1 and No. 2 selected by the harvesting firms. In pattern 1, the rule converged at Harvest-rule No. 1, under which the harvesting firm does not take certification. In pattern 2, the rule converged at Harvest-rule No. 2, under which the harvesting firm takes certification. In Fig. 7, rule No. 3 was omitted, because it converged at zero in both cases.

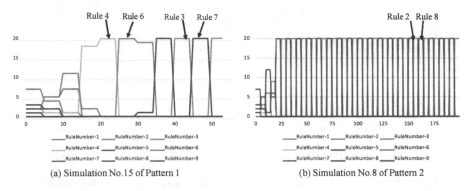

(a) Simulation No.15 of Pattern 1   (b) Simulation No.8 of Pattern 2

Fig. 6. Time change of the rules selected by the processing firm in both patterns.

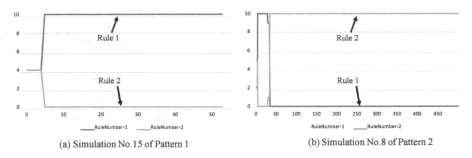

(a) Simulation No.15 of Pattern 1   (b) Simulation No.8 of Pattern 2

Fig. 7. Time change of the rules selected by the harvesting firm in both patterns.

In both cases, the rules of the consumer did not converge and remained diverse. This figure is therefore omitted from this paper.

Figure 8 shows the time change for the profit of the store for each period. In both cases, the profit of the store increased rapidly and stayed at a certain level. Comparing the two cases, it is found that the store profit in simulation No. 15 of pattern 1 is higher than that of simulation No. 8 of pattern 2.

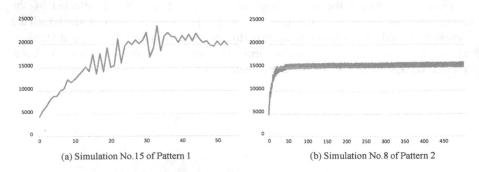

(a) Simulation No.15 of Pattern 1   (b) Simulation No.8 of Pattern 2

Fig. 8. Time change of the store profit for every period in both patterns.

Figure 9 shows the time change for the product waste that occurred in the store. In both cases, the volume of product waste increased. Comparing the two cases, it is apparent that the volume of product waste in simulation No. 15 of pattern 1 is higher than that in simulation No. 8 of pattern 2. In simulation No. 8 of pattern 2, the value converged at approximately 1,800.

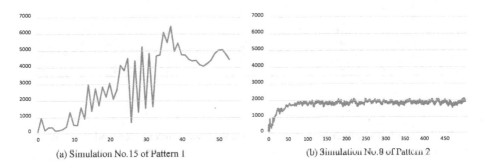

(a) Simulation No.15 of Pattern 1   (b) Simulation No.8 of Pattern 2

Fig. 9. Time change of the product waste that occurred in the store for both patterns.

4.4   Simulation Results: Converged Rules of Agents in Both Patterns

Table 5 shows the converged rules of the harvesting firm in both patterns.

In all cases of pattern 2 in which the resource was sustainable, the rules of the harvesting firm converged at No. 2 under which the harvesting firm takes certification. In 11 cases of pattern 1 in which the resource was exhausted, the rules of the harvesting firm converged at No. 1 under which the harvesting firm does not receive certification. In simulations of No. 2 and No. 4 of pattern 1, the rule converged at No. 2. In these two cases the resource was exhausted after the 100th period, while it was exhausted at approximately the 50th period in the other cases of pattern 1.

Table 5. Converged rules of the harvesting firm in the two patterns

Rule Number	Contents of rule		Number of occurrences as convergence	
	Certification	Value	Pattern 1	Pattern 2
1	No	0	11	0
2	Yes	1	2	7
3	Random	1 or 0 at random	0	0

Table 6 shows the converged rules of the processing firm in both patterns.

In pattern 1, in which the resource was exhausted, rules under which the eco-level is not changed or lowered were selected. In the pattern 2, in which the resource was sustainable, rules under which the eco-level is raised were selected.

Table 6. Converged rules of the processing firm in the two patterns

Rule Number	Change variable		Number of occurrences as convergence	
	Price-level	Eco-level	Pattern 1	Pattern 2
1	0	0	2	0
4	1	0	3	0
7	-1	0	4	1
3	0	-1	4	1
6	1	-1	3	0
9	-1	-1	2	0
2	0	1	1	5
5	1	1	0	1
8	-1	1	1	5

With regards to consumers, the rule did not show convergence and was diverse in all 20 simulations.

5 Discussion

5.1 Possibility of the Two Kinds of the Society

From the results of the simulation the basic model, two patterns were obtained, representing the possibility of two kinds of society.

The first is the pattern where neither the harvesting firm nor the processing firm select the environmentally conscious rules, leading to the exhaustion of resources. The second is the pattern of resource sustainability where both the harvesting firm and the processing firm follow environmentally conscious rules.

As a result, in the first pattern the resource was depleted rapidly and was not sustained, although all harvesting firms and some processing firms gained profit. In the second pattern the resource reached sustainable levels, while the economy cannot be regarded as sustainable because the profits of both the processing firm and the harvesting firm decreased.

In both patterns, although the store gained profit, product waste occurred. The amount of product waste in pattern 1 was greater than that in pattern 2.

5.2 Validity of the Basic Model

The results from the simulation of the basic model show that two different kinds of society can occur. One is a society where resources are exhausted early due to the action of harvesting resources and manufacturing without considering sustainability. The other is a society where sustainable management is carried out in both resource harvesting and manufacturing and as a result the society is sustainable.

Trade-offs between the economy and the environment occur in the real world and measures have been considered to avoid this. The basic model can therefore be assumed as valid because it represents a practically possible society.

In addition, the level of product waste in the sustainable society is smaller than that in the society where resources are exhausted. Such results can be considered to illustrate a link in the sustainable management between several processes in the supply chain. In this research one of the purposes was to provide a model to represent the link between the sustainable management of a resource and the waste of the resource. The basic model is also valid from this point of view.

5.3 Implications of the Simulation Results

From the results of the simulation, it was demonstrated that compliance with an appropriate level for gathering by the harvesting firm ensures sustainability in the management of resources, and indicates that a certification system is effective for the management of sustainable resources.

However, in all cases, product waste occurs at the store, and it is suggested that measures for decreasing waste at this point in the process should be taken simultaneously. In addition, the preferences of the consumer remained diverse in all simulations. It can be considered that the environmental education of consumers is therefore necessary.

6 Applications to Scenario Analysis and to Gaming Simulation

6.1 Application to Scenario Analysis

The basic model can be modified by changes to the parameters or the introduction of new roles for agents. However, before scenario analysis, an analysis of the sensitivity of the parameters is necessary to design a robust basic model. This includes a re-examination of the number of agents. In the basic model the number of agents is fixed. Even if a harvesting or processing firm goes bankrupt, it does not exit the market and no new firms occur. For applied models, the entry and exit of firms will be introduced. The number of stores and consumers included can also be re-considered.

Scenario analysis can be implemented in order to consider measures for resource management and food loss, which are the main objectives of this research. The following three applied models will be considered. First, the storage period is changed. In the basic model, products displayed in the store are wasted after the 3 periods following production. In an applied model, the storage period is extended. This applied model corresponds to a re-examination of the practice of the "one-third rule" that is implemented by businesses in Japan. Second, a financial penalty to be imposed on a processing firm if a product is sold out will be considered. This can be expressed as changes to the parameter for cost. Third, environmental policies, such as a tax against the production of large volumes of waste, subsidies for environmental measures, and the promotion of purchase of environmentally friendly products, will be added to the design of applied models.

6.2   Application to Gaming Simulation

Two types of gaming simulation can be designed based on the ABM used in this research. One is a gaming simulation for consumer education and the other is for business gaming.

In this basic model, the preference of the consumer remains diverse after the learning process among agents. A gaming simulation can be designed to find out the effects of consumer behavior. Participants are divided into several groups and the portfolio of priority rules for the selection of products are determined as in Table 3. Each group implements a simulation under the condition that the initial rate of consumer rules is determined by the portfolio of the group. Participants compete whether the simulated society is sustainable or not. Participants are then facilitated to discuss the differences in the results and to consider factors that could lead to a sustainable society.

Business gaming using this ABM can be designed as a hybrid between the human agent and an AI agent. Lee and Deguchi [16] produced leading research on hybrid gaming. The participant enters as a firm agent and decides a rule at each period in the simulation. They then compete the extent for sustainability of the society. It is necessary to design a human interface for hybrid gaming.

The Beer Game and the Bakery Game are well known business gaming systems concerning the management of supply chain. The former was developed in the MIT Sloan School of Management and the latter in Yokohama Business Games of Yokohama National University. Although those games do not include natural resource management, gaming based on this ABM include both natural resource and waste management for an economically and environmentally sustainable society.

7   Conclusions

This study was carried out to develop an agent-based model including both supply chain and resource management in order to investigate the effects of changing business rules and policy. In this paper, the basic model was suggested and the results of its simulation were demonstrated. Two patterns were obtained from the simulations of the basic model. The first pattern showed that the resource depletes rapidly and the economy is not sustainable. The second pattern demonstrated the situation where a resource reaches a sustainable level, but the society is not sustained economically. In both patterns, product waste occurred in the store, although the levels of product waste were different. It can be said that the basic model can reproduce an accurate situation of the trade-off between the environment and the economy.

For further research, the following three challenges must be overcome to improve the basic model and for its application for the sustainable design of society. The first is to incorporate parameter settings into the basic model for sensitivity analysis that can create a more robust model. The second is to incorporate settings for a scenario analysis that can investigate the measures and policies against current business practice such as the "one third rule" and penalties for creating product shortage. The third is to construct a gaming simulation based on the agent-based model. Two types of gaming simulation can be created for consumer education and hybrid business gaming with interaction between the human agent and the computer agent.

Acknowledgements. The author wishes to acknowledge the financial supports of a Japan Society for the Promotion of Science (JSPS) KAKENHI Grant-in-Aid for Scientific Research (C) (Grant Number 18K11764).

References

1. Botkin, D.B., Edward, A.K.: Environmental Science: Earth as a Living Planet, 8th edn. Wiley, Hoboken (2011)
2. Food and Agriculture Organization of the United Nations: Global food losses and food waste; Extent, causes and prevention, Rome, Italy (2011). http://www.fao.org/3/mb060e/mb060e00.htm
3. Heckbert, S., Baynes, T., Reeson, A.: Agent-based modeling in ecological economics. Ann. N. Y. Acad. Sci. Issue Ecol. Econ. Rev. **1185**, 39–53 (2010). https://doi.org/10.1111/j.1749-6632.2009.05286.x
4. Zaima, K.: Agent-based modeling for designing the environmental conscious society: a review and future researches. (Kankyo-hairyo-kata shakai wo dezainsuru agent-based modeling: Kenkyu no genjou to kongo no kadai). Oper. Res. **53**(12), 678–685 (2008). https://ci.nii.ac.jp/naid/110007005004. (in Japanese)
5. Kuscsik, Z., Horváth, D., Gmitra, M.: The critical properties of the agent-based model with environmental-economic interaction. Phys. A **379**, 199–206 (2007). https://doi.org/10.1016/j.physa.2007.01.003
6. Matthews, R.B., Gilbert, N.G., Roach, A., Polhill, J.G., Gotts, N.M.: Agent-based land-use models: a review of applications. Landscape Ecol. **22**(10), 1447–1459 (2007). https://doi.org/10.1007/s10980-007-9135-1
7. Mosler, H.-J., Martens, T.: Designing environmental campaigns by using agent-based simulations: strategies for changing environmental attitudes. J. Environ. Manag. **88**, 805–816 (2008). https://doi.org/10.1016/j.jenvman.2007.04.013
8. Janssen, M.A., Jager, W.: Simulating diffusion of green products: co-evolution between firms and consumers. J. Evol. Econ. **12**, 283–306 (2002). https://link.springer.com/article/10.1007/s00191-002-0120-1
9. Zaima, K.: Effects of structural and behavioral strategies toward the environmentally conscious society: agent based approach. In: Terano, T., Kita, H., Kaneda, T., Arai, K., Deguchi, H. (eds.) Agent-Based Simulation from Modeling Methodologies to Real-World Applications, vol. 1, pp. 233–246. Springer, Tokyo (2005). https://doi.org/10.1007/4-431-26925-8_21
10. Zaima, K.: Agent-based simulation on the diffusion of research and development for environmentally conscious products. In: Arai, K., Deguchi, H., Matsui, H. (eds.) Agent-Based Modeling Meets Gaming Simulation. ASS, vol. 2, pp. 119–138. Springer, Tokyo (2005). https://doi.org/10.1007/4-431-29427-9_12
11. Schwoon, M.: Simulating the adoption of fuel cell vehicles. J. Evol. Econ. **16**, 435–472 (2006). https://doi.org/10.1007/s00191-006-0026-4
12. Zhang, T., Gensler, S., Garcia, R.: A study of the diffusion of alternative fuel vehicles: an agent-based modeling approach. J. Prod. Innov. Manag. **28**, 152–168 (2011). https://doi.org/10.1111/j.1540-5885.2011.00789.x

13. Kiesling, E., Gunther, M., Stummer, C., Wakolbinger, L.M.: Agent-based simulation of innovation diffusion: a review. CEJOR **20**(2), 183–230 (2012). https://doi.org/10.1007/s10100-011-0210-y

14. Yamagata, Y., Mizuta, H.: Agent-based simulation on Kyoto Protocol and global emission permits. (Kyouto-giteisho to okusai haishuturyou torihiki no e-jentobesu simulaishon). Oper. Res. **46**(10), 555–560 (2001). (in Japanese)

15. Zaima, K.: Conditions to diffuse green management into SMEs and the role of knowledge support: agent-based modeling. J. Adv. Comput. Intell. Intell. Inform. (JACIII) **17**(2), 252–262 (2013). https://doi.org/10.20965/jaciii.2013.p0252

16. Lee, H., Deguchi, H.: The gaming of firm strategy in high-tech industry: human agents and artificial intelligence agents intermingled in a simulation model. In: Arai, K., Deguchi, H., Matsui, H. (eds.) Agent-Based Modeling Meets Gaming Simulation. ASS, vol. 2, pp. 31–38. Springer, Tokyo (2005). https://doi.org/10.1007/4-431-29427-9_4

Wonders of the World Simulation Program by Virtual Reality

Naraphol Deechuay[✉], Ratchadawan Nimnual, Panya Makasorn,
and Supanat Permpoon

King Mongkut's University of Technology, Thonburi, Bangkhuntien, Bangkok
10150, Thailand
ratchadawan.nim@kmutt.ac.th, iratnual@chaiyo.com

Abstract. Wonders of the World Simulation Program by Virtual Reality was
created to design and build up four 3D tourist destination models, namely, Eiffel
Tower, Petra, Great Pyramid of Giza, and Stonehenge. Unreal Engine 4 was
used to simulate these locations and their surroundings in order to help tourists
select a destination for their vacation. Twenty samples were recruited to participate in this study, based on a voluntary basis. The results demonstrated that
the participants were very satisfied with the appropriateness of the models in the
scenes (mean = 4.6/SD = 0.50). The simple operating system was highly rated
among the experts (mean = 4.5/SD = 0.75). The atmospheric features, sound
effects, and simulated scenes of these four Wonders, in general, provided users
novel experiences and realistic feelings.

Keywords: Wonder word · Simulation and Virtual Reality

1 Introduction

There are several tourist destinations scattering around the world. The information
about those places can be conveniently retrieved in order to decide for traveling during
vacations. Oftentimes, the journeys can be impeded due to in accurate available
information, inconvenient transportation, and limited budgets. Virtual Reality (VR) has
been introduced to implement entertaining experiences by generating realistic feelings
to users. This leads to the creation of Wonders of the World with VR. Unreal Engine 4
is used to simulate these Wonders through VR. Traveling to one location requires
planning processes and raises many concerns, such as budgets, means of transportation,
time, desirable destinations, and mishaps during journeys. Consulting various sources,
for example, Google Street View, YouTube 360, traveling reviews, and destination
photos.

2 Literature Review

Virtual Reality (VR) is one of the recent technological integration [1]. VR allows
learners to explore and broaden their knowledge through 3D virtual simulation [2–4].
The VR integration has attracted researchers to examine and develop VR software for

M. Wardaszko et al. (Eds.): ISAGA 2019, LNCS 11988, pp. 441–446, 2021.
https://doi.org/10.1007/978-3-030-72132-9_37

medical education, such as anatomy [5], surgery [6], and [7]. Prior studies have focused on a single dimension of the integrated contents, particularly anatomical learning [7–10]. In Thailand, VR have been applied to certain educational development, such as engineering and general education [11–13].

3 Material and Methodology

The data collected in the current study were collected through a survey. In order to accurately validate contents and reliability of the survey, the designing processes are illustrated as follows (Fig. 1 and Table 1).

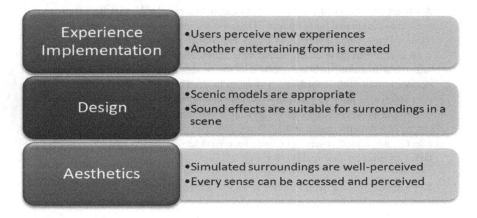

Fig. 1. The design process of the Wonder World Simulation Program.

Table 1. The satisfaction of the participants towards the Wonders of the World Simulation Program by Virtual Reality.

Measured factor	Categories	Indicators	Scales
Wonders of the World Simulation Program by Virtual Reality	Experience implementation	Users perceive new experiences	Mean
		Another entertaining form is created	Mean
		Feelings after testing	Mean
	Design	Scenic models are appropriate	Mean
		Sound effects are suitable for surroundings in a scene	Mean
	Aesthetics	Simulated surroundings are well-perceived	Mean
		Every sense can be accessed and perceived	Mean

The Wonders of the World Simulation Program by Virtual Reality was tested by the participants, aged ranging from below 15, 15–19, and 20–29 years old. The satisfaction questionnaire was distributed after the testing process. The test results from the participants are summarized as follows (Figs. 2 and 3):

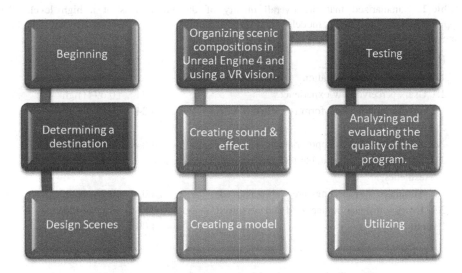

Fig. 2. The diagram of the VR WOW processes.

Fig. 3. Wonders of the World Simulation.

4 The Results

(See Tables 2 and 3).

Table 2. Summarized that the overall quality of the program is at a high level. The appropriateness of the models arranged in the scenes is rated the highest (mean = 4.6/SD = 0.50).

Evaluation questions	(mean)	S.D.	Quality level
1. Experience implementation			
1.1 Users perceive new experiences	4.2	0.69	High
1.2 Another entertaining form is created	4.04	0.82	High
2. Design			
2.1. Scenic models are appropriate	4.6	0.50	Very high
2.2. Sound effects are suitable for surroundings in a scene	4	0.45	High
3. Aesthetics			
3.1. Simulated surroundings are well-perceived	4.05	0.75	High
3.2. Every sense can be accessed and perceived	3.65	0.93	Moderate
Overall	4.09	0.18	High

Table 3. Shown that the overall quality of the program is at a moderate level. The simple and easy-to-use system is rated the highest (mean = 4.5/SD − 0.75). In the mean-time, the sound effects compatible with the scenes, the model arrangement, and the beauty of the scenes obtain the lowest rates (mean = 3.5/SD − 0.70).

Evaluation questions	x (mean)	S.D.	Quality level
1. Design			
1.1 Scenic compositions are appropriate	4	0	High
1.2 Sound effects are suitable for scenic surroundings	3.5	0.70	Moderate
1.3 Model arrangements generate realistic feelings	3.5	0.70	Moderate
2. Artworks and illustrations			
2.1. Scenic models are compatible with scenes	3.5	0.70	Moderate
2.2. Scenes are beautifully designed and illustrated	3.5	0.70	Moderate
2.3. Models and textures are realistic	4	1.41	High
3. Operating system			
3.1. The system is simple and easy-to-use	4.5	0.75	High
3.2. The program functions effectively	4	0	High
3.3. Scene shifting works smoothly - without lagging or freezing	4	0	High

5 Conclusion

The Wonders of the World Simulation Program by Virtual Reality was tested and evaluated by twenty participants. The quality evaluation consisted of Experience implementation, Design, and Aesthetics. The test results manifest that, among the participants, the appropriateness of the model in the scenes was reported very satisfying. Moreover, the novel experience generation, the sound effects compatible with the scenic surroundings, the sensory perceptions towards the surrounding simulation, the new form of media entertainment, and the accessibility of sensory perceptions were rated at a moderate level. Regarding the experts' evaluations, the appropriateness of the scenic compositions, the realistic models and textures, the simple and easy-to-use system, the effectively functioning program, and the smoothly scene shifting were rated at a high level. The sound effects and model arrangements were appropriate to the scenes and surroundings. According to the findings, the program is, hence, considered practical and applicable for VR Wonders of the World travel.

References

1. Falah, J., Harrison, D.K., Wood, B., Evans, D.: The characterisation of an IT system to reduce the gap between information technology and medical education. In: International Conference on Manufacturing Research (ICMR), vol. 2, pp. 360–365 (2012)
2. Al Falah, S.F., Harrison, D.K., Charissis, V., Evans, D.: An investigation of a healthcare management system with the use of multimodal interaction and 3D simulation: a technical note. J. Enterp. Inf. Manage. **26**, 183–197 (2013)
3. Craig, A.B., Sherman, W.R., Will, J.D.: Developing Virtual Reality Applications, pp. 145–189. Elsevier, Amsterdam (2009)
4. Oestergaard, J., et al.: Instructor feedback versus no instructor feedback on performance in a laparoscopic virtual reality simulator: a randomized educational trial. BMC Med. Educ. **1**, 7 (2012)
5. Izard, S.G., Juanes Méndez, J.A., Palomera, P.R.: Virtual reality educational tool for human anatomy. J. Med. Syst. **41**(5), 1–6 (2017). https://doi.org/10.1007/s10916-017-0723-6
6. Pensieri, C., Pennacchini, M.: Overview: virtual reality in medicine. J. Virtual Worlds Res. **7**, 1 (2014)
7. Alahmari, K.A., Sparto, P.J., Marchetti, G.F., Redfern, M.S., Furman, J.M., Whitney, S.L.: Comparison of virtual reality based therapy with customized vestibular physical therapy for the treatment of vestibular disorders. IEEE Trans. Neural Syst. Rehabil. Eng. **22**(2), 389–399 (2014)
8. Falah, J., et al.: Virtual Reality medical training system for anatomy education. In: 2014 Science and Information Conference, pp. 752–758. IEEE (2014). https://doi.org/10.1109/sai.2014.6918271
9. Maresky, H.S., Oikonomou, A., Ali, I., Ditkofsky, N., Pakkal, M., Ballyk, B.: Virtual reality and cardiac anatomy: exploring immersive three-dimensional cardiac imaging, a pilot study in undergraduate medical anatomy education. Clin. Anat. **32**(2), 238–243 (2019). https://doi.org/10.1002/ca.23292

10. Marks, S., White, D., Singh, M.: Getting up your nose: a virtual reality education tool for nasal cavity anatomy. In: Proceedings of the Special Interest Group on Computer Graphics and Interactive Techniques (SIGGRAPH Asia 2017) Symposium on Education; Bangkok, Thailand, 27–30 November 2017. Art 1. Association for Computing Machinery (ACM), New York (2017)
11. Itsarachaiyot, Y., Pochanakorn, R., Nillahoot, N., Suthakorn, J.: Force acquisition on surgical instruments for virtual reality surgical training system. In: Proceedings of the 2011 International Conference on Computer Control and Automation (ICCCA 2011), Jeju Island, South Korea, 1–3 May 2011, pp. 173–176 (2011)
12. Lertkulvanich, S., Buranajant, N., Sombunsukho, S.: A development of portable three dimensional position data measurement device for character or object modeling in computer animation, pp. 38–40 (2011)
13. Nimnual, R., Suksakulchai, S.: Virtual reality for packaging folding practice. In: Proceedings of the International Conference on Control, Automation and Systems. Seoul, Korea (2007)

Framework and Application of Live Video Streaming as a Virtual Reality Gaming Technology: A Study of Function and Performance

Zhengyu Wang, Yousuf Al-Shorji, and Cevin Zhang$^{(\boxtimes)}$ (iD)

Division of Health Informatics and Logistics, KTH Royal Institute
of Technology, 14156 Huddinge, Sweden
chenzh@kth.se

Abstract. Live video streaming of outdoor and built environment could be a source of scenarios generations for training games, especially when scenarios are on real-time dynamics of the environment. Such so-called live virtual reality (LVR) is, among other things, one of the most recent gaming technologies. There is an increasing need for effective solutions that can be utilized to process videos in attempts to gain desirable result, as the requirement of video quality is becoming higher and higher. The issue at the core of real-time transcoding is to control the right combination of transmission bitrate and resolution. This work aims to develop a prototypical workflow for dewarping videos from fisheye camera to the cloud and re-stream it to a client. This prototype is used for testing combinations of bitrate and resolution in various living scenarios of indoor, outdoor and street traffic environments. The study of performance is enabled by KTH students who supply feedbacks about quality of experience. Comments of observers prove the promising use of LVR in training and education games. The results reveal that the combination of bitrate 3.5–4.5 Mbps and resolution 720p is best suited for transmission in order to avoid noticeable lagging.

Keywords: Virtual reality gaming · Live video streaming · Quality of experience

1 Introduction

Training curriculum providers are working towards high-fidelity scenarios in game-based learning. Facilitators in simulation gaming sessions may have to consume paramount time and resources for instrumental development [1]. However, the perception of games may still be unsatisfactory because active learning and immersive experience are not evident [2]. Computer-assisted instruction is introduced in order to fulfill the growing requirement of quality experience.

Traditional spreadsheet-based and static training scenarios are entitled to some concerns for not bringing in the dynamics of the real world into the competency development of participants. Although the efficiency could benefit from the nature of being a problem-based solving exercise [3], a lack of visual explanation might hinder

© Springer Nature Switzerland AG 2021
M. Wardaszko et al. (Eds.): ISAGA 2019, LNCS 11988, pp. 447–457, 2021.
https://doi.org/10.1007/978-3-030-72132-9_38

the participants from establishing a mental connection with the model and therefore hurts the quality of training. On the part of role-play field studies, the environment might not be sufficiently safe for being qualified or might be subject to the low return of investments. Meanwhile, there is a need to provide multiple scenarios as approaching reality, but such practices of utilizing actual resources might not be flexible to obtain a training efficiency in the making.

Virtual, augmented and mixed reality are being used in logistics and medical training that require a workforce of safety and operation management [4, 5]. With computer-assisted visualization and processing, the potential of such emerging technologies is enormous to increase the quality of experience and therefore training efficiency [6]. With reality-related instruments properly designed and transcoded, the participants can be reasonably challenged to develop the skillset but without any risks of the real dynamic work.

Live virtual reality (LVR) is a powerful tool with apparent advantages in situations where a panoramic view and an interactive live action is desired, including warehouse monitors and live broadcasting at sports events. By live streaming from multiple fisheye cameras simultaneously to a Real Time Messaging Protocol (RTMP) or Real Time Streaming Protocol (RTSP) server, which transcodes the distorted pictures, even a 360-degree live broadcasting view can be obtained. In virtual reality scenarios that could be used by high-fidelity simulation game, but problematic user experiences might rise as long as the received video had been unsuitably dewarped by incompetent algorithms or methods transmission, or speed of the live streaming video from the cameras to the server had been inappropriately configured.

This contribution is to develop a technological framework and a complete prototypical solution for streaming live video from a 180-degree fisheye lens camera to a cloud game server with functions of undistortion and upstreaming the perspective videos to virtual reality games.

2 Products to Support Live Virtual Reality Deployment

At Stellaton AB, one of the Swedish startups working on computer vision and cutting-edge video technologies, there is a rough industrial idea of such a live streaming solution. To handle the critical function of LVR, a prototype of a dewarping application has previously been developed, with the help of open-source tools including Open Graphics Library (OpenGL) and OpenGL Shading Language (GLSL), see Fig. 1. The application receives a video stream from the fisheye camera as input, uses GLSL together with the OpenGL library to dewarp the video and sends undistorted video as output. The algorithm processes an image as a matrix and applies the values of the undistorted matrix to correct the image. The work emphasizes the video quality and user experience of the final product. The evaluation of the system is to be carried out under various conditions such as in-house built environment, road traffic, and terrains. The evaluation should take parameters, such as bitrates and resolutions of both input and output video streams, into consideration.

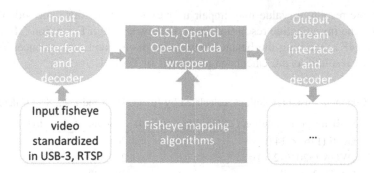

Fig. 1. Workflow of the live streaming solution at Stellaton AB

2.1   Comparison Between RTMP and RTSP Live Streaming Servers

The standard protocols of live streaming, for the time being, are RTMP and RTSP. RTMP is for high-performance transmissions of both audio and video between Adobe Flash Platforms [7]. This protocol uses TCP at the transport node and allows three variations: simple RTMP, which operates on TCP and uses port 1935; RTMPT (RTMP tunneled), which is encapsulated in Hypertext Transfer Protocol (HTTP), requests to overpass firewalls; and RTMP Secure, which operates as RTMP but with a secure Hypertext Transfer Protocol Secure (HTTPS) connection [8].

RTSP is a no-connection-oriented protocol to stream real-time data that defines how the information is delivered between the client and the server. RTSP allows for the transmission of previous stored or live multimedia content, defining different connection types and sets of requirements to guarantee that the data is sent over Internet Protocol networks as efficiently as possible. Independent from the transport protocol, RTSP may operate on User Datagram Protocol (UDP) or Transmission Control Protocol (TCP). Nevertheless, in the majority of cases, the TCP protocol is used to control the player and the UDP protocol for RTP data transmission. In a session, a client can establish and interrupt reliable transport connections with the server using RTSP requests. The cache function of the proxy server is also suitable for RTSP, as RTSP owns the ability to redirect and select the proper server based on its load capacities, to avoid network delay by overloading on a single server. Although RTSP operates like HTTP/1.1, it does not highlight simultaneous transmission but has excellent tolerance of network delay [9].

2.2   Defining Bitrate, Resolution and Frame Rate

Live streaming video in most situations operates at a constant bitrate (CBR) of about 2 Mbps for high-quality contents. However, variable bitrate (VBR) generally supplies more superior video quality than CBR in practice. As a rule of thumb, the bitrate is proportional to the video quality, i.e., the higher bitrate, the better quality, but the effect abides by the law of diminishing marginal utility [10].

The increasing resolution, which is the size of a video frame, may increase the video quality if the frame rate and clarity remain unchanged; otherwise, solely a more considerable resolution value may impair user experience of the same video [11]. In this study, the investigative resolution range is between High Definition (HD) and 4K resolution (4K) regarding the balance between economy and performance. The commonly used resolutions are calculated and listed in Table 1.

Table 1. Commonly used resolutions, calculated by Image Type and Data Size Calculator [12]

RGB Image Resolution (24-bit, 3 bytes/pixel)	Amount of data (byte)
QCIF (176 × 144)	76,032
QVGA (320 × 240)	230,400
CIF (352 × 288)	304,128
VGA (640 × 480)	921,600
SVGA (800 × 600)	1,440,000
SD-PAL (720 × 576)	1,244,160
SD_NTSC (720 × 480)	1,036,800
HD (1280 × 720)	2,764,800
FHD (1920 × 1080)	6,220,800
UHD/4K (3840 × 2160)	24,883,200
8K (7680 × 4320)	99,532,800

3 Methodology

This section elaborates methodology, solving methods and tooling. The system should consist of a camera, a server and a client with seamless integration. Figure 2 shows how the different components should be organized. The server prototype needs to receive a video stream from the camera, process real-time the video and live stream it to the client. Various ready-to-use media servers can receive streams and re-stream the streams to clients. However, the problem is that such servers offer no functions of video processing which is critical for its LVR usage potential.

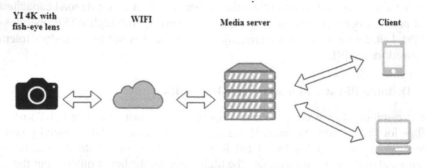

YI 4K with fish-eye lens   WIFI   Media server   Client

Fig. 2. System architecture diagram

3.1   Server Development

The server works as both receiver and sender with receiving raw data, i.e. video from the camera, undistorting the video by OpenCV and sending the video again by FFmpeg to the video player. To allow the server to receive a stream from a camera, it needs to be provided with the RTMP module. The server with RTMP module is installed on an Ubuntu Linux host running on a cloud server. The transmission of processed frames is carried out with the help of the Linux pipeline system. In the configuration files of the server, OpenCV library is applied together with the Python programming language; OpenCV makes it possible to receive and read a video stream in the form of the captured frames. Also, the NumPy library is also needed to offer support for multi-dimensional arrays and matrices.

The CameraMatrix and the Coefficients are determined when calibrating the fisheye camera. The processed frames are sent as raw data to the video player using FFmpeg. The FFmpeg command runs FFmpeg with several arguments that specify the input data and how the video and audio files are to be encoded and decoded.

3.2   Client Development

A client web application is developed for registering, logging in, generating & scanning QR-code, generating URL of live streaming and playing back the live streaming video in an embedded HTML5 player. This web application takes advantage of Java Servlet and Java Server Pages (JSP) for web page interactions, i.e. user management and Hibernate for MySQL database connection and CRUD operations. Users must enter several necessary parameters such as Wi-Fi SSID, password of the Wi-Fi network, URL of the RTMP server, resolution and bitrate to generate the QR-code in the web application; it is the camera that scans the code, extracts all the provided data in a JSON format and starts the Wi-Fi connection and live streaming to the target URL (see Fig. 3).

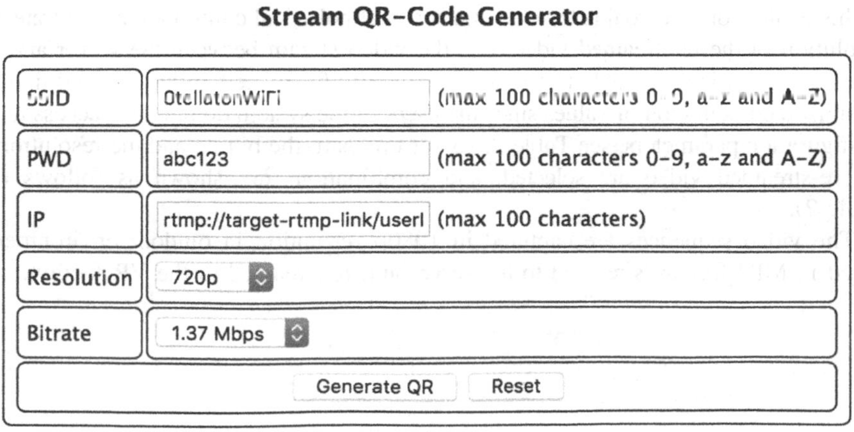

Stream QR-Code Generator

SSID	OtellatonWiFi	(max 100 characters 0-9, a-z and A-Z)
PWD	abc123	(max 100 characters 0-9, a-z and A-Z)
IP	rtmp://target-rtmp-link/userI	(max 100 characters)
Resolution	720p	
Bitrate	1.37 Mbps	
	Generate QR Reset	

Fig. 3.   QR-code generation

For the live streaming playbacks, a player framework Video.js is embedded in a JSP web page, and the RTMP live streaming URL with the type specified. The framework is Content Delivery Network enabled so that users only include two links referring to the source script of video.js in the web page. Video.js is also compatible for many other live streaming protocols including RTSP and HLS, and the protocols should be explicitly declared in the source tag like the above example. As to the panorama views, a plugin to Videojs "Videojs-panorama" is applied. Users are optional to drag the video on computers or tablets.

3.3   Subjective Evaluation

A subjective video quality evaluation is designed by applying the comparative performance analysis with Mean Opinion Score. The criteria for selecting the nine videos are different combinations of bitrates and resolutions of the input and output videos, the built environments for shooting the video sequences, and LVR experiences of scenarios.

Respectively, the aims are to determine the best combination for user experience in live streaming, understand the influences of various conditions for both static and dynamic video shootings and transmissions, and explore the possibility of using the videos for LVR technology based on their quality for constructing different bitrate and resolution combinations, selecting different environments and comparing different LVR experiences. In order to avoid bias during the surveys, the observers are met as both non-professionals of video/image processing or related domains, and young potential users of LVR products at ages between 20 and 40. The observers are prompted to watch each video sequence and rate each sequence by a score from 1 (poor) to 5 (excellent). Because most video samples are collected outdoor with unstable internet situations, the evaluation for outdoor scenarios in the VR survey has been carried out by live streaming the pre-recorded video samples. With Google Forms, two Absolute Category Rating style surveys are prepared and distributed as a link to the observers.

Evaluation Between the Server and the Player at the Client
In this evaluation, the goal is to select the best technological combination of bitrate and resolution of the re-streamed video, i.e., the video stream between the server and the client player. It is reasonable to test different values for related arguments and find the optimized combination of values since the users of the system do not have access to the configuration parameters, see Table 2. As for this part, the bitrate and the resolution of the re-streamed video are selected, and combinations are shown as follows (see Table 2).

The video sequences are captured in 1080p resolution in outdoor environments, saved in MP4 format, streamed to the server and re-streamed to the VR facility.

Table 2. Combination of bitrate and resolution for the evaluation between the server and client

# Combination	Bitrate	Resolution	Sample video sequence
1	2.0 Mbps–2.5 Mbps	1080p	Video 1
2	3.5 Mbps–4.5 Mbps	1080p	Video 2
3	5.5 Mbps–6.5 Mbps	1080p	Video 3
4	2.0 Mbps–2.5 Mbps	720p	Video 4
5	3.5 Mbps–4.5 Mbps	720p	Video 5
6	5.5 Mbps–6.5 Mbps	720p	Video 6

Evaluation of the Dewarping and LVR Effect

In this evaluation, the goal is to investigate the output of the dewarping function and the potential usage of the live streamed and dewarped videos for VR scenarios. The survey includes both three original videos from the fisheye lens and the similar three processed dewarped videos. The original video sequences and the dewarped sequences are shown in pair for the observers. The three scenarios are indoor parking place, outdoor lake and trees and street view of moving vehicles (See Table 3).

Table 3. Combination of bitrate and resolution for evaluation between the camera and server

# Scenario	Situation description
1	Indoor, parking place with structures of straight lines, moving automobiles and weak interior illuminations
2	Indoor, parking place with structures of straight lines, moving automobiles and weak interior illuminations
3	Streetview of buildings, moving vehicles and pedestrians

According to G. Blom [13], this work uses the most normal confidence level in practice, i.e. 95%. For each video sequence, the ratings of the observers, quantified from 1 to 5, are the sample data, and after that, the confidence interval has been calculated by the same confidence coefficient.

4 Results

With the help of the prototype, results are obtained as shown in Fig. 4 and 5. The result of previous works is shown for comparison. The original straight lines in the undistorted images look much straighter and reasonable than those in the previous works. In order to make the image look more as perspective, the undistorted images have been tailored more edge areas off, which makes them to fewer view scopes and thus less information than those of the current images.

Fig. 4. Result of the undistorting outdoor environment

Fig. 5. Result of the undistorting indoor built environment

For the part of dewarping function, the focus is user experience and suggestions about future LVR usage of the dewarped videos. Based on the theoretical foundation and the collected raw data from the survey, the confidence intervals of each video sequence are listed as follows (Table 4). Scenario Outdoor has 16 of 20 (80%) of the observers who agreed that the dewarped video could be used for VR purposes. Scenario Streetview has 15 of 20 (75%), and scenario Indoor has 12 of 20 (60%).

Table 4. Confidence intervals of the ratings on the three pairs of sample video sequences and opinions about LVR usage in the survey

# Scenario	Mean value (X)	Lower limit	Upper limit	LVR usage (Yes)	LVR usage (No)
1 Indoor	2.85	2.44	3.26	12	8
2 Outdoor	3.95	3.51	4.39	16	4
3 Streetview	3.10	2.65	3.55	15	5

The outdoor scenario, of the lake, trees, and rocks, is an entitled the best score. One possible interpretation is that human eyes are more sensitive to distortion of straight lines than that of already curved lines. In an outdoor environment, neither the water waves in the lake nor the profiles of trees and rocks are straight lines by nature, so that human brains expect the video images, after the dewarping, are still full of curved lines; whereas in indoor and streetview environments, there are a large number of straight lines and established patterns. Utterly the same opinions have been obtained when the observers are inquired whether these dewarped video sequences can be used for VR purposes: the Outdoor scenario is most suitable. The main reason is that the water surface is vast in the middle and occupied a majority of the video images so that after stitching the water surface seems continuous as if has never been cut in two parts before.

Typically, at least two 180-degree fisheye lenses are required to collect, stitch and reconstruct 3D panorama scenes for the playback, whereas only one 180-degree is proved to be useful in this work so that the dewarped images need to be stretch to the corners of each frame in the process of stitching. The observers also have written positive comments such as:

'The water movement is pretty clear.'
'The movement of vehicles seems as clear as that in a live show on TV.'
'The vehicles, the objects, and the buildings are clear enough to give an overview of the surrounding.'
'The colors and shapes of all objects in the video seem quite natural and vivid.'
...

These comments from a user survey demonstrate that live video streaming has tremendous potential usage for VR scenarios. The critical functions are a more precise calibration for the camera and a more efficient algorithm for undistortion. Camera calibration is needed in order to increase the sharpness of video images. On the computation side, due to the discard of peripheral areas of undistorted images, the valid areas of shown video images consequently contains less information than that of the original images and the edges of the processed video images look blurred after stitching, so that a more accurate algorithm for undistortion is on-demand in order to obtain an even more substantial proportion of remained valid image area than that of the previous industrial protocol.

5 Discussion and Future Work

In summary, a complete prototype solution, with functions of user management, QR-code generation, and video playback, has been developed based on complete open-source tools. The different point of using this technology for the virtual reality game is that scenarios could be obtained lively without reducing the video qualities. The major difference between previous research and this contribution is that the connection is from a 180-degree fisheye lens camera to a cloud game server. In this work, the performance of the result by the solution has been tested on three aspects: transmission of input and output video sequences, undistortion of images and playback of 3D panoramic scenes for future VR usage. As an output, the proper combination of bitrate and resolution, the suitable calibration arguments for undistortion as well as the causes of both the positive and the negative user experiences for 3D panoramic playback have been listed as the critical functions, which can be in line with previous works [14]. The defects found in the solution include the relatively unacceptable lagging of video playback, the blurred and overstretched video images as well as the error sporadically occurred during the playbacks in our own developed media player. Given more resources and time budgets, however, the defects above may be eliminated by increasing the number of fisheye lenses, developing own algorithms and libraries matching to the hardware and dewarped video formats. It is highly motivating that most feedback does not reflect upon the unnatural feeling to behave and communicate in this contribution's setup. This is due to the fact that only an easy-to-implement role playing mechanism is introduced for the player in the built environment. It needs to be kept in mind that that quality experience in gaming simulation is not subject to the visual aspect only, but more importantly, to put context with content is critical besides preventing delay and loss [15], which amongst other things, opens one of the interesting questions for future research.

The limitations of the current work exist mainly in the hardware side, undistortion algorithm and media player library as described, thus a suggestion to future works is

- Improve hardware, i.e. multiple lenses or larger than the 300-degree lens on a single camera.
- Embed 180-degree images in a 360-degree sphere, so that the images are not to be stretched when played back in a media player for 360-degree videos except that only 180-degree images are presented, but the rest of the sphere is in black.
- Develop an efficient algorithm for undistortion precisely based on the available hardware, which results in a better match and playback result after the dewarping process.
- Develop own JavaScript library for the media player that suits the specific format of the dewarped video by the undistortion algorithms described above.
- Perform experiments for camera calibration, image undistortion, more detailed survey questions and more precisely selected observers for the evaluation of the quality experience.

Acknowledgment. Funding and resource support from Stellaton AB are acknowledged for enabling this study.

References

1. Escher, C.: Field studies in simulation-based team training (2018)
2. Pedram, S., Perez, P., Palmisano, S., Farrelly, M.: A qualitative evaluation of the role of virtual reality as a safety training tool for the mining industry. In: Naweed, A., Wardaszko, M., Leigh, E., Meijer, S. (eds.) ISAGA/SimTecT -2016. LNCS, vol. 10711, pp. 188–200. Springer, Cham (2018). https://doi.org/10.1007/978-3-319-78795-4_14

3. Azer, S.A.: Problem-based learning: where are we now? Guide supplement 36.1 – viewpoint. Med. Teach. **33**(3), e121–e122 (2011)
4. Watcharasukarn, M., Page, S., Krumdieck, S.: Virtual reality simulation game approach to investigate transport adaptive capacity for peak oil planning. Transp. Res. Part A: Policy Pract. **46**(2), 348–367 (2012)
5. Kuehn, B.M.: Virtual and augmented reality put a twist on medical education. JAMA **319** (8), 756–758 (2018)
6. Bang, Y.-S., Son, K.H., Kim, H.J.: Effects of virtual reality training using Nintendo Wii and treadmill walking exercise on balance and walking for stroke patients. J. Phys. Ther. Sci. **28** (11), 3112–3115 (2016)
7. Lei, X., Jiang, X., Wang, C.: Design and implementation of streaming media processing software based on RTMP. In: 2012 5th International Congress on Image and Signal Processing (CISP), Chongqing, China, pp. 192–196 (2012)
8. Campo, W.Y., Arciniegas, J.L., García, R., Melendi, D.: Análisis de Trá-fico para un Servicio de Vídeo bajo Demanda sobre Recles HFC usando elProtocolo RTMP. Inf. Tecnológica **21**(6), 37–48 (2010)
9. Urbano, F.A., Chanchí, G., Campo, W.Y., Bermúdez Orozco, H.F., Astaiza, H.E.: Testing environment for video streaming support using open source tools. Ingeniería y Desarrollo **34** (2), 33–53 (2016)
10. Cermak, G., Pinson, M., Wolf, S.: The relationship among video quality, screen resolution, and bit rate. IEEE Trans. Broadcast. **57**(2), 58–62 (2011)
11. Barten, P.G.J.: The effects of picture size and definition on perceived image quality. IEEE Trans. Electron. Devices **36**(9), 5–9 (1989)
12. Fulton, W.: Understanding Color Photo Bit Depth and Image Data Size and RGB color. Calculator for MB and GB Conversion. https://www.scantips.com/basics1d.html. Accessed 30 Apr 2018
13. Blom, G., Enger, J., Holst, L., Englund, G., Grandell, J.: Sannolikhctsteori och statistikteori med tillämpningar, pp. 88–98. Studentlitteratur AB (2004). ISBN 978-9-1440-2442-4, 5/e
14. Konrad, R., Dansereau, D.G., Masood, A., Wetzstein, G.: SpinVR: towards live-streaming 3D virtual reality video. ACM Trans. Graph. **36**(6), 1–2 (2017)
15. Jarschel, M., Schlosser, D., Scheuring, S., Hoßfeld, T.: Gaming in the clouds: QoE and the users' perspective. Math. Computer Model. **57**(11), 2883–2894 (2013)

Author Index

Printed in the United States
by Baker & Taylor Publisher Services